Stan Lee Presents:

ESSENTIAL THE MIGHTY THOR VOL. 1

Collecting Journey Into Mystery #83-112

THIS HAMMER, IF HE
WORTHY, SHALL
POSSESS THE POWER OF

Stan Lee Presents:

ESSENTIAL THE MIGHTY THOR VOL. 1

JOURNEY INTO MYSTERY #83:
PLOT: STAN LEE
SCRIPT: LARRY LEIBER
PENCILS: JACK KIRBY
INKS: JOE SINNOTT
LETTERS: ART SIMEK

JOURNEY INTO MYSTERY #84:
PLOT: STAN LEE
SCRIPT: LARRY LEIBER
PENCILS: JACK KIRBY
INKS: DICK AYERS
LETTERS: ART SIMEK

JOURNEY INTO MYSTERY #85:
PLOT: STAN LEE
SCRIPT: LARRY LEIBER
PENCILS: JACK KIRBY
INKS: DICK AYERS
LETTERS: ART SIMEK

JOURNEY INTO MYSTERY #86:
PLOT: STAN LEE
SCRIPT: LARRY LEIBER
PENCILS: JACK KIRBY
INKS: DICK AYERS
LETTERS: ART SIMEK

JOURNEY INTO MYSTERY #87:
PLOT: STAN LEE
SCRIPT: LARRY LEIBER
PENCILS: JACK KIRBY
INKS: DICK AYERS
LETTERS: ART SIMEK

JOURNEY INTO MYSTERY #88:
PLOT: STAN LEE
SCRIPT: LARRY LEIBER
PENCILS: JACK KIRBY
INKS: DICK AYERS
LETTERS: ART SIMEK

JOURNEY INTO MYSTERY #89:
PLOT: STAN LEE
SCRIPT: LARRY LEIBER
PENCILS: JACK KIRBY
INKS: DICK AYERS
LETTERS: RAY HOLLOWAY

JOURNEY INTO MYSTERY #90:
PLOT: STAN LEE
SCRIPT: LARRY LEIBER
ART: AL HARTLEY
LETTERS: TERRY SZENICS

JOURNEY INTO MYSTERY #91:
PLOT: STAN LEE
SCRIPT: LARRY LEIBER
ART: JOE SINNOTT
LETTERS: TERRY SZENICS

JOURNEY INTO MYSTERY #92:
PLOT: STAN LEE
SCRIPT: ROBERT BERNSTEIN
ART: JOE SINNOTT
LETTERS: MARTINE EPP

JOURNEY INTO MYSTERY #93:
PLOT: STAN LEE
SCRIPT: ROBERT BERNSTEIN
PENCILS: JACK KIRBY
INKS: DICK AYERS
LETTERS: RAY HOLLOWAY

JOURNEY INTO MYSTERY #94:
PLOT: STAN LEE
SCRIPT: ROBERT BERNSTEIN
ART: JOE SINNOTT
LETTERS: SAM ROSEN

JOURNEY INTO MYSTERY #95:
PLOT: STAN LEE
SCRIPT: ROBERT BERNSTEIN
ART: JOE SINNOTT
LETTERS: SAM ROSEN

JOURNEY INTO MYSTERY #96:
PLOT: STAN LEE
SCRIPT: ROBERT BERNSTEIN
ART: JOE SINNOTT
LETTERS: ART SIMEK

JOURNEY INTO MYSTERY #97:
SCRIPT: STAN LEE
PENCILS: JACK KIRBY
INKS: DON HECK
LETTERS: ART SIMEK

TALES OF ASGARD:
SCRIPT: STAN LEE
PENCILS: JACK KIRBY
INKS: GEORGE ROUSSOS

JOURNEY INTO MYSTERY #98:
SCRIPT: STAN LEE
ART: DON HECK
LETTERS: ART SIMEK

TALES OF ASGARD:
SCRIPT: STAN LEE
PENCILS: JACK KIRBY
INKS: DON HECK
LETTERS: ART SIMEK

JOURNEY INTO MYSTERY #99:
SCRIPT: STAN LEE
ART: DON HECK
LETTERS: ART SIMEK

TALES OF ASGARD:
SCRIPT: STAN LEE
PENCILS: JACK KIRBY
INKS: DON HECK
LETTERS: ART SIMEK

JOURNEY INTO MYSTERY #100:
SCRIPT: STAN LEE
ART: DON HECK
LETTERS: ART SIMEK

TALES OF ASGARD:
SCRIPT: STAN LEE
ART: JACK KIRBY

JOURNEY INTO MYSTERY #101:
SCRIPT: STAN LEE
ART: DON HECK
LETTERS: SAM ROSEN

TALES OF ASGARD:
SCRIPT: STAN LEE
PENCILS: JACK KIRBY
INKS: PAUL REINMAN
LETTERS: ART SIMEK

JOURNEY INTO MYSTERY #102:
SCRIPT: STAN LEE
PENCILS: JACK KIRBY
INKS: G. BELL
LETTERS: SAM ROSEN

TALES OF ASGARD:
SCRIPT: STAN LEE
PENCILS: JACK KIRBY
INKS: G. BELL
LETTERS: ART SIMEK

Stan Lee Presents:

ESSENTIAL THE MIGHTY THOR VOL. 1

JOURNEY INTO MYSTERY #103:
SCRIPT: STAN LEE
PENCILS: JACK KIRBY
INKS: CHIC STONE
LETTERS: SAM ROSEN

TALES OF ASGARD:
SCRIPT: STAN LEE
PENCILS: JACK KIRBY
INKS: CHIC STONE
LETTERS: ART SIMEK

JOURNEY INTO MYSTERY #104:
SCRIPT: STAN LEE
PENCILS: JACK KIRBY
INKS: CHIC STONE
LETTERS: SAM ROSEN

TALES OF ASGARD:
SCRIPT: STAN LEE
PENCILS: JACK KIRBY
INKS: DON HECK
LETTERS: ART SIMEK

JOURNEY INTO MYSTERY #105:
SCRIPT: STAN LEE
PENCILS: JACK KIRBY
INKS: CHIC STONE
LETTERS: ART SIMEK

TALES OF ASGARD:
SCRIPT: STAN LEE
PENCILS: JACK KIRBY
INKS: G. BELL
LETTERS: ART SIMEK

JOURNEY INTO MYSTERY #106:
SCRIPT: STAN LEE
PENCILS: JACK KIRBY
INKS: CHIC STONE
LETTERS: ART SIMEK

TALES OF ASGARD:
SCRIPT: STAN LEE
PENCILS: JACK KIRBY
INKS: VINCE COLLETTA
LETTERS: ART SIMEK

JOURNEY INTO MYSTERY #107:
SCRIPT: STAN LEE
PENCILS: JACK KIRBY
INKS: CHIC STONE
LETTERS: ART SIMEK

TALES OF ASGARD:
SCRIPT: STAN LEE
PENCILS: JACK KIRBY
INKS: VINCE COLLETTA
LETTERS: ART SIMEK

JOURNEY INTO MYSTERY #108:
SCRIPT: STAN LEE
PENCILS: JACK KIRBY
INKS: CHIC STONE
LETTERS: ART SIMEK

TALES OF ASGARD:
SCRIPT: STAN LEE
PENCILS: JACK KIRBY
INKS: VINCE COLLETTA
LETTERS: ART SIMEK

JOURNEY INTO MYSTERY #109:
SCRIPT: STAN LEE
PENCILS: JACK KIRBY
INKS: CHIC STONE
LETTERS: SAM ROSEN

TALES OF ASGARD:
SCRIPT: STAN LEE
PENCILS: JACK KIRBY
INKS: VINCE COLLETTA
LETTERS: SAM ROSEN

JOURNEY INTO MYSTERY #110:
SCRIPT: STAN LEE
PENCILS: JACK KIRBY
INKS: CHIC STONE
LETTERS: ART SIMEK

TALES OF ASGARD:
SCRIPT: STAN LEE
PENCILS: JACK KIRBY
INKS: VINCE COLLETTA
LETTERS: ART SIMEK

JOURNEY INTO MYSTERY #111:

SCRIPT: STAN LEE
PENCILS: JACK KIRBY
INKS: CHIC STONE
LETTERS: ART SIMEK

TALES OF ASGARD:
SCRIPT: STAN LEE
PENCILS: JACK KIRBY
INKS: VINCE COLLETTA
LETTERS: ART SIMEK

JOURNEY INTO MYSTERY #112:

SCRIPT: STAN LEE
PENCILS: JACK KIRBY
INKS: CHIC STONE
LETTERS: SAM ROSEN

TALES OF ASGARD:
SCRIPT: STAN LEE
PENCILS: JACK KIRBY
INKS: VINCE COLLETTA
LETTERS: ART SIMEK

SPECIAL THANKS:
Roger Bonas & the guys at Repro, Tom Brevoort, Doreen Mulryan, Jared Osborne, Jacob Chabot & Ralph Macchio

REPRINT CREDITS:
COVER COLORS: STEVE BUCCELLATO
COVER DESIGN: JOHN "JG" ROSHELL OF COMICRAFT
INTERIOR DESIGN & RETOUCH: MIKHAIL BORTNIK
ASSITANT EDITOR: MATTY RYAN
COLLECTION EDITOR: BEN ABERNATHY
EDITOR IN CHIEF: JOE QUESADA

ESSENTIAL THOR® Contains material originally published in magazine form as JOURNEY INTO MYSTERY Vol. 1 #'s 83-112 and The Official Handbook of the Marvel Universe #7. Published by MARVEL COMICS, Bill Jemas, President; Frank Fochetta, Senior Vice President, Publishing; Joe Quesada, Editor-in-Chief; Stan Lee, Chairman Emeritus. OFFICE OF PUBLICATION:387 PARK AVENUE SOUTH, NEW YORK, N.Y. 10016. Printed in the U.S.A. First Printing, February, 2001. ISBN: 0-7851-0761-4. GST #R127032852. MARVEL COMICS is a division of MARVEL ENTERPRISES, INC. Peter Cuneo, Chief Executive Officer; AviArad,Chief Creative Officer.

10 9 8 7 6 5 4 3 2 1

IND.
12¢
JOURNEY INTO
APPROVED BY THE COMICS CODE CA AUTHORITY
MYSTERY
MC
83
AUG.
INTRODUCING... THE MIGHTY THOR!
THE MOST EXCITING SUPER HERO OF ALL TIME!!
BEGIN THE SAGA OF THOR IN THIS ISSUE!

THOR THE MIGHTY!
and "THE STONE MEN from SATURN!"
THE LEGEND HAS COME TRUE! BY THE WILL OF THE GODS, I AM ALIVE! I AM INVINCIBLE! I AM--THOR!!!
OUR STORY OPENS ON THE WINDY COAST OF NORWAY, WHERE WE SEE A FRAIL FIGURE SILHOUETTED AGAINST THE BLEAK SKY! HE IS DR. DON BLAKE, AN AMERICAN VACATIONING IN EUROPE!
AND, AS DOCTOR BLAKE TURNS AND LEAVES THE SITE, HE DOESN'T SEE THE STRANGE ALIEN SPACE-SHIP WHICH SILENTLY LANDS BEHIND HIM!
V-786
1

TWO PRINCIPALS IN A GRIM PAGEANT ...NEITHER ONE NOTICING THE OTHER! BUT HOW DIFFERENT WOULD THINGS BE IF THEY WERE TO MEET AT THIS MOMENT! HOW DIFFERENT WOULD BE THE FUTURE OF ALL MANKIND!

BUT OURS IS A DRAMA DECREED BY THE FATES TO BE ACTED OUT! NOTHING CAN STOP IT! NOTHING CAN CHANGE IT! WATCH AND SEE...
AH! AT LAST WE ARE ON EARTH!
THIS ATMOSPHERE--IT IS SO DIFFERENT FROM OUR OWN PLANET!

THAT IS TO OUR ADVANTAGE! ON SATURN, WE ARE MIGHTY BEINGS! BUT HERE, IN THIS OXYGEN ATMOSPHERE, OUR STRENGTH IS EVEN **GREATER!**

BEHOLD HOW EASILY I LIFT THIS PLANT-THING OUT OF THE GROUND!

HAH! **WELL DONE,** GORR!
NOW WATCH, AS **I** PROVE THE INVULNERABILITY OF OUR STONE BODIES!

WITHOUT THE SLIGHTEST HESITATION, I JUMP...

...FOR I KNOW THAT NOTHING ON THIS PUNY EARTH...

...CAN **HARM** ME!

BUT, ONE PAIR OF EYES **DOES** SEE THE AWESOME ALIENS! THE EYES OF AN AGED FISHERMAN!
BY THE BEARD OF ODIN, WHAT HAVE I STUMBLED **ONTO**?!!
AND IF OUR STRENGTH WERE NOT ENOUGH, WE COULD RELY UPON OUR **WEAPONS**!
IT WILL BE CHILD'S PLAY TO CONQUER THIS PLANET WHEN OUR MAIN INVASION FORCE ARRIVES!

I MUST RUN TO THE VILLAGE AND SOUND THE ALARM!!

BUT, WHEN THE OLD FISHERMAN TELLS HIS STORY...
STONE CREATURES FROM OUTER SPACE? WHAT NONSENSE DO YOU SPEAK?!!
BEGONE, OLD MAN! DO NOT WASTE OUR TIME WITH FAIRY TALES!
IT SOUNDS FANTASTIC! AND YET, THE MAN DOESN'T APPEAR MAD! I WONDER...?

THE FOLLOWING DAY, DR. DON BLAKE DECIDES TO EXPLORE THE COASTAL AREA DESCRIBED BY THE FISHERMAN...
SO FAR I'VE SEEN NO SIGN-- WAIT--WHAT'S THIS? FOOTPRINTS!! THEY LEAD AROUND THE BEND!

IT'S THEM--THE ALIENS!! THEY'RE JUST AS HE SAID THEY WERE-- MEN OF STONE!
REMEMBER... DEATH TO ANY WHO DISCOVER OUR PRESENCE!

IF THEY FIND ME HERE, THEY'LL KILL ME! I'D BETTER LEAVE WHILE--BLAST IT, I STEPPED ON A TWIG!
LO! AN EARTHLING! HE HAS SEEN US!!
AFTER HIM! DO NOT LET HIM ESCAPE!
SNAP!

I--I CAN'T RUN FAST ENOUGH! THEY'LL SOON CATCH UP TO ME!

OOH!! I TRIPPED...

I'M HELPLESS WITHOUT MY CANE--WAIT! PERHAPS I CAN HIDE IN THOSE CAVES--

MADE IT! BUT THEY'RE BOUND TO FIND ME SOON! IF ONLY THERE WERE A WAY OUT--!
BACK THERE! THERE IS ANOTHER EXIT!

...BUT IT'S BLOCKED BY THIS BOULDER! UHHH--IT'S HOPELESS! I CAN'T BUDGE IT AT ALL!

THE CAVE IS SO DANK--SO GLOOMY--AND AIRLESS! IT SEEMS NO HUMAN HAS SET FOOT IN HERE FOR AGES!! -SIGH- I MIGHT AS WELL WAIT FOR THE STONE MEN TO FIND ME--I-I'M **TRAPPED!**

BUT, SUDDENLY...
THE WALL IS **OPENING!!** I MUST HAVE PRESSED SOME KIND OF HIDDEN LEVER WHEN I LEANED AGAINST IT!

IT'S A SECRET CHAMBER! BUT THERE'S NOTHING INSIDE... EXCEPT THAT GNARLED WOODEN STICK--LIKE AN ANCIENT CANE!

I WONDER? PERHAPS BY USING THIS AS A LEVER, I CAN **MOVE** THE BOULDER!

UHHH... I...I **STILL** CAN'T BUDGE IT! BUT I **MUST** KEEP TRYING... MUSTN'T GIVE UP... IT'S MY ONLY CHANCE TO ESCAPE!

NO! IT--IT'S **HOPELESS!** EVEN A **BULL DOZER** COULDN'T MOVE THAT GIANT ROCK!

IN HELPLESS ANGER, DON BLAKE STRIKES THE USELESS CANE AGAINST THE IMMOVABLE BOULDER, AND, AS HE DOES SO...

WHA--?!!

THE CAVE IS BATHED IN BLINDING LIGHT!! LIKE A FIERY BOLT OF LIGHTNING! AND THE ANCIENT CANE--IT--IT'S CHANGING SHAPE!

AND--I'M CHANGING TOO!!
CAN THIS BE REALLY HAPPENING --OR AM I GOING MAD?!!

NO! IT ISN'T MAD!! I CAN FEEL MY BODY BURSTING WITH POWER--POWER SUCH AS I'VE NEVER KNOWN!!

THE CANE!! IT HAS BECOME A MIGHTY HAMMER!! AND I HAVE BEEN TRANSFORMED INTO--INTO--WAIT! THERE ARE WORDS INSCRIBED ON THE HAMMER!!

"WHOSOEVER HOLDS THIS HAMMER, IF HE BE WORTHY, SHALL POSSESS THE POWER OF... THOR"

THOR!! THE LEGENDARY GOD OF THUNDER!! THE MIGHTIEST WARRIOR OF ALL MYTHOLOGY!! THIS IS HIS HAMMER!! AND I--I AM THOR!!!

PART 2

"the POWER of THOR!

I CAN LIFT IT AS IF IT WERE CARDBOARD!

THE STONE CREATURES WILL NEVER SUSPECT THAT THEIR FRAIL QUARRY ESCAPED THROUGH THIS REAR EXIT!

BUT WHAT HAPPENS NOW? DO I WALK AMIDST THE CIVILIZED WORLD AS A MYTHOLOGICAL GOD?? OR--? IT IS TOO BEWILDERING! I MUST PAUSE... AND THINK THIS OUT!

THOR... THE GOD OF THUNDER! WHAT DO I REMEMBER OF HIM FROM MY SCHOOL DAYS? HE WAS THE NOBLEST AND STRONGEST OF ALL THE NORSE GODS!

THE FOURTH DAY OF THE WEEK, THURSDAY WAS NAMED IN HIS HONOR! HE WAS--WHA--? WHAT'S HAPPENING TO ME?? I'M-- I'M CHANGING AGAIN!!

I'M BACK TO NORMAL ONCE MORE! BUT HOW?? WHAT CAUSED IT?? WAIT-- THE INSCRIPTION ON THE HAMMER--

"WHOSOEVER HOLDS THIS HAMMER, IF HE BE WORTHY, SHALL POSSESS THE POWER OF THOR!"
SO THAT'S IT! I MUST CONTINUALLY HOLD THE HAMMER TO RETAIN THOR'S STRENGTH!

IF I LET GO OF IT, IN ABOUT SIXTY SECONDS I REVERT BACK TO MY NORMAL SELF!

ACCORDING TO THE LEGEND, THOR'S HAMMER HAD OTHER CHARACTERISTICS! ONE, IS THAT IT WAS SO HEAVY, NONE BUT MIGHTY THOR COULD LIFT IT!

THE LEGENDS ALSO SAY THAT THE HAMMER IS ENCHANTED! WHENEVER THOR HURLS IT FROM HIM...

...IT MUST RETURN!

ALSO, THE HAMMER IS INVINCIBLE!

NOTHING CAN RESIST IT!

CRASH

NOTHING!!

HIS BLOOD BOILING WITH EXCITEMENT, THE TRANSFORMED DOCTOR CONTINUES TO EXPERIMENT WITH HIS MYSTIC WEAPON...
BY STAMPING THE HANDLE TWICE ON THE GROUND...
THUMP
THUMP

...I CAN CREATE RAIN OR SNOW...

...WHICH SOON GROW INTO A RAGING TORNADO! ALL THE POWER OF THE STORM IS THOR'S TO COMMAND!
BOOM!

THEN, TO END THE STORM, I MERELY STAMP THIS HANDLE THREE TIMES ON THE GROUND!!!
THUMP
THUMP
THUMP

BUT, IF I SHOULD STAMP IT BUT ONCE...

THE HAMMER CHANGES BACK INTO A CANE... AND I ONCE AGAIN BECOME DR. DON BLAKE!

TO THINK, THE MOST INCREDIBLE POWER OF ALL TIME HAS BEEN HIDDEN IN THAT CAVE, WAITING TO BE FOUND!! BUT... I'VE WASTED ENOUGH TIME! THE WORLD MUST BE WARNED OF THE PRESENCE OF THE STONE MEN!

BUT EVEN AT THAT MOMENT, ON A NATO AIR BASE...
IT'S A FLEET OF UNIDENTIFIED FLYING OBJECTS!
ALERT ALL MILITARY UNITS--AND SCRAMBLE THE JETS!

THE HUMANS HAVE SENT UP ARMED AIRCRAFT!
WE SHALL SOON DISPOSE OF THEM! SET UP THE MONSTER-IMAGE!

A MOMENT LATER, A HUGE, THREE-DIMENSIONAL PICTURE FLASHES ACROSS THE SKY!
WHA--? WHAT IN THE NAME OF HEAVEN IS IT??
IT'S HEADING RIGHT FOR US! WE CAN'T BANK IN TIME!!
BAIL OUT!!
HIT THE SILK!!

HOW EASILY WE TRICKED THE EARTHLINGS!
NATURALLY-- THE HUMANS ARE A PRIMITIVE RACE!
IT SHALL BE CHILD'S PLAY TO CONQUER THEM!

BEHOLD HOW THEY TRY TO STOP US WITH MISSILES!
AS THOUGH MERE ROCKETS COULD PENETRATE OUR ATOMIC FORCE FIELDS!
THE EARTHLINGS HAVE NOTHING THAT CAN KEEP US FROM DESCENDING UPON THEM! NOTHING!!

EARTH'S WEAPONS ARE USELESS AGAINST THE INVADERS! BUT, PERHAPS WHAT TWENTIETH CENTURY SCIENCE CAN'T DO...
THUMP

...THE GOD OF THUNDER CAN!!

STRANGE--A MOMENT AGO THE SKY WAS CLEAR! YET NOW THERE IS A STORM BREWING!
HOW CAN THIS BE? ...OUR WEATHER INSTRUMENTS DID NOT FORECAST IT!

THE ENEMY IS A LONG DISTANCE FROM ME! YET, BY USING THE MIGHT OF THOR, AND WHIRLING MY HAMMER WITH THE SPEED OF LIGHTNING, I MAY YET BE ABLE TO STREAK THRU THE SKY, AS THE THUNDER GOD SHOULD!

THERE! I RELEASE MY WHIRLING HAMMER FOR A SPLIT-SECOND, CATCHING THE UNBREAKABLE THONG, AND THEN--I AM PULLED ALONG AFTER IT LIKE THE TAIL OF A ROCKET!!

PART 3
THOR THE MIGHTY
STRIKES BACK!

BEHOLD! AN EARTHLING! FLYING THRU THE AIR! TO ATTACK US!
DO NOT SLAY HIM! HE MUST BE CAPTURED, AND STUDIED!

CAPTURE HIM? HOW??
HIS WHIRLING WEAPON HOLDS US AT BAY!

WAIT! HE IS DIRECTLY BENEATH OUR CAPTIVE CAGE! IN A MOMENT, HE WILL BE OUR HELPLESS PRISONER!

HAH! HE IS OURS!
THUD!

THE EARTHLING IS POWERLESS...
NO! OBSERVE...
IT IS IMPOSSIBLE!
IRON BARS DO NOT A PRISON MAKE!

...NOT WHEN THE PRISONER HAS THE MIGHT OF THOR!!

THE EARTHLING IS TOO POWERFUL TO BE CAPTURED ALIVE!
HE MUST BE SLAIN! PREPARE TO DISINTEGRATE HIM!

BUT, BEFORE THE RUTHLESS INVADERS CAN FIRE...

OUR WEAPONS!!
THE EARTHLING CANNOT BE STOPPED!

YES HE CAN! SET THE MECHANO-MONSTER FREE! BE SWIFT!!
IT IS DONE, SIRE! NOW THE ENEMY WILL SURELY MEET HIS MASTER!

THERE IS YOUR FOE!! ATTACK HIM! DESTROY HIM!!
THAT MONSTROSITY LOOKS LIKE IT HAS EVERYTHING IN ITS FAVOR! EVERYTHING, EXCEPT...

...THE HAMMER OF THOR!

CLANG!

HE HAS VANQUISHED THE MECHANO-MONSTER!
THE HUMAN IS TOO MIGHTY --TOO SKILLED IN THE ART OF BATTLE!
AND WE KNOW NOT HOW MANY **MORE** THERE ARE LIKE HIM ON EARTH!

BACK!! BACK TO THE SHIPS AT ONCE!! WE MUST **FLEE** THIS ACCURSED PLANET!!

I'VE **BEATEN** THEM! I HAVE PROVEN THAT THE POWER OF THE HAMMER AND THE MIGHT OF THE THUNDER-GOD ARE **INVINCIBLE!** NOTHING CAN CONQUER THOR! **NOTHING!!**
HERE COMES THE INFANTRY! IF I REMAIN HERE, THEY'LL QUESTION ME!! THEY WON'T REST TILL THEY'VE LEARNED MY SECRET! I'LL BECOME AN INTERNATIONAL CURIOSITY!
BUT, ALL THAT CAN BE AVOIDED BY ONE GESTURE...
THUMP

LOOK! THE INVADERS ARE FLYING AWAY!
BUT **WHY??** WHAT COULD HAVE DRIVEN THEM OFF??
I DON'T **KNOW!** THERE'S NO ONE IN SIGHT...
NAT
13
...EXCEPT THAT LAME PASSER-BY, WITH A GNARLED OLD CANE!
WELL, IT'S A CINCH **THAT** SKINNY GENT ISN'T EARTH'S SECRET WEAPON!
THE MENACE IS ENDED! NOW, IT'S TIME FOR ME TO GO BACK TO THE STATES... TAKING WITH ME THE GREATEST POWER EVER KNOWN TO MORTAL MAN!
the END

EDITOR'S NOTE:
THORR THE MIGHTY, THE GREATEST NEW SUPER-HERO OF ALL TIME, WILL APPEAR REGULARLY IN JOURNEY INTO MYSTERY!
RESERVE NEXT MONTH'S ISSUE AT YOUR NEWSDEALER **NOW!** IT'S SURE TO BE A SELL-OUT!

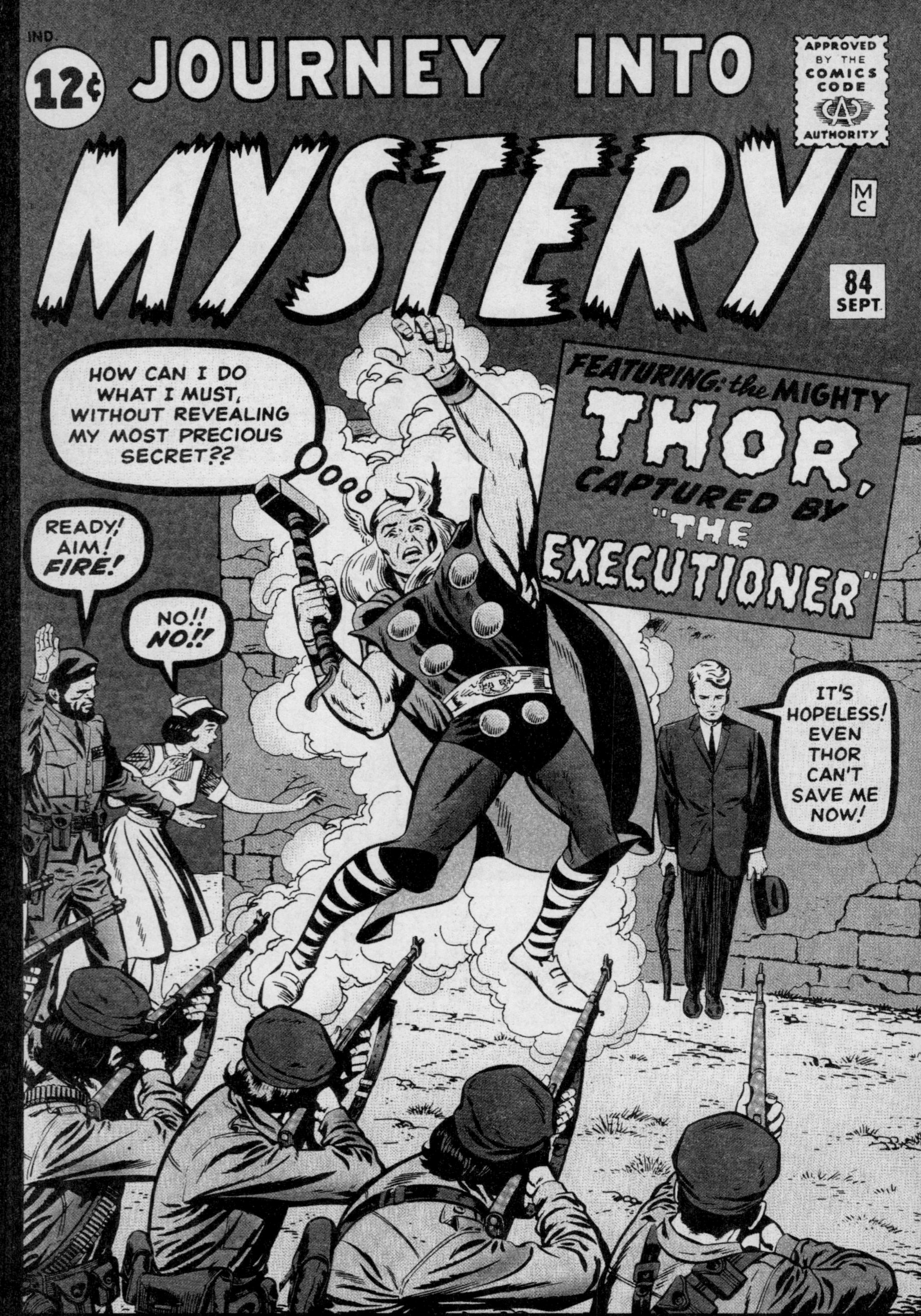

IND.
12¢
JOURNEY INTO
APPROVED BY THE COMICS CODE AUTHORITY
MYSTERY
MC
84
SEPT.
HOW CAN I DO WHAT I MUST, WITHOUT REVEALING MY MOST PRECIOUS SECRET??
FEATURING: the MIGHTY THOR, CAPTURED BY "THE EXECUTIONER"
READY! AIM! FIRE!
NO!! NO!!
IT'S HOPELESS! EVEN THOR CAN'T SAVE ME NOW!

THE MIGHTY THOR
VS. THE EXECUTIONER
ONLY I AND MY HAMMER STAND BETWEEN THE EXECUTIONER'S LEGIONS AND... DISASTER!
KIRBY AYERS
1

INTRODUCTION: IN THE LAST ISSUE OF JOURNEY INTO MYSTERY, WE BROUGHT YOU THE FANTASTIC TALE OF DR. DON BLAKE, A LAME AMERICAN VACATIONING IN NORWAY... WHO DISCOVERED AN ANCIENT CANE IN A REMOTE CAVE...
IT MUST HAVE BEEN HIDDEN HERE FOR CENTURIES!

UPON ACCIDENTALLY STRIKING THE CANE, THE LAME PHYSICIAN FOUND HIMSELF CHANGING INTO...
I'M BECOMING THOR, THE LEGENDARY THUNDER-GOD... AND THE CANE IS TURNING INTO A GIANT HAMMER!

IT WAS AN INCREDIBLE MYTH COME TO LIFE! AND, LIKE IN THE MYTH, THE MIGHTY HAMMER COULD ONLY BE LIFTED BY THOR... AND WHEN IT WAS HURLED, IT ALWAYS RETURNED TO ITS MASTER!
NOTHING CAN HARM THE HAMMER! NOTHING!!
CRACK

BUT, SCARCELY HAD THOR BEEN BORN, WHEN HE FOUND HIMSELF PITTED AGAINST AN INVASION FORCE OF MENACING STONE MEN FROM SATURN!

MIGHTY AS THEY WERE, THE STONE MEN COULD NOT MATCH THE POWER OF THE THUNDER-GOD...

AND FINALLY, IN UTTER DEFEAT, THEY FLED FROM EARTH!
NOW I MERELY STAMP THE MAGIC HAMMER ONCE... AND INSTANTLY I REVERT BACK TO MY ORIGINAL FORM!

I CARRY WITHIN THIS CANE THE GREATEST POWER EVER KNOWN TO MORTAL MAN! A POWER I SHALL NEVER USE, EXCEPT IN THE CAUSE OF JUSTICE AGAINST THE FORCES OF EVIL!

AND NOW, BACK TO THE PRESENT: DR. DON BLAKE HAS RETURNED TO THE STATES TO RESUME HIS MEDICAL PRACTICE...
HIS HEARTBEAT IS STRONGER, MRS. JONES! HE'S RECOVERING!
THANKS TO YOU, DOCTOR! WITHOUT YOUR TREATMENT, WHO KNOWS **WHAT** MIGHT HAVE HAPPENED?

YES, DON BLAKE IS A SUCCESSFUL PHYSICIAN! BUT IN **ANOTHER** AREA, HE'S SOMEWHAT **LESS** SUCCESSFUL...
JANE IS SO BEAUTIFUL! IF ONLY I COULD TELL HER HOW MUCH SHE MEANS TO ME! BUT I DAREN'T...

...FOR A GIRL SO LOVELY WOULD NEVER MARRY A--A LAME MAN! AND IF SHE **KNEW** I LOVED HER, SHE'D PROBABLY QUIT HER JOB! THEN I WOULD NEVER SEE HER AT ALL!

BUT, UNKNOWN TO THE DOCTOR, NOT ONLY DOES HIS NURSE NOT MIND HIS LAMENESS, BUT...

I COULD CARE FOR HIM DEEPLY, IF ONLY HE WOULD SHOW SOME AFFECTION TOWARD ME... IF EVEN ONCE HE WOULD TAKE ME IN HIS ARMS AND-- AND TELL ME HE CARES!

BUT NO-- NOT **HIM**! HE'S TOO DARN STUFFY TO EVER BE ROMANTIC!

AN IRONIC SITUATION... AND ONE THAT WILL SOON BE COMPLICATED BY AN INTERNATIONAL EVENT...
EXTRA! FIGHTING CONTINUES IN SAN DIABLO!
WHAT'S **THAT** ALL ABOUT?
WHILE YOU WERE IN EUROPE, A REVOLUTION BROKE OUT IN SAN DIABLO! TWO FACTIONS ARE BATTLING FOR POWER!

ONE FACTION IS DEMOCRATIC, THE OTHER IS PRO-COMMUNIST! ITS LEADER IS A RUTHLESS WARLORD KNOWN AS *"THE EXECUTIONER"*, BECAUSE OF THE MANY VICTIMS HE'S SENT TO THE FIRING SQUAD!

AND AS FATE WOULD HAVE IT, THE FOLLOWING WEEK AT A MEDICAL MEETING...
BECAUSE OF THE FIGHTING, THERE'S A GREAT SHORTAGE OF MEDICAL HELP IN SAN DIABLO! DISEASE IS RAMPANT, AND THEY'VE ASKED FOR VOLUNTEER DOCTORS!
I'LL GO THERE!
SO WILL I!
ME TOO!

AND SO, AN AMERICAN SHIP OF MERCY SOON SETS SAIL FOR THE WAR-TORN SOUTH AMERICAN COUNTRY...
I SHOULDN'T HAVE LET YOU COME, JANE! IF WE RUN INTO TROUBLE, I'LL NEVER FORGIVE MYSELF!
BUT SURELY THERE'LL BE NO TROUBLE FOR US! WE'RE JUST GOING TO HELP THOSE WHO ARE SICK!

YET, EVEN AS JANE NELSON SPEAKS...
OUR TARGET IS BELOW US!
WHY DOES THE EXECUTIONER ORDER US TO SINK IT? THERE ARE ONLY DOCTORS ABOARD!
THE EXECUTIONER DOES NOT WANT THE PEASANTS TO BE CURED! HE WANTS THEM TO REMAIN ILL, SO THEY WILL BE UNABLE TO OPPOSE US!

LOOK--JETS! THEY'RE ATTACKING US!!
THIS SHIP IS UNARMED! WE HAVEN'T A CHANCE!

NO ONE IS AROUND! NOW I CAN UNLEASH THE POWER OF THE MAGIC CANE!

A SINGLE BLOW OF THE ENCHANTED CANE PRODUCES A FLASH OF LIGHTNING! AND IN THAT AWESOME INSTANT, THE INCREDIBLE TRANSFORMATION TAKES PLACE...
I'M CHANGING...

...INTO THE MIGHTIEST OF ALL WARRIORS...

...INTO THOR!

NOW SHALL THE ATTACKERS FEEL THE WRATH OF THE THUNDER-GOD!

GREAT CAESAR'S GHOST--WHO'S THAT??!
THAT HAMMER! HE WHIRLED IT AROUND AND HELD ONTO THE END!! HE--HE'S ACTUALLY FLYING!

HAH!! I HAVE REACHED MY OBJECTIVE!

ONE SWING OF THE INVINCIBLE HAMMER...
AND THIS JET WILL NEVER-MORE ATTACK A HARMLESS VICTIM!

NOW TO WHIRL MY HAMMER BEFORE THE OTHER TWO PLANES CAN REACH ME!

WITH MY ENCHANTED HAMMER, I CAN CONTROL THE ELEMENTS AND MAKE THEM DO MY BIDDING!
HE'S WHIRLING THE HAMMER SO FAST, IT'S CREATING AN AIR POCKET!
WE'RE BEING SUCKED INTO IT!

MY PLANE'S OUT OF CONTROL! I'M GOING TO CRASH!
BAIL OUT-- QUICKLY!!

NEVERMORE WILL THESE PLANES MENACE INNOCENT MEN!
CRACK
6

IT IS DONE! NOW, I SHALL CHANGE BACK TO MY RIGHTFUL SELF UNDER-WATER, WHERE NONE CAN SEE ME!

I HAVE BUT TO STAMP THE HAMMER ONCE, AND--
THUMP!

AND A MOMENT LATER...
HELP! HELP!!
IT'S-- DR. BLAKE!!
THROW HIM A LINE!!
HURRY! HE'S LAME! I DON'T KNOW HOW LONG HE CAN STAY AFLOAT!

IN ALL THE EXCITEMENT, I ACCIDENTALLY FELL OVER-BOARD!
THANK HEAVENS YOU'RE SAFE!

WHAT--WHAT HAP-PENED TO THE JETS?
IT WAS INCREDIBLE! OUT OF NOWHERE, THERE APPEARED A FIGURE LIKE A LEGENDARY FLYING GOD!
HE WIELDED A MIGHTY HAMMER--JUST LIKE THOR, THE MYTHICAL GOD OF THUNDER!
HE DOWNED ALL FOUR PLANES!
AND HE WAS SO --SO HANDSOME!

MEANWHILE, AT SAN DIABLO...
WHAT!!! FOUR JET FIGHTERS FAILED TO SINK ONE UNARMED SHIP!! THOSE IMBECILE PILOTS WERE IN YOUR COMMAND! YOU WILL PAY FOR THEIR BUNGLING!
GUARDS! TAKE THIS FOOL TO THE WALL!
NO-- COMRADE EXECUTIONER-- SPARE MY LIFE!

READY... AIM... FIRE!
LISTEN WELL! I WANT THE YANKEE DOCTORS PREVENTED FROM TREATING THE SICK PEASANTS! IF YOU FAIL YOU ALSO SHALL FACE THE FIRING SQUAD!
Y-YES, COMRADE EXECUTIONER!
KA-POW
KA-POW
KA-POW
KA-POW

COMRADE-- WORD HAS JUST ARRIVED! THE YANKEES HAVE LANDED!
FEAR NOT! WE WILL DRIVE THEM BACK BEFORE THEY CAN CURE ANYONE!
DO NOT DARE FAIL.!!

LATER...
LOOK! THE YANKEES ARE COMING THROUGH THE PASS!
HOLD YOUR FIRE...WAIT... WAIT...

NOW! OPEN FIRE!
IT'S AN AMBUSH!
TAKE COVER!!
SNIPERS HIDDEN ALL OVER THE MOUNTAIN! EVEN THOR COULDN'T FIND THEM ALL IN TIME!
TWANNNG
PNNNNG
POW POW POW

THERE'S ONLY ONE THING TO DO-- CREATE A THUNDERSTORM!!*
THUD
THUD
NOTE: WHEN THE ANCIENT CANE IS STAMPED TWICE, IT CREATES WIND, RAIN, LIGHTNING AND THUNDER... THE SYMBOLS OF MIGHTY THOR!*

IT'S STARTING! IT'S BUILDING UP! COME, YOU FURIES--COME!!

THE WIND HOWLS... THE THUNDER ROARS... THE LIGHTNING FLASHES ...THE MOUNTING STORM RAGES ON AND ON...
IT'S RAINING SO HARD, I CANNOT SEE THE YANKEES!
I-I CAN'T SEE ANYTHING!

ALL THE RAIN IS MAKING THE GROUND SOFT!
THE MUD IS TOO SLIPPERY!
I'M SLIDING DOWN THE MOUNTAIN!! HELP!!

FINALLY, WHEN THE AMERICANS ARE SAFELY THROUGH THE MOUNTAIN PASS, DON BLAKE STRIKES THE MAGIC CANE THREE TIMES, BRINGING THE VIOLENT STORM TO A SUDDEN END!
I DON'T KNOW WHAT COULD HAVE CAUSED THE SUDDEN STORM, BUT WHATEVER IT WAS, IT SAVED OUR LIVES!
YES, BUT WE'RE NOT OUT OF DANGER YET! LOOK!

COMMIE TANKS! THEY MUST BELONG TO THE EXECUTIONER!
HE'S OUT TO GET US! AND THIS TIME HE MAY!
ONCE AGAIN, I MUST TAKE THE ASPECT OF THE MIGHTIEST OF ALL WARRIORS!

HEY, IT--IT'S HIM AGAIN!!
QUICKLY--FLEE!! I'LL HOLD THE TANKS BACK!!

ALL I NEED IS A LEVER, ABOUT AS LARGE...

...AS THIS TREE!

RACING SILENTLY BEHIND THE FIRST TANK, THE THUNDER-GOD STRIKES SWIFTLY...
JUST IN TIME!!

JUMP FOR YOUR LIVES!!
OUT OF THE TANK!! QUICK!

CRASH!
CRA-A-ASH!

NOW TO PUT THE LAST OF THE TANKS OUT OF ACTION!
POWM
SCREEE!

AN INSTANT LATER, THOR SMASHES HIS INVINCIBLE HAMMER INTO THE TANK WITH SUCH FORCE...

BONG!
TWANNNNNGG!

...THAT THE VIBRATION CAUSES THE VERY MOLECULES OF THE STEEL ITSELF TO DISSEMBLE AND FALL APART!

BUT THEN THE THUNDER-GOD TURNS... AND SEES THAT ALL THE AMERICANS HAVE ESCAPED... EXCEPT ONE!

THEY-- THEY'VE CAPTURED JANE!!
YOU FIGHT WITH THE STRENGTH OF A DOZEN DEMONS! BUT EVEN YOU CANNOT KEEP US FROM HOLDING THIS GIRL!
UNLESS YOU LEAVE, SHE WILL DIE!
DON'T LISTEN TO THEM! DEFEAT THEM ALL!

I CAN'T RISK JANE'S LIFE! I'LL FIND A PLACE TO HIDE ...AND CHANGE BACK TO DON BLAKE!
HAH! EVEN SO MIGHTY A WARRIOR AS HE, CANNOT IGNORE THE PLIGHT OF A HELPLESS WOMAN!
HE IS A FOOL!
COME-- LET US TAKE HER TO THE EXECUTIONER!

LATER...
THE OTHER YANKEES ESCAPED-- BUT WE WILL CAPTURE THEM BEFORE NIGHTFALL!
THIS AMERICAN GIRL... SHE QUITE A PRIZE! SUCH LOVELY EYES ...SUCH SOFT HAIR! SHE IS BEAUTIFUL!
JUST AS YOU ARE UGLY!

COMRADE EXECUTIONER --WE CAUGHT THIS YANKEE PROWLING OUTSIDE!
SO! A SPY!
DR. BLAKE!!!
I'M DOCTOR DON BLAKE! SHE'S MY NURSE! YOU'VE NO RIGHT TO HOLD HER! RELEASE HER AT ONCE!

SO, YOU DARE COMMAND THE EXECUTIONER! GIVE ME YOUR CANE! YOU WILL HAVE NO FURTHER NEED FOR IT! WE WILL TEST YOUR COURAGE AS YOU FACE MY FIRING SQUAD!

NO! DON'T SHOOT HIM! YOU MUSTN'T!
YOU LIKE HIM, EH? TELL ME WHAT YOU WOULD DO TO SAVE HIS LIFE? WOULD YOU MARRY ME??

YES, I'LL MARRY YOU! ONLY SPARE HIM--PLEASE--
NO! I CANNOT ALLOW JANE TO SACRIFICE HERSELF FOR ME! BUT I'M HELPLESS WITHOUT THOR'S HAMMER!

EXECUTIONER! YOU'RE A LILY-LIVERED COWARD! IF YOU WEREN'T, YOU'D FIGHT ME MAN TO MAN!

WHY, YOU PUNY YANKEE! YOU DARE INSULT THE MIGHTY EXECUTIONER!!!
MIGHTY? DO YOU NEED THAT CUDGEL TO ATTACK ONE LAME MAN??

DISDAINFULLY, THE EXECUTIONER STARTS TO TOSS THE ROUGH-HEWN WALKING STICK ASIDE, BUT A SLENDER ARM REACHES OUT, AND...

WHA--?
GOT IT!

ONCE AGAIN IN POSSESSION OF THE AMAZING CANE, DON BLAKE STRIKES IT AGAINST THE WALL, PRODUCING A BLINDING LIGHTNING BOLT!
THAT FLASH--
MY EYES--I CANNOT SEE...

AND IN THAT BLAZING INSTANT, AN INCREDIBLE TRANSFORMATION AGAIN TAKES PLACE!
THE YANKEE IS GONE! HE ESCAPED!
BUT THOR IS HERE! HERE... TO METE OUT VENGEANCE!
BAH! HE IS BUT ONE MAN! HE CANNOT OPPOSE AN ENTIRE ARMY! DESTROY HIM!!

BUT, BEFORE THE TROOPS CAN ACT, THE MIGHTY THOR HURLS HIS HAMMER AT A NEARBY SUPPLY TENT...

...AND THE INVINCIBLE OBJECT RETURNS TO ITS MASTER... PULLING THE GREAT TENT BACK WITH IT...
WHOOOOSH!

...DROPPING IT ON THE TROOPS WHO HAVE BEEN ORDERED TO ATTACK THOR!
SSSWISSH!

BUT THEN, ANOTHER ARMY APPEARS IN VIEW! THE ARMY OF THE DEMOCRATIC FACTION OF SAN DIABLO!
IT IS THE ENEMY! THEY ARE ON THE MARCH!
WE ARE NOT PREPARED TO ENGAGE THEM IN COMBAT! WE MUST RETREAT TO THE MOUNTAIN!

AS THE EXECUTIONER'S TROOPS FLEE, THE GOD OF THUNDER STAMPS HIS HAMMER FOUR TIMES-- BEFORE POINTING IT AT THE VOLCANIC MOUNTAIN!
A FEW LIGHTNING BOLTS ARE ALL IT WILL TAKE!

...TO MAKE THE VOLCANO ERUPT!!
LAVA!! HURRY-- BACK DOWN THE MOUNTAIN!
BETTER TO BE CAPTURED BY THE ENEMY THAN TO BE TRAPPED BY THE LAVA!

HIS ARMY CONFUSED AND DEFEATED, THE EXECUTIONER NOW TRIES TO ESCAPE...
LOOK-- OUR LEADER FLEES WITH OUR GOLD!
HE IS THE CAUSE OF OUR DOWNFALL, AND NOW HE TRIES TO DESERT US!
HE MUST PAY FOR HIS FAILURE!

HE BETRAYED US! HE BETRAYED OUR NATION! IT IS THE AMERICANS WHO ARE TRULY OUR FRIENDS...NOT THOSE WHO WOULD PLUNGE US INTO WAR!
KA-POW!
POW!

AND SO, IRONICALLY, THE MAN WHO CAUSED SO MANY OTHERS TO PERISH IN FRONT OF THE EXECUTION WALL, IS HIMSELF ITS FINAL VICTIM!

THE REVOLUTIONARY ARMY IS CRUSHED! IT'S THE END OF COMMUNIST INFILTRATION IN OUR LAND!
WE OWE OUR VICTORY TO THAT FANTASTIC FIGHTER WITH THE HAMMER! SAY, WHERE DID HE DIS-APPEAR TO!
HE SEEMS TO HAVE VANISHED!
HE WAS SO STRONG-- SO MASCULINE-- SO WONDERFUL!
13

SOMETIME LATER...
WELL, WE FINALLY GOT TO TREAT THE ILL PEOPLE OF SAN DIABLO! NOW WE CAN RETURN HOME TO THE STATES!
BY THE WAY, DOCTOR, WHERE WERE YOU WHILE ALL THE FIGHTING WAS GOING ON?

I WAS... AHH... HIDING BEHIND THE EXECUTION WALL! I FIGURED IT WAS THE SAFEST PLACE TO BE!
OH, I SEE...!
HIDING! GOLLY, WHY COULDN'T YOU BE BRAVE AND ADVENTUROUS LIKE--THOR! BUT NO...THAT WOULD JUST BE TOO MUCH TO HOPE FOR!
the END

IND.
12¢
JOURNEY INTO
MYSTERY
MC
APPROVED BY THE COMICS CODE AUTHORITY
85 OCT
I CHALLENGE YOU TO MATCH YOUR POWERS AGAINST MINE, THOR!
NEVER BEFORE HAS THE MIGHTY THOR FACED A FOE AS DANGEROUS AS LOKI, THE GOD OF MISCHIEF!!
TAKE THESE OTHER JOURNEYS INTO MYSTERY IN THIS GREAT ISSUE...
"FILBERT'S FRIGHTFUL FUTURE!"
"OFF-LIMITS!"
IT IS LOKI, MY SWORN ENEMY! HE HAS FOUND ME AT LAST!

THOR THE MIGHTY
AT LAST YOU'VE MET YOUR MATCH, THOR! THE POWER OF LOKI IS EVER GREATER THAN YOURS!
"TRAPPED BY LOKI, THE GOD OF MISCHIEF!"
1

BEYOND OUR SEGMENT OF TIME AND SPACE, THERE EXISTS ***ASGARD,*** THE CITADEL OF THE NORSE GODS, WHICH IS CONNECTED TO EARTH BY A RAINBOW BRIDGE CALLED ***BIFROST!***

AND, IN A REMOTE PART OF ASGARD, THERE STANDS A TREE, IN WHICH IS IMPRISONED LOKI, THE GOD OF MISCHIEF!

AGES AGO, THE GODS CONDEMNED ME TO BE TRAPPED WITHIN THIS TREE! HERE AM I DESTINED TO REMAIN UNTIL MY PLIGHT CAUSES SOMEONE TO SHED A TEAR!

BUT NO INHABITANT OF ASGARD WILL WEEP FOR ME...FOR I AM HATED BY ALL!

HOWEVER, FOR CENTURIES I HAVE BEEN IMPOSING MY WILL UPON THIS TREE...UNTIL AT LAST I CAN ***CONTROL*** IT!

AH, HEIMDALL, THE WARDER OF BIFROST APPROACHES!

HAVING BECOME MASTER OF THE TREE, THE VILLAINOUS LOKI COMMANDS ONE OF ITS LEAVES TO BREAK OFF AND FALL DOWN, INTO THE EYE OF THE PASSING DEITY...

...THE IMPACT OF WHICH CAUSES HEIMDALL'S EYE TO SMART AND SHED A TEAR...

I HAVE SUCCEEDED!

BECAUSE OF MY PLIGHT, I WAS ABLE TO GAIN CONTROL OF THIS TREE! AND THUS I WAS ABLE TO AFFECT HEIMDALL'S EYE! THEREFORE MY PLIGHT DID INDEED CAUSE HIM TO SHED A TEAR!

AND NOW, BY MY CUNNING WIT, I AM AT LAST FREE! FREE TO CAUSE MISCHIEF--TO CREATE DISCORD--AND TO SEEK REVENGE AGAINST THE ONE RESPONSIBLE FOR MY CAPTURE--***THOR,*** THE THUNDER GOD!

THOR HAS NOT BEEN IN ASGARD FOR AGES! NO ONE KNOWS WHERE HE IS! BUT I SHALL FIND HIM THROUGH HIS HAMMER!
HIS MALLET IS MADE OF URU, THE MAGIC MINERAL! BEFOR I WAS IMPRISONED, I ESTABLISHED A MENTAL "LINK" WITH IT! NOW, I SHALL USE THAT LINK TO LOCATE THE HAMMER!

THE IMAGE IS APPEARING... I CAN SEE THE URU HAMMER...

AH, THERE IS THE MIGHTY THUNDER-GOD! HE IS ON EARTH...IN A HOSPITAL...ENTERTAINING CHILDREN! HE ALWAYS DID HAVE A SOFT HEART...
...TOWARDS ALL EXCEPT ME!

WELL NOW, MY ANCIENT ENEMY IS IN FOR A SURPRISE! PREPARE YOURSELF, THOR... FOR LOKI IS COMING!!

TRAVELLING ACROSS THE RAINBOW BRIDGE AT THE SPEED OF THOUGHT, THE GOD OF MISCHIEF REACHES OUR UNSUSPECTING PLANET...
IT HAS BEEN AGES SINCE I WAS LAST ON EARTH! I HAD BEST ALTER MY ATTIRE TO MODERN-DAY CLOTHES, WHILE I SEARCH FOR THOR!

MOMENTS LATER, IN HUMAN GUISE, LOKI REACHES THE HOSPITAL HE HAD SEEN...
YES, THOR WAS HERE... BLESS HIS HEART... HE MADE OUR CHILDREN SO HAPPY! BUT HE LEFT AND I DON'T KNOW WHERE HE IS NOW!

I DON'T WANT TO REVEAL MYSELF YET, BY CONJURING UP ANOTHER IMAGE OF THE MAGIC HAMMER! HMMM, I KNOW... I'LL CREATE A DISTURBANCE THAT WILL MAKE THOR COME TO ME!
3

AND A FEW BLOCKS FROM LOKI, DR. DON BLAKE AND HIS NURSE ARE RETURNING FROM A HOUSE CALL, WHEN...
IT--IT'S HORRIBLE!!
HELP US! SOMEBODY-- HELP!!
OYS

HOLY HANNAH!! LOOK!!
THOSE PEOPLE--THEY'VE ALL BEEN TRANSFORMED INTO NEGATIVES!!

BUT HOW?? WHAT COULD HAVE CAUSED IT??
THEY'RE UNDER SOME KIND OF MAGIC SPELL! SOMEHOW I MUST HELP THEM, BUT I CAN'T DO IT AS DON BLAKE!

GOLLY, DOCTOR, I--!! WHY, HE'S GONE!

ONCE AGAIN I MUST CHANGE THE CANE INTO THE MAGIC HAMMER...

...AND MYSELF INTO--THOR!!

AND, A MOMENT LATER...
LOOK-- IT'S THOR!!
AH, MY LITTLE FEAT OF MAGIC FLUSHED OUT THE GREAT THUNDER-GOD HIMSELF!
CLEAR THE STREET! SOME SINISTER ENCHANT-MENT IS AT WORK!
4

IF I ROTATE MY HAMMER FAST ENOUGH, IT WILL EMIT ANTI-MATTER PARTICLES! THERE-- IT IS WORKING!

NOW I'LL JUST USE THE HAMMER AS A SUPER FAN, TO BLOW THE ANTI-MATTER PARTICLES AT THE "NEGATIVE" VICTIMS!

AND, AS THE ANTI-MATTER REVERSES THEIR ATOMS, IT TRANSFORMS THEM BACK INTO "POSITIVE" PEOPLE AGAIN!

THE SPELL IS OVER!! WE--WE'RE NORMAL AGAIN!!
THANKS TO THOR!
WHAT A GREAT PERFORMANCE!!
YOU WERE WONDERFUL!!

GREETINGS, THOR! IT HAS BEEN A LONG TIME, HASN'T IT?
A LONG TIME?

I SEE YOU DO NOT REMEMBER ME! VERY WELL, PERHAPS THIS WILL REFRESH YOUR MEMORY!
CRACK!

NOW DO YOU RECOGNIZE ME?? THE GOD YOU IMPRISONED--THE GOD WHO IS YOUR ETERNAL ENEMY, AND WHO HAS COME TO EARTH SEEKING VENGEANCE!!
LOKI!
5

PART 2
THOR THE MIGHTY
"THE VENGEANCE OF LOKI!"

LOKI, THE NORSE GOD OF MISCHIEF! ACCORDING TO THE ANCIENT LEGENDS, THE MOST CUNNING AND WICKED OF ALL THE GODS!
I CHALLENGE YOU TO BATTLE!
THE GUY MUST BE NUTS TO TAKE ON THOR!
LOKI... UMMM, A LOVELY NAME! AND HE SEEMS SO DASHING, AND ROMANTIC!

COME, THOR-- LET US BATTLE IN THE AIR, ABOVE THESE INSIGNIFICANT MORTALS!
LOOK! HE'S MAKING THE CARPET FLOAT!
I MUST ACCEPT HIS CHALLENGE! I HAVE NO OTHER CHOICE!
HOTEL ROYALE
BE CAREFUL, THOR... BE REAL CAREFUL...

WHIRLING HIS HAMMER ABOVE HIS HEAD, THE THUNDER GOD RISES AS SMOOTHLY AS A HELICOPTER...
MY PLAN IS WORKING...HE'S FOLLOWING ME UP...

BEING SUPER-HUMAN LIKE MYSELF, THOR CANNOT BE CONQUERED BY MY MAGIC ALONE! BUT, THERE ARE OTHER WAYS!
I'VE MANEUVERED HIM INTO A POSITION WHERE THE SUN'S RAYS REFLECT OFF HIS HAMMER INTO HIS EYES EACH TIME THE HAMMER PASSES IN FRONT OF HIM!

THE BLINKING REFLECTION PLUS MY POWER OF SUGGESTION WILL SOON HAVE HIM HYPNOTIZED!
YOU ARE TIRED, THOR... TOO TIRED TO REMAIN AWAKE...YOU MUST SLEEP... SLEEP...
I MUST SLEEP...

YOU ARE IN MY POWER...I AM YOUR MASTER... YOU MUST OBEY ME...
I MUST... OBEY YOU...

I HAVE TRIUMPHED! NOW TO HAVE MY REVENGE! I SHALL USE THOR AS MY INSTRUMENT FOR CREATING MISCHIEF!
DESCEND TO EARTH, THOR!
YES, LOKI!

BUT, WHEN THE TWO LIVING LEGENDS TOUCH THE GROUND, ONE SUDDEN FEAR SWEEPS THROUGH LOKI...
SOME ACCIDENTAL SHOCK MIGHT SUDDENLY SNAP HIM OUT OF HIS TRANCE! IF THAT HAPPENED AND HE HAD HIS HAMMER WITH HIM, IT WOULD BE TOO DANGEROUS FOR ME!
I MUST GET THOR'S HAMMER AWAY FROM HIM!

I COMMAND YOU TO GIVE ME THE ENCHANTED HAMMER!
I...I CANNOT OBEY YOU, LOKI! BY THE WILL OF ODIN* THE MAGIC WEAPON MUST NEVER BE WRESTED FROM THOR!

EDITOR'S NOTE! *ODIN IS THE RULER OF ALL NORSE GODS!

HIS ATTACHMENT TO THE HAMMER IS TOO STRONG FOR EVEN HYPNOSIS TO OVERCOME!
I WILL HAVE TO RESORT TO TRICKERY!
LOOK, THOR--THERE IS A SEA BEAST BENEATH THE SURFACE! IT IS ATTACKING THAT SMALL BOAT!

INSTINCTIVELY, THE GOD OF THUNDER HURLS HIS MIGHTY HAMMER IN THE DIRECTION INDICATED BY LOKI...
HAH! IT WORKED! HE BELIEVED THERE REALLY WAS A MENACE AND HE TRIED TO DESTROY IT!

BUT, AN INSTANT LATER...
OHH--I FORGOT--THE HAMMER'S GREATEST POWER---WHENEVER THOR THROWS IT, IT RETURNS TO HIM!

I MUST GET THE HAMMER AWAY FROM HIM! WAIT-- I HAVE A PLAN! I SHALL CONJURE UP ANOTHER THOR!

IN HIS HYPNOTIC TRANCE, HE MIGHT JUST BE DECEIVED BY THE IMAGE I'VE CREATED!
BEHOLD THOR, THE MIGHTY-- THE THUNDER GOD! THE HAMMER IS HIS! GIVE IT TO HIM!
YES, LOKI! THE HAMMER BELONGS TO THOR!

IT WORKED!
NOW GO TO YONDER HOUSE OF ANIMALS AND SET FREE THE BEASTS!
SET FREE THE BEASTS...

BUT AS THOR REACHES THE ANIMAL HOUSE, LOKI'S ATTENTION IS DIVERTED FOR A MOMENT...
FOOLISH MORTALS! STRAINING TO LIFT THE MAGIC HAMMER! IN ALL OF HEAVEN AND EARTH, NONE BUT THOR HAS STRENGTH ENOUGH TO LIFT IT!

AND, IN THAT FATEFUL MOMENT, THE TRANSFORMATION TAKES PLACE! FOR WHEN THE GOD OF THUNDER AND HIS HAMMER ARE SEPARATED FOR MORE THAN SIXTY SECONDS, HE REVERTS BACK TO HIS NORMAL FORM...

...AND THE HYPNOTIC SPELL WHICH THOR WAS UNDER HAS NO EFFECT UPON THE PERSON OF DR. DON BLAKE...
WHAT CAN BE TAKING THOR SO LONG? WHY HAS HE NOT RELEASED THE BEASTS?
I MUST MANAGE TO TOUCH THE HAMMER AGAIN!
ANIMAL HOUSE

I DON'T GET IT! I CAN'T LIFT THIS THING CLEAR OFF THE GROUND!
WHEW! I STRAINED EVERY MUSCLE IN MY ARM AND STILL COULDN'T BUDGE IT!
LET ME TRY!
8

ARE YOU KIDDIN'?? WE COULDN'T LIFT IT, SO HOW CAN A SKINNY GUY LIKE YOU DO IT?
LET THE POOR SAP TRY! IT'LL BE GOOD FOR A LAUGH!

BUT, THE INSTANT DON BLAKE TOUCHES THE MAGIC HAMMER, THERE IS A BLINDING FLASH OF LIGHT...
MY EYES!!
I CAN'T SEE!

WHERE'D THAT SKINNY GUY GO?
I DUNNO! BUT LOOK WHO'S HOLDING THE HAMMER NOW!
IT'S THOR!!
NOW LOKI, WE'RE GOING TO FINISH OUR BATTLE!
YOU'VE BROKEN THE HYPNOTIC SPELL!

AS HE FLEES FROM HIS FOE, THE GOD OF MISCHIEF USES HIS MAGIC POWERS TO GATHER TOGETHER ALL THE PIGEONS IN THE AREA...
I MUST ESCAPE THOR AND THINK UP A NEW PLAN TO DEFEAT HIM!

FLY, LITTLE BIRDS... FLY QUICKLY...
CLEVER TRICK! BUT IT WILL DO HIM NO GOOD!!

THOR HAS HURLED HIS HAMMER--AND HE'S HOLDING ON TO IT! HE'S FLYING AFTER ME!
HE--HE'S OVERTAKING ME! I MUST LAND!

I CAN USE THIS CROWDED THEATER TO MY ADVANTAGE!
BEGONE, PIGEONS!
LOOK! WHAT-- WHO IS IT??
MUST BE AN ADVERTISING STUNT!

TOO MANY PEOPLE AROUND! THERE'S NO ROOM TO SWING MY HAMMER!
THOR! HERE I AM! COME AND GET ME-- IF YOU DARE!

BAH! HAMMER OR NO HAMMER-- MY STRENGTH IS STILL THE GREATEST OF ALL THE GODS!

BUT ONCE AGAIN, LOKI USES HIS CRAFTY TALENT TO BEST THE GOD OF THUNDER...
WITH A SIMPLE BIT OF MAGIC, I RELEASE THE CURTAIN FROM ITS SUPPORTS!

...AND WHILE MY MIGHTY OPPONENT STRUGGLES TO FREE HIMSELF, I AGAIN MAKE MY ESCAPE! HA! HA! HA!

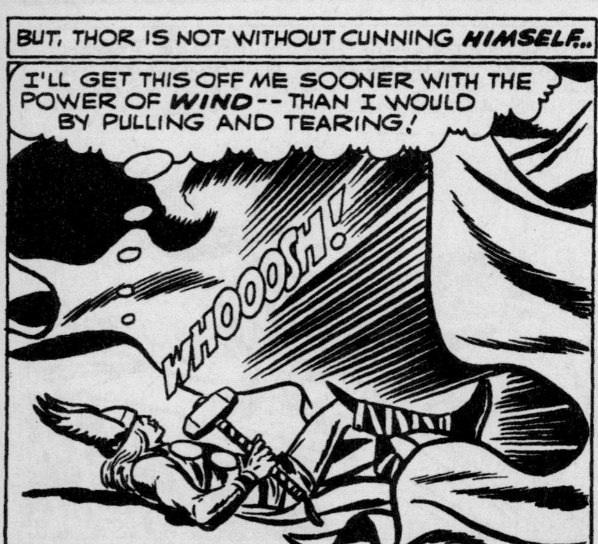
BUT, THOR IS NOT WITHOUT CUNNING HIMSELF...
I'LL GET THIS OFF ME SOONER WITH THE POWER OF WIND-- THAN I WOULD BY PULLING AND TEARING!
WHOOOSH!

AND MOMENTS LATER, THE FANTASTIC BATTLE IS RESUMED...
AN UNDERGROUND TUNNEL! I'LL SURELY DEFEAT THOR DOWN THERE!
ENTRANCE
SUBWAY

HE'S PUSHING THOSE PEOPLE OFF THE PLATFORM--AND A TRAIN'S COMING!
AWAY, PUNY MORTALS!

HAH! I KNEW THE SOFT-HEARTED THOR WOULD STOP TO HELP THE USELESS HUMANS!
NO TIME TO LOSE! THE TRAIN WILL PASS WITHIN SECONDS!

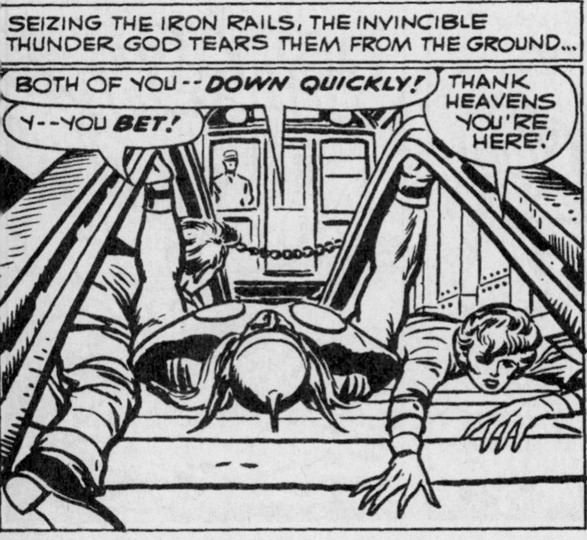
SEIZING THE IRON RAILS, THE INVINCIBLE THUNDER GOD TEARS THEM FROM THE GROUND...
BOTH OF YOU--DOWN QUICKLY!
Y--YOU BET!
THANK HEAVENS YOU'RE HERE!

IF I DIDN'T SEE IT WITH MY OWN EYES--
I DO SEE IT AND I STILL DON'T BELIEVE IT!
NOBODY CAN DO THAT!
NOBODY EXCEPT--THOR!!

WE'RE SAVED!!
NOW TO FIND LOKI, BEFORE HE DOES ANY MORE HARM!

UP THERE! HE'S BROUGHT THE WINGED HORSE OF A GASOLINE SIGN TO LIFE! NOW HE CAN FLY AGAIN!
AND IN THIS TIMES SQUARE CROWD, I CAN'T SWING MY HAMMER! I CAN'T FLY AFTER HIM!
TIMES

AND, WHILE THOUSANDS WATCH THE GOD OF MISCHIEF...
HE'S RUNNING AMOK--SMASHING THE DISPLAYS... LIKE A SPOILED CHILD IN A FIT OF ANGER!
2 BIG 2
FEATURES

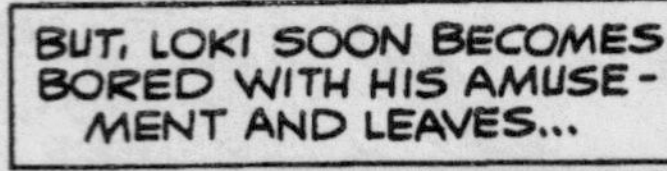

BUT, LOKI SOON BECOMES BORED WITH HIS AMUSEMENT AND LEAVES...

WHILE I'M APPROACHING YONDER STATUE, I'LL THINK OF A WAY TO DEFEAT THOR ONCE AND FOR ALL!

MEANWHILE...
THOSE SECTIONS OF PIPE... *THAT'S* THE ANSWER!

GRABBING ONE OF THE SECTIONS, THE MIGHTY THOR HURLS IT HIGH INTO THE AIR...

I PRAY MY AIM IS AS SUPERHUMAN AS MY STRENGTH!

GLUB!!
IT *WORKED!*
HOORAY!
HE *DID* IT!

SPLASH!

ACCORDING TO LEGEND, LOKI'S MAGIC POWERS ARE USELESS IN WATER! HE'LL *DROWN* UNLESS I RESCUE HIM!

SWIMMING FASTER THAN THE FASTEST FISH, THE THUNDER-GOD SOON REACHES HIS HELPLESS FOE...

YOU--*YOU* WOULD SAVE *ME??!*
I CAN NOT STAND BY AND LET *ANYONE* PERISH! --EVEN *YOU!*

MOMENTS LATER, BACK ON SHORE...
WHERE ARE YOU TAKING ME ?? STOP! GIVE ME A CHANCE TO DRY MYSELF!
WE'RE GOING TO THE EMPIRE STATE BUILDING...AND I'M KEEPING YOU WET SO YOU CAN'T USE YOUR MAGIC AGAINST ME!

SOON, ATOP THE WORLD'S TALLEST SKYSCRAPER!
WHY HAVE YOU TIED ME TO YOUR HAMMER ?? NO! STOP!! DON'T!
I'M SENDING YOU BACK TO ASGARD, LOKI--THE FASTEST WAY POSSIBLE!

FAREWELL, GOD OF MISCHIEF! MAY WE NEVER MEET AGAIN!

HURLED AT ALMOST THE SPEED OF THOUGHT, THE MAGIC HAMMER CARRIES ITS LIVING BURDEN HIGHER AND HIGHER... UNTIL IT REACHES THE RAINBOW BRIDGE AND THE CITADEL OF THE GODS, WHERE IT SWEEPS DOWN IN A GREAT ARC, BEFORE ODIN, BALDER, TYR, AND THE OTHER ASTONISHED GODS...
BEHOLD! IT IS THE HAMMER OF THOR!
IT BRINGS LOKI BACK TO US!
...AND RETURNS TO ITS MASTER!
ONCE AGAIN, MY ELDEST SON--THE LORD OF THUNDER, HAS VANQUISHED LOKI!

THE HAMMER RETURNS JUST IN TIME! ANOTHER FEW SECONDS AND IT WOULD HAVE BEEN GONE A FULL MINUTE, CAUSING ME TO LOSE MY POWERS!
THEN DON BLAKE WOULD HAVE BEEN STANDING HERE, TRYING TO CATCH IT... A FEAT HE COULD NEVER PERFORM!
13

A SHORT TIME LATER...
IMAGINE, THE GOD OF THUNDER--AND THE GOD OF MISCHIEF! BOTH BATTLING HERE ON EARTH, BEFORE OUR EYES!! HOW ROMANTIC! IT MAKES OUR OWN ORDINARY LIVES SEEM SO DULL, DOESN'T IT, DOCTOR BLAKE?
WELL, EH--IT'S ALL IN YOUR POINT OF VIEW!
THE END

IND.
12¢
JOURNEY INTO
MYSTERY
MC
APPROVED BY THE COMICS CODE AUTHORITY
86
NOV.
STARRING the MIGHTY
THOR!
HOW CAN I DEFEAT THE TOMORROW MAN, WHEN HE CAN FADE INTO A DIFFERENT YEAR BEFORE I CAN REACH HIM??

THOR THE MIGHTY

"ON THE TRAIL OF THE *TOMORROW MAN!*"

BEHOLD, THUNDER-GOD... YOU PURSUED ME INTO THE FUTURE, ONLY TO MEET YOUR DOOM AT THE HANDS OF MY STEEL SLAVES!

PLOT: STAN LEE *SCRIPT:* LARRY LIEBER *ART:* JACK KIRBY *INKS:* DICK AYERS

NO, WHAT YOU ARE LOOKING AT IS NOT ANOTHER WORLD! IT IS OUR VERY OWN EARTH, THREE CENTURIES FROM NOW! MANKIND HAS ABOLISHED WAR AND SCRAPPED ITS WEAPONS! PEACE AND CONTENTMENT PREVAIL THROUGHOUT THE GLOBE...

BUT THERE IS ONE WHO IS NOT PEACE-LOVING! HE IS A SCIENTIST NAMED ZARRKO... AND WITHIN HIS HEART LURKS AN EVIL AMBITION...
MY FELLOW MEN ARE WEAK, TENDER-HEARTED FOOLS! IT WILL BE EASY TO CONQUER THEM!

OTHER SCIENTISTS DEVOTE THEMSELVES TO HELPING CIVILIZATION... BUT I HAVE INVENTED A WAY OF LEAVING OUR CIVILIZATION! I HAVE CONSTRUCTED EARTH'S ONLY TIME MACHINE!
FIRST, I MUST VIEW THE PAST, THROUGH MY TIME-SCOPE! I MUST DISCOVER AN AGE WHEN MANKIND POSSESSED MIGHTY WEAPONS!

AHHH--AN ANCIENT EXPLOSION OF A NUCLEAR BOMB! THE PERFECT DEVICE WITH WHICH TO CONQUER THE TWENTY-THIRD CENTURY!
THOSE BOMBS EXISTED ON EARTH DURING THE TWENTIETH CENTURY! I SHALL GO BACK THERE AT ONCE!

MEANWHILE, TRAVELING AT THE STILL FASTER SPEED OF OUR IMAGINATION, LET US RETURN TO 1962! THE SCENE IS A REMOTE DESERT AREA...
WE APPRECIATE YOUR HELPING US TEST OUR NEWEST EXPERIMENTAL WEAPONS, THOR!
I'M HAPPY TO PLAY A PART IN KEEPING THE FREE WORLD STRONG AND SECURE AGAINST THE FORCES OF TYRANNY!

SUDDENLY, WITH A TREMENDOUS ROAR...
THE MISSILE'S BEEN FIRED!
GET READY, THOR...

THERE GOES THE ANTI-MISSILE MISSILE!

AND THERE GOES THOR!!

WITH FANTASTIC SPEED, MAN AND MISSILE SOAR HIGHER AND HIGHER IN PURSUIT OF THE ROCKET...

BUT IT IS THE THUNDER GOD WHO REACHES THE TARGET FIRST...
THE MISSILES ARE GETTING FASTER! I ALMOST LOST THIS ROCKET!

THOR WAS FASTER THAN THE ANTI-MISSILE MISSILE!
YES, BUT THIS TIME HE BEAT IT ONLY BY AN INSTANT!
USING HIM AS A MEASURING DEVICE, WE'RE ABLE TO CONSTANTLY IMPROVE OUR WEAPONS!

SOON PREPARATIONS ARE MADE FOR ANOTHER TEST...
WE ARE CERTAINLY LUCKY TO HAVE THE SERVICES OF THE MIGHTY THOR!
THIS IS A DIFFERENT TYPE OF TEST! THE MOST DANGEROUS OF ALL!

THERE! HE'S ALL WIRED UP!
NOW WE'LL BE ABLE TO TEST A HUMAN'S PHYSIOLOGICAL REACTIONS!
AN ORDINARY MAN WOULD BE KILLED, STANDING THAT CLOSE TO A COBALT BOMB EXPLOSION! BUT THOR BELIEVES HE CAN SURVIVE IT!
IF HE DOES, HE'LL PROVIDE US WITH INVALUABLE INFORMATION!

START THE COUNTDOWN!
9...8...7... 6...5...
WAIT! WHAT'S THAT APPEARING NEAR THE C-BOMB ??!

IT--IT'S SOME KIND OF MACHINE!!
IT MATERIALIZED OUT OF EMPTY SPACE!!
LOOK! SOMEONE IS STEPPING OUT OF IT!

HE'S GRABBED THE C-BOMB!
STOP THE COUNT-DOWN!

I DON'T KNOW WHAT THIS IS ALL ABOUT, BUT THAT BOMB IS TOO DANGEROUS TO BE ALLOWED TO FALL INTO THE WRONG HANDS!

THIS IS ONE SURE WAY TO STOP THE THIEF!

BUT THE TIME CABINET DEMATERIALIZES SO SWIFTLY THAT THOR'S HAMMER HARMLESSLY PASSES RIGHT THRU IT...

PULLED ALOFT BY HIS SOARING HAMMER, THOR FLIES FROM THE DESERT TO A DISTANT MOUNTAIN RANGE...

ATOP THE HIGHEST MOUNTAIN... THAT WILL BE THE PERFECT PLACE FOR MY TASK!

AS SOON AS HE'S LANDED, THOR STAMPS HIS HAMMER TWICE ON THE GROUND...*

EDITOR'S NOTE:** WHEN THE MAGIC URU HAMMER IS STAMPED TWICE, IT BRINGS ON A ***THUNDERSTORM!

FLIGHT TO THE FUTURE

GOD OF THUNDER... WHY HAST THOU SUMMONED ME...?

PART 2

I ASK OF MY FATHER, LORD OF ASGARD,* THE POWER TO JOURNEY INTO THE FUTURE... TO THE UNKNOWN WHENCE THIS METAL COMES!

***EDITOR'S NOTE:** ODIN IS MONARCH OF THE NORSE GODS! THE CITADEL IN WHICH THEY DWELL IS CALLED ASGARD!

MY JOURNEY IS OVER! I HAVE ARRIVED IN THE FUTURE!
WHAT YEAR IS THIS?
IT IS 2262!
WHO ARE YOU?
HOW HANDSOME HE IS!

THERE ARE EXPLANATIONS, INTRODUCTIONS, AND THEN...
ZARRKO RETURNED WITH THE COBALT BOMB LAST MONTH!
HE THREATENED TO DESTROY US IF WE DIDN'T MAKE HIM OUR RULER!
WE HAD NO WEAPONS WITH WHICH TO OPPOSE HIM! WE HAD TO OBEY HIS COMMAND!

SINCE THEN HE'S BEEN GOVERNING US LIKE A TYRANT!
HE IS AN EVIL DICTATOR! AND SO LONG AS HE HOLDS THE COBALT BOMB, WE ARE IN HIS POWER!
THEN HEAR ME WELL, FOR I HAVE COME TO WREST THE BOMB FROM HIM! HERE IS MY PLAN...

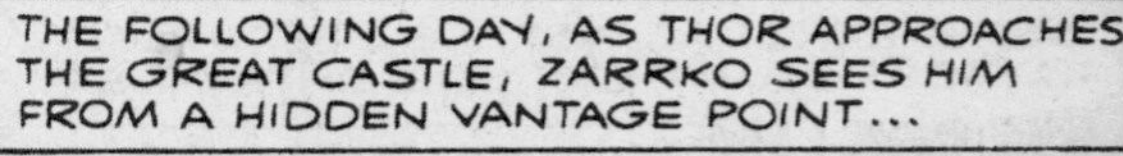

THE FOLLOWING DAY, AS THOR APPROACHES THE GREAT CASTLE, ZARRKO SEES HIM FROM A HIDDEN VANTAGE POINT...

HE IS THE ONE WHO TRIED TO PREVENT MY STEALING THE BOMB! I DON'T KNOW HOW HE FOLLOWED ME INTO THE FUTURE, BUT HE WAS A FOOL TO DO SO!

GUARDS-- SEIZE THAT MAN!!

SHALL WE OBEY?

WE HAVE NO CHOICE! ZARRKO HOLDS THE ONLY WEAPON ON EARTH! WE DARE NOT DEFY HIM!

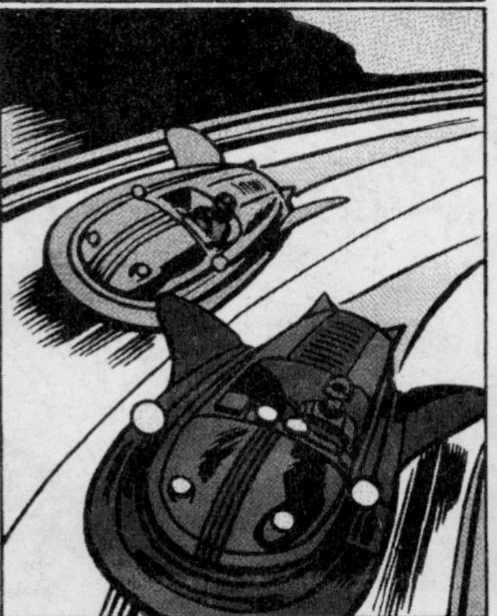

AND SO, THE GUARDS RACE FROM THE CASTLE TO APPREHEND THOR...

BUT, BEFORE THEY CAN REACH HIM, A BLACK-ROBED FIGURE HURLS A MIGHTY TREE IN THEIR PATH...

LOOK OUT!
JUMP!

THOR HAS GOTTEN PAST US!! BUT---
BUT WHO IS THE FIGURE FOLLOWING IN THE BLACK ROBE?! AND HOW COULD HE BE STRONG ENOUGH TO PUSH A GIANT OAK IN OUR PATH!

SO, ZARRKO! AT LAST WE MEET--FACE TO FACE! I AM THOR, GOD OF THUNDER!
BAH! YOU GOT PAST MY GUARDS BECAUSE THEY ARE FOOLS! BUT YOU SHALL NEVER TRIUMPH OVER ME!

GOODBYE, GOD OF THUNDER! HA, HA, HA!
A TRAP DOOR!

WELCOME TO MY ROOM OF MAGNETIC MIRRORS!
THEY'RE POWERFULLY MAGNETIZED AS YOU CAN SEE--AND FEEL! HA, HA, HA!
THUD!

BY TURNING OFF THE MAGNETISM OF ONE MIRROR...AND TURNING ON THAT OF ANOTHER... I CAN DASH YOU AGAINST THEM UNTIL YOU ARE HELPLESS!
THUMP!
8

BUT BEFORE ZARRKO CAN CONTINUE HIS DEADLY GAME...

ANOTHER THOR! BUT HOW...?
THE MAN IN YOUR TRAP WAS A DECOY! I AM THE ONE YOU HAVE TO FEAR! THE ONE WHO SHALL DE-FEAT YOU!!

I AM THE REAL THOR!
WHEW AND JUST IN TIME, TOO!

SO YOU TRICKED ME! BUT I HAVE OTHER RESOURC-ES, AS YOU SHALL NOW SEE!
NEVER! NOTHING SHALL STOP ME FROM REGAINING THE COBALT BOMB!

FOOL! THIS DELTA-ELECTRON GUN WILL SEND YOU INTO AN-OTHER DIMENSION... FROM WHICH YOU CAN NEVER ESCAPE!!

BEFORE THOR CAN HURL HIS HAMMER, HE BE-GINS TO FADE AWAY! BUT THE MIGHTIEST MAN-GOD OF ALL TIME IS NOT WITHOUT RE-SOURCES HIMSELF! HE DRAWS IN A GREAT BREATH, AND THEN HE EXHALES IT, WITH HURRICANE FORCE!!

THE SUPERNATURAL FURY OF THE GALE PIERCES THE DIMENSION-VEIL BEFORE IT CAN BE FULLY CLOSED, AND THOR AGAIN RETURNS TO THE THIRD DIMENSION-- AND HIS PURSUIT OF ZARRKO...
STOP, ZARRKO! NO MATTER WHERE YOU RUN, YOU CAN NEVER ESCAPE THOR!

BUT BEFORE THOR CAN OVERTAKE THE TYRANT FROM TOMORROW, HE ENCOUNTERS ***ANOTHER*** PERIL...

WHA--?
THESE ARE GIANT ROBOTS, THE LABORERS OF THE 23RD CENTURY! I HAVE CONVERTED THEM INTO MY OWN PRIVATE ARMY!

SUDDENLY, A HUGE METALLIC HAND REACHES DOWN AND GRABS THE MAGIC HAMMER...

DISARM HIM!!
WHA...?

IT TOOK ME BY SURPRISE! BUT NOW, WITHOUT THE HAMMER, I'LL ONLY REMAIN AS THOR FOR ANOTHER SIXTY SECONDS! THEN I'LL REVERT BACK TO MY NORMAL HUMAN SELF!
AS DON BLAKE, I'LL BE POWERLESS TO DEFEAT ZARRKO! I MUST REGAIN MY HAMMER WITHIN THE NEXT MINUTE! BUT--HOW??

59 SECONDS... 58...57...56...55...54...

THE STRENGTH OF THOR IS STILL MINE FOR THE NEXT 54 SECONDS! I'LL USE THAT STRENGTH--
--TO RIP UP THE FLOOR WITH MY BARE HANDS!

AND WITH EACH PASSING SECOND, THE ROBOTS COME CLOSER... CLOSER...

53 SECONDS...52 SECONDS...51 SECONDS...50 S
IF I'M LUCKY, I'LL FIND WHAT I NEED BENEATH MY FEET...

42 SECONDS... 41 SECONDS... 40 SECONDS...

HERE IT IS! A WATER PIPE!

SEIZING THE STEEL WATER PIPE, THE THUNDER GOD FLOODS THE ROOM ...
19 SECONDS...18 SECONDS...17 SECONDS...16 SE
THE WATER IS SEEPING INTO THE ROBOTS! IT'S SHORT-CIRCUITING THEIR MECHANISM! THEY'RE SLOWING DOWN!!

11 SECONDS...10 SECONDS...9 SECONDS...8 SEC
THEY'VE COME TO A COMPLETE STANDSTILL!!
MY HAMMER!! THE ROBOT IS RELEASING IT--IT'S FALLING...

4 SECONDS...3 SECONDS...2 SECONDS...1 SECOND...
GOT IT--AND NOT A SECOND TOO SOON!!

HAVING RENDERED THE ROBOTS HELPLESS, THOR NOW CONTINUES HIS GRIM PURSUIT...
HE'S RUNNING INTO A SPACE-SHIP! AND HE'S GOT THE C-BOMB WITH HIM!!
I'VE BEEN BEATEN AT EVERY TURN! BUT THERE IS STILL ONE LAST CARD TO PLAY!

IF I CAN'T USE THE COBALT BOMB TO ENSLAVE THE WORLD--THEN I'LL USE IT TO DESTROY THE WORLD!

HE'S GONE MAD! IF HE DROPS THE BOMB, IT WILL BE A CATASTROPHE! I MUST STOP HIM!
LET THERE BE STORM! STORM! STORM!!
THUMP!
THUD!

SECONDS AFTER THE MAGIC HAMMER IS STAMPED AGAINST THE GROUND, THE RAIN BEGINS! THEN COMES THE WIND, THUNDER AND LIGHTNING...
THE STORM IS RAGING SO HARD, IT'S BUFFETING THE SHIP!

I--I CAN'T GET OVER TO THE BOMB, TO DROP IT ON THE EARTH!

THEN THE GOD OF THUNDER RAISES HIMSELF INTO THE AIR BY WHIRLING HIS HAMMER... AND IN SO DOING, CREATES A SUCTION OF AIR THAT SPINS THE LITTLE SPACECRAFT AROUND AND AROUND, UNTIL...
IF I CAN JUST JAR THE BOMB LOOSE...

THERE IT IS! IT'S FALLING!

I'VE GOT IT!!

AND AS THOR DESCENDS SAFELY TO THE GROUND, THE SPACESHIP, OUT OF CONTROL, CRASH-LANDS...

AND, THOUGH ZARRKO EMERGES FROM THE WRECKAGE STILL ALIVE...
WHO--WHO AM I ?? WHAT AM I DOING HERE...??
WE'LL BE ABLE TO CURE HIS PHYSICAL INJURIES!
BUT HIS MEMORY WILL NEVER RETURN!

YOU DEFEATED A TYRANT! AND YOU SAVED OUR WORLD FROM DESTRUCTION!
WE SHALL BE FOREVER GRATEFUL!
LONG LIVE THE MIGHTY THOR!
NOW I MUST RETURN THE C-BOMB TO MY OWN TIME!

ONCE AGAIN THOR WHIRLS HIS LEGENDARY HAMMER AT UNIMAGINABLE SPEED, AS TIME ITSELF IS BENT TO THE THUNDER-GOD'S WILL!
2053
2015
2000
198
1974
1962

SOON THE YEAR IS 1962 AND THE PLACE IS THE NEW MEXICAN DESERT...
YOU HAVE YOUR BOMB BACK! LET US MENTION IT NO MORE! YOU WOULD NEVER BELIEVE MY TALE!
MAYBE NOT! BUT WE'D STILL LIKE TO KNOW WHERE IT WAS--AND HOW YOU BROUGHT IT BACK!
FORGET IT, BOB! WE'VE GOT SOME WEAPONS TESTS TO PERFORM NOW!

A SHORT TIME LATER, AFTER THOR HAS TURNED BACK TO THE QUIET DR. DON BLAKE...
ANYTHING HAPPEN WHILE I WAS GONE, JANE?
ARE YOU KIDDING, DOCTOR? DON'T YOU READ THE PAPERS?!
THOR RESCUES C-BOMB
SURVIVES EXPLOSION
13

NO, JANE! NOTHING IN THE PAPERS INTERESTS ME... IT'S ALL TOO NERVE-WRACKING!
OH, IF ONLY I COULD WORK FOR THOR--INSTEAD OF COLORLESS DR. BLAKE!
PRIV

I WONDER IF JANE WILL EVER SUSPECT THAT SOME OF US READ ABOUT THE NEWS...
...WHILE SOME OF US ARE TOO BUSY MAKING IT!
THE END

IND.
12¢
JOURNEY INTO
MYSTERY
APPROVED BY THE COMICS CODE AUTHORITY
MC
87
DEC.
THESE CHAINS ARE ELECTRONICALLY TREATED! I CANNOT BREAK THEM!
Starring THE MIGHTY THOR! in
"PRISONER OF THE REDS!"

THE MIGHTY THOR!
"PRISONER OF THE REDS!"
BEHOLD, GOD OF THUNDER--MANY HAVE FOUGHT YOU! BUT ONLY I HAVE DEFEATED YOU!
PLOT: STAN LEE • SCRIPT: LARRY LIEBER
ART: JACK KIRBY • INKING: DICK AYERS
LETTERING: ART SIMEK
V-947
1.

FOR THOR, ADVENTURE OFTEN BEGINS IN UNEXPECTED WAYS... SUCH AS WHEN THE WIFE OF A FAMOUS SCIENTIST ARRIVES HOME AND FINDS HER HUSBAND MISSING...
THERE'S A NOTE! IT MUST BE FROM JOHN!
Sylvia

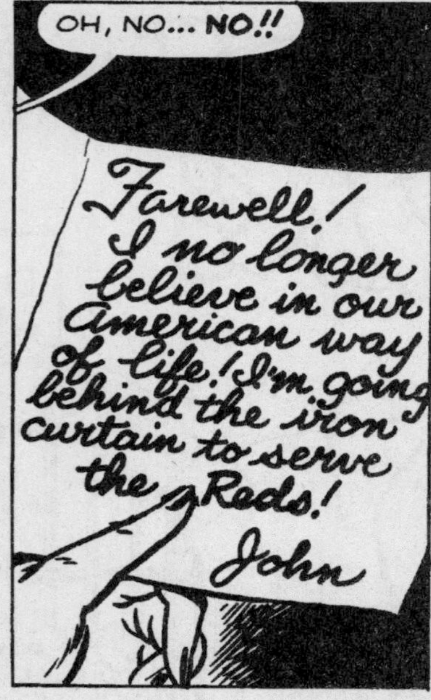
OH, NO... NO!!
Farewell! I no longer believe in our American way of life! I'm going behind the iron curtain to serve the Reds!
John

... JOHN BLANDINGS IS THE FIFTH SCIENTIST TO DEFECT TO THE REDS WITHIN THE PAST MONTH!
GOVERNMENT OFFICIALS ARE UNABLE TO EXPLAIN THESE SUDDEN DEFECTIONS! HOWEVER, THE F.B.I. IS WORKING DAY AND NIGHT...
NEWS

AND AT THAT MOMENT, IN THE HOME OF DR. DON BLAKE...
MISSING SCIENTISTS... HMMMM ...THIS MIGHT BE A JOB FOR THOR! I'D BETTER SEE MY OLD FRIEND, COLONEL HARRISON, IN WASHINGTON!

AND SO, THE LAME DOCTOR PACKS FOR AN OVERNIGHT TRIP...
HERE ARE YOUR ALLERGY PILLS AND VITAMIN TABLETS! DON'T FORGET TO TAKE THEM!
AND BE SURE TO STAY OUT OF DRAFTS! YOU KNOW HOW EASILY YOU CATCH COLD!
HOW CAN I FORGET? YOU NEVER LET ME!

WELL, YOU'RE SO FRAIL, THAT SOMEBODY HAS TO TAKE CARE OF YOU!
I HOPE YOU DON'T RESENT MY PLAYING "MOTHER HEN"!
THERE'S NOTHING ABOUT YOU THAT I RESENT, JANE!

GOSH, I WONDER IF HE EVER CATCHES COLD?
WHO??

OH-- EH-- NOBODY!
WELL, GOODBYE, JANE! I'LL SEE YOU WHEN I RETURN!

IF ONLY I COULD TELL JANE THAT I LOVE HER, BUT I DAREN'T! SHE MIGHT PITY A WEAKLING LIKE ME... BUT SHE COULD NEVER LOVE ME!
IF SHE KNEW HOW I FELT, SHE'D QUIT HER JOB! THEN I WOULD LOSE HER FOREVER!

SOON, DON BLAKE IS IN THE OFFICE OF COLONEL EDWARD HARRISON, U.S. ARMY INTELLI-GENCE...
I WANT TO SET MYSELF UP AS BAIT BY CLAIMING THAT I'VE INVENTED A NEW WEAPON IN BIOLOGICAL WARFARE! MAYBE THEN I CAN LEARN HOW THE REDS ARE MAKING OUR SCIENTISTS DEFECT!
WHY ARE YOU DOING THIS, DON?

CAN'T TELL HIM THAT I'M REALLY THOR! MUST MAKE UP A CONVINC-ING STORY!
MY BUM LEG KEPT ME OUT OF THE KOREAN WAR ...AND WELL, THIS IS MY CHANCE TO MAKE UP FOR IT-- TO SERVE MY COUNTRY!
OKAY, I'LL BUY YOUR PLAN!

LATER, IN A LONELY ALLEYWAY...
NOW TO GET HOME, THE FASTEST WAY POSSIBLE!
CRACK!

STRIKING HIS ENCHANTED CANE SHARPLY ON THE GROUND, THE PUNY DOCTOR IS SUDDENLY TRANSFORMED...

...INTO THE MIGHTY THOR!

MOMENTS LATER, THE GOD OF THUNDER STREAKS ACROSS THE SKY!
I DON'T KNOW WHAT MADE ALL THOSE TOP SCIENTISTS SUDDENLY DEFECT... BUT I'LL SOON FIND OUT!

ONCE AGAIN BACK IN HIS OFFICE, DON BLAKE PRE-TENDS TO EMBARK ON A SECRET PROJECT...
I HAVEN'T TOLD JANE WHY I'M DOING THIS! THE LESS SHE KNOWS, THE SAFER SHE'LL BE!

FINALLY, AFTER DAYS OF FAKE SCIENTIFIC EXPERIMENTATION...
HMMMM... THIS DOCTOR BLAKE COULD BE ANOTHER USEFUL SCIENTIST FOR OUR CAUSE!
DAILY-BULLETIN
DOCTOR DEVELOPS NEW VIRUS FOR GERM WARFARE!
DR. DON BLAKE

THE FOLLOWING DAY...
DOCTOR, THERE'S A PHOTOGRAPHER HERE TO SEE YOU!
MAYBE THIS IS IT... WHAT I'VE BEEN WAITING FOR...

I'M FROM A NATIONAL MAGAZINE! WE'RE DOING A STORY ON YOUR NEW BIOLOGICAL WEAPON AND I'VE BEEN SENT TO TAKE SOME PHOTOS OF YOU!
FINE! I'LL BE GLAD TO OBLIGE!

I KNOW YOU'RE BUSY, DOCTOR, SO I'LL DO THIS AS QUICKLY AS I CAN! THAT'S IT! HOLD IT... HOLD IT...

THERE-- FOOL!!
WHA-? GAS!! I--UHHHH--
CLICK!

BEFORE DON BLAKE CAN ACT, THE STRANGE FUMES ENTER HIS NOSTRILS AND IMMEDIATELY TAKE EFFECT...

IT WORKED! THE GAS HAS HYPNOTIZED HIM, JUST AS IT DID ALL THE OTHERS!

HIS WILL OVERCOME BY THE GAS, THE HELPLESS DOCTOR FOLLOWS THE COMMANDS OF HIS CAPTOR...
WRITE A FAREWELL NOTE!

NO ONE WILL SEE US LEAVE BY THE BACK DOOR!
NO ONE-- WILL-- SEE--

THE PLANE IS WAITING!
PLANE... WAITING...

SOON WE WILL BE BEHIND THE IRON CURTAIN!
BEHIND... IRON... CURTAIN...

SEVERAL JET HOURS LATER...
TOO BAD YOU DO NOT REALIZE WHAT IS HAPPENING TO YOU! BUT YOU WILL KNOW SOON ENOUGH!

THIS IS TO BE YOUR NEW HOME! A HOME THAT YOU WILL NEVER LEAVE!

AND FINALLY, WHEN THE HYPNOTIC TRANCE WEARS OFF...
UHHH... MY HEAD... I... I...
HE'S COMING AROUND NOW!
POOR GUY, THEY SNARED HIM THE SAME WAY THEY GOT US!

WHERE-- WHERE AM I?
YOU'RE IN A COMMIE FORTRESS!
WE'RE AMERICAN SCIENTISTS LIKE YOURSELF!
THE REDS ABDUCTED US! BUT MADE IT APPEAR AS IF WE DEFECTED!

THE COMMIES WANT US TO DO SCIENTIFIC WORK FOR THEM!
SO FAR, WE'VE REFUSED! BUT THEY'RE MAKING IT ROUGHER ON US!
I DON'T KNOW HOW LONG WE CAN HOLD OUT!

I SEE...
NOW IT'S TIME FOR ME TO CHANGE INTO THOR! BUT IF I DO, THESE MEN WILL SEE ME! MY SECRET IDENTITY WILL BE REVEALED! I MUST THINK OF SOME WAY...

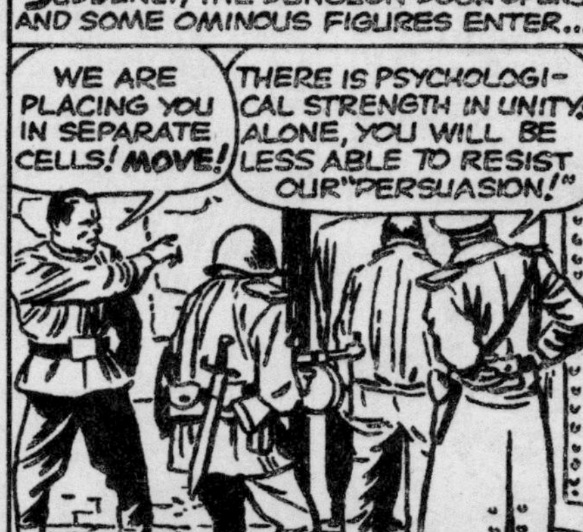
SUDDENLY, THE DUNGEON DOOR OPENS, AND SOME OMINOUS FIGURES ENTER...
WE ARE PLACING YOU IN SEPARATE CELLS! MOVE!
THERE IS PSYCHOLOGICAL STRENGTH IN UNITY! ALONE, YOU WILL BE LESS ABLE TO RESIST OUR "PERSUASION!"

THEN, AS SOON AS DON BLAKE IS ALONE IN A CELL...
THEY SOLVED MY PROBLEM FOR ME! NOW TO LET THE REDS FACE THE FURY OF--THOR!!
KA-RACK!

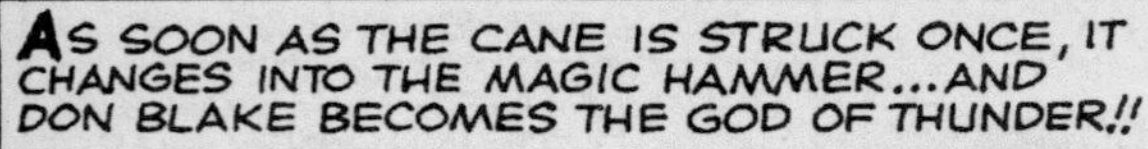
AS SOON AS THE CANE IS STRUCK ONCE, IT CHANGES INTO THE MAGIC HAMMER...AND DON BLAKE BECOMES THE GOD OF THUNDER!!

I'LL BREAK OUT OF HERE BY SPINNING MY HAMMER FAST ENOUGH TO CREATE SHOCK WAVES...

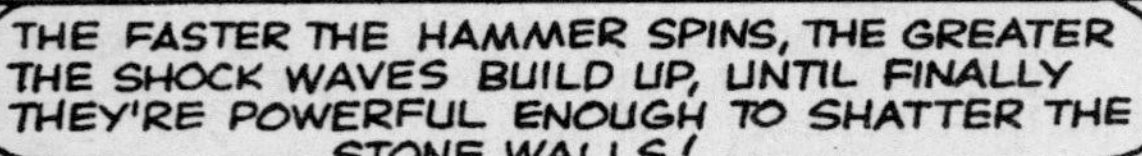
THE FASTER THE HAMMER SPINS, THE GREATER THE SHOCK WAVES BUILD UP, UNTIL FINALLY THEY'RE POWERFUL ENOUGH TO SHATTER THE STONE WALLS!

THERE--I AM FREE! FREE TO DO WHAT ONLY THE MIGHTY **THOR** CAN DO!

HE CARRIES A HAMMER, LIKE OUR HAMMER AND SICKLE EMBLEM! IS HE ONE OF **US??**
FOOL! HE IS THE ONE THE WESTERN WORLD CALLS THOR-- **THE THUNDER GOD!!**
HE IS OUR ENEMY! **STOP HIM!!**

BUT BEFORE THE GUARDS CAN FIRE, THE MIGHTY THOR RUBS HIS HANDS AGAINST THE MAGIC HAMMER, CREATING SUCH INTENSE **FRICTION**, THAT IT EMITS SPARKS, AS HOT AND BLINDING AS A BLAST FURNACE!
MY EYES-- I CANNOT SEE!
GET BACK! QUICKLY!

HAVING ROUTED THE GUARDS, THOR RUSHES ALONG THE TUNNEL, UNWITTINGLY PASSING AN ELECTRIC EYE BEAM...

THE INSTANT THE BEAM IS SEVERED, IT TRIGGERS THE RELEASE OF A TRAP DOOR!
WHA--??
I'VE STUMBLED INTO A TRAP!

MAN-EATING SHARKS! CAN'T FIGHT THEM ALL AT ONCE! ONLY ONE WAY TO BEAT THEM!

SPINNING HIS HAMMER RAPIDLY, THE MIGHTIEST FIGURE ON EARTH CREATES A WHIRLPOOL...
IT'S WORKING! THE SHARKS ARE BEING DRAWN INTO IT!

BY THE TIME THE WHIRLPOOL SPINS ITSELF OUT, THOSE MAN-EATERS WILL BE TOO DIZZY TO MENACE ANYONE ELSE!
NOW TO ATTEND TO THE REDS-- ESPECIALLY THAT ONE WHO BROUGHT ME HERE!

SEARCHING THE FORTRESS, THOR SOON COMES UPON HIS FOES...
HEAR ME, THUNDER-GOD! IF YOU TAKE ANOTHER STEP, I'LL THROW THE SWITCH, SMASHING THE ENTIRE DUNGEON AREA!
EVERYONE WILL BE DESTROYED, INCLUDING THE AMERICAN SCIENTISTS!

YOUR CHOICE IS SIMPLE! EITHER YOU SURRENDER, OR THEY ALL DIE!
I-I CAN'T LET THOSE INNOCENT MEN BE HARMED! I MUST DO WHAT HE SAYS!

AND SO, FOR ONE OF THE RARE TIMES IN HIS FANTASTIC CAREER, THE MIGHTY THOR IS TAKEN PRISONER...
THESE CHAINS ARE ELECTRONICALLY TREATED! EVEN YOU WILL NOT BE ABLE TO SEVER THEM!
NOW I SHALL SEND FOR OUR LEADERS! I SHALL SHOW THEM MY VALUABLE CAPTIVE!
I CANNOT BUDGE THE HAMMER!
IT IS SAID THAT NONE BUT THOR CAN LIFT IT!

BAH! IT'S FUTILE! LEAVE THE HAMMER! WE MUST GO NOW! THOR IS HELPLESS!
WITHOUT THE MAGIC OF MY HAMMER, I CAN ONLY REMAIN AS THOR FOR SIXTY SECONDS! IN LESS THAN A MINUTE, I'LL CHANGE BACK TO DON BLAKE!

WHEN THE SIXTIETH SECOND HAS PASSED...
I'M TRANSFORMING! AND THE CHAINS THAT HELD THOR SO SECURELY, FIT LOOSELY AROUND THE FRAIL FORM OF DR. BLAKE!

CLIMBING OUT OF THE SLACK CHAINS, THE LAME DOCTOR HOBBLES OVER TO THE MAGIC HAMMER...
ONCE AGAIN I FEEL THE POWER OF THE THUNDER GOD ENTERING MY BODY!

MINUTES LATER, THOR LOCATES THE CELLS WHERE THE SCIENTISTS ARE BEING HELD...
LOOK! IT'S-- IT'S--
SHHHH--I WANT TO GET YOU SAFELY OUT OF THE FORTRESS, BEFORE THE REDS FIND OUT!

B-BUT HOW DID YOU KNOW WE WERE HERE??
NO TIME FOR EXPLANATIONS! JUST FOLLOW BEHIND ME!

SWINGING HIS HAMMER WITH UNBELIEVABLE SPEED, THE THUNDER GOD HOLLOWS AN UNDERGROUND TUNNEL...
LOOK HOW FAST HE'S DIGGING! IT'S-- SCIENTIFICALLY IMPOSSIBLE!
HIS POWER COMES FROM A SOURCE BEYOND SCIENCE! IT IS THE POWER OF A NORSE GOD!

WE'RE FREE!
WAIT! WHERE'S DR. BLAKE?
HE'S NOT WITH US! WE MUST HAVE LEFT HIM BACK THERE!
ALL OF YOU KEEP UNDER COVER! I'LL GO BACK AND GET BLAKE!

I CAN'T REVEAL THAT BLAKE AND I ARE THE SAME PERSON... BUT IF THINGS WORK OUT RIGHT, I WON'T HAVE TO!
ARE YOU SURE YOU'VE CAPTURED THOR?
OF COURSE, COMRADE! WAIT UNTIL YOU SEE HIM! HE IS BOUND AS HELPLESS AS A CHILD!

NOT QUITE, COMRADE!
T-THOR!! BUT HOW--? HOW--??
YOU BLUNDERING FOOL!!
STOP HIM... BEFORE HE CAN USE THAT ACCURSED HAMMER!

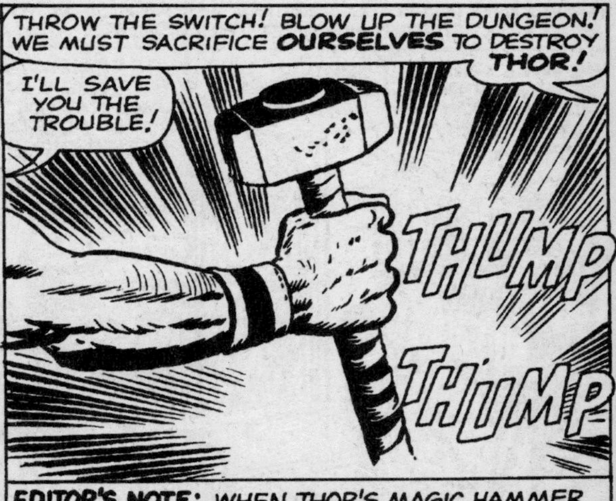
THROW THE SWITCH! BLOW UP THE DUNGEON! WE MUST SACRIFICE OURSELVES TO DESTROY THOR!
I'LL SAVE YOU THE TROUBLE!
THUMP
THUMP
EDITOR'S NOTE: WHEN THOR'S MAGIC HAMMER IS STAMPED TWICE ON THE GROUND, IT CREATES A THUNDERSTORM!

AND THEN, AS THE RAIN AND WIND POUND AGAINST THE STRONGHOLD, THOR RAISES HIS ARMS TO THE HEAVENS...
OH, MIGHTY ODIN, GREATEST OF THE NORSE GODS--HEAR THY ELDEST SON!
UNLEASH THY FURY, FATHER! DESTROY THIS CITADEL OF EVIL!

FROM THE HEAVENS, BLAZE THE MIGHTY FLASHES OF LIGHTNING--HURTLING FROM THE SKY--CRASHING INTO THE FORTRESS--SHATTERING STONE AND MORTAR...

AND, WITH A FURY THAT IS BEYOND BELIEF, THE STORM RAGES ON... ON AND ON UNTIL THE DEBACLE IS COMPLETE...

THE FORTRESS-- REDUCED TO RUINS!

SO THOR WAS YOUR HELPLESS PRISONER, WAS HE?! IMBECILE! YOU WILL **PAY** FOR THIS BLUNDERING!

I COULD CAPTURE THEM ALL, BUT I **WON'T**! I'LL LET THEM PUNISH **EACH OTHER** FOR THEIR DEFEAT!

SOON, THE STORM ENDS, AND DR. DON BLAKE JOINS THE OTHER AMERICANS...

WHERE IS **THOR??**

I DON'T KNOW! AFTER HE RESCUED ME, HE LEFT!

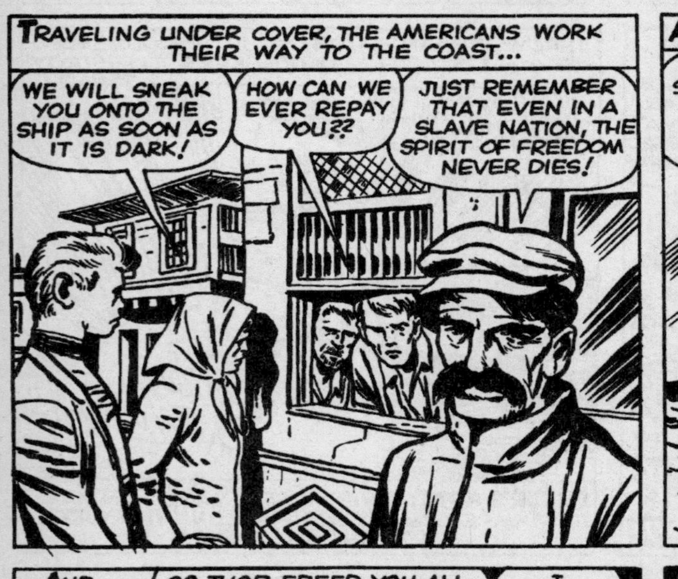

TRAVELING UNDER COVER, THE AMERICANS WORK THEIR WAY TO THE COAST...
WE WILL SNEAK YOU ONTO THE SHIP AS SOON AS IT IS DARK!
HOW CAN WE EVER REPAY YOU??
JUST REMEMBER THAT EVEN IN A SLAVE NATION, THE SPIRIT OF FREEDOM NEVER DIES!

AND SO, THE SCIENTISTS SOON SAIL FOR HOME...
THE COMMIE'S SCHEME TO MAKE US WORK FOR THEM ALMOST SUCCEEDED!
NO TELLING **WHAT** WOULD HAVE HAPPENED IF NOT FOR **THOR**!
WHATEVER HE IS-- MORTAL, OR IMMORTAL... HE SURE IS THE **GREATEST**!

AND FINALLY...
SO THOR FREED YOU ALL, AND THEN DESTROYED THE FORTRESS! IS IT ANY **WONDER** THAT I'M SO IN LOVE WITH HIM?!
I SUPPOSE NOT, JANE!

JANE, MY DARLING! HOW I LONG TO TAKE YOU IN MY ARMS-- TO TELL YOU HOW THOR LOVES YOU!! BUT I DARE NOT! HEAVEN HELP ME... I DARE NOT!
I KNOW I'LL NEVER FIND THOR... BUT I'LL NEVER STOP DREAMING... AND HOPING-- AND PRAYING!
THE END

IND.
12¢
JOURNEY INTO
MYSTERY
MC
APPROVED BY THE COMICS CODE AUTHORITY
88
JAN.
HEED MY WORDS, THOR! THOUGH BOTH OF YOU ARE MY SONS, YOU MUST DEFEAT THE EVIL LOKI... FOR THE SAKE OF MANKIND!
NOTHING CAN SAVE YOU, THUNDER GOD! FOR NOW I KNOW THE SECRET OF YOUR HAMMER!
I SHALL NOT FAIL, NOBLE ODIN! NO MATTER WHAT THE COST, LOKI SHALL NOT MENACE EARTH!
SEE THOR, THE MIGHTIEST HERO OF ALL, AS HE DARES FACE "THE TERRIBLE VENGEANCE OF LOKI!"

THE MIGHTY THOR! STARRING IN:
"THE VENGEANCE OF LOKI!"
ONCE AGAIN, LOKI, MOST DANGEROUS OF THE NORSE GODS, RETURNS TO GIVE THE MIGHTY THOR HIS GREATEST CHALLENGE!!
PLOT: STAN LEE
SCRIPT: L.D. LIEBER
ART: JACK KIRBY
INKING: DICK AYERS
LETTERING: ART SIMEK
1

IN THEIR LAST EARTHLY ENCOUNTER, THOR DEFEATED THE SINISTER LOKI, AND DISPATCHED HIM TO ASGARD, THE HEAVENLY CITADEL OF THE NORSE GODS...
IT IS THE GOD OF MISCHIEF-- ONCE AGAIN VANQUISHED BY THE MIGHTY THOR!

NOW THE ENCHANTED HAMMER RETURNS TO EARTH--AND TO ITS MASTER, THE LORD OF THUNDER!

AND THEN SPOKE ODIN, RULER OF ASGARD...
NEVER AGAIN ARE YOU TO LEAVE OUR HOME! YOU WILL REMAIN HERE FOREVER!
YES, FATHER...

BUT LOKI CANNOT FORGET HIS BITTER TASTE OF DEFEAT! EACH DAY HIS ANGER TOWARD THOR MOUNTS, UNTIL FINALLY...
I THIRST FOR REVENGE... AND I SHALL NOT REST UNTIL IT IS MINE!

THE GOD OF MISCHIEF THEN TAKES SOME STRANGE LEAVES AND COVERS THEM WITH THE SAP FROM A SACRED TREE...
ACCORDING TO THE ANCIENT RITUAL, I SUBJECT THE LEAVES TO FIRE...

AND AS THE SMOKE RISES, I CONCENTRATE ON MY FOE... THOR... THOR...

HE APPEARS! I SEE THAT AT THIS MOMENT HE IS BOUND HELPLESSLY IN A DUNGEON!
EDITOR'S NOTE: LOKI HAS "TUNED IN" ON THOR DURING HIS ADVENTURE LAST MONTH, "THOR--PRISONER OF THE REDS!"

BUT WAIT--NOW HE IS CHANGING! THE THUNDER GOD IS BECOMING AN ORDINARY MORTAL!

IN HIS HUMAN GUISE, THE CHAINS NOW FIT HIM LOOSELY! HE IS SLIPPING OUT OF THEM!

AGAIN HE TOUCHES HIS HAMMER...

...AND CHANGES BACK TO HIS ACCURSED TRUE SELF!
SO THAT IS HIS SECRET! HE'S THE ALL-POWERFUL GOD OF THUNDER, ONLY WHILE HE HOLDS THE HAMMER!
ONCE THE MALLET IS OUT OF HIS HANDS, HE BECOMES AN ORDINARY MORTAL!

HE IS COMPLETELY DEPENDENT ON THE HAMMER! THAT IS HIS WEAKNESS--HIS ACHILLES' HEEL --THROUGH WHICH I SHALL DEFEAT HIM AT LAST!!

IN THE DAYS THAT FOLLOW, LOKI MAKES FURTHER STUDIES OF THE THUNDER GOD AND HIS HUMAN COUNTERPART, DR. DON BLAKE! AND THEN, FINALLY, THOR'S ARCH-ENEMY TAKES ACTION!!
TO REACH EARTH, I MUST CROSS BIFROST, THE RAINBOW BRIDGE!

BUT HEIMDALL, THE GUARDIAN OF THE BRIDGE, KNOWS THAT ODIN HAS ORDERED ME TO REMAIN HERE! HE WILL NEVER ALLOW ME TO PASS!
SO I MUST USE MY MAGIC POWER TO ASSUME ANOTHER FORM...

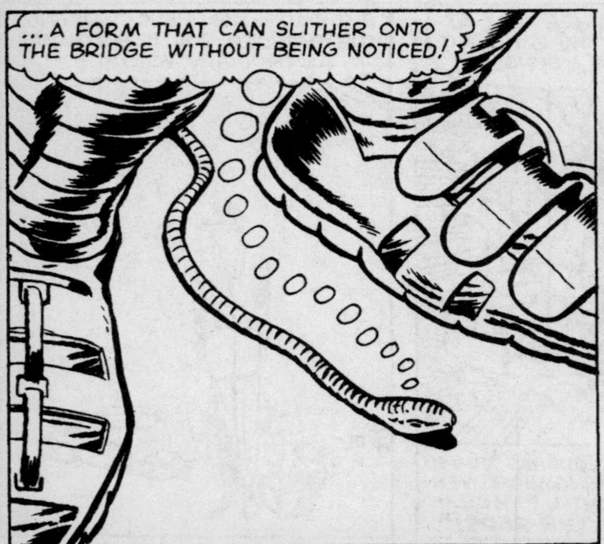
...A FORM THAT CAN SLITHER ONTO THE BRIDGE WITHOUT BEING NOTICED!

ONCE PAST HEIMDALL, LOKI REVERTS BACK TO HIS TRUE FORM! THEN, AT ALMOST THE SPEED OF THOUGHT...
ONCE AGAIN DO I MAKE THE FORBIDDEN JOURNEY TO EARTH! AND THIS TIME, I SHALL NOT RETURN UNTIL I HAVE BESTED THOR!
3

MINUTES LATER, AN OLD MAN ENTERS THE RECEPTION ROOM OF DR. DON BLAKE...
YOU!! COME TO ME! I COMMAND YOU!

WHEN THE OLD MAN SPEAKS TO NURSE JANE FOSTER, SHE FINDS HERSELF TRANSFIXED BY HIS STRANGE, UNHUMAN EYES...WHICH OVERWHELM HER WILL...WHICH MAKE HER OBEY ...OBEY...

I MUST SEE DR. BLAKE AT ONCE!
AT--AT ONCE! GO RIGHT IN!

BUT BEFORE ENTERING THE OFFICE, THE STRANGER WHISPERS A COMMAND TO HIS DAZED SUBJECT...
HEAR MY INSTRUCTIONS! REMEMBER THEM! AND WHEN THE TIME COMES--OBEY!

MOMENTS LATER...
YOU ARE DOCTOR BLAKE?
YOU'RE NOT ONE OF MY PATIENTS! HOW DID YOU GET PAST MISS FOSTER?

GETTING PAST A MERE MORTAL IS NO PROBLEM FOR...

...THE GOD OF MISCHIEF!!
LOKI!

WITH REFLEX-ACTION SWIFTNESS, THE LAME PHYSICIAN SEIZES HIS CANE, STAMPING IT SWIFTLY ON THE FLOOR...
THUMP!

YOU DARE COME--HERE?!

TRANSFORMED INTO THE MOST POWERFUL FIGURE EVER TO WALK THE EARTH, THE THUNDER GOD NOW CONFRONTS HIS FOE!
HOW DID YOU DISCOVER MY SECRET IDENTITY?
THAT IS MY SECRET, HATED ONE! AND NOW--I HAVE COME TO DO BATTLE WITH YOU!

AND IF YOU REFUSE MY CHALLENGE, I'LL CAUSE SUCH HAVOC THROUGHOUT THIS PUNY WORLD, THAT YOU WILL HAVE TO FIGHT ME!
YOU LEAVE ME NO CHOICE! THE GOD OF THUNDER HAS DEFEATED YOU ONCE, AND HE WILL DO IT AGAIN!

NO, THOR, THIS TIME LOKI SHALL BE THE VICTOR! MEET ME AT CENTER PARK, IN ONE HOUR! THERE, SHALL WE TEST OUR METTLE!
SO BE IT!

WITH THE DISAPPEARANCE OF LOKI, THOR AGAIN BECOMES DR. DON BLAKE, AND THEN...
I'LL BE GONE THE REST OF THE AFTERNOON, JANE!
YES, DOCTOR!
AFTER HE LEAVES, I MUST LEAVE TOO, AS I HAVE BEEN COMMANDED!

MINUTES LATER, A GODLIKE FIGURE HURLS HIS HAMMER INTO THE SKY, FLYING AFTER IT AS HE GRIPS THE LEATHER THONG WITH FINGERS OF STEEL!
LOOK! IT'S THE MIGHTY THOR!
THE WAY HE'S SPEEDING ACROSS THE SKY--YOU CAN BET HE'S ON THE TRAIL OF SOMEONE!
I'M SURE GLAD IT'S NOT ME!

HE COMES! NOW VENGEANCE SHALL BE MINE!

PREPARE TO BATTLE, THOR! AND PREPARE TO BE VANQUISHED BY LOKI!
YOU DECEIVE YOURSELF, LOKI! THOUGH I CANNOT MATCH YOU, POWER FOR POWER, I HAVE ONE WEAPON WHICH YOU CANNOT MATCH...

...THE INVINCIBLE HAMMER OF THOR!

SUDDENLY, WITH GODLIKE DEFTNESS, LOKI SIDE-STEPS THE ONCOMING MALLET... AND, AT THAT INSTANT, A SLENDER FEMALE ENTERS THE SCENE!
THE NURSE HAS FOLLOWED MY INSTRUCTIONS! NOW FOR THE REST OF MY PLAN!

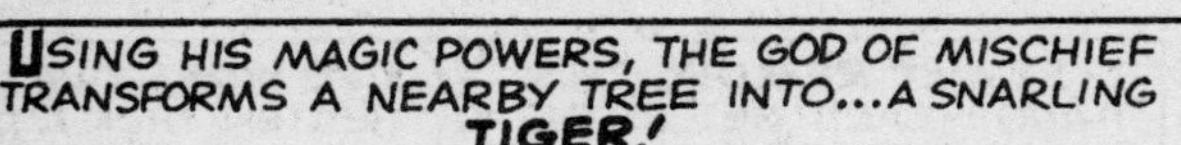
USING HIS MAGIC POWERS, THE GOD OF MISCHIEF TRANSFORMS A NEARBY TREE INTO...A SNARLING TIGER!

THEN, BEFORE THE ENCHANTED HAMMER CAN RETURN TO THOR...
BEHOLD! YOUR NURSE IS IN DIRE DANGER! SAVE HER... OR SEIZE YOUR HAMMER!! THERE IS TIME TO DO ONLY ONE! WHICH SHALL IT BE, THUNDER GOD?!!
JANE--!!

WITHOUT AN INSTANT'S HESITATION, THE MIGHTY IMMORTAL LEAPS TO THE GIRL'S DEFENSE...
HAH! I KNEW THAT WOULD BE YOUR CHOICE! FOOL!

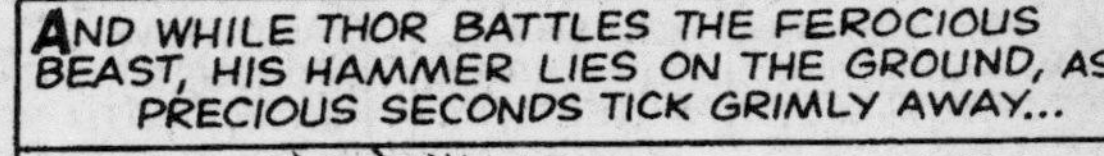
AND WHILE THOR BATTLES THE FEROCIOUS BEAST, HIS HAMMER LIES ON THE GROUND, AS PRECIOUS SECONDS TICK GRIMLY AWAY...

I'VE SLAIN THE TIGER! BUT THE HAMMER --IT'S BEEN OUT OF MY HAND FOR ALMOST SIXTY SECONDS! UNLESS I TOUCH IT AGAIN BEFORE THE MINUTE IS UP, I'LL LOSE THE POWER OF THOR!

TOO LATE! THE MINUTE HAS PASSED! I'M TURNING BACK TO MY NORMAL SELF!

THEN, BEFORE THE HUMAN DON BLAKE CAN REACH THE HAMMER, LOKI CREATES A MAGICAL FORCE FIELD AROUND IT...

I-I CAN'T REMOVE THIS THING--CAN'T GET TO THE HAMMER!!
I'VE WON! I'VE BEATEN THOR! AT LAST!

NO ONE--NOTHING--CAN PIERCE MY FORCE FIELD! THE HAMMER IS FOREVER BEYOND YOUR REACH!
YOU SHALL NEVER AGAIN POSSESS THE POWER OF THOR! THUS HAVE I DEFEATED YOU!

AND NOW, TO CELEBRATE MY CONQUEST, I SHALL HAVE SPORT WITH YOUR HELP-LESS PLANET!

FAREWELL!!
NO! COME BACK!!

HELPLESS TO STOP HIS EVIL FOE, DR. DON BLAKE TURNS TO HIS UNCONSCIOUS NURSE...

SHE ONLY FAINTED! LUCKY IT HAPPENED BEFORE I LOST THE POWER OF THOR! OTHERWISE, SHE, TOO, WOULD HAVE DISCOVERED MY DUAL IDENTITY!

DR. BLAKE! WHAT HAPPENED?? WHERE-- WHERE IS--THOR??
THOR IS GONE! EASY NOW, JANE, I'LL TAKE YOU HOME!

MEANWHILE, THE TRIUMPHANT LOKI BEGINS HIS RAMPAGE...

SO MANY MORTALS IN THE CITY! IT WILL BE AMUSING TO WATCH THEIR REACTIONS WHEN I TRANSFORM THEM INTO BLANK BEINGS!!

AND, AT A GESTURE FROM THE SINISTER LOKI...

CHARLIE-- WHERE ARE YOU??
WHAT'S HAPPENED TO US??!
WE--WE'RE TURNING INTO NOTHINGS!!

IT'S MADNESS! IMPOSSIBLE!
HELP!! SOMEONE HELP US!
HA! HA! LISTEN TO THE FOOLS PANIC! I'LL WAIT ANOTHER FEW MINUTES BEFORE I RETURN THEM TO NORMAL!

AGAIN ASSUMING THE FORM OF A BIRD, LOKI FLIES TO ANOTHER CITY...

THIS TIME I'LL TAMPER WITH NON-LIVING OBJECTS!

ONCE MORE, THE UNBELIEVABLE COMES TO PASS...
THE BUILDING-- ALL THE BRICK AND CEMENT--IT'S TURNING INTO C-CANDY!!
I DON'T BELIEVE IT! THERE'S NO SUCH THING AS A CAR MADE OF ICE CREAM!

THE SUN IS MELTING MY CONVERTIBLE!
HEY! STOP LICKING MY BICYCLE! SHOO!
PRICELESS! I HAVEN'T HAD THIS MUCH FUN IN CENTURIES!

AND SO THE GOD OF MISCHIEF AMUSES HIMSELF, WHILE THE GREATEST POWER IN THE UNIVERSE-- THE ONE POWER THAT CAN STOP HIM--LIES IMPRISONED WITHIN A MAGIC FORCE FIELD!

LOKI TRAVELS ON AND ON, SPANNING THE CONTINENT --WINGING NORTH TOWARD THE ARCTIC...UNTIL...
SOMETHING HAS FALLEN FROM THAT AIRCRAFT! IT IS A BOMB!

THIS WILL BE OUR GREATEST ATOMIC TEST!!
IT WILL BE THE MOST POWERFUL EXPLOSION IN HISTORY!
THE AMERICANS WILL TREMBLE WHEN THEY HEAR OF IT!
DA!

BUT, AS THE BOMB HURTLES DOWN, LOKI EXERCISES HIS MAGIC POWER UPON IT!

IT-IT WAS A DUD!
WE FAILED!! HOW CAN WE FACE NIKITA NOW?
PLINK!

AS LOKI CONTINUES HIS RAMPAGE, FEAR AND CONFUSION MOUNT...
BUT HE'S JUST AN ANCIENT MYTH! LOKI DOESN'T REALLY EXIST!
HE MAY NOT BE FOR REAL, BUT THE THINGS HE'S DOING CERTAINLY ARE!
HOW DO YOU DEFEAT A SUPER BEING?
THE ONLY WAY IS WITH ANOTHER SUPER BEING ---THOR!!

AND ELSEWHERE AT THAT MOMENT...
WHERE IS THOR?? WHY DOESN'T HE STOP LOKI, AS HE DID ONCE BEFORE??
PERHAPS HE WILL --SOMEHOW--

LOKI IS ONLY TOYING WITH MANKIND NOW... PLAYING FOOLISH, SENSELESS PRANKS! BUT SOON, HIS PRANKS MAY GROW MORE SERIOUS--MORE DEADLY!!
HE MUST BE DRIVEN FROM EARTH! AND YET, WITHOUT THE POWER OF MY ENCHANTED HAMMER, I AM COMPLETELY HELPLESS!

MEANWHILE, EARTHLY WEAPONS ARE BROUGHT INTO PLAY AGAINST THE MASTER OF MISCHIEF!
PREPARE TO FIRE!
FOOLS! YOU CANNOT MATCH THOSE TOYS AGAINST THE MAGIC OF LOKI!

FIRE!
MY RIFLE! IT'S SPROUTED WINGS!!
THE BAZOOKA'S FLYING AWAY!!
HA! HA! HA!

AND AT THAT VERY MOMENT, DON BLAKE GETS THE IDEA!
THAT'S THE ANSWER! IT'LL WORK! I'M CERTAIN OF IT!

THE NEXT DAY, THE DYNAMIC DOCTOR PUTS HIS DESPERATE PLAN INTO EFFECT...
EXTRA! THOR VOWS TO DEFEAT LOKI BEFORE END OF WEEK! EXTRA!
THOR??! BUT THAT'S IMPOSSIBLE! WITHOUT THE HAMMER, THAT PUNY DOCTOR CAN NEVER AGAIN BECOME THE THUNDER GOD!

AND THE HAMMER IS SURROUNDED BY MY IMPENETRABLE FORCE FIELD! NOTHING CAN GET THROUGH IT! YET, WHAT IF I AM WRONG? WHAT IF HE DISCOVERED A WAY??
I MUST FIND OUT AT ONCE!

AND SO, ONCE AGAIN LOKI FLIES TO THE SITE OF HIS BATTLE WITH THOR!
THE FORCE FIELD IS STILL THERE, AND-- NO!! IT ISN'T POSSIBLE--!!

WELCOME, LOKI!! I'VE BEEN EXPECTING YOU!
THOR!! YOU HAVE REGAINED YOUR HAMMER! BUT-- IT IS IMPOSSIBLE! YOU COULDN'T! I-I MUST REMOVE THE FORCE FIELD AND SEE!!

BUT, THE INSTANT LOKI REMOVES THE MAGIC BARRIER, A SLENDER FIGURE REACHES OUT, AND--
YOU-YOU'RE NOT THOR! IT IS ONLY A PLASTIC DUMMY!
RIGHT! I WAS HIDING BEHIND IT, WAITING FOR YOU TO REMOVE THE FORCE FIELD!

STOP!! DON'T TOUCH THAT HAMMER!!
YOU'RE TOO LATE, LOKI!

AT LAST THE POWER OF THOR SURGES THROUGHOUT MY BODY! ONCE AGAIN I HAVE BECOME--THE GOD OF THUNDER!!

YOU HAVEN'T WON YET! I SHALL ESCAPE AND DEVISE ANOTHER PLAN!
WHA--??

HE HAS TRANSFORMED HIMSELF INTO A PIGEON! BUT WHICH ONE IS HE???
I MUST NOT LET HIM ESCAPE ME AGAIN!

SUDDENLY, WITH SUPERHUMAN SPEED, THOR RACES ACROSS THE PARK!
THERE'S ONE WAY TO FIND OUT!

IF THERE'S ANYTHING PIGEONS LIKE, IT'S PEANUTS!
PEANUTS

THEY'RE ALL GATHERED AROUND THE PEANUTS...EXCEPT THAT ONE WHO HAS MORE IMPORTANT THINGS ON HIS MIND!
BLAST IT! THOR TRICKED ME INTO REVEALING MYSELF!

HE'S FLYING OFF! BUT HE WON'T GET FAR!

SORRY, GENTLEMEN! BUT RIGHT NOW I NEED THIS NET MORE THAN YOU DO!

THOR IS A FOOL IF HE THINKS HE CAN CATCH ME! I'LL LET HIM GET CLOSE, JUST TO FRUSTRATE HIM, THEN I'LL CHANGE INTO A ROCKET AND VANISH!

BUT, BEFORE LOKI CAN ACT...
A PERFECT CATCH!
THAT NET!! HOW--??

A MOMENT LATER, THE THUNDER GOD RETURNS TO EARTH WITH HIS CAPTIVE FOE...

BITTER IN DEFEAT, LOKI REVERTS TO HIS NATURAL FORM...
THEY LAUGH AT ME NOW... WHEN JUST HOURS AGO THE MERE MENTION OF MY NAME SENT A WAVE OF FEAR AROUND THE WORLD!

WHERE ARE YOU TAKING ME NOW? OH NO--NOT THERE! YOU CAN'T TAKE ME THERE!!
I MUST! YOU ARE TOO DANGEROUS TO REMAIN AMONG THE HELPLESS MORTALS OF EARTH!

LATER... AT THE PORTALS OF ASGARD, CITADEL OF THE IMMORTAL NORSE GODS...
I AM MOST PLEASED TO SEE MY FAVORITE SON AGAIN! BUT, AS FOR LOKI...
13

...I KNOW NOT WHAT TO DO WITH HIM! HE GROWS MORE WILY, MORE DANGEROUS, MORE UNCONTROLABLE EACH HOUR! WE MUST PRAY THAT THE WORLD WILL NEVER SEE THE DAY WHEN HIS POWER EXCEEDS THAT OF--THE MIGHTY THOR!!
THE END

IND.
12¢
JOURNEY INTO
MYSTERY
MC
APPROVED BY THE COMICS CODE AUTHORITY
89
FEB.
STARRING THE MIGHTY...
THOR!
THE MOST COLORFUL SUPER HERO OF ALL!!!
SEE THE HEROIC THUNDER GOD BATTLE THE FORCES OF EVIL!!

THE MIGHTY THOR!
The THUNDER-GOD AND THE THUG!
WHAT HAPPENS WHEN, AIDED BY GUNS AND GOONS, A MORTAL GANGSTER DARES TO DEFY A THUNDER-GOD!??
OUR STORY OPENS WITH THE MIGHTY GOD OF THUNDER STREAKING THRU THE SKY AFTER THE COMPLETION OF HIS MOST RECENT ADVENTURE...
IT IS TIME FOR ME TO RETURN TO MY OFFICE AND ONCE AGAIN TO ASSUME THE ROLE OF DON BLAKE, DOCTOR OF MEDICINE!
PLOT: STAN LEE
SCRIPT: L.D. LIEBER
ART: JACK KIRBY
INKING: DICK AYERS
LETTERING: RAY HOLLOWAY
... AND THE NEWSPAPER SAID THAT THOR FLEW AWAY BEFORE THE CROWD COULD EVEN THANK HIM!
WHAT A GUY! I'D SURE LIKE TO SEE HIM IN PERSON SOME DAY INSTEAD OF JUST READING ABOUT HIM!
X-29
LOOK! IT'S HIM—THOR!!
HE FLEW RIGHT PAST US!
OH, OH... THE PATIENTS IN MY WAITING ROOM HAVE SPOTTED ME!
IF THEY SEE ME ENTER THE OFFICE, THEY MIGHT SUSPECT THAT THOR AND DR. DON BLAKE ARE ONE AND THE SAME PERSON!
SO I'LL HAVE TO DIVERT THEIR ATTENTION!

SINCE NOBODY'S IN THE MANNEQUIN SHOP AT THIS HOUR, I'LL JUST USE SOME OF THEIR MATERIAL AND PAY THEM FOR IT LATER!

THERE! IT'S FINISHED! A SOMEWHAT CRUDE IMITATION OF ME, BUT IT'LL BE MOVING SO FAST THAT NO ONE WILL BE ABLE TO TELL IT ISN'T THE REAL THOR!

LIFTING THE DUMMY AS THOUGH IT WERE WEIGHTLESS, THE MIGHTY THUNDER-GOD HURLS IT THRU THE WINDOW...

HEY! IT'S THOR AGAIN!
HE'S FLYING AWAY!
THE DUMMY WILL COME DOWN OVER THE OPEN SEA, WHERE IT WON'T INJURE ANYONE!

AND WHILE THE UNSUSPECTING PATIENTS WATCH THE MANNEQUIN THRU *ONE* WINDOW, THOR HIMSELF ENTERS THRU *ANOTHER*...

WOW! LOOK AT HIM GO!
HE'S AS FAST AS A ROCKET!

IN THE PRIVACY OF HIS OFFICE, THE MIGHTIEST FIGURE TO STRIDE THE EARTH REVERTS BACK TO THE FORM OF

... THE LAME DOCTOR DONALD BLAKE!

SORRY TO KEEP YOU WAITING, JANE! YOU CAN SEND IN THE FIRST PATIENT NOW!
YES, DOCTOR!

BUT AT THIS POINT, LET US PAUSE BRIEFLY AND REVIEW THE FANTASTIC *ORIGIN* OF THOR, FOR THE BENEFIT OF THOSE READERS WHO MIGHT HAVE MISSED THE EARLIER ISSUES OF

JOURNEY INTO MYSTERY

MANY MONTHS AGO, VACATIONING IN NORWAY, DR. DON BLAKE FOUND AN ANCIENT CANE IN A HIDDEN CAVE...

IT MUST HAVE BEEN HIDDEN HERE FOR CENTURIES!!

AND, WHEN THE LAME PHYSICIAN ACCIDENTALLY POUNDED THE CANE AGAINST THE GROUND...

I'M BECOMING ***THOR,*** THE LEGENDARY THUNDER-GOD! AND THE CANE IS TURNING INTO A GIANT ***HAMMER!***

IT WAS AN INCREDIBLE MYTH COME TO LIFE! AND, LIKE IN THE MYTH, THE MIGHTY HAMMER COULD ONLY BE LIFTED BY THOR... AND WHEN IT WAS HURLED, IT WOULD ALWAYS RETURN TO ITS MASTER!

NOTHING CAN WITHSTAND THE ENCHANTED HAMMER! ***NOTHING!!***
POW

AIDED BY HIS POWERFUL WEAPON, THE GOD OF THUNDER COULD EVEN CONTROL THE VERY ELEMENTS THEMSELVES!

BY STAMPING THE HAMMER TWICE, I'VE CREATED A RAGING THUNDER STORM!

AND THEN, BENEATH THE WATCHFUL EYE OF ODIN, MASTER OF THE NORSE GODS AND FATHER OF THOR, A VOW WAS MADE...

I CARRY WITHIN THIS HAMMER THE GREATEST POWER EVER KNOWN TO MORTAL MAN! A POWER I SHALL NEVER USE, EXCEPT IN THE CAUSE OF JUSTICE AND AGAINST THE FORCES OF EVIL!

THUS WAS BORN THE MIGHTY THOR! BUT WHAT OF DON BLAKE, THE SECRET COUNTERPART OF THOR? ***HE*** IS A SUCCESSFUL PHYSICIAN, ALTHOUGH SOMEWHAT ***LESS*** SUCCESSFUL IN ANOTHER AREA...

I LOVE JANE, BUT I DAREN'T TELL HER! A GIRL SO BEAUTIFUL WOULD NEVER MARRY A-- A WEAKLING LIKE ME!

BUT, AS THE POET ROBERT BURNS ONCE SAID... "OH, FOR THE GIFT THE GIFTIE GIE' US... TO SEE OURSELVES AS OTHERS SEE US!"

I COULD CARE FOR HIM SO DEEPLY, IF ONLY HE WOULD SHOW SOME AFFECTION TOWARD ME!
BUT NO... NOT ***HIM!*** HE'S TOO DARN STUFFY TO EVER BE ROMANTIC!

AND SO, THINKING DON BLAKE HAS NO ROMANTIC INTEREST IN HER, HIS LOVELY NURSE FILLS HER LONELY HOURS WITH DAY-DREAMS!

OH... THAT THOR! WHAT A MAN! I'LL BET HE'D NOTICE A GAL WHO WAS RIGHT UNDER HIS NOSE!

"AND ALTHOUGH HE'S BIG AND STRONG, I'D LOVE TO LOOK AFTER HIM! HE'D COMPLAIN ABOUT MY FUSSING, BUT I KNOW THAT HE'D SECRETLY ENJOY IT..."

YOU NEEDN'T BOTHER...
NONSENSE! YOUR HAMMER WILL LOOK MORE IMPRESSIVE POLISHED!

I'D BE ASHAMED IF MY BOSS WERE SEEN IN PUBLIC WITH A WRINKLED CLOAK!
I NEVER GAVE IT A THOUGHT BEFORE!

YOU'LL FEEL LOTS COOLER DURING THE SUMMER WITH YOUR HAIR SHORTER!

I FEEL BETTER ALREADY!

BUT, LET US LEAVE JANE FOSTER TO HER DAY-DREAMS AND RETURN TO THE PRESENT ONCE MORE...

HEY, ISN'T THAT THUG THATCHER, THE MOB LEADER?
YEAH! HE TRIED TO MUSCLE IN ON THE STEEL INDUSTRY!
THEY CAUGHT HIM SELLING SUB-STANDARD STEEL! NOW HE'S HEADED FOR PRISON!

BUT THE OCTOPUS OF CRIME HAS MANY TENTACLES...
HERE COMES THE CAR! GET READY!
DON'T WORRY, WE'LL HAVE THE BOSS FREE IN NO TIME!

IT'S THATCHER'S MOB!

I KNEW MY BOYS WOULDN'T LET ME DOWN!

BAM

MEANWHILE, IN DON BLAKE'S OFFICE...

THAT'S THE LAST PATIENT! YOU MAY GO HOME NOW, JANE!

THAT NOISE OUTSIDE... SOUNDS LIKE GUNFIRE!

BANG BANG BANG

IT IS A GUN BATTLE! AND THE POLICE SEEM TO BE OUT-NUMBERED!
IF ONLY JANE WEREN'T HERE, I COULD CHANGE INTO THOR AND GO INTO ACTION! BUT NOW IT'S IMPOSSIBLE!
BANG!
BANG!

WE BLEW OUT THEIR TIRES! THEY WON'T BE ABLE TO FOLLOW US! LET'S GET BACK INTO THE TRUCK!
UHHH--MY SHOULDER!

HURRY--HEAD FOR OUR HIDEOUT!
THE BOSS HAS BEEN HIT!
GOOD THING WE STAYED OUTA THE ACTION! WE GOTTA FETCH HIM A SAWBONES!

WE'RE IN LUCK! LOOK! A DOCTOR RIGHT IN THIS BUILDING!
H. SYKES
DON BLAKE M.D.

MOMENTS LATER...
THE MOBSTERS ESCAPED!
IT DOESN'T MATTER... THE POLICE WILL TRACK THEM DOWN! AT ANY RATE, THERE'S NOTHING YOU OR I CAN DO ABOUT IT!
BUT THOR WOULD HAVE DONE PLENTY IF YOU HADN'T BEEN HERE!

SUDDENLY...
YOU'RE COMIN' WITH US, DOC!
TIE UP THE DAME, VINCE!

STOP! LET ME GO! DR. BLAKE-- HELP ME!
GET A LOAD OF HER, MAX! SHE EXPECTS HELP FROM THAT SKINNY SAWBONES!
SOME CHANCE!
ONE STAMP OF THE CANE-- THAT'S ALL IT WOULD TAKE-- BUT THEN THEY'D LEARN MY DUAL IDENTITY! I CAN'T DO IT YET!
SNAP

LEAVING JANE LOCKED IN THE OFFICE, THE GANGSTERS DRIVE DON BLAKE OUT OF THE CITY...

WHERE ARE YOU TAKING ME?

TO SUNDAY SCHOOL! HA! HA! HA!

SOON, THEY REACH THUG THATCHER'S HIDEOUT!

WE SAW YA GET HIT, BOSS! WE BROUGHT A SAWBONES!

GOOD! I KNEW I COULD COUNT ON YOU!

THUG'S IN BAD PAIN! YOU MUST FIX HIM UP, DOC! PLEASE...
KNOCK IT OFF, RUBY! I DON'T NEED MY GIRL BEGGIN' FOR ME!
I'LL TREAT YOU--NOT BECAUSE OF YOUR THREATS--BUT BECAUSE IT'S MY DUTY AS A PHYSICIAN!

OKAY, BIG MOUTH--GET TO WORK!
I'LL HOLD THAT CANE OF YOURS, DOC! YOU'LL NEED BOTH HANDS TO TAKE THE SLUG OUT!
MY CANE! BUT...NO TIME TO WORRY ABOUT IT NOW!

I MUST REMOVE THE BULLET AND CLEANSE THE WOUND BEFORE GANGRENE SETS IN!
HURRY, DOCTOR!
REAX, BABY--EVERYTHING'S GONNA BE FINE!

FINALLY...
THERE, IT'S FINISHED! NOW ALL YOU HAVE TO WORRY ABOUT IS THE POLICE!
WELL, IF THEY CATCH ME, IT'S GONNA BE WITHOUT YOUR HELP!
TAKE CARE OF THE GOOD DOCTOR, BOYS!
NO, THUG! YOU CAN'T HARM HIM!! NOT AFTER HE SAVED YOUR LIFE!

YOU'RE WRONG, RUBY! I CAN'T RISK ANYONE SQUEALIN' TO THE COPS!
DON'T WORRY, BOSS--I'LL MAKE SURE HE WON'T TALK!
MY CANE--WITHOUT IT I'M HELPLESS!

BUT WAIT--EVEN THOUGH I HAVEN'T THE BODY OF THOR, I STILL HAVE HIS BRAIN--HIS THOUGHT PROCESSES!
IF I CONCENTRATE INTENSELY, PERHAPS I CAN ESTABLISH MENTAL CONTACT WITH--ODIN!

DESPERATELY, THE DOOMED DOCTOR FOCUSES HIS THOUGHTS --AND SENDS HIS PLEA UPWARDS, BEYOND EARTH, ACROSS THE RAINBOW BRIDGE TO THE CITADAL OF THE NORSE GODS...

...WHERE IT IS RECEIVED BY THE ALL-POWERFUL RULER OF THE NORSE GODS...THE NOBLE ODIN!
MY SON, THE LORD OF THUNDER, IS IN DANGER! HE CALLS FOR HELP! I MUST RESPOND AT ONCE!

USING HIS SUPREME POWER, ODIN CREATES FIRE AND LIGHTNING...

I HAVE BUT TO FUSE THESE ELEMENTS WITHIN MY BODY TO TRANSFORM THEM INTO A FORCE WAVE!

THEN, THE MIGHTY ODIN WILLS THE FORCE WAVE TO EARTH, WHERE IT STRIKES ITS HUMAN TARGET, SHOCKING HIM INTO DROPPING THE CANE, AS THOUGH IT WERE A RED HOT POKER!

YEEOWW--
ODIN HAS HEARD MY PLEA!! I'M SAVED!

AT LAST!! I'VE GOT MY CANE!
ALL OF A SUDDEN, I FELT A SUDDEN SHOCK!
HEY! WHAT'S THE DOC DOIN'?

STRIKING THE FLOOR WITH ALL HIS MIGHT, THE ONCE-PUNY DOCTOR AGAIN UNDERGOES THE WORLD'S MOST AWESOME TRANSFORMATION!

IF I'M LUCKY, THE FLASH WILL BE TOO BRIGHT FOR THEM TO SEE ME CHANGE!
WHA--?? WHAT'S HAPPENIN'?!

LOOK! IT'S-- IT'S THOR!!
WHERE'D THE DOC GO?
GOT TO MAKE UP AN EXCUSE FAST!!
GOOD THING I WAS PASSING BY AN SAW THIS LITTLE SCENE! I'VE TOSSED YOUR INTENDED VICTIM TO SAFETY! AND NOW I'LL DEAL WITH YOU!

AS THE MOBSTERS DRAW THEIR WEAPONS, THOR THUNDERS INTO ACTION... AS ONLY HE CAN!

LOOK OUT!
HELP!!!
BOSS-- STOP 'IM!!

THUG, IT'S USELESS! NOBODY CAN DEFEAT THOR!
YEAH? WE'LL SEE ABOUT THAT! GET HIM, BOYS!
ALRIGHT, STRONG-MAN, WE KNOW YA CAN DISH IT OUT! NOW LET'S SEE HOW YA TAKE IT!

BUT THE GUNMEN ARE NOT DESTINED TO FIND OUT... FOR BEFORE THEY CAN FIRE, THE MIGHTY THOR EXHALES WITH THE POWER OF A HURRICANE...
WOOOSH!

HEY, STOP! LEMME OUTA HERE!
I CAN'T SEE! WHAT'S GOIN' ON?
I'LL JUST TIE YOU ALL IN A NICE, COSY BUNDLE...

...AND PUT YOU OUT THERE ON THE SHELF!

MAN, OR LEGEND--- WHATEVER THAT GUY IS, HE'S TOO MUCH FOR US!
YOU AIN'T KIDDIN'! LET'S HEAD FOR THE HILLS!
IF THEY THINK THEY CAN ESCAPE...

...THEN THEY HAVEN'T RECKONED WITH THE ENCHANTED HAMMER OF THOR!

THE TREES ARE BLOCKING THE ROAD! WE CAN'T GO FORWARD!
WE CAN'T GO BACK EITHER!
THE DOORS ARE JAMMED! WE CAN'T EVEN GET OUT OF THE CAR! WE'RE TRAPPED!

BUT IN ALL THE EXCITEMENT, TWO PEOPLE HAVE MANAGED TO ESCAPE...

I SHOULDN'T BE HELPING YOU! I SHOULD HAVE LEFT YOU BACK THERE WITH THE REST OF THE MOB! BUT I COULDN'T! I LOVE YOU TOO MUCH!
YEAH--AND THAT'S WHY YOU'LL ALWAYS STICK BY ME, NO MATTER WHAT! NOW BE QUIET--I GOTTA THINK!

BUT THOR WILL CATCH UP TO YOU SOONER OR LATER, AND THEN...
DON'T BE TOO SURE! I REMEMBER READIN' THAT THOR AND THAT CREEP DR. BLAKE ALWAYS SEEM TO BE IN THE SAME PLACE AT ABOUT THE SAME TIME!

I FIGGER THERE'S SOME KINDA BOND BETWEEN THEM! SO, IF I TAKE THE DOC HOSTAGE, I MAY BE ABLE TO KEEP HIS BUDDY OFF MY BACK!

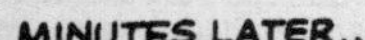
MINUTES LATER...

THE MOBSTERS ARE IN CUSTODY! NOTHING MORE FOR ME TO DO HERE! I'LL GO BACK TO MY OFFICE AND FREE JANE! THEN I'LL TRY TO TRACK DOWN THUG THATCHER!

FINDING ONE LONE GANGSTER SHOULDN'T BE TOO DIFFICULT FOR THOR!

BUT WHEN THE THUNDER-GOD REACHES THE OFFICE...
TOO BAD YOUR PUNY BOSS AIN'T HERE! THAT MEANS YOU'LL HAVTA BE MY HOSTAGE!
NO--LET ME GO--
THUG, LOOK!! IT'S THOR!!

ALRIGHT, BIG MAN!--DROP THE HAMMER, OR I SHOOT!! GO ON... DO WHAT I SAY! I'M NOT FOOLIN' AROUND!
I--I CAN'T LET HIM HARM JANE...

THAT'S IT! FROM WHAT I READ, MOST OF YOUR POWER COMES FROM THAT BLAMED HAMMER! WITHOUT IT, YOU MAY NOT BE SO TOUGH TO HANDLE!
HE'S SACRIFICING HIMSELF TO SAVE ME! BUT WHY? HE DOESN'T EVEN KNOW ME?!!
9

WHEN THE HAMMER IS OUT OF MY HANDS FOR SIXTY SECONDS, I'LL BECOME DON BLAKE AGAIN! I'VE GOT TO ACT BEFORE THEN, WHILE I'M STILL THOR! BUT WHAT CAN I *DO??*

AS THE PRECIOUS SECONDS TICK RAPIDLY AWAY, AN IDEA SUDDENLY COMES TO THOR! USING HIS SUPER-DEVELOPED VOCAL CORDS, HE THROWS HIS VOICE ACROSS THE ROOM...

DROP THE GUN, THATCHER! WE HAVE YOU COVERED!

AND, AS THE STARTLED MOBSTER TURNS AROUND...

WHO--WHO *SAID* THAT??
HIS GUN ISN'T TRAINED ON JANE! THIS IS THE MOMENT TO ACT!

GUIDED UNERRINGLY BY THOR'S KICK, THE HAMMER KNOCKS THE GUN FROM THATCHER'S HAND...

...AND RETURNS TO ITS MASTER!

THE POWER OF THE HAMMER IS AGAIN MINE!

HE'S REACHING FOR THE GUN AGAIN!

THE FIRST THING I MUST DO IS GET JANE TO A SAFE PLACE!

AND THE THUNDER-GOD SPINS HIS MAGIC MALLET SO FAST, THAT IT CREATES A MIGHTY UPDRAFT...

OHH--

BLAST IT! THEY'RE MOVIN' TOO FAST! I CAN'T GET A BEAD ON 'EM!
DO NOT BE AFRAID, JANE!
BANG!
I *COULDN'T* BE-- WITH *YOU* HERE!
BANG!
BANG!

HOLY HANNAH! THERE'S A WOMAN *FLOATING IN THE AIR!*
AND THAT CLOAKED FIGURE FLYING UP AFTER HER-- IT'S *THOR!!*

THERE! YOU'LL BE SAFE NOW!
OH-- THOR!!

I HAD TO GET YOU AWAY FROM THATCHER, AND THIS WAS THE QUICKEST WAY TO DO IT!
IS THERE NOTHING YOU CANNOT DO, THOR?

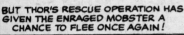

BUT THOR'S RESCUE OPERATION HAS GIVEN THE ENRAGED MOBSTER A CHANCE TO FLEE ONCE AGAIN!

IT'S USELESS! THOR HAS SEEN US! HE'S COMING AFTER US AGAIN!
HE WON'T GET ME! NOT WHILE I'M STILL PACKIN' A ROD!

THUG! YOU CAN'T ESCAPE! COME BACK! GIVE YOURSELF UP-- TAKE YOUR MEDICINE! I'LL WAIT FOR YOU... I SWEAR IT!
SHUDDUP, RUBY! GET LOST!

PLEASE... DO IT FOR ME! (SOB!) I--I LOVE YOU!
YA DUMB DAME! YOU'RE NUTHIN' BUT A MILLSTONE AROUND MY NECK!

LOOK OUT, RUBY!
BANG! BANG!
BANG!

ARE YOU ALL RIGHT??
Y-YES... HE... HE MISSED...
THE CRAZY FOOL MIGHT HAVE HIT THE GIRL!
WHO IS THAT MAN, ANY-WAY?
I RECOG-NIZE HIM FROM THE NEWS-PAPERS! IT'S THUG THATCHER!
11

THATCHER THE MOBSTER?
YEAH! HE WAS MUSCLING IN ON THE STEEL INDUSTRY-- SELLING SUB-STANDARD STEEL!
HE ESCAPED FROM THE COPS ON THE WAY TO PRISON!
BUT NOW HIS CRIME CAREER HAS COME TO AN END! I VOW IT!

THOR STAMPS THE ENCHANTED HAMMER ON THE GROUND FOUR TIMES* AND THEN AIMS IT UPWARD...
THE MALLET IS SHOOTING OUT LIGHTNING BOLTS!
THEY'RE HITTING THE CABLES OF THE ELEVATOR! MELTING 'EM!

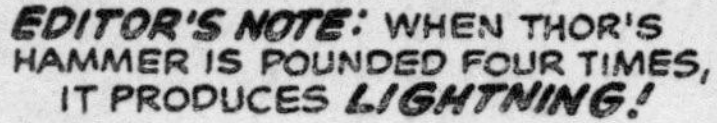
EDITOR'S NOTE: WHEN THOR'S HAMMER IS POUNDED FOUR TIMES, IT PRODUCES LIGHTNING!

YOU WON'T FIND SAFETY ON THE GIRDERS, THATCHER! I CAN MELT THEM TOO! YOU'D BETTER SURRENDER WHILE YOU STILL CAN!
YOU CAN'T SCARE ME, THOR!

ALL RIGHT THEN... WE'LL DO IT THE HARD WAY!
HE'S HITTING THE GIRDERS WITH LIGHTNING!
THEY'RE BEGINNING TO MELT!

BUT SUDDENLY, THE FUGITIVE SEES...
RIVETS! THEY'RE RED HOT!! THAT'S MY OUT! I'M GONNA WIN AFTER ALL!! HA! HA! HA!

THOR-- HEAR ME! THIS BUCKET IS FILLED WITH HOT RIVETS! UNLESS YOU LET ME GO FREE AND KEEP ME SAFE FROM THE COPS, I'LL DUMP 'EM ON THE CROWD!
HE MEANS IT! LET'S GET OUT OF HERE!
NO! IF HE SEES US RUN, HE'LL DROP THE RIVETS! WE COULD NEVER GET AWAY IN TIME!

I CAN'T LET HIM ESCAPE! BUT I CAN'T ALLOW THESE INNOCENT PEOPLE TO BE HARMED! WHAT WILL I-- WAIT-- I SEE IT!! THAT'S THE ANSWER!
ALL RIGHT, THATCHER-- I PROMISE NOT TO TRY TO CAPTURE YOU!

I'VE WON! I'M FREE! WHA-- WHAT'S HAPPENING TO THE GIRDER??! OH, NO-- NO-- IT'S COLLAPSING!!

I'M FALLING! AIIIEEE---
I VOWED NOT TO TRY TO CAPTURE YOU... BUT I MAY ATTEMPT TO SAVE YOU!

AND THUS DOES A CAREER IN VIOLENCE COME TO ITS END.
HOLD HIM! DON'T LET HIM FALL!! DON'T LET HIM FALL!! I--I STILL LOVE HIM ≥SOB≤! I CAN'T HELP MYSELF!
DON'T WORRY, LADY-- THOR'S GOT HIM! BUT A CRUMB LIKE THAT SURE DON'T DESERVE ANYONE AS LOYAL AS YOU!
THOR SAVED HIS LIFE--BUT HE'LL BE SPENDING MOST OF IT BEHIND BARS!

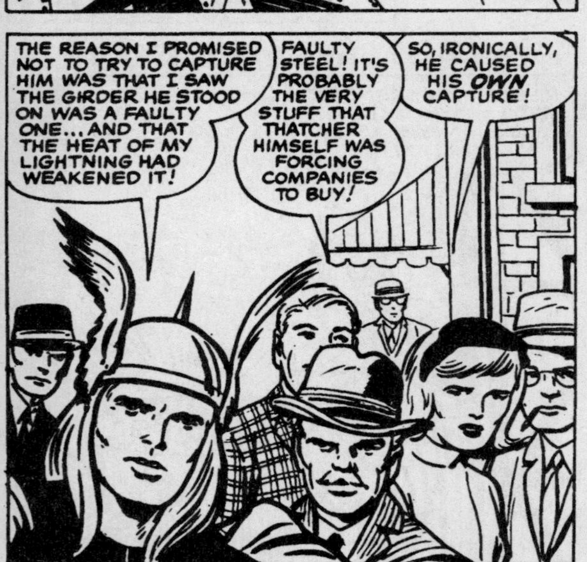

THE REASON I PROMISED NOT TO TRY TO CAPTURE HIM WAS THAT I SAW THE GIRDER HE STOOD ON WAS A FAULTY ONE... AND THAT THE HEAT OF MY LIGHTNING HAD WEAKENED IT!
FAULTY STEEL! IT'S PROBABLY THE VERY STUFF THAT THATCHER HIMSELF WAS FORCING COMPANIES TO BUY!
SO, IRONICALLY, HE CAUSED HIS OWN CAPTURE!

THEN THOR LIFTS HIS GAZE UPWARD, SILENTLY ASKING ODIN, THE LORD OF ASGARD, FOR ONE MORE BOON...

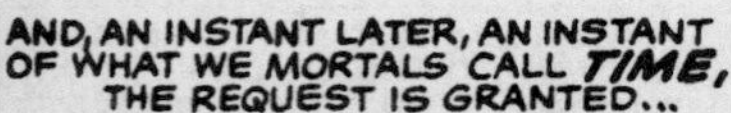

AND, AN INSTANT LATER, AN INSTANT OF WHAT WE MORTALS CALL TIME, THE REQUEST IS GRANTED...

THE MEMORY OF THUG THATCHER IS FOREVER REMOVED FROM HER MIND! SHE IS FREE OF HER TRAGIC LOVE! FREE TO FIND ONE WHO WILL BE WORTHY OF HER!
13

AS FOR ME, MY WORK HERE IS FINISHED! I MUST RETURN TO MY OTHER LIFE... AND TO THE GIRL WHO HOLDS MY HEART... ALTHOUGH I'D NEVER DARE ADMIT IT!

NEXT ISSUE: THOR BATTLES A FOE WHOSE POWERS SEEM TO BE GREATER THAN THOSE OF THE THUNDER-GOD HIMSELF!! DON'T MISS THOR AS HE FACES:

"THE CARBON-COPY MAN!"

The End

IND.
12¢
JOURNEY INTO
MYSTERY
APPROVED BY THE COMICS CODE AUTHORITY
MC
90
MAR.
Starring THE MIGHTY THOR
--BATTLING THE SUPER-CREATURE FROM SPACE... THE CARBON COPY MAN!
IN ANOTHER SECOND YOU WILL BE ETERNALLY TRAPPED IN A BLOCK OF UNBREAKABLE ICE! THIS IS THE END OF MIGHTY THOR!

THE MIGHTY THOR! "TRAPPED BY THE CARBON-COPY MAN!"

I CAN'T BUDGE! I'M FROZEN SOLID! AND THE ICE-GIANT IS COMING NEARER... *NEARER*...

·*PLOT* —— STAN LEE
·*SCRIPT* —— LARRY LIEBER
·*ART* —— AL HARTLEY
·*LETTERING* — TERRY SZENICS

FAR BEYOND OUR GALAXY IS THE WARLIKE PLANET XARTA...
OUR MIGHTY WAR LORD APPROACHES
WITH HIS SON AT HIS SIDE!
THIS IS A PROUD MOMENT FOR OLD UGARTH!
X-70

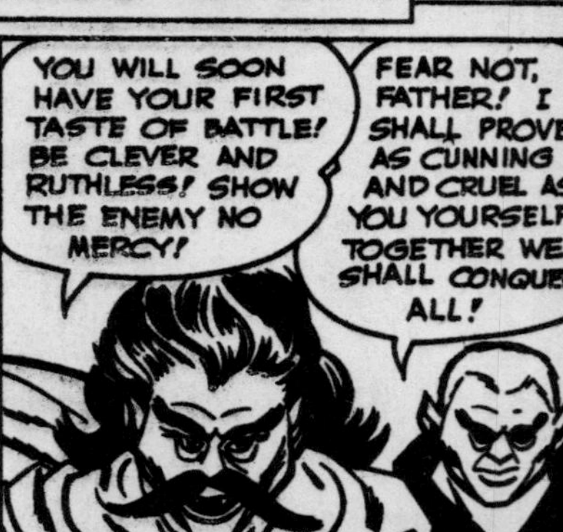

YOU WILL SOON HAVE YOUR FIRST TASTE OF BATTLE! BE CLEVER AND RUTHLESS! SHOW THE ENEMY NO MERCY!
FEAR NOT, FATHER! I SHALL PROVE AS CUNNING AND CRUEL AS YOU YOURSELF. TOGETHER WE SHALL CONQUER ALL!

THIS CAMPAIGN WILL BE MY LAST! AFTER THIS CONQUEST, I RETIRE! THEN YOU, MY SON ZANO, WILL BE WAR LORD OF XARTA!
I SHALL PROVE A WORTHY SUCCESSOR, FATHER!

SUPPOSE UGARTH AND ZANO DO NOT LEAD US TO VICTORY? SUPPOSE WE ARE DEFEATED?!
NONSENSE! DO WE XARTANS NOT POSSESS THE GREAT POWER??
THE GREAT POWER HAS NEVER FAILED US BEFORE! IT WILL NOT FAIL US NOW!

THE SCENE IS SOMETIME LATER, ON OUR OWN PLANET, WHERE WE FIND DR. DON BLAKE IN A TROUBLED STATE.
OTHER MEN REVEAL THEIR FEELINGS! WHY DON'T I? WHY DON'T I JUST UP AND TELL JANE THAT I LOVE HER?? WHAT AM I AFRAID OF??

BLAST IT!! AM I A MAN OR A MOUSE?!!
THUMP

I, WHO POSSESS THE GREATEST STRENGTH ON EARTH... WHO WOULD BATTLE ENTIRE ARMIES... WHO WOULD DEFY THE HEAVENS THEMSELVES! I FEAR NOTHING! ...NOTHING!!
ONE BLOW OF HIS ENCHANTED CANE TRANSFORMS THE PUNY DOCTOR INTO THE MIGHTIEST CREATURE IN ALL THIS UNIVERSE... THOR, THE THUNDERGOD!

NOTHING... EXCEPT THE MOCKING LAUGTER OF A BEAUTIFUL WOMAN, UPON LEARNING THAT A FRAIL, TIMID DOCTOR IS HOPELESSLY IN LOVE WITH HER!

WELL I'M NOT JUST A FEARFUL HUMAN! I'M ALSO THE MIGHTY THOR!! AND TOMORROW, I SHALL TELL JANE THE TRUTH ABOUT BOTH MY IDENTITY, AND MY LOVE!
2

AND SO, THE FOLLOWING MORNING...
JANE, I MUST SPEAK WITH YOU! I'VE SOMETHING IMPORTANT TO SAY...
YES, DR. BLAKE?

BUT SUDDENLY, THERE'S A LOUD THUNDERCLAP...
CAAARRRAACK

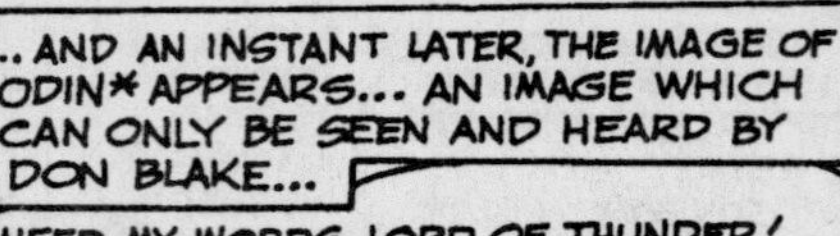

...AND AN INSTANT LATER, THE IMAGE OF ODIN* APPEARS... AN IMAGE WHICH CAN ONLY BE SEEN AND HEARD BY DON BLAKE...

HEED MY WORDS, LORD OF THUNDER! YOU ARE BOUND *NEVER* TO REVEAL YOUR IDENTITY TO ANY OTHER MORTAL! I HAVE SPOKEN!

**EDITORS NOTE:* ODIN IS MONARCH OF THE NORSE GODS AND FATHER OF THOR!!

WHAT'S THE MATTER? YOU LOOK PALE! DID THE THUNDER FRIGHTEN YOU?
NO, I'M ALL RIGHT! UH... WHAT I WANTED TO TELL YOU... IT WAS REALLY NOTHING IMPORTANT... FORGET IT!
I'M DUE AT CENTER HOSPITAL NOW! I'LL BE WORKING IN THE CHARITY WARD TILL THE AFTERNOON!
ALAS, THAT I SHOULD BE FORBIDDEN TO REVEAL THE TRUTH! IT MUST FOREVER BE KEPT HIDDEN FROM THE WOMAN I LOVE!
I'LL BET THE THUNDER *DID* FRIGHTEN HIM! THE POOR SOUL! IF ONLY HE WEREN'T SO TIMID! IF ONLY HE WERE LIKE... BUT WHAT AM I THINKING... THERE'S *NO ONE* AS BRAVE AS MY *IDOL* THOR!

BUT MINUTES LATER, THE DOCTOR'S ANGUISH IS FORGOTTEN, AS HE COMES UPON A STARTLING SIGHT...
WHAT *IS* THIS... SOME KIND OF GAG??
BUT I DON'T *WANT* TO WALK IN THE GUTTER!
SORRY, BUDDY, IT'S THE COMMISSIONER'S ORDERS! HE SAYS CAR OWNERS ARE RICHER AND MORE IMPORTANT THAN PEDESTRIANS! SO *THEY* GET TO USE THE SIDEWALK!
BUS

FROM NOW ON, ALL PEDESTRIANS WILL HAVE TO FOOT IT IN THE GUTTER!
THIS IS *OUTRAGEOUS!*
I WON'T *STAND* FOR IT! I'LL SUE THE CITY!
BUS STOP

AS HE LIMPS ALONG, DON BLAKE *SEES OTHER* STRANGE, UNBELIEVABLE EVENTS OCCURING THROUGHOUT THE CITY...

HEY!! YOU GUYS ARE SUPPOSED TO PASTE THAT ON THE *BILLBOARD*, NOT ON THIS SIDE OF OUR *BUILDING!!*

SORRY, MAC! WE GOT OUR ORDERS!

A BRIDGE PAINTED WITH POLKA DOTS! IT'S *NUTTY!*

PUFFIE CIGARE

DRUGS

THIS IS "TRUST PEOPLE WEEK"! LOCKED DOORS AREN'T ALLOWED!

AND THAT AFTERNOON, WHEN THE DOCTOR RETURNS TO HIS OFFICE...

A SUMMONS... FOR TREATING CHARITY PATIENTS! IT SAYS ITS AGAINST THE LAW!

THE PEOPLE DOWN AT CITY HALL MUST HAVE LOST THEIR SENSES!

NO! THEY ARE PERFECTLY *RIGHT!!*

WHAT?!! YOU, TOO?

YOU HAVE NO BUSINESS TREATING PEOPLE WITHOUT CHARGE! IF THEY'RE TOO POOR TO PAY, YOU SHOULD LET THEM *REMAIN* SICK! THEY *DESERVE* TO BE ILL!

I REFUSE TO WORK FOR A SOFT-HEARTED FOOL! ESPECIALLY WHEN HE'S A QUACK WHO DOESN'T KNOW THE FIRST THING ABOUT MEDICINE! *GOOD-BYE!!*

JANE, WHAT ARE YOU SAYING?!! *JANE!!!*

HAS THE WHOLE CITY GONE MAD...OR IS IT SOMETHING MORE SINISTER?!... *MAYOR HARRIS!!* IF ANYONE WOULD HAVE THE ANSWER, *HE* WOULD!

HE AND I ARE GOOD FRIENDS! TOGETHER, WE MAY BE ABLE TO LEARN WHAT IS MAKING EVERYONE ACT INSANE!

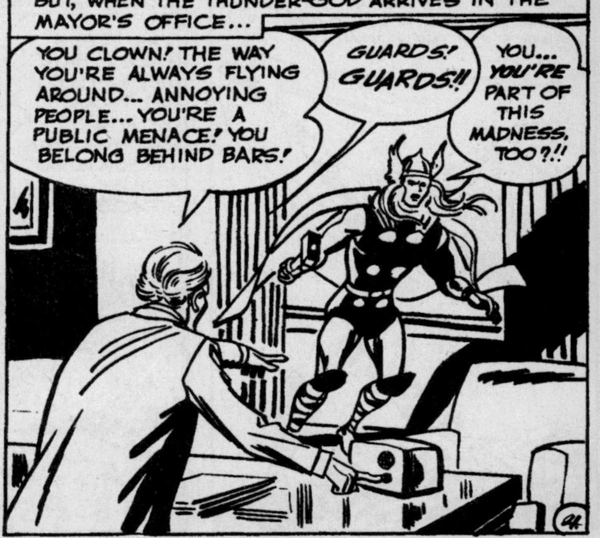

BUT, WHEN THE THUNDER-GOD ARRIVES IN THE MAYOR'S OFFICE...
YOU CLOWN! THE WAY YOU'RE ALWAYS FLYING AROUND... ANNOYING PEOPLE... YOU'RE A PUBLIC MENACE! YOU BELONG BEHIND BARS!
GUARDS! GUARDS!!
YOU... YOU'RE PART OF THIS MADNESS, TOO?!!

ARREST THAT COSTUMED PEST! HURRY! ARREST HIM!!
SORRY--- BUT I HAVE OTHER PLANS!
HIS HAMMER IS EVERYWHERE AT ONCE! ---CAN'T GET NEAR HIM!

HE'S HURLED THE MALLET OUT THE WINDOW! HE'S ESCAPING!
HE'S MOVING SO FAST I CAN'T GET A BEAD ON HIM!

LATER, ON THE OUTSKIRTS OF THE CITY...
I'LL REST AWHILE AND TRY TO FIND THE ANSWER TO A CITY GONE MAD!
I HAVE AN IDEA... I'LL SEND MY MIND BACK IN TIME AND SPACE, TO ASGARD* ON A DAY WHEN ODIN COUNSELED HIS SONS!
* EDITOR'S NOTE: ASGARD IS THE CITADEL OF THE NORSE GODS!

AND, USING THE POWER OF THE ENCHANTED HAMMER, THOR CONJURES UP A LONG FORGOTTEN EVENT...

WHEN SOMETHING PUZZLES YOU, ALWAYS SEEK THE SIMPLEST, MOST OBVIOUS EXPLANATION ...NO MATTER HOW IMPOSSIBLE IT MAY SEEM!

FOR, REMEMBER... NOTHING IS TRULY IMPOSSIBLE.

THE SIMPLEST, MOST OBVIOUS EXPLANATION! IF PEOPLE ARE NOT ACTING LIKE THEMSELVES, THEN THEY MUST NOT BE THEMSELVES! THEY MUST BE IMPOSTERS!!
BUT WHO ARE THE IMPOSTORS??? WHY ARE THEY DOING IT?? AND HOW??

ONLY ONE WAY TO FIND OUT! I MUST MAKE A THOROUGH SEARCH OF THE CITY!

LATER, AS TWILIGHT FALLS...
THE TREES BELOW HAVE BEEN FELLED, AS THOUGH BY A HUGE SCYTHE... OR A LARGE AIRCRAFT.. PERHAPS--- A SPACESHIP!!

I WAS RIGHT! THERE IT IS ... HALF HIDDEN FROM VIEW!

IT'S MADE OF A METAL NOT FOUND ON EARTH! IT MIGHT EVEN BE FROM ANOTHER GALAXY!
BUT I SEE NO DOOR TO THE SHIP! IT MUST BE HIDDEN!

I'LL JUST LAY DOWN MY HAMMER FOR A FEW SECONDS, WHILE I FEEL ALONG THE HULL TO LOCATE THE DOOR!

THEN, SUDDENLY...
THERE'S SOME KIND OF MAGNETIC FORCE HOLDING ME FAST TO THE HULL! I CANNOT PULL AWAY!
BUT I MUST GET FREE WITHIN A MINUTE! I MUST... OR I'LL LOSE THE POWER OF THOR*!!
*EDITOR'S NOTE: IF THE ENCHANTED MALLET IS OUT OF THOR'S HAND FOR SIXTY SECONDS, HE AUTOMATICALLY CHANGES BACK TO DON BLAKE!

BUT, THE STRANGE MAGNETIC FORCE IS TOO POWERFUL FOR EVEN THE MIGHTY THOR...AND, AS SOON AS THE FATEFUL MINUTE HAS PASSED...
I'M REVERTING BACK TO MY NORMAL FORM!

SO! THE ION-MAGNET HAS CAPTURED ANOTHER HUMAN!
TURN OFF THE CURRENT! I WILL BRING THIS PUNY EARTHLING TO UGARTH!

DR. BLAKE! THEY'VE CAPTURED YOU, TOO!
JANE! MAYOR HARRIS! THEN I WAS RIGHT! THE OTHERS WERE IMPOSTERS!
YES, WE XARTANS HAVE A GREAT POWER...

... THE POWER TO IMPERSONATE ANYONE! BEHOLD!!
HE ... HE'S CHANGING!

HE'S ASSUMING *MY* FEATURES!

NOTICE HOW SWIFTLY AND EFFORTLESSLY HE CHANGES!

HE'S A PERFECT *DUPLICATE* OF ME! BUT *WHY?* WHAT'S *BEHIND* IT ALL?

REGAIN YOUR NORMAL FORM AND THEN *TELL* HIM, MY SON!

WE ARE PLANTING IMPERSONATORS IN KEY JOBS THROUGHOUT THE CITY! THEIR TASK IS TO MAKE FOOLISH LAWS...TO CAUSE CONFUSION AND PANIC! THEN, ONCE THEY THROW YOUR CITY INTO CHAOS...

... THE *REST* OF OUR WAITING ARMADA WILL LAND AND REPEAT THE SAME DISRUPTIVE PROCESS IN EVERY CORNER ON EARTH!

AND AFTER WE HAVE CONFUSED AND FRIGHTENED YOUR ENTIRE CIVILIZATION, THEN WE SHALL ATTACK AND CONQUER YOU!

YOU'LL *NEVER* CONQUER EARTH... NOT WHILE THE MIGHTY THOR LIVES!

HE'LL SAVE US! *HE'LL* DEFEAT YOUR ENTIRE RUTHLESS ARMY!

WHAT!! ONE MERE HUMAN WILL BEAT *US?* YOU SPEAK LIKE *MADMEN!*

NO! THEY SPEAK THE *TRUTH!*

LOOK! IF YOU GRANT ME MY FREEDOM, I SHALL *LEAD YOU* TO THOR! PERHAPS YOU CAN CATCH HIM OFF GUARD AND CAPTURE HIM!

VERY WELL, IT SHALL BE *YOUR* FREEDOM FOR THIS *THOR'S!*

NO, DR. BLAKE! DON'T DO IT!

THE COWARDLY TRAITOR! HE'S SELLING OUT MANKIND'S ONLY HOPE, JUST TO SAVE HIS OWN SKIN!

I LAST SAW THOR JUST BEYOND THOSE TREES!

COME, ZANO -- LET US ENCOUNTER THIS SO-POWERFUL EARTHLING!

HAH! HE WILL SOON BE OUR HELPLESS PRISONER!

NOW IS MY CHANCE... WHILE THEY'RE ALL LOOKING THE OTHER WAY!
AND, AS DESPERATE FINGERS CLUTCH THE ENCHANTED HAMMER, THERE IS A TREMENDOUS LIGHTNING FLASH, TURNING THE LAME HUMAN INTO THE INVINCIBLE GOD OF THUNDER!
LOOK! AN EARTHLING IN STRANGE GARB!
SPEAK! WHO ARE YOU?
I AM THE ONE YOU SEEK! I AM... THOR!
SO, THAT IS THEIR CHAMPION. EH! LET ME BATTLE HIM ALONE, FATHER! I SHALL PROVE MY METTLE! I SHALL HAND HIM OVER TO YOU AS A HELPLESS CAPTIVE, WHIMPERING FOR HIS LIFE!
WELL SAID, MY SON!
BRING OUT THE HUMANS! I WANT THEM TO WITNESS THE DEFEAT OF THEIR MIGHTY THOR!
ENOUGH TALK!.. LET'S SEE IF YOU FIGHT AS WELL AS YOU SPEAK!
FOOL! YOU HAVE NO CHANCE AGAINST ME! FOR WE XARTANS CAN CHANGE OURSELVES AT WILL! THUS DO I BECOME...
... A FROZEN WARRIOR, ABLE TO ENCASE YOU IN A TRAP OF ICE!!
BUT, AS THE ICE POURS OVER THOR, HE HURLS HIS MAGIC HAMMER...
8.

BEHOLD! THE HUMAN IS HELPLESSLY FROZEN IN THE ICE!
HE CANNOT MOVE HIS MUSCLES, MIGHTY AS THEY ARE!
WELL DONE, ZANO!
BAH! IT WAS NOT EVEN A CONTEST!
BUT THE XARTANS HAVE FAILED TO RECKON WITH THE INVINCIBLE MAGIC MALLET, WHICH, WHEN THROWN, NEVER FAILS TO RETURN TO ITS MASTER!
HE'S FREE!
NOTHING CAN WITHSTAND THE MIGHT OF THE ENCHANTED HAMMER! AND NOW, IT'S MY TURN TO STRIKE!

HOWEVER, BEFORE THOR CAN ACT, HIS FOE UNDERGOES ANOTHER FANTASTIC TRANSFORMATION, THIS TIME BECOMING A GIANT GLADIATOR!
I'VE HEARD THAT YOUR ANCESTORS USED THESE WEAPONS IN ANCIENT TIMES! WE WILL SEE HOW YOU YOURSELF FARE AGAINST THE SWORD AND STEEL NET!
IT TAKES GREAT SKILL TO HURL THE DEADLY NET SWIFTLY AND ACCURATELY... LIKE SO!!
HE'S CAUGHT HIM!
BRAVO, ZANO!

NOW EARTHLING, I HAVE FINISHED TOYING WITH YOU!
DON'T COUNT YOUR LAURELS YET! I CAN TURN YOUR VICTORY INTO DEFEAT MERELY BY STAMPING MY HAMMER*!
* EDITOR'S NOTE: WHEN THE URU MALLET IS STAMPED FOUR TIMES, IT EMITS AWESOME LIGHTNING!
HERE, ZANO... HAVE A THUNDERBOLT! COMPLIMENTS OF YOUR "DOOMED CAPTIVE"!
YAAIIII.....
9.

AND, AS THE XARTAN SINKS TO HIS KNEES, THE HUMANS CHEER WILDLY...
HE BEAT HIM! HE DID IT WITH HIS LIGHTNING!
I KNEW MY THOR WOULD WIN! NOBODY CAN DEFEAT HIM!
LOOK AT HIM BREAK THE STEEL NET... LIKE IT'S ONLY CARDBOARD!

I... I HAVE SHAMED YOU, FATHER!
REST EASY! I SHALL AVENGE YOUR DEFEAT! WE XARTANS WILL YET BE THE MASTERS OF EARTH! I VOW IT!

ALL RIGHT, CHAMPION... YOU WERE ABLE TO BEAT A CALLOW YOUTH! BUT NOW YOU FACE A BATTLE-HARDENED WARRIOR, THE VICTOR OF A THOUSAND GALACTIC CAMPAIGNS!
AND YOU, VILLAIN, FACE THE SON OF ODIN... WHO FEARS NO CREATURE IN ALL THE UNIVERSE!

SO BE IT!!
LOOK! HE'S STARTING TO VANISH!
HE MUST BE AFRAID OF THOR! HE'S NOT GOING TO FIGHT HIM!
IT CAN-NOT BE!
YOUR FATHER NEVER FLED FROM BATTLE IN HIS LIFE! JUST WATCH...

YOU CANNOT SEE ME, EARTHLING... BUT I AM HERE! AN INVISIBLE FOE WITH IRON FISTS!

HERE... FEEL THEM!!
UHHHH....

IT'S DIFFICULT TO FIGHT AN ENEMY THAT YOU CANNOT SEE, ISN'T IT?! YOU CAN NEVER TELL WHEN OR WHERE HE WILL STRIKE NEXT! YOU'RE AT HIS MERCY!
OHH, I CAN'T LOOK! OHHHH!
THOR DOESN'T HAVE A CHANCE! EVEN HIS STRENGTH CAN HOLD OUT MUCH LONGER!

AS THE INVISIBLE UGARTH STRIKES THOR AGAIN AND AGAIN, THE THUNDER GOD SEEMS DESTINED TO BE DEFEATED FOR THE FIRST TIME IN HIS FANTASTIC CAREER.
MUSTN'T GIVE UP?! THERE HAS TO BE A WAY TO WIN! WAIT... I HAVE IT! I KNOW HOW TO SEE THE INVISIBLE!

STAMPING HIS HAMMER TWICE, THE LORD OF THUNDER CREATES A STORM!
RAIN CAN'T PASS THROUGH A SOLID FIGURE, WHETHER IT'S VISIBLE OR INVISIBLE! AND WHERE THERE IS NO RAIN...

...THERE I SHALL FIND MY FOE!
UHHH...

NOW UGARTH... YOU SHALL KNOW THE WRATH OF THOR!

STOP! RELEASE ME!!
NOTHING CAN SAVE YOU NOW! NOTHING!!

HE'S WHIRLING HIM ABOVE HIS HEAD... JUST AS HE DOES HIS HAMMER!
BUT, WHY??
WE'LL SOON FIND OUT!

AND NOW, UGARTH... FAREWELL!!

AS THE HELPLESS XARTAN SOARS HIGHER AND HIGHER, HE AUTOMATICALLY REVERTS BACK TO HIS NORMAL FORM...
LOOK! IT IS OUR WAR LORD!
BY THE STARS OF JUPITER ... WHAT COULD HAVE HAPPENED?!?

REVERSE ALL ENGINES! FOLLOW UGARTH! PREPARE FOR SPACE RESCUE!

BY THE TIME THEY CATCH UP TO HIM, THEY'LL BE OUTSIDE OUR SOLAR SYSTEM!
OH, YOU WERE SO WONDERFUL!!
THANK HEAVENS YOU WERE ABLE TO DEFEAT THEIR LEADER!

BUT WHAT ABOUT THESE JOKERS?
WE SHALL KEEP UGARTH'S SON AND HIS COMPANIONS AS HOSTAGES... TO MAKE CERTAIN THE XARTANS NEVER AGAIN INVADE US!
12

BUT THE ALIENS CAN CHANGE THEMSELVES INTO ANYTHING! THEY'RE TOO DANGEROUS TO KEEP AROUND!
DO NOT FEAR! THEY WILL BE RENDERED HARMLESS!
YOU, ZANO, RECALL YOUR AGENTS FROM THE CITY!

NOT DARING TO INCUR THE VICTORIOUS THUNDER GOD'S WRATH, HIS CAPTORS OBEY HIM IMMEDIATELY AND.....
I COMMAND YOU ALL TO TRANSFORM YOURSELVES INTO TREES! OBEY, OR YOU WILL AGAIN FEEL THE MIGHT OF THOR!
DO AS HE SAYS! HE FORGOT WE CAN CHANGE BACK AGAIN ANY TIME WE WISH!
YES..... ONCE HE LEAVES, WE WILL FREE OURSELVES!

THEY'RE DOING IT!
AS TREES THEY'RE HARMLESS! BUT FOR HOW LONG WILL THEY REMAIN TREES? THE XARTANS CAN ASSUME ANOTHER FORM, WHENEVER THEY WISH!
YES, I KNOW!

BUT, THIS IS THE LAST CHANGE THEY SHALL EVER MAKE! FOR, WHEN THEY IMPERSONATE SOMETHING, THEY TAKE ON ALL ITS TRAITS!
AND SINCE TREES CANNOT THINK, NEITHER CAN THE XARTANS!
THEREFORE, THE IDEA OF CHANGING CAN NEVER AGAIN OCCUR TO THEM!
OF COURSE! WE SHOULD HAVE REALIZED THAT!

AND SO, WE'RE SAFE... THANKS TO YOU!
ONE THING MORE... DO NOT BE HARSH WITH DR. BLAKE! HE ONLY PRETENDED TO BETRAY ME! BY SO DOING, HE ACTUALLY HELPED ME!
I DON'T UNDERSTAND, BUT I'LL TAKE THE WORD OF THOR ANY TIME!

WITH THE MENACE ENDED, THINGS SOON RETURN TO NORMAL...
AND HE SAID YOU HELPED HIM, THOUGH I CAN'T REALLY SEE HOW!
IT WAS PROBABLY BY KEEPING OUT OF HIS WAY!
WELL, DON'T BE TOO DISAPPOINTED IN ME! AFTER ALL, JANE...

...WE CAN'T ALL BE AS BRAVE AS THOR!

-THE END-

12¢
JOURNEY INTO
MYSTERY
MC
91
APR.
APPROVED BY THE COMICS CODE AUTHORITY
THOUGH I AM FAR FROM EARTH I, LOKI, SHALL STILL DEFEAT THOR WITH THE HELP OF... SANDU!
"SANDU, MASTER OF THE SUPERNATURAL"
WAS ONLY A MORTAL... BUT, HIS POWERS WERE THE POWERS OF LOKI HIMSELF!
EVEN MY GREAT STRENGTH WILL NOT BE ENOUGH TO SAVE ME IF SANDU COVERS ME WITH THAT CONCRETE BUILDING!

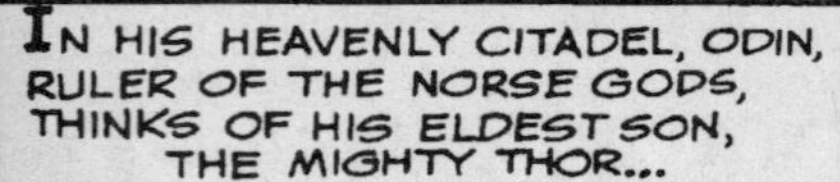

IN HIS HEAVENLY CITADEL, ODIN, RULER OF THE NORSE GODS, THINKS OF HIS ELDEST SON, THE MIGHTY THOR...

THIS IS HIS BELT OF STRENGTH! IF HE WERE TO GIRD IT ABOUT HIM, HIS AWESOME STRENGTH WOULD BE *INCREASED!*

BUT THUS FAR HE HAS NEEDED IT NOT! HIS *OWN* STRENGTH HAS BEEN MORE THAN ENOUGH TO DEAL WITH WRONG DOERS! SO THE ENCHANTED BELT REMAINS IN MY TRUST UNTIL THE FATEFUL DAY WHEN THE LORD OF THUNDER HAS NEED OF IT!

BUT, UNKNOWN TO ODIN, THAT DAY IS CLOSE AT HAND! EVEN NOW AS THOR RETURNS FROM HIS LAST ADVENTURE, HOPING FOR A PERIOD OF PEACE AND QUIET...
WHAT'S HAPPENING BELOW? SOME KIND OF ADVERTISING STUNT?

THE MIGHTY THOR! BATTLES... "SANDU, MASTER OF THE SUPERNATURAL!"

NO U TURNS

IT-IT JUST STARTED TO RISE IN THE AIR BY *ITSELF!*

IT'S NOT STOPPING! IT'S FLOATING *HIGHER!*

ALL THOSE PEOPLE INSIDE THE BANK! WHAT WILL *HAPPEN* TO THEM?

LOOK! HERE COMES *THOR!!* *HE'LL* SAVE THE BANK!

PLOT — STAN LEE
SCRIPT — LARRY LIEBER
ART — JOE SINNOTT
LETTERING — TERRY SZENICS

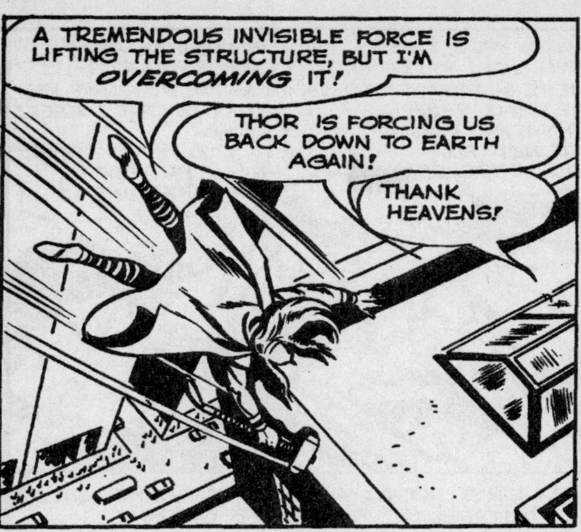
A TREMENDOUS INVISIBLE FORCE IS LIFTING THE STRUCTURE, BUT I'M OVERCOMING IT!
THOR IS FORCING US BACK DOWN TO EARTH AGAIN!
THANK HEAVENS!

BUT, IN THE NEXT AWESOME INSTANT...
THE BANK...IT'S GONE!!
IT JUST VANISHED INTO THIN AIR!
B-BUT HOW?!?

AND THEN, MOMENTS LATER..
LOOK! ALL THE PEOPLE IN THE BANK HAVE REAPPEARED!!
NOTHING MORE FOR THOR TO DO! TIME FOR DOCTOR DON BLAKE TO TAKE OVER!

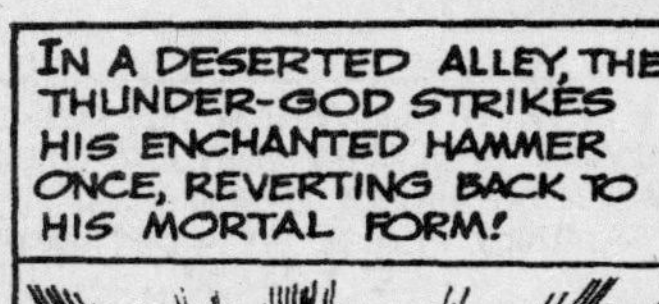
IN A DESERTED ALLEY, THE THUNDER-GOD STRIKES HIS ENCHANTED HAMMER ONCE, REVERTING BACK TO HIS MORTAL FORM!

WHERE DID YOU ALL VANISH TO!
WE DON'T KNOW! BUT I--I HAD MY LIFE SAVINGS IN THAT BANK!
YEAH! WHAT HAPPENED TO ALL THE MONEY?!?
IT'S ALL LIKE A FANTASTIC DREAM!

I CAN'T REMEMBER ANYTHING THAT HAPPENED AFTER WE VANISHED!
I'M A DOCTOR! TELL ME... DO YOU HAVE HEADACHES, OR ANY HEAD PAINS WHATSOEVER!
ME NEITHER!
NO! IT'S JUST THAT MY MEMORY'S GONE!
SAME HERE!

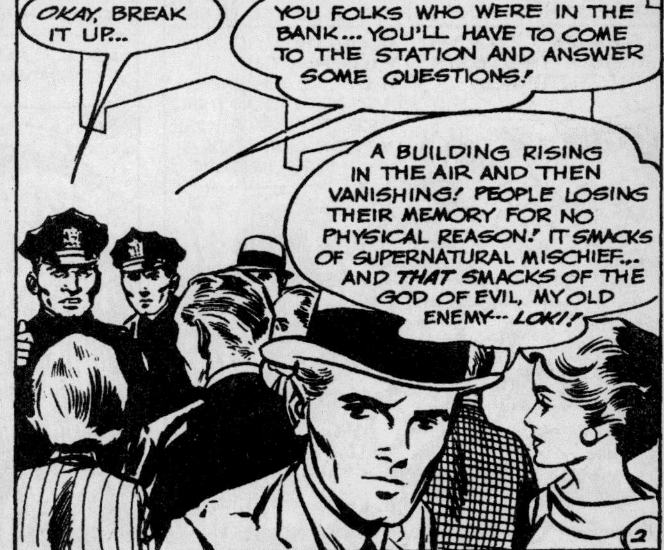
OKAY, BREAK IT UP...
YOU FOLKS WHO WERE IN THE BANK... YOU'LL HAVE TO COME TO THE STATION AND ANSWER SOME QUESTIONS!
A BUILDING RISING IN THE AIR AND THEN VANISHING! PEOPLE LOSING THEIR MEMORY FOR NO PHYSICAL REASON! IT SMACKS OF SUPERNATURAL MISCHIEF... AND THAT SMACKS OF THE GOD OF EVIL, MY OLD ENEMY-- LOKI!
2

ONCE AGAIN, DON BLAKE BECOMES THOR... AND, FLYING TO A LONELY MOUNTAIN, HE INVOKES THE NAME OF HIS LEGENDARY NORSE FATHER...
ODIN, HEAR ME! I, THY ELDEST SON, SEEK THE WHEREABOUTS OF THE SINISTER LOKI!

BY MY WILL, THE EVIL LOKI IS CONFINED HERE IN ASGARD*, WHERE HE SHALL REMAIN UNTIL HE HAS ATONED FOR HIS MISDEEDS!
THEN HE HAS NOT COME TO EARTH AGAIN! THEN HE IS NOT THE ONE I SEEK!
I THANK THEE, FATHER! FAREWELL!
*EDITOR'S NOTE: ASGARD IS THE HEAVENLY CITADEL OF THE NORSE GODS!

BUT IF IS NOT LOKI, THEN WHO IS RESPONSIBLE FOR WHAT HAS HAPPENED? WHO ELSE HAS THE POWER TO MAKE A BUILDING RISE IN THE AIR AND THEN VANISH!??

EVEN WHILE THOR PONDERS OVER THE MYSTERY, ANOTHER ASTONISHING EVENT IS TAKING PLACE AT A DISTANT RACE TRACK...
ALL OUR MONEY... IT'S FLOATING IN THE AIR!
STOP IT! STOP IT!!
HOW??

IT'S THE ENTIRE DAY'S TAKE... FLYING AWAY!
BUT THERE'S NO WIND! WHAT'S MAKING ALL THE BILLS MOVE? WHAT'S KEEPING THEM IN THE AIR??
I DUNNO! I ONLY WISH I COULD FLOAT TOO! I'D GO AFTER ALL THAT BEAUTIFUL LOOT!
EDSON

BUT, IN THE CITADEL OF THE GODS, THE MOST DANGEROUS IMMORTAL OF ALL WATCHES THE EARTHLY SCENE WITH UNDISGUISED GLEE!
I HAVEN'T ENJOYED MYSELF THIS MUCH IN CENTURIES!
POOR THOR! ODIN TOLD HIM THE TRUTH! I AM IN ASGARD! BUT THERE ARE OTHER THINGS WHICH ODIN DOES NOT KNOW!

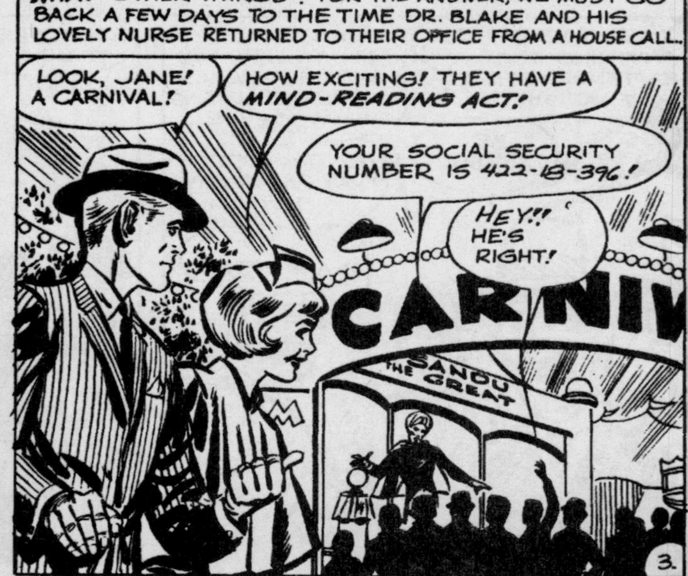

WHAT "OTHER THINGS"? FOR THE ANSWER, WE MUST GO BACK A FEW DAYS TO THE TIME DR. BLAKE AND HIS LOVELY NURSE RETURNED TO THEIR OFFICE FROM A HOUSE CALL...
LOOK, JANE! A CARNIVAL!
HOW EXCITING! THEY HAVE A MIND-READING ACT!
YOUR SOCIAL SECURITY NUMBER IS 422-18-396!
HEY!! HE'S RIGHT!
CARNIV
SANDU THE GREAT

GEE! I WONDER WHAT THE TRICK OF MIND-READING IS?
IT MAY NOT BE A TRICK! SANDU MAY REALLY HAVE EXTRA-SENSORY MENTAL POWERS! SOME PEOPLE DO! BUT ONLY TO A SLIGHT DEGREE!

YOU ARE CORRECT, SIR! I HAVE JUST DETECTED YOUR THOUGHTS! THUS I KNOW YOU ARE IN LOVE WITH A WOMAN WHOSE INITIALS ARE J.F.!

WHY--- THOSE ARE MY INITIALS!
HE--EH,--- HE MUST HAVE MADE A MISTAKE...I MEAN, THEY OFTEN TRY TO EMBARRASS PEOPLE! IT'S PART OF THEIR ACT!

I SHOULD'VE KNOWN THAT DR. BLAKE WOULD NEVER BE INTERESTED IN ME ROMANTICALLY! HE'S TOO STUFFY TO FALL FOR ANY GIRL!
SANDU REALLY SCORED A BULL'S EYE, BUT I COULDN'T ADMIT IT TO JANE!

IF SHE KNEW I LOVED HER, I'D BE ABLE TO KEEP NO SECRETS FROM HER! SHE'D SOON LEARN I WAS THOR... AND ODIN HAS FORBIDDEN ME TO REVEAL THAT TO ANY OTHER MORTAL!

MEANWHILE, IN A REALM BEYOND MORTAL MEN, LOKI IS PLOTTING REVENGE AGAINST THE ONE WHO HAD TWICE DEFEATED HIM ON EARTH...

ODIN FORBIDS ME TO GO TO EARTH! BUT, IF I WERE TO INCREASE THE EXTRASENSORY POWERS OF THAT MIND READER, I COULD MAKE HIM ALMOST AS POWERFUL AS I AM!

AND IF I'M ANY JUDGE OF MORTALS... SANDU, GIVEN SUPER MENTAL POWERS WOULD USE THEM FOR EVIL!
HE MIGHT EVEN DEFEAT THOR, THUS GIVING ME THE VENGEANCE I SEEK!

SO BE IT! I SHALL INCREASE THE HUMAN'S MEAGER EXTRA-SENSORY ABILITY! I SHALL MAKE IT A THOUSAND TIMES STRONGER!!!

THEN, WHEN LOKI HAD WORKED HIS MAGIC SPELL...

STRANGE... BUT SUDDENLY I KNOW JUST HOW MUCH MONEY EACH SPECTATOR IS CARRYING!

YES, LOKI HAD CHOSEN HIS SUBJECTS WELL! FOR THEN SANDU SELECTED THE PERSON WITH THE MOST MONEY...

NEVER BEFORE COULD I LEVITATE THINGS! BUT NOW I MERELY CONCENTRATE...

...AND NOT ONLY CAN I MAKE THE MONEY RISE, I CAN ALSO TELEPORT IT INSTANTLY FROM ONE PLACE...

... TO ANOTHER!

AND THAT FIRST ACT OF CRIME ONLY WHETTED SANDU'S APPETITE...

SUCH FANTASTIC MENTAL POWERS MUST NOT BE WASTED ON SMALL FEATS! I SHALL COMMIT SPECTACULAR CRIMES! THERE WILL BE NO STOPPING ME! I'LL BECOME AS RICH AS MIDAS!

AHHH, I HAVE INDEED CHOSEN THE RIGHT MORTAL! THAT VILLAINOUS SANDU WILL CREATE AS MUCH HAVOC ON EARTH AS I EVER DID!
AND SOONER OR LATER HE WILL BATTLE THOR! HOW I LONG FOR THAT MOMENT WHEN SANDU DEFEATS MY ANCIENT ENEMY! NOT UNTIL THEN SHALL I REST!

SO, WHILE LOKI WATCHED GLEEFULLY...

IN A MOMENT, THESE FOOLS WILL WITNESS THE MOST AMAZING BANK ROBBERY OF ALL TIME... THE LEVITATION OF AN ENTIRE BANK!

BUT, AS LUCK WOULD HAVE IT, JUST AS SANDU PERFORMS HIS FANTASTIC FEAT...

IT'S THOR!!

HE'S FORCING THE FLOATING BANK DOWN AGAIN!

BAH! THAT MEDDLESOME OAF WON'T STOP ME...

... NOT WHILE I ALSO HAVE THE POWER OF TELEPORTATION!
HOLY HANNAH! IT'S VANISHING!!

BY SHEER MENTAL CONCENTRATION, SANDU TELEPORTED THE BANK AND HIMSELF TO A SECLUDED AREA OUTSIDE THE CITY...

HOW... HOW DID WE GET HERE??
FIRST WE WERE FLOATING IN AIR... AND NOW THIS!!
IT IS MERELY ONE OF MANY MENTAL FEATS THAT I INTEND TO PERFORM!

YOU CAUSED THIS??
OKAY, MAC, I DON'T KNOW HOW YOU DID IT, BUT YOU'D BETTER UNDO IT!
AND NO FUNNY STUFF, SEE!!
HAH!! YOU THINK PUNY WEAPONS FRIGHTEN ME! ... GO AHEAD... SHOOT!

ANGRY AND DESPERATE, THE GUARDS OPENED FIRE! BUT, TO THEIR ASTONISHMENT...
MY BULLET... IT JUST DROPPED TO THE GROUND!
MINE TOO!
WITH MY MENTAL POWER OF LEVITATION, I CAN CONTROL THE MOVEMENT OF ANYTHING.. ...EVEN BULLETS!
AND I'M NOT FINISHED YET...

THE REVOLVER--- IT FLOATED OUT OF MY HAND!
MY GUN'S TURNED AROUND! IT'S AIMING AT ME!
I COULD EASILY "WILL" THE TRIGGERS TO MOVE AGAIN---BUT I WON'T! I'VE NO NEED TO HARM SUCH HELPLESS FOES!

INSTEAD, I'LL SIMPLY TELEPORT YOU ALL BACK TO THE CITY... AND AT THE SAME TIME REMOVE TELEPATHICALLY THE MEMORY OF THIS INCIDENT FROM YOUR MINDS!
THUS, YOU SHALL NEVER BE ABLE TO REVEAL THE WHEREABOUTS OF THE BANK!

SECONDS LATER...
THEY'RE BACK!
WHERE DID YOU VANISH TO?
I... I CAN'T REMEMBER!!
WHAT ABOUT THE BANK... ALL THE MONEY... WHERE IS IT?
STRANGE! I-I CAN'T RECALL A THING!

AND THAT WAS ONLY THE BEGINNING OF SANDU'S SUPERNATURAL CRIME WAVE...
WE SAW THE TRAIN CARRYING GOLD BULLION, RISE OFF THE TRACKS AND FLY AWAY!
EVERY PAINTING IN THE MUSEUM... VANISHED!!
THERE'S NOT A THING TO GO ON! NO LEADS!! NO CLUES!

AND SO WE RETURN TO THE PRESENT...
I'VE EXPLORED THE ENTIRE STATE, BUT IT'S USELESS! I CAN FIND NO TRACE OF THE VANISHED BANK OR TRAIN OR ANYTHING!
OF COURSE NOT, FOOL! FOR AFTER SANDU EMPTIED THEIR VALUABLE CONTENTS INTO AN UNDERGROUND VAULT...

... HE TELEPORTED THE REMNANTS OF HIS CRIMES TO ... THE MOON!
BUT SOON, SANDU WILL GROW MORE CONFIDENT! HE WILL COMMIT EVEN BOLDER ACTS!
JEWELRY

AND SO, IT HAPPENS...
A MAN WITH MY POWERS SHOULD LIVE IN A PALACE... EVEN IF IT MEANS TELEPORTING HIMSELF HALFWAY AROUND THE WORLD TO FIND ONE!

AND, AFTER LEVITATING ITS OCCUPANTS OUTSIDE, SANDU MOVES THE GREAT EDIFICE---
NOW TO RETURN HOME... AT THE SPEED OF THOUGHT!

FROM NOW ON, I'M THROUGH CONCEALING MYSELF! I'M READY TO FACE THE WORLD AND BECOME ITS MASTER!!!
7

REVEALING HIS DEEDS TO THE AUTHORITIES, SANDU INFORMS THEM THAT HIS NEXT TARGET WILL BE IN NEW YORK CITY...
THEY DIDN'T BELIEVE ME UNTIL THEY SAW ME LEVITATE MYSELF! NOW THEY'VE SENT JET FIGHTERS TO STOP ME!
IF HE DOESN'T SURRENDER AND RETURN TO THE GROUND, OUR ORDERS ARE TO OPEN FIRE!

BUT THE MENTAL MARVEL SCOFFS AT THE AIRMEN'S COMMANDS! AND WHEN THEY LET LOOSE WITH MACHINE GUNS AND ROCKETS...
I MERELY CONCENTRATE, TO TURN THEIR OWN WEAPONS AGAINST THEM!
HE'S MAKING THE SHELLS COME RIGHT BACK AT US!
WE CAN'T DODGE THEM! BAIL OUT!!
USAF

GOOD THING OUR EJECTOR SEATS WORKED IN THE NICK OF TIME!
MAN, NOTHING'S GONNA STOP THAT GUY... NOT WITH HIS POWER!
AND IF THEY DARE ATTACK ME WITH NUCLEAR BOMBS, I'LL SIMPLY TELEPORT THEM TO SOME OTHER CONTINENT!

REACHING NEW YORK, SANDU HEADS FOR THE UNITED NATIONS BUILDING! AND AMONG THOSE WATCHING THE SPECTACLE...
NOW THAT HE HAS COME INTO THE OPEN, IT WON'T BE LONG BEFORE HE ENCOUNTERS THOR! THEN I SHALL HAVE THE PLEASURE OF SEEING HIM DEFEAT THE THUNDER-GOD, WITH THE POWERS I HAVE GIVEN HIM!

LOOK! HE'S MAKING THE U.N. BUILDING RISE!!
IT HAPPENED SO FAST! ALL THE DELEGATES ARE STILL INSIDE! THEY DIDN'T HAVE A CHANCE TO GET OUT!

MEANWHILE IN ANOTHER CITY...
WHERE ARE YOU RUSHING OFF TO DOCTOR?
TO THE--EH--HOSPITAL! THERE'S AN--EH--EMERGENCY CASE! THEY WANT ME FOR CON-SULTATION!

BUT, MOMENTS LATER, IN A DESERTED ALLEYWAY...
THERE'S AN EMERGENCY, ALRIGHT.. BUT IT'S NOT AT THE HOSPITAL, AND IT CAN'T BE HANDLED BY A MEEK MORTAL! IT NEEDS THE POWER OF... THE MIGHTY THOR!!

THEN, WHILE THOR TAKES TO THE AIR, THE MAN WITH THE INVINCIBLE MIND CARRIES OUT HIS GRIM PLAN...
HEAR ME, DELEGATES OF THE UNITED NATIONS! I SHALL LEVITATE THIS BUILDING BEYOND THE ATMOSPHERE OF EARTH!
BUT THERE'S NO OXYGEN IN OUTER SPACE! WE WON'T BE ABLE TO BREATHE!
YOU MUST NOT DO IT! YOU MUST RETURN US TO THE GROUND!

I'LL SPARE YOUR LIVES ON ONLY ONE CONDITION... THAT YOU MAKE ME ABSOLUTE RULER OF EARTH!!
BUT WE'RE ONLY REPRESENTATIVES! WE HAVEN'T THE POWER TO DO THAT!
THE MAN IS MAD! HUMOR HIM!
LOOK! HERE COMES THOR!!

AT LAST... THE MOMENT I HAVE AWAITED!
SANDU, THOSE PEOPLE ARE NOT WARRIORS, BUT I AM! RETURN THEM SAFELY TO THE GROUND AND PREPARE TO BATTLE ONE WHO IS YOUR EQUAL!
NO ONE THAT BREATHES IS MY EQUAL! WE SHALL SOON SEE IF YOUR DEEDS CAN MATCH YOUR WORDS!

TELEPORTING THE BUILDING BACK TO EARTH, SANDU HIMSELF DESCENDS, WITH THE THUNDER-GOD IN PURSUIT...
COME, THOR...CATCH ME IF YOU CAN!
I CAN, AND I WILL!

THAT DERRICK AND THOSE GIRDERS... ALL I HAVE TO DO IS CONCENTRATE AND I CAN TELEPORT THEM INTO THE AIR RIGHT BEHIND ME...

"...LIKE SO!!"
THOSE GIRDERS! I'M GOING TO... UGH!!
CLANG!

IT WAS A CLEVER TRICK AND IT WORKED LIKE A CHARM! THERE GOES THE MIGHTY THOR... PLUMMETING TO THE GROUND... UNCONSCIOUS!

AND SANDU'S MENTAL POWERS ARE SO GREAT THAT HE SENSES LOKI'S FRANTIC ADVICE...
MUST SEPARATE HIM FROM THE HAMMER... MY ONLY CHANCE!
OTHERS MAY FEAR YOU, THOR... BUT NOT I! TO ME, YOU'RE A COWARD!! YOU FEAR ME SO MUCH THAT YOU DARE NOT HURL YOUR MALLET AT ME!

IMPUDENT CLOD! THE MIGHTY THOR FEARS NOTHING THAT LIVES!

A SPLIT-SECOND BEFORE THE SPEEDING HAMMER CAN REACH HIM, SANDU TELEPORTS HIMSELF OUT OF ITS DEADLY PATH!
IT MISSED ME!

THEN, PERFORMING THE MOST SPECTACULAR FEAT OF HIS FANTASTIC CAREER, THE MENTAL MARVEL TELEPORTS HIMSELF AND THE ENTIRE SURROUNDING AREA INTO ANOTHER DIMENSION!!
I DID IT! I'VE SEPARATED THOR FROM HIS HAMMER! NOW THEY'RE IN TWO DIFFERENT DIMENSIONS!
WITHOUT THE MALLET, I'LL LOSE MY POWER! IN SIXTY SECONDS I'LL BE DON BLAKE AGAIN!

THERE'S NO WAY FOR THOR TO ENTER THE OTHER DIMENSION---TO RETRIEVE HIS MALLET! THE THUNDER-GOD IS FINISHED!
THE LEGENDARY MAGIC HAMMER! NOW IT BELONGS TO ME! NOW I, SANDU, SHALL WIELD IT!

BUT, WHEN THE EVIL HUMAN ATTEMPTS TO LIFT THE ENCHANTED MALLET...
UHHH... THE THING WON'T BUDGE... I DON'T UNDERSTAND! I'LL HAVE TO USE MY MENTAL POWERS AND LIFT IT BY LEVITATION!

BUT EVEN THEN...
I... STILL CAN'T MOVE IT, NO MATTER HOW HARD I CONCENTRATE!
BUT I WON'T GIVE UP! MY MENTAL POWERS ARE SUPREME! I'LL ALLOW NOTHING TO DEFY THEM! I'LL STRAIN MYSELF TO THE UTMOST!
NO! STOP! NOBODY BUT THOR CAN LIFT THE HAMMER DON'T TRY IT!
12

THE MINUTE IS ALMOST UP! AS SOON AS IT'S OVER, I'LL CHANGE BACK TO MY MORTAL FORM!
I WON'T BE THWARTED! I'LL FORCE THE HAMMER TO RISE! I MUST DO IT! I MUST!
STOP! YOU FOOL! THE MALLET'S ENCHANTMENT IS INVINCIBLE! THERE'S NO POWER THAT CAN DEFY IT!

BUT THE FRUSTRATED SANDU KEEPS STRAINING HIS POWER OF CONCENTRATION...FORCING IT... TRYING TO MAKE IT DO THE IMPOSSIBLE...UNTIL FINALLY, HE CAUSES...A MENTAL SHORT CIRCUIT!!

WHA... WHAT HAPPENED?? I'M BACK IN MY OWN DIMENSION AGAIN!
THE HAMMER!! IT RETURNED JUST IN TIME!

AND NOW TO SETTLE A SCORE!
YOU CAN'T HARM ME! I HAVE BUT TO CONCENTRATE AND... I...I... I CAN'T DO IT! I CAN'T TELEPORT MYSELF OR EVEN LIFT MYSELF IN THE AIR! ALL MY POWER IS GONE!

I COULD MAKE YOU FLY! I COULD HURL YOU HALFWAY AROUND THE WORLD! BUT I WON'T BOTHER! YOU'RE NO LONGER A FOE WORTHY OF THE MIGHTY THOR!
WE'LL TAKE HIM, THOR! FROM NOW ON, HE'LL GIVE US NO TROUBLE!
HE'S DUE FOR A LONG STRETCH IN PRISON!

LATER, ATOP A LONELY MOUNTAIN...
...AND WHEN SANDU LOST HIS MENTAL POWERS, ALL HIS FEATS WERE UNDONE! EVERY THING IS NOW AS IT WAS BEFORE, OH NOBLE ODIN!
THE BELT OF STRENGTH SERVED YOU WELL! I HOPE YOU HAVE NO NEED OF IT AGAIN! BUT IF YOU DO, IT IS YOURS!

AND, IN A REMOTE PART OF ASGARD...
THAT BRAINLESS MORTAL! IF HE HAD NOT TRIED TO LIFT THE HAMMER, THOR MIGHT HAVE BEEN DEFEATED!
BUT I SHALL STILL FIND A WAY TO DEFEAT THOR! FOR I HAVE ALL ETERNITY IN WHICH TO SCHEME!

– THE END –

JOURNEY INTO MYSTERY
MARVEL COMICS GROUP 12¢
APPROVED BY THE COMICS CODE AUTHORITY
92 MAY
I'VE DONE IT! I'VE STOLEN THOR'S HAMMER! NOW THE THUNDER GOD IS AT MY MERCY!
THE MIGHTY THOR CANNOT REACH HIS ENCHANTED HAMMER! IS THIS TO BE LOKI'S FINAL VICTORY??
I CANNOT REACH IT! WITHIN SECONDS ALL MY SUPER POWERS WILL BE GONE ...FOREVER!

THE MIGHTY THOR!
WITHOUT HIS MAGIC HAMMER, MIGHTY THOR IS AS BEREFT OF POWER AS MIGHTY SAMSON WITHOUT HIS HAIR! AND YET...WELL, BRACE YOURSELF FOR A HAMMER-BLOW OF SURPRISE WHEN YOU LEARN WHAT HAPPENS ON...
THE DAY LOKI STOLE THOR'S MAGIC HAMMER
BY THE GODS! THOSE MOVING TREES ARE ACTUALLY ATTACKING ME! AND I HAVE NO MAGIC HAMMER WITH WHICH TO REPEL THEM!!
PLOT: STAN LEE SCRIPT: R. BERNS ART: JOE SINNOTT LETTERING: M. EPP
THOR DOESN'T SUSPECT THAT I, LOKI, HAVE STOLEN HIS ENCHANTED HAMMER! NOW HE'S HELPLESS TO BATTLE ANY MENACE I CHOOSE TO SEND AGAINST HIM!

BEYOND OUR SEGMENT OF TIME AND SPACE THERE EXISTS *ASGARD*, HOME OF THE NORSE GODS, WHICH CAN ONLY BE REACHED FROM EARTH BY THE RAINBOW BRIDGE CALLED *BIFROST!*

THE POWERFUL GUARDIAN OF THE BRIDGE IS *HEIMDALL*, THE WARDER, WHO OBEYS NONE BUT *ODIN*, KING OF THE GODS.

HALT AND IDENTIFY YOURSELF!

COME, HEIMDALL! DO YOU NOT RECOGNIZE NERI, HAND-MAIDEN TO FRICKA, QUEEN OF *ASGARD*?

AYE! BUT YOU COULD ALSO BE THAT ROGUE SON OF ODIN'S... *LOKI*, WHO BY MAGIC CAN EVEN TRANSFORM HIMSELF INTO A LOVELY MAIDEN LIKE YOURSELF!

INDEED, LOKI ONCE TOOK THE SHAPE OF A WRIGGLING *SNAKE* TO SLIP BY ME AND VENTURE DOWN TO *EARTH* TO WORK HIS MISCHIEF AGAINST HAPLESS MORTALS!

BUT I *COULDN'T* BE LOKI! I MYSELF *SAW* LOKI ON YONDER HILL!
WHERE? I SEE HIM *NOT!*

THEN, NERI LEADS HEIMDALL TO A RISE OF LAND...

THERE! FASTENED TO A ROCK WITH TEN CHAINS! THUS LOKI MUST REMAIN, ON ODIN'S ORDERS, TILL THE END OF TIME!

HMM... SO I SEE, LASS! AND WELL DOES LOKI *DESERVE* THAT FATE!

HE IS THE VERY SPIRIT OF EVIL, AND THE DEADLY ENEMY OF THOR, ODIN'S FAVORITE SON! FREE LOKI AND DISASTER WILL SURELY BEFALL BOTH EARTH AND *ASGARD!*

NOW THAT I KNOW LOKI HAS NOT ESCAPED HIS BONDS, YOU MAY PASS ON TO BIFROST, SWEET NERI, AS LONG AS YOU LIKE!
THANK YOU, NOBLE HEIMDALL!

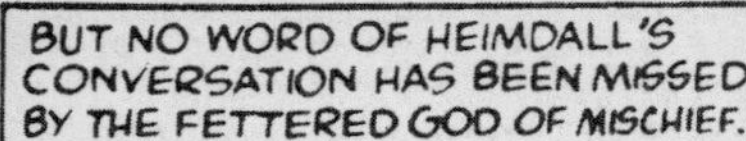

BUT NO WORD OF HEIMDALL'S CONVERSATION HAS BEEN MISSED BY THE FETTERED GOD OF MISCHIEF...

"SWEET NERI"! "NOBLE HEIMDALL"! BAH! HOW I HATE THOSE WELL-MEANING, VIRTUOUS INHABITANTS OF ASGARD! THEY THINK I'M IMPRISONED FOREVER ON THIS ROCK, DO THEY!?

BUT THEY UNDERESTIMATE MY POWERS! SOONER OR LATER I SHALL SHATTER THESE HUMILIATING CHAINS WHICH MY FATHER, ODIN, PERSONALLY FORGED TO PREVENT ME FROM SEEKING VENGEANCE ON THOR!

THEN THEY'LL LEARN I'M NOT CALLED GOD OF EVIL FOR NOTHING! THAT SUPREME DO-GOODER, THOR, WILL YET PERISH BY MY HAND! I SO VOW.

MEANWHILE, AN INFINITY AWAY FROM ASGARD, AT THE OFFICE OF DR. DON BLAKE...

NOW THAT YOUR OFFICE HOURS ARE OVER, DR. BLAKE, I'LL DELIVER THESE BLOOD-SAMPLES TO THE LAB!
THANKS, JANE! MEANWHILE, I'LL ANALYZE THIS SET OF X-RAYS!

AS NURSE JANE FOSTER LEAVES THE OFFICE, BEADY EYES WATCH HER...

OKAY, CHIEF... BLAKE'S ALONE IN HIS OFFICE NOW!
IT'S ABOUT TIME! (GROAN!) WITH THESE TWO POLICE SLUGS IN MY STOMACH, I'LL DIE OF LEAD POISONIN' BEFORE I REACH AN OPER-ATING TABLE!

I GOT NO LUCK! WHY COULDN'T ONE OF YOU MUGGS HAVE CAUGHT THE SLUGS DURING THE GETAWAY INSTEAD OF ME?

DON'T WORRY, BOSS! BLAKE'S A TOP SURGEO HE'LL EXTRACT THE BULLETS! AFTER ALL, WE COULDN'T RUSH YOU TO A HOSPITA AFTER THE STICKUP...

DR. BLA

THEY'D ONLY SIC THE POLICE ON US! BUT BLAKE'S A WEAKLING! HE'LL DO WHAT WE TELL HIM TO...
AND HE WON'T FILE NO REPORT TO THE COPS, EITHER! BECAUSE AFTER BLAKE FIXES YOU UP, WE'LL POLISH HIM OFF!

BLAKE, WE BROUGHT YOU A PATIENT! HE CAUGHT TWO BULLETS! TAKE 'EM OUT... OR ELSE!
SO! THAT POLICE FLASH I HEARD AN HOUR AGO OVER THE RADIO! THEY SAID ONE CROOK WAS WOUNDED IN A JEWEL ROBBERY...

THAT'S *ME*, BLAKE! NOW GET TO WORK...AN' DON'T MAKE NO MISTAKES, UNDERSTAND?
ER..SURE! TAKE OFF YOUR SHIRT, PLEASE!
HMM...FATE BROUGHT THEM TO THE RIGHT DOCTOR! AFTER I SAVE THIS THUG'S LIFE, I'LL MAKE SURE THAT HE RECUPERATES IN *PRISON*!

PRESENTLY, AS DR. BLAKE FINISHES THE OPERATION...
BY THE WAY. THE BROADCAST ALSO SAID THAT *THOR* IS HELPING THE POLICE TRACK YOU DOWN! AREN'T YOU AFRAID HE'LL CATCH UP WITH YOU?
HERE...IN A LAME DOCTOR'S OFFICE? DON'T MAKE US LAUGH!

IT'S NO LAUGHING MATTER, MY FRIEND! THOR'S ENTERING THE ROOM NOW!
(GASP!) *WH-WHERE?*

AS THE GUNMEN WHIRL IN PANIC, THE HANDICAPPED PHYSICIAN SEIZES HIS CANE AND STAMPS IT ON THE FLOOR...
A NOISE... *BEHIND US!*

THOR!
IN PERSON, GENTLEMEN!

HEY! WHAT HAPPENED TO *DR. BLAKE*?
HE'S HIDING...FOR FEAR THERE MAY BE SOME WILD SHOOTING! NOW CLIMB ABOARD THE OPERATING TABLE, BOYS! YOU'RE GOING FOR A *RIDE*!

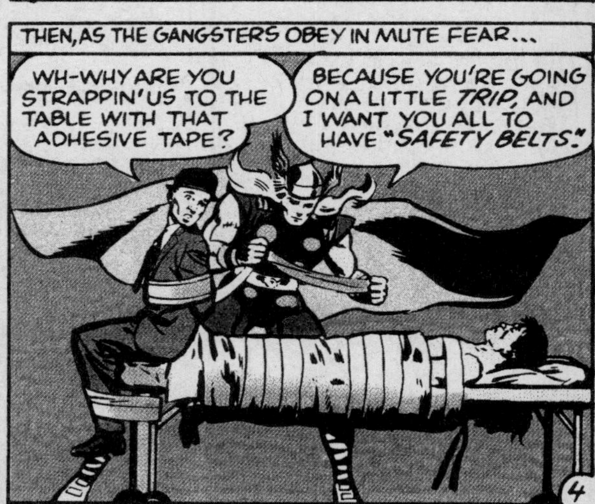
THEN, AS THE GANGSTERS OBEY IN MUTE FEAR...
WH-WHY ARE YOU STRAPPIN' US TO THE TABLE WITH THAT ADHESIVE TAPE?
BECAUSE YOU'RE GOING ON A LITTLE *TRIP*, AND I WANT YOU ALL TO HAVE "*SAFETY BELTS*."

YOU GONNA PUSH THIS THING TO THE POLICE PRECINCT?
OH, NO! THAT WOULD TAKE TOO LONG! YOU'RE GOING TO FLY THERE! FIRST I'LL TAPE MY HAMMER TO THE TABLE...

...THEN GIVE IT A FEW RAPID SPINS...

...AND AWAY YOU GO!

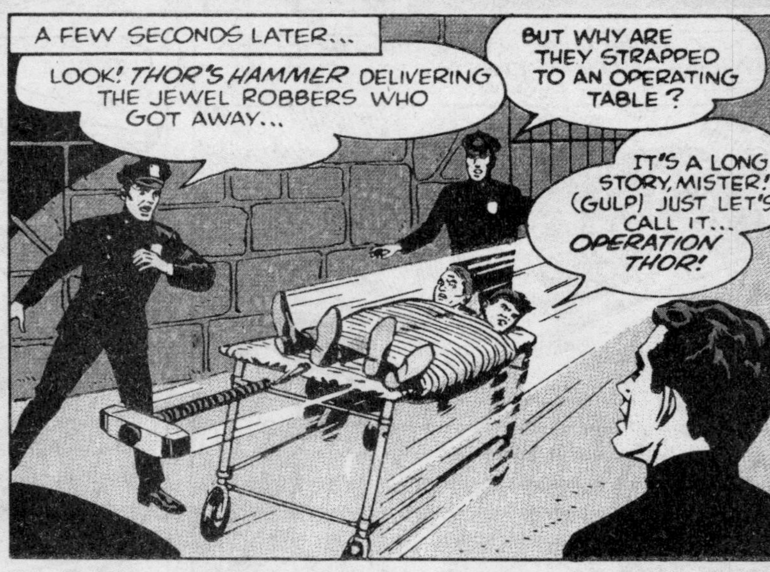
A FEW SECONDS LATER...
LOOK! THOR'S HAMMER DELIVERING THE JEWEL ROBBERS WHO GOT AWAY...
BUT WHY ARE THEY STRAPPED TO AN OPERATING TABLE?
IT'S A LONG STORY, MISTER! (GULP) JUST LET'S CALL IT... OPERATION THOR!

THEN, AS THE ENCHANTED HAMMER RETURNS TO ITS MASTER.
HERE COMES JANE, RETURNING FROM THE LAB! I'D BETTER SLIP AWAY AND SWITCH BACK TO MY DR. BLAKE IDENTITY BEFORE SHE GETS SUSPICIOUS!

AND SO, BY THE TIME JANE ENTERS THE OFFICE...
THE CROWD OUTSIDE TOLD ME THOR CAPTURED SOME THUGS IN HERE..
YES, JANE! IN FACT, I OWE MY LIFE TO THOR! IF HE HADN'T SUDDENLY APPEARED, THEY'D HAVE KILLED ME AFTER FORCING ME TO OPERATE ON THEIR GANG LEADER!

SO THE PEOPLE WEREN'T LYING WHEN THEY SAID THOR TURNED YOUR OPERATING TABLE INTO AN AERIAL PATROL WAGON!
NO, JANE! THOR'S A PRETTY INGENIOUS FELLOW..
HE'D BETTER BE...TO KEEP JANE AND THE WORLD, FROM REALIZING THAT DR. DON BLAKE AND THOR ARE THE SAME MAN!

A WEEK LATER, AT A NORWEGIAN SEA PORT...
THANKS, THOR, FOR AGREEING TO PROVIDE THE SPECIAL EFFECTS WE NEED IN THIS VIKING PICTURE!
SINCE THE PROCEEDS FOR MY CONTRIBUTION WILL GO TO VARIOUS CHARITIES, I'M GLAD TO HELP OUT!

IT INVOLVES THAT SEA SERPENT! DO YOU RECALL THE SCRIPT I SHOWED YOU?
PERFECTLY! ACTIVATE YOUR MECHANICAL SERPENT AND ROW YOUR SHIPS INTO THE FJORD WHILE I TAKE OFF WITH MY MAGIC HAMMER!

AS THE "SERPENT ATTACK" SCENE BEGINS...
IN THE FILM STORY, I'VE SWORN PROTECTION TO A GOOD TRIBE OF VIKINGS! THUS, WHEN THEY'RE MENACED BY A SEA SERPENT CONJURED UP BY EVIL LOKI, WHO HATES THE MORTALS...

...I'M SUPPOSED TO DEFEAT LOKI'S SCHEME BY FLYING RIGHT INTO THE SERPENTS MOUTH.

THEN, BECAUSE THE SERPENT CAN'T CLOSE ITS JAWS ON MY POWERFUL BODY...

...I PROCEED TO DRAG IT DOWN TO THE BOTTOM OF THE FJORD WHERE THE MONSTER DROWNS!
WOW! WHAT AN UNDERWATER SHOT! AND TO THINK WE'VE GOT THOR HIMSELF ENACTING IT!!

AN HOUR LATER...
NOW, ACCORDING TO THE SCRIPT, LOKI SENDS A FLEET OF WICKED VIKINGS WHO WORSHIP HIM, TO ATTACK THE GOOD VIKING VILLAGE! I PREVENT THIS BY STAMPING MY HAMMER TWICE, THUS CREATING A THUNDER STORM!
THUMP!
THUMP!

NEXT INSTANT, AS A TEMPEST ENGULFS THE INVADERS...
THOSE "EVIL VIKINGS" ARE JUST DUMMY FIGURES TO BE DE-STROYED BY THE CHURNING SEAS AND LIGHTNING BOLTS! NOW TO FILM THE FLEET'S DESTRUCTION BY FLYING INTO THE TEETH OF THE STORM WHERE NO HUMAN CAMERAMAN CAN GO!

THUNDERATION! WHAT FILM COMPANY EVER BEFORE HAD A MYTHOLOGICAL GOD DO ITS CAMERA-WORK FOR THEM?
YOU BET, B.J.! IT'S A MOVIE FIRST! THIS SEA-DISASTER SCENE WILL MAKE FILM HISTORY!

BUT, IN ANOTHER DIMENSION, ANOTHER PAIR OF EYES BALEFULLY WATCHES THE MIGHTY GOD AT WORK...
MY BODY IS TRAPPED HERE...BUT NOT MY SUPERNATURAL VISION! THERE'S MY ENEMY THOR AT HIS USUAL INSIPID JOB OF HELPING WORTHY CAUSES! AND THE IRONY OF IT...EVEN IN AN EARTH FILM HE'S WRECKING MY EVIL SCHEMES!

BUT, AS LOKI CONTINUES TO EAVESDROP FROM AFAR...
GREAT WORK, THOR! NOW, IN THIS LAST SEQUENCE, YOU HURL YOUR HAMMER AT THAT MOUNTAIN, CAUSING AN AVALANCHE TO BURY THE VILLAINOUS VIKING VILLAGE!
AHHH! THIS IS MY BIG OPPORTUNITY...

THOR'S HAMMER IS MADE OF THE SAME MAGIC MINERAL AS MY CHAINS... THE METAL URU! THAT'S WHY MY CHAINS ARE UNSHATTERABLE!

UNSHATTERABLE, THAT IS, BY ANYTHING EXCEPT THE GREATER FORCE OF THOR'S HAMMER! NOW I KNOW HOW TO FREE MYSELF! DEAR NOBLE THOR... ARE YOU IN FOR A SURPRISE!

AND SO, ON EARTH, AS THOR'S MIGHTY WEAPON STRIKES THE FJORD...
LOOK AT THAT IMPACT! EQUAL TO HALF A MILLION TONS OF T.N.T.! NOW THE AVALANCHE WILL BURY THE VIKING VILLAGE BELOW!
PWAAAMM!

BY ODIN'S BEARD... THE HAMMER IS NOT RETURNING TO MY HAND! IT'S STREAKING AWAY! BUT... HOW?

WITHOUT THE SPEED OF THE HAMMER TO CARRY ME ALONG, I'M LOSING FORWARD MOMENTUM! I'M... FALLING!

BLAMM!
CRACK!

MEANWHILE, IN ASGARD, A FLYING OBJECT APPEARS!
MY POWERS OF SORCERY HAVE WORKED! I'VE CAUSED THE URU METAL OF MY CHAINS TO ATTRACT THE URU METAL OF THE HAMMER WITH IRRESISTIBLE MAGNETISM!!

THE HAMMER IS SMASHING MY CHAINS TO BITS! I'M FREE!
SPANG!

I'VE TRIUMPHED! AND THOR'S HAMMER LIES HERE... CLINGING MAGNETICALLY TO THE DEBRIS OF CHAINS IT SHATTERED!

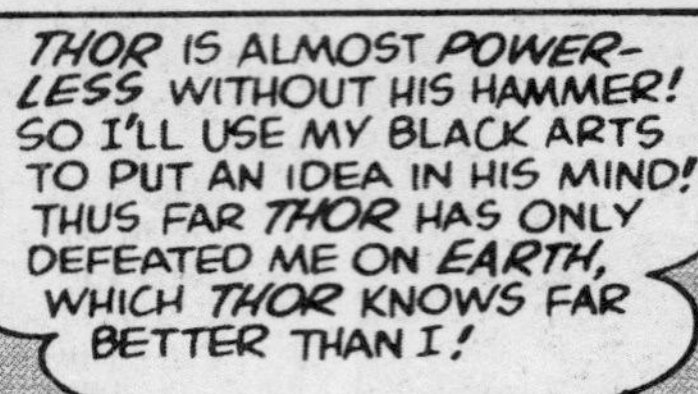
THOR IS ALMOST POWERLESS WITHOUT HIS HAMMER! SO I'LL USE MY BLACK ARTS TO PUT AN IDEA IN HIS MIND! THUS FAR THOR HAS ONLY DEFEATED ME ON EARTH, WHICH THOR KNOWS FAR BETTER THAN I!

BUT, IN ASGARD I AM ON HOME GROUND! I HAVE A BETTER CHANCE TO VANQUISH HIM HERE...SO I WILL LURE THOR TO ASGARD... TO HIS DOOM!
FUNNY... AN IDEA JUST ENTERED MY MIND... TO SUMMON ODIN! AND I MUST DO IT BEFORE SIXTY SECONDS ELAPSE!

IN THE PAST, WHEN I'VE BEEN IN DANGER, I'VE CALLED UPON THE KING OF THE GODS, ODIN, MY FATHER, TO HELP ME! AND HE HAS NEVER FAILED ME!
OH, GREAT ODIN, WISEST OF ALL THE GODS! HEAR YOUR SON'S PLEA AND APPEAR BEFORE ME!

YOUR APPEAL HAS REACHED MY EARS, THOR! WHAT TROUBLE BESETS MY FAVORITE SON?
MY HAMMER HAS MYSTERIOUSLY DISAPPEARED! HELP ME FIND IT FOR I KNOW NOT WHERE TO LOOK!

THE SOLUTION OF THIS PROBLEM REQUIRES THE COMBINED POWERS OF ALL THE GODS! SINCE YOUR HAMMER CANNOT NOW TAKE YOU THROUGH THE SEGMENTS OF TIME AND SPACE, I SHALL TRANSPORT YOU TO ASGARD MYSELF!

WHAT A STROKE OF FORTUNE! WHEN ODIN APPEARS ON EARTH, TIME STANDS STILL.. SO I SHALL NOT TURN BACK TO DR. BLAKE, EVEN THOUGH MY HAMMER HAS NOW BEEN GONE FOR SIXTY SECONDS! ONCE IN ASGARD, I CAN REMAIN THOR INDEFINITELY!

MY PLAN IS WORKING OUT PERFECTLY! ODIN IS BRINGING THOR TO ASGARD! NOW TO USE MORE SORCERY TO PUT MY "SOLUTION" INTO THE BRAINS OF THE SUPREME COUNCIL OF THE GODS!

PRESENTLY, AT ODIN'S PALACE, AS THE RULER OF ASGARD CALLS AN EMERGENCY MEETING...
WE HAVE PONDERED YOUR PREDICAMENT, THOR, AND WE OFFER THIS ADVICE! YOUR HAMMER MUST SOMEHOW HAVE RETURNED TO ASGARD! THEREFORE, SEARCH FOR IT HERE!

UNFORTUNATELY, WE CANNOT HELP YOU WITH YOUR QUEST, FOR WE ARE EACH BURDENED WITH THOUSANDS OF TASKS OF OUR OWN! BUT WE ALL WISH YOU SUCCESS!
THANK YOU, NOBLE ODIN! I SHALL BEGIN MY SEARCH IMMEDIATELY!

EVERYTHING IS HAPPENING AS I DESIRED! NOW, I HAVE THOR AT MY MERCY...ON MY HOME GROUND... WITH NO MAGIC HAMMER TO HELP HIM! VERILY, THOR HAS COME HOME TO PERISH!

SOON AFTER, AS THOR ENTERS A FOREST...
THAT'S IT, THOR...ENTER MY WILDERNESS...WHERE I WILL MAGICALLY TRANSFORM THOSE GIANT TREES INTO THE INSTRUMENTS OF YOUR DESTRUCTION!

NOW, MY BRAWNY BEAUTIES!! ATTACK THE ACCURSED THUNDER-GOD!
BY THE GODS! I'VE STUMBLED INTO LOKI'S FOREST---AND HIS OBEDIENT TREES ARE SURROUNDING ME!

WITH MY ENCHANTED HAMMER I COULD REPULSE THIS MENACE WITH EASE! I HAD BETTER FASHION ANOTHER KIND OF HAMMER QUICKLY, FOR EVEN MY MIGHTY STRENGTH CANNOT WITHSTAND SUCH ODDS FOREVER!

THAT'S ONE DOWN! NOW TO FELL A SMALLER TREE WITH ONE SLASH OF MY PALM!

THEN, AS THOR TWISTS STOUT VINES AROUND THE FALLEN TREES, BINDING THEM TOGETHER...
THIS WOODEN MALLET WON'T BE AS POWERFUL AS MY URU HAMMER, BUT IT MAY SUFFICE TO KEEP THESE ENCHANTED NIGHTMARES AT BAY!

THANK THE GODS I SELECTED TIMBER OF MUCH TOUGHER GRAIN THAN THE LUMBERING BRUTES ATTACKING ME!

BLAST MY LUCK! I FORGOT HOW POWERFUL THOR IS, EVEN WITHOUT HIS MAGIC WEAPON! I MUST DEVISE A STILL MORE FOOLPROOF METHOD OF DESTROYING HIM, ONCE AND FOR ALL! AND I CAN DO IT... FOR HOME ON ASGARD, MY POWER IS AS GREAT AS HIS!

MEANWHILE, I'LL SOON DISPOSE OF HIS WOODEN HAMMER!
MY WEAPON IS BURNING UP, AS IF BY MAGIC!

MAGIC!? WHY DIDN'T I THINK OF THAT BEFORE? LOKI, THAT MASTER OF MAGIC, MIGHT HAVE HAD SOMETHING TO DO WITH MY HAMMER'S DISAPPEARANCE!

THE LAST I HEARD OF LOKI, ODIN HAD HIM CHAINED TO A ROCK NEAR THE RAINBOW BRIDGE! I'LL SEE IF HE'S STILL THERE!
THOR'S HEADING TOWARD BIFROST! I MUST ACT QUICKLY!

I'LL CHANGE THOSE CLOUDS INTO FLYING DRAGONS...AND ORDER THEM TO DESTROY THOR BY SHEER WEIGHT OF NUMBER AND STRENGTH!

THOR CAN'T IMPROVISE A HAMMER NOW! HIS BACK IS TO THE WALL! THERE IS NO WOOD ANYWHERE!
THIS NEW PERIL CAN ONLY BE LOKI'S WORK! NOBODY BUT HE COULD TRANSFORM MERE CLOUDS INTO SNARLING, DEADLY DRAGONS!

BUT, I'M NOT FINISHED YET! MY FINGERS ARE STRONG ENOUGH TO GOUGE A STONE WEAPON OUT OF THE CLIFF SIDE!

BLAST HIM! THOR'S THE STRONGEST MAN IN CREATION! HE'S MADE ANOTHER HAMMER FOR HIMSELF...THIS TIME OUT OF SHEER ROCK!
AND NOW, ATTACK ME-- IF YOU DARE!

A PLAGUE ON THOR! I THOUGHT HE'D BE HELPLESS WITHOUT HIS HAMMER! BUT HE KEEPS CREATING A SUBSTITUTE TO MEET EACH NEW DANGER!

THEN, AS THE LAST DEFEATED CREATURE FLEES...
I'M SEEING THINGS! AFTER STRIKING THE DRAGON, THE HAMMER IS NOT FALLING TO THE GROUND!! IT'S FLYING ON... TOWARD THE RAINBOW BRIDGE!
12

SUDDENLY, AS THOR NOTICES SOMETHING ELSE...
THIS GLEAMING CLIFF WALL IS NOT COMPOSED OF ORDINARY STONE! IT CONTAINS THE MAGIC METAL, URU, OF WHICH MY MAGIC HAMMER AND LOKI'S CHAINS WERE BOTH CONSTRUCTED!

I'LL WAGER THAT'S HOW I LOST MY HAMMER! SOMEHOW LOKI MUST HAVE MAGNETIZED IT, AND IT WAS DRAWN IRRESISTIBLY TOWARD ASGARD... EVEN AS THE STONE MALLET I JUST FASHIONED IS BEING ATTRACTED TO THE SAME SPOT!

MOMENTS AFTER...
I WAS RIGHT! THERE'S MY MAGIC HAMMER LYING ON THE DEBRIS OF LOKI'S CHAINS! I MUST CONTACT ODIN INSTANTLY AND TELL HIM THAT LOKI IS ON THE LOOSE AGAIN!

THEN, AS THE GODS RESPOND TO THOR'S SIGNAL...
ODIN! HEIMDALL! FRICKA!
YES, YOU VILLAIN! THOR HAS SUMMONED US! YOU USED YOUR BLACK ARTS TO ATTRACT THOR'S HAMMER TO ASGARD, IN ORDER TO SMASH YOUR UNSHATTER-ABLE CHAINS...

THEN YOU INFLUENCED THOR'S MIND TO LURE HIM TO ASGARD.. AND OUR MINDS TO KEEP HIM HERE...SO THAT YOU COULD DESTROY HIM!
AYE, ODIN...BUT LUCKILY, I CONSTRUCTED OTHER KINDS OF HAMMERS TO REPEL THE MENACES HE SENT AGAINST ME!

SOON, NEAR BIFROST...
RETURN AGAIN TO EARTH, MY SON, AND FEAR NOT! WE SHALL FIND A BETTER WAY TO IMPRISON THE SINISTER LOKI!
I HOPE SO, FATHER! FOR, IF LOKI EVER REALLY BREAKS FREE, ALL THE HAMMERS IN THE WORLD MIGHT NOT STOP HIM!

THAT NIGHT, AT DR. BLAKE'S OFFICE...
GOSH, DOC, TAKE IT EASY! YOU COULD HURT A GUY WITH THAT RUBBER HAMMER!
DON'T WORRY, MR. JONES! DR. BLAKE IS VERY EXPERIENCED IN USING A MALLET!!
JANE, HONEY...YOU DON'T KNOW THE HALF OF IT!

JOURNEY INTO
MYSTERY
APPROVED BY THE COMICS CODE AUTHORITY
MARVEL COMICS GROUP 12¢
93 JUNE
EVEN THE MIGHTY THOR IS FORCED TO OBEY THE SINISTER COMMANDS OF THE AWESOME "RADIO-ACTIVE MAN!"
THROW AWAY YOUR ACCURSED HAMMER, THOR! YOU HAVE NO CHOICE... YOU ARE MY SLAVE!
I--AM--YOUR SLAVE!
WITHOUT HIS HAMMER, THOR CANNOT STOP THE RADIO-ACTIVE MAN! WE'RE ALL DOOMED!

OUT OF THE SINISTER, SCIENTIFIC LABORATORIES OF RED CHINA IS SPAWNED A NEW KIND OF MENACE, DESIGNED ONLY FOR ONE PURPOSE... TO DESTROY MIGHTY THOR, PROTECTOR OF DEMOCRACY! THAT IS THE BACKGROUND, AND THIS IS THE STORY! THE TITANTIC TALE OF...
THE MIGHTY THOR! VERSUS...
"The mysterious RADIO-ACTIVE MAN!"
BY ODIN! SOMETHING HAS DEFLECTED MY HAMMER! I CAN NOT INJURE YOU!
EXACTLY, THOR! THE RADIATIONS OF MY BODY HAVE TURNED YOUR NOW-USELESS WEAPON ASIDE!
GREAT GUNS! THOR IS DONE FOR! HE'S AT THE RADIO-ACTIVE MAN'S MERCY... AND THAT MEANS WE ARE, TOO!!!
PLOT: STAN LEE
SCRIPT: R. BERNS
ART: JACK KIRBY
INKING: DICK AYERS
LETTERING: R. HOLLOWAY
X-202
1

INDIA!! VAST, REMOTE, MENACED BY THE RED CHINESE ATTACKERS!! INTO THIS WAR-TORN LAND COMES AN AMERICAN MEDICAL MISSION, LED BY...
DR. BLAKE, WHAT'S YOUR ESTIMATE OF THE SITUATION?
WELL, IF THE INDIANS ARE TO TURN BACK THE RED CHINESE INVADERS IN THIS BORDER WAR, THEY'LL NEED MORE THAN AMERICAN ARMS AND MILITARY ADVISERS!

THEY NEED ALL THE MEDICAL SUPPLIES AMERICA CAN SEND THEM... AMBULANCES, NURSES, DOCTORS, SURGICAL INSTRUMENTS, MEDICINE TO TAKE CARE OF THE WOUNDED BEHIND THE FRONT!
YOU'RE RIGHT, DOCTOR!

SUDDENLY...
RUN FOR YOUR LIVES! RED TANKS HAVE PENETRATED OUR DEFENSES AND ARE COMING THROUGH THE CHOGI PASS!
TAKE COVER!

SECRETLY, DR. DON BLAKE HOBBLES INTO THE WOODS, AND THEN...
IF THOSE CHINESE TANKS AREN'T STOPPED THEY'LL PULVERIZE THIS HOSPITAL BASE! I MUST SWITCH FROM DR. DON BLAKE TO... THE MIGHTY THOR!

INSTANTLY, BOTH DR. BLAKE AND AND HIS ANCIENT CANE CHANGE SHAPE!
NOW I CAN HALT THE REDS DEAD IN THEIR TRACKS!

AS THOR SOARS SKYWARD AT FANTASTIC SPEED...
MY HAMMER CAN DO THE WORK OF MANY ANTI-MISSILE MISSILES!!

NOW, I COULD EASILY DESTROY THE RED TANKS, BUT I'D RATHER DELIVER THEM TO THE HINDUS!!

SO I'LL MERELY WRECK THEIR FIRE-POWER...

NEXT, I'LL CHAIN THEM ALL TOGETHER...
AND THEN...

...I'LL ATTACH THE CHAIN TO MY HAMMER...

AND OFF TO THE NEAREST INDIAN ARMY CAMP!

BUT THOR'S STUPENDOUSLY EPIC FEAT DOES NOT GO UNOBSERVED BY ENEMY EYES...
THIS IS DISASTEROUS, COLONEL! THOR IS HELPING THE HINDUS AND HAS GIVEN THEM OUR OWN TANKS!
THOR!! THEN THERE IS SUCH A ONE!! WE MUST REGROUP... MUST MAKE NEW PLANS! HIS POWERS MAKE HIM THE EQUAL OF AN ARMY DIVISION!

SOON, AT A HINDU BASE...
HERE! WITH A FEW MINOR REPAIRS, YOUR FORCES CAN OPERATE THESE RED TANKS!
WE ARE GRATEFUL, MIGHTY THOR! BUT ALAS, THERE IS NO WAY TO PREVENT THE CHINESE FROM SENDING MORE TANKS AGAINST US!

YES, THERE IS! JUST WATCH!
3

THEN, AS THE RED CHINESE GAPE IN HELPLESS DISMAY...

AS GOD OF THUNDER, I CAN CONTROL LANDSLIDES AND AVALANCHES!
RRRRRRRRRR

KRAMM
ONCE I CLOSE THIS PASS, NO RED TANKS WILL EVER GET THRU AGAIN!

NEXT, AS THOR STAMPS HIS HAMMER TWICE ON THE GROUND...

THIS THUNDERSTORM WILL IMPEDE THE CHINESE ARMY! SOON THEIR MOTORIZED EQUIPMENT WILL BOG DOWN IN A SEA OF MUD!

NOW I CAN RETURN TO HINDU TERRITORY! THE RED HORDES WON'T BE THREATENING THE INDIAN OUTPOSTS FOR A LONG TIME TO COME!
GET ME PEKING AT ONCE!... WHAT DO YOU MEAN YOU CAN'T HEAR ME? I'M SHOUTING, YOU IDIOT!

BUT GENERAL FU, I ONLY HEAR THE SOUND OF BIG GUNS, FIRING ROUND AFTER ROUND! THE NOISE IS DROWNING OUT YOUR WORDS!

FOOL!! OUR GUNS ARE SILENT! WHAT YOU HEAR IS THE POUNDING OF THE THUNDER CREATED BY THOR... THOR, I SAID! HE'S STOPPED OUR ADVANCE... AND IT'S NOT MY WORDS WHICH ARE DROWNING! IT'S US!

WE CAN'T MOVE FORWARD ONE INCH, BECAUSE OF THOR! NOW PUT ME THROUGH TO PEKING, TO OUR GREAT LEADERS THEMSELVES, OR SO HELP ME, YOU NUMB-SKULL, YOU'LL FACE A FIRING SQUAD BEFORE SUNDOWN!

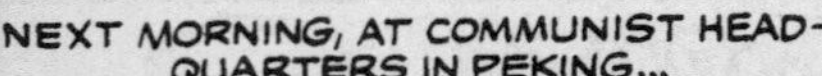

NEXT MORNING, AT COMMUNIST HEAD-QUARTERS IN PEKING...

... NOW THAT YOU'VE HEARD THE LATEST NEWS ABOUT THOR'S VICTORY OVER OUR ARMY... WHAT ARE YOU GOING TO **DO** ABOUT IT?

WHAT **CAN** WE DO ABOUT IT? THOR IS THE MIGHTIEST FIGHTING FORCE ON EARTH!

SILENCE! SUCH TALK IS **TREASON! COMMUNISM** IS THE MIGHTIEST FORCE ON EARTH... AND IT WILL DESTROY EVEN **THOR!!** I DEMAND SOLUTIONS, RESULTS... NOT WHINING EXCUSES!

YOU ARE OUR GREATEST MILITARY STRATEGISTS... OUR MOST INGENIOUS SCIENTISTS! SPEAK UP! HOW DO WE GET **RID** OF THOR? I DEMAND IMMEDIATE SUGGESTIONS!

OUR GREAT LEADER IS RIGHT! SOONER OR LATER WE MUST FIGHT THE DEMOCRACIES, AND WE MUST PREPARE FOR IT NOW BY SHAKING THEIR MORALE! WE CAN MAKE FREE MEN TREMBLE BY DESTROYING THEIR HERO-PROTECTOR, THOR!

OH, GREAT ONE, I, CHEN LU, SHALL SPEAK FOR OUR SCIENTISTS! WE'LL WORK DAY AND NIGHT IN OUR SECRET LABORATORIES UNTIL WE CREATE **SOME-THING** TO DEFEAT THOR!
SO BE IT CHEN! BUT REMEMBER MY WARNING...

... EITHER **YOU** ERADICATE THOR, OR I WILL ERADICATE **YOU!** THAT GOES FOR **ALL** OF YOU! THE PENALTY FOR FAILURE IS DEATH! AM I UNDERSTOOD?
PERFECTLY, GREAT ONE! THOR'S DAYS ARE NUMBERED!

WHAT ARE YOU GOING TO DO, CHEN LU? DO **YOU** KNOW OF ANY WAY TO ERADICATE THOR?
YES, COMRADE! AS IT HAPPENS, I **DO!** NOW IF YOU'LL EXCUSE ME, I'LL RETURN TO MY RESEARCH!

WHEN I FINISH MY EXPERIMENTS, NOT ONLY THOR, BUT THE **WHOLE WORLD** WILL COWER BEFORE MY INVINCIBLE POWER!

AN HOUR LATER, AS CHEN LU ARRIVES AT THE CONVERTED BUDDHIST TEMPLE WHICH IS HIS PRIVATE LAB...
EVERYBODY KNOWS ATOMIC POWER CAN BE LIMITLESSLY DESTRUCTIVE!

BUT RADIO-ACTIVITY... ENOUGH OF IT... IS POTENTIALLY THE GREATER MENACE! AND I HAVE DISCOVERED THROUGH MY RADIO-ACTIVE EXPERIMENTS, HOW TO MAKE A HUMAN BEING SUPER-POWERFUL BY SUBJECTING HIM TO SUFFICIENT RADIO-ACTIVITY TO CHANGE HIS ENTIRE ATOMIC STRUCTURE!

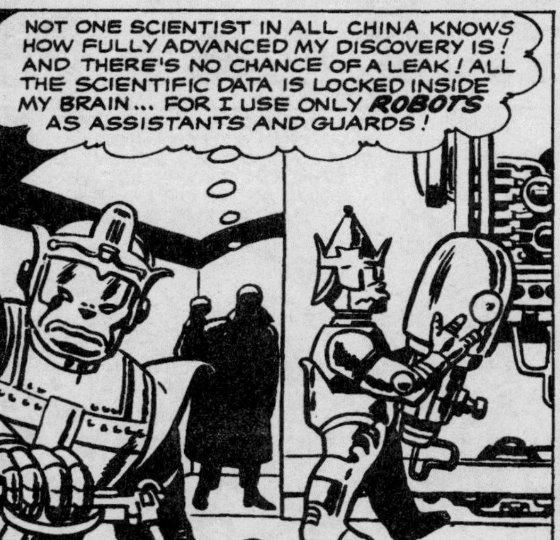
NOT ONE SCIENTIST IN ALL CHINA KNOWS HOW FULLY ADVANCED MY DISCOVERY IS! AND THERE'S NO CHANCE OF A LEAK! ALL THE SCIENTIFIC DATA IS LOCKED INSIDE MY BRAIN... FOR I USE ONLY ROBOTS AS ASSISTANTS AND GUARDS!

AT FIRST, I THOUGHT I'D ENDOW SOME HUMAN GUINEA PIG WITH RADIO-ACTIVE POWER! BUT THEN I DECIDED... WHY SHOULD I MAKE SOMEONE ELSE SO STRONG? WHY SHOULDN'T I MYSELF BECOME... THE RADIO-ACTIVE MAN?

STRAIGHT AWAY I DECIDED THAT CHEN LU WOULD BECOME THE MOST AWE-INSPIRING HUMAN ON EARTH... INVULNERABLE TO ALL MENACES... UNCONQUERABLE EVEN BY THOR THE MIGHTY!

AND NOW... IN A FEW MOMENTS... MY AMBITIONS WILL BE REALIZED! I HAVE, FOR MANY MONTHS, INCREASINGLY IMMUNIZED MYSELF AGAINST THE DEADLY EFFECTS OF RADIATION!

THEREFORE, I CAN ABSORB AN INFINITE AMOUNT OF RADIO-ACTIVITY WITHOUT INJURING MYSELF!

ON THE CONTRARY, I WILL BECOME AN AMAZING HUMAN RESERVOIR OF RADIO-ACTIVE POWER WHICH I CAN USE AS I PLEASE! AH! THE TINGLING RAYS ARE SUFFUSING MY BODY FROM HEAD TO TOE...

AN ORDINARY MAN WOULD BE INCINERATED BY THESE SUPER-INTENSE RADIATIONS... BUT I AM MERELY WARMED BY THEM AS IF THEY WERE ORDINARY SUN-BEAMS!

I HAVE BUT TO EXUDE A LITTLE RADIO-ACTIVE FORCE AND THIS ENTIRE LAB... EQUIPMENT, ROBOTS, AND THE BUILDING ITSELF... WILL CRUMBLE INTO SMOKING RUINS!

I HAVE NO FURTHER USE FOR IT! LET IT VANISH SO THAT NO OTHER SCIENTIST CAN RECONSTRUCT MY EQUIPMENT OR LEARN MY SECRET FORMULAS!

NOW I'LL CONTACT OUR GREAT LEADERS AND SHOW THEM WHAT CHEN LU HAS ACCOMPLISHED WITH HIS SCIENTIFIC GENIUS!

THAT AFTERNOON...
UNBELIEVABLE! AND YOU CAN TURN ON THIS RADIO-ACTIVE POWER AT WILL?
AYE, GREAT ONE! I AM NOW GLOWING ONLY SLIGHTLY SO THAT YOU WILL NOT BE HARMED, BY MY PRESENCE!

CHEN LU, YOU ARE A GENIUS! WITH SUCH POWER, YOU WILL BECOME OUR GREATEST NATIONAL HERO!
AYE, MASTER... ESPECIALLY AFTER I GET RID OF THOR! LET ME TELL YOU HOW I INTEND TO DISPOSE OF HIM...

A WEEK LATER, IN A RED CHINESE SUBMARINE OFF THE U.S. COAST...

CHEN LU, WE ARE ONLY A FEW MILES NOW FROM THE AMERICAN SHORE-LINE!
GOOD! STAY OUT-SIDE THE THREE MILE LIMIT AND FIRE ME OUT OF AN EMPTY TORPEDO TUBE!

GOOD LUCK ON YOUR GLORIOUS MISSION!
I NEED NO LUCK! I AM INVINCIBLE! NOW... FIRE!!

I NEED ONLY TURN ON MY RADIO-ACTIVE HEAT AND THE TORPEDO CASING WILL MELT AWAY!

ALLOWING ME TO SWIM THE REMAINING DISTANCE!

NEW YORK CITY... LITTLE DO THEY SUSPECT WHAT IS IN STORE FOR THEM!! I'LL GIVE THE AMERICANS THE SHOCK OF THEIR LIVES!

SOON, AS CHEN LU WALKS BRAZENLY THROUGH A CUSTOMS STATION...
HEY! STOP THAT MAN! HE HAS NO PASSPORT... NO PAPERS!
PASSPORT! PAPERS! BAH! USE YOUR GUNS ON ME! THEY CANNOT STOP ME! NOTHING CAN!
CUSTOMS

OMIGOSH! LOOK! H-HE'S TURNED INTO A MASS OF BLINDING LIGHT!

OUR SLUGS ARE MELTING! SO'S THE CONCRETE FLOOR!
CORRECT, YOU DOLTS! SO I ADVISE YOU TO KEEP YOUR DISTANCE! I AM HERE FOR ONLY ONE PURPOSE ... TO SEEK OUT AND DESTROY THOR!

PRESENTLY, AS THE BIZARRE FIGURE TRUDGES UP BROADWAY...
I HEREBY ISSUE A CHALLENGE TO THOR, WHEREVER HE IS, TO COME FORWARD AND MEET ME IN BATTLE!
THIS IS UNCANNY! MACHINE-GUN BULLETS CAN'T HARM HIM! AND NOBODY DARES TOUCH HIM BECAUSE OF HIS RADIO-ACTIVE BODY!

THEN, IN TIMES SQUARE...
LET IT BE BROADCAST THROUGHOUT THE WORLD THAT I AM WAITING HERE FOR THOR TO SHOW UP TO FIGHT ME! MEAN-WHILE, DON'T TRY ANY TRICKS! EVEN ARTILLERY SHELLS OR POISON GAS CAN'T HARM ME!
WHAT'S MORE, WE CAN'T EVEN DROP A BOMB ON HIM! HE'S IN THE HEART OF MANHATTAN! TOO MANY INNOCENT PEOPLE WOULD BE HURT!

AS HOURS PASS AND THOR DOESN'T APPEAR...
WHERE'S THOR? SURELY HE KNOWS ABOUT THE RADIO-ACTIVE MAN'S CHALLENGE!
MAYBE THOR'S AFRAID OF HIM... N-NOT THAT I BLAME HIM! HOW CAN ANYTHING DEFEAT THE RADIO-ACTIVE MAN??
YOU SEE? YOUR ESTEEMED THOR IS A COWARD! HE MUST HAVE SEEN ME AND REALIZED THAT HE HAS MET HIS MASTER AT LAST!

BUT, THOR'S REASON FOR NOT APPEARING IS A SECRET TO EVERYONE EXCEPT DR. DON BLAKE!
THE WHOLE HOSPITAL IS BUZZING ABOUT THE RADIO-ACTIVE MAN'S CHALLENGE! BUT I CAN'T ACCEPT IT... YET! THIS OPERATION IS A LIFE-AND-DEATH MATTER AND I CAN'T LEAVE THE OPERATING TABLE TILL MY PATIENT IS OUT OF DANGER!

AN HOUR LATER...
CONGRATULATIONS, BLAKE! YOUR OPERATION WAS A MASTERPIECE OF MEDICAL SKILL! IF ANY OTHER SURGEON THAN YOU HAD OPERATED, THE MAN WOULD NEVER HAVE PULLED THRU!
I'M GLAD I WAS SUCCESSFUL!
NOW I MUST TACKLE ANOTHER LIFE-AND DEATH MATTER... THIS MYSTERIOUS PERSON CALLED THE RADIO-ACTIVE MAN! I MUST CHANGE TO THOR AT ONCE!
9

MOMENTS LATER DR. BLAKE SWITCHES TO THOR IN A DESERTED ROOM IN THE HOSPITAL...

LOOK! THERE'S THOR NOW!
AH! SO YOU FINALLY DARE TO CONFRONT ME, THOR!
WHY SHOULD I NOT? WHAT'S SO INVINCIBLE ABOUT YOU?

MY RADIO-ACTIVE POWER! I'LL DESTROY YOU WITH IT!
SAY THAT AFTER YOU FEEL MY HAMMER'S STING!

BUT, AMAZINGLY...
BY ODIN! SOMETHING HAS DEFLECTED MY HAMMER!
BEHOLD, THOR! THE RADIATIONS OF MY BODY TURNED IT ASIDE! PERHAPS YOU CAN THINK OF SOMETHING ELSE TO HARM ME?

THE FORCES OF THE ELEMENTS ARE MINE TO CONTROL! NO ONE CAN WITHSTAND MY LIGHTNING BOLTS!
NO ONE BUT... ME!

HA! HA! ELECTRICAL SHOCKS HAVE NO EFFECT WHATEVER ON ME!
THEN I WILL TAKE YOU ON MYSELF! I'M STILL THE MIGHTIEST OF IMMORTALS! I'LL DEFEAT YOU, IF I MUST, WITH MY BARE HANDS!

THINK AGAIN, MY HELPLESS FOE! MY RADIO-ACTIVE MOLECULES ARE SO ARRANGED THAT IF I WERE SUBJECTED TO ANY SUDDEN PHYSICAL VIOLENCE I WOULD REACH CRITICAL MASS AND THEN... POOF... I'D BLOW UP LIKE AN H-BOMB AND TAKE THE WHOLE CITY WITH ME!
BY THE GODS! MY HANDS ARE TIED! BUT THERE MUST BE SOME WAY TO FIGHT YOU!!

STYMIED, EH? YOU DON'T KNOW WHAT TO DO ABOUT ME! BUT I KNOW HOW TO HANDLE YOU! I'LL SIMPLY USE MY RADIO-ACTIVE POWERS TO PUT YOU INTO A HYPNOTIC-TRANCE! AND SO, THOR, IN JUST ONE SPLIT-SECOND, YOU WILL BECOME... MY SLAVE!
THAT LIGHT!! MY EYES!! OHHH...
10

YOU CANNOT RESIST MY HYPNOTIC INFLUENCE, THOR! YOU ARE HYPNOTIZED EVEN NOW! IN FACT, YOU NO LONGER KNOW WHO YOU ARE! AM I RIGHT?
YES, MASTER! I DO NOT KNOW WHO I AM!

GOOD! NOW TO GET RID OF THE SOURCE OF YOUR POWER! TOSS AWAY YOUR HAMMER, THOR! NOW!!
YES, MASTER!
GREAT GUNS! THOR'S DONE FOR! HE'S THROWN AWAY HIS MIGHTY HAMMER! NOW HE'S AT THAT CHARACTER'S MERCY AND SO ARE WE! RUN FOR YOUR LIVES!

IDIOT? DID I SAY THROW IT SO FAR?!! NOW I MUST SEARCH FOR IT, CURSE YOU!
YES MASTER!

BUT, AS THE RADIO-ACTIVE MAN RUNS OFF, LITTLE DOES HE SUSPECT THAT THOR CANNOT BE WITHOUT HIS URU HAMMER FOR MORE THAN SIXTY SECONDS WITHOUT CHANGING BACK TO DR. DON BLAKE! AND SO, AS A SINGLE MINUTE PASSES...

HOLY HYPOS! I-I'VE BECOME DR. BLAKE AGAIN! IT'S A GOOD THING EVERYONE'S FLED IN PANIC, OR ELSE SOMEBODY WOULD HAVE SEEN THOR'S SECRET IDENTITY!

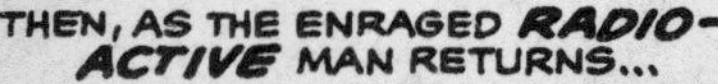

THEN, AS THE ENRAGED RADIO-ACTIVE MAN RETURNS...

BLAST IT! I COULD NOT FIND THOR'S HAMMER... AND NOW HE'S DISAPPEARED, TOO! BUT THAT'S IMPOSSIBLE! I HAD HIM HYPNOTIZED AND HE COULDN'T DO ANYTHING WITHOUT A COMMAND FROM ME! YOU! PUNY ONE... DID YOU SEE WHERE THOR WENT?

ALTHOUGH THOR WAS HYPNOTIZED, DR. BLAKE WAS NOT! NOW THAT I'M BLAKE AGAIN, THE HYPNOTIC SPELL IS BROKEN! BUT THE RADIO-ACTIVE MAN CANNOT KNOW THAT! NOW TO THROW HIM OFF THE TRAIL...
WELL, FOOL? SPEAK... OR I'LL DESTROY YOU!

HE--HE RAN THAT WAY! UPTOWN!
GOOD! THOR WON'T GET FAR IN HIS HYPNOTIZED CONDITION... AND WITHOUT HIS HAMMER, HE'S HELPLESS!

WHEN I CATCH UP WITH HIM, I'LL TAKE NO MORE CHANCES! I'LL DESTROY HIM ON THE SPOT!
THE RADIO-ACTIVE MAN WILL NEVER FIND THOR, BECAUSE "THOR" IS NOW HEADING FOR THE OFFICE OF DR. DON BLAKE AS FAST AS HE CAN GET THERE!

MINUTES LATER, AS NURSE JANE FOSTER LISTENS ANXIOUSLY TO THE RADIO...
JANE, I'M GOING INTO MY PRIVATE LAB AND I DON'T WANT TO BE DISTURBED FOR THE NEXT TWO HOURS!
BUT HOW CAN YOU WORK CALMLY IN YOUR LAB WHEN THAT RADIO-ACTIVE MAN IS RUNNING AMOK IN THE CITY?

HE JUST ANNOUNCED TO THE POLICE THAT HE CAME FROM RED CHINA TO DESTROY THOR, AND IF THE AUTHORITIES DON'T HELP HIM LOCATE THOR, HE'LL BLOW UP ALL OF NEW YORK!
SO HE'S FROM RED CHINA, EH? THAT EXPLAINS WHY HE'S AFTER THOR!
WELL, THERE'S NOTHING I CAN DO ABOUT IT, JANE! FOR ME, IT'S BUSINESS AS USUAL!
DR. DON BLAKE
PRIVATE LAB
NO ADMITTANCE

IF I LIVE TO BE A MILLION, I'LL JUST NEVER UNDER-STAND WHAT MAKES DON BLAKE TICK!!
I'M SURE JANE DESPISES ME FOR MY ATTITUDE! BUT I CAN'T CONFESS THAT I'M ABOUT TO CREATE A DEVICE TO ENABLE ME TO LOCATE THOR'S HAMMER!! FOR WITHOUT IT, I CAN NEVER BECOME THOR AGAIN!

AFTER AN HOUR OF FRANTIC ELECTRONIC EXPERIMENTING...
AH, I'M IN LUCK! THIS X-RAY-TYPE DEVICE CAN MONITOR ANY AREA WITHIN TEN MILES! I TRAINED IT ON THE WEST SIDE WHERE RADIO REPORTS SAY THOR FLUNG HIS HAMMER. AND THERE IT IS, LYING AT THE BOTTOM OF THE HUDSON RIVER, NEAR A PIER!

THIS IS THE PIER ALL RIGHT! MY VIEWER REVEALED THAT THE URU HAMMER IS LYING BELOW IN 80 FEET OF WATER! THE BIG QUESTION IS... CAN DON BLAKE SURVIVE A DIVE LIKE THAT??!

WELL, NOBODY IN THIS CITY WILL SURVIVE IF I CAN'T RETRIEVE THE HAMMER! SO HERE GOES...

GOSH, THE PRESSURE IS TERRIFIC! BUT I MUST DIVE STILL FURTHER DOWN! I MUST...

I--I SEE THE HAMMER!...(GASP!)... IT'S ONLY 20 FEET AWAY NOW...

...(GASP!)... BUT I CAN'T BREATHE ANY MORE!...(GASP!)... I-I'M BLACKING OUT...

GOT TO HOLD ON... ANOTHER SECOND... NOW!

I DID IT!! REACHED THE HAMMER IN TIME! NOW TO GET RID OF THAT RADIO-ACTIVE MENACE FOREVER!

SOON, ON THE WEST SIDE...

THE TIME IS UP! NOW TO BLOW UP NEW YORK, AND--WHA...? THOR!!

IN PERSON! AND NOW IT'S TIME TO CREATE YOUR OWN PRIVATE TORNADO, WHICH WILL WHISK YOU BACK OVER THE SEA TO RED CHINA!

NO...DON'T!! I'M MOVING TOO FAST! WHEN I LAND, I'LL REACH CRITICAL MASS, AND...
THAT'S YOUR PROBLEM, MY RADIO-ACTIVE FRIEND! YOUR RED MASTERS GAVE YOU A MISSION ...NOW THEY CAN HAVE YOU BACK, INTACT OR OTHERWISE!!

HOURS LATER, IN RED CHINA...

GREAT ONE... LOOK! A TORNADO IS HEADING FOR YONDER MOUNTAINS!
YET, IT IS UNLIKE ANY TORNADO I HAVE EVER SEEN!
13

BEHOLD--AN ATOMIC EXPLOSION!!! CAN IT BE--??
THERE IS ONLY ONE ANSWER... EVEN THE RADIO-ACTIVE MAN COULD NOT DEFEAT THOR!
BARRRROOOOOMM

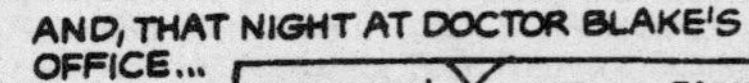

AND, THAT NIGHT AT DOCTOR BLAKE'S OFFICE...

IMAGINE! WHILE YOU WERE DOING YOUR ROUTINE WORK IN YOUR LAB, THE MIGHTY THOR SAVED US ALL... SIGH
WELL, JANE, YOU KNOW HOW IT IS--WE CAN'T ALL BE HEROES!
DAILY BULLETIN
THOR RIDS CITY OF RADIO-ACTIVE MAN!

The End

JOURNEY INTO
MYSTERY
IND.
APPROVED BY THE COMICS CODE AUTHORITY
MARVEL COMICS GROUP 12¢
94 JULY
ANY MAN WHO LIFTS HIS HAND AGAINST LOKI, WILL HAVE TO BATTLE THOR AS WELL!!!
SEE MIGHTY THOR AND EVIL LOKI UNITE, TO BATTLE THE HUMAN RACE, AS THE MARVEL COMICS GROUP USHERS IN THE MARVEL AGE OF COMICS!
I'VE SUCCEEDED IN MAKING THOR THINK I'M HIS FRIEND! BUT WHEN HE'S SERVED HIS PURPOSE HE SHALL BE MY NEXT VICTIM!

THE MIGHTY THOR!
"THOR AND LOKI ATTACK THE HUMAN RACE!"
LOOK, LOKI! BY A SLIGHT PRESSURE OF MY LITTLE FINGER, I CAN TOPPLE THE LEANING TOWER OF PISA!
RUN FOR YOUR LIVES! THOR IS NO LONGER HUMANITY'S PROTECTOR! HE HAS JOINED FORCES WITH EVIL LOKI TO DESTROY MANKIND!
PLOT:....STAN LEE
SCRIPT:...R. BERNS
ART:......J. SINNOTT
LETTERING:..S. ROSEN
X-228
1.

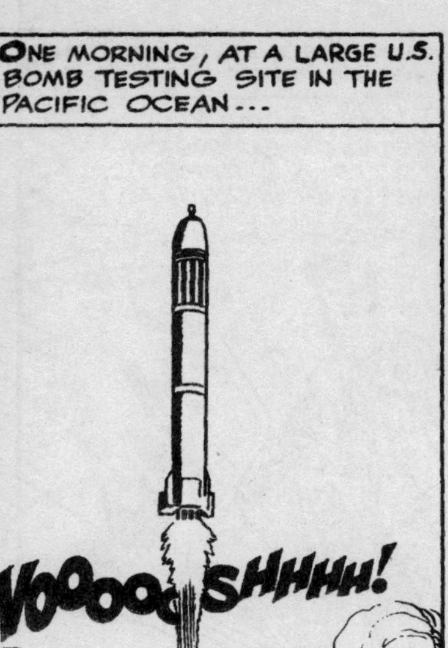
ONE MORNING, AT A LARGE U.S. BOMB TESTING SITE IN THE PACIFIC OCEAN...
WHOOOOOSHHHH!

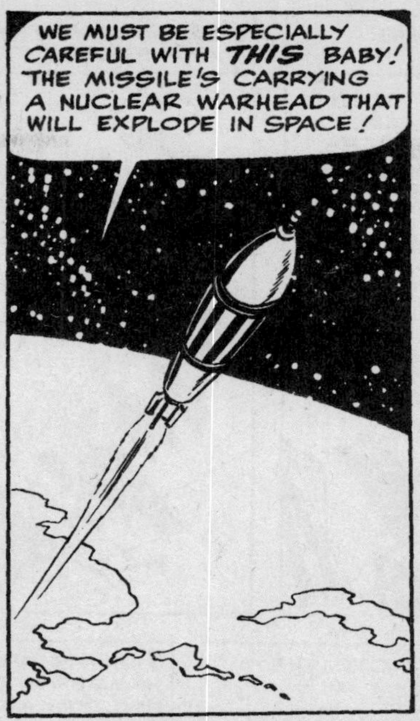
WE MUST BE ESPECIALLY CAREFUL WITH THIS BABY! THE MISSILE'S CARRYING A NUCLEAR WARHEAD THAT WILL EXPLODE IN SPACE!

SUDDENLY, IN THE CONTROL ROOM...
GENERAL! SOMETHING'S WRONG! THE MISSILE IS CHANGING COURSE! IT'S NOT HEADING AWAY FROM EARTH! IT'S JUST FLYING WILD!
GREAT SCOTT! THEN THERE'S NO TELLING WHERE IT'LL STRIKE OR WHAT DAMAGE IT WILL DO!!

WE MUST GET RID OF IT! PUSH THE DESTRUCT BUTTON!
YES, SIR!
CLICK!
DESTRUCT

GENERAL!! (GASP)... WE CAN'T DESTROY THE MISSILE!
BUT THAT'S IMPOSSIBLE! EVERY DEVICE IN OUR TESTING PROGRAM IS SET UP SO THAT IT CAN BE DES-TROYED INSTANTLY ON COMMAND!

I KNOW... BUT RIGHT NOW WE HAVE NO CONTROL WHATEVER OVER THAT MISSILE!
WELL, IF OUR ELECTRON-IC EQUIPMENT CAN'T BLOW IT UP WHERE IT'LL DO NO HARM, ONLY ONE PERSON CAN DES-TROY IT BEFORE IT'S TOO LATE! SEND OUT AN IMMEDIATE S.O.S. FOR MIGHTY THOR!!

AND SO, AN URGENT, WORLD-WIDE MESSAGE IS RADIOED AROUND THE EARTH...
ATTENZIONE, THOR!
ACHTUNG, THOR!
ATTENTION, THOR! NUCLEAR MISSILE FLYING OUT OF CON-TROL! CONTACT PENTAGON AT ONCE!
THOR!
ATTENDEZ, THOR!!

IN HIS MEDICAL OFFICE, AS DR. BLAKE HEARS THE RADIO FLASH ---
CALLING THOR! THOR, YOUR ASSISTANCE IS NEEDED DESPERATELY!
IT'S A GOOD THING MY NURSE, JANE FOSTER, IS OFF-DUTY TODAY! I CAN SWITCH TO THOR INSTANTLY!

AS THE LAME PHYSICIAN HOBBLES TO HIS CANE AND STAMPS IT ONCE ON THE FLOOR ---
THOR... PHONE THE PENTAGON EXTENSION 2715-A ... REPEAT... EXTENSION 2715-A...
THUMP!
THUMP!

MOMENTS AFTER, AS THOR CONTACTS THE PROPER AUTHORITIES ---
THANK GOODNESS YOU HEARD OUR DISTRESS CALL, THOR! HERE'S THE EXACT POSITION OF THE RUNAWAY MISSILE ---
DON'T WORRY! I'LL REACH IT BEFORE IT HITS THE GROUND...

THEN, AS THE MIGHTY NORSE GOD HURLS HIS HAMMER INTO SPACE, GRASPING ITS UNBREAKABLE THONG ---
I'M SPEEDING SO FAST I'M PRACTICALLY INVISIBLE! NOBODY SAW ME LEAVE DR. BLAKE'S OFFICE, NOR CAN ANYONE SPOT ME AS I STREAK SKYWARDS...

MEANWHILE, IN ASGARD, THE HEAVENLY CITADEL OF THE NORSE GODS, LOKI, GOD OF MISCHIEF, THE ONE WHO CAN SEE THOR, GAZES EARTHWARD AND GLOATS!
EVERYTHING IS WORKING OUT PERFECTLY! IT WAS MY REMOTE CONTROL MAGIC WHICH FIRST TAMPERED WITH THE MISSILE'S COURSE! THEN I SHATTERED THE MISSILE'S AUTOMATIC "DESTRUCT" DEVICE!

I KNEW THAT IF THE DEADLY MISSILE BEGAN TO FLY WILD, BEYOND ANY HUMAN CONTROL, THEY'D HAVE TO CALL UPON THOR TO SAVE THE DAY... AND HERE HE COMES!
3.

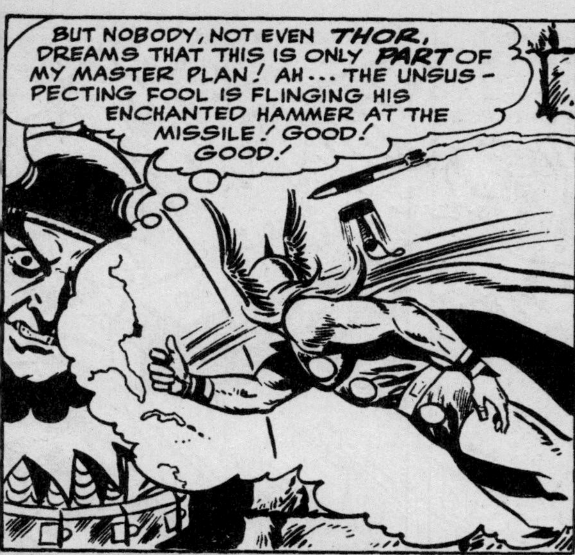
BUT NOBODY, NOT EVEN THOR, DREAMS THAT THIS IS ONLY PART OF MY MASTER PLAN! AH... THE UNSUSPECTING FOOL IS FLINGING HIS ENCHANTED HAMMER AT THE MISSILE! GOOD! GOOD!

ODIN AND HIS COUNCIL OF GODS THOUGHT THAT SHACKLING ME TO THIS CLIFF WITH ULTRA-POWERFUL URU MENACLES WOULD KEEP ME ETERNALLY IMPRISONED AS PUNISHMENT FOR MY WICKED DEEDS...

BUT THEY RECKONED WITHOUT MY SUPER-CUNNING AND REMOTE CONTROL MAGIC! HMM... THOR'S HAMMER HAS EXPLODED THE MISSILE AT A SAFE DISTANCE FROM THE GROUND...
SO FAR, SO GOOD!
BAROOM!

NOW... AS THE HAMMER RETURNS TO THOR... I WILL IMPLEMENT THE SECOND PART OF MY PLAN! I MAY COMPLETELY EXHAUST MY MAGICAL ENERGY TO ACCOMPLISH THIS FEAT... BUT THE RESULT WILL JUSTIFY THE EFFORT!

...GASP! I..I FEEL THE STRAIN ON MY BODY... BUT I MUST CONTINUE! I MUST CREATE A SUPERNATURAL INTERRUPTION... TO CAUSE THOR TO TURN HIS HEAD AT THE CRUCIAL SPLIT-SECOND BEFORE THE HAMMER RETURNS TO HIM!

...'TIS DONE! BUT... (GROAN)... I'M DRAINED OF ALL STRENGTH... I- I CANNOT REMAIN CONSCIOUS... OHHH

A FLAME-BREATHING DRAGON... BEHIND ME!

BUT THERE ARE NO DRAGONS ON EARTH IN THIS AGE! WHAT SORCERY CAN THIS BE??

GASP! IT IS SOME SUPERNATURAL MENACE! I'M STRIKING AN ILLUSION-- THAT NOW ASSUMES THE APPEARANCE OF A CLOUD!

I... OWWWWWW!
WHACK!

SIMULTANEOUSLY, ON ASGARD, AS LOKI COMES OUT OF HIS FAINT...
MY DIVERSION WORKED! THOR CLUTCHES HIS HEAD IN AGONY AS HE REACHES OUT FOR THE HAMMER WHICH BOUNCES OFF HIS HELMET!

THAT MEANS I TIMED THE INCIDENT SO PERFECTLY THAT THE HAMMER HIT HIS CHROMOSOMATIC GLAND, WHICH DETERMINES AND CHANGES PERSONALITY!

I'LL SOON SEE WHETHER THOR'S NATURE HAS CHANGED FROM GOOD TO BAD, DUE TO THE BLOW ON HIS HEAD! I'LL CONTACT HIM MENTALLY...

AH! THOR HAS UNDERGONE A TOTAL CHANGE OF PERSONALITY! HE'S OBEYING THE IDEA I'VE PUT INTO HIS HEAD TO FLY TO ASGARD AND RESCUE ME!
5

MOMENTS AFTER, IN ANOTHER DIMENSION...
THOR! WHY HAVE YOU RETURNED TO ASGARD?
NONE OF YOUR BUSINESS, HEIMDALL! YOU'RE JUST THE GUARDIAN OF BIFROST, THE RAIN-BOW BRIDGE WHICH CONNECTS ASGARD WITH EARTH!

OUT OF MY WAY, YOU FLUNKY!
OWWWW!!

SOMETHING IS AMISS! THOR, THE MIGHTIEST OF THE GODS, HAS NEVER ABUSED HIS STRENGTH BEFORE! HE ACTUALLY SNEERED AS HE PUSHED ME ASIDE! I MUST ALERT ODIN IMMEDIATELY!

LOKI... MY BROTHER... WHAT'S HAPPENED TO YOU? WHY ARE YOU FETTERED WITH THESE URU BONDS?
HA! THOR DOESN'T EVEN REMEMBER THAT I'M HIS ARCH-ENEMY! THIS IS MY GREATEST TRIUMPH!

OUR FATHER, ODIN, DID THIS TO ME, NOBLE BROTHER! ODIN ORDERED THE OTHER GODS TO IMPRISON ME TO KEEP THE TWO OF US APART!
HE DID, DID HE? WELL, I'LL UNDO HIS LITTLE SCHEME!
I'LL RIP OUT THE MENACLES AND CRUMBLE THEM TO METALLIC DUST!
THIS IS DELIGHTFUL! NOW THAT THOR'S NATURE IS LIKE MINE, I CAN CONVINCE HIM TO USE HIS POWER TO AID MY OWN SINISTER SCHEMES!

NOW YOU ARE FREE, LOYAL BROTHER!
THANKS TO YOU, THOR! I VALUE YOUR SUPPORT... FOR WE MUST STAND TOGETHER AGAINST YONDER GODS WHO APPROACH US IN ANGER!

HAVE YOU LOST YOUR MIND, THOR? HOW COULD **YOU,** OF ALL PERSONS, FREE **LOKI,** THE EVIL ONE?
SILENCE, ODIN! SPEAK NOT AGAINST MY BROTHER, LOKI! I RESENT YOUR CHAINING HIM HERE LIKE SOME WILD BEAST!
DARE I BELIEVE MY EARS? IT WAS **YOU** YOURSELF WHO FORGED THE URU BONDS WHICH IMPRISONED LOKI!
NEVER, ODIN! I WOULD NEVER HARM THE LOYAL LOKI!
NO, THOR.. BUT ODIN AND HIS BOOT-LICKING COUNCIL OF YES-MEN WOULD HARM US!

THEY FEAR THAT OUR COMBINED POWERS COULD TAKE OVER ASGARD ITSELF AND WREST SUPREME CONTROL FROM ODIN! AND **THAT'S** WHY THEY SEEK TO DIVIDE US!
SO, YOU'RE UP TO YOUR OLD TRICKS, EH, LOKI? AND YOU'VE MANAGED TO DUPE MIGHTY **THOR** INTO JOINING YOU?

YOUR NATURE THRIVES ON CONFLICT AND CRISES! THUS YOU SPEND YOUR LIFE FOREVER TRYING TO CAUSE TROUBLE! SOME-HOW YOU'VE USED YOUR MAGIC POWERS TO CHANGE THOR'S PERSONALITY...FOR NORMALLY HE WOULD **NEVER** SIDE WITH HIS AGE-OLD ENEMY!

WHAT IS YOUR SCHEMING MIND UP TO **THIS** TIME? WHY HAVE YOU BEWITCHED THOR INTO THINKING AS **YOU** DO?
THOR...HELP! DO NOT LET ODIN PRY MY PLANS FROM ME!
NONE MAY RAISE A HAND TO LOKI WHILE **THOR** LIVES!
ODIN! FOR **THIS** THOR SHALL...
NO! STAY.. BACK! THOR IS **BEWITCHED!** HE KNOWS NOT WHAT HE DOES!
HA! YOU **KNOW** THAT EVEN **YOUR** STRENGTH CANNOT MATCH MIGHTY **THOR'S!**

NOW...THOR AND I INTEND TO **RULE** ASGARD ...BUT, WE REALIZE THAT SINCE WE ARE EACH POWERFUL IN DIFFERENT WAYS WE MAY NOT BE STRONG ENOUGH TO DEFEAT **ALL** OF YOUR LOYAL GODS! ANY STRUGGLE WOULD END IN A STALEMATE ... **BUT...**

BUT WHAT IF THOR AND I SHOULD HOLD A GRAVE THREAT OVER YOUR HEAD? YOU'D HEAR US THEN, EH?
WHAT THREAT, LOKI? WHAT IS THAT SLY BRAIN OF YOURS CONCOCTING NOW?

EARTH AND MANKIND ARE CLOSE TO YOUR HEART, ODIN! SO SUPPOSE THOR AND I WERE TO GO TO EARTH AND CAUSE TERRIBLE HAVOC THERE? THINK WHAT WE TWO COULD DO AGAINST THE HELPLESS EARTHLINGS!
LOKI... YOU WOULDN'T!!

WOULDN'T I? THAT'S MY PLAN, ODIN... TO MAKE EARTH MY HOSTAGE TILL YOU YIELD CONTROL OF ASGARD TO THOR AND ME!
VILLAIN!! HAVE YOU NO PITY FOR THE HELPLESS HUMANS YOU MAY INJURE?

AND YOU, THOR, WHO SPENT MOST OF YOUR LIFE ON EARTH... HOW CAN YOU LEND YOURSELF TO LOKI'S SINISTER SCHEMES?

WHATEVER LOKI WANTS, I WANT, FOR HE IS MY BROTHER!

ENOUGH TALK! YOU KNOW OUR TERMS, ODIN! IF YOU WANT TO SAVE THE HUMAN RACE, SURRENDER ASGARD TO US!
COME, LOKI! HOLD TIGHT TO MY WAIST WHILE MY INVINCIBLE HAMMER TRANSPORTS US TO THE MORTAL WORLD!

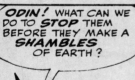

ODIN! WHAT CAN WE DO TO STOP THEM BEFORE THEY MAKE A SHAMBLES OF EARTH?

I DO NOT KNOW! BUT WHAT TROUBLES ME MOST IS THE CHANGE IN THOR! TILL NOW THOR WAS MY FAVORITE SON... NOBLEST OF ALL THE NORSE GODS!

NOW HIS NATURE HAS BECOME THE OPPOSITE OF HIS FORMER SELF... UNDOUBTEDLY BECAUSE OF SOME OF LOKI'S EVIL MAGIC! BUT HOW COULD LOKI HAVE WROUGHT SUCH A TERRIBLE CHANGE?? I MUST PONDER...

SOON, AS LOKI AND THOR REACH THE EARTH ...
THIS IS THE MOMENT, THOR... CREATE THUNDERSTORMS ALL OVER THIS PUNY PLANET!
IT IS CHILD'S PLAY FOR ME, LOKI! BEHOLD!
THUMP!

NOW PRODUCE LIGHTNING BOLTS TO DESTROY MAN'S PROUDEST ACHIEVEMENTS!
AS YOU COMMAND, MY BROTHER!
THUMP! THUMP! THUMP! THUMP!

NOW LET THE EARTH TASTE YOUR FULL WRATH! CAUSE EARTHQUAKES WHICH WILL BRING ALL MANKIND TO ITS KNEES!
IT SHALL BE DONE!
CRRRRAACKKKK!

AND SO, DISASTER STRIKES IN EVERY QUARTER OF THE GLOBE ...
WHY HAS THOR DONE THIS TO US?
WE THOUGHT THOR WAS THE FRIEND OF HUMANKIND, NOT ITS ENEMY!
WHAT... WHAT HAVE WE DONE TO ANGER MIGHTY THOR?

HA! MORE! MORE! WHAT FURTHER DAMAGE CAN YOU DO WITH YOUR POWERS?
BY TWIRLING MY HAMMER LIKE A GIANT FAN, I CAN COMMAND THE POWER OF THE TORNADO, A POWER WHICH CAN BLOW ANYTHING AWAY... EVEN THE TAJ MAHAL!
9

I CAN CREATE ENOUGH SUCTION TO WHISK FAMOUS LANDMARKS ... LIKE THE EIFFEL TOWER ... INTO THE ATMOSPHERE ...

AND THEN CUT THE EMPTY, FLYING STRUCTURES INTO RIBBONS, AS IF THEY WERE MERE SAUSAGES FED INTO A SLICING MACHINE!

WITH THIS CRUSHING POWER OF MY URU HAMMER I CAN GRIND THE PROUDEST STONE PYRAMID INTO A PILE OF RUBBLE!

...TEAR THE GOLDEN GATE BRIDGE TO SHREDS ...

SEAL UP THE PANAMA CANAL SO THAT IT BECOMES WORTHLESS!
CRASH!

... AND, BY THE MERE PRESSURE OF A FINGER ... PUSH OVER THE LEANING TOWER OF PISA!
KKKRRAAK!

THERE! I'VE DONE MY SHARE OF WRECKING! NOW, LOKI, SEE WHAT YOU CAN DO TO MAKE MANKIND TREMBLE!
VERY WELL, THOR! SINCE I HAVE MAGI-CAL POWERS...
10.

I CAN CONJURE UP ALL SORTS OF ILLUSIONS AND TRANSFORMATIONS! FOR EXAMPLE, I CAN TURN AN ORDINARY WHALE INTO A FEARFUL **SEA SERPENT!**

"BRING THE SPHINX TO A SEMBLANCE OF LIFE AND MAKE IT GALLOP THROUGH THE STREETS OF CAIRO!"

"ANIMATE STRUCTURES LIKE THE EMPIRE STATE BUILDING AND HAVE THEM ROCK THEMSELVES AWAY FROM THEIR FOUNDATIONS..."

"AND PERFORM SIMPLER FEATS SUCH AS AWAKENING PREHISTORIC BEHEMOTHS IN MUSEUMS..."

SO YOU SEE, THOR, WE MAKE A GREAT TEAM! BETWEEN US, WE CAN ACCOMPLISH **ANYTHING!**
AYE, LOKI! EVEN **NOW,** STRANGELY GARBED HUMANS APPROACH, BEARING THE WHITE FLAG OF SURRENDER!

WE ARE A SPECIAL COMMITTEE FROM THE UNITED NATIONS... ALL OF US ARE SCHOLARS OF THE ANCIENT NORSE LEGENDS! WE CANNOT UNDERSTAND WHY YOU ARE ATTACKING HUMANITY SO MERCILESSLY!

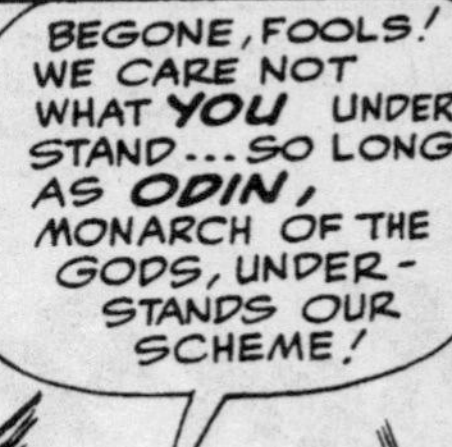
BEGONE, FOOLS! WE CARE NOT WHAT **YOU** UNDERSTAND... SO LONG AS **ODIN,** MONARCH OF THE GODS, UNDERSTANDS OUR SCHEME!

WE WILL CONTINUE TO BLACKMAIL ODIN BY WREAKING HAVOC ON EARTH TILL HE YIELDS CONTROL OF ASGARD TO THE TWO OF US!

THEN LET US TRY TO INTERCEDE WITH ODIN.. FOR OUR PLANET CANNOT LONG ENDURE YOUR ASSAULT!

COME TO OUR U.N. BUILDING, HOME OF ALL EARTH NATIONS, AND HEAR US REQUEST ODIN TO SURRENDER TO YOU!
SOUNDS LIKE A GOOD IDEA, EH, THOR? SENTIMENTAL ODIN WON'T BE ABLE TO RESIST MANKIND'S DESPERATE APPEAL FOR HIM TO SAVE THEIR PUNY PLANET!

VERY WELL, MORTAL! WE'LL OBSERVE THE OUTCOME OF YOUR MESSAGE TO ODIN!
WE THANK YOU! THE U.N. ASSEMBLY HAS BEEN PREPARED FOR THIS SOLEMN OCCASION! FOLLOW US, PLEASE!

AND SO...
NOW TELL US, THOR, HOW CAN WE CONTACT THE OMNIPOTENT ODIN?
ONLY AN IMMORTAL CAN SUMMON THE KING OF THE GODS! IT WILL REQUIRE A SIGNAL... AND THE MOST FITTING SIGNAL OF ALL WILL BE THE DESTRUCTION OF THE U.N. EMBLEM WHICH STANDS BEHIND ME!

THEN, AS THOR HURLS HIS AWESOME HAMMER...
PWANNNGG!
SWOOSH!

... A TRAPDOOR SUDDENLY OPENS BENEATH HIS FEET AND...
OHH...
WHAT DEVILTRY IS THIS? THOR HAS BEEN TAKEN BY SURPRISE! HIS HAMMER RETURNS, BUT HE CANNOT CATCH IT!

NOW THE HAMMER HOVERS OVER THE PLACE WHERE THOR HAS FALLEN! BUT HOW? WHY? WHO IS CONTROLLING IT??

I CONTROL IT! AND NOW IT WILL DROP, STRIKING THIS EXACT PART OF HIS BRAIN ... HIS CHROMOSOMATIC GLAND ... WHERE, OWING TO YOUR TRICKERY, HE HAD RECEIVED SUCH A FATEFUL BLOW ONCE BEFORE!

HOW DID YOU KNOW THAT?
AS I TOLD YOU, WE ARE EXPERTS ON THE NORSE GODS! WE CAN EVEN UNDERSTAND THE SUBTLE, SINISTER SCHEMES OF LOKI!

DO YOU RECOGNIZE US NOW?
ODIN! AND THE GODS OF ASGARD!!
AYE, LOKI! IT TOO US A WHILE TO FIGURE OUT HOW YOU TRANSFORMED THOR'S PERSONAL TY INTO ONE AS EV AS YOURS, BUT WHEN WE DID...

WE PLANNED THIS MEANS OF RESTORING THOR TO HIS ORIGINAL NOBLE, HEROIC SELF... MY TRUE SON AND HEIR!
BUT YOU'LL NEVER RECAPTURE ME, ODIN! I'LL VANISH FROM SIGHT!
NAY, LOKI! MY MAGIC HAMMER NOW FLIES MORE SWIFTLY THAN YOU CAN WORK YOUR MAGIC!

I KNOW YOU NOW FOR THE ROGUE YOU ARE, LOKI! THOUGH YOU ARE MY BROTHER IN NAME, MY BROTHER IN FACT, YOU SHALL ALWAYS BE MY ENEMY IN SPIRIT!
QUICK, LORDS OF ASGARD! SEIZE LOKI WHILE HE REMAINS STUNNED!

MOMENTS LATER, MIGHTY THOR MOUNTS THE ASSEMBLY ROSTRUM...

FORGIVE ME, PEOPLE OF EARTH, FOR THE DESTRUCTION I WROUGHT WHILE UNDER LOKI'S SPELL! WE GODS OF ASGARD VOW, WITH OUR SUPERNATURAL POWERS, TO REPAIR ALL THE DAMAGE DONE TO YOUR PLANET! EVERYTHING SHALL BECOME ONCE AGAIN AS IT WAS!
AND THE MEMORY OF THESE EVENTS SHALL BE ERASED FROM THE MINDS OF MEN!

LATER, ON ASGARD...
NOW THAT LOKI IS ONCE AGAIN IMPRISONED, ONE THING STILL TROUBLES ME, FATHER ODIN! WHAT IF HE SHOULD ESCAPE AGAIN? AND WHAT IF WE SHOULD BE UNABLE TO THWART HIS PLANS?
DO NOT FRET, MY SON! NO MATTER HOW STRONG, OR HOW SLY EVIL MAY BE, THERE WILL ALWAYS BE A CHAMPION TO CHALLENGE AND DEFEAT IT! A CHAMPION SUCH AS MIGHTY THOR... NOBLEST OF THE GODS, PROTECTOR OF MANKIND!
THE END.

JOURNEY INTO
MYSTERY
APPROVED BY THE COMICS CODE AUTHORITY
IND.
MARVEL COMICS GROUP 12¢
95 AUG.
MIGHTY THOR!
YOU HAVE FINALLY MET THE ONE ENEMY YOU CAN NEVER DEFEAT, THOR! YOU HAVE MET...
...A FAR MORE POWERFUL DUPLICATE OF --YOURSELF!

THE MIGHTY THOR! FACES THE MENACE OF... "THE DEMON DUPLICATORS!"
IT CAN'T BE!! ZAXTON'S DEMON DUPLICATE OF ME, POSSESSING TWO MAGIC HAMMERS TO MY ONE, HAS TWICE MY STRENGTH AND POWER!
FAREWELL, THOR! WITHIN SECONDS I SHALL DESTROY YOU... WITH A DOUBLE-HAMMER BLOW!
STORY PLOT: STAN LEE
SCRIPT: R.BERNS
ART: JOE SINNOTT
LETTERING: S.ROSEN
1

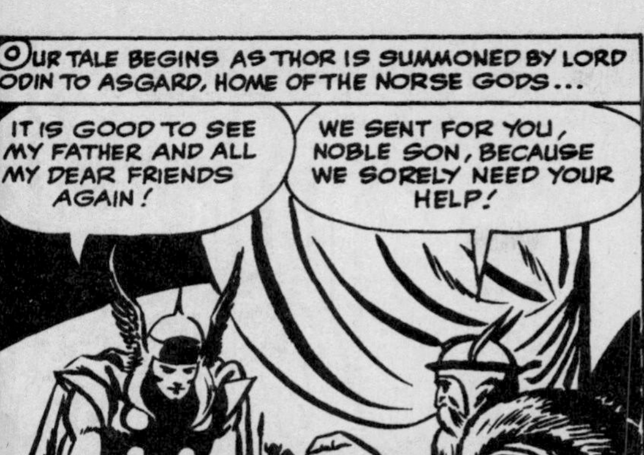
OUR TALE BEGINS AS THOR IS SUMMONED BY LORD ODIN TO ASGARD, HOME OF THE NORSE GODS...
IT IS GOOD TO SEE MY FATHER AND ALL MY DEAR FRIENDS AGAIN!
WE SENT FOR YOU, NOBLE SON, BECAUSE WE SORELY NEED YOUR HELP!

A TERRIBLE DROUGHT HAS AFFLICTED ASGARD! OUR LAND IS PARCHED... CROPS, PLANTS AND FLOWERS HAVE WITHERED! OUR WATER SUPPLY HAS VANISHED! WE MUST HAVE RAIN, THOR... TORRENTS OF IT!

THEN RAIN YOU SHALL HAVE, ODIN! TO CREATE A THUNDERSTORM, I NEED BUT STAMP MY ENCHANTED HAMMER TWICE ON THE GROUND!
THUD!
THUD!

WE ARE GRATEFUL, MY SON! HOW LONG WILL THIS THUNDER-STORM LAST?
FOR A FULL SEVEN DAYS, FATHER! AT THE END OF THE WEEK, I'LL RETURN TO ASGARD, STAMP MY HAMMER THREE TIMES AND THE STORM WILL END!

NOW I MUST RETURN TO EARTH TO AID A HUMAN SCIENTIST WITH A VITAL EXPERIMENT!
FAREWELL, MY SON! MAY YOUR DEEDS BRING AS MUCH BENEFIT TO THE HUMANS AS YOU HAVE TODAY BROUGHT TO ASGARD!

AND SO, AS MIGHTY THOR HURLS HIS HAMMER, AND HANGS ON TO IT...
FAITHFUL HEIMDALL, GUARDIAN OF THE RAINBOW BRIDGE WHICH CONNECTS EARTH WITH ASGARD, IS WAVING GOODBYE! IF I WERE NOT SO USED TO MANKIND, I WOULD GLADLY DWELL IN THIS DIMENSION FOREVER!

I'LL HEAD STRAIGHT FOR THE SCIENTISTS' CONVENTION WHERE PROFESSOR ZAXTON IS SCHEDULED TO DEMONSTRATE THE STRANGE ANDROID WHICH MY OTHER IDENTITY, DR. DON BLAKE, INVENTED!

LOOK! THOR HAS ARRIVED!
ALL RIGHT, PROFESSOR ZAXTON... PROCEED WITH THE EXPERIMENT!

THOR REQUIRES NO INTRODUCTION, GENTLEMEN! THE WHOLE WORLD KNOWS HIM AS THE MIGHTIEST FIGURE ON EARTH! FOR INSTANCE, IT IS SIMPLE FOR THOR ...

...TO RIP OFF THE DOOR OF A SPECIALLY CONSTRUCTED SAFE THAT COULD RESIST A TON OF T.N.T. OR THE MOST POWERFUL ACETYLENE TORCH EVER INVENTED!
RIPPP!

NOW OBSERVE THE ***OCCUPANT*** OF THE SAFE! ***A GREEN ANDROID***... AN AUTOMATON RESEMBLING A HUMAN BEING... CREATED BY THAT MEDICAL GENIUS, DR. DON BLAKE!

DR. BLAKE'S FANTASTIC ANATOMICAL KNOWLEDGE ENABLED HIM TO CONSTRUCT THIS SYNTHETIC CREATURE DOWN TO ITS LAST CELL! BUT WHAT CELLS! WHAT AN AUTOMATON!

UNFORTUNATELY, DR. BLAKE COULDN'T BE PRESENT TO EXPLAIN HIS CREATION HIMSELF ...

HOW ***COULD*** HE BE... WHEN ***I*** SECRETLY AM BLAKE HIMSELF!

THEREFORE I AM HONORED THAT DR. BLAKE ASKED ME TO DEMONSTRATE HIS INVENTION FOR HIM!
I KNEW WHAT I WAS DOING! ZAXTON IS ONE OF THE WORLD'S FOREMOST THEORETICAL PHYSICISTS!

HE EASILY UNDERSTOOD THE INCREDIBLE POTENTIAL OF MY ANDROID!
USING THIS PALM-SIZE REMOTE CONTROL PANEL, I WILL SIGNAL THE ANDROID TO STEP FORWARD!

FIRST, I WILL ILLUSTRATE HIS UNEARTHLY INTELLIGENCE! WILL SOME EXPERT ON PHYSICS COME FORWARD AND GIVE THE ANDROID A SEEMINGLY IMPOSSIBLE PROBLEM?
I'VE GOT ONE, ZAXTON!

IF BLAKE'S ANDROID CAN SOLVE THIS BRAIN-TWISTER, HE'LL HAVE PUZZLED OUT AN EQUATION I HAVEN'T BEEN ABLE TO SOLVE IN ALL MY YEARS!
ANDROID! WORK PROFESSOR VLACH'S EQUATION!

GOOD HEAVENS! H-HE'S DOING IT! HE'S SOLVED THE WORLD'S MOST COMPLICATED MATHEMATICAL PROBLEM!
NATURALLY! BLAKE BUILT INTO THE ANDROID AN I.Q. OF 375...TWICE THAT OF THE BRIGHTEST HUMAN BEING!

NOW FOR A TEST NO MERE HUMAN COULD PASS... RESISTANCE TO THOR'S MIGHTY HAMMER! THOR!!
READY, PROFESSOR ZAXTON!

RWWAMMMNGGG!

AMAZING, EH? THOR'S HAMMER CAN SPLIT A MOUNTAIN, BUT IT CAN'T EVEN SCRATCH THE ANDROID'S SKULL!

WHY NOT? BECAUSE DR. BLAKE GAVE THIS SYNTHETIC CREATURE AN UNBREAKABLE SKIN! ONLY DR. BLAKE KNOWS THE SECRET FORMULA FOR THE ANDROID'S IMPENETRABLE PLASTIC TISSUE!
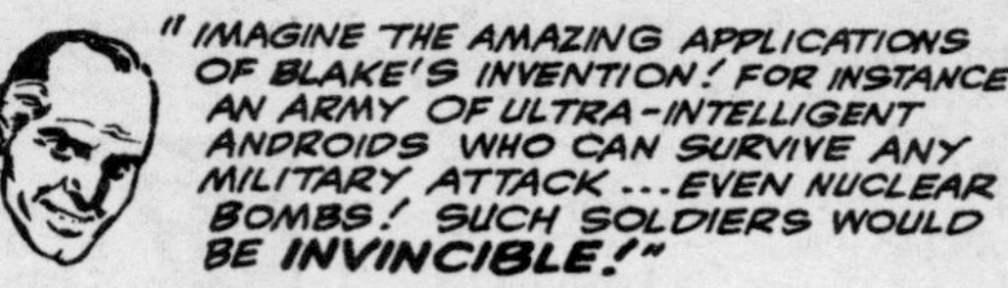
"IMAGINE THE AMAZING APPLICATIONS OF BLAKE'S INVENTION! FOR INSTANCE, AN ARMY OF ULTRA-INTELLIGENT ANDROIDS WHO CAN SURVIVE ANY MILITARY ATTACK... EVEN NUCLEAR BOMBS! SUCH SOLDIERS WOULD BE INVINCIBLE!"

SUDDENLY...
WAIT! ZAXTON'S HAND MUST'VE SLIPPED AND TWISTED ALL THE DIALS AT ONCE! MY ENTIRE MECHANISM IS BEING SHORT-CIRCUITED!
WHAT?!!

DON'T WORRY, THOR! IF THE ANDROID BLOWS UP, IT WILL ONLY BE INTERNALLY! HIS INDESTRUCTIBLE SKIN WILL CONTAIN THE EXPLOSION!
YOU'RE WRONG, ZAXTON!

DR BLAKE CONSTRUCTED MY ANATOMY OUT OF THE SAME PLASTIC SUBSTANCE! WHEN I EXPLODE, MY SKIN WILL DISINTEGRATE LIKE SHRAPNEL!
FOR PETE'S SAKE, THOR, DO SOMETHING!

THERE'S ONLY ONE THING TO DO! GET RID OF THIS SUPER-GRENADE!
RRIIPPP!
5.

I'LL STRAP HIM TO MY HAMMER WITH THESE TWO METAL SECTIONS FROM THE DEMOLISHED VAULT DOOR!
HURRY, THOR! THE MOLECULAR CHANGE IS ALMOST COMPLETED INSIDE ME!

I'M READY TO...

...EXPLODE!

BARROOOOMMM!

MOMENTS AFTER...
WHEW! IF THAT HAD HAPPENED HERE, WE'D ALL HAVE BEEN GONERS! I DIDN'T KNOW AS MUCH ABOUT BLAKE'S INVENTION AS I THOUGHT!
OBVIOUSLY NOT! I GUESS THIS ENDS THE DEMONSTRATION!

LATER THAT DAY, AS THOR STREAKS UNOBSERVED TO DR. BLAKE'S OFFICE, AND SWITCHES TO HIS HUMAN IDENTITY...
THAT BUNGLER, ZAXTON! I SHOULD NEVER HAVE ENTRUSTED THE DEMONSTRATION TO HIM! HIS SIMULTANEOUS TWISTING OF DIALS SEEMED ALMOST DELIBERATE!
THUMP!

HMM... JANE ISN'T HERE! MAYBE SHE WENT OUT FOR COFFEE OR SOMETHING... ALTHOUGH IT ISN'T LIKE HER TO TAKE OFF WITHOUT LEAVING A NOTE!
LOOKING FOR YOUR NURSE, JANE FOSTER, DOCTOR?
6.

ZAXTON! WHAT ARE YOU DOING HERE? DID YOU SEE JANE?
FORGET MISS FOSTER! WE HAVE SOMETHING MORE IMPORTANT TO DISCUSS! MY NEW INVENTION...

THOR TOLD ME HOW YOU BOTCHED MY ANDROID EXPERIMENT! HOW COULD YOU MAKE SO STUPID A MISTAKE?
WE'LL GET TO THAT PRESENTLY! THIS, MY DEAR DOCTOR, IS A DUPLICATING MACHINE! IT DUPLICATES ANY-THING IT IS AIMED AT!

TAKE THAT EASY CHAIR! I PRESS THE DUPLICATING BUTTON, AND PRESTO! YOU'VE GOT A CARBON COPY OF IT!

SPEAKING OF "CARBON COPIES"... IF I KEEP PRESSING THE BUTTON, I CAN CREATE TWELVE TYPEWRITERS WITHIN SECONDS! FANTASTIC... AND YET, BLAKE, I NEED YOUR HELP TO PERFECT THE RAY!
CLICK! CLICK!
CLICK! CLICK!

MY HELP? YOU'RE CRAZY, ZAXTON! YOUR MACHINE WORKS PERFECTLY! BESIDES, I'M NOT YOUR EQUAL IN THE PHYSICAL SCIENCES! I SPECIALIZE IN THE HUMAN BODY!
NONSENSE! YOUR ANDROID WAS A MECHANICAL MIRACLE!

WHETHER YOU LIKE IT OR NOT, YOU'RE GOING TO HELP ME TO ADVANCE TO PHASE TWO OF MY INVENTION! YOU'RE GOING TO HELP ME DUPLICATE HUMAN BEINGS!
BUT YOU CAN'T DO THAT! YOU CAN'T TAMPER WITH HUMAN LIFE!

I THOUGHT YOU WERE AN HONORABLE MAN, ZAXTON! BUT I NOW SEE THERE'S AN EVIL STRAIN IN YOU! I REFUSE TO HELP YOUR MAD SCHEMES!
NOT SO FAST, BLAKE! MISS FOSTER IS MY PRISONER!

YOU'LL NEVER SEE HER ALIVE AGAIN UNLESS YOU HELP ME COMPLETE MY MACHINE SO THAT IT CAN DUPLICATE HUMAN LIFE! I'M A DESPERATE MAN, BLAKE! I'LL DO ANYTHING TO GET MY WAY!

TAKE YOUR ANDROID! I WAS JEALOUS OF YOUR INVENTION, SO I DELIBERATELY MADE IT BLOW UP... NOT REALIZING THE EXPLOSION MIGHT'VE DESTROYED ME, TOO! LUCKILY, THOR WAS THERE...

THOR IS ALSO HERE! I COULD SWITCH TO THOR AND FORCE THIS MADMAN TO REVEAL WHERE HE HID JANE ... BUT IT'S AGAINST MY CODE TO HARM HUMAN BEINGS EXCEPT IN SELF-DEFENSE!

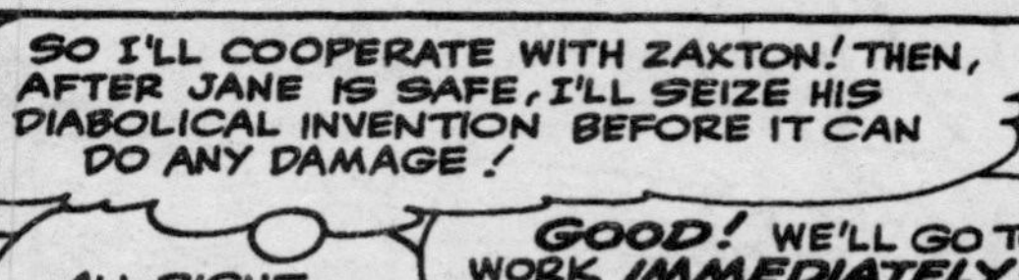
SO I'LL COOPERATE WITH ZAXTON! THEN, AFTER JANE IS SAFE, I'LL SEIZE HIS DIABOLICAL INVENTION BEFORE IT CAN DO ANY DAMAGE!

ALL RIGHT, ZAXTON, YOU WIN!
GOOD! WE'LL GO TO WORK IMMEDIATELY!

AND SO, THROUGH THE LONG, LONG NIGHT, IN DR. BLAKE'S LAB ...
ONE LAST ADJUSTMENT AND WE ARE THROUGH, ZAXTON!
NO, BLAKE! WE'RE NOT FINISHED TILL I MAKE SURE THE MACHINE WORKS! ONLY THEN WILL I TELL YOU WHERE JANE FOSTER IS IMPRISONED!

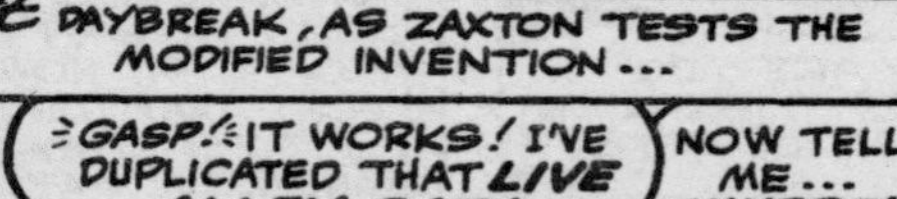
AT DAYBREAK, AS ZAXTON TESTS THE MODIFIED INVENTION...

GASP! IT WORKS! I'VE DUPLICATED THAT LIVE ALLEY CAT!
NOW TELL ME... WHERE'S JANE?
CLICK!

LOCKED IN THE CELLAR OF MY HOUSE! IT'S ASTOUNDING!! I CAN PRODUCE DUPLICATES WITH MACHINE-GUN RAPIDITY!

HMM... WHILE ZAXTON IS ADMIRING HIS INVENTION I'LL SLIP INSIDE AND CHANGE TO THOR AND RESCUE JANE!
CLICK
CLICK
CLICK
CLICK
8.

BUT, SECONDS LATER, AS DON BLAKE STAMPS HIS CANE...
I..I DIDN'T EXPECT ZAXTON TO WALK IN ON ME! NOW HE'S THE FIRST AND ONLY HUMAN TO KNOW MY DUAL IDENTITY!
GREAT SCOTT! I'M SEEING THINGS! YOU, BLAKE, HAVE TRANSFORMED YOURSELF INTO... THOR!!

BUT, BEFORE THOR CAN ACT...
W-WAIT!
TOO LATE, THOR! YOU'VE BEEN DUPLICATED! AND WHAT A DUPLICATION! YOU SEE, I PURPOSELY DIDN'T MENTION ONE THING ABOUT MY INVENTION!
CLICK!

WHILE IT DUPLICATES AN OBJECT'S EXACT PHYSICAL STRUCTURE, IT CREATES THE OPPOSITE OF THE ORIGINAL'S PERSONALITY AND BRAINS UNDER MY TELEPATHIC CONTROL!
YOU MADMAN! I'LL SMASH YOUR MACHINE TO BITS!

OHHHHH!
HA! SEE THE FIX YOU'RE IN, THOR? YOUR DUPLICATE PROTECTS ME! INDEED, YOU'RE EQUALLY MATCHED IN ALL POWERS EXCEPT ONE...

... I WILL AID THE DUPLICATE, THOR! FOR EXAMPLE, BY GIVING HIM AN EXTRA MAGIC HAMMER!

NOW YOU'RE OVER-MATCHED, THOR, BECAUSE TWO MAGIC HAMMERS POSSESS TWICE THE STRENGTH OF ONE! AND I'LL HELP MY EVIL CHAMPION IN COUNTLESS WAYS AS HE GOES ABOUT DESTROYING YOU!
WHY ARE YOU DOING THIS, ZAXTON? WHAT ARE YOU AFTER?
TOTAL, ABSOLUTE POWER! BUT I NEVER DREAMT I COULD ACHIEVE IT SO SOON! WHO'D THINK THAT THE LAME DR. BLAKE WAS REALLY MIGHTY THOR? AND HOW LUCKY THAT YOU PLAYED INTO MY HANDS THE WAY YOU DID!!

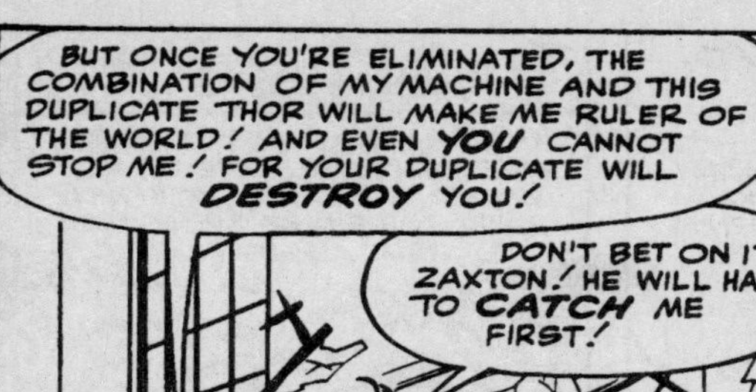
BUT ONCE YOU'RE ELIMINATED, THE COMBINATION OF MY MACHINE AND THIS DUPLICATE THOR WILL MAKE ME RULER OF THE WORLD! AND EVEN YOU CANNOT STOP ME! FOR YOUR DUPLICATE WILL DESTROY YOU!
DON'T BET ON IT, ZAXTON! HE WILL HAVE TO CATCH ME FIRST!

I'LL SEE TO IT THAT THOR DOES NOT ELUDE HIS PURSUER! I'LL CREATE A DUPLICATE OF THAT OFFICE BUILDING!
CLICK!

NEXT SECOND...
OHHHHH!
SMASSHHHH!
CRANDA

THE IMPACT FLOORED ME! AND HERE COMES MY DUPLICATE...MUSTN'T LET HIM STRIKE ME WITH THOSE TWO MIGHTY HAMMERS!

IF I STAMP MY HAMMER FOUR TIMES, IT WILL SHOOT FORTH LIGHTNING BOLTS!
THUMP!
THUMP!
THUMP!
THUMP!

YEEOWWW!
THE MAGIC HAMMERS ARE MADE OUT OF THE MINERAL, URU, AN EXCELLENT CONDUCTOR OF ELECTRICITY!

THE SHOCK WOULD'VE KILLED TEN ORDINARY MEN... BUT IT'S WEAKENED MY STUNNED "TWIN" ENOUGH TO RENDER HIM VULNERABLE TO MY HAMMER!
MY DUPLICATE IS AT THOR'S MERCY! I MUST SAVE HIM!

BY ODIN! ZAXTON'S CREATED YET ANOTHER THOR... TO RECEIVE MY HAMMER BLOW!

THE FIGURE VAPORIZED, LEAVING MY ORIGINAL TARGET UNTOUCHED!
I'VE FOILED THOR! BY THE TIME THE HAMMER RETURNS TO HIM, HIS EVIL DUPLICATE WILL REGAIN HIS TWO HAMMERS!

THEN, AS THE LIFE-AND-DEATH CHASE RESUMES...
HMM... SINCE BOTH THORS HAVE IDENTICAL RATES OF SPEED, MY DUPLICATE WILL NEVER OVERTAKE THOR WITH-OUT ASSISTANCE!
CLICK! CLICK!
CLICK! CLICK!
CLICK!

FOR THE LOVE OF ASGARD!! ZAXTON IS DUPLICATING DOZENS OF AIRLINERS! THEY'RE BLOCKING MY PATH! IF I SUSTAIN MY SPEED, I'LL COLLIDE, WITH THEM!

BUT IF I SLOW UP, AS I'M DOING... I'M CORNERED! ZAXTON'S DEMON DUPLICATE WILL HAVE ME AT HIS MERCY!

HA! I KNEW THAT TENDER-HEARTED CHARACTER WOULDN'T SMASH THROUGH AN AIRLINER TO SAVE HIS OWN LIFE! MY DUPLICATE HAS HIM TRAPPED!
11.

NO WAY OUT! IN A SPLIT-SECOND BOTH HAMMERS WILL STRIKE ME... OVERPOWERING ME BY THE DOUBLE BLOW!

BUT AMAZINGLY, AS THE DUPLICATE'S HAMMERS STRIKE THOR...
IT'S UNCANNY! I FELT NOTHING...NOTHING WHATEVER! I WONDER WHAT'S CAUSING MY ENEMY'S HAMMERS TO LOSE THEIR IMPACT?
THUD!
THUD!

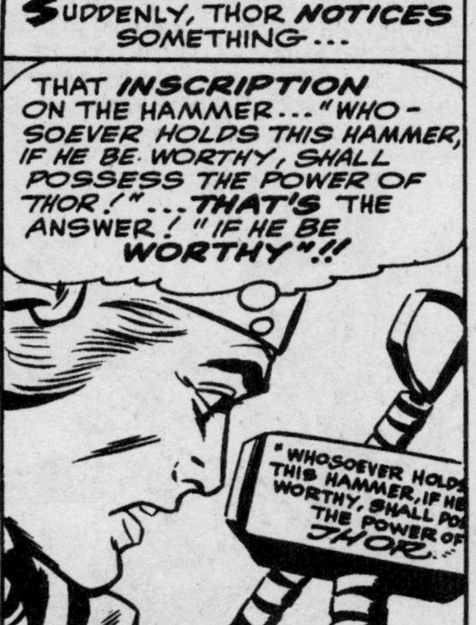
SUDDENLY, THOR NOTICES SOMETHING...
THAT INSCRIPTION ON THE HAMMER..."WHOSOEVER HOLDS THIS HAMMER, IF HE BE WORTHY, SHALL POSSESS THE POWER OF THOR!"...THAT'S THE ANSWER! "IF HE BE WORTHY"!!
"WHOSOEVER HOLDS THIS HAMMER, IF HE WORTHY, SHALL PO THE POWER OF THOR.

THAT'S WHY MY DUPLICATE, EVEN IF HE HELD A HUNDRED HAMMERS, WOULDN'T BE ABLE TO DEFEAT ME WITH THEM! HE IS AN EVIL COPY OF ME, THEREFORE UNWORTHY TO POSSESS MY HAMMER'S POWER!

SO, IRONICALLY, FROM THE START I HAD NOTHING TO FEAR FROM ZAXTON'S DUPLICATE! AND NOW, AS MY OWN ENCHANTED MALLET STRIKES HIM HE'S FADING AWAY...INTO THE NOTHINGNESS FROM WHENCE HE CAME!

NOW TO GET ZAXTON!
FOR SOME REASON, MY DUPLICATE COULDN'T HARM THOR! I-I MUST MAKE A DUPLICATE OF MYSELF SO THOR WON'T KNOW WHICH IS THE REAL PROFESSOR ZAXTON TO PUNISH!
CLICK!

OH...NO!! IN MY NERVOUSNESS, THE MACHINE SLIPPED OUT OF MY HANDS! I MUST GRAB IT BEFORE IT FALLS OVER THE PARAPET!

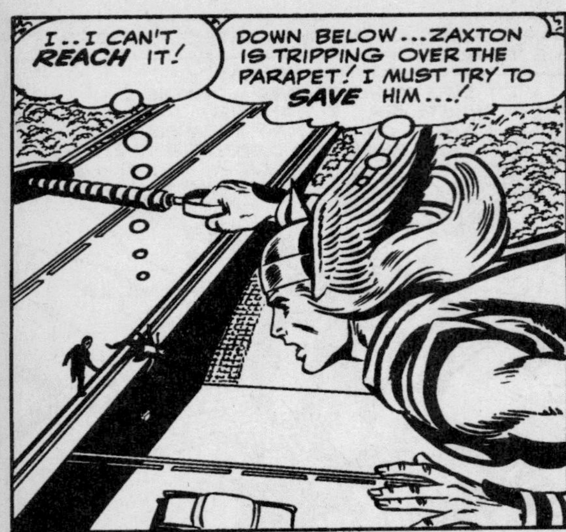
I..I CAN'T REACH IT!
DOWN BELOW...ZAXTON IS TRIPPING OVER THE PARAPET! I MUST TRY TO SAVE HIM...!

EEIIIIII!
TOO LATE! I CAN'T REACH HIM IN TIME!

HE'S DONE FOR! AND THE SECRET OF HIS SINISTER INVENTION IS GONE WITH HIM!

BUT, BY A TWIST OF FATE, ANOTHER PROFESSOR ZAXTON LIVES ON! A DUPLICATE OF THE ORIGINAL ONE, BUT WITH AN OPPOSITE PERSONALITY! WITHOUT HIS STREAK OF VILLAINY!

IT'S FOR THE BEST! THE WORLD HAS RID ITSELF OF A CRUEL MENACE...AND IN HIS PLACE STANDS A SCIENTIFIC GENIUS WHO SHALL DO GOOD WHERE THE ORIGINAL DID BAD!

AFTER THOR DISPOSES OF THE DEAD MAN AND FREES JANE FOSTER...
THANK GOOD-NESS YOU'VE FOUND ME! PRO-FESSOR ZAXTON MUST HAVE GONE MAD!
I KNOW, JANE... BUT NOW HE'S..UH..SNAPPED OUT OF IT AND HE'S SORRY FOR WHAT HE'S DONE!
I WON'T RUIN THE "NEW" PROFESSOR'S REPUTA-TION! IN HIS NEW MENTAL STATE HE CAN BECOME A BOON TO HUMANITY!

DAYS LATER, IN ASGARD...
AH, GOOD! YOU'VE ENDED THE RAINFALL! FOR A WHILE I THOUGHT YOU'D FORGOTTEN US, THOR!
FORGET ASGARD? NEVER, MY FATHER! FOR NO MATTER WHAT ADVENTURES MAY SUMMON ME TO THE WORLD BELOW, THIS IS THE LAND MY HEART CALLS HOME!
THUMP! THUMP! THUMP!
The END

JOURNEY INTO MYSTERY
IND.
APPROVED BY THE COMICS CODE AUTHORITY
MARVEL COMICS GROUP 12¢
96 SEPT.
THRILL TO THE BATTLE OF TITANS-- AS MIGHTY THOR FACES THE AWESOME POWER OF MERLIN THE MAD!
BEHOLD, THOR... YOUR POWER IS NOTHING COMPARED TO THE MYSTIC ARTS AT MY COMMAND!
MERLIN'S ENCHANTMENT HAS STILLED MY ARM!! I CANNOT MOVE! HOW CAN I BREAK HIS SPELL ?
SUPER HEROES! SUPER-VILLAINS! IN THE MARVEL-OUS MARVEL STYLE!

THE MIGHTY THOR!
DEFYING THE MAGIC OF...
MAD MERLIN!
HMM... SO "MERLIN" IS VISITING AMERICA! IT'S A GOOD THING HE'S IN NO CONDITION TO PRACTICE HIS STRANGE SORCERY NOW!
HEY, PROFESSOR! WHAT'S INSIDE THAT BIG, STONE SARCOPHAGUS?
THE BODY OF MERLIN, THE MAD WIZARD OF KING ARTHUR'S COURT! MERLIN'S CRYPT WAS JUST DISCOVERED IN ENGLAND, AND IT'LL BE OPENED BY ARCHEOLOGICAL EXPERTS AT THE NEW YORK MUSEUM TOMORROW!
STORY PLOT: STAN LEE
SCRIPT: R. BERNS
ART: JOE SINNOTT
LETTERING: ART SIMEK
1

I HOPE I LEFT THE REAR WINDOW OF MY OFFICE OPEN SO THAT I CAN FLY INTO MY PRIVATE LAB WITHOUT ANY DIFFICULTY...

YES! EVERYTHING IS AS I LEFT IT WHEN I TOOK OFF AN HOUR AGO TO HANDLE THAT BUS ACCIDENT!

I LEFT AN OFFICE FULL OF PATIENTS! I WONDER WHETHER THEY'RE STILL WAITING FOR ME!
THUMP! THUMP!

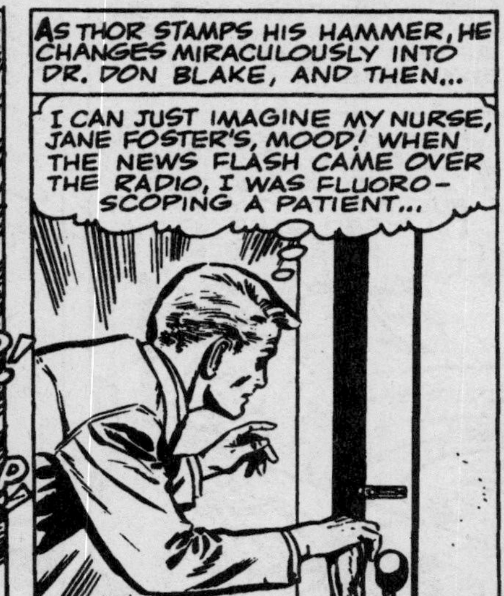
AS THOR STAMPS HIS HAMMER, HE CHANGES MIRACULOUSLY INTO DR. DON BLAKE, AND THEN...
I CAN JUST IMAGINE MY NURSE, JANE FOSTER'S, MOOD! WHEN THE NEWS FLASH CAME OVER THE RADIO, I WAS FLUORO-SCOPING A PATIENT...

I LEFT THE PATIENT WITH HER AND BOLTED MYSELF IN THIS LAB TO SWITCH TO THOR! I'LL BET JANE'S AS SORE AS A BOIL ABOUT MY LEAVING HER IN THE LURCH FOR THE HUNDREDTH TIME!

BUT IT CAN'T BE HELPED! FIRST THING'S FIRST! I CAN ALWAYS FLUORO-SCOPE A PATIENT! BUT I'LL NEVER GET A SECOND CHANCE TO RESCUE A BUS-LOAD OF PASSENGERS PLUNGING OFF A BRIDGE!

OH, SO YOU FINALLY DE-CIDED TO COME OUT OF YOUR LAB! ALL YOUR PATIENTS HAVE GONE HOME...OR TO OTHER DOCTORS!
IT COULDN'T BE HELPED JANE! I...UH...HAD SOMETHING MORE IMPOR-TANT TO DO IN THE LAB AT THE TIME!

WHAT? A CHEMICAL EXPERI-MENT? AN URGE TO TAKE A NAP? I HAMMERED ON THE LAB DOOR FOR A HALF HOUR... YET YOU DIDN'T EVEN DO ME THE COURTESY OF ANSWERING!

I KEPT MAKING LAME EXCUSES TO YOUR PATIENTS! FINALLY, ONE BY ONE, THEY BECAME DISGUSTED AND WALKED OUT! AND I DON'T BLAME THEM! THIS IS NO WAY TO CONDUCT A MEDICAL PRACTICE!

IF YOU HAVE OFFICE HOURS, USE THEM FOR DOCTORING YOUR PATIENTS... NOT FOR BEAUTY SLEEPS OR LAB EXPERIMENTS! YOU WON'T HAVE A PRACTICE LEFT IF YOU KEEP SHOWING NO SENSE OF RESPONSIBILITY!
NO RESPONSIBILITY, EH?

"JANE DOESN'T KNOW THAT, AS THOR, I WAS AT THE SCENE OF THE TRAGEDY A MINUTE AFTER I HEARD THE NEWS FLASH...
LOOK! THOR'S HERE! MAYBE HE CAN RAISE THE BUS IN TIME!
THAT WIDENING RIPPLE MARKS THE SPOT WHERE THE BUS WENT DOWN! HMM... I'LL NEED SOME OF THIS STEEL CABLE!

I CAN SAVE EVERY PASSENGER IF NOT TOO MANY WINDOWS WERE OPEN... AND THE BUS DIDN'T FILL TOO RAPIDLY WITH WATER!

BY ODIN! I DIDN'T ARRIVE A SECOND TOO SOON! THE FRANTIC PASSENGERS WILL NEVER CLAW THEIR WAY OUT AT THE RATE THE WATER IS POURING IN! I MUST WRAP THIS CABLE AROUND THE BUS!

I-I MUST TIE THIS STEEL CABLE INTO A KNOT! BUT... -GASP!-... I CAN'T HOLD MY BREATH MUCH LONGER! MY LUNGS ARE READY TO BURST!...

NOW TO SECURE MY HAMMER TO THE CABLE, AND THEN...

...WHIRL THE BUS AROUND, DESPITE THE RESISTANCE OF THE WATER PRESSURE...

...AND AWAY IT GOES, ON ITS WAY TO THE EAST SIDE BUS TERMINAL!
...THE HAMMER WILL GUIDE IT TO A SMOOTH, GLIDING LANDING!

A FEW INSTANTS LATER...
HOLY CATS!!! IT'S THE BUS THAT SKIDDED OVER THE BRIDGE! HOW'D IT SUDDENLY BECOME AIR-BORNE?
BECAUSE OF THAT HAMMER! IT'S THOR'S! SOMEHOW THOR MUST'VE REACHED IT JUST IN THE NICK OF TIME!
EAST SIDE BUS TERMINAL

THEN, AS THE MYSTIC MALLET RETURNS TO ITS MASTER...
I JUST REMEMBERED! I LEFT AN OFFICE FULL OF PATIENTS BEHIND ME!
I'D BETTER BE RUSHING BACK BEFORE JANE THREATENS TO QUIT ...FOR THE MILLIONTH TIME! I SOMETIMES THINK I WORRY MORE ABOUT HER, THAN ABOUT ANY OF THE SUPER-VILLAINS I'VE EVER BEEN THREATENED BY!

FLASH! THE EAST SIDE BUS COMPANY JUST REPORTED THAT THOR HAS RESCUED THE SUNKEN BUS WITH ALL ITS OCCUPANTS!
THERE! THAT'S WHAT I CALL RESPONSIBILITY! YOU WOULDN'T CATCH THOR NAPPING IN HIS LAB!
POOR JANE! IF SHE ONLY KNEW...

AS THE NEWS BULLETINS CONTINUE...
THIS SEEMS TO BE A DAY FOR UNUSUAL HAPPENINGS! TODAY, THE STONE CRYPT OF MERLIN, FAMED WIZARD OF KING ARTHUR'S COURT, WAS UNLOADED ON A WEST SIDE PIER!
MERLIN? I THOUGHT HE WAS JUST A LEGEND!

BUT IF THEY'VE DISCOVERED HIS CRYPT, HE MUST HAVE REALLY EXISTED! I WONDER IF MERLIN USED HIS MAGIC FOR GOOD... OR EVIL?
WHO KNOWS, JANE? CERTAINLY HIS DUSTY OLD BONES WON'T REVEAL WHETHER HE WAS A VILLAIN OR NOT! IN ANY CASE, IT'S NO CONCERN OF OURS!

BUT, LITTLE DOES DR. BLAKE DREAM OF WHAT GREAT CONCERN MERLIN WILL SOON BE TO THOR! FOR, THE NEXT MORNING, AT THE MUSEUM, AS THE EXPERTS OPEN MERLIN'S CRYPT...
IT-- IT'S IMPOSSIBLE!
I-I CAN'T BELIEVE MY EYES!

HIS BODY IS IN PERFECT CONDITION... AS IF HE HAD DIED ONLY YESTERDAY! COULD HE HAVE USED MAGIC POWERS TO PRESERVE HIMSELF FOR 1,000 YEARS?
NONSENSE! THERE'S NO SUCH THING AS MAGIC!

THERE MUST BE SOME SCIENTIFIC EXPLANATION FOR THIS! THE CRYPT MAY HAVE BEEN ABSOLUTELY AIR-TIGHT!
CORRECT! OR ELSE, MERLIN'S KEEN MIND HIT UPON SOME EMBALMING PROCESS WE KNOW NOTHING ABOUT! LET'S RETIRE TO THE CONFERENCE ROOM TO DISCUSS THIS AMAZING DISCOVERY!

THEN, AFTER THE EXPERTS LEAVE, AND THE CRYPT REMAINS ALONE AND UNGUARDED IN THE VAST CHAMBER...
THEY'VE GONE! MY MASTER PLAN IS WORKING PERFECTLY!

THEY THINK I'M DEAD! BUT I NEVER DIED... NEVER!

I WAS **PREPARED** FOR MY ENEMIES! WHEN THEY CAME TO KILL ME, THEY FOUND ME IN A COMATOSE STATE! THEY THOUGHT I'D **POISONED** MYSELF! BUT I HAD MERELY USED A MAGIC SPELL WHICH ONLY **MY GENIUS** COULD CREATE!

THE SPELL ARRANGED THAT WHEN MY CRYPT WOULD BE OPENED, THE RUSH OF AIR WOULD REVIVE ME AFTER A SLEEP OF CENTURIES!

AND MANY CENTURIES IT HAS BEEN! ACCORDING TO THIS NEWSPAPER, IT IS THE YEAR 1963... AND THE KING... **PRESIDENT**, THEY CALL HIM... OF THIS LAND IS A CERTAIN JOHN F. KENNEDY!
JFK SPEAKS TO NATION ON TV TONIGHT!
PRESIDENT'S MESSAGE WILL CONTAIN

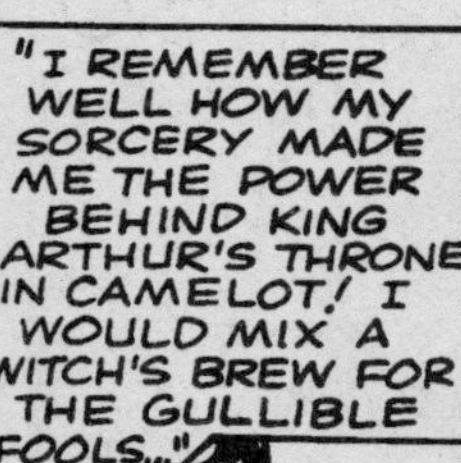
"I REMEMBER WELL HOW MY SORCERY MADE ME THE POWER BEHIND KING ARTHUR'S THRONE IN CAMELOT! I WOULD MIX A WITCH'S BREW FOR THE GULLIBLE FOOLS..."

NOW I SHALL READ THE FUTURE IN THE SWIRLING, MURKY CONCOCTION! **AHA!** ENEMIES APPROACH THY CASTLE, KING ARTHUR! TO ARMS! DEFEND THYSELF AGAINST A SNEAK ATTACK!

"THE KNIGHTS OF THE ROUND TABLE DID NOT KNOW I USED WITCH'S BREWS AND OTHER WEIRDLY DRAMATIC EFFECTS ONLY TO **IMPRESS** THEM! IT WAS **I** WHO POSSESSED THE POWERS, NOT THE SMELLY SOUPS I BREWED!"
BLESS MERLIN! IF NOT FOR HIS MAGIC FORESIGHT, WE WOULDN'T HAVE BEEN READY FOR THIS FOUL ASSAULT!

"NOT ONLY DID I POSSESS **TELEPATHY...** BUT UNIQUE POWERS OF LEVITATION!"
LOOK, MERLIN CAUSES THE CONTENDER TO FLY AND WHIRL ABOUT IN THE AIR! FANTASTIC!
THE PEOPLE ARE AWED, AMUSED, AND TERRIFIED BY WHAT THEY SEE! THE SUPERSTITIOUS NUMBSKULLS THINK I'M THE MASTER OF MAGIC, THE WIZARD OF WITCHCRAFT!

NOBODY IN MEDIEVAL TIMES SUSPECTED I WAS ONE OF THE MUTANTS ON EARTH... DERIVING MY POWERS NOT FROM ANY OCCULT MAGIC... BUT FROM WITHIN MY OWN BODY!

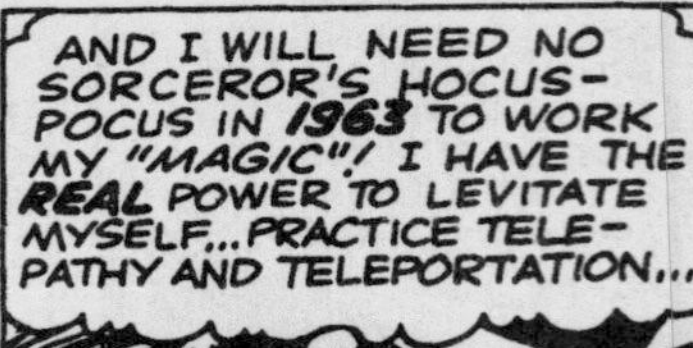
AND I WILL NEED NO SORCEROR'S HOCUS-POCUS IN 1963 TO WORK MY "MAGIC"! I HAVE THE REAL POWER TO LEVITATE MYSELF... PRACTICE TELEPATHY AND TELEPORTATION...

...WITHIN LIMITS, OF COURSE, JUST AS I AM NOW TRANSFERRING MYSELF TO CAPE D'OR!
NEW SATELLITE TO BE FIRED INTO ORBIT TODAY AT CAPE D'OR!

HMMM... ALL MY UNIQUE SKILLS STILL WORK! BUT I MUST CONVINCE THIS GOVERNMENT OF THAT! FOR, JUST AS IN OLDEN TIMES, I INTEND TO BECOME THE REAL POWER BEHIND THE COUNTRY'S LEADER!

THE EYES OF THE ENTIRE WORLD ARE ON THE MISSILE WHICH THEY'RE FIRING INTO SPACE! IT WILL ATTRACT A LOT OF ATTENTION IF I CAUSE THE ROCKET TO CHANGE ITS COURSE!
HEY! SOMETHING'S WRONG! THE MISSILE TOOK A SUDDEN ZIG-ZAG!

IF THAT DARN THING GOES OFF COURSE, WE MAY HAVE TO PRESS THE DESTRUCT BUTTON AND BLOW IT TO SMITHEREENS!
HA! AFTER THEY'VE DESTROYED IT, I'LL COME FORWARD AND REVEAL THIS WAS JUST A SAMPLE OF THE THINGS I CAN DO IF I'M NOT GIVEN THE POWER I SEEK!
MISSILE CONTROL ROOM

AT THAT MOMENT, AS DR. BLAKE WATCHES THE LAUNCHING ON HIS OFFICE TV SET...

HOLD YOUR BREATH, FOLKS! IT'LL BE A TERRIBLE LOSS TO THE U.S. IF THAT VALUABLE MISSILE MUST BE DESTROYED!

IT WON'T BE, IF I CAN BECOME THOR IN TIME, THEN ZIP INTO THE SKY AND FIND SOME WAY TO PUT THAT ROCKET INTO PROPER ORBIT!

SECONDS LATER, AS U.S. ARMY PURSUIT PLANES WATCH THOR STREAK SPACEWARD...

HOLD EVERYTHING! THOR IS ADJUSTING THE CAPSULE'S TRAJECTORY! THE ALTITUDE ANGLE IS NOW OKAY!

THERE SEEMS TO BE NO MECHANICAL FAILURE! SOME OUTSIDE FORCE MUST HAVE AFFECTED THIS ROCKET! CAN IT BE--LOKI!??

SOON AFTER, AS THOR FLIES TO ASGARD, HOME OF THE NORSE GODS...

YOU WASTED YOUR TIME, THOR! THIS TIME I'M NOT GUILTY! NOT THAT I WOULDN'T LIKE TO MAKE MAN-KIND MISERABLE... BUT THE REAL CULPRIT HAPPENS TO BE MERLIN!

YOU'RE WRONG, LOKI! MERLIN LIES IN A CRYPT AT THE MUSEUM, DEAD AS A DOORNAIL!

NOT SO! HE'S TRICKED EVERY-BODY FOR 1,000 YEARS! HE'S AS ALIVE AS YOU ARE! I'VE BEEN WATCHING HIM FOR THE PAST HOUR! HE'S AT CAPE D'OR RIGHT NOW!

GREAT ODIN!! IF MERLIN'S ALIVE, I'VE GOT MY WORK CUT OUT FOR ME! WITH HIS FANTASTIC POWERS, HE COULD BE A TERRIBLE MENACE TO THE EARTH!

WITHIN MINUTES, THOR STREAKS TO THE MUSEUM TO CHECK ON LOKI'S TIP...

IT'S TRUE, THOR! MERLIN HAS VANISHED... AND WE CAN'T ACCOUNT FOR HIS WEIRD "RESURRECTION"!

BECAUSE HE WASN'T DEAD TO BEGIN WITH! HMM... SO FOR ONCE, LOKI TOLD THE TRUTH! I MUST FIND MERLIN BE-FORE HE HAS GONE TOO FAR TO STOP!

BUT, AS THOR FLIES TO CAPE D'OR, MERLIN MATERIALIZES IN A WASHINGTON, D.C. POLICE STATION...
SINCE I OVERHEARD THAT IT WAS THOR WHO RUINED MY SCHEME, I MUST GET RID OF HIM AS SOON AS POSSIBLE! IF I MATERIALIZE HERE, THE POLICE WILL SEND FOR THOR! THEN I'LL TAKE CARE OF HIM... FOR GOOD!
TURN, AND BEHOLD--MERLIN!
H-HUH?

I REPEAT... I AM MERLIN! CONTACT THOR IMMEDIATELY AND TELL HIM I CHALLENGE HIM TO A DUEL OF POWERS!
LISTEN TO THE NUT! THE "SILLY SEASON" MUST BE WITH US AGAIN!
YEAH! ALL SORTS OF CRANKS WILL START SHOWING UP SINCE THAT RADIO BROADCAST ANNOUNCED THAT THE BODY OF MERLIN WAS GONE FROM HIS CRYPT!

LOOK, PAL... DO ME A FAVOR AND GET LOST! WE'RE TOO BUSY TO WASTE TIME ON ODDBALLS!
FOOLS! BY TOMORROW YOU WILL TREMBLE AT THE MERE MENTION OF MY NAME!
HMMM... I HAVE A MUCH BETTER IDEA ABOUT HOW TO LURE THOR TO ME SO I CAN DESTROY HIM! I WILL LEVITATE MYSELF DIRECTLY TO THE WHITE HOUSE!
MINUTES LATER, IN WASHINGTON, D.C....
EXCUSE ME, MR. SECRETARY... BUT THIS SCREWBALL JUST TURNED UP! SAYS HE'S MERLIN, AND HE WANTS TO SEE THE PRESIDENT!
FIRST, NOBODY CAN SEE THE PRESIDENT WITHOUT AN APPOINTMENT! SECOND, THE PRESIDENT HAS ENOUGH PROBLEMS WITHOUT BEING BOTHERED BY CRACK-POTS! THAT WILL BE ALL, OFFICER!
PRESS SECRETARY
IT WILL NOT BE ALL! I SHALL NOW DE-MATERIALIZE AND INTRODUCE MYSELF TO THE PRESIDENT!
GREAT SCOTT! H-HE'S VANISHING BEFORE OUR VERY EYES!
HE MUST REALLY BE MERLIN, THE ONE WHO VANISHED FROM THE CRYPT-- IMPOSSIBLE AS IT SEEMS! WE-WE'VE GOT TO NOTIFY THE F.B.I.! AND ---SEND FOR THOR!
SOON, IN A WHITE HOUSE CORRIDOR...
ALL RIGHT, DEAR... I'LL TAKE YOU TO YOUR MOTHER AND TELL HER TO LET YOU RIDE "MACARONI"!
PERHAPS THAT MAN WITH HIS DAUGHTER IS-- NO! HE LOOKS TOO YOUNG! I'LL HAVE TO SEARCH FURTHER TILL I FIND THE PRESIDENT!
MEANWHILE, AT CAPE D'OR, THOR HEARS A STRANGE COAST-TO-COAST NEWS FLASH...
SO, THAT SUPER-NATURAL MADMAN IS SOMEWHERE IN THE WHITE HOUSE! I MUST GET THERE AS QUICKLY AS POSSIBLE!
AND, FINALLY...
LOKI TOLD THE TRUTH! IT IS YOU, MERLIN!
AH, THE MIGHTY THOR! AT LAST I'M FACE TO FACE WITH THE ONE MAN I MUST ELIMINATE BEFORE BECOMING THE SUPREME POWER IN THIS TWENTIETH CENTURY!
K-RASH!
9

SORRY, MERLIN! YOU'RE GOING BACK TO THE CRYPT WHERE YOU BELONG!
SO, THOR! YOU HURL YOUR HAMMER AT ME! APPARENTLY YOU DON'T REALIZE THE SORT OF ANTAGONIST YOU'RE UP AGAINST!

YOU VANISHED! MY MAGIC HAMMER WENT THROUGH YOU, AS IF YOU WERE A GHOST!
BUT I'M NO GHOST, I ASSURE YOU! I SIMPLY HAVE TELE-PORTATION POWERS, WHICH I CAN ALSO TRANSMIT TO OTHERS!

YOU WON'T GET THE CHANCE, MERLIN... NOT AFTER I SEIZE YOU!
YOU'LL NEVER REACH ME, THOR! I'M CONCEN-TRATING... CONCENTRATING ...TO MAKE YOUR FEET STOP MOVING!

IT MAY TAKE ALL MY ENERGY... BUT I WILL STOP YOU... I WILL!!

THERE! YOU ARE ROOTED TO THE FLOOR... WHILE I ESCAPE AS FREE AS A BIRD! BY THE TIME YOUR "PARALYSIS" WEARS OFF, I'LL BE READY WITH THE WEAPON THAT WILL DESTROY YOU!
GREAT ODIN! HE MAY SUCCEED AT THAT! HIS POWER IS ALMOST EQUAL TO LOKI'S!

HOLY MACKERAL! LOOK AT THAT CHARACTER! HE'S APPEARED OUT OF NOWHERE! AND--AND--
HMM... THE AMERICANS CALL THIS HUGE OBELISK WASHINGTON MONUMENT! JUST WHAT I NEED!
WASHINGTON MONUMENT

...FOR I WILL CONVERT IT INTO A JAVELIN THAT WILL FINISH THOR!

AT THAT MOMENT, AS THOR REGAINS THE USE OF HIS LIMBS...
BY THE GODS! HE'S TURNED WASHINGTON MONUMENT INTO A SUPER-LANCE! I COULD SHATTER IT WITH MY HAMMER, BUT I DARE NOT ATOMIZE A NATIONAL SHRINE!

INSTEAD, I'LL LASSO ITS TIP WITH MY MAGIC MALLET AND DEFLECT ITS COURSE!

BACK IT GOES TO ITS ORIGINAL RESTING PLACE!
BLAST THOR! HE OUTWITTED ME! BUT NOT NEXT TIME! I'LL FIND SOMETHING ELSE THAT WILL PERMANENTLY ERASE HIM!

THEN, AS THOR RACES AFTER THE MAD MAGICIAN...
YOU'RE DONE FOR NOW, THOR! I'VE LEVITATED THAT BUILDING! IN AN INSTANT IT WILL COME CRASHING DOWN UPON YOU!
CAN'T GET OUT OF THE WAY IN TIME! IT'S MOVING TOO FAST!
PENTAGON
(ONLY AUTHORIZED PERSONS ADMITTED)

...BUT I SURE CAN GET OUT FROM UNDER!

LO! THOR LIES VANQUISHED BENEATH THE PENTAGON!
-WHEW- THAT WAS CLOSE! AT THE LAST INSTANT, I CAUSED THE EARTH TO CRACK OPEN WIDE ENOUGH TO LET ME SLIDE INTO AN EARTH FAULT! NOW TO HACK MY WAY OUT!

MINUTES LATER, AS MERLIN EXULTS...
THOR!! Y-YOU ESCAPED! BUT HOW? BY WHAT MAGIC?
THE SORCERY OF MY OWN WITS, AND AN ALL-POWERFUL HAMMER! GOT ANY NEW SCHEMES, MERLIN?

THAT HUGE, SEATED FIGURE! I'LL MAKE IT COME TO LIFE AND IT WILL TRAMPLE THOR INTO THE GROUND!
YOU SHALL NOT HAVE LONG TO WAIT, MY DOOMED FOE!

L-LOOK! LINCOLN'S STATUE IS GETTING UP!
IT'S COME TO LIFE! IT-IT'S MOVING!
FORWARD, MIGHTY STATUE! FORWARD, AND CRUSH THOR--AS I SHALL CRUSH ALL WHO DEFY ME!

IT'S THE END, THOR! IF YOU TRY TO FLY AWAY, I'LL MAKE THE BRONZE STATUE FLY AFTER YOU! I CAN TELEPORT LIFELESS MATTER AS WELL AS LIVING THINGS.
ONLY ONE THING TO DO! SPIN MY HAMMER AROUND AT TERRIFIC SPEED!

AHH! JUST AS I PLANNED! I'VE CREATED A FAN WHICH HAS ENOUGH FORCE TO BLOW "HONEST ABE" BACK ONTO HIS SEAT!
BAH!! IS THERE NOTHING HE CANNOT DO TO WRECK MY PLANS?
PLOP!

SOON, AS THOR CORNERS MERLIN IN A WOODED SPOT NEAR THE POTOMAC RIVER...
THIS DUEL WILL END IN A STALEMATE UNLESS I CAN TRICK MERLIN WITH A LITTLE "MAGIC" OF MY OWN!
MERLIN! BEFORE YOU VANISH AGAIN, I'VE GOT A CONFESSION TO MAKE TO YOU!
12

IF MERLIN SEES THROUGH MY RUSE, I'M FINISHED! BUT IT'S JUST POSSIBLE I MIGHT WIN THIS LIFE-AND-DEATH GAMBLE RIGHT NOW!
YOU-YOU'VE CHANGED YOUR SHAPE! YOU'VE BECOME AN ORDINARY HUMAN--AND YOUR HAMMER HAS BECOME A WALKING STICK!

CORRECT! BUT THIS IS ONLY ONE OF A THOUSAND FORMS I CAN ASSUME, MERLIN! FOR MY MAGIC IS TEN TIMES MORE POWERFUL THAN YOURS! IF I SO DESIRE, I CAN DESTROY YOU RIGHT NOW!
NO! NO!... STOP!! WAIT!

IT WORKED! MERLIN KNOWS NOTHING ABOUT MY SECRET IDENTITY! HE BELIEVES I CAN CHANGE MYSELF INTO ANYTHING!
VERY WELL, MERLIN! I'LL LET YOU LIVE! BUT ONLY ON CONDITION YOU DO EXACTLY AS I SAY!
I'LL DO ANYTHING, THOR! ANYTHING!

THEN RETURN TO YOUR CRYPT AND CAST ANOTHER SPELL, OR WHATEVER IT WAS THAT ENABLED YOU TO SLEEP FOR CENTURIES! THE STONE LID WILL BE SEALED OVER YOUR BODY WHILE YOU SLEEP FOR ANOTHER THOUSAND YEARS!
HOW DO I KNOW YOU WILL NOT SLAY ME WHILE I AM HELPLESS?

YOU HAVE THOR'S WORD! BUT REMEMBER... IF YOU SHOULD EVER AWAKEN TO MENACE MANKIND, I'LL BE WAITING FOR YOU... AND I VOW TO SHOW YOU NO MERCY!
SO BE IT, MIGHTY THOR! I'LL RETURN IMMEDIATELY TO MY CRYPT!

A HALF HOUR LATER, AT THE MUSEUM...
WE DON'T KNOW HOW IT HAPPENED, THOR, BUT SUDDENLY WE LOOKED INTO THE CRYPT AND THERE WAS MERLIN INSIDE AGAIN, DEAD TO THE WORLD!
CONSIDER YOURSELVES LUCKY HE'S NOT ON THE LOOSE, AND SEAL THIS CRYPT FOREVER! SOMETIMES THERE ARE THINGS SCIENCE CAN'T EXPLAIN!
13

THAT NIGHT, IN A HOSPITAL OPERATING ROOM...
WELL, I MUST ADMIT THAT IF YOU DO LOSE A FEW PATIENTS AT THE OFFICE, YOU LOSE NO ONE AT THE OPERATING TABLE! AS A SURGEON, DR. BLAKE, YOU'RE A MAGICIAN!
THANKS, JANE...
YOU DON'T KNOW IT, HONEY, BUT THERE'S MORE TRUTH THAN FICTION TO WHAT YOU SAID!

THE END

JOURNEY INTO MYSTERY
IND.
APPROVED BY THE COMICS CODE AUTHORITY
MARVEL COMICS GROUP 12¢
97 OCT.
SUPER SPECIAL ISSUE!
LEE AND KIRBY COMBINE TALENTS TO BRING YOU MIGHTY THOR BATTLING THE AMAZING LAVA MAN!
Also: BEGINNING IN THIS ISSUE: "TALES OF ASGARD"
FANTASY AND LEGEND FROM THE HOME OF THE MIGHTY THOR!

THE MIGHTY THOR! BATTLES... THE LAVA MAN

THAT JET FIGHTER IS IN TROUBLE! I'VE GOT TO DO SOMETHING BEFORE IT CRASHES INTO THE CITY!

WRITTEN BY: STAN LEE
DRAWN BY: JACK KIRBY
INKED BY: DON HECK
LETTERED BY: ART SIMEK

SWINGING HIS ENCHANTED MALLET, AND HOLDING FAST TO THE UNBREAKABLE THONG, THE MIGHTY THUNDER GOD TAKES TO THE AIR!

NO MATTER HOW INGENIOUS MORTALS ARE, THERE IS ALWAYS A CHANCE OF HUMAN ERROR!
BUT, SO IT IS WITH ALL OF LIFE! EVEN WE GODS OF ASGARD ARE NOT TRULY PERFECT!

THERE! I'VE FREED HIM IN TIME! NOW TO SET UP AN IRRESISTIBLE WIND CURRENT TO BLOW THE PLANE SAFELY OUT TO SEA!

THOR! YOU SAVED THE PILOT--AND PREVENTED THE PLANE FROM CRASHING INTO THE CITY!
QUICKLY--HE NEEDS MEDICAL ATTENTION!
WE'LL TAKE OVER NOW, THOR! YOU'VE DONE YOUR SHARE!

BOY, WHAT A STORY! "THOR SAVES PILOT IN MID-AIR!"
I OWE MY LIFE TO YOU, THOR! HOW--HOW CAN I EVER--??
SAY NO MORE! IT IS THE PEOPLE WHO OWE MUCH TO SUCH AS YOU FOR GUARDING OUR SHORES!

AND THEN, THE MIGHTY THOR, THE POWERFUL, DAUNTLESS GOD OF THUNDER WHO FEARS NOTHING THAT LIVES, NOTHING THAT BREATHES, RACES FROM THE SCENE NERVOUSLY BEFORE THE ONSLAUGHT OF HERO-WORSHIPPING REPORTERS AND WELL-WISHERS!
NO! DON'T CLOSE IN ON ME! I CAN'T BE SURROUNDED! I MUST HAVE SPACE --ROOM TO MOVE!
WE'RE TOO LATE! HE'S TAKIN' TO THE AIR AGAIN!
THOR, WAIT! WE WANT SOME MORE PICTURES OF YOU IN ACTION!
HOLD IT! HOW ABOUT AN INTERVIEW?? COME BACK!
2

SECONDS LATER, ATOP THE MIDTOWN BUILDING WHICH HOUSES THE MEDICAL OFFICES OF DR. DON BLAKE, PHYSICIAN...
I ALWAYS FEAR TOO MUCH PUBLICITY--TOO MANY PEOPLE GETTING CLOSE TO ME!
FOR THERE IS ALWAYS THE CHANCE THAT ONE MAY ACCIDENTALLY STUMBLE UPON THE SECRET OF MY HUMAN IDENTITY!

THEN, THE MOST AWE-INSPIRING FIGURE IN ALL THE WORLD STAMPS HIS LEGENDARY MALLET ONCE UPON THE ROOFTOP BENEATH HIS FEET, AND...

...WHERE THE MIGHTY THOR HAD KNELT BUT A SECOND BEFORE, THE SLIM, LAME FIGURE OF DR. DON BLAKE NOW RISES IN HIS PLACE!
SO FAR, SO GOOD! NOW TO GO DOWN-STAIRS, WALK AROUND THE BLOCK, AND ENTER MY OFFICE NORMALLY, SO AS TO AROUSE NO SUSPICIONS!

AS THE LAME DOCTOR SLOWLY CIRCLES THE BLOCK, HE IS LOST SO DEEPLY IN THOUGHT THAT HE IS OBLIVIOUS TO THE CRIES OF THE CORNER NEWSBOY...
EXTRA! EXTRA! ALL ABOUT THE STRANGE MONSTER OF THE VOLCANO!!
Star-Bulletin
INHUMAN CREATURE STALKS SCENE OF NEW VOLCANIC ERUPTION!
STRANGE ACTS OF VIOLENCE

FOR DOCTOR BLAKE HAS ANOTHER MATTER ON HIS MIND--ONE WHICH DEALS WITH HIS LOVELY NURSE, JANE FOSTER...
HELLO, JANE! ALTHOUGH IT'S MY DAY OFF, I THOUGHT I'D COME AND SPEAK TO YOU...
I CAN'T PUT IT OFF ANY LONGER! I'VE GOT TO TELL HER HOW I FEEL ABOUT HER! EVEN A THUNDER GOD HAS FEEL-INGS--EMOTIONS--EVEN THOR CAN FALL VICTIM TO--LOVE!
I WAS JUST FINISHING AN INVENTORY OF YOUR MEDICAL SUPPLIES, DOCTOR!
3

NOW, WHAT WAS IT YOU WANTED TO SAY TO ME?
AND YET, I DON'T DARE TELL HER MY TRUE FEELINGS! IF, BY SOME WONDERFUL MIRACLE, SHE SHOULD AGREE TO MARRY ME, I WOULD HAVE TO REVEAL THAT THOR AND I ARE ONE AND THE SAME!

AND THAT SECRET IS NOT MINE TO DIVULGE-- NOT WITHOUT THE PERMISSION OF ODIN, MY FATHER--LORD OF THE GODS OF ASGARD!
COME TO THINK OF IT, JANE, PERHAPS THIS IS NOT THE RIGHT TIME!
I THINK I KNOW WHAT IT IS THAT YOU'RE TRYING TO SAY, DOCTOR--

YOU'VE WANTED TO SAY IT TO ME FOR MONTHS! I CAN FEEL IT! BUT--WHY DON'T YOU?
OH, JANE--MY DARLING! IF ONLY I COULD! BUT--GIVE ME JUST ONE MORE DAY! THERE IS ONE THING I MUST DO FIRST! AND THEN--

YES, DOCTOR, I KNOW! THERE IS ALWAYS JUST ONE MORE THING! WELL, A GIRL CAN'T WAIT FOREVER, DON BLAKE--NOT FOR A MAN WHO HASN'T ENOUGH GUMPTION TO SPEAK HIS OWN MIND! GOOD NIGHT, DOCTOR!

AND, AT THAT SOUL-SEARING MOMENT, THE TORTURED HUMAN WITH THE GNARLED WALKING STICK MAKES HIS DECISION! GRIMLY, HE STAMPS HIS CANE UPON THE FLOOR, AS A POWERFUL THUNDER-CLAP FILLS THE ROOM...
I CAN POSTPONE IT NO LONGER! IT MUST BE DONE!
BUT I MUST DO IT AS THOR, SON OF ODIN!

A MICROSECOND LATER, THE MIGHTY THUNDER GOD FACES A HALF-OPEN WINDOW, AND THEN...
NOBLE ODIN-- SHOW THYSELF TO THY SON! I SUMMON THEE, OH MY IMMORTAL FATHER!

SPEAK THEN, MIGHTY THOR! I GRANT THEE LEAVE TO PETITION ME!
MY HEART IS TORN WITH LOVE, MY FATHER! I CRAVE PERMISSION TO MARRY A MORTAL GIRL-- THE NURSE OF DOCTOR BLAKE-- THE ONE KNOWN AS JANE FOSTER!

HAVE YOU TAKEN LEAVE OF YOUR SENSES??! THE GOD OF THUNDER MARRYING A MORTAL?? IT IS IMPOSSIBLE! PETITION REFUSED!!
MY FATHER-- WAIT! HEAR ME OUT--YOU MUST -- TOO LATE! HE HAS GONE!

SHOCKED--DISAPPOINTED--THE STUNNED SUPER-HERO TURNS FROM HIS WINDOW, STILL UNAWARE OF THE COMMOTION IN THE STREETS BELOW...
LOOKS GRIM, DOESN'T IT?
LAVA MAN!?? WHO IS HE? WHAT IS HE?
EXTRA! MORE ABOUT LAVA MAN! GOVERNOR SUMMONS NATIONAL GUARD! READ ALL ABOUT IT! LAVA MAN NEARING CITY! EXTRA!
METROPOLITAN NEWS
MENACE FROM VOLCANO IDENTIFIED AS LAVA MAN!
FIRST PHOTOS OF STRANGE CREATURE FROM UNDER EARTH'S SURFACE
METROPOLITAN NEWS
HAVOC WIDESPREAD
THOUSANDS FLEE!
CHRONICLE-S
RALLY TROOPS TO STOP LAVA MAN

BUT ONE PAIR OF EARS DO NOT HEAR! ONE ACHING HEART DOES NOT RESPOND!
HE HAS NEVER REFUSED ME BEFORE!
I-I CANNOT GIVE HER UP! AND YET-- I MUST! I MUST!

WHILE IN ASGARD ITSELF, ANOTHER SON OF ODIN SURVEYS THE DRAMATIC TABLEAU ON EARTH! LOKI, GOD OF MISCHIEF, SWORN ENEMY OF HIS BROTHER THOR, GLOATS WITH EVIL GLEE AT THE THUNDER GOD'S DILEMMA!
NOW IS THE TIME FOR ME TO STRIKE AGAINST THE HATED THOR! NOW WHEN HIS HEART IS HEAVY-- WHEN HIS HAND WILL BE UNSURE!
BUT I AM STILL A PRISONER OF ASGARD, UNABLE TO LEAVE! AGAIN I MUST FIND A CATSPAW, AN AGENT TO DO THE TASK FOR ME!

BUT WAIT-- THAT DEVASTATED AREA BELOW! IT IS THE WORK OF A NEW MENACE WHO HAS APPEARED UPON EARTH! A MENACE KNOWN AS--

--THE LAVA MAN! I HAD FORGOTTEN ABOUT HIM-- ALTHOUGH IT WAS I WHO BROUGHT HIM TO THE SURFACE AS A SINISTER PRANK WHEN I MENTALLY CAUSED A LONG-DEAD VOLCANO TO ERUPT!
I SHALL WATCH IN AMUSEMENT AS HE DEFEATS THE HEARTSICK THOR!

MEANTIME, WE FIND THOR ONCE AGAIN IN HIS EARTHLY IDENTITY AS DR. BLAKE...
THERE IS ONLY ONE THING I CAN DO-- I MUST DISAVOW MY HERITAGE! I MUST GIVE UP MY ROLE AS THOR!
ONLY IF I BECOME TRULY HUMAN, WILL I BE ABLE TO MARRY THE GIRL I LOVE! AND YET... HOW CAN I FORSAKE MY LIFE AS GOD OF THUNDER??

DOCTOR, MAY I SPEAK TO YOU FOR A MOMENT?
JANE! I-I WAS JUST THINKING OF YOU! I WAS TRYING TO COME TO A-- DECISION!

I'M AFRAID IT'S TOO LATE FOR ANY DECISIONS NOW, DOCTOR!
I'M LEAVING! I HAVE ACCEPTED A POSITION AS NURSE WITH DOCTOR BASIL ANDREWS!
ANDREWS! THAT WOLF WHO HAS ALWAYS TRIED TO DATE YOU--TO TAKE YOU FROM ME!! WHY? WHY, JANE??

BECAUSE I KNOW WHAT YOU WANTED TO ASK ME, DON! AND I KNOW HOW I FEEL ABOUT YOU! AND-- I WON'T TAKE THE CHANCE-- THE CHANCE OF SAYING "YES" TO--A MAN WHO IS TOO WEAK TO SPEAK HIS MIND!
THEN--THIS IS GOODBYE, JANE!
6

MINUTES LATER, DAZED AND DEFEATED, DON BLAKE WALKS THE STREETS OF THE CITY, HIS HEAD ACHING--HIS HEART RACKED WITH ANGUISH...
GOT TO RUN! GOT TO LEAVE THE CITY!
ALL MY STRENGTH-- MY POWER--USELESS TO ME NOW!
NEWS-LEDGER
BULLETIN:
LAVA MAN NEARS CITY!
RESIDENTS FLEE SUBURBS!
LAST CHANCE
LAVA MAN

CITIZENS! TAKE COVER! CLEAR THE STREETS! THIS IS AN EMERGENCY! THE LAVA MAN IS APPROACHING!
TROOPS IN THE CITY?? AN EMERGENCY?? LAVA MAN?? WHA-WHAT IS HAPPENING??
US ARMY

THE NEXT SIGHT HE SEES IS SO STARTLING, SO FEARFUL, THAT IT DRIVES HIS PERSONAL PROBLEM FROM HIS MIND, AS DR. BLAKE BEHOLDS...
THE LAVA MAN! FIRE!!
HUMANS! THIS IS MY FINAL WARNING! EVACUATE THE CITIES! TAKE TO THE SEA! I CLAIM ALL THE DRY SURFACE OF EARTH FOR THE LAVA PEOPLE!
IT'S USELESS! OUR SHELLS ARE CHARRED BEFORE THEY CAN REACH HIM!

TOO LONG HAVE WE DWELLED BELOW, WHILE YOU PUNY HUMANS ENJOYED THE FRUITS OF THE SURFACE!
YOUR WEAPONS ARE DISTASTEFUL TO ME! I SHALL DESTROY THEM--SO!

ALL HE DID WAS POINT HIS HAND!
OUR RIFLES-- BAZOOKAS--THEY'VE ALL TURNED TO-- TO VOLCANIC ASH!!
FALL BACK! REGROUP! WE'VE GOT TO MAKE NEW DEFENSE PLANS!

BUT SUDDENLY, LIKE A BLAZING STREAK OF UNCHAINED FURY, THOR, GOD OF THUNDER, LEAPS TO THE ATTACK!!
BACK, YOU DEMON FROM THE NAMELESS DEPTHS! THE SURFACE BELONGS TO MANKIND, AND THOR IS THEIR PROTECTOR!!
YOUR WORDS IS AS FUTILE AS YOUR DEEDS, COSTUMED ONE! THE DAY OF THE HUMANS IS OVER! DO NOT PROLONG THEIR AGONY!!

THIS IS WHAT I NEEDED!! ACTION! COMBAT! A FOE TO LASH OUT AT!
NOT FOR ME ARE THE ROMANTIC PURSUITS OF HUMAN BEINGS! I WAS BORN FOR BATTLE!! MY LIMBS ACHE TO SMASH AND SHATTER!!

HE'S GONE! CAN I HAVE--? NO! I FELT NO IMPACT! I DID NOT STRIKE HIM!
ONLY ONE ANSWER--HE HAS THE POWER TO MELT THE GROUND BENEATH HIS FEET!

SECONDS LATER, THE MIGHTY THUNDER GOD DISCOVERS ANOTHER POWER OF THE AMAZING LAVA MAN, AS A POWERFUL UNDERWATER GEYSER SPOUTS UP FROM THE BOTTOMLESS CHASM BELOW!!
THE DEPTHS ARE HIS TO COMMAND! HE IS A FOE WORTHY OF MY METTLE! BUT HE MUST BE DEFEATED!
DO MY EARS DECEIVE ME, OR DO I SEEM TO HEAR LAUGHTER--SINISTER CHORTLES RINGING DOWN FROM ABOVE!

YOU HEAR CORRECTLY, DESPISED ONE! LOKI IS WATCHING... AND I APPLAUD THE FACT THAT YOU HAVE AT LAST MET YOUR MATCH!
UGH! NOT YET, GOD OF EVIL!
THE FINAL BLOW HAS YET TO BE STRUCK! THE FINAL NOTE YET TO BE SOUNDED!

THE CITY HAS BEEN EVACUATED! ALL THAT REMAIN ARE THE LAVA MAN--AND ME! BUT BEFORE DARKNESS FALLS, ONE OF US SHALL REMAIN NO MORE!

LOOK WELL, EVIL LOKI! SEE HOW THE THUNDER GOD FIGHTS, WHEN HUMANITY IS IN PERIL!

FLY, MY ENCHANTED MALLET! SEEK OUT MY ENEMY!
LET YOUR IRRESISTIBLE FORCE FLUSH HIM OUT INTO THE OPEN--WHERE HE CAN FEEL THE FULL FURY OF THE WRATH OF THOR!

THE COSTUMED ONE'S WEAPON!! I MUST NOT LET IT STRIKE ME!

RETURN TO YOUR MASTER, MY URU HAMMER! YOU HAVE DONE YOUR WORK WELL!
YOUR FLIGHT IS USELESS, INHUMAN ONE! THERE IS NO PLACE ON EARTH WHERE YOU CAN BE SAFE FROM THE POWER OF THE THUNDER GOD!
BAH! NO MERE SURFACE DWELLER CAN DEFEAT ME!

OBSERVE, HELPLESS THOR! NOTE HOW HIS POWER IS ALMOST LIMITLESS! SEE HOW HE HURLS A MASS OF QUICK-DRYING, CLINGING LAVA AT YOU!
LET HIM HURL WHAT HE WILL, LOKI! I WELCOME HIS ATTACK! FOR MY HEART LONGS FOR BATTLE!
YOU FIGHT FOR YOUR CAUSE, MIGHTY ONE! BUT I FIGHT FOR MINE! MY PEOPLE HAVE EARNED THE RIGHT TO CLAIM EARTH'S SURFACE FOR THEIR OWN!

NOT SO! THE UNIVERSE IS HUGE--ENDLESS! THERE IS ROOM FOR ALL!
THERE IS STILL TIME FOR YOU TO FOLLOW THE PATH OF PEACE! YOUR PEOPLE AND THE HUMANS MAY YET EXIST SIDE-BY-SIDE, IN FRIENDSHIP!

NEVER! HUMANITY IS WEAK! IT CANNOT DEFEND ITSELF! IT HAS NO PLACE ON EARTH!
ONLY THE STRONG SHALL SURVIVE! JUST AS I AM STRONG --AND YOU ARE DEFEATED!

YOU HAD YOUR CHANCE, LAVA MAN! NOW, YOU CAN EXPECT NO MERCY! AND IF LOKI STILL GLOATS ABOVE, HE IS DOOMED TO BITTER DISAPPOINTMENT!
SILENCE! I NOW DISPOSE OF YOU AS EASILY AS I SHALL DESTROY ALL OF HUMANITY! NOTHING CAN FREE ITSELF OF THAT THICK COAT OF LAVA!

NOW THAT I HAVE STILLED HIS EMPTY WORDS, I CAN TURN TO THE TASK AT HAND! I MUST LEAD MY PEOPLE TO THE SURFACE, SO THAT WE MAY TAKE POSSESSION OF ALL THE EARTH!
FOR YEARS MEN HAVE ACCLAIMED MY MIGHT! NOW, AS NEVER BEFORE, MUST IT PROVE ITSELF!

EVEN AS I LIE HERE, I CAN FLEX MY MUSCLES UNTIL THEY BECOME ALMOST ROCK-HARD! NOW, BY MARSHALLING ALL MY STRENGTH, BY MAKING ONE SUPREME EFFORT...
...I CAN FEEL MY BODY THROB-- MY SINEWS STRAIN --THE MOMENT IS AT HAND--THE ONE FATEFUL SURGE OF ENERGY--!!

AT THAT INCREDIBLE INSTANT, IF ANY HUMAN EYE COULD HAVE WITNESSED THE SIGHT, THEY WOUL HAVE SEEN THE BODY OF THOR ACTUALLY GLOW ING, AS THOUGH CHARGED WITH UNIMAGINABLE FORCE, AS HE SHATTERED THE CRUSHING MASS WHICH SURROUNDED HIM!
I'M FREE!

NO! IT ISN'T POSSIBLE! NOTHING HUMAN COULD HAVE ESCAPED MY LAVA TRAP!!
THIS IS NO HUMAN YOU FACE, LAVA MAN! THIS IS THOR, GOD OF THUNDER -- SON OF ODIN, LORD OF ASGARD!

CALL YOURSELF WHAT YOU WILL, I SHALL STILL CRUSH YOU INTO NOTHINGNESS! EVEN YOUR FLYING HAMMER CANNOT STOP ME FROM TURNING INTO A TOWER OF LAVA--WHICH NOTHING CAN SHATTER!

MY ENCHANTED HAMMER CAN DO MORE THAN STRIKE--IT CAN CREATE STORM, THUNDER--AND WHIRLWIND!!!

A WHIRLWIND STRONG ENOUGH TO CARRY YOU HIGH INTO SPACE... TO KEEP YOU HELPLESS AS YOU SPIN FASTER THAN THE SPEED OF SOUND!
MY HAMMER MUST RETURN WITHIN SIXTY SECONDS...
...BUT I SHALL JOIN YOU BEFORE YOU CAN FALL! FOR I HAVE NOT DONE WITH YOU YET!
ARE YOU WATCHING LOKI??? DO YOU SEE HOW EASILY THOR IS DEFEATED?? ARE YOU STILL GLOATING--STILL SNEERING??
NO! YOU ARE SILENT NOW--AS I KNEW YOU WOULD BE, MY FRUSTRATED FOE!
AS FOR THE LAVA MAN, HE WAS SPAWNED BY AN ERUPTING VOLCANO, AND HE SHALL RETURN FROM WHENCE HE CAME!
POUNDING THE TOP OF A NEARBY MOUNTAIN WITH HIS AWESOME HAMMER, THE MIGHTY THOR CAUSES THE ENTIRE PEAK TO FALL UPON THE TOP OF THE VOLCANO, SEALING IT --AND THE STRANGE RACE WHICH DWELLS WITHIN--FOREVER!!!
THUS DO I RETURN THE LAVA MAN TO HIS OWN KIND!! FOR EARTH'S SURFACE SHALL NEVER BE VIOLATED WHILE THOR ENDURES!
12

MOMENTS LATER, A DRAMATIC FLYING FIGURE HURTLES BACK TO THE HEART OF THE CITY, AND THE MEDICAL OFFICE OF DR. DON BLAKE...

NOW THAT THE MENACE OF THE **LAVA MAN** IS ENDED, I MUST SEE JANE AGAIN! THERE MUST BE **SOME** WAY I CAN PREVENT HER FROM LEAVING ME...

BUT, BY THE TIME THE LAME DOCTOR CAN REACH HIS OFFICE...
JANE! DR. BRUCE ANDREWS! WHAT--?
I'M GLAD YOU'VE COME, DON! I WAS WAITING FOR YOU! I DIDN'T WANT TO LEAVE WITHOUT SAYING--GOODBYE!
JANE IS GOING TO WORK FOR ME, BLAKE! I'M SURE YOU UNDERSTAND!

JANE, I KNOW I'VE NO RIGHT TO INSIST-- TO PLEAD --BUT--
IT'S TOO LATE FOR THAT NOW! I WAITED--HOPING YOU'D RETURN-- HOPING YOU'D FINALLY SAY WHAT I'VE LONGED TO HEAR--BUT, WHILE THE CITY WAS THREATENED BY THE LAVA MAN, YOU DIDN'T EVEN CARE ENOUGH TO FIND ME--

DOCTOR ANDREWS DROVE ME TO THE SUBURBS-- LOOKED AFTER ME! A WOMAN WANTS A MAN, DOCTOR BLAKE--NOT A TIMID MOUSE! AND SO, I'M LEAVING...
DON'T WORRY, BLAKE --YOU'LL FIND ANOTHER NURSE!
AFTER THE TWO HAVE DEPARTED, A BITTER FIGURE STARES SADLY OUT OF THE WINDOW, THINKING THOUGHTS THAT NO HUMAN WOULD EVER SUSPECT...
OF ALL THOSE WHO WALK THE EARTH, THOR IS THE MIGHTIEST! AND YET...
...I'M POWERLESS TO WIN THE ONE PRIZE I WANT MORE THAN ANY OTHER! IS THIS TO BE MY DESTINY? MUST THE THUNDER GOD LIVE OUT HIS DAYS-- ALONE??
NEXT ISSUE: MORE EPIC SUPER-ADVENTURE, MINGLED WITH STARK, GRIPPING DRAMA, AS THOR MAKES HIS MOST IMPORTANT DECISION!!!

THE END

TALES OF... ...ASGARD!
HOME OF THE MIGHTY NORSE GODS
BEFORE MAN COULD READ OR WRITE, HE HAD HIS LEGENDS! AND NO LEGENDS WERE MORE THRILLING, MORE COLORFUL, MORE FILLED WITH FANTASY AND HIGH ADVENTURE THAN THE LEGENDS OF ASGARD, HOME OF THE GODS! THUS, WITH GREAT PRIDE, WE PRESENT THIS NEW, TREND-SETTING SERIES, BASED UPON HIGHLIGHTS OF NORSE MYTHOLOGY-- TALES OF ASGARD, THE BIRTHPLACE OF THE MIGHTY THOR!!
WRITTEN BY: STAN LEE
DRAWN BY: JACK KIRBY
INKED BY: G. BELL
LETTERED BY: ART SIMEK
1

HEROIC LEGENDS CAN ONLY ORIGINATE FROM A HEROIC PEOPLE... AND NONE WERE MORE HEROIC THAN THE ANCIENT NORSEMEN WHO STRUGGLED VALIANTLY AGAINST WILD BEASTS AND WILDER WEATHER!

NO NORSEMAN COULD EVER RELAX HIS VIGIL! ALMOST DAILY, THE HARDY FARMERS AND THEIR WOMENFOLK WERE FORCED TO TAKE UP ARMS AGAINST SAVAGE RAIDERS FROM THE MOUNTAINS!

AND THOSE WHO TURNED TO THE SEA WERE THE MOST FEARLESS OF ALL! THEIR COURAGE AND DARING WILL LIVE ON AS LONG AS MEN TELL OF VALOR--FOR WHO AMONG US HAS NOT THRILLED TO THE TALES OF THE ANCIENT VIKINGS??!

YES, SUCH ARE THE NORSEMEN... THE BRAVE, STOUT-HEARTED WARRIORS WHO CHANTED THE LEGENDS OF ASGARD AROUND THEIR CAMPFIRES --WHO CREATED HEROES AND GODS AND DEMONS WHICH STILL FIRE THE IMAGINATION OF MEN!

TO THE NORSEMEN, THEIR LEGENDARY CHARACTERS WERE EITHER ALL GOOD OR ALL BAD! THEIR GOOD GODS WERE CALLED THE ÆSIR--AND THEY FOUGHT FOR AGES AGAINST THE TOTALLY EVIL FRONT GIANTS!

AND THE PLACE WHERE THEY DWELLED WAS BOUNDED BY THE LAND OF FIRE ON THE SOUTH, AND THE LAND OF MIST ON THE NORTH!

AT THE WORLD'S END SAT SURTUR, THE DEMON OF FIRE, WHO WAITED, WITH HIS FLAMING SWORD, FOR THE END OF THE WORLD, WHEN HE MIGHT GO FORTH TO DESTROY GODS AND MEN ALIKE!

AND BENEATH ALL LAY THE MAGICAL WELL OF LIFE! IT WAS FROM THIS WELL THAT ALL THE RIVERS FLOWED--RIVERS WHICH WERE TURNED INTO HUGE BLOCKS OF ICE BY THE CRUEL, NORTHERN WINDS!

FINALLY, AFTER COUNTLESS CENTURIES, A STRANGE FORM OF LIFE MAGICALLY APPEARED! THE TONS OF ICE WHICH HAD BEEN FORMING ABOVE THE WELL OF LIFE CHANGED THEIR SHAPE, AND TURNED INTO YMIR, GREATEST OF ALL THE EVIL FROST GIANTS!

SECONDS LATER, ANOTHER FORM OF LIFE APPEARED -- THIS WAS A GIGANTIC MAGIC COW, WHOSE MILK PROVIDED NOURISHMENT FOR THE MONSTROUS YMIR! AND, FOR AGES, YMIR AND THE MAGIC COW ROAMED THE FROZEN WASTES, UNTIL...

...ONE DAY THE MAGIC COW FOUND SOMETHING STIRRING IN THE ICE! AT FIRST, IT WAS UNRECOGNIZABLE...

...BUT THEN, SLOWLY, POWER-FULLY, A NOBLE HEAD APPEARED ABOVE THE ICE...

AND THUS THE FIRST OF THE GOOD ÆSIR CAME INTO BEING! LOOK WELL AT HIM! LOOK WELL AT THE ONE CALLED BURI! FOR THOSE WHO FOLLOW HIM SHALL BE GODS!
4

BURI GREW WISE, AND STRONG, AND ONE DAY TOOK HIM A WIFE! THEN HE HAD A SON NAMED **BORR!** AND YEARS LATER BORR WAS MARRIED AND HAD THREE SONS OF HIS OWN! BUT OH, WHAT SONS THEY WERE! FOR ONE WAS NAMED -- **ODIN!!!**

ODIN!! CALLED THE ALL-FATHER! **ODIN!!** GREATEST OF ALL NORSE GODS! **ODIN!** SUPREME WARRIOR WHO SLAYED THE LAST OF THE ICE GIANTS, THUS BRINGING ABOUT THE FIRST TRIUMPH OF GOOD OVER EVIL!

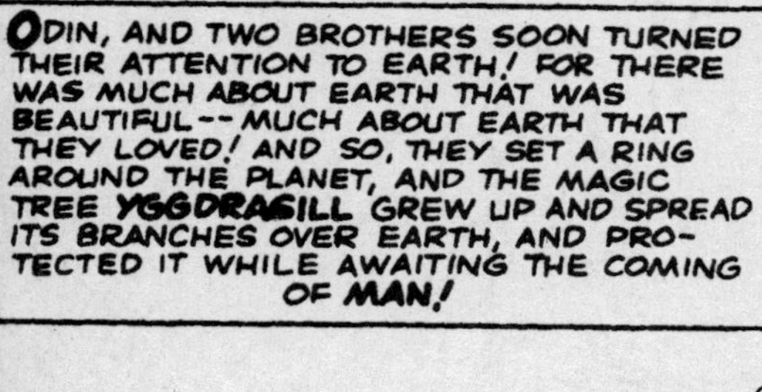
ODIN, AND TWO BROTHERS SOON TURNED THEIR ATTENTION TO EARTH! FOR THERE WAS MUCH ABOUT EARTH THAT WAS BEAUTIFUL-- MUCH ABOUT EARTH THAT THEY LOVED! AND SO, THEY SET A RING AROUND THE PLANET, AND THE MAGIC TREE **YGGDRASILL** GREW UP AND SPREAD ITS BRANCHES OVER EARTH, AND PROTECTED IT WHILE AWAITING THE COMING OF **MAN!**

NEXT ISSUE: WE SHALL GO BACK STILL FURTHER TO BRING YOU, IN FASCINATING DETAIL, THE **BATTLE** BETWEEN ODIN AND THE EVIL **ICE GIANTS**-- THE MOST EPIC BATTLE OF ALL TIME!
The END

JOURNEY INTO
MYSTERY
IND.
APPROVED BY THE COMICS CODE AUTHORITY
98 NOV.
MARVEL COMICS GROUP 12¢
THINK YOU HAVE TROUBLES WAIT TILL YOU SEE WHAT HAPPENS TO...
THOR WHEN HE MEETS... THE HUMAN COBRA!
EVEN A THUNDER GOD CANNOT MATCH MY GREAT POWER... AS YOU ARE NOW ABOUT TO LEARN!!
also: "TALES OF ASGARD!"---"ODIN BATTLES THE ICE GIANTS!"

THE MIGHTY THOR!

"CHALLENGED BY THE HUMAN COBRA!"

IT ISN'T **FAIR!** IT ISN'T **JUST!** I'VE LOST THE ONE THING I WANT MOST IN THE WORLD --LOST IT BECAUSE I'M **THOR**-- BECAUSE I DARE NOT DISOBEY THE COMMAND OF **ODIN**, RULER OF THE GODS!

EVEN A **THUNDER GOD** CAN GO ON THE RAMPAGE! EVEN THE MIGHTY **THOR** CAN LASH OUT IN A FIT OF UNCONTROLLABLE TEMPER! PERHAPS YOU NEVER THOUGHT OF SUPER HEROES POSSESSING THE ALL-TOO-HUMAN QUALITIES OF JEALOUSY, FRUSTRATION, AND VIOLENT ANGER... BUT **THOR** HAS EMOTIONS, EVEN AS YOU AND I! AND SO, AS OUR THRILLING TALE BEGINS, WE FIND HIM GIVING VENT TO A RAGING BURST OF FURY...

WRITTEN BY: **STAN LEE**
ILLUSTRATED BY: **DON HECK**
LETTERED BY: **ART SIMEK**

X-451

WHY MUST I REMAIN THE MIGHTY THUNDER GOD?? MY IDENTITY HAS BROUGHT ME NOTHING BUT GRIEF, AND LONELINESS!
ALL I NEED DO IS STAMP MY ENCHANTED HAMMER TO RETURN TO MY HUMAN FORM AS DOCTOR DON BLAKE!
THUMP!

BUT, EVEN AS DR. BLAKE, HAPPINESS CANNOT BE MINE! NOT WITHOUT JANE FOSTER, THE GIRL I LOVE!
BUT SHE'S GONE NOW! SHE'S LEFT ME, NEVER TO RETURN! AND ALL BECAUSE OF THOR!

THOR! THE VERY MENTION OF THAT NAME MAKES MY BLOOD BOIL!
CRASH!

IF ONLY I HAD BEEN ABLE TO TELL HER THAT THOR AND DR. BLAKE WERE ONE AND THE SAME! BUT I COULDN'T! ODIN FORBADE IT!
EVEN WHEN I LEARNED SHE LOVED ME, HE SAID WE COULD NEVER MARRY! A THUNDER GOD MAY NEVER MARRY A MORTAL!

"AND SO, THOUGH MY HEART ACHED FOR THE WANT OF HER--THOUGH MY ARMS LONGED TO EMBRACE HER-- I COULD NEVER TELL HER MY TRUE FEELINGS! I COULD NEVER SPEAK OF MY LOVE!"
YOU SAID THERE WAS SOMETHING YOU WANTED TO TELL ME, DOCTOR! AND NOW--YOU'RE SO STRANGELY SILENT!
I'M SORRY, JANE! IT--IT SEEMS TO HAVE SLIPPED MY MIND!

"IT WAS INEVITABLE THAT SHE WOULD ONE DAY LEAVE ME--INEVITABLE THAT SHE WOULD THINK MY SILENCE MEANT I DIDN'T CARE! AND THEN, IT HAPPENED..."
GOODBYE, DOCTOR! YOU MAY REACH ME AT DR. ANDREWS' OFFICE IF YOU NEED ME!
I KNOW YOU'LL BE HAPPY AS MY NURSE, JANE!

SUDDENLY, DR. BLAKE'S REVERIE IS BROKEN BY A RESOUNDING THUNDERCLAP, AND A RUMBLING, DISTANT VOICE, HEARD ONLY BY THE MAN WHO IS THOR!
MY SON! I SUMMON THEE TO ASGARD, THY HOME! FOR I HAVE WORDS TO SPEAK WITH THEE!
IT IS ODIN! I CANNOT DISOBEY HIM! I MUST RETURN TO ASGARD!

AN INTERVAL LATER, FOR TIME AS WE KNOW IT MEANS NOTHING TO THE GODS OF ASGARD, MIGHTY THOR STANDS BEFORE THE THRONE OF HIS FATHER!
I CAN SENSE THY GRIEF, MY SON! AND SO, I HAVE CALLED THEE TO ME TO RECEIVE MY ADVICE...
PUT ALL THOUGHTS OF THE HUMAN JANE FOSTER FROM OUT OF THY MIND! FORGET HER! ELSE, YOU WILL NEVER KNOW PEACE!
NO, LORDLY ODIN! THAT I CAN NEVER DO!

EVEN THE GOD OF THUNDER CANNOT CLOSE HIS HEART UPON COMMAND!
HE DARES TURN HIS BACK ON THEE, ODIN!!
STAY THY HAND! I FORGIVE HIM! FOR I MUST SHARE THE SORROW OF MY FAVORITE SON!

RETURNING TO HIS LONELY OFFICE AGAIN, AS THE LAME DR. BLAKE, THE HEARTSICK MAN COMES TO A MOMENTOUS CONCLUSION...
I MUST GET AWAY--TO FORGET! I'LL GO TO SOME DISTANT LAND, WHERE NOTHING WILL REMIND ME OF THE GIRL I'VE LOVED--AND LOST!

BUT FATE WORKS IN MYSTERIOUS WAYS! AT THE OTHER SIDE OF THE GLOBE, AS DON BLAKE WINGS HIS WAY TOWARDS THE EAST, A BITTER, JEALOUS MAN WATCHES HIS KINDLY EMPLOYER WITH HATE-FILLED EYES...

I THINK WE ARE CLOSE TO FINDING THE TOTAL CURE FOR SNAKE-BITE WHICH WE HAVE BEEN SEEKING, KLAUS!
THAT IS GRATIFYING, PROFESSOR SHECKTOR! YOU MUST BE VERY PLEASED!
BAH! ANOTHER GREAT DISCOVERY WILL BE CREDITED TO THE FAMOUS PROFESSOR SHECKTOR, WHILE I, HIS ASSISTANT, SLAVE FOR A MEASLY WAGE!

BUT, IF SOMETHING WERE TO HAPPEN TO THE GOOD PROFESSOR... IF I COULD GET THE CREDIT FOR HIS DISCOVERY....!
WELL, WHY NOT?? IN THIS LONELY, ISOLATED REGION OF INDIA, WHO COULD PROVE IT WAS NOT AN--ACCIDENT?!!

IT WILL BE SO EASY! I WILL LET THE COBRA BITE BOTH SHECKTOR AND ME! BUT I WILL TAKE THE ANTIDOTE--AND I WILL NOT GIVE IT TO HIM!
IT WILL BE FOOLPROOF... IT WILL SEEM LIKE AN ACCIDENT, BECAUSE WE WILL BOTH HAVE BEEN BITTEN--AND I CAN SAY I COULD NOT GET THE SERUM TO SHECKTOR IN TIME!

LATER, IN BOMBAY, AN INTERESTED TOURIST OVER-HEARS A STARTLING BIT OF NEWS...
IT IS TRUE! THE GOOD PROFESSOR SHECKTOR IS DYING--FROM THE BITE OF A POISONOUS SERPENT!
PROFESSOR SHECKTOR! MY OLD TEACHER! THE MAN THEY CALL THE ALBERT SCHWEITZER OF INDIA! IT CAN'T BE!
HE HAS DONE SO MUCH GOOD FOR OUR PEOPLE! THIS IS A TRAGIC DAY FOR OUR BELOVED INDIA!

I HAD HOPED I'D NEVER AGAIN FIND THE NEED TO BECOME THOR! AND YET --PERHAPS I CAN HELP MY OLD FRIEND, IF I GET TO HIM IN TIME...
THUMP!

AND NONE CAN TRAVEL AS FAST-- OR AS UNERRINGLY, AS THE GOD OF THUNDER!

IT SEEMS I CAN NEVER ABANDON MY LEGENDARY IDENTITY! FOR, WHEN THERE IS A NEED, THOR MUST RESPOND!
DRIVER, YOU WILL FIND THE PAYMENT FOR THIS RIDE ON THE BACK SEAT OF YOUR VEHICLE! I MUST NOW SEEK A FASTER METHOD OF TRAVEL!

HUH? WHO SAID-- ?? WHERE'D HE GO??
OUT THE WINDOW... I MUST BE SEEING THINGS! A FLYING MAN!

ONWARD, MY TRUSTY MALLET! LET YOUR SURGING POWER CARRY ME TO THE MOUNTAIN VILLAGE WHERE DOCTOR SHECKTOR LIES DYING!

MOMENTS LATER, AFTER A SKYBORNE FLIGHT AT ALMOST UNIMAGINA-BLE SPEED...
THERE IS THE VILLAGE BELOW ME! I HOPE I HAVE ARRIVED IN TIME!

WITHIN SECONDS, THOR REACHES THE BEDSIDE OF THE FATALLY STRICKEN PROFESSOR...
HEED MY WORDS WELL, MIGHTY THOR... A FEARSOME NEW MENACE IS AT LARGE IN THE WORLD ...AND HE MUST BE FOUND... AND STOPPED... BEFORE HE CAN BRING UNTOLD HARM TO MANKIND... I SPEAK OF... THE COBRA...
THE COBRA ??

"YES! ONCE HE WAS MY ASSISTANT, AN ENVIOUS, UNTALENTED EX-CONVICT NAMED KLAUS, WHOM I HAD TRIED TO REHABILITATE! BUT HE PLOTTED MY MURDER, ALLOWING A POISONOUS COBRA TO BITE ME, AND DENYING ME THE LIFE-SAVING ANTIDOTE! HOWEVER, THERE WAS ONE THING HE DID NOT KNOW..."
YOU FOOL! YOU TRIED TO MAKE IT LOOK LIKE AN ACCIDENT BY HAVING THE COBRA BITE YOU, TOO...
BUT YOU DIDN'T KNOW THAT I HAD BEEN EXPERIMENTING ON THAT COBRA--HE IS RADIOACTIVE!
I'VE BEEN BITTEN BY A RADIO-ACTIVE COBRA ??!!

"EVEN THOUGH THE ANTIDOTE MANAGED TO SAVE HIS LIFE--IT CHANGED HIM! BY SOME FREAK OF CHANCE, HE SEEMED TO DEVELOP THE INSTINCTS, THE POWERS OF A COBRA ITSELF!"

MOMENTS LATER, A SADDENED, VENGEFUL THUNDER GOD LEAVES THE PROFESSOR'S DEATHBED...
I SHALL FIND THE COBRA--AND DESTROY HIM!

NO MATTER WHERE HE FLEES--NO MATTER HOW GREAT HIS NEW-FOUND POWER... HE SHALL FEEL THE WRATH OF THOR!
I KNOW NOW THAT THIS IS WHAT I NEEDED! THE THRILL OF BATTLE! THE MENACE OF A DEADLY FOE! THE PROMISE OF DANGER AND HIGH ADVENTURE AWAITING ME!

AT THE NEAREST AIRPORT, THOR LEARNS HE IS MINUTES TOO LATE...
AH YES, SAHIB! THE ONE YOU DESCRIBE DID BOARD A JET PLANE A SCANT FEW MINUTES EARLIER! HE FORCED THE PILOT TO CHANGE COURSE AND HEAD FOR AMERICA!
THERE ARE NO OTHER JETS HERE THAT I MAY FOLLOW IN! THEREFORE, THERE IS ONLY ONE WAY FOR ME TO OVERTAKE MY QUARRY! STAND BACK, ALL OF YOU, WHILE I WHIRL MY HAMMER!

AND NOW FOR THE COBRA!

BUT, AFTER A FEW MILES OF FLIGHT...
MIGHTY AS MY HAMMER IS, THERE IS YET A FASTER WAY FOR THE GOD OF THUNDER TO TRAVEL!
I SHALL CREATE AN UNBRIDLED TYPHOON, OF ALMOST LIMITLESS SPEED AND BLINDING FORCE... AND THEN...

RIDING THE TYPHOON AS ONLY A THUNDER GOD CAN, MIGHTY THOR TRAVELS ACROSS HALF THE GLOBE AT SPEEDS WHICH MATCH THOSE OF THE FLEEING JET ITSELF!
IT IS ONLY FITTING THAT THE GOD OF THUNDER SHOULD TRAVEL ON THE WINGS OF THE WIND!

FINALLY, AT IDLEWILD AIRPORT, WHEN THE CREATURE WHO NOW CALLS HIMSELF THE COBRA MAKES A DRAMATIC EXIT FROM HIS COMMANDEERED JET, A PAIR OF PIERCING EYES FOLLOW HIS EVERY MOVE...
I SHALL FOLLOW MY FOE, AND LEARN OF HIS PLANS BEFORE I STRIKE!

HE SLITHERS UP AND DOWN WALLS LIKE THE SERPENT WHOSE NAME HE HAS TAKEN! HE SHALL TRULY BE A FORMIDABLE OPPONENT!
BUT WHY HAS HE CHOSEN TO ENTER THAT CHEMICAL MANU-FACTURING PLANT?

HEAR ME, YOU PUNY HUMANS! I, THE COBRA, DEMAND COMPLETE CONTROL OF THIS ENTIRE PLANT!
HERE SHALL I MANUFACTURE GALLONS OF COBRA SERUM, TO CREATE A VAST ARMY OF OTHERS LIKE MYSELF -- TO DO MY BIDDING AND SERVE ME WITHOUT QUESTION!
ARE WE SEEING THINGS??! IT-IT LOOKS LIKE A HALF-MAN AND HALF-SERPENT! A THING OF UNIMAGIN-ABLE EVIL!

MY POWER FAR EXCEEDS THAT OF MORTAL MAN! I HAVE THE SPEED AND CUNNING OF A SERPENT -- THE DEADLY STING OF THE KING COBRA ITSELF, COUPLED WITH THE BRAIN AND CUN-NING OF A HUMAN BEING!
AND SO I COMMAND YOU TO OBEY MY EVERY ORDER, OR ELSE FEEL MY FATAL STING!

I HAVE HEARD ENOUGH! YOU ARE DESERVING OF NO MERCY, COBRA! AND THE ONLY STING TO BE FELT THIS DAY SHALL BE THAT OF MY HAMMER, WHICH HUNGERS FOR YOUR DEFEAT!
WHAT A STROKE OF LUCK! IT'S THOR!
PREPARE FOR A SURPRISE, OVER-RATED THUNDER GOD! FOR MY POWER IS STILL GREATER THAN YOURS -- AS YOU ARE ABOUT TO FIND OUT!

NOT FOR NOTHING DO I CALL MYSELF THE COBRA!
FOR ONE SINGLE BITE FROM MY NAMESAKE BRINGS CERTAIN DEATH...

...AS YOU SHALL LEARN WHEN MY COBRA DARTS FIND THEIR MARK!

LIKE SO MANY OTHERS BEFORE YOU WITH NEW-FOUND POWERS, YOU TALK ABOUT THEM TOO MUCH, COBRA!
AND WHILE YOU BOAST, I HAVE TIME TO PREPARE--TO HURL MYSELF OUT OF HARM'S WAY--LIKE THIS!

FOOL! DO YOU THINK I LIMIT MYSELF TO MERELY ONE WEAPON! EVEN A THUNDER GOD, WITH ALL YOUR SPEED, CANNOT DODGE THESE...

FOR THEY ARE CAPSULES OF DEADLY COBRA GAS, MADE BY TRANSFORMING THE COBRA VENOM INTO A DENSE, FAST-SPREADING VAPOR!
MY LUNGS--FILLING WITH THE FATAL VAPORS! MUST DISPEL THEM... BEFORE IT'S TOO LATE...

NO MATTER HOW DENSE A VAPOR MAY BE, THE POUNDING GUSTS OF WIND I CAN CREATE WILL BLOW EVERY TRACE AWAY WITHIN SECONDS!
YOU THINK FAST, THOR--BUT TO NO AVAIL! YOU ARE MERELY POSTPONING THE INEVITABLE OUTCOME OF OUR BATTLE, FOR MY POWER IS STILL FAR GREATER THAN YOURS!
7

HAVE YOU EVER SEEN A SNAKE WRAP ITSELF AROUND ITS VICTIM, THOR? IN THE SAME WAY CAN THE HUMAN COBRA REDUCE YOU TO COMPLETE HELPLESSNESS WITH A LIGHTNING-LIKE TOSS OF MY UNBREAKABLE COBRA-CORD!
IS THERE NO LIMIT TO HIS DIABOLICALLY INGENIOUS DEVICES??!
SO UNEXPECTED WAS HIS SUDDEN MANEUVER, THAT I CARELESSLY DROPPED MY HAMMER IN SURPRISE! WITHOUT IT, MY MAIN SOURCE OF POWER IS DENIED ME!

ONLY IF THROWN WILL THE ENCHANTED MALLET RETURN TO ME! IF IT IS DROPPED, IT REMAINS WHERE IT FELL!! I MUST FIND A WAY TO RETRIEVE IT MYSELF!
COBRA, YOU WILL GAIN NOTHING BY THIS USELESS FEAT! YOU HAVE NOT EVEN ENOUGH STRENGTH TO HURL ME THRU THE WINDOW!

OH NO?? I'LL SHOW YOU HOW MUCH STRENGTH THE COBRA HAS!

HE SWALLOWED THE BAIT! HE DID NOT KNOW THAT I TURN BACK TO DON BLAKE IF MY ENCHANTED HAMMER IS OUT OF MY GRASP FOR MORE THAN SIXTY SECONDS!
AND, AS THE THINNER BLAKE, IT IS A SIMPLE MATTER TO SLIDE OUT OF HIS COBRA CORD!

RUSHING OUTSIDE TO RESUME HIS BATTLE WITH MIGHTY THOR, THE UNSUSPECTING COBRA PAYS NO ATTENTION TO THE LAME, PUNY MAN WHO HOBBLES BACK INTO THE BUILDING...
THOR IS GONE! BUT, THAT'S IMPOSSIBLE! HOW DID HE FREE HIMSELF???

QUICKLY, DON BLAKE SEIZES THE FALLEN HAMMER, STAMPS IT ONCE UPON THE GROUND, AND THEN...
TURN, EVIL COBRA!
TURN AND FACE THOR AGAIN! FACE THE ONE WHO WILL NOW DEFEAT YOU!
THOR!
8

HE IS PLUMMETING TOWARDS ME--ABOUT TO STRIKE WITH THAT ACCURSED HAMMER! I MUST WARD HIM OFF SOMEHOW--OR I AM LOST!
HOW GOOD IT FEELS TO LEAP INTO BATTLE AGAIN--TO HURL MYSELF AGAINST A CREATURE OF EVIL!

JUST WHAT I NEED! THIS VALVE--WHICH ACTIVATES THE FLOW OF A LIQUID CHEMICAL FORCE-BLAST PIPE!

BY A BLIND STROKE OF LUCK, THE CHEMICAL RELEASED BY THE COBRA'S SUDDEN MOVE IS A BLINDING, STINGING, ACID-BASE FORMULA, WHICH STRIKES THE THUNDER GOD WITH ENOUGH FORCE TO DESTROY A DOZEN MORTAL MEN!
WHOOM!

RECOVERING FROM THE TREMENDOUS IMPACT WITH SUPERHUMAN SPEED, THE BATTLE-HARDENED THOR ONCE AGAIN HURLS HIS INVINCIBLE HAMMER, AS A BLOOD-CURDLING WAR CRY RINGS OUT FROM HIS LIPS IN A THUNDEROUS CRESCENDO!
BY THE BEARD OF NOBLE ODIN, OH TRUSTY HAMMER--STRIKE! STRIKE IN THE NAME OF ASGARD!

AND THEN, AMAZINGLY, THE ALMOST IMPOSSIBLE HAPPENS! MOVING WITH BLINDING SPEED, AS SWIFTLY AND AS UNERRINGLY AS THE SERPENT WHOSE NAME HE HAS TAKEN, THE COBRA, HAVING BEEN BITTEN BY A RADIO-ACTIVE SNAKE, IS ONE OF THE FEW LIVING CREATURES EVER TO BE ABLE TO DODGE THOR'S MIGHTY HAMMER!

BY THE GODS! MY HAMMER HAS MISSED THE COBRA AND CRASHED INTO THAT TANK OF CHEMICAL TEST GAS ABOVE HIM!

HAH! EVEN YOUR MUCH-VAUNTED HAMMER IS NOT FAST ENOUGH TO MATCH MY SUPERHUMAN SPEED!

THE SWIFTLY SPREADING GAS VAPORS TEMPORARILY BLIND THE SURPRISED THUNDER GOD BEFORE HIS HAMMER CAN RETURN, ALLOWING HIM TO DISPEL THEM!
MY EYES! I CAN-NOT SEE!
CRASH!

AND, BY THE TIME THE SMOKY FUMES HAVE BLOWN AWAY...
THE COBRA HAS ESCAPED!
BUT I MUST FIND HIM! SOMEWHERE, SOMEHOW--HE MUST BE FOUND!

MEANTIME, FATE DISPLAYS A GRIM TOUCH OF IRONY AS WE FIND THE COBRA ABOUT TO ENTER A WINDOW --A VERY SPECIAL WINDOW...
JUST WHAT I HAVE BEEN SEEKING--A DOCTOR'S OFFICE!

YES, YOU GUESSED IT! OF ALL THE DOCTORS IN THE SPRAWLING CITY OF NEW YORK, THE SERPENTINE MENACE ENTERS THE OFFICE OF DOCTOR ANDREWS, CONFRONTING BOTH THE STARTLED PHYSICIAN AND HIS NEW NURSE, JANE FOSTER!
DR. ANDREWS! WHO--WHAT IS THAT???
I-I DON'T KNOW, JANE! BUT HE LOOKS DANGEROUS--TERRIFYING!
EVEN MORE DANGEROUS THAN YOU CAN SUSPECT, MY GOOD DOCTOR! FOR I AM THE COBRA! BUT, IF YOU OBEY MY EVERY COMMAND TO THE LETTER, I MAY PERMIT YOU TO LIVE--A WHILE LONGER!
FIRST, YOU MUST PROVIDE ME WITH SERUMS FROM YOUR MEDICINE CABINET--SERUMS WITH WHICH I CAN ACHIEVE MY ULTIMATE OBJECTIVE!

DOCTOR, YOU MUSTN'T! NO MATTER HOW HE THREATENS US, YOU MUST NOT AID HIM!
QUIET, YOU YOUNG FOOL! IF YOU DON'T WISH TO CONTINUE LIVING, I DO!

OF COURSE I WILL DO WHAT YOU SAY, COBRA! I-I AM NOT LOOKING FOR ANY TROUBLE! WH-WHAT DO YOU REQUIRE?
I CAN'T BELIEVE IT! YOU'RE NOTHING BUT A-A COWARD!
AND TO THINK I LEFT DOCTOR BLAKE IN ORDER TO WORK FOR YOU!
ALTHOUGH HE IS LAME, AND UN-GLAMOROUS, YOU'LL NEVER BE HALF THE MAN THAT HE IS!

SECONDS LATER, THE DISILLUSIONED GIRL SEES A MIGHTY FIGURE STREAKING PAST THE WINDOW, SEARCHING FOR HIS VANISHED FOE!
IT'S THOR! IF ONLY I CAN ATTRACT HIS ATTENTION!

YOU MUST NOTICE THIS, MIGHTY THOR! YOU MUST!
CRASH!

THE COBRA SAW ME! HE-HE'S LIVID WITH RAGE!
SO! YOU TRIED TO DEFY THE COBRA, DID YOU? YOU SHALL LIVE TO REGRET THAT FOOLISH DEED!

...BUT NOT FOR LONG! NOT AFTER YOU HAVE FELT THE STING OF MY COBRA DARTS!
NO! NO! YOU MUSTN'T!
HELP ME, SOMEBODY-- HELP!

AT THAT SPLIT-SECOND, AN AWESOME, FIGHTING-MAD BLUE AND GOLD CLAD FIGURE STOPS THE FLIGHT OF THE DEADLY COBRA-DARTS IN MIDAIR!
THIS TIME, YOU MERCILESS FIEND, THERE SHALL BE NO ESCAPE!
THOR!

I STILL SHALL WIN THE FINAL BATTLE, THUNDER GOD! FOR IF YOU MAKE ANOTHER MOVE, AN INNOCENT GIRL WILL PERISH!
DON'T WORRY ABOUT ME, THOR! YOU MUST STOP THE COBRA-- NO MATTER WHAT!
NO, JANE FOSTER-- I SHALL NOT ALLOW YOU TO BE INJURED!

HARM ONE HAIR OF HER HEAD, COBRA-- AND THERE WILL NOT BE A PLACE IN THE KNOWN UNIVERSE WHERE YOU WILL BE SAFE FROM MY VENGEANCE!
AND REMEMBER, IF YOU TRY TO STOP ME, YOU WILL BE RESPONSIBLE FOR THIS FEMALE'S TRAGIC FATE!
THAT'S JUST WHAT I HOPED YOU'D SAY, YOU SPINELESS FOOL! AND NOW, FAREWELL!! I'LL LEAVE AS ONLY THE COBRA CAN!

WORDS! THAT'S ALL YOU ARE GOOD FOR, THUNDER GOD-- SPOUTING HIGH-SOUNDING WORDS! BUT I DO NOT FEAR YOU-- FOR I HAVE PROVEN MYSELF TO BE YOUR MASTER!
I'VE GOT TO FREE JANE FROM THAT MADMAN WITHOUT INJURING HER! BUT HOW?!

WAIT! PERHAPS THERE IS A WAY! IT'S A LONG CHANCE--BUT I MUST TAKE IT!

EVERYTHING DEPENDS UPON THE COBRA NOT SEEING ME AS I PLUNGE FROM THE WINDOW!
NOW THAT I HAVE DEFEATED THOR, THERE IS NO ONE WHO CAN STOP ME!
YOU'LL NEVER DEFEAT THE THUNDER GOD, COBRA! JUST WAIT!

SO FAR, SO GOOD! NOW--EVERYTHING DEPENDS UPON SPLIT-SECOND TIMING!

MADE IT!
NOW, COBRA--NOW LET ME HEAR YOU BOAST HOW YOU HAVE DEFEATED ME!
YOU HAVEN'T GOT ME YET! I WARNED YOU THE GIRL WOULD DIE...
NO! DON'T DROP ME!

FEAR NOT, JANE FOSTER! NO HARM SHALL BEFALL YOU WHILE THOR LIVES!
BUT THE COBRA-- HE'S ESCAPING!

TIME ENOUGH FOR HIM AT SOME LATER DATE! FIRST, I MUST TAKE YOU TO SAFETY!

IN LESS TIME THAN IT TAKES TO TELL, THE DISILLUSIONED GIRL IS RETURNED TO HER OFFICE, WHERE SHE REMAINS JUST LONG ENOUGH TO PACK HER BELONGINGS, AND...
GOODBYE, DOCTOR ANDREWS! I AM GOING TO RETURN TO A REAL MAN, AND ASK HIS FORGIVENESS--BEG HIM TO LET ME WORK FOR HIM AGAIN, IF HE'LL HAVE ME!
JANE! WAIT-- YOU CAN'T-- JANE!

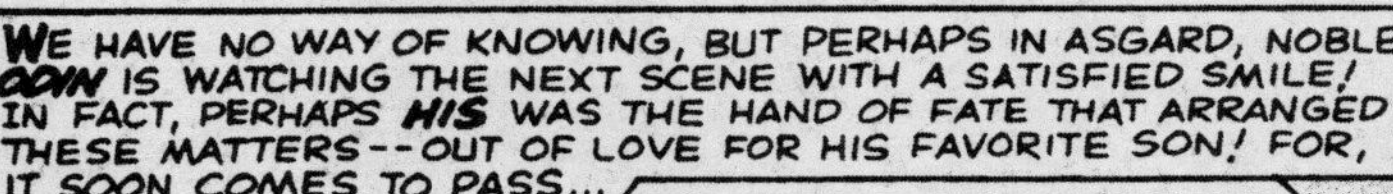

WE HAVE NO WAY OF KNOWING, BUT PERHAPS IN ASGARD, NOBLE ODIN IS WATCHING THE NEXT SCENE WITH A SATISFIED SMILE! IN FACT, PERHAPS HIS WAS THE HAND OF FATE THAT ARRANGED THESE MATTERS--OUT OF LOVE FOR HIS FAVORITE SON! FOR, IT SOON COMES TO PASS...

DR. BLAKE--DON--IT'S SO GOOD OF YOU TO TAKE ME BACK! I'VE BEEN SUCH A FOOL!
NOT ANOTHER, WORD, JANE! WE'RE TOGETHER AGAIN, AND THAT'S ALL THAT MATTERS! IN FACT, I'M SURE THAT THOR HIMSELF WOULD BE PLEASED AT HOW THIS EPISODE ENDED--IF HE ONLY KNEW!
13

AND SO THE SAGA OF THE COBRA DRAWS TO AN END... BUT ONLY FOR NOW! FOR THE COBRA STILL LIVES! AND WHILE HE WALKS THE EARTH, PLOTTING NEW DARK DEEDS, WHO KNOWS WHAT THE FUTURE HOLDS FOR MANKIND--AND FOR THOR!??

The End!

TALES OF ASGARD, HOME OF THE GODS!
ODIN BATTLES YMIR, KING OF THE ICE GIANTS
WRITTEN BY: STAN LEE
DRAWN BY: JACK KIRBY
INKED BY: DON HECK
LETTERED BY: ART SIMEK
IN THE DAYS OF THE GODS, WHEN THE WORLD WAS YOUNG, ASGARD WAS MENACED BY THE RAMPAGING ICE GIANTS, DETERMINED TO BRING FROST, DESOLATION, AND ETERNAL NIGHT TO THE LAND OF THE GODS! THIS IS THE TALE OF THEIR ATTACK, ONE OF THE GREATEST BATTLES OF ALL TIME!
BASED UPON THE IMMORTAL LEGENDS OF THE NORSE GODS!
X-452
1

IN HIS IMPERIAL CASTLE, ON THE HIGHEST PEAK OF THE TALLEST MOUNT IN ALL OF ASGARD, NOBLE **ODIN**, LORD OF THE GODS, HEARS THE CALL TO BATTLE!

THE TRUMPET BLARES! THE TIME HAS COME! I MUST DESTROY THE ICE GIANTS!

RIDING A GOLDEN CHARIOT, DRAWN BY HIS MAGNIFICENT WINGED STALLIONS, THE RULER OF ALL THE GODS THUNDERS THRU THE SKIES...

FASTER, MY MIGHTY MOUNTS! MY BLADE HUNGERS FOR COMBAT... MY SOUL THIRSTS FOR REVENGE!

BEHOLD! ODIN JOINS THE BATTLE!
WHEN HE IS SLAIN, ALL OF ASGARD SHALL BE OURS!

BUT, THOUGH DWARFED IN SIZE BY HIS GIGANTIC FOES, THE VALIANT ODIN DRAWS BACK HIS MAGIC SWORD AS HIS DEAFENING WAR CRY REVERBERATES THRU THE HEAVENS...

DEATH TO THE ENEMIES OF ASGARD!

SUMMONING THE AWESOME FORCES OF NATURE TO HIS BEHEST, THE MONARCH OF ASGARD HURLS MIGHTY METEOR BOLTS AT THE FEARSOME FRIGID BEHEMOTHS WHO ARE MENACING HIS DOMAIN!

BUT, THOSE OF THE ICE GIANTS WHO SURVIVE THE MIGHTY BLASTS USE THEIR DEADLY ICE-CLUBS AGAINST ODIN, TRYING TO BATTER HIM FROM THE SKIES!

UNABLE TO STRIKE THE SWIFTLY-DARTING CHARIOT, THEY THEN RESORT TO THEIR MOST POTENT POWER... IN UNISON, THE ICE GIANTS UNLEASH A TITANIC GUST OF FROZEN NORTH WIND, HURLING THEIR NOBLE FOE FROM HIS CRAZILY-SPINNING CHARIOT!

AS THE GRACEFUL WINGED STALLIONS FLY OFF, ODIN LANDS ATOP THE MOUNTAIN ON WHICH THE ICE GIANTS STAND...

THEN, AS HIS CONFIDENT FOES CREEP SLOWLY TOWARDS HIM, MIGHTY ODIN DRAWS BACK HIS MAGIC SWORD...

...AND STRIKES, SPLITTING THE ENTIRE MOUNTAIN IN TWO, WITH ONE INCREDIBLE BLOW!

UNPREPARED FOR ODIN'S SUDDEN MANEUVER, THE CONFUSED TITANS FALL INTO THE NEWLY-FORMED CHASM, WHERE THE DEMONS OF SURTUR WAIT GREEDILY BELOW, TO MAKE THEM PRISONERS FOR ALL TIME!
DOWN, YOU MARAUDING MONSTERS! SO PLUNGE YOU TO SURTUR'S FIERY DOMAIN... WHERE YOU SHALL MENACE ASGARD NO MORE!

BUT ONE FROZEN BEHEMOTH STILL REMAINS! THIS, THE MIGHTIEST, THE MOST SAVAGE OF ALL, IS YMIR, KING OF THE ICE GIANTS!
VICTORY IS NOT YET YOURS, ACCURSED ODIN! MY ICY SPEAR SHALL YET BRING YOU TO YOUR KNEES!

HAH! I HAVE DISLODGED THE PEAK ON WHICH YOU HIDE LIKE A FEARFUL FLEA! AND NOW, I SHALL END YOUR REIGN FOREVER!
NOT SO, EVIL YMIR! WHILE BREATH REMAINS IN ME I SHALL FIGHT YOU! AND, BY MY BEARD, THE VICTORY SHALL YET BE MINE!

YOUR WORDS ARE BRAVE, BUT YOUR DEEDS MAKE A MOCKERY OF THEM! EVEN NOW, AS YOU RETREAT IN COWARDLY PANIC, I SHALL SEIZE YOU... AND DESTROY YOU!

BUT, REACHING THE ARID, VOLCANIC AREA HE SEEKS, THE MONARCH OF THE GODS SUDDENLY STOPS, TURNS, AND THEN...
I HAVE TRAPPED YOU, YMIR! BEFORE YOU CAN MAKE ANOTHER MOVE, I STRIKE THIS VERY SPOT...

...RELEASING THE ONE FORCE WHICH CAN DEFEAT YOU... THE FIERY, SMOLDERING FLAMES FROM THE DEPTHS BELOW!

AND SO YMIR, THE LAST OF THE DREADED ICE GIANTS, BECOMES AN ETERNAL PRISONER ON THAT BARREN SPOT, SURROUNDED BY A WALL HE CAN NEVER PENETRATE!

WHILST NOBLE ODIN, RULER OF THE GODS, RETURNS TO HIS THRONE IN ASGARD!
THE END
NEXT ISSUE: SURTUR the FIRE DEMON!
5

JOURNEY INTO MYSTERY
IND.
APPROVED BY THE COMICS CODE AUTHORITY
MARVEL COMICS GROUP 12¢
99 DEC.
THE MIGHTY THOR
MEETS THE MOST DRAMATIC SUPER-FOE OF THE YEAR.....
THE MYSTERIOUS MISTER HYDE!
IT IS TIME FOR MIGHTY THOR TO BECOME WEAK DOCTOR BLAKE AGAIN...
...I HOPE NO NEW MENACE SHOWS UP NOW... FOR I'D BE HELPLESS TO FIGHT IT!
MISTER HYDE! STRONGER THAN A DOZEN MEN! MORE DANGEROUS THAN ANY MERE MORTAL!
Also: YOU WILL MEET SURTUR, THE FIRE DEMON IN THIS ISSUE'S "TALES of ASGARD!"

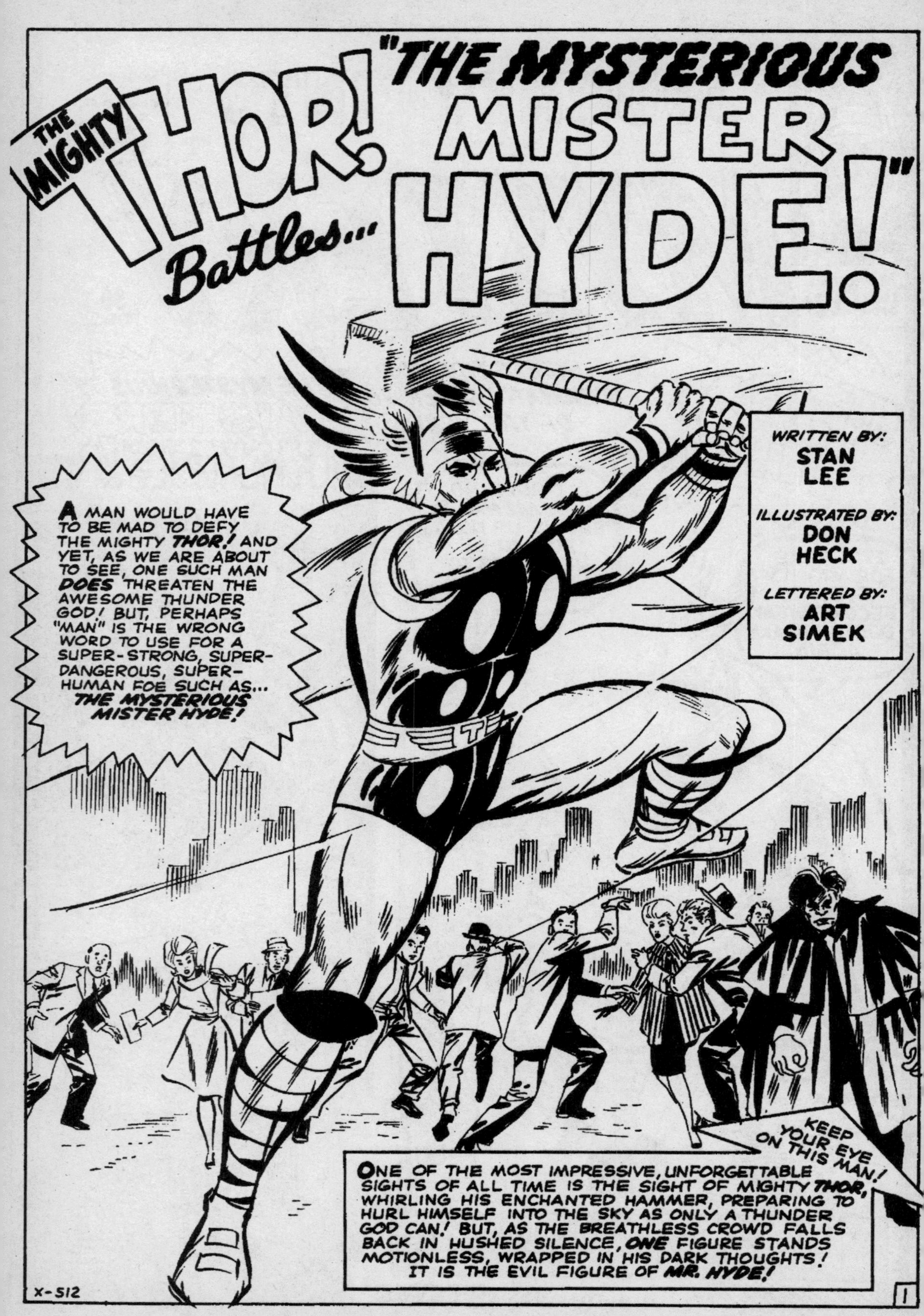
THE MIGHTY THOR! Battles... "THE MYSTERIOUS MISTER HYDE!"
WRITTEN BY: STAN LEE
ILLUSTRATED BY: DON HECK
LETTERED BY: ART SIMEK
A MAN WOULD HAVE TO BE MAD TO DEFY THE MIGHTY THOR! AND YET, AS WE ARE ABOUT TO SEE, ONE SUCH MAN DOES THREATEN THE AWESOME THUNDER GOD! BUT, PERHAPS "MAN" IS THE WRONG WORD TO USE FOR A SUPER-STRONG, SUPER-DANGEROUS, SUPER-HUMAN FOE SUCH AS... THE MYSTERIOUS MISTER HYDE!
KEEP YOUR EYE ON THIS MAN!
ONE OF THE MOST IMPRESSIVE, UNFORGETTABLE SIGHTS OF ALL TIME IS THE SIGHT OF MIGHTY THOR, WHIRLING HIS ENCHANTED HAMMER, PREPARING TO HURL HIMSELF INTO THE SKY AS ONLY A THUNDER GOD CAN! BUT, AS THE BREATHLESS CROWD FALLS BACK IN HUSHED SILENCE, ONE FIGURE STANDS MOTIONLESS, WRAPPED IN HIS DARK THOUGHTS! IT IS THE EVIL FIGURE OF MR. HYDE!
X-512
1

THEN, LIKE A RAGING THUNDERBOLT, THE POWERFUL COSTUMED FIGURE HURTLES INTO THE SKY, ON A MISSION KNOWN ONLY TO HIMSELF, AS THE WIDE-EYED CROWD STARES IN UNDISGUISED WONDER!
THIS IS A SIGHT I'LL REMEMBER AS LONG AS I LIVE!!
IT'S SOMETHING WE'LL TELL OUR CHILDREN -- AND THEY'LL REPEAT TO THEIR CHILDREN!

WHERE DO YOU THINK HE'S HEADING FOR?
WHO KNOWS? WITH SOMEONE LIKE THOR IT COULD BE ANY PLACE!
LOOK! HE'S ALMOST OUT OF SIGHT ALREADY! IF ONLY WE COULD HAVE GOTTEN A LONGER LOOK AT HIM-- -SIGH-!

BUT, WITHIN THE CROWD, ONE MAN--IF MAN HE IS--FEELS NO REGRET AT SEEING THOR VANISH INTO THE BLUE...
I'VE--I'VE GOT TO GET AWAY! I'VE NEVER SEEN ANYONE SO REPULSIVE--SO FRIGHTENING!!
HE'S GONE! GOOD! THIS MAKES EVERYTHING PERFECT!

WITH THOR OUT OF THE CITY, THERE IS NO ONE STRONG ENOUGH TO FRUSTRATE MY PLANS!

AND NOW, IT IS TIME FOR DOCTOR DON BLAKE TO RECEIVE A VISIT!! AN UNEXPECTED VISIT FROM-- MISTER HYDE!

MEANWHILE, TRAVELING AT SPEEDS FASTER THAN THE HUMAN MIND CAN COMPREHEND, THE MIGHTY THOR REACHES HIS DESTINATION! HE HAS ARRIVED AT ASGARD, HOME OF THE LEGENDARY NORSE GODS-- THRONE CITY OF ODIN, THE ALL-POWERFUL, FATHER OF THOR!
AGAIN I COME TO PLEAD MY CAUSE!
BUT THIS TIME I SHALL NOT LEAVE WITHOUT THE ANSWER I CRAVE!

THEN, WITHIN THE GOLDEN THRONE ROOM OF ODIN...
AGAIN YOU PLAGUE ME WITH YOUR IMPOSSIBLE DEMAND?? BEWARE, THOR! THOUGH YOU BE MY FAVORITE SON, YOU WEAR MY PATIENCE THIN!

AS THE SON OF ODIN, AND HEIR TO THE THRONE OF ASGARD, I HAVE THE PRIVI-LEGE OF REPEATING A REQUEST! AND YOU KNOW THAT WELL, NOBLE FATHER!

YOU MUST LET ME MARRY THE EARTH-BOUND FEMALE, JANE FOSTER! THOUGH HE BE MAN OR THUNDER-GOD, EVERYONE THAT BREATHES MUST ANSWER TO HIS HEART!
ENOUGH! I WILL HEAR NO MORE! AN IMMORTAL MAY NEVER MARRY AN EARTHLING! THAT IS THE FINAL WORD OF ODIN!

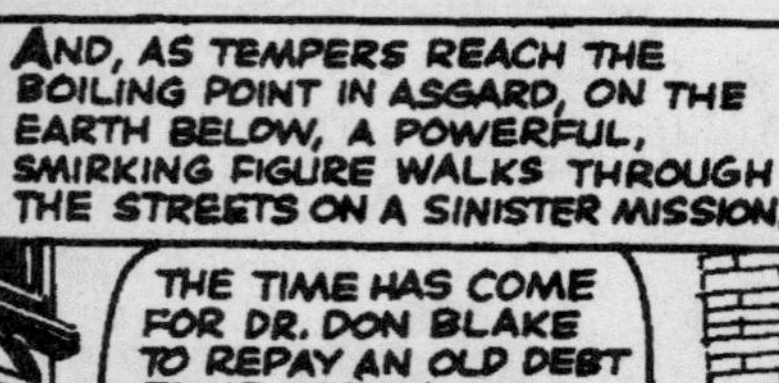
AND, AS TEMPERS REACH THE BOILING POINT IN ASGARD, ON THE EARTH BELOW, A POWERFUL, SMIRKING FIGURE WALKS THROUGH THE STREETS ON A SINISTER MISSION...

THE TIME HAS COME FOR DR. DON BLAKE TO REPAY AN OLD DEBT TO MR. HYDE! AND I SHALL SEE THAT I AM PAID IN FULL!

JUST A FEW BLOCKS AWAY, IN DR. BLAKE'S OUTER OFFICE, HIS LOVELY NURSE, JANE FOSTER, IS WRAPPED IN HER OWN THOUGHTS... UNAWARE OF THE LURKING MENACE WHICH IS COMING EVER CLOSER...
IF ONLY I COULD STOP LOVING DON BLAKE!! I KNOW MY FEELINGS FOR HIM ARE IN VAIN-- AND YET, MY HEART CAN'T FORGET HIM!
I FEEL HE LOVES ME, TOO... BUT THERE SEEMS TO BE SOME TERRIBLE SECRET WHICH HE NEVER DARES SPEAK OF... BUT WHICH WILL ETERNALLY KEEP US APART!
BUT LITTLE DOES JANE FOSTER DREAM THAT WITHIN MINUTES, A NEW MENACE WILL APPEAR, A MENACE GRAVE ENOUGH TO MAKE HER FORGET HER ROMANTIC LONGINGS!
3

FOR, IN THE STREET BELOW, MR. HYDE PAUSES BEFORE ENTERING BLAKE'S BUILDING... PAUSES TO REFLECT UPON THE PAST...
BLAKE DOES NOT SUSPECT WHAT I HAVE BECOME!

"HE HAS NO WAY OF KNOWING THAT MY STRENGTH HAS BEEN MAGNIFIED A DOZEN TIMES, SO THAT I AM AS POWERFUL AS ANY TWELVE NORMAL HUMAN BEINGS! BUT, HE IS SOON TO LEARN OF MR. HYDE--AND SO IS THE REST OF MANKIND!"
HA! HA! HA!

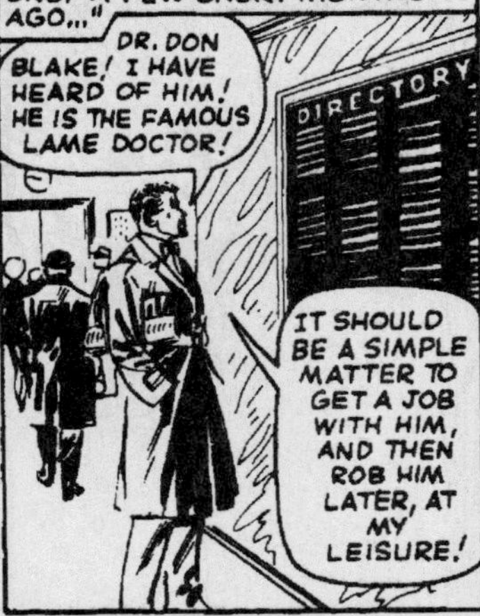

"NOR WILL HE SUSPECT THAT I AM THE SAME MAN WHO ONCE CALLED HIMSELF CALVIN ZABO, AND WHO CAME TO SEE HIM ONLY A FEW SHORT MONTHS AGO..."
DR. DON BLAKE! I HAVE HEARD OF HIM! HE IS THE FAMOUS LAME DOCTOR!
DIRECTORY
IT SHOULD BE A SIMPLE MATTER TO GET A JOB WITH HIM, AND THEN ROB HIM LATER, AT MY LEISURE!

"BUT BLAKE PROVED TO BE LESS UNSUSPECTING THAN I THOUGHT!"
I'VE HEARD ABOUT YOU, ZABO! YOU'RE NO GOOD! YOU'VE BEEN FIRED FROM EVERY JOB YOU'VE EVER HELD! I CAN'T USE YOU! SHOW HIM OUT, MISS FOSTER!
SO! YOU DARE HUMILIATE CALVIN ZABO THIS WAY!! YOU'LL PAY FOR THIS, BLAKE! I PROMISE YOU!

"I HATED HIM! HE HAD EVERYTHING! WEALTH, FAME, A BEAUTIFUL NURSE! I KNEW I HAD TO FIND A WAY TO HARM HIM --SOMEHOW!"

"AND AS I LEFT, THE GERM OF AN IDEA BEGAN TO HATCH IN MY BRAIN AS I VOWED BITTER VENGEANCE UPON DR. DON BLAKE!"
SLAM

(EDITOR'S NOTE: NATURALLY, THE MAN CALLED CALVIN ZABO HAS NO WAY OF KNOWING THAT THE FRAIL DOCTOR WHOM HE HATES, AND THE MIGHTY THOR, ARE ONE AND THE SAME!! FOR, IF HE SUSPECTED... BUT, MORE OF THAT LATER....!)

"FOR YEARS, I HAD BEEN FASCINATED BY THE TALE OF DR. JEKYLL AND MR. HYDE! I HAD ALWAYS FELT IT WAS MORE THAN JUST AN IMAGINARY STORY-- I FELT IT COULD HAPPEN! AND SO..."
I KNOW IT MUST BE POSSIBLE TO CHANGE A HUMAN BEING--CHANGE HIM SO THAT HIS BASER NATURE TAKES OVER, JUST AS HAPPENED TO DR. JEKYLL! AND IF MY CALCULATIONS ARE CORRECT...

"AND SO I DRANK THE POTION I HAD CREATED! AND THEN, THE CHANGE BEGAN! JUST AS ROBERT LOUIS STEVENSON HAD DESCRIBED IT IN HIS CLASSIC TALE, IN HIS TALE WHICH WAS ***TRUER*** THAN HE HAD DREAMT! I CHANGED! I BECAME WHAT I HAD ***WANTED*** TO BECOME -- I BECAME ***MISTER HYDE!***"

"AND, WITH THAT CHANGE, CAME A HATRED OF HUMANITY--AND A DESIRE TO TRIUMPH OVER THE WEAKER HUMAN RACE!"

"BUT, EVEN AS MY PERSONALITY CHANGED, SO DID MY STRENGTH! THE POWER OF A DOZEN MEN FLOWED THRU MY VEINS! I COULD ACCOMPLISH ANY FEAT I DESIRED! I COULD DEFEAT ANYONE, ANYTHING!"

"THEN, I REALIZED THE MOST WONDERFUL THING! NO MATTER WHAT CRIME I COMMITTED, NO ONE WOULD EVER SUSPECT MY TRUE SELF, CALVIN ZABO--FOR EVEN MY ***FINGERPRINTS*** HAD CHANGED WHEN I BECAME MR. HYDE! THIS MEANT I COULD DO ***ANYTHING*** AS MISTER HYDE, AND ONCE CHANGING BACK TO CALVIN ZABO, I WOULD BE SAFE FROM ARREST!"

"AND, WITH MY NEW-FOUND STRENGTH, WHAT MASSIVE CRIMES I COULD COMMIT! EVEN THE STRONGEST BANK VAULT DOORS WOULD CRUMBLE BEFORE MY MIGHTY GRASP--"

"AND, ONCE I TURNED BACK TO CALVIN ZABO, NONE WOULD EVER SUSPECT I WAS THE ONE WHO CALLED HIMSELF MR. HYDE! IT WOULD BE THE PERFECT MEANS OF ESCAPE --THE ABILITY TO CHANGE TO A COMPLETELY DIFFERENT PERSON! NOTHING COULD EVER STOP ME!"
BANK

BUT MR. HYDE'S MUSINGS COME TO A SUDDEN HALT AS HE EASILY SMASHES DOWN THE DOOR TO DR. DON BLAKE'S OUTER OFFICE...
BUT NOW TO THE TASK AT HAND-- MY REVENGE UPON DR. BLAKE!

MEANWHILE, IN ASGARD, THOR DOES NOT REALIZE THAT AN ENEMY HAS INVADED THE OFFICE OF HIS EARTHLY ALTER EGO!

NOBLE ODIN, YOU MUST NOT TURN AWAY FROM ME! YOU MUST HEAR MY PETITION!

IT IS USELESS! AN IMMORTAL MAY NOT MARRY A MORTAL! THAT IS THE LAW! NOTHING MORE REMAINS TO BE SAID!

BUT I HAVE AN ANSWER FOR THAT, MY FATHER! YOU HAVE A POWER WHICH YOU HAVE NEVER USED BEFORE! THE POWER TO MAKE A HUMAN BEING AN IMMORTAL-- JUST AS MY ENCHANTED HAMMER HAS MADE ME THE GOD OF THUNDER!
WHAT??! YOU DARE SUGGEST I USE THAT GREAT POWER ON A MERE EARTH GIRL-- FOR NO OTHER PURPOSE THAN TO MAKE HER YOUR WIFE!!!

TO BECOME AN IMMORTAL, ONE MUST BE PROVEN TO BE NOBLE, UNSELFISH, FEARLESS, AND POSSESSING VIRTUES FAR IN EXCESS OF THOSE WHICH THE ORDINARY EARTHBOUND HUMAN POSSESSES! AND THIS YOU KNOW FULL WELL, MY SON!

YOU CANNOT DISMISS ME SO CASUALLY! YOU SEEK TO THWART ME AT EVERY TURN! BUT I DO NOT ACCEPT YOUR ANSWER, ODIN!
WHAT?!! YOU DARE RAISE YOUR HAMMER TO ME??!

FORGIVE ME, MY FATHER! IT WAS AN INVOLUNTARY GESTURE! I MEANT YOU NO HARM! I-- OHHH!
SILENCE! EVEN A THUNDER GOD MUST BE TAUGHT HUMILITY!

STUNNED MOMENTARILY BY ODIN'S MIGHTY POWER-BLAST, THOR STAGGERS BACK--AND THE SIGHT OF HIS REPENTFUL SON TOUCHES THE HEART OF THE NOBLE MONARCH...
I AM SADDENED THAT I MUST CAUSE ANGUISH TO THE SON I LOVE! PERHAPS I YET MAY LEAVE A CRUMB OF HOPE FOR HIM TO CLING TO...

AND SO...
GO NOW, THOR, AND HEED MY FINAL WORDS: SHOULD THE EARTHLING YOU LOVE PROVE HERSELF WORTHY OF IMMORTALITY, THEN YOU MAY COME TO ME AGAIN AND I SHALL LISTEN TO YOUR PETITION!
THEN THERE IS STILL HOPE, MY FATHER! I THANK YOU FOR THAT!

THEN, JOYOUSLY, LIKE A FLYING, FLASHING STREAK, THE MIGHTY THOR HURTLES EARTHWARD...
THERE STILL IS HOPE! SHE MAY YET BE MINE!

WHERE A HUMAN CAN BE STRONG, A THUNDER GOD IS MIGHTY! WHERE A HUMAN CAN BE FAST, A THUNDER GOD IS LIGHTNING SWIFT! AND, WHERE A HUMAN MIGHT BE HAPPY, A THUNDER GOD'S UNBRIDLED JOY KNOWS NO LIMITS!!!
SHE MAY YET BE MINE! HA HA-- MINE!

AND SO, AS FATE WOULD HAVE IT, THE MIGHTY THOR SWINGS INTO DR. BLAKE'S PRIVATE OFFICE THROUGH AN OPEN WINDOW, AT THE VERY SAME INSTANT AS ANOTHER DRAMATIC EVENT TAKES PLACE...

NOW TO CHANGE TO DR. BLAKE BEFORE JANE CAN ENTER THE ROOM AND DISCOVER ME!

IN THE OUTER OFFICE, AT THAT SPLIT-SECOND, THE REPELLENT FORM OF MR. HYDE SMASHES THROUGH THE LOCKED DOOR, AND NOW OUR TALE BEGINS TO MOVE INTO HIGH GEAR...
TAKE ME TO DOCTOR BLAKE, AT ONCE! MISTER HYDE COMMANDS YOU!
THAT FACE! THAT INHUMAN STRENGTH!! WHO--WHAT ARE YOU??!

AND, HEARING THE HARSH VOICE DEMANDING TO SEE HIM, BUT NOT DREAMING OF THE MENACE WHO POSSESSES THAT VOICE, THOR STAMPS HIS ENCHANTED HAMMER ONCE UPON THE FLOOR, AND HIS TRANSFORMATION IS COMPLETED INSTANTANEOUSLY!
IT IS TIME TO BECOME DON BLAKE AGAIN...
AND NOW TO SEE WHAT THAT COMMOTION IS, IN MY OUTER OFFICE!

BUT, AS DON BLAKE, THOR'S SENSES ARE NOT AS ALERT AS WHEN HE IS THE GOD OF THUNDER, AND SO HE MAKES A CARELESS MISTAKE AS HE THOUGHTLESSLY DROPS HIS ENCHANTED WALKING STICK, LETTING IT FALL OUT OF REACH!
THAT VOICE-- I DON'T RECOGNIZE IT!
IT SOUNDS HARSH, GUTTERAL--FROUGHT WITH HATRED AND MENACE!

CRRASSSH!

DOCTOR! I WANTED TO WARN YOU-- BUT HE DIDN'T GIVE ME THE CHANCE! HE--
SILENCE, WOMAN!! IT IS TOO LATE FOR WORDS! MY MOMENT IS AT HAND!
I DON'T KNOW WHO YOU ARE, FELLA, BUT I'M NOT USED TO HAVING MY DOORS BASHED IN LIKE THAT!!
HAVE TO DISTRACT HIM WITH TALK-- TILL I CAN GRAB MY CANE!

THEN, SUDDENLY, DON BLAKE LUNGES DESPERATELY FOR HIS ENCHANTED STICK! BUT MR. HYDE MISTAKES THE GESTURE, THINKING BLAKE WANTS TO ATTACK HIM WITH THE SIMPLE OBJECT!
FOOL! YOU THINK YOU CAN SAVE YOURSELF BY GRAB-BING A CANE!
IF I CAN ONLY GET MY FINGERS ON IT-- THERE! I'VE GOT IT!

BUT, BEFORE BLAKE CAN POUND IT ON THE FLOOR--
I DIDN'T MEAN TO FINISH YOU SO SOON-- BUT IT'S YOUR OWN FAULT!
THE WINDOW! I-I'M FALLING-- TOO LATE TO SAVE MYSELF!
8

WHILE INSIDE THE ROOM, JANE FOSTER RECOILS IN SHOCK AT THE SIGHT OF THE MAN SHE LOVES, PLUMMETING TO ALMOST CERTAIN DEATH THROUGH THE OPEN WINDOW--!

DON! DON!! OH, NO!

AND THEN, BECAUSE SHE IS A FEMALE...
SHE FAINTED! IT IS JUST AS WELL! NOW I WILL NOT BE FORCED TO--SILENCE HER!

THEN, RIPPING BLAKE'S PRIVATE WALL VAULT DOOR OFF ITS HINGES AS EASILY AS IF IT IS MADE OF PAPER MACHE...
WHAT COULD BE MORE FITTING THAN FOR THE ONE WHO VANQUISHED HIM TO TAKE BLAKE'S MONEY, HIS PAPERS, AND THE RESULTS OF HIS LIFETIME OF RESEARCH AND STUDY!!
IT IS ONLY FITTING THAT MR. HYDE SHOULD GAIN BY BLAKE'S DEATH! AND NOW, MY REVENGE IS COMPLETE!
RRIP!

MEANWHILE, OUTSIDE THE BUILDING, DON BLAKE CONTINUES TO PLUMMET TOWARDS THE GROUND...
ONLY ONE CHANCE...
...IF I CAN JUST TOUCH THE WALL WITH MY CANE!! I-I'VE GOT TO!!

AND THEN, A SCANT FEW STORIES FROM THE WAITING PAVEMENT BELOW...
I'LL HAVE TIME FOR ONLY ONE TRY--MUST DO IT NOW--NOW!

I--I DID IT!
THUMP!

AS DON BLAKE, MORTAL, I WAS FORCED TO FALL TOWARDS THE GROUND...
BUT, AS MIGHTY THOR, THE THUNDER GOD, WITH THE AID OF MY ENCHANTED HAMMER, I CAN LAND SAFELY BY FLYING!

AND NOW, MISTER HYDE, WE SHALL FACE EACH OTHER AGAIN--ON MY TERMS!

BY TWIRLING MY MALLET IN THIS MANNER, I CAN RISE STRAIGHT INTO THE AIR, IN THE FASHION OF AN EARTHLY HELICOPTER!

BUT, UPON REACHING BLAKE'S OFFICE AGAIN...
HYDE IS GONE! HE MADE GOOD HIS ESCAPE! BUT, NOT FOR LONG!
JANE, ARE YOU ALRIGHT?? WHAT HAPPENED?? WHO WAS HE??
I DON'T KNOW! HE CALLED HIMSELF MR. HYDE! HE SEEMED TO KNOW DR. BLAKE-- OH!
DR. BLAKE!! HE-HE FELL FROM THE WINDOW-- HE--!!!

NO, DO NOT FEAR FOR HIS SAFETY! HE IS ALL RIGHT! LUCKILY, I WAS PASSING BY AND SAW HIM FALLING! I MANAGED TO SAVE HIM BEFORE HE STRUCK THE GROUND!
OH, THANK HEAVENS! I-I WAS SO WORRIED--!!

SHE SEEMS TO LOVE BLAKE AS MUCH AS I LOVE HER! IF ONLY I COULD TELL HER MY SECRET! BUT, IN TIME, PERHAPS I SHALL! ONCE ODIN IS CONVINCED THAT SHE IS WORTHY!

AND THEN...
THOR--WAIT! BEFORE YOU GO-- WHERE IS DOCTOR BLAKE?? I WANT TO SEE HIM!
EH, I'M NOT QUITE SURE NOW! BUT DON'T WORRY --HE SAID HE'D CALL YOU! YOUR PHONE SHOULD BE RINGING ANY MINUTE NOW!

TRUE TO HIS WORD, ONCE OUT OF SIGHT, THOR CHANGES AGAIN TO DON BLAKE AND HURRIES TO THE NEAREST PHONE BOOTH...
JANE? YES--YES MY DEAR, IT'S REALLY ME! THANKS TO THOR, I WASN'T INJURED! I'LL BE BACK IN THE OFFICE IN A LITTLE WHILE!
AFTER I'VE ATTENDED TO THE MYSTERIOUS MR. HYDE!
ELEPHONE

MEANWHILE, IN ANOTHER PART OF TOWN...
NOW THAT I HAVE HAD MY REVENGE ON DON BLAKE, I CAN CONCENTRATE ON MY PLANS-- PLANS FOR COMMITTING THE GREATEST CRIMES OF THE CENTURY!

WITH MY SUPER-HUMAN STRENGTH, MY NEWLY-FORMED DEVIOUS, SCHEMING BRAIN, AND MY ABILITY TO CHANGE IDENTITIES, I CAN NEVER FAIL!
THE MONEY I STOLE FROM BLAKE IS BUT A PITTANCE TO WHAT I SOON SHALL POSSESS! IT IS NO MORE THAN ---- A SYMBOL! A SYMBOL OF MY POWER--MY DESTINY!

BUT SUDDENLY, A NEWS BROADCAST INTERRUPTS THE BACKGROUND MUSIC WHICH HAD BEEN PLAYING ON HYDE'S RADIO, AND HE LEARNS...
WE BRING YOU A SPECIAL BULLETIN FROM OUR NEWS ROOM! IT HAS BEEN REPORTED THAT DR. DONALD BLAKE, THE EMINENT NEURO-SURGEON, WAS MIRACULOUSLY SAVED FROM A PLUNGE FROM HIS OFFICE WINDOW TODAY BY THE ARRIVAL OF THE MIGHTY THOR WHO SNATCHED HIM FROM SUDDEN DEATH IN A DRAMATIC RESCUE...
WHAT??!! BLAKE STILL LIVES!!

THEN THOR HAS RETURNED!! AND HE HAS FOILED MY REVENGE!

I FEARED THAT THOR WAS THE ONLY ONE WHO COULD FOIL ME! SO THIS IS ONLY ONE COURSE FOR ME TO FOLLOW! MY FIRST TASK-- MY MOST IMPORTANT TASK SHALL BE-- THE DESTRUCTION OF THOR--BY MR. HYDE!!

NO MATTER HOW STRONG HE IS, MY STRENGTH WILL MATCH HIS!
AND I SHALL HAVE THE ADVANTAGE OF SURPRISE-- FOR THOR, IN HIS ARROGANT SELF-CONFIDENCE, CANNOT SUSPECT THAT I AM CAPABLE OF DEFEATING HIM--UNTIL IT IS TOO LATE!
SNAP

THE NEXT DAY, IN THE MAIN LOBBY OF ONE OF NEW YORK'S LARGEST SAVINGS AND LOAN INSTITUTIONS...
OH NO! IT--IT ISN'T POSSIBLE!
LOOK--LOOK WHO IT IS!!

CRASH!
BACK! ALL OF YOU! LET NONE INTERFERE WITH THE MIGHTY THOR!

YOU ALL KNOW ME--AND YOU KNOW MY POWER! I DO NOT WANT TO HARM ANYONE UNLESS IT IS NECESSARY! SO I WARN YOU--STAY BACK AND DO NOT FORCE ME TO SLAY ANY OF YOU PUNY MORTALS!
WHAT HAS HAPPENED TO THOR?
THE WORST THING POSSIBLE, FOR MAN-KIND!! HE--HE SEEMS TO HAVE TURNED BAD!!

I SHALL DO WHAT I MUST QUICKLY, AND EFFORTLESSLY! THERE ARE NONE WHO WOULD DARE TRY TO STOP ME!
RRIIP

HE'S ROBBING THE BANK! RIGHT BEFORE OUR EYES! I CAN'T BELIEVE IT--NOT OF THOR!
I WON'T BE GREEDY! I'LL ONLY TAKE AS MUCH AS I CAN CARRY! AND THOR CAN CARRY A FORTUNE!

EVEN IF YOU ARE THE MIGHTY THOR, I CAN'T STAND BY AND LET YOU--OHHH...
YOU DARE POINT A GUN AT ME!!! I'LL CRUMPLE IT TO DUST BEFORE YOUR EYES!

THEN, BEFORE ANYONE CAN MAKE ANOTHER MOVE, THE THUNDER GOD TURNS AND RACES FROM THE BANK WITH BLINDING SPEED, CARRYING THE HEAVY MONEY BAGS AS THOUGH THEY ARE ***WEIGHTLESS!***

WITHIN MINUTES, THE NEWS IS FLASHED TO AN INCREDULOUS WORLD, AS A STARTLED HUMANITY FINDS ITSELF UNABLE TO BELIEVE WHAT IT HAS HEARD--UNABLE TO IMAGINE THE DIRE CONSEQUENCES FOR MANKIND IF THE REPORTS ARE ***TRUE!!***

LOOK, CHIEF, WE CAN'T MAKE ANY EXCEPTIONS! IF THOR HAS TURNED BAD, WE'VE GOT TO GET HIM!
YOU'RE RIGHT, CLARK! IT'S OUR DUTY, AND WE MUST DO IT! BUT HAVE YOU STOPPED TO CONSIDER, MAN--?? HOW DO YOU BRING IN A BEING WHO CAN FLY--WHO CAN CONTROL THE VERY ELEMENTS THEMSELVES--AND WHOSE STRENGTH IS SO GREAT IT HAS NEVER BEEN ACCURATELY MEASURED!??

IN THE HOURS THAT FOLLOW, THOR BECOMES PAGE ONE NEWS! HIS NAME IS ON EVERYONE'S LIPS, AND HIS DEEDS WIPE REPORTS OF WARS AND REVOLUTIONS FROM THE FRONT PAGES!

ARE THERE ANY FURTHER LEADS ON THE ***THOR*** CASE CHIEF?

HOW SOON DO YOU EXPECT AN ARREST CHIEF?? CAN YOU TELL US YOUR PLANS FOR CAPTURING THOR?

SORRY, BOYS... NO COMMENT! THIS IS MORE THAN A LOCAL POLICE MATTER! WE EXPECT AID FROM THE FEDERAL AUTHORITIES WITHIN A FEW HOURS!

COMMISSIONER

THE CHIEF'S REMARKS RECEIVE WIDE CIRCULATION! *"THIS IS* ***MORE*** *THAN A LOCAL POLICE MATTER!"* AND SUDDENLY THE CITY SEEMS HELD IN A GRIP OF FEAR! ALERT POLICE OFFICERS PATROL EVERY STREET--CRUISING POLICE CARS SLOWLY DRIVE THROUGH EVERY NEIGHBORHOOD--AND THE ORDINARY CITIZEN REMAINS AT HOME, BEHIND LOCKED DOORS, UNLESS HIS BUSINESS IS URGENT!

ANY SIGN OF HIM YET, JOE?
NO, BUT LOOK SHARP! WE DON'T WANT TO TAKE ANY CHANCES WITH HIM!!
POLICE

AND, AS THE GREATEST CITY IN THE WORLD TAKES ON THE ASPECT OF A TOWN UNDER SIEGE, WE HALT OUR STORY! BUT THERE IS MUCH MORE TO COME! NEXT ISSUE YOU WILL MARVEL AT THE AMAZING CONCLUSION AS ***THOR*** AND THE ***MYSTERIOUS MISTER HYDE*** MEET AGAIN, FACE-TO-FACE, IN A FIGHT TO THE FINISH! SO, FOR THE STARTLING EXPLANATION TO THE STRANGE EVENTS YOU HAVE JUST WITNESSED--AND ONE OF THE MOST THRILLING CLIMAXES YOU HAVE EVER WITNESSED, DON'T DARE MISS THE EPIC 100TH ISSUE OF ***JOURNEY INTO MYSTERY!!*** SEE YOU THEN!

the END

TALES of ASGARD
HOME OF THE MIGHTY NORSE GODS!
SURTUR the FIRE DEMON!
EDITOR'S NOTE: ACCORDING TO NORSE LEGEND, THE TROLLS LIVE UNDER HILLS WHICH THEY CRANK UP IN ORDER TO SEE THE OUTSIDE WORLD!
THERE ARE NO SECRETS FROM ODIN, KING OF THE GODS! WHEN HE HEARS THAT THE TROLLS HAVE JOINED SURTUR TO REBEL AGAINST ASGARD, THE MIGHTY ODIN PERSONALLY INVADES THE LAND OF THE TROLLS, AND THUS BEGINS OUR LEGENDARY EPIC...
PRESENTED WITH PRIDE BY STAN LEE AND JACK KIRBY
X-498
1

ODIN PRESSES ON, EVEN THOUGH THE TROLL KING THREATENS HIM WITH DEATH IF HE DOES NOT LEAVE THE FORBIDDEN LAND!

AND THEN, THE TROLLS ATTACK HEROIC ODIN! ODIN, WHOSE POWER IS THE ONLY FORCE IN THE UNIVERSE THAT CAN SHATTER THE UNBREAKABLE GRIP OF A DEADLY TROLL!

SUDDENLY, THERE IS A BLINDING, SEARING, NERVE-SHATTERING BLAST, AND...

ODIN IS FREE! FOR WHEN HE PLUNGES HIS SWORD INTO THE GROUND, ANCHORING IT THERE, HE DRAWS UNTO HIMSELF THE LIMITLESS POWERS OF THE GODS!

THEIR WILL TO FIGHT CRUMBLES BEFORE ODIN'S SHOW OF FORCE, AND THE TROLLS TELL HIM WHERE TO FIND SURTUR! SO, ODIN VENTURES FORTH ONCE MORE--INTO THE SEA OF FLAME!

SLOWLY, PONDEROUSLY, THE GIGANTIC HEAD OF EVIL SURTUR, KING OF THE FIRE DEMONS, RISES FROM BENEATH THE SWIRLING MASS OF MOLTEN LIQUID--AS ODIN FACES THE MONSTROUS CREATURE--UNAFRAID!

THEN, BEFORE THE VERY EYES OF THE RULER OF THE GODS, SURTUR'S LEFT HAND UNDERGOES AN AWESOME CHANGE--AS HIS FINGERS ARE MAGICALLY TRANSFORMED INTO SINISTER SERPENTS!

BUT, BEFORE THE HUNGRY APPARITIONS CAN STRIKE, ODIN'S GREAT SWORD GESTURES SKYWARD--REACHING THROUGH THE EMPTINESS OF SPACE ITSELF...REACHING TO THE VERY END OF INFINITY!

AND, IN A SPLIT-SECOND, THE FROZEN REMNANTS OF LONG-DEAD PLANETS COME HURTLING DOWN TO SURTUR'S EVIL LAND OF FIRE!

AT THE MOMENT THEY ARE HIT WITH THE ICY SPACE WASTE, THE SERPENTS SHRIVEL UP AND BECOME HARMLESS, FOR FLAME CANNOT ENDURE SUCH BITTER COLD!

FOR LONG, SILENT MOMENTS, THE TWO MIGHTY ENEMIES FACE EACH OTHER, AS ODIN COMMANDS SURTUR TO OBEY HIS ROYAL COMMANDS--WHILE SURTUR KEEPS HIS DISTANCE, FEROCIOUSLY PLANNING HIS NEXT ATTACK!

AND THEN, SURTUR MAKES HIS MOVE! HE KNOWS HE CANNOT HARM ODIN HIMSELF, SO HE WILL STRIKE AT THE KING OF THE GODS BY DESTROYING THE ONE THING ODIN LOVES... THE PLANET EARTH!

SURTUR REACHES EARTH BEFORE ODIN CAN STOP HIM! EARTH, AROUND WHICH THE MAGIC TREE YGGDRASILL HAS SPREAD ITS BRANCHES, WHILE AWAITING THE COMING OF MAN!

BORING DEEP INTO THE CENTER OF THE PLANET, SURTUR RELEASES A HUGE CHUNK OF MATTER--A CHUNK WHICH FLIES INTO THE SKY WHERE IT WILL SPIN AROUND THE EARTH--AND BE FOREVER KNOWN AS--THE MOON!

BUT, AT THE HOME OF THE GODS, ODIN FORMS THE SPARKLING RAINBOW BRIDGE, FOR THE FIRST TIME, TO SPEED HIS WAY TO EARTH!

THEN, AFTER REACHING HIS FAVORITE PLANET, ODIN HOLDS HIS GREAT SWORD ABOVE IT, DRAWING ON ALL THE ELECTRO-MAGNETIC PARTICLES OF THE COSMOS-- AND CONCENTRATING THEM ABOVE THE FERTILE PLANET...

SOON, THE POWERFUL FORCES CAUSE THE EARTH TO BEGIN SPINNING, FASTER AND FASTER AROUND THE SUN--AN ENDLESS ROTATION WHICH CONTINUES TO THIS VERY DAY...

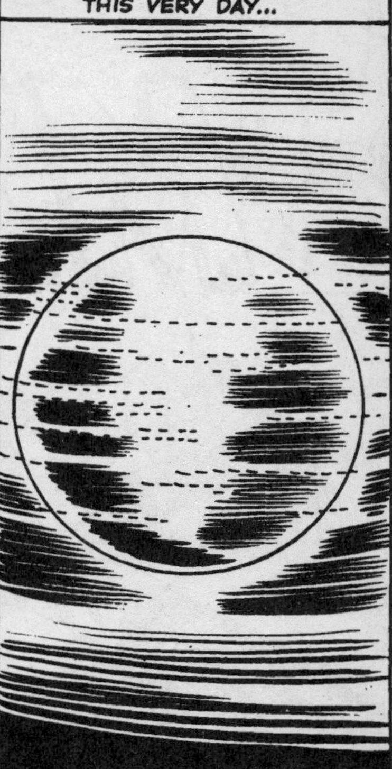

AND WHICH TRAPS SURTUR IN THE CENTER OF THE PLANET, HOLDING HIM THERE BY CENTRIFUGAL FORCE-- KEEPING HIM AN ETERNAL PRISONER, WHERE HE FURNISHES HEAT AND ENERGY TO THE PLANET HE HAD HOPED TO DESTROY!

HOPING TO CAUSE ODIN TO SET HIM FREE, SURTUR SENDS A GIFT TO THE VICTORIOUS GOD... A GIFT WHICH FLIES THROUGH THE MOUTH OF A SPOUTING VOLCANO ...IT IS A WONDERFUL WINGED HORSE WHICH ODIN KEEPS--AS THE EVIL SURTUR HOPES THAT ONE DAY ODIN'S WRATH WILL BE APPEASED AND HE'LL BE FREED!

SURTUR CARES NOT HOW LONG IT TAKES... HE HAS ALL ETERNITY TO WAIT!

NEXT ISSUE: YOU'LL MARVEL AT-- THE BOYHOOD OF THOR!

THE END

JOURNEY INTO MYSTERY
IND.
APPROVED BY THE COMICS CODE AUTHORITY
MARVEL COMICS GROUP 12¢
100 JAN.
YOU WILL NEVER FORGET
"THOR'S SHOWDOWN WITH MR. HYDE!"
Also: "THE BOYHOOD OF THOR" featured in TALES OF ASGARD!

THE MIGHTY THOR!
"The MASTER PLAN of MR. HYDE!"
LAST ISSUE, WE MET MR. HYDE, ONE OF THE MOST SINISTER MENACES OF ALL TIME! POSSESSING THE STRENGH OF A DOZEN NORMAL MEN, MR. HYDE HAS SWORN TO DESTROY HIS MOST DANGEROUS ENEMY... MIGHTY THOR!! AND NOW, WE FIND THE HEROIC THUNDER GOD ACCUSED AND CONDEMNED BY THOSE HE HAS SWORN TO PROTECT! LET US PICK UP THE THREAD OF THIS EPIC TALE NOW, AND FOLLOW IT TO ITS SPELLBINDING CONCLUSION!!
HAS THE CITY GONE MAD?!! WHEREVER I TURN, I SEE HATRED AND FEAR IN THE EYES OF MEN! AND IT IS ALL DIRECTED AGAINST... ME!!
IT'S THOR! HOW DOES HE DARE SHOW HIS FACE HERE AGAIN??!
SOMEONE CALL THE POLICE, BEFORE HE GETS AWAY!
GET BACK! STAY AWAY FROM HIM! THERE IS NO TELLING WHAT HE'LL DO NEXT!!
Written by: STAN LEE
Illustrated by: DON HECK
Lettered by: S. ROSEN
ANOTHER MARVEL AGE PRODUCTION BY THE MIGHTY MARVEL COMICS GROUP!
X-513

STAND BACK! WE'LL HANDLE THIS!
SURRENDER, THOR! DON'T FORCE US TO SHOOT YOU!
HE'S SWINGING HIS HAMMER! FIRE.. BEFORE HE HURLS IT AT US!!
LUCKILY I CAN DEFLECT THEIR SHELLS WITH MY ENCHANTED MALLET BEFORE THEY CAN STRIKE ME!
BUT I'VE GOT TO GET AWAY! GOT TO GO SOME-PLACE WHERE I CAN PUZZLE THIS OUT, AND FIND OUT WHY I'M BEING TREATED LIKE A PUBLIC ENEMY!

I'LL FLY TO ANOTHER PART OF THE CITY WHERE I'LL BE SAFE FROM THEIR BULLETS!
LOOK! HE'S ZOOMING OFF INTO THE SKY!
DOESN'T MATTER! WE'LL GET HIM WHEN HE LANDS! THERE'S AN "ALL POINTS" ALARM OUT FOR HIM!

A FEW SECONDS LATER...
WHAT WOULD HAVE MADE THOR TURN CRIMINAL?? IMAGINE HIM ROBBING A BANK!
BEATS ME! BUT WHO CAN FIGURE OUT A CHARACTER LIKE HIM?!
THEY CALL ME A CRIMINAL... SAY I'VE ROBBED A BANK! THIS IS INSANE!

I KNOW I'M NOT A CRIMINAL ... I HAVEN'T ROBBED ANY BANKS! SO THE ONLY ANSWER IS THAT SOMEONE HAS BEEN IMPERSONATING ME! BUT WHO?... WAIT!! WHAT A FOOL I AM!!
------I HAD FORGOTTEN ABOUT MR. HYDE! IT WAS HE WHO SMASHED HIS WAY INTO MY OFFICE THE OTHER DAY! HE HAS THE STRENGTH OF A DOZEN MEN!... AND THE INSTINCTS OF A BEAST!

"I REMEMBER HOW HE CALLOUSLY HURLED ME THROUGH MY OFFICE WINDOW DURING OUR STRUGGLE..."

"AND HIS EVIL VOICE WAS THE LAST THING I HEARD AS I PLUNGED DOWNWARD..."

"IT WAS ONLY BY A MIRACLE THAT I MANAGED TO STRIKE MY CANE AGAINST THE WALL AS I FELL, TRANSFORMING MYSELF TO THOR AGAIN, THUS SAVING MY LIFE!"
2

THERE'S ONLY ONE THING TO DO!..ONLY ONE PLACE WHERE I'LL BE SAFE!

I'VE GOT TO RETURN TO MY OFFICE AND BECOME DR. BLAKE AGAIN! MUSTN'T TAKE A CHANCE OF ANYONE GETTING HURT IF THOR MUST BATTLE ANY HUMANS!
STRANGE, HOW HYDE ENTERED MY LIFE JUST WHEN I THOUGHT MY BIGGEST PROBLEM HAD BEEN SOLVED! I FINALLY FOUND A WAY TO GET ODIN'S PERMISSION TO MARRY JANE.

ALTHOUGH AN IMMORTAL MAY NOT MARRY A HUMAN, MY NOBLE FATHER MIGHT MAKE HER AN IMMORTAL, TOO, IF SHE PROVED HERSELF WORTHY!
THOSE ARE MY FINAL WORDS, THOR!
THANK YOU, FATHER! THEN I STILL MAY HOPE!

MOMENTS LATER, AT THE OFFICE OF DOCTOR DON BLAKE...THE VALIANT THUNDER GOD STAMPS HIS MIGHTY HAMMER ONCE AND...
NOW LET THOR, GOD OF THUNDER, VANISH!...
...TO BE REPLACED BY THE MORTAL DR. BLAKE..
THUMP!

OH, THERE YOU ARE, DON! FOR A MOMENT, I THOUGHT YOU HAD FORGOTTEN YOUR PROMISE TO TAKE ME TO DINNER TONIGHT, ON MY BIRTHDAY!
I...I HAD FORGOTTEN... BECAUSE OF MY PROBLEM AS THOR! BUT I CAN'T DISAPPOINT JANE...
OF COURSE, JANE DEAR! I'VE BEEN LOOKING FORWARD TO IT ALL WEEK!

I'LL PICK YOU UP AT EIGHT AND WE'LL HAVE DINNER AT THE RITZ TERRACE!
I HOPE IT WON'T BECOME NECESSARY FOR ME TO BECOME THOR AGAIN BEFORE THAT TIME!
THE RITZ TERRACE! OH, DON... IT'S THE MOST GLAMOROUS PLACE IN TOWN! I'M SO THRILLED!

But OTHER EARS HAVE ALSO HEARD THAT BRIEF CONVERSATION! THE EARS OF THE MYSTERIOUS MR. HYDE!
THE RITZ TERRACE, EH? WELL, MISS FOSTER... YOU WILL BE EVEN MORE THRILLED THAN YOU EXPECT!
3.

THAT NIGHT, A FEW MINUTES PAST EIGHT, AT THE RITZ TERRACE, A HANDSOME COUPLE ENJOY THE DINNER MUSIC AS THEY PREPARE TO ORDER...
IT'S SO WONDERFUL BEING HERE WITH YOU LIKE THIS, DON!.. AWAY FROM THE OFFICE, WHERE WE CAN BE DON AND JANE, RATHER THAN DR. BLAKE AND NURSE FOSTER!
JANE, MY DARLING.. IF ONLY IT COULD BE THIS WAY FOREVER! BUT, I DARE NOT SPEAK OF MY LOVE UNTIL ODIN CONSENTS TO MAKE YOU AN IMMORTAL!
YOU LOOK BEAUTIFUL TONIGHT, MY DEAR! AND WHETHER YOU ARE MISS FOSTER, OR JANE TO ME, IT'S ALWAYS HEAVEN BEING WITH YOU!

I JUST WISH I COULD FORGET ABOUT THAT HORRID MR. HYDE! THE WAY HE BROKE INTO THE OFFICE, AND ATTACKED YOU, FOR NO REASON! WHAT IF THE BRUTE SHOULD EVER RETURN?
TRY TO PUT IT OUT OF YOUR MIND, JANE! I'M SURE WE'VE HEARD THE LAST OF HIM!

AFTER ALL, WHEN THOR SAVED MY LIFE... BY A LUCKY MIRACLE... HE SCARED HYDE AWAY! NO MATTER HOW POWERFUL HYDE MAY BE, I'M SURE HE'D NEVER REMAIN IN THE SAME CITY AS THE MIGHTY THOR!
I'LL TAKE YOUR ORDER NOW, SIR!

YOU!
DON! WHAT IS IT??

DO AS I SAY AND I MAY LET YOU BOTH LIVE A WHILE LONGER! GET UP AND WALK OUT OF THE RESTAURANT! AND REMEMBER, I'M RIGHT BEHIND YOU!
DON!! WHAT...?!
WE CAN'T REASON WITH HIM, JANE! WE'VE GOT TO OBEY!

WHY DO YOU HOUND US THIS WAY, HYDE?? WHAT IS YOUR PURPOSE??
YOU'LL FIND OUT SOON ENOUGH! NOW GET INTO YOUR CAR AND DRIVE WHERE I TELL YOU TO!
I CAN'T TURN INTO THOR NOW... NOT WITH JANE WATCHING! ALSO, I'M ANXIOUS TO LEARN WHAT HIS PLANS ARE FIRST!

YOU REPRESENT EVERYTHING I HATE, BLAKE! YOU ARE HONEST... HARD-WORKING... SUCCESSFUL! WHILE I... I AM THE EVIL NATURE OF MAN, PERSONIFIED!
OH, DON, MY DARLING... IF ONLY YOU WERE STRONG ENOUGH TO COPE WITH THIS BRUTE... BUT YOU'RE NOT!

DRIVE STRAIGHT UP TO THE TOP OF THAT HILL! THAT OLD DESERTED CASTLE IS THE HOME OF MR. HYDE!
THE FACT THAT HE LETS JANE AND ME SEE HIS HIDEOUT IS PROOF THAT HE EXPECTS WE'LL NEVER BE ABLE TO TELL THIS TO ANYONE!

WHY HAVE YOU BROUGHT US HERE? WHAT DO YOU PLAN TO DO?
WALK! NO ONE QUESTIONS MR. HYDE! I SHALL EXPLAIN EVERYTHING TO YOU IN MY OWN GOOD TIME!

FIRST, I SHALL LASH YOU TO THIS POST, BLAKE! YOU ARE SO FRAIL AND WEAK THAT YOU MIGHT INJURE YOURSELF IF I LET YOU RUN FREE!
MY CANE! WHERE DID HE PUT IT??
DON'T... DON'T HURT HIM! ...I BEG OF YOU! HE HAS DONE NOTHING TO YOU!
IF ONLY THOR WERE HERE! BUT, MIRACLES DON'T OCCUR TWICE! AND WITH THE POLICE SEARCHING THE CITY FOR HIM, HE WOULDN'T HAVE TIME TO WORRY ABOUT SAVING ANYONE ELSE!

NOW, BEFORE I GO, I SHALL ARRANGE THIS TIME BOMB HERE! IT IS SET TO GO OFF IN EXACTLY TWENTY-FOUR HOURS! ONLY I KNOW HOW TO STOP IT FROM EXPLODING! SO, IF ANYTHING HAPPENS TO ME WITHIN THE NEXT TWENTY-FOUR HOURS, YOU ARE DOOMED, BLAKE!

YOU AND I ARE LEAVING NOW! AND IF YOU DEFY ME, OR IF ANY HARM COMES TO ME...IT WILL BE THE END OF DON BLAKE!
I MUST DO WHAT THIS CREATURE SAYS...FOR THE SAKE OF THE MAN I LOVE!
5.

A SHORT TIME LATER, MR. HYDE AND HIS RELUCTANT CAPTIVE COME TO A STOP BEFORE THE EAST RIVER NAVAL YARD...
THIS IS WHERE I SHALL EXECUTE THE CRIME OF THE CENTURY! AND YOU, JANE FOSTER, WILL BEAR WITNESS TO IT!
WHA...WHAT DO YOU PLAN TO DO?

WHAT NO OTHER LIVING BEING WOULD EVER DARE TO ATTEMPT! I AM ABOUT TO STEAL A POLARIS SUBMARINE!
YOU'RE MAD! IT ISN'T POSSIBLE!
MAD, AM I? YOU SHALL SEE THAT ANYTHING IS POSSIBLE FOR MISTER HYDE!

WITH MY FANTASTIC STRENGTH, I CAN TEAR THROUGH THIS STEEL FENCE AS EASILY AS IF IT WERE PAPER!
I COULD TRY TO ESCAPE HIM NOW BUT I DARE NOT... FOR DON'S SAKE!

ONCE THE SUB IS MINE, I SHALL ROAM THE SEVEN SEAS LIKE A KING...AND YOU SHALL BECOME MY QUEEN!

HALT!! WHO GOES THERE?! THIS AREA IS CLOSED TO UNAUTHORIZED PERSONNEL!
THAT IS A VERY IMPRESSIVE SPEECH, MY UNSUSPECTING FRIEND!

BUT NO AREA CAN BE CLOSED TO...MISTER HYDE!
HE'S FLINGING THAT GUARD ASIDE AS THOUGH HE'S WEIGHTLESS! I WONDER IF HE COULD EVEN BE BEATEN BY THOR??

MEANTIME, BACK AT THE LONELY CASTLE WHERE DON BLAKE IS IMPRISONED...
MY CANE IS ON THE FLOOR...ONLY A FEW INCHES AWAY...BUT JUST BEYOND MY REACH!
BUT I MUSTN'T GIVE UP! I'VE GOT TO KEEP TRYING TO REACH IT!

JUST A LITTLE FURTHER ... IF ONLY I COULD STRETCH ANOTHER INCH ...
MY ARM FEELS AS THOUGH IT'S BREAKING.. BUT I'VE GOT TO KEEP STRETCHING... STRETCHING...

I..I DID IT! IT'S MINE!

NOW, ALL THAT REMAINS IS TO POUND IT ONCE UPON THE FLOOR...

...AND, THE HEAVY ROPES WHICH BOUND DON BLAKE SO SECURELY...
...ARE LIKE THIN PIECES OF THREAD.. TO THE MIGHTY THOR!

ALTHOUGH I DO NOT KNOW WHERE HYDE HAS GONE...

...I'LL SCOUR THE CITY UNTIL I FIND HIM...
...FOR FIND HIM I MUST!

AND AT THE OTHER SIDE OF TOWN, PANDEMONIUM REIGNS!
BACK, YOU HELPLESS FOOLS! ... BACK!! DO NOT COME A STEP CLOSER TO ME IF YOU VALUE THIS GIRL'S LIFE!
HOLD YOUR FIRE, MEN! THAT CHARACTER DOESN'T LOOK LIKE HE'S KIDDIN'!

HELLO! HELLO! PUT ME THROUGH TO WASHINGTON! HYDE IS MORE THAN WE CAN HANDLE! THIS CALLS FOR THE MILITARY!
SECURITY

AND AT THAT MOMENT, AN UNIMAGINABLE DISTANCE AWAY, IN ASGARD...
IT IS TIME I GAZED AT EARTH TO WATCH MY FAVORITE SON...
I SEE THERE IS GRAVE TROUBLE BREWING! A POWER-FUL NEW MENACE NAMED HYDE THREATENS MANKIND!
AND THOR IS ABOUT TO CONFRONT HIM! EVEN NOW HE FLIES TOWARD THE DOCK, ATTRACTED BY THE CROWDS AND THE COMMOTION!

THERE! ON THE DOCK BELOW... I HAVE FOUND MY PREY!
INCREDIBLE THOUGH IT MAY SEEM, HE IS ATTEMPTING TO STEAL A POLARIS SUBMARINE, SINGLE-HANDED! WITH HIS GREAT STRENGTH, USING JANE AS A HOSTAGE, HE SEEMS ON THE VERGE OF SUCCEEDING!

TURN AND FACE ME, HYDE! FACE THE ONE WHO WILL DESTROY YOU!
THOR!
SO! YOU STILL DARE TRY TO FOIL MY PLANS, DO YOU? WELL, THIS TIME I'LL MAKE SURE I STOP YOU... FOR GOOD! THIS TIME YOU'RE NOT SCARING SOME PUNY HUMAN... YOU'RE TACKLING THE SUPER-POWERFUL MR. HYDE!

IF YOU WANT ME, THUNDER GOD... COME AND GET ME!
RRIP!

TRY AND STOP ME, MISTER!

YOU MEAN... LIKE THIS??
OOOFF!!
WHUMPH!

THAT WOULD HAVE KILLED ANYONE ELSE... BUT IT MERELY SLOWED THOR DOWN! WELL, NO MATTER... IT GAVE ME THE TIME I NEED!

YOU'RE TOO LATE, THOR!

NOTHING CAN STOP ME NOW!
PWANG!

HE'S LOCKED HIMSELF WITHIN THE SUB! BUT HE STILL IS HOLDING JANE AS A HOSTAGE!

AND NO METAL ON EARTH IS STRONG ENOUGH TO STOP ME FROM REACHING HER SIDE WHEN SHE NEEDS ME!
RRI-IP!

NO MATTER WHERE YOU RUN, THOR WILL FIND YOU, HYDE!
QUIET! YOU'LL SEE THAT I'M MORE THAN A MATCH FOR HIM!

I KNOW YOU'RE DOWN HERE, HYDE! YOU CAN'T ESCAPE FROM ME!
NO ANSWER! THAT MEANS HE STILL HOPES TO BATTLE ME ... AND TO DEFEAT ME!

BUT NO MATTER WHAT HIS PLAN IS, I MUST SEE THAT NO HARM COMES TO JANE!
THAT'S IT, THOR... COME CLOSER... STILL CLOSER, YOU BUNGLING FOOL! CLOSER TO YOUR DOOM!

HAH! I'VE GOT YOU! AND NOW, WITH MY ALMOST UNLIMITED STRENGTH, I'LL FINISH YOU OFF FOREVER!

YOU DARE MENTION YOUR STRENGTH WHEN YOU SPEAK TO MIGHTY THOR?!!

THANK HEAVENS! THOR IS BEATING HIM!
WAIT! WHAT AM I THINKING?! IF ANY-THING HAPPENS TO HYDE, THAT BOMB WILL EXPLODE IN HIS CASTLE... THE CASTLE WHERE DON IS IMPRISONED!

THOR'S GREATEST WEAPON IS HIS HAMMER! IF I COVER IT WITH THIS CANVAS HE MAY NOT BE ABLE TO FIND IT QUICKLY, AND THAT WILL GIVE HYDE A CHANCE TO ESCAPE!
I.. I KNOW I SHOULDN'T HELP HYDE... BUT DON'S LIFE IS AT STAKE... I HAVE NO OTHER CHOICE!

ALL RIGHT, THOR! I HATE TO RESORT TO ANYTHING SO COMMONPLACE AS A GUN, BUT I'M FINISHING YOU OFF HERE AND NOW!
MY HAMMER! IT'S BEEN OUT OF MY HAND FOR ALMOST SIXTY SECONDS! IF I DON'T GET IT IMMEDIATE-LY, I'LL REVERT BACK TO DON BLAKE, AND BE AN EASY PREY FOR HYDE'S BULLETS!
BUT WHERE IS IT?! I DROPPED IT... BUT WHERE??

ONLY A FEW SECONDS LEFT! CAN'T WASTE THEM LOOKING FOR THE HAMMER! GOT TO PROTECT MYSELF!!

MOVING WITH BLINDING SPEED, THE THUNDER GOD WHIRLS HIS CRIMSON CAPE ABOUT HIM, AND...
EVEN WITHOUT MY HAMMER, I'M STILL THE GOD OF THUNDER AND THE STORM...
USING MY CAPE, I'LL CREATE A TORNADO WITHIN THIS SMALL AREA...

THEN, AS THE SUDDEN FURY OF THE STORM BLOWS THE DEADLY WEAPON FROM THE HAND OF MR. HYDE, THE FATEFUL SIXTY SECONDS ARE UP...

...AND MIGHTY THOR TURNS BACK TO THE MORTAL DON BLAKE...
LUCKILY, UNDER COVER OF THE SWIRLING WINDSTORM, NO ONE COULD HAVE SEEN THE SUDDEN TRANSFORMATION!

NOW I'VE GOT TO FIND MY HAMMER BEFORE HYDE SEES ME!
IT MUST BE HERE SOMEWHERE! NO ONE COULD HAVE LIFTED IT...NOT EVEN HYDE!

AND THEN, JUST AS THE EVIL HYDE DIMLY SEES BLAKE'S FORM THROUGH THE HAZE OF THE TORNADO...
SOMEONE IS CRAWLING ACROSS THE FLOOR!
I'VE GOT IT! IT WAS UNDER THIS CANVAS!

EXACTLY ONE SECOND LATER...
LET THE WIND CEASE! THE GOD OF THUNDER COMMANDS!
THOR!

YOU HAVE YOUR HAMMER AGAIN! OH, NO...YOU MUST LET HYDE ESCAPE! IF YOU DON'T, DON BLAKE WILL DIE!!
JANE... DON'T! STAND ASIDE!

NO! LET HIM GO! YOU MUST!
POOR JANE! I CANNOT TELL HER THAT I AM BLAKE!..AND I AM SAFE! SHE IS ONLY DOING THIS OUT OF LOVE FOR ME!
THANKS TO THE WITLESS FEMALE, I SHALL MAKE GOOD MY ESCAPE!

LOOK! IT'S HYDE! HE'S ESCAPING!
IMPOSSIBLE! THOR WOULD NEVER LET HIM GO! YOU...YOU DON'T THINK HE BEAT THOR, DO YOU?

NO, I DIDN'T BEAT THOR THIS TIME!
...BUT NEXT TIME WE MEET, IT WILL BE A DIFFERENT STORY!

WE NOW KNOW HYDE IMPERSONATED YOU! BUT HE MUST HAVE DROWNED! WE'VE BEEN WATCHING, BUT HE DIDN'T COME UP FOR AIR!
THAT MEANS NOTHING WITH A SUPER-MENACE LIKE HIM! I FEAR WE HAVE NOT SEEN THE LAST OF MR. HYDE!!

YOU ARE SAFE NOW, WOMAN! WHY DO YOU LOOK SO WORRIED?
IT'S DON BLAKE! I.. I DON'T KNOW WHETHER HE'S STILL ALIVE, OR...!!

I HAVE TO SET HER MIND AT EASE, WITHOUT REVEALING MY TRUE IDENTITY!

DO NOT FEAR! I SHALL FLY TO HYDE'S CASTLE AND SET HIM FREE! NO HARM WILL COME TO DON BLAKE WHILE THOR LIVES!

B-BUT HOW DOES THOR KNOW WHERE HYDE'S CASTLE IS?? OR EVEN THAT DON IS IN THE CASTLE?
I'M AFRAID THAT THOR WILL ALWAYS BE AN ENIGMA TO ME!

SUDDENLY, THE SCOWLING FACE OF ODIN APPEARS BEFORE THOR...
YOU DARED ASK ME TO MAKE THAT FEMALE AN IMMORTAL?!!
ODIN! WAIT! HEAR ME OUT!

SILENCE!! I SAW HER THWART YOUR EFFORTS TO CAPTURE AN EVIL-DOER!! PETITION DENIED! SHE IS NOT WORTHY!
BUT, NOBLE FATHER...
TOO LATE! HE'S GONE!

AGAIN I HAVE LOST THE ONE I LOVE MOST IN ALL THE UNIVERSE!! AGAIN MY VICTORY HAS A HOLLOW RING!
BUT I SHALL NEVER DESPAIR! IF MORTAL MAN CAN FIND HAPPINESS, SOME-DAY THE GOD OF THUNDER SHALL FIND IT, TOO!

NEXT ISSUE: ANOTHER GRIPPING SAGA OF THOR, THE MOST DRAMATIC SUPER-HERO OF ALL TIME!!

Tales of ASGARD
HOME OF THE MIGHTY NORSE GODS!
The BOYHOOD of THOR!
"THE STORM GIANTS"
WRITTEN BY: STAN LEE
DRAWN BY: JACK KIRBY
INKED BY: P. REINMAN
LETTERED BY: ART SIMEK
LOOK, LOKI! THERE ARE THE TWO SONS OF THE STORM GIANT! THEY HAVE STOLEN THE GOLDEN APPLES OF THE GODDESS IDUNA! IT IS OUR DUTY TO RETURN THEM TO THEIR RIGHTFUL OWNER!
DO NOT SPEAK TO ME OF DUTY, THOR! I DO WHAT I WILL!
AS A YOUTH, FROM THE DAY HE WAS STRONG ENOUGH TO WIELD A SWORD, THOR HAD DREAMED OF ONE DAY IN-HERITING THE ENCHANTED BATTLE HAMMER OF ODIN! BUT ODIN'S HAMMER COULD ONLY BE WON BY ACCOMPLISH-ING DEEDS OF VALOR--DEEDS SUCH AS THE ONE YOU ARE ABOUT TO SEE...!
X-520
1

STEALTHILY, SILENTLY, THOR STEALS INTO THE HUGE CASTLE OF THE TOWERING STORM GIANTS, FOLLOWED BY HIS RELUCTANT BROTHER!

MORE MEAT, MY FATHER! MY HUNGER IS RAVENOUS!

SUDDENLY, THE MALICIOUS LOKI MAKES A SURPRISE MOVE, PUSHING THE STARTLED THOR INTO FULL VIEW OF THE GIANTS!
IF YOU'RE SO ANXIOUS TO BE A HERO, THOR, I'LL GIVE YOU THE CHANCE! THIS IS THE TIME TO ATTACK-- WHILE THEIR THOUGHTS ARE ON THEIR FOOD!
YOU FOOL! THEY'LL SEE ME!

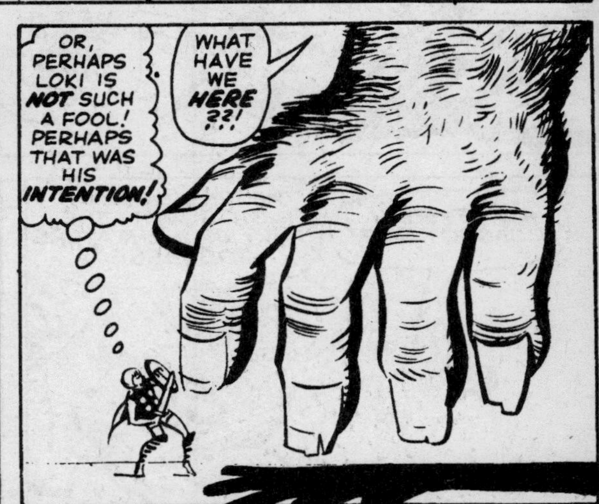

OR, PERHAPS LOKI IS NOT SUCH A FOOL! PERHAPS THAT WAS HIS INTENTION!
WHAT HAVE WE HERE ??!

IT IS A PUNY ONE-- FROM THE LAND OF ASGARD! LET US SLAY HIM AS A WARNING TO OTHERS NOT TO ENTER OUR DOMAIN!
HOLD YOUR TONGUE, INSOLENT ONE! YOU SPEAK TO THOR, SON OF ODIN! I AM HERE TO RETURN THE GOLDEN APPLES TO IDUNA!

SO! THAT IS YOUR PURPOSE?!
HE WAS A FOOL TO TELL US!
DROWN THE YOUNG FOOL IN A TORRENT OF BROTH!

BUT, THOUGH YOUNG, **THOR** IS STILL A **GODLING** --WITH THE **STRENGTH** OF AN IMMORTAL!

GLUBBB!
IT IS **YOU** WHO SHALL PARTAKE OF THE BROTH--NOT **ME!**

MOVING WITH BLINDING SPEED AND UNBELIEVABLE STRENGTH, THE YOUNG PRINCE HURLS A CRUDE **PEPPER** RECEPTACLE IN THE DIRECTION OF THE DAZED STORM GIANTS BEFORE THEY CAN MAKE A MOVE!

THE TINY GODLING FIGHTS WITH THE FURY OF A CREATURE POSSESSED!

BUT THEN, A PRODIGIOUS SNEEZE, FROM LUNGS ENORMOUS ENOUGH TO TOPPLE A MOUNTAIN, BOWLS OVER THE HANDSOME YOUNG BATTLER!

AND, BEFORE THOR CAN REGAIN HIS BALANCE, HIS SWORD IS RENDERED USELESS BY A TITANIC FIST!
I'M TRAPPED!

HAH! SO THIS IS THE ONE WHO DARED DEFY US!
SEE HOW HELP-LESS HE IS NOW!
PERHAPS I SHALL KEEP HIM AND WEAR HIM TIED TO MY BELT AS AN ORNAMENT!

BUT, AT THAT MOMENT, THE WILY LOKI, WHO HAS NOT YET BEEN SEEN, TOSSES A PILE OF WET LEAVES INTO THE HUGE, FLAMING FIREPLACE...

AND, WITHIN SECONDS, THICK CLOUDS OF BLIND-ING SMOKE FILL THE VAST CHAMBER!
THERE MUST BE ANOTHER TINY ONE HIDDEN AMONG US!
WAIT NO LONGER! KILL HIM! SLAY THEM ALL!

BUT, UNDER COVER OF THE DENSE SMOKE, THE VALIANT THUNDER GOD STRIKES OUT AGAIN, WITH TELLING EFFECT!
AHH! I KNEW THIS WOULD MAKE YOU RELEASE YOUR HOLD ON ME!

THAT WAS QUICK THINKING, LOKI! NOW QUICKLY-- WE MUST FIND THE GOLDEN APPLES AND FLEE!
BAH! I DID NOT DO IT TO SAVE YOU-- MERELY TO CREATE A DIVERSION FOR ME! FOR I KNOW WHERE THE APPLES ARE HIDDEN!

SEE? THEY ARE HERE, ATOP AGNAR, KING OF THE EAGLES ...THE ETERNAL PRISONER OF THE STORM GIANTS!
BUT I SHALL ESCAPE ON HIS BACK NOW, AND LEAVE YOU BE-HIND TO SAVE YOURSELF FROM THE STORM GIANTS AS BEST YOU CAN!
NO! YOU SHALL NOT LEAVE WITHOUT ME!

THEN, AS THE STORM GIANTS COME LUMBERING UP TOWARDS THEM, THOR FREES THE KING OF EAGLES WITH ONE MIGHTY STROKE OF HIS SWORD, LEAP-ING UPON ITS HUGE CLAW AT THE SAME INSTANT!

THEY HAVE SET OUR EAGLE FREE --TAKEN OUR GOLDEN APPLES!!
STOP THEM! STOP THEM! HOW COULD SUCH TINY ONES HAVE DEFEATED US???
5

BUT NOTHING CAN STOP THE YOUNG GODLINGS! AND LATER, BACK IN ASGARD...
BAH! I HOPED THAT I WOULD RECEIVE CREDIT FOR THIS DEED, BUT ODIN IS TOO WISE TO BE DECEIVED!
AFTER EACH DEED OF VALOR, MY SON THOR, YOU ARE ABLE TO LIFT MY HAMMER A LITTLE HIGHER! UNTIL FINALLY, SOME DAY...

BUT THOR STILL HAS MANY STRANGE ADVEN-TURES AHEAD OF HIM... MANY POWERFUL FOES TO DEFEAT BEFORE ODIN'S HAMMER WILL BE TRULY HIS! MORE ABOUT THE BOYHOOD OF THE MIGHTY THUNDER GOD IN OUR NEXT GREAT ISSUE!

THE END

JOURNEY INTO
IND.
APPROVED BY THE COMICS CODE AUTHORITY
MYSTERY
MARVEL COMICS GROUP 12¢
101 FEB.
THE MIGHTY
THOR
THRILLS YOU AS NEVER BEFORE IN...
"THE RETURN OF ZARRKO, THE TOMORROW MAN!"
A MIGHTY MARVEL MASTERWORK!

THE MIGHTY THOR
"The RETURN OF ZARRKO, The TOMORROW MAN!"
STAND BACK, FOLKS! WE DON'T KNOW WHAT IT'S ALL ABOUT, BUT THOR'S ON A RAMPAGE AND IT ISN'T SAFE TO GET NEAR HIM!
ODIN! I'VE GOT TO SEE ODIN!
DID YOU SEE THAT? HIS FOOT CHIPPED A PIECE OUT OF THAT LAMPPOST AS HE PASSED BY!
AND LOOK HOW HE SCRUNCHED THE STEEL LITTER BASKET THAT WAS IN HIS WAY!! WOW!
WRITTEN BY: STAN LEE
DRAWN BY: JACK KIRBY
INKED BY: G. BELL
LETTERED BY: S. ROSEN

SUDDENLY, AS THOUGH SNAPPING OUT OF A DREAM, THE MIGHTY THUNDER GOD SEEMS TO SEE THOSE SURROUNDING HIM FOR THE FIRST TIME, AND...
AWAY, ALL OF YOU!! LET NONE INTRUDE UPON THOR!

MORTALS! HOW LIKE CHATTERING MONKEYS YOU ARE!! ALWAYS GATHERING ABOUT THOSE WHO WANT TO BE ALONE!
WELL, THOR HAS HAD ENOUGH OF YOU! I HAVE LOST INTEREST IN YOUR PETTY, PUNY LIVES!

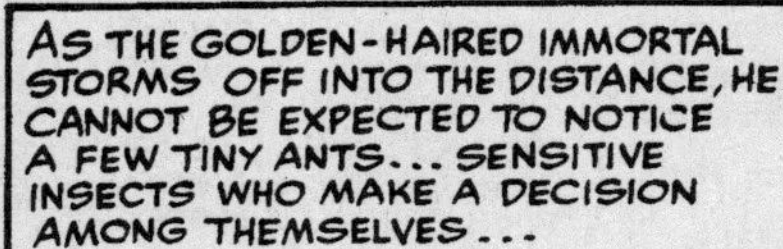
AS THE GOLDEN-HAIRED IMMORTAL STORMS OFF INTO THE DISTANCE, HE CANNOT BE EXPECTED TO NOTICE A FEW TINY ANTS... SENSITIVE INSECTS WHO MAKE A DECISION AMONG THEMSELVES...

AND SOME DISTANCE AWAY, THE RESULT OF THAT DECISION CAN NOW BE SEEN!
QUIET, JAN! A MESSAGE FROM THE ANTS IS JUST COMING IN! SOUNDS URGENT!
WHAT DO THEY SAY, HANK?

IT'S THOR! HE SEEMS TO BE IN A RAGE! THERE'S A CHANCE SOMEONE MIGHT GET HURT! I'LL CONTACT IRON MAN! IT MAY TAKE US BOTH TO CALM THOR DOWN!
WILL YOU CHANGE TO GIANT-MAN OR ANT-MAN, HANK?
GIANT-MAN! I'LL NEED ALL THE STRENGTH I CAN MUSTER!

WELL, WHAT ARE YOU WAITING FOR? LET'S GO!
STOP SNARLING, BOSS MAN! YOU CAN'T GO WITHOUT YOUR SIZE-CAPSULES BELT!

MUCH OBLIGED, WASP! IT WAS CARELESS OF ME TO FORGET THAT! NOW FOLLOW ME!
TO THE ENDS OF THE EARTH, YOU BIG DREAM-BOAT!

MEANTIME, THE SECRET CODED NUMBER WHICH GIANT-MAN HAD CALLED ACTIVATES AN ALARM SIGNAL IN THE HOME OF MILLIONAIRE TONY STARK... BETTER KNOWN TO THE WORLD AS IRON MAN!
IF I HURRY, I SHOULD BE ABLE TO RENDEZ-VOUS WITH GIANT-MAN AND THE WASP IN THE NEXT FEW MINUTES!

MINUTES LATER, OVER AN INTERSECTION AT THE VAN WYCK EXPRESSWAY...
THERE'S THOR NOW! BUT...HE DOESN'T EVEN NOTICE THAT TRUCK BEARING DOWN ON HIM!
HEY, FANCY PANTS! WATCH OUT!! I CAN'T STOP!!

THOR WATCHES OUT FOR NOBODY!!
WHAM!
HOLY COW!

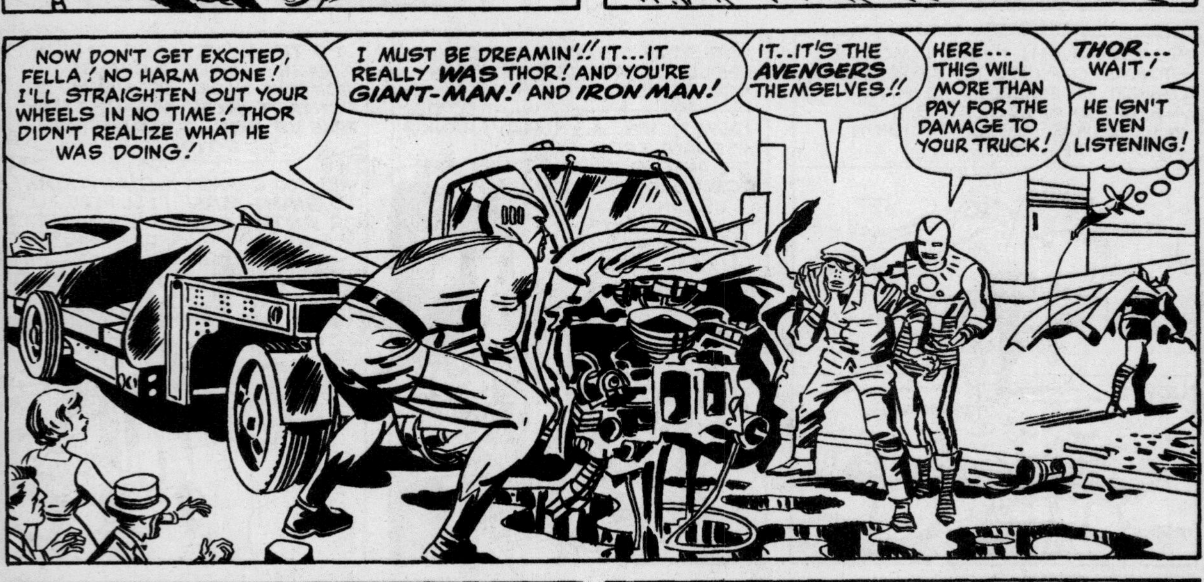
NOW DON'T GET EXCITED, FELLA! NO HARM DONE! I'LL STRAIGHTEN OUT YOUR WHEELS IN NO TIME! THOR DIDN'T REALIZE WHAT HE WAS DOING!
I MUST BE DREAMIN'!! IT...IT REALLY WAS THOR! AND YOU'RE GIANT-MAN! AND IRON MAN!
IT..IT'S THE AVENGERS THEMSELVES!!
HERE... THIS WILL MORE THAN PAY FOR THE DAMAGE TO YOUR TRUCK!
THOR... WAIT!
HE ISN'T EVEN LISTENING!

THOR! LISTEN...THIS IS GIANT-MAN! YOU CAN'T ROAM AROUND THE CITY THAT WAY, TRAMPLING ON ANYTHING THAT GETS IN YOUR WAY!
WHAT'S WRONG, PARTNER?? WE'RE ALL ON THE SAME TEAM! WE WANT TO HELP YOU! THOR... WAIT!
NO ONE CAN HELP ME!

WHAT I HAVE TO DO MUST BE DONE ALONE! WHERE I HAVE TO GO, NONE CAN ACCOMPANY ME! SO LEAVE ME! THIS IS NO CONCERN OF YOURS! I SAY GO!!

NOW, **LOOK**, THUNDER GOD!! PARTNER OR NOT, **NOBODY** TALKS TO **US** THAT WAY! IF YOU'VE GOTTEN TOO BIG FOR YOUR BOOTS, THEN IT'S TIME...

COOL IT, GIANT-MAN! THOR'S RIGHT! IT'S NONE OF OUR BUSINESS! IF HE HAS A PERSONAL PROBLEM, **WE** CAN'T HELP! COME ON, BIG FELLA ... HE KNOWS WHAT HE'S DOING!

AND SO, THE AVENGERS RELUCTANTLY TAKE THEIR LEAVE... AS A SILENT, TROUBLED FIGURE FINDS HIS WAY TO THE WATERFRONT, WHERE HE STANDS ALONE WITH HIS DARK, BROODING THOUGHTS...

WITHOUT THE ONE I LOVE, LIFE IS EMPTY AND MEANINGLESS!

BUT MY FATHER, NOBLE ODIN, WILL NOT GRANT ME PERMISSION TO MARRY JANE FOSTER!

AND I DARE NOT DEFY THE WISHES OF ALL-POWERFUL ODIN! SO I MUST AGAIN VISIT ASGARD, TO PLEAD MY CAUSE!

BUT AS HE STANDS IN THE SHADOWS, LITTLE DOES THOR SUSPECT THAT HE IS CLOSER TO ODIN THAN HE THINKS... AND TO EVIL **LOKI** AS WELL ...

THERE, NOBLE ODIN! I GIVE YOU A THOUGHT-PROJECTION OF THOR, AS YOU REQUESTED!

MY FAVORITE SON **STILL** IS TROUBLED! IF ONLY I COULD DRIVE THAT GIRL FROM HIS HEART!

YOU HAVE ORDERED HIM TO FORGET HER... BUT STILL HE BROODS! IS THIS NOT RANK DISOBEDIENCE?
YES, LOKI... IT **IS**! AND, BY THUNDER, IT SHALL BE **PUNISHED**!!

FROM THIS INSTANT HENCE, THOR'S **POWER** IS REDUCED BY HALF! NO LONGER SHALL HE HAVE CONTROL OF THE STORM AND THE ELEMENTS!! AND NO LONGER MAY HE COME TO ASGARD! NOT UNTIL HE GIVES UP ALL THOUGHTS OF THE MORTAL GIRL HE LOVES!
4.

HOW WELL I REMEMBER HOW UNWORTHY THE MORTAL NAMED JANE FOSTER PROVED HERSELF TO BE! IT WAS ONLY ONE SHORT MONTH AGO, WHEN THOR WAS CONFRONTED BY THE MENACE OF MR. HYDE...*
* JOURNEY INTO MYSTERY #100... EDITOR

"I CAN STILL SEE THAT LAST SCENE VIVIDLY IN MY MIND'S EYE... STILL SEE HOW JANE FOSTER CAME BETWEEN MY SON, THOR, AND MR. HYDE..."

"...AND THEN SHE PLEADED WITH MY SON TO LET THE ARCH-VILLAIN GO FREE! IF I HAD NOT SEEN IT, I MIGHT NEVER HAVE BELIEVED IT!"

YET, THOR DARES TO STILL DESIRE SUCH A WOMAN! NEVER! HE SHALL NEVER WED HER WHILST ODIN LIVES!
OF COURSE NOT, SIRE! YOU ARE MOST WISE!

JUST THEN, UNAWARE OF ODIN'S WORDS...UNAWARE THAT HIS POWER HAS BEEN HALVED, THOR APPROACHES HEIMDALL, GUARDIAN OF THE RAINBOW BRIDGE...
STAND ASIDE, LOYAL HEIMDALL! I CRAVE AUDIENCE WITH MY FATHER!
YOU MAY NOT PASS, THOR! THOSE ARE THE ORDERS OF ODIN HIMSELF!

YOU LIE! NONE MAY REFUSE ADMITTANCE TO THE GOD OF THUNDER!
ODIN MAY! ...HIS WORD IS LAW!

I WARN YOU, HEIMDALL...LET ME PASS! MY HAMMER KNOWS NAUGHT OF MERCY!!

THOR... WAIT! ODIN HAS TAKEN HALF YOUR POWER! YOUR HAMMER CAN NO LONGER TRIUMPH!
I'LL HEAR NO MORE!! STAND ASIDE... OR I STRIKE!!

NO, GOD OF THUNDER... IT IS I, WHO SHALL STRIKE FIRST!... WITH ALL THE COSMIC FORCE OF THE UNIVERSE IN THE BLADE OF MY SWORD!!

YOU TOPPLED ME!! BUT IT CANNOT BE! NOTHING CAN STOP MY ENCHANTED HAMMER!!
I WARNED YOU, THOR! ODIN HAS REDUCED YOUR POWER! YOU ARE NO LONGER INVINCIBLE!

BUT STILL I SHALL TRIUMPH!
SEE HOW MY HAMMER HEAD GLOWS WITH THE UNTAPPED POWER OF THE NETHER WORLDS.. A POWER WHICH WILL BRING ME WITHIN ASGARD'S GATES!

NOW ARE YOU CONVINCED, MIGHTY THOR??
ONCE THAT BLOW WOULD HAVE HUMBLED ME... NOW IT BARELY SPLINTERS MY SHIELD!

IT IS TRUE, THEN... ODIN HAS TAKEN HALF MY POWER! I AM NO LONGER IN FAVOR IN ASGARD!

BUT HE CANNOT DENY ME! HE MUST NOT REFUSE TO HEAR MY WORDS!!
ODIN!! NOBLE FATHER! DO NOT SPURN ME! HEAR ME, ODIN!
6.

I HEAR... BUT I MUST NOT ANSWER!
THOUGH IT BREAKS MY HEART, MY SON MUST BE TAUGHT NEVER TO DEFY MY WILL!

BUT, THERE IS ONE HEART IN ASGARD WHICH IS HAPPY... THE HEART OF LOKI, THE EVIL ONE!
I MAY NEVER AGAIN HAVE SUCH A GOLDEN OPPORTUNITY! AT LAST I HAVE THE CHANCE TO DESTROY THOR, FOREVER!

AND THIS TIME, I MUST BE EQUAL TO THE TASK! AT LAST I CAN MAKE UP FOR ALL THE DEFEATS, ALL THE INDIGNITIES WHICH THOR HAS HEAPED UPON ME THROUGHOUT THE AGES!

BUT ODIN MUST NEVER SUSPECT MY MOTIVES! I MUST USE ANOTHER TO DO THE JOB FOR ME! BUT WHO...?
NORN HAG, I COMMAND YOU.. SHOW ME THE WELL OF CENTURIES!
AS YOU WISH, MY LORD LOKI!

I SHALL SEARCH THE CENTURIES THROUGH THESE ENCHANTED WATERS UNTIL I FIND THE ONE I SEEK...

AHHH! THIS IS THE AGE I WANT! EARTH'S FAR DISTANT FUTURE!

AND THERE IS MY MAN! ZARRKO, THE SCIENTIST WHO ALMOST DEFEATED THOR WHEN LAST THEY MET! IN PUNISHMENT, THOR TOOK AWAY HIS MEMORY...*
* JOURNEY INTO MYSTERY #86 "THE TOMORROW MAN!" ..EDITOR

BUT I SHALL GIVE IT BACK! REMEMBER, ZARRKO, REMEMBER!!
IT WAS THOR WHO BEAT YOU! IT WAS THOR WHO TURNED A BRILLIANT SCIENTIST INTO A MENIAL FLUNKY!
MY MEMORY! IT... IT'S RETURNING!

I AM ZARRKO, ONCE THE GREATEST SCIENTIST OF THIS CENTURY! WHY AM I WORKING HERE AS A LOWLY CLERK? WAIT! I REMEMBER NOW! IT WAS THOR'S DOING!

WITHOUT A SECOND THOUGHT, ZARRKO LEAVES HIS JOB AND SPEEDS TO THE MUNICIPAL SCIENCE CENTER...
I REMEMBER IT ALL NOW!

I HAD STOLEN THE COBALT BOMB FROM 20 TH CENTURY EARTH AND BROUGHT IT TO MY OWN CENTURY, FAR IN THE FUTURE! WE HAD NO WEAPONS IN THE FUTURE, AND I KNEW I COULD RULE THE WORLD WITH SUCH A BOMB!

"TRY AS HE MIGHT, THOR COULDN'T STOP ME FROM LEAVING THE TWENTIETH CENTURY AND REACHING MY OWN TIME..."

"BUT HE DID THE ONE THING I NEVER EXPECTED...HE FOLLOWED ME INTO THE FUTURE, AND REGAINED THE DREADED BOMB!"

"THEN IN OUR FINAL BATTLE, AN ACCIDENT MADE ME LOSE MY MEMORY... AND I'VE BEEN UNABLE TO REMEMBER UNTIL NOW! BUT... WHAT BROUGHT MY MEMORY BACK TO ME NOW?"
HE REMEMBERS NOTHING! HE'S HARMLESS NOW!
DO NOT FEAR! WE WILL GIVE YOU A JOB ...LOOK AFTER YOU!

BUT THE TOMORROW MAN'S THOUGHTS ARE BROKEN AS HE FINALLY REACHES THE MUNICIPAL SCIENCE CENTER...
ANY CITIZEN OF THE TWENTY-THIRD CENTURY HAS THE RIGHT TO USE THESE MATERIALS! AND WHAT USE I SHALL MAKE OF THEM!!!

I SHALL AGAIN RETURN TO THE TWENTIETH CENTURY... AND AGAIN STEAL THEIR MOST POWERFUL WEAPON!
BUT THIS TIME I SHALL NOT FAIL, FOR I SHALL BRING AN INDESTRUCTIBLE MINING ROBOT WITH ME...AFTER I HAVE ALTERED IT SLIGHTLY TO SUIT MY OWN PLANS!

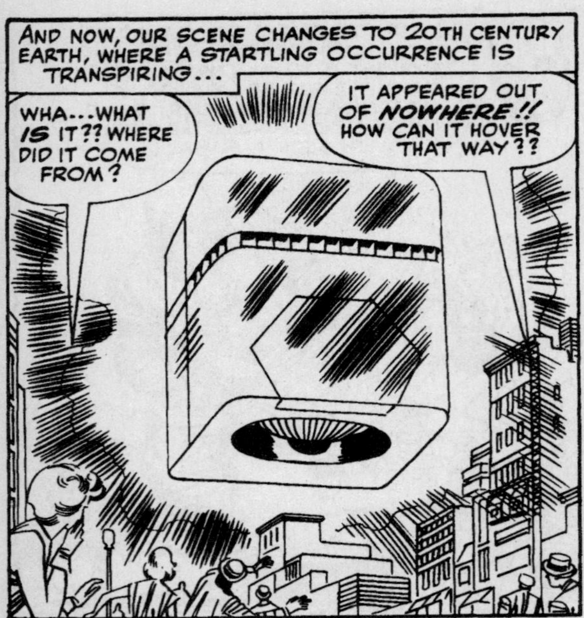
AND NOW, OUR SCENE CHANGES TO 20TH CENTURY EARTH, WHERE A STARTLING OCCURRENCE IS TRANSPIRING...
WHA...WHAT IS IT?? WHERE DID IT COME FROM?
IT APPEARED OUT OF NOWHERE!! HOW CAN IT HOVER THAT WAY??

SUDDENLY, A STRANGE-LOOKING RAMP OPENS UP, AND TWO FIGURES, ONE HUMAN, THE OTHER INHUMAN, GLIDE TO THE GROUND ON STREAMS OF PURE ENERGY!
IT'S A MAN... AND SOME SORT OF GIGANTIC ROBOT!!

ALL RIGHT, MISTER... WHAT'S GOING ON HERE?
STAY BACK! I AM ZARRKO, THE TOMORROW MAN! I AM YOUR MASTER!

LOOK! HIS MACHINE IS MOVING! IT'S OPENING ITS EYES!
KEEP YOUR GUN ON IT! DON'T TAKE ANY CHANCES! I DON'T LIKE THE LOOKS OF THIS!

A BEAM IS COMING OUT OF HIS EYES! IT'S...
OH, NO!! IT CAN'T BE!!

IT..IT'S TURNED MY GUN TO FINE DUST!! JUST BY LOOKIN' AT IT!

HELLO, CHIEF? SEND REINFORCEMENTS, QUICK!! I DON'T KNOW...IT'S SOME KINDA NUTTY SPACE SHIP WITH A ROBOT THAT CAN MELT GUNS!!
NO! I HAVEN'T BEEN IN THE SUN TOO LONG!!

SLOWLY, CALMLY, THE TOMORROW MAN ORDERS HIS ROBOT TO GIVE A LITTLE SHOW OF STRENGTH, TO DEMONSTRATE HIS GREAT POWER FOR THE AWE-STRICKEN MULTITUDES!

ENOUGH! REPLACE THE BUILDING NOW! WE MUST BE READY... FOR THOR IS CERTAIN TO HEAR OF OUR COMING! AND WHEN HE DOES...!!

MEANWHILE WHAT OF THOR?? IN HIS MORTAL IDENTITY AS DR. DON BLAKE, HE WATCHES THE EVENING NEWSCAST..
AND THE CITY HAS BEEN ORDERED EVACUATED AS SOON AS POSSIBLE!

A MAN WHO CLAIMS TO BE FROM THE FUTURE... WITH AN INDESTRUCTIBLE GIANT ROBOT!
IT MIGHT BE MY OLD ENEMY, THE TOMORROW MAN!

BUT NO MATTER WHO IT IS... I CAN'T SIT HERE AND BROOD ALL NIGHT! PERHAPS A BATTLE IS WHAT I NEED... A CHANCE TO PIT MY STRENGTH AGAINST OTHERS... AS THE MIGHTY THOR!

WITHIN SECONDS, THE LAME DOCTOR RISES AND POUNDS HIS WALKING STICK ON THE FLOOR!

NOW FOR THE TOMORROW MAN!

THOUGH MY STRENGTH HAS BEEN REDUCED BY HALF, I AM STILL MIGHTY THOR! STILL MORE THAN A MATCH FOR ANY MORTAL HERE ON EARTH!

HURLING HIS ENCHANTED HAMMER WITH BLINDING SPEED, AND WHIRLING THROUGH THE AIR AFTER IT, WHILE HOLDING ONTO ITS UNBREAKABLE THONG, THOR SOON REACHES HIS DESTINATION...
THERE HE IS! THE ROBOT IS FAR LARGER... FAR STRONGER THAN I WOULD HAVE IMAGINED!

HE HAS PLACED A DESERTED BUILDING ACROSS THE HIGHWAY, TO BLOCK TRAFFIC!!
BUT THOR WILL CRUMBLE THE BRICKS TO ASHES WITH ONE HAMMER STROKE!

I FAILED! ALL I DID WAS CHIP OFF SOME BRICKS!
THE POWER OF MY HAMMER HAS BEEN HALVED ALSO! AND JUST WHEN I NEED IT THE MOST!

SUDDENLY, A POWERFUL BLAST OF AIR CATCHES THE THUNDER GOD AND LIFTS HIM HIGH OFF HIS FEET.

...WHERE HE IS CAUGHT IN THE VISE-LIKE GRIP OF ZARRKO'S GIANT ROBOT!
IN THE 23RD CENTURY THESE ROBOTS ARE USED FOR DIGGING MINES THROUGH ROCK-HARD EARTH! BUT HERE, IT SERVES A STILL BETTER PURPOSE...IT HAS CAUGHT THOR FOR ME!!

CATCHING THE GOD OF THUNDER AND HOLDING HIM, TOMORROW MAN, ARE TWO DIFFERENT THINGS!!

THERE! I THOUGHT THAT WOULD OPEN YOUR FINGERS!
CLANG!

YOUR CHILDISH DISPLAY WILL DO YOU NO GOOD, THOR!
MY ENEMY HAS BROKEN FREE! STOP HIM! AND THIS TIME HE MUST NOT ESCAPE!

BUT, BEFORE THE TITANIC ROBOT CAN MAKE A MOVE, THOR DRAWS THE MAGNETIC FORCES OF THE GALAXY INTO HIS HAMMER HEAD! AND THEN...
BY POSITIONING THIS CORRECTLY, I'LL MAGNETIZE THAT MONSTER INTO A HARMLESS PILE OF TIN!

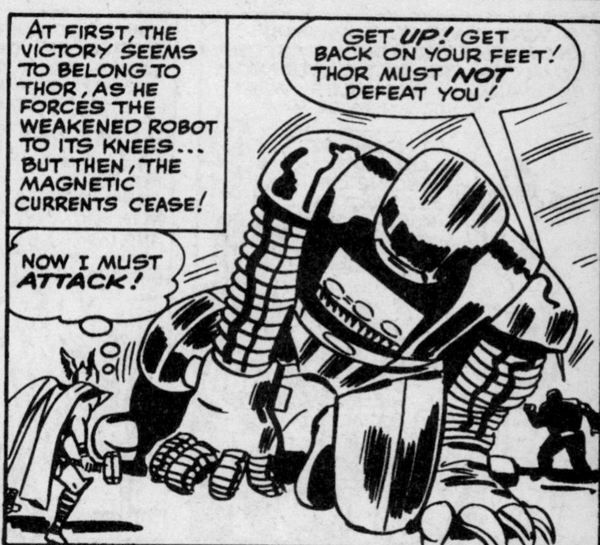
AT FIRST, THE VICTORY SEEMS TO BELONG TO THOR, AS HE FORCES THE WEAKENED ROBOT TO ITS KNEES... BUT THEN, THE MAGNETIC CURRENTS CEASE!
GET UP! GET BACK ON YOUR FEET! THOR MUST NOT DEFEAT YOU!
NOW I MUST ATTACK!

IT'S NOW, OR NEVER!

BUT SUDDENLY, THOR IS HIT WITH THE SAME EXPLOSIVE FORCE WHICH THE ROBOT USES TO BLAST ENTIRE MOUNTAINS IN THE FUTURE!! AND, DUE TO THE FACT THAT HIS STRENGTH HAS BEEN REDUCED BY HALF...
CAN'T HELP MYSELF! BEING HURLED BACK-WARDS LIKE A TOY!
12.

THAT'S IT! HURL HIM FROM WALL TO WALL!! GOOD! GOOD! SHOW HIM HOW POWERLESS HE IS AGAINST YOU!

AND NOW, THOR...DO YOU REALIZE THAT YOU HAVE MET YOUR SUPERIOR AT LAST??
BUT I SHALL NOT ORDER MY ROBOT TO ATTACK YOU ANY MORE! I HAVE NO WISH TO INJURE YOU... FOR I HAVE NEED OF YOU!

IF YOU GIVE ME YOUR WORD TO RETURN TO THE 23RD CENTURY WITH ME, AND DO MY BIDDING, I SHALL DO NO FURTHER HARM HERE IN THIS CENTURY!
BUT IF YOU REFUSE... I'LL ORDER MY ROBOT TO GO ON THE RAMPAGE, DESTROYING UNTIL NOTHING REMAINS ON THE SURFACE OF YOUR PLANET!

IF YOU CAN'T STOP HIM, YOU KNOW THAT NOBODY CAN! ONLY YOU CAN PREVENT EARTH FROM BECOMING A SHAMBLES! WHAT IS YOUR ANSWER?
I CANNOT LET THAT ENGINE OF DESTRUCTION RUN AMOK ON EARTH!

SINCE ODIN HAS REDUCED MY STRENGTH, I CANNOT SAVE EARTH FROM THAT ROBOT! I MUST GIVE IN TO ZARRKO'S TERMS!
YOU WIN, ZARRKO! I WILL GO TO THE 23RD CENTURY WITH YOU.. AND DO YOUR BIDDING!
HAH! I KNEW IT! WE LEAVE IMMEDIATELY!!

TRIUMPHANTLY I SHALL RETURN TO BECOME RULER OF MY ENTIRE WORLD! AND MY REVENGE WILL BE DOUBLY SWEET BECAUSE YOU MUST HELP ME!

WHILE BACK IN ASGARD, NOT KNOWING THE REASON FOR THOR'S SURRENDER, ODIN IS THUNDERSTRUCK!
THIS IS TOO MUCH TO BEAR! MY SON HAS GIVEN UP TO A MORTAL!
YES, SO HE HAS, SIRE!
13.

ALL GOES PERFECTLY! IF THOR HELPS THE EVIL TOMORROW MAN CONQUER THE 23RD CENTURY, ODIN WILL NEVER FORGIVE HIM! AND NONE WILL KNOW THAT LOKI HAS ARRANGED IT ALL!

DON'T DARE MISS THE CONCLUSION, NEXT ISSUE, WHEN THOR MAKES ZARRKO EMPEROR OF THE FUTURE! WE PROMISE YOU AN ENDING YOU WILL NEVER FORGET!

THE BOYHOOD OF THOR!
TALES of ASGARD HOME OF THE MIGHTY NORSE GODS!
"the INVASION of ASGARD!"
HERE STANDS HEIMDALL! HEIMDALL, GUARDIAN OF THE RAINBOW BRIDGE TO ASGARD! HEIMDALL, THE ETERNALLY VIGILANT! HEIMDALL THE IMMOVABLE!
HEIMDALL, I HAVE HEARD THAT THE FORCES OF EVIL* ARE ABOUT TO ATTACK ASGARD! I CAME TO HELP YOU GUARD THE RAINBOW BRIDGE!
WRITTEN BY: STAN LEE
DRAWN BY: JACK KIRBY
INKED BY: G. BELL
LETTERED BY: ART SIMEK
* "FORCES OF EVIL": ALL THE SINISTER, POWERFUL MENACES WHICH WOULD DESTROY NOBLE ASGARD!
-568
1

LEAVE ME, YOUNG THOR! THERE IS MAN'S WORK TO BE DONE HERE! GO!
BUT I MUST DO NOBLE DEEDS, THAT I MAY EARN THE MIGHTY URU HAMMER OF ODIN!
PSSST, THOR! COME HERE! LOKI WILL TELL YOU HOW TO WIN YOUR FATHER'S HAMMER!

WHERE ARE YOU LEADING ME, LOKI?
FOLLOW ME! I HAVE FOUND A HOLE IN ASGARD'S DEFENSES! YOU MUST GUARD IT WHILE I GO FOR HELP!

SEE? HERE IT IS! IF THE EVIL ONES FIND THIS UNGUARDED OPENING, THEY WILL OVERRUN OUR LAND!
BUT, IF YOU GUARD IT WELL, YOU WILL CERTAINLY COME CLOSER TO HAVING EARNED ODIN'S HAMMER!
LOKI, YOU HAVE DONE ME A SERVICE WHICH I SHALL NOT SOON FORGET!

TRUSTING FOOL! I KNOW YOU WON'T SOON FORGET THIS -- FOR IT IS I WHO MADE THAT HOLE -- AND IT IS I WHO TOLD THE EVIL ONES IT IS THERE -- SO THAT THEY WILL COME AND DEFEAT YOU!
AND THEN, IT WILL BE LOKI'S TURN TO TRY TO WIN THE ENCHANTED HAMMER!

AND, NO SOONER HAS LOKI RUN OFF THEN THE *EVIL ONES* ATTACK! *NEVER* HAS THERE BEEN SO AWE-SOME AN ARRAY OF IMMORTAL FOES....!!

the NORN HAG riding ULFRIN the DRAGON

the MERCILESS RIME GIANTS

I MUST PROTECT ASGARD --WITH MY *LIFE* IF NEED BE!

LAST of the ICE GIANTS

SKOLL & HATI, the WOLF GODS!

GEIRRODUR the TROLL

KNOWING HIS SWORD ALONE CANNOT HOLD BACK THE SURGING ATTACK OF THE EVIL ONES, THOR RESORTS TO CUNNING--TO TRICKERY--AS HE CAUSES A GEYSER TO ERUPT WITH ONE BLOW OF HIS UNBREAKABLE BLADE!

I MUST DO WHAT I CAN TO GAIN TIME TILL HELP ARRIVES!

THESE MIGHTY ROCKS, STRUCK WITH ALL MY FORCE BY THE FLAT OF MY BLADE, WILL CAUSE SOME OF THE EVIL ONES TO DRAW BACK!! IF ONLY LOKI CAN BRING THE WARRIORS OF ASGARD IN TIME!

BUT, LITTLE DOES BRAVE THOR REALIZE, AS HE FACES THE ATTACK OF THE NORN HAG ON HER INCREDIBLE DRAGON, THAT LOKI HAS SUMMONED NO HELP!
WELL DONE, HAG! HE IS TRAPPED!
NOTHING THAT LIVES CAN WITHSTAND MY DRAGON'S ENCHANTED BREATH!

WEAKENED BY THE SMOKEY FUMES, HIS STRENGTH WANING--THOR SINKS TO HIS KNEES AS THE MIGHTY RIME GIANT WEAVES A SPELL ABOUT HIM...

AND, AT THE CONCLUSION OF THE SPELL, THE SON OF ODIN FINDS HIMSELF INEXORABLY TURNING INTO--A TREE!
WHERE ARE THE WARRIORS?? IN ANOTHER FEW MINUTES, IT WILL BE TOO LATE FOR ANYTHING TO SAVE ME!!

BUT THEN, AS THOUGH IN ANSWER TO THOR'S IMPASSIONED PLEA, A MIGHTY WAR CRY IS HEARD...
FOR ODIN, AND ASGARD!!!

AS THE FIRST BLOW IS STRUCK, THE SPELL FALLS FROM YOUNG THOR, AND HE BECOMES THE IMMORTAL GODLING ONCE AGAIN!!

WE HEARD THE SOUNDS OF BATTLE, MY SON! IT WAS THE CLANGING OF YOUR SWORD THAT ALERTED US!

OH, BUT, FATHER, I HAVE FAILED! THE EVIL ONES WOULD HAVE *DEFEATED* ME IF NOT FOR YOUR ATTACK!

SPEAK NOT SO, YOUNG THOR! WITHOUT YOUR VALIANT DEFENSE, THEY WOULD HAVE BROKEN THROUGH THIS OPENING TO ASGARD! YOU HAVE GIVEN US THE TIME TO DEFEND OURSELVES! YOU HAVE *SAVED* ASGARD!

THEN, REALIZING THEY HAVE LOST THE ADVANTAGE OF SURPRISE... SEEING THE FURY WITH WHICH THE GODS OF ASGARD BATTLE -- THE EVIL ONES SLOWLY TURN AND STUMBLE BACK TO THE DARKNESS FROM WHENCE THEY HAVE COME!

5

WHILE HE WHO WILL ONE DAY BE GOD OF THUNDER LIFTS THE URU HAMMER HIGHER THAN IT HAS EVER BEEN LIFTED BEFORE!!
I HAVE BEEN REWARDED WITH ADDITIONAL STRENGTH! SOON PERHAPS, SOON I SHALL BE ABLE TO LIFT THE MIGHTY HAMMER ABOVE MY HEAD! AND, ON THAT GLORIOUS DAY, IT WILL BE *MINE* TO CLAIM!
THAT DAY WILL NEVER COME, THOR! NOT SO LONG AS *LOKI* CAN LIFT A FINGER TO PREVENT IT!
THE END

MANY ARE THE SAGAS OF ASGARD, THE MYSTICAL LAND WHERE TITANS DWELL!! NEXT ISSUE WE BRING YOU ANOTHER IN THIS, THE MOST WIDELY-ACCLAIMED SERIES IN MODERN COMIC MAGAZINE HISTORY!

JOURNEY INTO
IND
APPROVED BY THE COMICS CODE AUTHORITY
MYSTERY
MARVEL COMICS GROUP 12¢
102 MAR.
the MIGHTY THOR!
SLAVE OF "THE TOMORROW MAN!"
ANOTHER TITANIC TRIUMPH FROM THE MARVEL AGE OF COMICS!

THE MIGHTY THOR!
"SLAVE OF ZARRKO, The TOMORROW MAN!"
YOU ARE ABOUT TO ENTER THE WORLD OF THE FUTURE, WHERE THE MIGHTY THOR MUST DO THE BIDDING OF A MASTER VILLAIN!! ANOTHER MARVEL TRIUMPH!
LET YOUR THUNDERING HAMMER SERVE ME, THOR! I AM YOUR MASTER! YOU ARE MY SLAVE!
CUNNINGLY CONCEIVED BY: STAN LEE
DARINGLY DRAWN BY: JACK KIRBY
INGENIOUSLY INKED BY: CHIC STONE
LOVINGLY LETTERED BY: ART SIMEK
X-573
1

LAST ISSUE WE SAW HOW AN ANGRY ODIN, LORD OF THE NORSE GODS, REFUSED THOR ENTRY INTO ASGARD AND TOOK AWAY HALF OF HIS INVINCIBLE POWER! ALL BECAUSE OF THOR'S LOVE FOR A MORTAL EARTH GIRL!
NO MATTER WHAT PUNISHMENTS I MAY RECEIVE, I CAN NEVER PUT JANE FOSTER OUT OF MY HEART! MY LOVE FOR HER WILL NEVER DIE!

ALTHOUGH ODIN'S HEART IS HEAVY BECAUSE THOR IS IN TRUTH HIS FAVORITE SON, THERE IS ONE WHO REJOICES AT THE THUNDER GOD'S PREDICAMENT! THE EVIL LOKI, GOD OF MISCHIEF, AND THOR'S HALF-BROTHER, DECIDES THE TIME HAS COME TO PLAY HIS HAND!
NOW, WHILE THOR IS WEAKER THAN HE HAS EVER BEEN, I MUST FIND A MORTAL TO DEFEAT HIM FOR ME!
AH, THERE IS THE ONE I SEEK! THERE--IN THE 23RD CENTURY!

LOKI HAS FOUND ZARRKO, THE SINISTER SCIENTIST FROM THE FUTURE WHOM THOR HAD DEFEATED ONCE BEFORE!* LOKI RESTORES ZARRKO'S MEMORY TO HIM, AND THE TOMORROW MAN RETURNS TO THE 20TH CENTURY WITH A FANTASTICALLY POWERFUL ROBOT...
WE MEET AGAIN, THUNDER GOD! BUT THIS TIME THE VICTORY SHALL BE MINE!
EVEN YOUR GREAT STRENGTH IS NOT ENOUGH TO OVERCOME THE RAW POWER OF MY ROBOT SLAVE!!
DEFEND YOURSELF, ZARRKO! I BEAT YOU ONCE--AND I SHALL DO IT AGAIN!

BUT, BECAUSE ODIN HAS TAKEN HALF HIS POWER FROM HIM, THE MIGHTY THOR FINDS HE CANNOT STOP THE GIGANTIC ROBOT FROM THE FUTURE!!

NEVER HAVE MORTAL EYES WITNESSED SUCH A BATTLE! NEVER HAS ONE LONE CHAMPION FOUGHT SO VALIANTLY IN THE FACE OF HOPELESS ODDS... BUT THE FINAL OUTCOME IS INEVITABLE...

TRY AS I MAY, I CANNOT DELIVER ONE FINAL SHATTERING BLOW!!

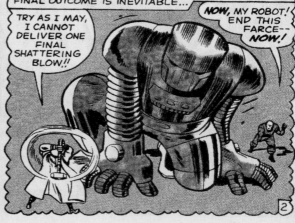

NOW, MY ROBOT! END THIS FARCE-- NOW!

(* JOURNEY INTO MYSTERY #86 -- EDITOR)

IT'S NO USE! WITH MY POWER REDUCED TO HALF BY MY FATHER ODIN, I AM NO MATCH FOR THE ROBOT'S MIGHT!

HEAR ME, THOR! NOTHING ON EARTH CAN STOP MY ROBOT! ONCE YOU ARE DEFEATED, I CAN PILLAGE THE ENTIRE 20TH CENTURY! BUT I AM NOT INTERESTED IN THIS PRIMITIVE AGE! INSTEAD, I HAVE AN OFFER TO MAKE TO YOU!
WHAT KIND OF OFFER?

IF YOU RETURN TO THE 23RD CENTURY WITH ME, AND HELP ME CONQUER MY OWN FUTURE WORLD, THEN I PROMISE TO LEAVE THIS CENTURY AND CAUSE NO MORE HARM HERE!
I HAVE NO CHOICE! I CANNOT PUT THE 20TH CENTURY AT YOUR MERCY! I WILL SERVE YOU IN THE WORLD OF THE FUTURE!

IN FAR OFF ASGARD, NOBLE ODIN HEARS THE PROMISE OF THOR, AND IS SORELY GRIEVED!
MY OWN SON-- SURRENDERING TO A MORTAL!! HOW HE FILLS ME WITH SHAME!
ODIN FORGETS THAT HE HAS TAKEN HALF OF THOR'S POWER! THERE IS NOTHING ELSE THE GOLDEN-HAIRED ONE CAN DO!

MY PLAN IS PROCEEDING PERFECTLY! IF THOR HELPS ZARRKO CONQUER THE FUTURE, THEN ODIN IS SURE TO DISINHERIT HIM, AND THE MANTLE OF THOR WILL FALL ON MY SHOULDERS! LOKI WILL BECOME THE MOST POWERFUL OF GODS!

THIS TIME I CANNOT FAIL! THOR HAS GIVEN ZARRKO HIS PROMISE--A PROMISE WHICH CANNOT BE BROKEN! EVEN NOW THEY ARE RETURNING TO THE 23RD CENTURY...

AHHH, THEY HAVE ARRIVED! TRULY, THIS SHALL BE THE FINAL DEFEAT OF THOR, THE STEPBROTHER WHOM I DESPISE!

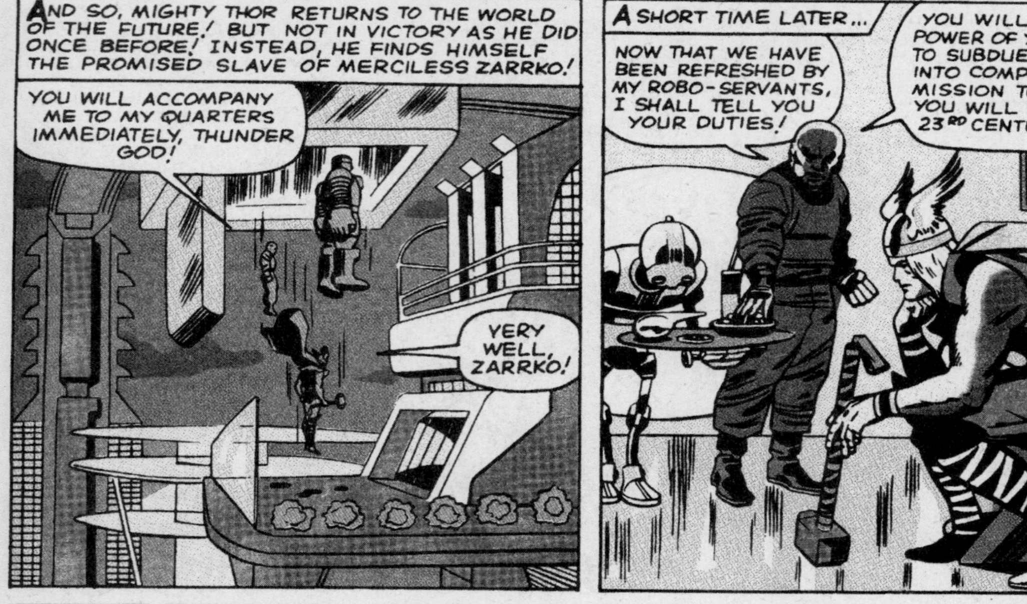
AND SO, MIGHTY THOR RETURNS TO THE WORLD OF THE FUTURE! BUT NOT IN VICTORY AS HE DID ONCE BEFORE! INSTEAD, HE FINDS HIMSELF THE PROMISED SLAVE OF MERCILESS ZARRKO!
YOU WILL ACCOMPANY ME TO MY QUARTERS IMMEDIATELY, THUNDER GOD!
VERY WELL, ZARRKO!
A SHORT TIME LATER...
NOW THAT WE HAVE BEEN REFRESHED BY MY ROBO-SERVANTS, I SHALL TELL YOU YOUR DUTIES!
YOU WILL USE THE POWER OF YOUR HAMMER TO SUBDUE THE POPULACE INTO COMPLETE SUB-MISSION TO MY WILL! YOU WILL CONQUER THE 23RD CENTURY FOR ME!

THERE ARE NO WEAPONS IN THIS ENLIGHTENED AGE--NO POLICE FORCES! WITH YOU FIGHTING FOR ME, NONE CAN RESIST ME!
I HAVE GIVEN YOU MY OATH, EVIL ZARRKO! I SHALL DO AS YOU COMMAND--THOUGH MY VERY SOUL CRIES OUT IN PROTEST!

AND SO, WE TURN TO A TYPICAL STREET SCENE, AS PEDESTRIANS RIDE THE MOVING SIDEWALKS OF THE FUTURE...

SUDDENLY, FOR THE FIRST TIME IN DECADES, SOMETHING GOES WRONG --AS THOUGH A MIGHTY HAMMER HAS SMASHED THE CENTRAL CONTROL MECHANISM!

ACCIDENTS BEGIN TO OCCUR WITH ALARMING FRE-QUENCY! REMOTE CONTROL AIRBORNE DELIVERY VEHICLES ARE SUDDENLY SMASHED FROM THE SKY, AS IF BY MAGIC!

HIGHLY SOPHISTICATED ROBOTS, WHICH PERFORM MENIAL TASKS, SUDDENLY FIND THEIR ELECTRONIC GUIDANCE SYSTEMS NOT OPERATING CORRECTLY...
ROBOT POLICE AIR TRAFFIC DIVISION
STOP
GO

...CONFUSED, UNCERTAIN, RENDERED USELESS BY THE DESTRUCTION OF THEIR MAIN POWER DYNAMO STATIONS, THEY WHIRL OUT OF CONTROL...

...CAUSING TRAFFIC JAMS, PANIC, AND A GENERAL SLOWDOWN OF ALL THE VITAL SERVICES WHICH A CIVILIZATION NEEDS IF IT IS TO SURVIVE!

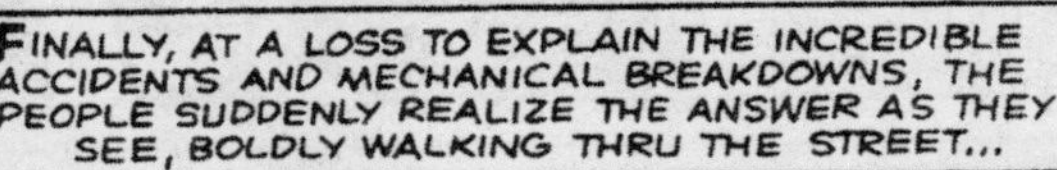
FINALLY, AT A LOSS TO EXPLAIN THE INCREDIBLE ACCIDENTS AND MECHANICAL BREAKDOWNS, THE PEOPLE SUDDENLY REALIZE THE ANSWER AS THEY SEE, BOLDLY WALKING THRU THE STREET...

LOOK! IT'S ZARRKO! THE EVIL SCIENTIST! HIS MEMORY MUST HAVE RETURNED!
BUT LOOK WHO'S WITH HIM! IT'S THE MIGHTY THOR-- THE ONE WHO DEFEATED ZARRKO MONTHS AGO! NOW HE SEEMS TO BE HIS ALLY!

BACK! STAND BACK! MAKE WAY FOR ZARRKO AND HIS INVINCIBLE SLAVE, THE MIGHTY THOR!
IT IS THOR WHO HAS CAUSED THE ACCIDENTS OF THE PAST FEW HOURS--AT MY COMMAND--TO DEMONSTRATE MY ABSOLUTE MASTERY OVER HIM!

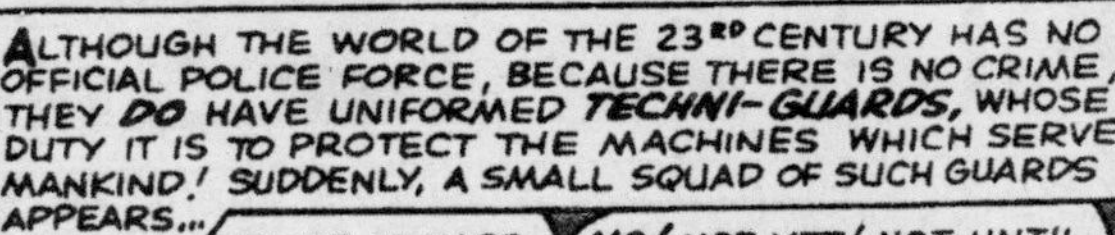
ALTHOUGH THE WORLD OF THE 23RD CENTURY HAS NO OFFICIAL POLICE FORCE, BECAUSE THERE IS NO CRIME, THEY DO HAVE UNIFORMED TECHNI-GUARDS, WHOSE DUTY IT IS TO PROTECT THE MACHINES WHICH SERVE MANKIND! SUDDENLY, A SMALL SQUAD OF SUCH GUARDS APPEARS...

STAND AT EASE, ZARRKO! WE SHALL TAKE YOU BEFORE THE WORLD COUNCIL!
NO! NOT YET! NOT UNTIL I AM READY! I OBEY NO OTHER COMMANDS!

THOSE INSTRUMENTS YOU HOLD ARE NOT REALLY WEAPONS! THEY ARE MEANT ONLY TO CONTROL DEFECTIVE MACHINES! THEY CANNOT THREATEN THOR! DESTROY THEM, THUNDER GOD!
I MUST DO AS I AM BIDDEN!

ALTHOUGH I POSSESS ONLY HALF MY NORMAL POWER, I CAN STILL HARNESS THE ALPHA PARTICLES FROM THE ATMOSPHERE AND FOCUS THEM WITH THE GLEAMING HEAD OF MY HAMMER...

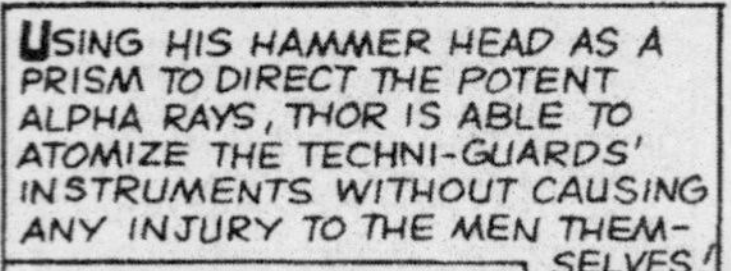

USING HIS HAMMER HEAD AS A PRISM TO DIRECT THE POTENT ALPHA RAYS, THOR IS ABLE TO ATOMIZE THE TECHNI-GUARDS' INSTRUMENTS WITHOUT CAUSING ANY INJURY TO THE MEN THEMSELVES!

HIS POWER IS BEYOND DESCRIPTION! THERE IS NO WAY TO FIGHT SUCH AN ENEMY!

YOU WERE TOO GENTLE WITH THEM, THOR! I WANT THEM COMPLETELY SUBDUED! YOU MUST OBEY ME!
AN IMMORTAL MAY NEVER BREAK HIS OATH! I MUST HEED ZARRKO'S COMMANDS!

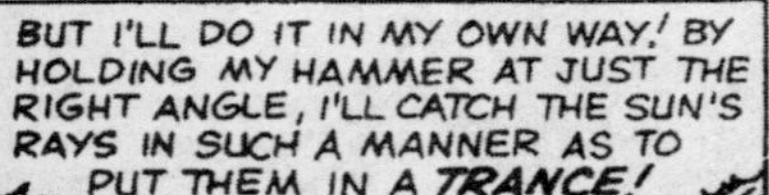

BUT I'LL DO IT IN MY OWN WAY! BY HOLDING MY HAMMER AT JUST THE RIGHT ANGLE, I'LL CATCH THE SUN'S RAYS IN SUCH A MANNER AS TO PUT THEM IN A TRANCE!

WE-- -ARE-- -AT-- -YOUR-- -SERVICE-- -ZARRKO!

I HAVE SUBDUED THEM, AS YOU ORDERED!

AND STILL WITHOUT CAUSING ANY BODILY HARM!

IT'S NOT QUITE WHAT I MEANT, BUT IT WILL DO--FOR NOW!

INASMUCH AS I AM IN THE DRIVER'S SEAT, I WILL NOW VISIT THE WORLD COUNCIL! TAKE ME THERE, AT ONCE!

ALTHOUGH I HAVE SAVED THE 20TH CENTURY FROM THIS MADMAN'S THREAT, WHAT HAVE I UNLEASHED UPON THE 23RD CENTURY??!

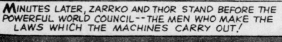

MINUTES LATER, ZARRKO AND THOR STAND BEFORE THE POWERFUL WORLD COUNCIL--THE MEN WHO MAKE THE LAWS WHICH THE MACHINES CARRY OUT!
WOC
YOU HAVE ALREADY SEEN EXAMPLES OF MY MIGHT! WITH THOR AT MY SIDE, NONE CAN STOP ME!
WE'LL BE THE JUDGES OF THAT, ZARRKO! NOW SPEAK-- WHAT IS IT YOU WANT??

POWER! I WANT TO KNOW WHERE THE MASTER MACHINE IS HIDDEN! THE ONE SUPREME MACHINE WHICH GIVES YOU YOUR ORDERS! ONCE I PUT THAT MACHINE UNDER MY COMMAND, THE WORLD IS MINE!
AND IF WE REFUSE TO TELL YOU WHERE IT IS???

YOU DARE NOT REFUSE ME--NOT WHILE MIGHTY THOR IS MY SLAVE!!
HE IS RIGHT, GENTLEMEN! DON'T DO ANYTHING TO FORCE ME TO USE MY POWER!

COME, THOR! WE'LL GIVE THEM ONE HOUR TO MAKE THEIR DECISION, AND IF THEY DO NOT ACCEPT MY DEMANDS, YOU'LL TURN YOUR HAMMER AGAINST THEM!
THE THUNDER GOD LEFT A NOTE ON THE TABLE, UNSEEN BY ZARRKO! WHAT CAN IT BE?

THEN, NO SOONER DO THOR AND ZARRKO WALK THRU THE DOOR, WHEN...
WE MUST STOP THEM NOW! THOR MUST NOT BE ALLOWED TO STRIKE THE FIRST BLOW!
IF THE MAXIMUM SECURITY OCTI-ROBOT CANNOT DEFEAT HIM, WE ARE DOOMED!

AT THE TOUCH OF A BUTTON BY THE CHIEF COUNCILMAN, A WALL PANEL SLIDES OPEN AND A POWERFUL, COMPLEX PROTECTO-ROBOT, IN THE FORM OF A GIANT OCTOPUS, HURLS ITSELF AT THE TWO DEPARTING FIGURES!

IF ODIN HAD NOT TAKEN HALF MY STRENGTH, I COULD SHATTER THIS MACHINE WITH ONE MIGHTY HAMMER BLOW! BUT NOW-- I FIND I CAN NO LONGER DEPEND ON NAKED STRENGTH ALONE!

SUDDENLY...
THE OCTI-ROBOT IS EMITTING A CLOUD OF POISONOUS VAPOR-- JUST LIKE THE OCTOPUS FOR WHICH IT IS NAMED EMITS CLOUDS OF INKY FLUID!!

SOMETIMES STRENGTH ALONE IS NOT ENOUGH!! IF I CAN JUST BEND THESE VENTS BACK-- FORCING THE VAPOR TO RETURN TO THE PLASTIC SACK--

I DID IT! NOW--THE MORE VAPOR THE ROBOT EMITS, THE MORE IT WILL STRETCH ITS OWN PLASTIC SACK, UNTIL...

...IT BURSTS, DESTROYING ITSELF!

I KNEW I COULDN'T FAIL WITH YOU AT MY SIDE, THOR! AND NOW, WE'LL TEACH THEM TO DEFY US!
WAIT! ONE OF THEM APPROACHES! LET US HEAR WHAT HE HAS TO SAY!

ZARRKO, WE REALIZE THAT THE PEACEFUL WORLD OF THE 23RD CENTURY IS NO MATCH FOR THOR'S MIGHT--OR YOUR OWN VILLAINY! TO SPARE OURSELVES FURTHER CONFLICT, WE SHALL GIVE YOU THE LOCATION OF THE MASTER ROBOT WHICH CONTROLS THE PLANET!
I KNEW IT! THAT MEANS I'VE WON!

MINUTES LATER, AFTER ZARRKO HAS RECEIVED THE INFORMATION HE DESIRES...
YOU MAY LEAVE NOW! AFTER I HAVE TAKEN OVER THE MASTER ROBOT, I SHALL RETURN TO RULE THE WORLD COUNCIL! PERHAPS, I SHALL LET YOU TOO REMAIN TO SERVE!
IF YOU SUCCEED IN GAINING CONTROL OF THE MASTER ROBOT, THE WHOLE HUMAN RACE WILL HAVE TO SERVE YOU, ZARRKO!

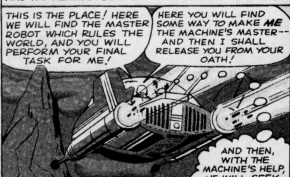

AND SO, WITH THE MIGHTY THOR STILL AT HIS SIDE, THE EVIL ZARRKO JOURNEYS TO A LONELY ISLE-- AND HIS RENDEZVOUS WITH A STRANGE DESTINY...
THIS IS THE PLACE! HERE WE WILL FIND THE MASTER ROBOT WHICH RULES THE WORLD, AND YOU WILL PERFORM YOUR FINAL TASK FOR ME!
HERE YOU WILL FIND SOME WAY TO MAKE ME THE MACHINE'S MASTER--AND THEN I SHALL RELEASE YOU FROM YOUR OATH!
AND THEN, WITH THE MACHINE'S HELP, HE WILL SEEK TO DESTROY ME! BUT I MUST SEE THIS THRU TO THE END!

THEN, AFTER LANDING...
THIS IS THE PLACE WHERE THE MASTER MACHINE IS HIDDEN! SMASH IT OPEN, THOR!
STAND BACK, ZARRKO!

WHOOM!

YOU DID IT! YOU OPENED THE CAVE! WHAT DO YOU SEE? WHAT'S INSIDE??
QUIET! I HEAR SOMETHING --SOMETHING OMINOUS!

AND THEN, UTTERLY WITHOUT WARNING, ONE OF THE STRANGEST DEVICES OF THE 23RD CENTURY COMES HURTLING PAST THEM--A SPEEDING, CAREENING TORPEDO-SHAPED OBJECT CALLED A C-BOMB!!

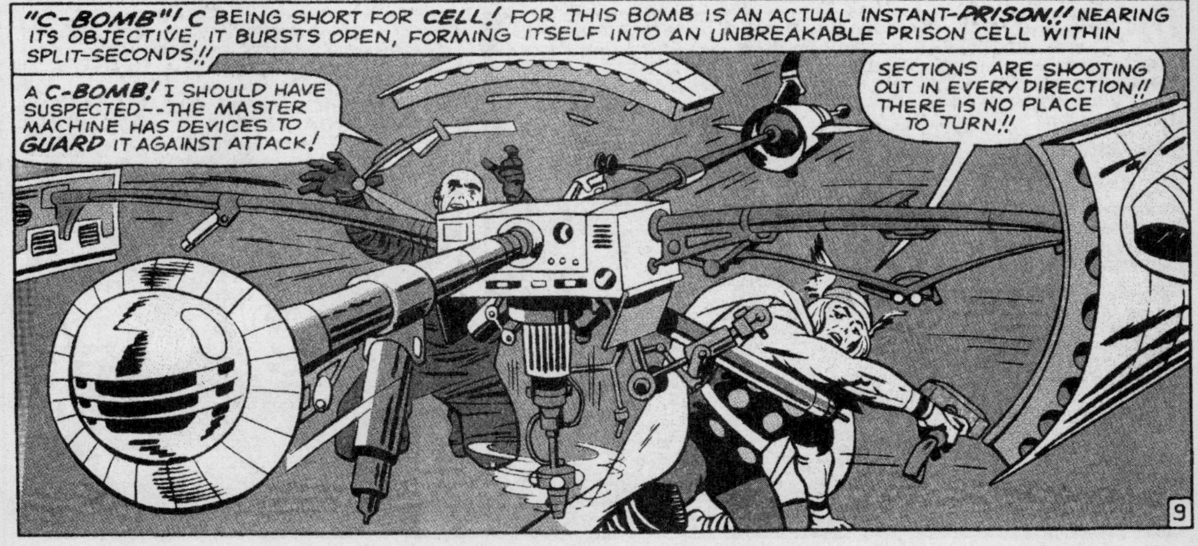
"C-BOMB"! C BEING SHORT FOR CELL! FOR THIS BOMB IS AN ACTUAL INSTANT-PRISON!! NEARING ITS OBJECTIVE, IT BURSTS OPEN, FORMING ITSELF INTO AN UNBREAKABLE PRISON CELL WITHIN SPLIT-SECONDS!!
A C-BOMB! I SHOULD HAVE SUSPECTED--THE MASTER MACHINE HAS DEVICES TO GUARD IT AGAINST ATTACK!
SECTIONS ARE SHOOTING OUT IN EVERY DIRECTION!! THERE IS NO PLACE TO TURN!!

THEN, AS QUICKLY AS IT HAD STARTED, ALL MOTION STOPS!
I'VE FAILED! ALL IS LOST! WE'RE DEFEATED-- HOPELESSLY TRAPPED!!
WHY? THERE IS PLENTY OF ROOM TO CRAWL OUT BETWEEN THE METAL LEGS!

NO SOONER ARE THE WORDS OUT OF HIS MOUTH THAN THE THUNDER GOD GETS HIS ANSWER! AN ATOM-POWERED REACTOR WITHIN THE C-BOMB BEGINS TO ALTER THE GRAVITY IN THE AREA, INCREASING IT UNTIL THE PRESSURE BECOMES ALMOST UNBEARABLE...
BEING PRESSED AGAINST THE GROUND--AS THOUGH PUSHED DOWN BY A GIGANTIC HAND...

EVEN THOUGH HE NOW POSSESSES ONLY HALF HIS NORMAL STRENGTH, THE MIGHTY THOR EXERTS EVERY OUNCE OF SUPERHUMAN POWER HE CAN MUSTER, AS HE SLOWLY RAISES HIS ENCHANTED HAMMER--HIGHER--HIGHER--BRINGING IT INTO POSITION FOR ONE THUNDEROUS BLOW!

JUST A LITTLE FURTHER-- A LITTLE MORE...

SMASH!
YOU DID IT, THOR! WE'RE FREE!

THAT WAS THE MACHINE'S DEFENSE! NOW THAT WE HAVE PENETRATED IT, NOTHING ELSE CAN STOP US! I HAVE WON!
THAT MUST BE THE MASTER MACHINE-- THAT ENORMOUS COMPLEX OF VAST ELECTRONIC CIRCUITS AHEAD OF US!

YES, THIS IS IT! IT CONTROLS EVERY HIGH-LEVEL DECISION MADE ON EARTH! IT ACTUALLY RULES THE WORLD FOR HUMANITY!
NOW ALL I NEED DO IS SET THE MAIN CIRCUIT TO TAKE ORDERS ONLY FROM ME, AND THEN I WILL BE THE ONE RULING THE HUMAN RACE! I HAVE REACHED MY GOAL! I AM MASTER OF MANKIND!
NEW YORK
TOKYO
PARIS
LONDON
BELGRADE
ATHENS
BANGKOK
OSLO
CAIRO
CAPETOWN
BRASILIA
CHICAGO
MOSCOW
NEW DELHI
LIMA
ANTARCTICA
TAHITI
MADRID
SAIGON
NOME
QUEBEC
BOMBAY
REKJAVIK
BERLIN

THEN I HAVE KEPT MY WORD! I HAVE GIVEN YOU MASTERY OF THE 23RD CENTURY!
YES, YOU FOOL--YOU KEPT YOUR WORD! AND I HAVE REALIZED MY DREAM! I'M THE MOST POWERFUL HUMAN WHO EVER LIVED!

AS FOR YOU, I SHALL KEEP YOU HERE IN THE 23RD CENTURY, AS A PERMANENT REMINDER OF MY TRIUMPH -- AND MY POWER!
ALAS, YOUR TRIUMPH IS ABOUT TO COME TO AN END, ZARRKO! NOW THAT I HAVE KEPT MY WORD, I AM FREE TO FOLLOW MY OWN WHIMS-- FREE TO BATTLE YOU!

I EXPECTED THAT SORT OF REACTION FROM YOU, MY UNSUSPECTING FRIEND! BUT NOW THAT ALL THE MIRACLE MACHINES OF THE 23RD CENTURY ARE AT MY COMMAND, I HAVE NO NEED TO FEAR YOU--OR ANYONE THAT LIVES!

ENOUGH OF YOUR WITLESS BOASTING! THE MOST THAT ANY MACHINE CAN DO IS STOP ME FOR A SECOND OR TWO--BUT THEN MY HAMMER STRIKES!

YOUR EVERY MOVE IS PREDICTABLE, THOR! KNOWING YOU WOULD HURL YOUR HAMMER, I HAD THIS ELECTRONIC REFRIGERATO-BEAM ALL READY TO STOP IT IN ITS FLIGHT!

AND WHAT MY QUICK-FREEZE RAY CAN DO TO YOUR HAMMER, IT CAN ALSO DO TO YOU! YOU CAN'T DODGE IT FOREVER, THUNDER GOD!
PERHAPS NOT-- BUT I CAN DODGE IT LONG ENOUGH--!

--LONG ENOUGH TO CATCH MY ENCHANTED HAMMER-- WHICH MUST ALWAYS RETURN TO ME, EVEN IF YOU HAD COVERED IT WITH THE MAJESTIC ALPS THEMSELVES!
NO-- NO!!
11

STAY BACK! YOU CAN'T GET ME! YOU MUSTN'T GET ME! NOT WHEN I HAVE REACHED MY GOAL! NOT WHEN I'M BEYOND THE LAW!

I ALONE, OF ALL THE SPINELESS MILKSOPS IN THIS CENTURY, DARED TO COMMIT A CRIME! AND IF YOU DO NOT HALT, I WILL PULL THIS LEVER AND COMMIT ANOTHER!

BY HARNESSING THE ENERGY OF THE MASTER MACHINE, I CAN DIRECT BEAMS OF PURE FORCE TO ANY PLACE ON EARTH, DESTROYING WHATEVER THEY TOUCH!

"OR I CAN SEND MY FORCE RAYS INTO THE VERY STRATOSPHERE, CAUSING VITAL SPACE STATIONS AND SATELLITES TO PLUNGE HELPLESSLY BACK TO EARTH!"

SO IF YOU COME A STEP CLOSER, I'LL PULL THIS SWITCH-- SIGNALING THE DEATH KNELL OF EARTH!
YOU SHALL PULL NO MORE SWITCHES, ZARRKO! YOUR DAYS OF THREAT-ENING ARE OVER!

WHILE YOU WERE TALKING, I HAVE BEEN GENTLY RUBBING MY HAMMER HEAD ALONG THE GROUND, PICKING UP VAST AMOUNTS OF NATURAL ENERGY --ENERGY WHICH I HAVE DIRECTED TOWARDS THE MASTER MACHINE-- SO THAT IT IS NOW ABLE TO AGAIN DEFEND ITSELF!
OHHH...

I-I CAN SEE-- HEAR--I CAN BREATHE! BUT --I CAN'T GET OUT! I'M EN-CLOSED IN SOME SORT OF A BALL OF SEMI-SOLID ENERGY MATTER!
AND THERE YOU WILL STAY, TILL THEY COME FOR YOU! DID YOU THINK THAT A MASTER MACHINE WHICH GOVERNS EARTH WOULD ONLY HAVE ONE DEFENSE WEAPON AT ITS DISPOSAL??

A SHORT TIME LATER, AN OFFICIAL SCOUT SHIP OF THE WORLD COUNCIL REACHES THE THUNDER GOD...
YOU HAVE COME IN TIME! THE BATTLE IS OVER!

THERE IS YOUR PRISONER! I HOPE YOU WILL BE ABLE TO HOLD HIM THIS TIME!
HE SHALL BE KEPT IN A MAXIMUM SECURITY AREA!

WHEN YOU LEFT YOUR NOTE ON THE TABLE, A SHORT TIME AGO, I WAS PUZZLED AT FIRST! BUT THEN, REMEMBERING WHAT OUR STUDY OF LEGENDS HAS SAID ABOUT YOU IN SCHOOL, I WAS SURE YOU COULD BE TRUSTED!
I AM GLAD YOU HONORED THE REQUEST I WROTE-- ASKING YOU TO LET ME HANDLE ZARRKO IN MY OWN WAY!

THOR, TO YOU THIS IS PROBABLY JUST ANOTHER ONE OF A THOUSAND VICTORIES --BUT TO THOSE OF US LIVING IN THIS CENTURY, YOU HAVE DONE SOMETHING WHICH WE SHALL NEVER FORGET!
EVERY VICTORY OVER THE FORCES OF EVIL IS AN IMPORTANT ONE, MY FRIEND! BUT NOW, I MUST RETURN TO MY OWN CENTURY...

STAND BACK! I HAVE NO TIME MACHINE TO TRAVEL IN, BUT MY HAMMER WILL SERVE ME WELL! BY SWINGING IT AT EXACTLY TWICE THE SPEED OF LIGHT, I CAN MOVE BACKWARD OR FORWARD IN TIME!

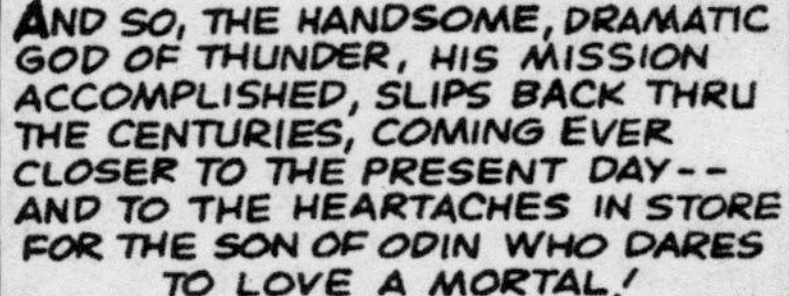

AND SO, THE HANDSOME, DRAMATIC GOD OF THUNDER, HIS MISSION ACCOMPLISHED, SLIPS BACK THRU THE CENTURIES, COMING EVER CLOSER TO THE PRESENT DAY-- AND TO THE HEARTACHES IN STORE FOR THE SON OF ODIN WHO DARES TO LOVE A MORTAL!

13

WHILE, HIGH ABOVE IN FABLED ASGARD...
DID YOU SEE, LOKI! MY FAVORITE SON DID NOT FAIL ME! HE ONLY SEEMED TO BE IN LEAGUE WITH THE MORTAL, UNTIL HE HAD CARRIED OUT HIS OATH!
BAH! EVERYTHING WENT WRONG WITH MY PLAN! THOR IS BACK IN FAVOR WITH ODIN AGAIN!

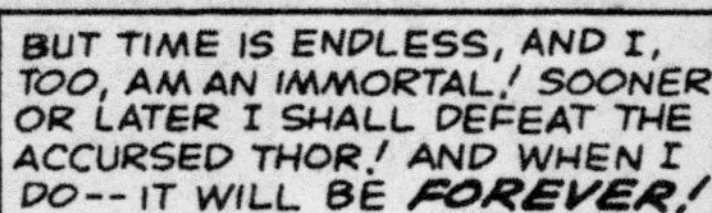

BUT TIME IS ENDLESS, AND I, TOO, AM AN IMMORTAL! SOONER OR LATER I SHALL DEFEAT THE ACCURSED THOR! AND WHEN I DO-- IT WILL BE FOREVER!

THE END

AND SO WE LEAVE ONE OF THE MOST COLORFUL OF ALL SUPER HEROES AS HE HURTLES BACK THRU THE CENTURIES TO ONE OF THE WEIRD-EST ADVENTURES OF ALL TIME! BUT THAT'S A TALE FOR NEXT ISSUE...

Tales of ASGARD
HOME OF THE MIGHTY NORSE GODS!
The BOYHOOD of THOR!
AT THE AGE OF EIGHTEEN!
"DEATH" COMES TO THOR!
AT LAST I'VE FOUND THE THREE FATES! THEY CAN TELL ME IF I SHALL EVER BE AWARDED ODIN'S MAGIC HAMMER!
WRITTEN BY: STAN LEE
ILLUSTRATED BY: JACK KIRBY
INKED BY: PAUL REINMAN
LETTERED BY: ART SIMEK
NOTE: THE EDITORS ARE PLEASED TO ANNOUNCE THAT "TALES OF ASGARD" HAS BECOME ONE OF THE MOST POPULAR SERIES IN COMICDOM, AND HAS WON ITSELF A PERMANENT PLACE AMONG THE MARVEL ROSTER OF FABULOUS FEATURES!
1

SEEING THOR, THE THREE FATES SENSE HIS REQUEST AND ANSWER HIM BEFORE HIS LIPS CAN FRAME THE QUESTION...
YOU CAN WIN ODIN'S ENCHANTED HAMMER-- BUT YOU WILL HAVE TO MEET DEATH FIRST!
THE FATES NEVER LIE! THIS MUST MEAN I'M DOOMED!

BUT I WILL NEVER STOP TRYING! I MUST HAVE THE MAGIC HAMMER!
AND IF I MUST DIE IN ORDER TO GET IT, THEN I SHALL FACE MY DESTINY WITH COURAGE-- AS THE SON OF ODIN SHOULD!

RETURNING TO ODIN'S PALACE, THE YOUNG GODLING ONCE MORE TRIES TO LIFT THE ALL-POWERFUL HAMMER-- BUT STILL CANNOT RAISE IT MORE THAN A FEW INCHES...
THIS IS THE HIGHEST I HAVE EVER RAISED IT-- BUT IT STILL IS NOT ENOUGH!

AT THAT MOMENT, BALDER, THE INNOCENT, STAGGERS INTO THE GREAT CHAMBER, COVERED WITH THE WOUNDS OF BATTLE...
THOR... THE STORM GIANTS-- AMBUSHED ME-- SEIZED MY SISTER-- SIF--
GENTLE SIF-- A PRISONER OF THE STORM GIANTS!! IT IS UNTHINKABLE!

HERE COME THE GUARDS TO ATTEND YOU, VALIANT BALDER! AS FOR ME, I SHALL RESCUE SIF FROM THE ENEMY, OR DIE TRYING! THIS I SWEAR TO YOU, MY FRIEND!!

THEN, FOR THE FIRST TIME IN HIS LIFE, THOR GRASPS THE MIGHTY HAMMER AND HOLDS IT HIGH OVER HIS HEAD!! BUT SO INTENT UPON HIS MISSION IS HE THAT HE DOESN'T REALIZE WHAT HE IS DOING!
LET THE STORM GIANTS **BEWARE!**

LATER, AT THE OUTER APPROACHES TO THE CASTLE WHERE SIF IS IMPRISONED...
BEHOLD! IT IS THE PUNY GODLING! **THIS** TIME HE WILL NOT ELUDE US AGAIN!
TAKE CAUTION, BROTHER! THOUGH HIS SIZE IS SMALL COMPARED TO OURS, HE HAS THE STRENGTH AND VALOR OF **MANY** MEN!

I HAVE NO TIME TO WASTE WITH MERE CASTLE GUARDS! I MUST FIND THE LOVELY SIF WITHIN THOSE WALLS!
THIS WILL ENABLE ME TO REACH THE CASTLE WITHOUT ANY FURTHER INTERFERENCE!

AND NOW TO RESCUE THE SISTER OF MY FRIEND BALDER!!

I KNOW THIS PLACE WELL! IT IS THE CASTLE OF KING RUGGA! THOUGH HE IS NOT A GOD HIMSELF, IT IS HIS DEAREST DESIRE TO BECOME ONE!

RUGGA, I HAVE COME FOR SIF!! FREE HER, OR SUFFER THE CONSEQUENCES!
WAIT, THUNDER GOD! LET ME EXPLAIN! HELA, THE GODDESS OF DEATH, HAS SWORN THAT SHE WOULD MAKE ME AN IMMORTAL IF I DELIVER SIF TO HER! SO-- I DID!

HEARTLESS ONE! YOU WOULD ACCEPT LIFE AT THE EXPENSE OF SOME-ONE ELSE'S DEATH??! TELL ME--WHERE CAN I FIND HELA! SPEAK!
DO NOT HARM ME! I SHALL TELL YOU WHERE TO FIND HER! BUT NO MAN IN HIS RIGHT MIND GOES TO FIND THE GODDESS OF DEATH!

BUT MIGHTY THOR IS NOT JUST A MERE MAN-- AND SO--
YOU KNOW THAT I AM HELA, GODDESS OF DEATH! AT MY TOUCH, EVEN A GOD MUST PERISH!
DO WITH ME WHAT YOU WILL-- BUT FREE THE INNOCENT SIF!

I OFFER MYSELF IN HER PLACE! LET ME FEEL YOUR FATAL TOUCH--I KNOW NO FEAR!! BUT SET SIF FREE!
YOU WOULD SACRIFICE YOURSELF FOR ANOTHER? NEVER HAVE I HEARD SUCH AN OFFER!

I CANNOT DO IT! I CANNOT TAKE A LIFE WHICH IS SO YOUNG, SO BRAVE, SO NOBLE! GO, THOR, SON OF ODIN... AND TAKE SIF WITH YOU! YOU HAVE EARNED HER FREEDOM!

AND SO IT WAS THAT THOR FIRST GAINED FULL POSSESSION OF HIS MAGIC HAMMER-- BY OFFERING TO MAKE THE SUPREME SACRIFICE-- GIVING UP HIS LIFE FOR THAT OF ANOTHER! AND THE IRONY OF THE TALE IS THIS-- NOT UNTIL DAYS LATER DID THE MIGHTY GOD REALIZE HE HAD WON HIS GOAL!
NEXT ISSUE: ANOTHER TALE OF ASGARD, FEATURING THE NOBLEST SUPER HERO OF THEM ALL--THE MIGHTY THOR!!

JOURNEY INTO MYSTERY
IND.
APPROVED BY THE COMICS CODE AUTHORITY
MARVEL COMICS GROUP 12¢
103 APR.
CAN MIGHTY THOR DEFEAT TWO OF THE STRANGEST SUPER-MENACES OF ALL TIME?
IMMORTAL VS. IMMORTAL!! THOR'S MOST TITANIC BATTLE!!
The ENCHANTRESS and The EXECUTIONER!
WE PROMISE THAT YOU WILL NEVER FORGET THE BREATH-TAKING ENCHANTRESS!

THE MIGHTY THOR! MENACED BY "THE ENCHANTRESS AND THE EXECUTIONER!"
SWINGING HIS ENCHANTED HAMMER AT TWICE THE SPEED OF LIGHT, THE MIGHTY THOR LEAVES THE FUTURE, WHERE WE LEFT HIM LAST ISSUE, AND TRAVELS BACK THROUGH TIME!! BACK... BACK... AT MIND-STAGGERING SPEED, UNTIL...
AT LAST!! I HAVE RETURNED TO THE TWENTIETH CENTURY!! I WONDER WHAT NEW PERILS AWAIT ME!!?
WRITTEN BY: STAN LEE MASTER OF FANTASY
ILLUSTRATED BY: JACK KIRBY MASTER OF PICTO-DRAMA
INKED BY CHIC STONE
LETTERED BY S. ROSEN
A Feature-Length Marvel Masterpiece of Compelling Excellence!!

EVEN A MIGHTY THUNDER GOD CAN FEEL THE STRAIN OF THE EXHAUSTING TRIP THROUGH SPACE-TIME! WEARILY, THE POWERFUL FIGURE OF THOR KNEELS WHERE HE LANDED, AS THE ALMOST INDESCRIBABLE POWER SURGES BACK INTO HIS MASSIVE, RIPPLING MUSCLES...
BEEP! BEEP!
HEY! QUIT BLOCKIN' TRAFFIC, MAC!

I'LL HAVE TO ASK YOU TO MOVE ON, THOR! YOU'RE CAUSING A TRAFFIC JAM!
I UNDERSTAND, OFFICER! MY STRENGTH HAS RETURNED! SO, STAY BACK...

... WHILE I SWING MY HAMMER! I'LL BE GONE WITHIN SECONDS!
WOW! IT FEELS LIKE A TORNADO BLOWING UP!

IT'S GOOD TO BE BACK IN MY OWN TIME ... MY OWN AGE!
HOW MY HEART AND SOUL ACHE TO SET EYES ONCE MORE ON JANE FOSTER, THE GIRL I LOVE!

THIS IS THE ROOF OF THE BUILDING WHERE DOCTOR DON BLAKE HAS HIS OFFICE! BEFORE ANY MORTAL KNOWS WHAT HAPPENS, A MIRACULOUS CHANGE WILL NOW TAKE PLACE...

ALL THE GOD OF THUNDER NEED DO IS POUND THE ENCHANTED URU HAMMER BUT ONCE UPON THE SURFACE BELOW, AND THEN...

...I RETURN TO MY MORTAL FORM AS DR. BLAKE...WITH THE SECRET OF MY DUAL IDENTITY STILL INTACT!
2.

WHERE THE MIGHTY THOR MIGHT HAVE BEEN SLIGHTLY WEARY, THE WEAKER, LAME DOCTOR FINDS HIMSELF COMPLETELY EXHAUSTED AFTER HIS GRUELLING ORDEAL! AND SO, SECONDS AFTER HIS RETURN TO HIS OFFICE...
THE POOR DEAR MUST HAVE BEEN ON CALL ALL NIGHT!

GENTLY WAKING THE MAN SHE LOVES, JANE FOSTER LEADS HIM TO HIS OFFICE COUCH...
LIE DOWN HERE, DOCTOR! YOU'LL BE MORE COMFORTABLE, AND I'LL SEE TO IT THAT YOU'RE NOT DISTURBED!
THANK YOU, JANE! I'VE HAD A, EH, RATHER TIRING EVENING!

IF ONLY I COULD DO THIS FOR HIM ALWAYS! BUT, THOUGH I'M SURE HE LOVES ME, FOR SOME STRANGE REASON HE NEVER SUGGESTS MARRIAGE!

SINKING INTO A DEEP SLEEP ALMOST INSTANTLY, THE WEARY DON BLAKE BEGINS TO DREAM OF THE EVENTS THAT HAVE JUST TRANSPIRED... BEGINNING WITH THE REAPPEARANCE OF THE TOMORROW MAN!*
* JOURNEY INTO MYSTERY #102... ED.

IN HIS DREAM, BLAKE REMEMBERS HOW ZARRKO HAD FORCED THOR TO GO TO THE FUTURE WITH HIM, TO AID IN HIS MAD PLAN OF CONQUEST!

ALL THE STRANGE AND STARTLING EVENTS OF THE PAST FEW HOURS SPEED BY, TRANSFORMING HIS DREAM INTO A STARTLING KALEIDOSCOPIC NIGHT-MARE!

BUT, EVEN AS THE UNHAPPY MAN DREAMS HIS TROUBLED DREAM, ANOTHER IS ALSO REMEMBERING BYGONE EVENTS! LET US TURN TO A FAR-OFF KINGDOM, HIDDEN IN THE VASTNESS OF INFINITY! THE LEGENDARY KINGDOM OF... ASGARD, HOME OF THE GODS!!

IT IS HERE THAT WE FIND NOBLE ODIN, LORD OF ASGARD, FATHER OF THOR, DEEP IN THOUGHT IN HIS THRONE ROOM, AS EVIL LOKI, HIS STEP-SON, PLANS NEW DEVILTRY...
ALTHOUGH I AM RULER OF THE GODS, I HAVE FAILED TO DRIVE THE LOVE FOR JANE FOSTER FROM THE HEART OF THOR!
I HAVE A PLAN WHICH MAY SUCCEED, NOBLE ODIN!

PERHAPS IF THOR MEETS ONE WHO IS MORE BEAUTIFUL, MORE DESIRABLE, HE WILL FORGET THE MORTAL GIRL!! AND HERE IN ASGARD IS JUST SUCH A ONE!
OF COURSE! THE ENCHANTRESS!

AND SO...
I SHOULD HAVE THOUGHT OF THIS LONG AGO! THE ENCHANTRESS MAY SUCCEED WHERE BRUTE FORCE HAS FAILED!

MINUTES LATER, LOKI SPEAKS TO ONE WHOSE BEAUTY IS DEEMED TO BE MORE THAN ANY MORTAL MAN CAN RESIST!
ONLY I KNOW THAT THE BEAUTY OF YOUR FORM AND FACE ARE MATCHED ONLY BY THE CRUELTY AND AMBITION OF YOUR SCHEMING HEART! AND SO, I HAVE A MISSION FOR YOU, MY LOVELY ONE!
ODIN COMMANDS YOU TO GO TO EARTH, AND WIN THE HEART OF ONE CALLED DON BLAKE! THUS WILL YOU ALSO GAIN THE LOVE OF THOR AS WELL!

HOW YOU MUST HATE THE MIGHTY THUNDER GOD, LOKI! I KNOW 'TWAS YOU WHO GAVE THIS PLAN TO ODIN! BUT NO MATTER... I SHALL CARRY OUT THIS MISSION... FOR LONG HAVE I WISHED TO CONQUER THE HEART OF HANDSOME THOR!

AH, MY BEAUTIFUL ONE! WHAT A TEAM WE WOULD MAKE, IF ONLY...
DO NOT SAY IT, LOKI! WE ARE TOO MUCH ALIKE! WE COULD NEVER TRUST EACH OTHER!
TRUE, ENCHANTRESS! FOR I KNOW YOU WOULD TURN AGAINST **ME**, TOO, ANY TIME IT SUITED YOUR MERCILESS FANCY!

SOMETIME LATER, A BREATHTAKINGLY GORGEOUS FEMALE APPEARS IN THE SALON OF ONE OF NEW YORK'S MOST EXCLUSIVE FASHION DESIGNERS...
CREATE A WARDROBE FOR ME! **IMMEDIATELY!** THE COST IS OF NO CONCERN!
I..I'LL **DO** IT! RIGHT **NOW!** ALL MY LIFE I HAVE DREAMED OF OUT-FITTING SUCH A PERFECT FEMININE FORM! SHE...SHE'S LIKE A **GODDESS!**

LATER...
"LIKE A GODDESS!" IF ONLY HE KNEW HOW CLOSE TO THE TRUTH HE WAS!
LOOK UP THE ADDRESS OF DR. DON BLAKE AND TAKE ME THERE!
LADY, I'D TAKE **YOU** TO THE **MOON**, IF YOU ASKED ME TO!

FINALLY, AT DON BLAKE'S OFFICE...
DOCTOR, THIS LADY WANTS TO SEE YOU! SHE WOULDN'T GIVE ME HER NAME!
MY NAME IS OF NO IMPORTANCE! YOU MAY **LEAVE** US NOW, NURSE!

PERHAPS IF YOU WERE TO LOOK AT MY FACE...
I..I SEEM TO KNOW THIS FACE! THAT FATAL APPEAL! OF COURSE! IT...IT'S...

STOP THIS PRETENSE! YOU'RE THE ENCHANTRESS! HOW DID YOU GET HERE?? WHY...??
IT'S ALL SO SIMPLE! YOU SEE...OH! MY ANKLE! I TWISTED IT! QUICK, DOCTOR ...HOLD ME!

DOCTOR, YOU HAVE ANOTHER... OHHH!
THIS IS THE MOMENT! I MUST FIND HIS LIPS... NOW!
CAN'T YOU SEE HE DOESN'T WANT TO BE DISTURBED, NURSE??!

SLAM!
JANE! WAIT! IT'S NOT WHAT YOU THINK! JANE!

HANDICAPPED BY HIS LAME LEG, BLAKE CANNOT CATCH THE HEARTBROKEN NURSE, AS THE ENCHANTRESS THINKS...
NEVER HAS ANYONE BROKEN FROM MY EMBRACE BEFORE!
JANE! MY DARLING...LET ME EXPLAIN!

EVEN THOUGH HE IS THE MORTAL DON BLAKE, HE STILL POSSESSES THE STRENGTH OF CHARACTER OF THOR! WELL, I AM STRONG, TOO! I SHALL NOT BE DEFEATED.. BY MAN OR THUNDER GOD!

THEN, AGAIN ASSUMING HER IMMORTAL GUISE, THE ENCHANTRESS RETURNS TO FABLED ASGARD...
SO LONG AS JANE FOSTER LIVES, THOR WILL NEVER SUCCUMB TO MY CHARMS! AND SO...
...THE ONLY SOLUTION IS... JANE FOSTER MUST NOT LIVE!!

HERE IN ASGARD DWELLS ONE WHO CAN REMOVE THE MORTAL GIRL FOR ME! HERE WILL I FIND... THE EXECUTIONER!!
6.

ENCHANTRESS! YOU HAVE COME TO ME AT LAST! DOES THIS MEAN YOU WILL BE MINE ??
NOT YET, MY POWERFUL FRIEND! BUT PERHAPS, IF YOU ACCOMPLISH A SIMPLE TASK FOR ME, I SHALL LOOK UPON YOU WITH GREATER FAVOR!

ANYTHING, BEAUTIFUL ONE! I AM YOURS TO COMMAND! I WOULD BATTLE ALL OF ASGARD TO WIN YOUR HEART!
THAT WILL NOT BE NECESSARY! I WANT YOU TO GO TO EARTH...

STUDY THAT PICTURE! I TOOK IT FROM THE DESK OF DON BLAKE! IT IS HIS NURSE, JANE! I WISH HIM NEVER TO BE ABLE TO SET EYES ON HER AGAIN!
IT SHALL BE DONE WITHOUT DELAY!

AND SO, THIS DEMI-GOD WITH THE HEART OF A SERPENT, THE POWER OF A GOLIATH, AND THE EYES OF A HUNTING FALCON, BEGINS HIS SINISTER MISSION...

MEANWHILE, A DISTRAUGHT DON BLAKE FRANTICALLY TRIES TO LOCATE THE GIRL HE LOVES...
BUT CAN'T YOU TELL ME..??
I'M HER LAND-LADY, NOT HER KEEPER! I DON'T KNOW WHERE SHE WENT!

I'M GETTING NOWHERE! BUT, WHERE A SLENDER, LAME DOCTOR MIGHT FAIL...

...THERE IS ANOTHER WHO MIGHT SUCCEED!

IF JANE FOSTER IS TO BE FOUND, THE MIGHTY THOR SHALL FIND HER!

WITHIN SECONDS, THE FAST-MOVING THUNDER GOD BURSTS INTO THE OFFICE OF THE POLICE COMMISSIONER ...
COMMISSIONER! I'D LIKE YOU TO ISSUE AN ALL-POINTS ALARM!
HOLD IT, THOR!

I JUST RECEIVED A CALL! IT MAY BE RIGHT UP YOUR ALLEY! THERE'S AN EIGHT-FOOT TALL CHARACTER IN STRANGE ARMOR, CARRYING A HUGE BATTLE-AX, CAUSING PANIC AMONG THE PEOPLE!
EIGHT FEET TALL? ARMOR? CARRYING A BATTLE-AX? IT SOUNDS LIKE... THE AWESOME EXECUTIONER!

ORDER YOUR MEN TO STAND BACK! HAVE THE CROWDS DISPERSED! IF IT IS THE ONE I SUSPECT, IT IS BETTER THAT I DEAL WITH HIM ALONE!
VERY WELL, THOR! I HOPE YOU KNOW WHAT YOU'RE DOING! I'LL GIVE YOU FIFTEEN MINUTES BEFORE WE MOVE IN!

MEANWHILE, THE EXECUTIONER STALKS THE CITY, OBLIVIOUS TO THE SURGING CROWDS AROUND HIM, USING HIS SUPER-HUMAN FALCON HUNTING VISION TO SINGLE OUT ONE FACE AMONG MANY MILLIONS...

AND THEN, THE INEVITABLE OCCURS! THE FACE OF JANE FOSTER IS OBSERVED, AS A GARGANTUAN ARM REACHES OUT, AND...
I HAVE FOUND YOU!

LIFE AND DEATH ARE ALMOST MEANINGLESS TO THOSE WHO DWELL IN ASGARD! TO THEM, THERE ARE MANY WAYS TO EXECUTE A VICTIM! IT IS NOT NECESSARY TO TAKE THEIR LIFE FROM THEM...

USING HIS AX TO CUT THROUGH TIME AND SPACE, RATHER THAN FRAIL HUMAN FLESH, THE EXECUTIONER WHIRLS IT ABOUT HIM AT FANTASTIC SPEED, CREATING A BLINDING, SPINNING VORTEX ...

... INTO WHICH JANE FOSTER IS HURLED... UNTIL THE VORTEX CEASES! AND THEN, AS THE SHADOWS LIFT, SHE FINDS HERSELF IN A LAND OF MIST... FAR REMOVED FROM EARTH OR ASGARD... TRAPPED IN LIMBO, THE HALF-WORLD BETWEEN HERE AND THERE!

BUT, NO SOONER DOES JANE FOSTER FADE FROM MORTAL SIGHT, THAN THE MIGHTY THOR APPEARS, RECOGNIZING HIS DANGEROUS FOE AT A GLANCE!
WHAT EVIL THING IS THIS YOU HAVE DONE, MERCILESS ONE?!!

THOR! YOU ARE TOO LATE! JANE FOSTER IS ALREADY TRAPPED IN THE LAND OF LIMBO!
SO THAT WAS YOUR MISSION! WELL, IT SHALL NOT SUCCEED... NOT SO LONG AS THE THUNDER GOD LIVES!!

THEN, SO BE IT, ACCURSED THOR! LET US SEE IF YOU CAN SURVIVE THE DEVASTATING ENERGY OF AN EXPLODING SUN, CREATED BY MY WHIRLING AX!

YOU STILL LIVE?!! BUT YOU ARE STUNNED, STUNNED ENOUGH SO THAT I CAN NOW FINISH THE JOB!!

HAVE YOU FORGOTTEN, EXECUTIONER, HOW QUICKLY THE THUNDER GOD CAN RECOVER HIS UNLIMITED STRENGTH?!
BAH! EVERYTHING HAS ITS LIMIT... EVEN YOUR STRENGTH! I SHALL PROVE THAT HERE AND NOW!

YOUR WORDS, AS EVER, BELIE YOUR POWER! ALWAYS SHALL THOR BE YOUR MASTER!!
OOOF!

DO NOT UNDERESTIMATE ME, THUNDER GOD! REMEMBER, MY BATTLE-AX STILL POSSESSES THE POWER TO SLASH THROUGH SPACE... AS IT NOW DOES TO BRING THE FROST FROM THE EARTH'S ARCTIC REGIONS!
YOU THINK TO CONQUER THOR WITH A COATING OF MERE FROZEN ICE ?!

THIS IS HOW I ANSWER YOUR FUTILE ATTACKS! AND NOW, UNLESS YOU RETURN JANE FOSTER FROM THE LAND OF LIMBO, MY WRATH WILL EXCEED ANY FURY YOU HAVE EVER KNOWN!

YOU HAVEN'T BEATEN ME YET! I CAN STILL CUT THROUGH SUB-SPACE ITSELF, PUTTING EVEN YOU IN ANOTHER UNIVERSE FROM WHICH YOU SHALL NEVER ESCAPE!

NOT WHILE MY URU HAMMER CAN BLAST YOUR BATTLE-AX FROM YOUR HAND BEFORE ANOTHER SPLIT-SECOND CAN FLY BY!

ON YOUR KNEES, EXECUTIONER! DOWN, I SAY! THE BATTLE IS OVER AND WON! THE TIME FOR THE RECKONING IS HERE!

STAY YOUR HAND, MIGHTY THOR! SLAYING ME WILL AVAIL YOU NOTHING! BUT IF YOU WOULD HAVE ME RETURN THE GIRL, I WILL MAKE YOU AN OFFER!
SPEAK THEN, WICKED ONE!

FOR AGES I HAVE LONGED FOR YOUR HAMMER! I DESIRE IT MORE THAN ANYTHING ON EARTH OR ASGARD! IF YOU PLEDGE IT TO ME, I SHALL RETURN THE GIRL! IF NOT, YOU LOSE HER... FOREVER!!

WITHOUT MY HAMMER, I SHALL BECOME DON BLAKE AGAIN, TO REMAIN SO FOR ALL TIME! AND YET, IF THOR MUST BE SACRIFICED SO THAT JANE FOSTER MAY LIVE, I HAVE NO OTHER CHOICE!
10.

RETURN THE GIRL... AND THE HAMMER SHALL BE YOURS! BY THE WORD OF THOR!!
THEN IT IS I WHO HAVE WON!! AFTER ALL THESE AGES! YOU MAY HAVE THE MORTAL FEMALE... SHE IS OF NO CON- SEQUENCE TO ME!

ONCE AGAIN THE EXECUTIONER WHIRLS HIS BATTLE-AX AND, AFTER HE STOPS...
I.. I'M BACK! I FEEL AS THOUGH I'VE AWAKENED FROM A BAD DREAM! THOR... IS IT YOU!?
ALAS, AFTER SIXTY SECONDS HAVE FLOWN BY, IT SHALL BE THOR NO LONGER!
AND NOW, THE HAMMER IS MINE!

WHAT HAS HAPPENED TO ME? WHERE WAS I? THOR, WHY DON'T YOU SPEAK?
I.. I CANNOT!
I FORGOT! NONE BUT THOR CAN LIFT THE URU HAMMER! BUT IT IS MINE, NOW! I MUST LIFT IT! I MUST!!

THIRTY SECONDS HAVE PASSED ALREADY!
I CAN RAISE THE HANDLE... BUT CANNOT LIFT IT OFF THE GROUND! THIS IS MADNESS! WHAT GOOD CAN IT DO ME??

SUDDENLY...
YOU HAVE BETRAYED ME! YOU VOWED TO REMOVE THE GIRL FOREVER!
THAT VOICE! IT IS THE ENCHANTRESS!

MY ARMS! MY LEGS! NO! NO!!
HAVE YOU FORGOTTEN MY POWERS OF SORCERY?? DID YOU THINK I AM CALLED THE ENCHANTRESS FOR NAUGHT!?

AS FOR YOU, THUNDER GOD...
THE ENCHANTRESS IS APPEARING! JANE MUST NOT WITNESS THIS!
YOU MUST FLEE, JANE FOSTER! NOW! YOUR VERY LIFE MAY BE AT STAKE!
YES! YES! I'LL GO!
11.

FIFTY-THREE SECONDS FROM THE TIME THOR SURRENDERED HIS HAMMER, AS JANE FOSTER DASHES OUT OF SIGHT, THE **ENCHANTRESS** TAKES FORM, AND THEN...

YOU STILL **LIVE,** EXECUTIONER ?? THEN I SHALL WORK **ANOTHER** SPELL ON YOU...!

THOR! SAVE ME! ONLY **YOU** CAN DO IT! TAKE BACK YOUR HAMMER... I RELEASE YOU FROM YOUR PLEDGE! BUT... **SAVE ME!!**

IT'S A **MIRACLE!** WITH ONLY SECONDS TO SPARE!

COME NO FURTHER, GOD OF THUNDER! REMEMBER, NOTHING CAN CONQUER THE **ENCHANTRESS!** THE SPELLS I CAN WEAVE ARE WITHOUT LIMIT!

I KNOW THAT ONLY TOO WELL, BEAUTIFUL ONE! BUT **THOR** FEARS NO SPELL... NO FOE THAT LIVES!

THEN NOW IS THE TIME FOR YOU TO **LEARN** THE MEANING OF FEAR! AT A GESTURE FROM ME, I SHALL TRANSFORM YOUR URU HAMMER INTO A DEADLY SERPENT!

YOU SPEAK OF THE HAMMER FORGED BY **ODIN** HIMSELF! NO POWER IN THE UNIVERSE, SAVE **HIS**, CAN AFFECT THIS ENCHANTED WEAPON!

Y-YOU ARE **RIGHT!** I HAVE **FAILED!** BUT IF MY **POWER** CANNOT MOVE YOU, WHAT OF MY **BEAUTY?**
WERE I ONLY HUMAN, I COULD NOT RESIST YOU! BUT MY HEART IS THE HEART OF A GOD ...AND IT KNOWS LOVE FOR ONLY **ONE!**
THE SPELL IS LIFTING... I'M BECOMING **MYSELF** AGAIN!

BUT YOU HAVE BOTH CAUSED **ENOUGH** DAMAGE... ENOUGH CONFUSION ON THIS HAPLESS PLANET! EARTH IS UNDER MY PROTECTION, AND SO I **BANISH** YOU! RETURN TO ASGARD... **RETURN,** I SAY!

THEN, BEFORE ANOTHER MOVE CAN BE MADE, BOTH THE ENCHANTRESS AND THE EXECUTIONER ARE CAUGHT UP IN THE VORTEX CAUSED BY THOR'S WHIRLING HAMMER, AND...

...THE TWO DEMI-GODS ARE HURLED BACK TO ASGARD WHERE THEY RETURN IN DEFEAT, THEIR MISSION A TOTAL FAILURE!

AS FOR THE MIGHTY THUNDER GOD HIMSELF, HE SOON FINDS A SECLUDED CORNER, WHERE HE MAKES SURE HE IS SAFE FROM PRYING EYES...
ONCE AGAIN I SHALL BECOME THE MORTAL DR. DON BLAKE AND RETURN TO MY BELOVED!

HAILING A PASSING TAXI, DON BLAKE OVERTAKES JANE FOSTER BEFORE SHE CAN REACH THEIR OFFICE BUILDING! AND SO...
WELL, IF IT ISN'T DR. BLAKE! HOW IS YOUR NEW BLONDE GIRL-FRIEND, DOCTOR?
JANE, SHE WAS NOTHING TO ME! LET ME EXPLAIN..

NO NEED TO EXPLAIN! YOU'RE NOT MARRIED TO ME! YOU'RE FREE TO KISS ANY GLAMOR GIRL YOU WANT TO! AS FOR ME, I HAPPEN TO BE WAITING FOR THOR!
PERHAPS YOU WON' MIND IF I WAIT WITH YOU, JANE...

FOR, SO LONG AS I AM DON BLAKE, IT'S LIABLE TO BE A LONG, LONG WAIT!
HOW I HOPED HE'D RETURN AND TRY TO MAKE UP WITH ME! BUT I WON'T ADMIT IT TO HIM! PERHAPS I CAN MAKE HIM JEALOUS WITH THOR!

MEANWHILE, A PAIR OF THE WISEST, MOST ALL-SEEING EYES IN THE GALAXY WITNESS THE TABLEAU YOU HAVE JUST SEEN, AS AN INDESCRIBABLE RAGE FILLS THE HEART OF ODIN!
SO! STILL THEY ARE IN LOVE!!

BY ASGARD! MY SON MAY NOT LOVE A MORTAL! THOR MAY NOT DEFY HIS FATHER ODIN! THE TIME FOR WORDS IS PAST! NOW I MUST ACT!!

SEE WHAT HAPPENS WHEN ODIN HIMSELF OPPOSES MIGHTY THOR! DON'T MISS ONE OF THE MOST SENSATIONAL FANTASY DRAMAS OF ALL TIME! OUR NEXT GREAT ISSUE IS A MUST!

THE EN

Tales of ASGARD HOME OF THE MIGHTY NORSE GODS!
"THOR'S MISSION to MIRMIR!"
THIS IS THE TALE OF THOR'S ODYSSEY TO MIRMIR... ONE OF THE STRANGEST MISSIONS EVER UNDERTAKEN BY MORTAL OR GODLING! OUR SAGA BEGINS WITH THOR'S ARRIVAL IN THE HEART OF THE ASGARD MOUNTAINS, WHERE DWELL THE SUBJECTS OF SINDRI, KING OF THE DWARFS...
TAKE ME TO SINDRI, YOUR KING!
HERE, IN THE LAND OF THE DWARFS, ARE FORGED ALL THE ENCHANTED WEAPONS OF ASGARD!
FOLLOW US, MIGHTY THOR! KING SINDRI AWAITS YOU!
MASTERFULLY WRITTEN BY: STAN LEE
MAGNIFICENTLY ILLUSTRATED BY: JACK KIRBY
MAJESTICALLY INKED BY: CHIC STONE
MERITORIOUSLY LETTERED BY: ART SIMEK
X-625
1

I HAVE CREATED THAT WHICH YOU REQUESTED, MIGHTY THOR! A MAGIC VESSEL WHICH YOU MAY CARRY WITH YOU--BUT, AT YOUR COMMAND, IT WILL GROW LARGE ENOUGH TO TAKE YOU TO ANY PLACE IN THE UNIVERSE!
I VOW TO USE IT WELL, KING SINDRI, ON MY MISSION TO MIRMIR!

AND NOW, MY WONDROUS SHIP, BRING ME TO THE LAND OF MIRMIR!
FOR IT IS *THERE* THAT NOBLE ODIN HAS SENT ME, ON MY MOST IMPORTANT MISSION!
SKIPBLADNIR

REACHING THE DANGEROUS DARK SEA WHICH SURROUNDS THE LAND OF MIRMIR, THE ENCHANTED VESSEL STOPS! FOR ONLY BY TRAVELING ON FOOT MAY ONE ENTER THE MYSTERIOUS REALM...
THIS LAND IS FRAUGHT WITH MACABRE DANGERS, BUT I DARE NOT SHIRK MY TASK!

SUDDENLY, THOR HEARS THE BEATING OF GIGANTIC WINGS, AS *SKORD*, THE FLYING DRAGON, SWOOPS DOWN TO ATTACK!
YOUR STRENGTH MAY EQUAL THAT OF MINE, BUT I SHALL DEFEAT YOU WITH MY *WITS!* FIRST, I SWING MY HAMMER...

BUT THOR DOES NOT STRIKE HIS AWESOME WINGED FOE WITH HIS MIGHTY MALLET! INSTEAD, WITH A SKILL WHICH ONLY A GODLING CAN MUSTER, HE SMASHES A BOULDER BELOW HIM, CAUSING ONE HUGE CHUNK TO FLY INTO THE MOUTH OF SKORD!
THERE! BY THE TIME YOU HAVE DISLODGED THAT MAMMOTH ROCK, I SHALL BE SAFELY ON MY WAY!

NOW TO CONTINUE MY JOURNEY! ODIN WARNED ME IT WOULD BE FRAUGHT WITH PERIL, BUT I MUST SUCCEED! WAIT-- I HEAR A VOICE--A THUNDEROUS, INHUMAN BELLOW--!
YOU SHALL GO NO FURTHER, PUNY GODLING --UNTIL YOU HAVE MET THE CHALLENGE OF GULLIN, MIGHTIEST OF THE BOAR GODS!

AND THOUGH YOU HAVE A HAMMER, I HAVE ONE, TOO! AND MINE IS FAR BIGGER!

AND THERE, ON THE OUTER FRINGES OF THE KINGDOM OF MIRMIR, ONE OF THE MOST TITANIC BATTLES OF ALL TIME TAKES PLACE, AS THE MIGHTY THOR AND THE GARGANTUAN GULLIN POUND AT EACH OTHER WITH PLANET-SHATTERING BLOWS-- NEITHER FOE MOVING BACK OR YIELDING A SINGLE INCH!
YOU HAVE COURAGE, THOR-- BUT IT IS USELESS AGAINST MY LARGER, MORE DEADLY HAMMER!
LARGER YOURS MAY BE, GULLIN-- BUT ONLY MY HAMMER WAS FORGED BY ODIN HIMSELF! NOTHING CAN WITHSTAND IT FOR LONG!

AND THE NEXT TREMENDOUS IMPACT DEMON-STRATES THE TRUTH OF MIGHTY THOR'S WORDS, AS GULLIN'S WEAPON IS SHATTERED TO BITS BEFORE HIS VERY EYES!
NOW YOU ARE DEFENSELESS, GULLIN! I ORDER YOU TO FLEE BEFORE MY HAMMER STRIKES AGAIN!

HE HAD NO CHOICE BUT TO ALLOW ME FREE PASSAGE! AND NOW, MY GOAL IS ALMOST AT HAND...

I MUST FOLLOW THIS MAIN STREAM WHICH WILL LEAD ME DIRECTLY TO KING MIRMIR HIMSELF!!

AND FINALLY, AT THE HEAD OF THE STREAM, BEHIND THE MYSTIC FOUNTAIN WHICH FEEDS ALL THE WORLD'S OCEANS, THOR FINDS THE ONE HE SEEKS!
THOR! IT IS YOU! DOES THAT MEAN MY MOMENT IS AT HAND?
YES! NOBLE ODIN HAS SENT YOU THIS MESSAGE --YOU MUST DO WHAT YOU ARE PLEDGED TO DO!

ODIN HAS SENT THIS BRANCH, FROM YGGDRASILL, THE TREE OF LIFE! YOU KNOW WHAT MUST BE DONE!
SO BE IT! MIRMIR WILL BE TRUE TO HIS SACRED TRUST! GIVE ME THE MAGIC BRANCH!

I PLACE THE BRANCH OF LIFE INTO THE ENCHANTED FOUNTAIN, AND SLOWLY STIR THE MYSTIC WATERS! NOW LET THEM SPILL INTO THE WORLD BELOW...

AND, FAR BELOW, IN THE PLACE CALLED MIDGARD, SOME OF THE MAGIC DROPS TRICKLE ONTO A PAIR OF TREES, AN ALDER AND AN ASH, PLANTED AGES BEFORE BY WISE ODIN...

...AND LO, THE TREES SLOWLY CHANGE FORM UNTIL... WHERE STOOD AN ALDER AND AN ASH, WE NOW SEE THE PROUD FIGURES OF ASKE AND EMBLA, DESTINED TO START A NEW RACE, IN THE IMAGE OF THE IMMORTALS OF ASGARD!

THUS, HIS MISSION ACCOMPLISHED, THE MIGHTY THOR RETURNS TO HIS HOME IN ASGARD, TO AWAIT THE NEWER AND MORE STARTLING TASKS WHICH ODIN HAS IN STORE!
THE END

EDITOR'S NOTE: FREELY TRANSLATED, THE TALE YOU HAVE JUST READ IS PART OF THE NORSE LEGENDS WHICH DEAL WITH THE BIRTH OF MAN-KIND AND THE DAYS BEFORE THE BEGINNING OF TIME!

NEXT ISSUE: THE START OF A NEW ASGARD SERIES! BIOGRAPHIES IN DEPTH OF THE DWELLERS OF ASGARD! OUR FIRST SUBJECT WILL BE **HEIMDALL**, GUARDIAN OF THE RAINBOW BRIDGE, AS ONLY STAN AND JACK CAN PRESENT HIM TO YOU!

JOURNEY INTO MYSTERY
WITH
THE MIGHTY THOR
APPROVED BY THE COMICS CODE AUTHORITY
IND.
MARVEL COMICS GROUP 12¢
104 MAY
THE MOST DRAMATIC HERO OF ALL TIME!
THE PRIDE OF THE MARVEL GROUP!
NOTHING YOU HAVE EVER SEEN BEFORE CAN EQUAL THE BREATH-TAKING SPECTACLE OF
"GIANTS WALK THE EARTH!"

THE MIGHTY THOR
"GIANTS WALK THE EARTH!"
THIS IS A TALE SO POWERFUL IN CONCEPT, SO DRAMATIC IN SCOPE, THAT ONLY THE INSPIRED TALENT OF STAN LEE COULD HAVE WRITTEN IT... ONLY THE GIFTED HAND OF JACK KIRBY COULD HAVE ILLUSTRATED IT!!
INKED BY: CHIC STONE
LETTERED BY: S.ROSEN
POSSIBLY ONE OF THE TEN ALL-TIME EPICS YOU WILL NEVER EVER FORGET!!
X-636.

AT THE END OF THE SHIMMERING RAINBOW BRIDGE, AS FAR AS OUR IMAGINATIONS WILL REACH, LIES THE FABLED LAND OF ASGARD, HOME OF THE LEGENDARY NORSE GODS...

AND, SOMEWHERE IN THAT ENCHANTED REALM, TWO DEMI-GODS REPORT TO EVIL LOKI...
THE EXECUTIONER AND THE ENCHANTRESS! YOU BOTH FAILED TO DEFEAT THOR!

MY PLAN WAS PERFECT! AND YET YOU BUNGLED IT! THOR OUTSMARTED THE TWO OF YOU!!*
* JOURNEY INTO MYSTERY #103: EDITOR.

THE MIGHTY THOR IS MORE POWERFUL, AND FAR WISER THAN YOU SUSPECT, LOKI!
BAH! OUT OF MY SIGHT, BOTH OF YOU! I WILL LISTEN TO NO SUCH TALK! NONE ARE WISER, CRAFTIER THAN LOKI!

BUT ONE THERE IS WHO IS THE WISEST, THE MOST POWERFUL OF ALL! BEHOLD ODIN, LORD OF ASGARD, RULER OF THE GODS!
ODIN HAS SUMMONED ME! THIS IS MY CHANCE TO TRY A NEW SCHEME TO DEFEAT THE HATED THOR!

WITHOUT TURNING, THE REGAL ODIN SENSES LOKI'S PRESENCE, AND HE SPEAKS...
LOKI, I AM SORELY TROUBLED! MY FAVORED SON, THOR, THE ONE CLOSEST TO MY HEART, CONTINUES TO DEFY ME! THOUGH I HAVE FORBIDDEN IT, HE HAS GIVEN HIS HEART TO THE MORTAL JANE FOSTER!

THE ONLY EMOTION I CANNOT CONTROL IS... LOVE! I CANNOT DRIVE HIS LONGING FOR THE EARTH WOMAN FROM HIS HEART! YET, I CANNOT PERMIT HIM TO DEFY ME! YOU ARE CLEVER, LOKI! I ASK FOR YOUR ADVICE!
2.

AT LAST! MY CHANCE HAS COME!
YOU HAVE BUT ONE COURSE TO TAKE, NOBLE ODIN! YOU YOURSELF MUST GO TO EARTH AND ASSERT YOUR AUTHORITY IN PERSON!
I? VISIT EARTH AFTER ALL THESE AGES??

BY ASGARD! YOUR SUGGESTION STRIKES MY FANCY! I SHALL DO IT!! AND IN MY ABSENCE, I INVEST YOU WITH A PORTION OF MY POWER, LOKI! YOU SHALL RULE ASGARD TILL MY RETURN!
AND IF MY PLAN SUCCEEDS, THAT MEANS I SHALL BE LORD OF ASGARD FOREVER!!

MEANWHILE, BACK ON EARTH, DR. DON BLAKE GAZES TENDERLY AT HIS LOVELY NURSE, JANE FOSTER...
SHE IS STILL WEARY FROM THAT TERRIBLE ORDEAL WITH THE EXECUTIONER AND THE ENCHANTRESS! HOW MY ARMS YEARN TO HOLD HER... COMFORT HER!

FORGIVE ME, DOCTOR! I DIDN'T MEAN TO DOZE OFF THAT WAY! I-I'M SO EXHAUSTED!
I UNDERSTAND, JANE! I'D LIKE YOU TO TAKE THE REST OF THE DAY OFF! GO HOME AND GET SOME SLEEP, MY DEAR! YOU NEED IT!

BUT WHAT ABOUT YOU?!
I'LL BE ALL RIGHT, JANE! I STILL HAVE SOME WORK TO FINISH UP!

THEN, AFTER JANE HAS LEFT...
I DON'T LIKE IT! IT'S TOO QUIET!... THE AIR IS TOO STILL... SOMETHING OMINOUS IS ABOUT TO HAPPEN! I CAN SENSE IT!

NOW THAT THE EXECUTIONER AND THE ENCHANTRESS HAVE FAILED, WHO KNOWS WHAT LOKI WILL TRY NEXT?! I HAD BETTER SEARCH THE CITY FOR ANY TELL-TALE SIGNS OF DANGER!
3.

DRAMATICALLY, THE SLENDER, LAME DOCTOR GRASPS HIS ROUGH-HEWN WALKING STICK IN HIS TWO HANDS, AND THEN, HE THUMPS IT ONCE UPON THE FLOOR...

AND, A SPLIT-SECOND LATER, THE MORTAL DR. BLAKE IS REPLACED BY THE MIGHTIEST OF IMMORTALS... THOR, GOD OF THUNDER!

WITH THE AID OF MY ENCHANTED HAMMER, I CAN SEARCH THE ENTIRE CITY IN LESS TIME THAN IT WOULD TAKE DON BLAKE TO CROSS A STREET!

I DARE NOT RELAX MY VIGILANCE FOR AN INSTANT... NOT WHILE LOKI STILL LIVES!

MEANTIME, IN A SHABBY SECTION OF TOWN...
WELL, WELL! A RICH-LOOKIN' OLD GEEZER!... AND HE'S ALL ALONE!

SAY, MAC, YOU GOT A MATCH?
MY NAME IS NOT MAC!
NOW AIN'T THAT INTERESTIN'?

HEY!! WHA...??!

FAR MORE INTERESTING THAN YOU SUSPECT, MORTALS!
NONE MAY TOUCH THE PERSON OF... ODIN!!
4.

BUT, LET US RETURN TO ASGARD ONCE AGAIN, WHERE WE FIND...
I'VE DONE IT! I'VE GOTTEN THE POWER I ALWAYS CRAVED!

ODIN'S THRONE!! I WAS BORN TO POSSESS IT!
IT MUST BE MINE FOREVER! I'LL NEVER GIVE THIS UP! NEVER!

I MUST MAKE SURE THAT ODIN CAN NEVER RETURN TO ASGARD! TO DO THAT, I'LL NEED HELP! I NOW HAVE THE POWER TO FREE HIS TWO MOST FEARSOME ENEMIES... THEY SHALL DEFEAT ODIN FOR ME!

FIRST, BY THE POWER WHICH ODIN SO FOOLISHLY GAVE ME, I RELEASE SKAGG, THE STORM GIANT, FROM THE CIRCLE OF FLAME IN WHICH ODIN HAD IMPRISONED HIM!

NEXT, I BREAK THE SPELL WHICH HAS KEPT SURTUR, THE FIRE DEMON, IMPRISONED WITHIN THE DEPTHS OF THE EARTH FOR ALL THESE CENTURIES!

BUT LOYAL HEIMDALL, GUARDIAN OF THE RAINBOW BRIDGE, WHOSE EARS ARE THE SHARPEST IN THE UNIVERSE, HEARS LOKI'S INCANTATIONS, AND HE SENDS FOR BALDER THE BRAVE...
I HAVE SWORN NEVER TO LEAVE MY POST... BUT BALDER SHALL ALERT NOBLE ODIN FOR ME!

YOU MUST FLY TO EARTH, BALDER, AND WARN ODIN OF THE TERRIBLE THREAT WHICH AWAITS HIM!
I SHALL NOT FAIL, HEIMDALL!

A JOURNEY SUCH AS THIS IS BUT THE WORK OF MINUTES WHILE I RIDE ODIN'S OWN WINGED BATTLE STATION!

I HAVE RENDERED MYSELF INVISIBLE TO ALL BUT IMMORTAL EYES! ODIN OR THOR SHALL SIGHT ME WITHIN SECONDS!

SUDDENLY, LIKE A FLASHING, FLYING STREAK, THE THUNDER GOD'S ENCHANTED HAMMER WHIZZES THROUGH THE SKY, CATCHING THE HARNESS OF BALDER'S STEED!
THOR! MY QUEST IS FULFILLED!

WHAT BRINGS YOU TO THE PLANET OF MORTALS, LOYAL BALDER?
THOR, THERE IS NO TIME TO LOSE! LORD ODIN IS HERE ON EARTH... IN THE GRAVEST DANGER!

IN ODIN'S ABSENCE, EVIL LOKI HAS FREED SURTUR AND SKAGG! YOU KNOW HOW POWERFUL THEY ARE!!
I PRAY YOUR WARNING HAS COME IN TIME!

IF MY FATHER IS ON EARTH, THERE IS ONLY ONE HE WOULD SEEK... DR. DON BLAKE!
FOLLOW ME, BALDER!
6.

MEANWHILE, AT DR. BLAKE'S OFFICE...
SORRY, SIR! THERE ARE OTHERS AHEAD OF YOU!
SILENCE, FOOLISH WOMAN!

NOW LOOK... LOOK INTO MY EYES!
Y-YOU MAY ENTER DR. BLAKE'S INNER OFFICE AT ONCE, SIR.!

BUT, NO SOONER DOES REGAL ODIN WALK INSIDE, THEN...
MY FATHER!
THOR! IT IS YOU!

NOBLEST OF LORDS, FORGIVE ME FOR SPEAKING FIRST, BUT GRAVE DANGER THREATENS! SURTUR AND SKAGG ARE ABOUT TO ATTACK THE EARTH!! BALDER HAS JUST BROUGHT THE NEWS FROM ASGARD!

THE HUMAN RACE MUST NOT WITNESS WHAT IS ABOUT TO OCCUR!! STAND BACK, MY SON! I HAVE AN AWESOME FEAT TO PERFORM!

THEN, AT A GESTURE FROM THE MONARCH OF ASGARD, THE VERY FABRIC OF TIME ITSELF STANDS STILL, AS THE ENTIRE HUMAN RACE, UNDER AN IRRESISTIBLE SPELL, IS INSTANTLY TRANSPORTED TO A DIMENSION BEYOND THE KEN OF THE HUMAN MIND!
FOR SO LONG AS MY SPELL LASTS, THEY SHALL KNOW NOTHING OF WHAT IS HAPPENING!
7.

THEN, NOT FAR FROM WHERE THE LEGENDARY FIGURES STAND, A GIGANTIC FORM APPEARS, BRANDISHING HIS TEN-TON WAR CLUB... THE WAR CLUB WHICH CAN SPLIT A MOUNTAIN WITH BUT ONE STROKE!! THUS DOES SKAGG, THE STORM GIANT ISSUE HIS CHALLENGE!
LO! THESE MANY AGES HAVE I WAITED TO STRIKE... TO SMASH AT MY ACCURSED ENEMIES, THE GODS OF ASGARD!! AND NOW... THE TIME HAS COME!

STAND BACK!! LET ME FLY TO HURL THOSE WORDS BACK INTO HIS COWARDLY THROAT!!
NO, MY SON! SEE HOW EAGERLY BRAVE BALDER CHARGES FORTH! LET HIS SWORD BE THE FIRST TO STRIKE!
DEFEND YOURSELF, SKAGG!! I FIGHT FOR THE HONOR OF ASGARD.. IN THE NAME OF LORD ODIN!!

PUNY ONE!! I SHALL SMASH YOU AS I WOULD SMASH A FLEA!!
NOTHING CAN WITHSTAND THE FORCE OF MY BATTERING WAR CLUB!

YOU ARE WRONG, VILLAINOUS SKAGG! ONE THING CAN DESTROY YOUR LUMBERING WEAPON!! A BLADE OF ENCHANTED STEEL... FORGED BY THE ETERNAL FLAMES OF ASGARD!

EVEN SO I SHALL DEFEAT YOU!! SEE HOW I FUNNEL THE WATERS OF THE OCEAN ITSELF THROUGH MY SHATTERED CLUB, CREATING A GIANT WATER SPOUT WHICH WILL TOSS YOU ASIDE LIKE THE TINY INSECT YOU ARE!

COURAGE, BALDER! YOU HAVE DONE YOUR SHARE!! BUT A STRONGER ARM THAN YOURS IS NEEDED TO FINISH THE JOB!! IT IS A TASK FOR THOR!!
8

BUT, BEFORE THE RAMPAGING THUNDER GOD CAN STRIKE WITH HIS IRRESISTIBLE HAMMER, A HUGE FIREBOLT HURTLES THROUGH THE SKY, FLASHING TOWARDS THE ENCHANTED MALLET...

EVEN YOUR HAMMER IS NO MATCH FOR ME, HATED ONE!
SURTUR, THE FIRE DEMON!! HE HAS JOLTED MY HAMMER, UN-BALANCING ME!

THEN, BEFORE MIGHTY THOR CAN REGAIN HIS BALANCE.....
I HAVE SEEN ENOUGH!! NO LONGER CAN I REMAIN MERELY A WITNESS...

...IT IS TIME FOR ODIN HIMSELF TO ENTER THE BATTLE!! FIRST, I COMMAND THE BED OF THE SEA TO SOFTEN BENEATH THE FEET OF SKAGG!!

SURTUR! I'M SINKING!! HELP ME!!
I MUST! I CANNOT BATTLE SUCH FOES ALONE!

HURRY!! I SINK DEEPER AND DEEPER!! FREE ME, SO THAT I CAN DESTROY THE POWER OF ODIN FOR ALL TIME!
MY FATHER MUST HAVE ENTERED THE FRAY! I MUST RETURN TO SHORE...TO FIGHT SHOULDER TO SHOULDER WITH HIM!

HOW GOES THE BATTLE, BRAVE BALDER?
IT HAS BUT BEGUN! BUT WE MUST TRIUMPH! FOR IF WE LOSE.. WE LOSE ALL!
9.

USING THE POWER OF HIS INTENSE FLAME, SURTUR FUSES THE EARTH AROUND SKAGG'S FEET, HARDENING IT ENOUGH TO SUPPORT THE TOWERING GIANT!!.
THERE!! I HAVE SAVED YOU! NOW SEE THAT YOU ARE WORTHY OF MY EFFORTS!!

YOU SHALL LEARN HOW WORTHY SKAGG CAN BE! NOTHING SHALL ESCAPE MY VENGEANCE!
BAH! BATTLES ARE NOT WON WITH WORDS OF THUNDER!

STAND BEHIND ME! I SHALL SHOW YOU HOW TO DEFEAT THE GODS OF ASGARD! I SHALL DESTROY THAT WHICH ODIN PRIZES MOST... EARTH ITSELF!!

THEY HAD GOOD REASON TO IMPRISON ME FOR ALL THESE AGES... FOR MY POWER IS THE POWER OF A THOUSAND BLAZING SUNS!! SEE HOW I SPIN AROUND, CREATING A CIRCLE OF PURE FLAMING ENERGY!!

ENERGY ENOUGH TO DESTROY AN ENTIRE GALAXY!!

NOW, ALL I NEED DO IS REACH THE ARCTIC CIRCLE, MELTING THE ICE FLOWS AT WILL, TILL THE WATERS RUN SOUTHWARD, FLOODING THE ENTIRE GLOBE AS THEY DID ONCE BEFORE, AT THE DAWN OF TIME!

GO THEN, SURTUR!! I SHALL REMAIN HERE, AND CAUSE SUCH DAMAGE THAT THEY WILL NOT DARE TO PURSUE YOU!!

TRUE TO HIS WORD, SKAGG, THE STORM GIANT, CREATES A STORM OF EVER-INCREASING INTENSITY, A STORM WHICH BEGINS TO DEMOLISH THE OLD DESERTED PIERS WHICH STAND AT ITS PERIPHERY...

IT IS I WHO AM GOD OF THUNDER, YET, SO SURE IS SKAGG OF HIS OWN POWER, THAT HE DARES DEFY US WITH MY OWN WEAPON!! NOW, BY YOUR LEAVE, FATHER, I SHALL TEACH HIM THE FOLLY OF CHALLENGING THOR!
PERMISSION GRANTED! AND NOW, I SHALL MOUNT MY BATTLE STALLION!

TO MY SIDE, BRAVE BALDER! THERE IS NOT MUCH TIME LEFT TO US!
SKAGG INCREASES THE FORCE OF HIS STORM... BUT HE KNOWS IT IS USELESS! FOR NOW... THOR SHALL STRIKE BACK!

LET THE FURY OF A THOUSAND LIGHTNING BOLTS BURST FORTH FROM MY ENCHANTED HAMMER!!

THOUGH THE POWER OF THOR'S ONSLAUGHT WOULD HAVE TOPPLED AN ARMY... THE GIGANTIC SKAGG IS ABLE TO SURVIVE IT! BUT, IT CAUSES HIM TO TURN FROM THE STORM HE HAD CREATED... IT WEAKENS AND STUNS HIM!!
WHAAM!

MEANWHILE, WISE ODIN RIDES OVER THE BESIEGED LAND ON HIS WINGED STALLION...
THERE! I HAVE PLACED A PROTECTIVE SHIELD OVER THE CITY! IT IS SAFE FROM THE FURY OF SKAGG!

THOR!! BALDER!! BEHOLD YOUR LIEGE!!

I'LL ATTACK SKAGG HEAD ON... DRAINING HIS EVIL POWER FROM HIM THROUGH THE MAGIC OF MY SHINING SWORD!

BUT, ODIN DOES NOT SUSPECT THAT HE IS OPPOSING TWO IMMORTAL FOES! FOR, WATCHING UNSEEN FROM ASGARD, THE CRAFTY LOKI KEEPS REPLENISHING THE STRENGTH OF SKAGG WHICH ODIN DRAINS AWAY!

FINALLY HOWEVER, EVEN LOKI'S POWER WANES, AS HE SEES THE STORM GIANT WEAKEN AND CRUMBLE BEFORE THE SUPREME POWER OF THE FATHER OF THOR!

PANIC BEGINS TO WELL UP WITHIN LOKI'S BREAST AS HE REALIZES PART OF HIS PLAN HAS FAILED!! HIS ONLY REMAINING HOPE IS... SURTUR!!

AS FOR ODIN...
MY FATHER! YOU HAVE EXHAUSTED YOURSELF! LET ME BE YOUR SUPPORT! LET MY STRENGH BE YOURS!
WORRY NOT ABOUT ME! FIND SURTUR... HE TOO MUST BE STOPPED ...BEFORE IT IS TOO LATE!

THOR! HE HEADED FOR THE FROZEN NORTH, MUTTERING THAT HE WOULD MELT THE ICE CAPS! IF HE SUCCEEDS, EARTH IS DOOMED!!
HE SHALL NOT SUCCEED! THOUGH WE CANNOT REACH HIM IN TIME, THERE ARE OTHER WAYS TO STOP HIM!!

SURTUR IS AN OLDER IMMORTAL THAN I, SO MY HAMMER MIGHT NOT PREVAIL AGAINST HIS POWER! BUT... THE SWORD OF ODIN... IT IS OLDER THAN ALL... AND ONLY ODIN'S SON CAN WIELD IT!

AT THAT MOMENT, MANY MILES TO THE NORTH, A GIGANTIC FIREBOLT IS ABOUT TO STRIKE THE ICECAPS, MELTING THEM...

...BUT IT IS DESTINED TO NEVER REACH ITS OBJECTIVE!! FOR SUDDENLY, IT IS DRAWN UP, FAR INTO OUTER SPACE, BY A POWER IT IS HELPLESS TO RESIST!
12

FURTHER AND FURTHER IT SPEEDS, HEADING TOWARDS A TINY ASTEROID IN ANOTHER GALAXY! A VERY SPECIAL ASTEROID!! AN ASTEROID WHICH IS COMPOSED OF MAGNETIC PARTICLES!

AND, THE INSTANT SURTUR COMES WITHIN RANGE, THE ATTRACTION OF THE ASTEROID HOLDS HIM... TRAPS HIM IN A GRIP WHICH GROWS EVER STRONGER...A MAGNETIC PULL WHICH WILL LAST FOR AGES TO COME!

AND BACK IN OUR OWN PRECIOUS GALAXY...
NOBLE ODIN, WE HAVE DISPATCHED EVIL SKAGG! HE IS AGAIN TRAPPED WITHIN THE ETERNAL CIRCLE OF FLAME!
AND SURTUR, IMPRISONED IN ANOTHER GALAXY, SHALL MENACE US NO MORE!

YOU HAVE DONE WELL, MY WARRIORS! AND NOW YOU SHALL RETURN WITH ME TO ASGARD! YOU HAVE BOTH EARNED YOUR REST! I SHALL SEND OTHERS TO WATCH OVER EARTH!
MY SON, WHY DO YOU LAG BEHIND?
I CANNOT GO!!

EARTH IS MY HOME, FATHER! AND THE HOME OF THE ONE I LOVE! I SHALL NEVER LEAVE! HERE SHALL I REMAIN...ALWAYS!
STILL YOU ARE OBDURATE! THEN WE HAVE SETTLED NOTHING! BUT THIS IS NOT THE TIME TO SPEAK OF SUCH THINGS! FAREWELL, MY SON!

RETURNING TO ASGARD, ODIN MAKES A SINGLE GESTURE, AND SUDDENLY ALL IS AS IT WAS BEFORE HE HAD COME TO EARTH...
OF THE BILLIONS OF MORTALS, ONLY I KNOW WHAT TRANSPIRED HERE WHILE TIME STOOD STILL!!

HELLO, JANE! SORRY TO BE REPORTING SO LATE...
NO NEED FOR YOU TO HAVE RUSHED, DOCTOR! ACTUALLY, IT'S BEEN A VERY QUIET DAY SO FAR!
13.

AND, IN THE GREAT HALL OF ASGARD...

HEIMDALL HAS TOLD ME OF YOUR TREACHERY, LOKI! YOU WILL SERVE THE TROLLS UNTIL I SET YOU FREE! NOW GO, UNFAITHFUL ONE!

IN ALL THE UNIVERSE, THERE IS NONE BRAVER, NONE WORTHIER THAN THOR! YET, I FEAR FOR HIM... FOR THE FUTURE IS FRAUGHT WITH DANGER, AND HIS HEART IS WEAKENED BY LOVE!

NEXT ISSUE: THE MIGHTY THOR BATTLES A NEW EARTHLY MENACE... IN A TALE OF STARTLING DRAMA AND STRANGE SUSPENSE! TILL THEN, MAY THE EYES OF ASGARD BE EVER ON YOU!

The End.

TALES of ASGARD
HOME OF THE MIGHTY NORSE GODS
BEGINNING: A NEW DIMENSION IN COMICS!
BIOGRAPHIES IN DEPTH OF ASGARD'S HEROES!
HEIMDALL
GUARDIAN of the MYSTIC RAINBOW BRIDGE!
A TALE TOLD IN SPLENDOR BY: STAN LEE
A DRAMA DRAWN IN GLORY BY: JACK KIRBY
ADDITIONAL PROOF, IF ANY BE NEEDED, THAT THE MARVEL AGE OF COMICS IS HERE!
INKED BY: DON HECK
LETTERING: ART SIMEK
1

AGES AGO THE RAINBOW BRIDGE SPANNED THE VAST DISTANCE FROM EARTH TO ASGARD WITH NONE TO GUARD IT! BUT THEN, ONE DAY, A VALIANT WARRIOR WAS SUMMONED TO THE THRONE ROOM OF MIGHTY ODIN...

YOU SENT FOR ME, MY LORD?

YES, LOYAL HEIMDALL! ASGARD HAS NEED OF YOUR COURAGE, YOUR FIDELITY, AND YOUR SKILL! HEAR THEN THE WORDS OF ODIN...

TOO LONG HAS THE RAINBOW BRIDGE REMAINED UNGUARDED! TOO MANY TIMES HAVE OUR ENEMIES ATTACKED ASGARD BY CROSSING ITS SHIMMERING SPAN! THE BRIDGE NEEDS A ***SENTRY!***

LOOK, YOU! MARK HOW EVEN ***NOW*** A LABOR FORCE OF TROLLS WORKS TO REPAIR THE DAMAGE DONE TO THE WALLS OF ASGARD WHEN THE STORM GIANTS LAST CROSSED THE BRIDGE!

ONLY ***THOR'S*** MIGHTY HAMMER AND THE VALOR OF MY WARRIORS, SUCH AS ***YOU***, SAVED ASGARD FROM BEING OVERRUN BY THE ENEMY!

AND ***THAT*** IS WHY I HAVE DECIDED TO APPOINT A ***GUARDIAN*** OF THE RAINBOW BRIDGE! I HAVE SELECTED ***THREE*** WARRIORS--AND NOW I SHALL CHOOSE ***ONE*** OF YOU!

AND SO...
I WANT EACH OF YOU TO TELL ME WHY YOU THINK YOU SHOULD BE CHOSEN! AGNAR THE FIERCE, YOU SPEAK FIRST!
MY LUNGS ARE THE STRONGEST, LORD ODIN! NONE HAS A CHEST AS MIGHTY AS MINE!
BAH! OF WHAT IMPORTANCE IS THAT?!!
SILENCE, GOTRON!! YOUR TURN WILL COME NEXT!
NONE BUT I HAVE THE POWER TO BLOW A WARNING OF ATTACK ON THE ENCHANTED DRAGON HORN OF ASGARD--LIKE THIS!!
HE SPEAKS THE TRUTH! FOR AGES THE HORN HAS BEEN SILENT--YET NOW, ITS ROAR REACHES TO THE VERY END OF INFINITY!!
AND WHAT OF YOU, GOTRON, THE AGILE??
MY DEEDS SPEAK FOR THEMSELVES, SIRE! SURELY YOU REMEMBER THAT I WAS NIMBLE ENOUGH TO DEFEAT SEVEN STORM GIANTS WHEN THEY ATTACKED ASGARD ONLY LAST YEAR!
THUS HAVE AGNAR AND GOTRON SPOKEN! AND NOW, HEIMDALL THE FAITHFUL MUST BE HEARD!
MY LORD ODIN, MY STRENGTH IS A MATCH FOR ANY-- BUT I HAVE OTHER ABILITIES --- I CAN SENSE APPROACHING DANGER BEFORE ANY OTHER! I SHALL PROVE IT IN YOUR GARDEN...
THEN, STEPPING OUT INTO THE LUSH GARDEN OF THE LORD OF ASGARD, HEIMDALL PUTS HIS EAR TO THE SOFT GRASS, AND SAYS...
EVEN AT THIS MOMENT, I CAN HEAR THE TINIEST PLANT GROWING IN THE HEART OF THE HIDDEN HILLS!
YOU LIE! YOU SHALL FEEL THE BITE OF AGNAR'S SWORD FOR THIS!!
AND OF GOTRON'S SPEAR!!
3

STAND FAST!! ONLY ODIN COMMANDS HERE! WE SHALL SEE IF HEIMDALL LIES! GO, MY GARDENER... FLEE TO THE EXACT PLACE HEIMDALL MENTIONED AND SEE IF THERE GROWS A TINY PLANT!!
I OBEY, MY LORD! BUT IT CANNOT BE! NOTHING CAN GROW IN THE HIDDEN HILLS SINCE ONCE A DRAGON BREATHED HIS FIERY BREATH UPON THAT LAND!
EVEN NOW I HEAR THE TINY BUDS REACHING FOR THE SURFACE --EAGER TO FIND THE SUN!

TENSE MOMENTS LATER...
BY THE GODS!! HEIMDALL SPOKE THE TRUTH! AT THE VERY SPOT HE DESCRIBED-- A NEW PLANT--WHICH HAS JUST THIS SECOND BLOSSOMED INTO LIFE!!

THEN, WHEN THE ALMOST SPEECHLESS GARDENER RETURNS...
YOUR EARS INDEED ARE WONDROUS SHARP, LOYAL HEIMDALL! BUT I HAVE HEARD THAT YOU HAVE STILL OTHER POWERS!
THAT IS SO, MY LORD ODIN! NOTHING CAN ESCAPE THE SCANNING OF MY EYES!

I CAN LOOK ACROSS TIME, AS WELL AS SPACE!! EVEN NOW I SEE THE FAR-OFF APPROACH OF AN INVADING PARTY, MARCHING TOWARDS THE RAINBOW BRIDGE! THEY ARE A SAVAGE BAND OF STORM GIANTS, STILL A FULL TWO DAYS AWAY!

NOT DARING TO IGNORE HEIMDALL'S DRAMATIC WARNING, ODIN IMMEDIATELY DISPATCHES A HEAVILY-ARMED WAR PARTY TO MEET THE INVADERS BEFORE THEY CAN REACH THE VITAL RAINBOW BRIDGE!
CAN HEIMDALL REALLY HAVE SEEN AN ENEMY TWO DAYS AWAY??
THE WORDS OF LOYAL HEIMDALL ARE ALWAYS CLOAKED IN TRUTH!

AND, BEFORE THE WEEK HAS PASSED, THE WAR PARTY RETURNS--WITH A VALUABLE PRISONER --THE KING OF THE STORM GIANTS!
AGAIN YOUR WORDS HAVE BORNE THE RING OF TRUTH, HEIMDALL! YOUR WARNING HAS SAVED ASGARD FROM A DANGEROUS ATTACK!

BEND THY KNEE, WARRIOR WITH EYES SHARPER THAN THE HAWK-- WITH EARS KEENER THAN THE ANTELOPE! NOW RISE, LOYAL HEIMDALL--GUARDIAN OF THE RAINBOW BRIDGE--FOREVER!

AND THUS STANDS HEIMDALL, THE ALL-SEEING, THE ALL-HEARING! HEIMDALL, THE EVER-VIGILANT! HEIMDALL, ETERNAL PROTECTOR OF THE FABLED LAND MEN CALL... ASGARD!
NEXT ISSUE-- THE NEVER-BEFORE-REVEALED ACCOUNT OF THE TIME HEIMDALL FAILED! AN EPIC SAGA YOU WON'T WANT TO MISS!

The END

JOURNEY INTO MYSTERY
WITH
THE MIGHTY
THOR
APPROVED BY THE COMICS CODE AUTHORITY
IND.
MARVEL COMICS GROUP 12¢
105
JUNE
A NEW MARVEL SUPER-SPECTACULAR!
BACK ON THE RAMPAGE AGAIN!!
"THE COBRA and MR. HYDE!"
DON'T MISS THE LATEST "TALE OF ASGARD"
"WHEN HEIMDALL FAILED!"

THE MIGHTY THOR!
"THE COBRA and MR. HYDE!"
OUR SCENE IS THE HEADQUARTERS OF THE AVENGERS, WHERE WE FIND EARTH'S MIGHTIEST TEAM OF SUPER HEROES AT THE CONCLUSION OF ONE OF THEIR REGULAR MEETINGS...
WRITTEN BY HAPPY STAN LEE
DRAWN BY HEALTHY JACK KIRBY
INKED BY HUSKY CHIC STONE
LETTERED BY HASTY ART SIMEK
WE HAVE NO FURTHER BUSINESS TO DISCUSS, IRON MAN!
MIGHT AS WELL ADJOURN, THOR, AND RETURN TO OUR NORMAL LIVES!
IT'S BEEN A QUIET FEW DAYS--TOO QUIET FOR CAPTAIN AMERICA!
LET'S GO, GIANT-MAN! YOUR LITTLE WASP IS GETTING HUNGRY!
OKAY, HONEY! THERE'S NOTHING MORE FOR US TO DO HERE!
A DOUBLE-LENGTH MODERN MARVEL MASTERPIECE!
X-681
1

N A WAY YOU ARE FORTUNATE, GIANT-AN! NOT MANY OF S CAN CARRY THE IRL WE LOVE ABOUT WITH US AS YOU DO!
DON'T YOU HAVE A GIRL-FRIEND, THOR??
HUSH, WASP! YOU KNOW OUR CODE! NONE OF US IS TO PRY INTO THE PERSONAL LIFE OF ANY OF THE OTHERS!

YOU'RE JUST AN OL' SPOIL SPORT, BIG MAN! I'M DYING TO LEARN MORE ABOUT ALL OF OUR GLAMOROUS PARTNERS!
I'LL BET YOU ARE, HONEY!
IF THE MEETING'S OVER, CAP AND I WILL REMAIN! HE PROMISED TO SHOW ME SOME NEW JUDO HOLDS!
LET US RETURN AGAIN, ONE WEEK FROM TODAY!
BUT THEY'LL NEVER REPLACE THAT IRON SUIT, PAL!

START FLYING, WASP! I'LL SHRINK DOWN TO ANT SIZE AND JOIN YOU!
OKAY, BLUE EYES! BUT HOW ABOUT GETTING ME A FLYING ANT, TOO! MY WINGS GET TIRED!

I HAD HIM WAITING OUTSIDE THE WINDOW, JAN! I WANTED TO SURPRISE YOU!
SOME SURPRISE! OTHER GIRLS GET FLOWERS, CANDY, JEWELRY! I GET A FLYING ANT!

NOW THAT MY TWO INSECT-SIZED PARTNERS ARE SAFELY AWAY, I TOO, SHALL TAKE TO THE AIR-- BUT IN A MATTER MORE BEFITTING THOR, GOD OF THUNDER!!

LIKE A MIGHTY HUMAN METEOR, THE SON OF ODIN STREAKS THRU THE SKY...

BUT SECONDS LATER...
I HAVE A STRANGE FEELING--AS THOUGH DANGER IS NEAR!!

THEN SUDDENLY, ATOP A NEARBY STEEPLE, THE THUNDER GOD SEES...
THE COBRA!! HE'S AT LARGE AGAIN!* WHAT NEW DEVILTRY IS HE PLANNING??
THOR!! I MUSTN'T LET HIM GET ME!!
*THE COBRA FIRST APPEARED IN JOURNEY INTO MYSTERY #98-EDITOR.

I MISSED! HE IS FASTER-- MORE SLIPPERY THAN EVER!
THOR WILL GET ME SOONER OR LATER--UNLESS I CAN STOP HIM WITH MY "SERPENT'S STING"!

SUDDENLY, FROM A SPECIALLY-DESIGNED WRIST DEVICE, THE COBRA EJECTS THREE FAST-MOVING DELAYED-ACTION VIALS!

AS THEY NEAR THE THUNDER GOD AT BLINDING SPEED, THEIR MINIATURIZED FIRST STAGES DROP OFF, AND...

...THREE DAZZLING LIGHTS OF GREAT INTENSITY FLASH IN FRONT OF MIGHTY THOR, BLINDING HIM FOR AN INSTANT...
THAT GLARE-- CAN'T SEE--

THEN, AS HIS SIGHT RETURNS, THE VIALS' SECONDARY EFFECT TAKES PLACE, AS THE THUNDER GOD FEELS HIS SENSES SPIN...

NOW, WHILE HE IS STILL DAZED, I'LL YANK HIM OFF BALANCE WITH MY "COBRA CABLE"!

AND BEFORE THE IMMORTAL AVENGER CAN MAKE ANOTHER MOVE...
SOMETHING CAUGHT MY LEG-- TUGGED ME OFF THE LEDGE!! I'M FALLING!!

BUT MAKING THOR LOSE HIS BALANCE, AND DEFEATING HIM, ARE TWO DIFFERENT THINGS!!
ALL I NEED DO WHILE FALLING IS SWING MY ENCHANTED HAMMER...

...AND THEN RETURN TO THE BATTLE!! BUT WHERE DID THE COBRA GO?? HE IS NOWHERE IN SIGHT!!

HE MIGHT HAVE SLIPPED INTO ANY ONE OF A HUNDRED WINDOWS! MY ONLY COURSE IS TO WAIT UNTIL HE APPEARS AGAIN! HE CAN'T STAY HIDDEN FOREVER!

NOW LET US LEAVE THE DEPARTING THUNDER GOD FOR A BRIEF TIME, AND FOLLOW THE SINISTER COBRA AS HE STEALS INTO A NEARBY APARTMENT...
I HEAR SOMEONE IN THE NEXT ROOM--BUT WHOEVER HE IS, HE'LL BE NO MATCH FOR ME!!

A SCIENTIST! WHAT AN EASY VICTIM HE WILL BE FOR THE POWERFUL COBRA!
I HOPE HE IS A SUCCESSFUL SCIENTIST--WITH A LOT OF MONEY IN HIS APARTMENT FOR ME TO SEIZE!!

BUT HIS INTENDED VICTIM'S EARS ARE FAR KEENER THAN THE COBRA SUSPECTS...
SOMEONE BEHIND ME! IT CAN ONLY BE AN ENEMY!

THEN, BEFORE THE SERPENTINE FIGURE REALIZES WHAT IS HAPPENING, THE MAN IN THE LAB RAISES HIS GLASS BEAKER TO HIS LIPS, AND DRINKS DEEP!!

AHHHH! I FEEL THE MIRACULOUS EFFECTS OF MY POTION BEGINNING TO AFFECT ME ALREADY!! NO LONGER WILL I REMAIN THE UNKNOWN AND UNIMPORTANT DR. CALVIN ZABO...

NO!! THANKS TO MY SECRET POTION, I'M NOW ONCE AGAIN MR. HYDE--WITH THE STRENGTH OF A DOZEN MEN AND THE CUNNING TO MATCH MY POWER!

HIS STARTLING TRANSFORMATION COMPLETED, THE SNARLING MR. HYDE TURNS TO FACE A MYSTIFIED COBRA!!
YOU CHANGED INTO ANOTHER MAN--RIGHT BEFORE MY EYES!! BUT HOW DID YOU DO IT--AND WHO DID YOU BECOME!??
CALL ME MR. HYDE!! IT'S THE NAME THE WORLD WILL KNOW ME BY BEFORE VERY LONG!

AND NOW I'LL SHOW YOU WHAT HAPPENS TO ANY COSTUMED FOOLS WHO DARE BREAK INTO THE LAIR OF MR. HYDE!!

THE COBRA! I'VE HEARD THAT NAME! YOU TOO WERE DEFEATED BY THOR!
YOU HAD THE ADVANTAGE OF SURPRISE--BUT NOW THE COBRA WILL FIGHT BACK--AS YOU FALL VICTIM TO MY "STING"!!

BUT NOW, MR. HYDE, IT IS YOU WHO WILL TASTE DEFEAT--AS MY NERVE GAS VIAL SHATTERS NEAR YOUR FACE, RELEASING ITS POTENT FUMES!

BUT THE COBRA'S NERVE GAS, POTENT ENOUGH TO STUN A HALF-DOZEN ORDINARY MEN, ONLY SLOWS THE SUPER-POWERFUL MR. HYDE FOR A SPLIT SECOND...
WHY DON'T YOU FALL ?!!

FALL, I SAY!! NO ONE CAN DEFY THE COBRA!!
YOU FOOL! I HAVE THE STRENGTH OF A DOZEN MEN! I'LL CRUSH YOU LIKE A FLEA!!

EXERTING SOME OF HIS TREMENDOUS POWER, THE VILLAINOUS MR. HYDE FORCES HIS EQUALLY-VILLAINOUS FOE BACK--BACK--UNTIL--
THERE!
UGH!!

I UNDERESTIMATED YOU, HYDE--BUT I SHALL STILL PROVE TO BE YOUR MASTER!
NEVER! I'LL FIGHT YOU TO A STANDSTILL THE WAY I DID WITH MIGHTY THOR!!

WHAT??!! YOU FOUGHT THOR ALSO?? DO YOU KNOW WHAT YOU'RE SAYING, HYDE??
I KNOW FULL WELL!! AND NEXT TIME WE MEET, HE'LL BE THE LOSER--DO YOU HEAR?!!

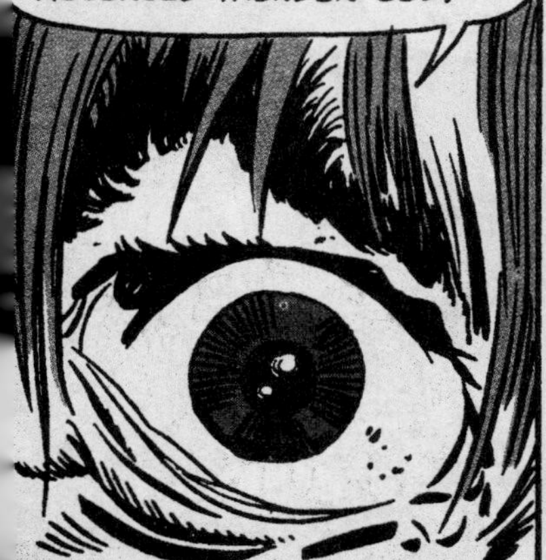
I'VE BEEN HIDING, WORKING, TRAINING ALL THESE MONTHS--MAKING MYSELF MORE POWERFUL THAN EVER--WAITING FOR MY NEXT MEETING WITH THE ACCURSED THUNDER GOD!

WELL THEN, YOU SHALL NOT FIGHT HIM ALONE! HE IS MY ENEMY TOO! ALONE, EACH OF US HAS ALMOST BEATEN HIM--TOGETHER, WE CANNOT FAIL!!
THE COBRA AND MR. HYDE!! YOU ARE RIGHT! WHY FIGHT EACH OTHER WHEN WE CAN JOIN FORCES TO CONQUER THOR!!?!

MEANWHILE, UNMINDFUL OF THE CONSPIRACY WHICH HAS BEEN FORMED AGAINST HIM, THE MIGHTY THOR STREAKS TOWARD HIS DESTINATION...
SOONER OR LATER I'LL FIND THE COBRA! HE SHALL NOT ELUDE ME FOR LONG!

BUT FIRST, I MUST RETURN TO MY WORK AS DR. DON BLAKE! I CANNOT REMAIN GONE TOO LONG WITHOUT AROUSING TOO MANY SUSPICIONS!

WITH A FIRM MUFFLED IMPACT, THOR'S ENCHANTED HAMMER STRIKES THE HARDWOOD FLOOR, AND THEN...

...IN THE SPACE OF A SINGLE HEART-BEAT, HE IS REPLACED BY THE MORTAL DR. DON BLAKE -- AND HIS HAMMER HAS BECOME THE WALKING STICK OF THE LAME PHYSICIAN!

OH, DR. BLAKE! I DIDN'T HEAR YOU COME IN!!

I PLANNED IT THAT WAY, JANE-- MY DARLING!

WERE THERE ANY IMPORTANT CALLS OR VISITORS TODAY?

HOW HARD IT IS TO SOUND BUSINESSLIKE WHEN I LONG TO TAKE HER IN MY ARMS AND TELL HER HOW I LOVE HER! BUT I DARE NOT!

NO, DOCTOR-- IT'S BEEN VERY QUIET ALL DAY!

BY THE WAY, DOCTOR--WOULD YOU MIND IF I LEAVE A LITTLE EARLY TONIGHT? I HAVE A DATE TO GO DANCING, AND I'D LIKE ENOUGH TIME TO GO HOME AND CHANGE!
THIS IS WHAT I ALWAYS FEARED! I KNEW SHE WOULDN'T WAIT FOR ME FOREVER! SOONER OR LATER SHE WAS BOUND TO FIND ANOTHER MAN...!!

I MUST ACT AS THOUGH I DON'T CARE--- FOR HER SAKE!
OF COURSE, JANE! I HOPE YOU HAVE A GOOD TIME!
I WAS RIGHT! -SOB- HE REALLY DOESN'T CARE! IF I MEANT ANYTHING TO HIM HE'D BE ANGRY -- JEALOUS! BUT HE'S NOT! MY LOVE MEANS NOTHING TO HIM!

BUT THERE IS ANOTHER, STILL MORE FATEFUL PROBLEM AWAITING THE TROUBLED MAN...
WHY BOTHER WITH YOUR COMPLICATED MACHINES?? WE CAN DEFEAT THOR BY FORCE!!
I'LL SHOW YOU WHY

WE CAN'T DESTROY THOR UNTIL WE **FIND** HIM--AND MY **TIME REVERSAL RAY** WILL FIND HIM **FOR** US!

IT WILL SHOW US WHERE HIS **HEADQUARTERS** IS--SO THAT WE MAY ATTACK HIM **THERE,** WHERE HE LEASTS EXPECTS IT! THIS IS MY GREATEST INVENTION!

TIME REVERSAL RAY?? WHAT DO YOU **MEAN?** WHAT IS--? **WAIT!!** DON'T POINT IT AT **ME!!**

QUIET! I'M JUST GOING TO DEMONSTRATE HOW IT WORKS! DON'T FORGET I'M A SCIENTIFIC RESEARCHER!! THAT'S HOW I DISCOVERED HOW TO CHANGE MYSELF INTO **MR. HYDE!** BUT NOW--**WATCH--**

BZZZZZZZZZZZZ

AFTER YOU AIMED IT AT ME AND FLIPPED THE SWITCH, IT STARTED TO PROJECT A PICTURE IN THE AIR! IT'S A PICTURE OF **US**--AS WE WERE A FEW SECONDS AGO!!

EXACTLY! NOW SEE HOW IT SHOWS TIME GOING **BACK,** AS THOUGH WE'RE SHOWING A MOVIE **BACKWARDS!** IF WE **KEEP** WATCHING, IT'LL TAKE US BACK TO THE TIME YOU WERE **BORN!**

I GET IT!! IF YOU AIM YOUR RAY AT THOR, IT'LL SHOW YOU ALL HIS ACTIONS BACKWARDS, TRACING HIM BACK IN TIME UNTIL WE CAN SEE WHERE HE COMES FROM!!
AND THEN, ONCE WE KNOW WHERE HE HOLES UP, WE CAN ATTACK HIM AT OUR LEISURE!!

A FEW HOURS LATER, TWO STRANGE-LOOKING FIGURES PREPARE FOR THE NEXT STEP OF THEIR INGENIOUS PLAN TO DEFEAT THE MIGHTY THOR!
YOU TAKE YOUR POSITION HERE ON THE ROOFTOPS! I'LL GO BELOW INTO THE STREET!
THE PLAN IS A CLEVER ONE, BUT THOR IS CLEVER, TOO! THERE MUST BE NO SLIP-UPS!

MEANWHILE, ALONE IN HIS OFFICE, HAVING DISMISSED JANE FOSTER FOR THE EVENING, DR. DON BLAKE TURNS HIS RADIO ON, TO LEARN THE EVENING'S NEWS...
I'VE GOT TO DO SOMETHING TO STOP ME FROM THINKING OF JANE! MY JANE--WITH ANOTHER MAN!

WE INTERRUPT TO BRING YOU AN URGENT BULLETIN! THE NOTORIOUS MR. HYDE HAS BEEN SIGHTED IN NEW YORK! HE IS ATTACKING A JEWELRY STORE AT THIS MOMENT! THE WINDOW IS COVERED WITH IRON BARS, BUT DUE TO HIS GREAT STRENGTH...
MR. HYDE!! AT LARGE AGAIN! HE MUST BE STOPPED!

FIRST THE COBRA-- AND NOW HYDE! CAN THERE BE ANY CONNECTION??

IF THERE IS-- THE GOD OF THUNDER WILL FIND OUT!

WITH LUCK, I SHOULD REACH THE SCENE EVEN BEFORE THE POLICE!! HYDE'S POWERFUL FRAME IS VIRTUALLY BULLETPROOF, AND I CAN'T LET ANY COURAGEOUS POLICEMEN BE INJURED!!

THOR!!
THERE HE IS! BENDING THOSE IRON BARS AS THOUGH THEY'RE PLYWOOD!

I KNEW HE'D SHOW UP! NOW TO FOLLOW MY PLAN!!
THESE CHEMICAL IRRITANT SPRAYS HIDDEN UNDER MY SHIRT WILL DELAY HIM LONG ENOUGH FOR ME TO BEGIN MY ESCAPE!

HYDE IS SHOOTING A STREAM OF CHEMICALS AT ME-- IRRITATING MY EYES!! BUT SURELY HE DOESN'T THINK THIS CAN STOP ME FOR LONG?!!!

BUT THE SINISTER MR. HYDE DOESN'T WANT THOR STOPPED! HE WANTS HIM TO PURSUE HIM!! AND SO...
NOW TO LEAD HIM TO WHERE THE COBRA IS WAITING!

SECONDS LATER, ONCE HE HAS BRUSHED THE CHEMICAL IRRITANT FROM HIS EYES, THE MIGHTY THUNDER GOD GIVES CHASE...
WHEREVER HYDE CAN GO, THOR CAN FOLLOW!

BUT UPON REACHING A CROWDED SECTION OF THIRD AVENUE...
STRANGE! THERE'S NOT A SIGN OF HIM! AND YET-- I WAS RIGHT AT HIS HEELS! WHERE COULD HE HAVE VANISHED TO??

UNFORTUNATELY, THE IMMORTAL AVENGER HAS NO WAY OF KNOWING ABOUT MR. HYDE'S OTHER IDENTITY-- NO WAY OF KNOWING THAT THE EVIL SCHEMER IS FACING HIM RIGHT NOW, APPEARING IN THE CROWD AS NORMAL-LOOKING CALVIN ZABO...
SO FAR, SO GOOD! THE COBRA IS IN THIS AREA SOMEWHERE! NOW, IF HE DOES HIS PART AS PLANNED, THOR WILL BE AS GOOD AS FINISHED!

NO SENSE IN WASTING TIME NEEDLESSLY! I CAN SEARCH FAR BETTER BY COVERING THE NEIGHBORHOOD FROM THE AIR!!
SO I'LL SWING MY ENCHANTED HAMMER AND BE ON MY WAY--!!!

IT WORKED! THERE HE IS! NOW, ALL I HAVE TO DO IS AIM AT THOR...

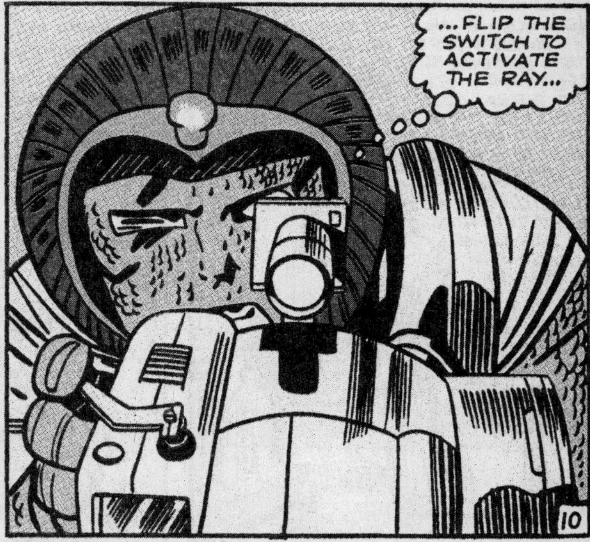
...FLIP THE SWITCH TO ACTIVATE THE RAY...

AHH, MR. HYDE!! YOU ARRIVED JUST IN TIME!! THERE IS A BACKWARD IMAGE OF THOR NOW! SEE?? HE'S FLYING BACKWARDS--WHIRLING HIS HAMMER--AND FINALLY--LOOK! HE MUST HAVE COME FROM THAT WINDOW!

THAT'S WHAT WE WANT! THAT WINDOW! TURN THE ZOOM LENS SWITCH ON MY RAY--IT WILL GIVE US A CLOSE-UP!!

TURN IT STILL ANOTHER NOTCH! THAT'S IT! NOW--ONCE MORE--
DR. DON BLAKE

PERFECT!! NOW WE KNOW THERE IS SOME CONNECTION BETWEEN THOR AND THAT DR. BLAKE!
DR. DON BLAKE
OFFICE HOURS

BAH! THE IMAGE STOPPED AT THAT POINT!! I DON'T UNDERSTAND!! WHY DIDN'T THE RAY KEEP GOING BACK--AS IT SHOULD?? WHY??!!
IT DOESN'T MATTER! WE KNOW ALL WE HAVE TO! LET'S GO!

HOW COULD MR. HYDE SUSPECT THAT THE IMAGE STOPPED BECAUSE AN INSTANT BEFORE THAT TIME THOR HAD NOT BEEN THOR--HE HAD BEEN DR. BLAKE--AND THE RAY COULD ONLY PROJECT A PICTURE OF THE ONE IT WAS ORIGINALLY FOCUSED UPON? BUT NOW, LET US TURN AGAIN TO DON BLAKE...

I CAN'T GO ON THIS WAY MUCH LONGER--PINING FOR JANE EVERY MINUTE!! EVEN NOW, I MAY HAVE LOST HER FOREVER!

IF THOR MAY NOT MARRY A MORTAL GIRL, DR. BLAKE MAY! ALL I HAVE TO DO IS GIVE UP MY OTHER IDENTITY--NEVER BECOME THOR AGAIN!! BUT--CAN I GIVE IT UP??
THERE'S ONLY ONE WAY TO FIND OUT...

I'LL LOCK MY CANE IN THIS STEEL CABINET FOR A FULL DAY! NO MATTER WHAT HAPPENS, I WON'T RETRIEVE IT! AND WITHOUT IT, I CANNOT BECOME THE GOD OF THUNDER!

JANE, MY BELOVED! IF ONLY YOU KNEW HOW I LOVE YOU-- IF YOU COULD SUSPECT THE SACRIFICE I PLAN TO MAKE FOR YOU!!
BLAST IT!! THOR ISN'T HERE!!
BUT BLAKE IS--GET HIM!

MR. HYDE!! THE COBRA!! HOW DID YOU GET HERE??
WE'LL ASK THE QUESTIONS, WEAK-LING!! WHERE'S THOR??

THOR?? HOW WOULD I KNOW ANYTHING ABOUT THOR??
DON'T LIE TO US IF YOU WANT TO LIVE! WE KNOW THOR WAS HERE!
IF YOU TELL US WHERE TO FIND THOR, WE'LL LET YOU GO FREE! YOU MEAN NOTHING TO US! BUT WE MUST FIND HIM!!

MEANWHILE, NOT FAR AWAY, JANE FOSTER REALIZES A DATE MEANS NOTHING TO HER IF IT ISN'T A DATE WITH DON BLAKE!
WOULD YOU MIND TAKING ME BACK, PAUL! I'M SORRY, BUT I SEEM TO HAVE DEVELOPED A SPLITTING HEADACHE!
PERHAPS I'M A FOOL... BUT I'D RATHER WORK IN THE OFFICE WITH DR. BLAKE THAN GO TO THE MOST ROMANTIC NIGHT CLUB WITH ANYONE ELSE!

MINUTES LATER...
BESIDES, DON LOOKED WORRIED! I'D BETTER MAKE SURE HE'S ALL RIGHT!

HAH! I SEE THE GOOD DOCTOR HAS A VISITOR! NOW WE'LL MAKE HIM TALK!
MPPFF!!!

JANE! YOU SHOULDN'T HAVE COME HERE!
I WAS WORRIED ABOUT YOU!! BUT-- I NEVER DREAMED--!!
NOW, BLAKE, IF YOU WANT NO HARM TO COME TO HER, TELL US WHERE TO FIND THOR!!
12

AS DON BLAKE I'M HELPLESS! AND WITHOUT MY CANE, I CAN'T BECOME THOR AGAIN! BUT I MUST DO SOMETHING! I DON'T CARE ABOUT MYSELF, BUT I MUST SAVE JANE!
VERY WELL! OPEN THE LOCKED STEEL CABINET BEHIND YOU, AND I'LL TELL YOU HOW TO FIND THOR!

LOCKS MEAN NOTHING TO ONE WITH MR. HYDE'S STRENGTH!
NOW TAKE THE WALKING STICK FROM THE CABINET!

TAP IT ONCE ON THE FLOOR AND LOOK OUT OF THE WINDOW! IT'S THOR'S SIGNAL--HE'LL APPEAR!
IF YOU'RE TRYING TO FOOL US, BLAKE, I'LL--
DO AS HE SAYS, HYDE! HE WOULDN'T DARE LIE TO US!!

I'LL TAP THE CANE NOW!
AND I'LL WAIT TO GRAB THOR WHEN HE FLIES IN!!

THEY'RE NOT LOOKING AT ME! THERE'S ONE SLIM CHANCE THAT I CAN ACCOMPLISH WHAT I MUST WITHOUT THEM SUSPECTING WHO I REALLY AM!
TAP!

GOOD! THEY STILL HAVEN'T TURNED!
NOW THEY'LL NEVER BE ABLE TO HOLD MY CANE, FOR IT'S TURNED INTO THOR'S ENCHANTED HAMMER!

EVEN THE TREMENDOUS STRENGTH OF MR. HYDE CANNOT HOLD THOR'S MALLET FOR A SINGLE SECOND, AND SO...
WHAT HAPPENED??
I DON'T KNOW!! SOMETHING SEEMS TO HAVE PULLED ME DOWN TO THE FLOOR!!

I'M IN LUCK! IT HAPPENED SO FAST THAT HE DOESN'T REALIZE THE CANE TURNED INTO MY HAMMER! AND NOW IT'S FLYING BACK TO ME!
WHERE'D THE CANE GO??
I MUST HAVE DROPPED IT OUT OF THE WINDOW!!
13

THOR!! WHERE DID YOU COME FROM??
THE GOD OF THUNDER EXPLAINS TO NO ONE!! BUT ONE THING I WILL TELL YOU...

DR. BLAKE OUT-SMARTED YOU BOTH!
WHILE YOU LOOKED OUT OF THE WINDOW, HE RAN TO CALL THE POLICE, AND I CAME IN THRU THE DOOR BEHIND YOU!!

DR. BLAKE TOOK A CHANCE LIKE THAT!! RISKING HIS LIFE-- FOR ME?!!??
BLAKE'S LOVE FOR YOU MUST BE GREATER THAN YOU DREAM!! BUT NOW, STAND ASIDE! I SHALL DEAL WITH THESE TWO IN MY OWN WAY!!

QUICK, HYDE-- SEPARATE! HE CAN'T GET US BOTH IF WE GO IN DIFFERENT DIRECTIONS!
STICK TO "PLAN B", COBRA!! WE'LL DEFEAT HIM YET! WE SIMPLY HAVE TO CHANGE OUR METHOD OF OPERATION!

THE COBRA IS SLIPPERY AS THE SERPENT HE IS NAMED FOR! HE SLITHERED RIGHT OUT FROM UNDER MY ARM!!
AND MR. HYDE IS FASTER THAN ONE WOULD SUSPECT BY LOOKING AT HIM! BUT THEY WON'T GET FAR!

HAH! ONLY SOMEONE WITH THE SERPENTINE QUALITY OF A COBRA COULD DODGE THE MIGHTY THOR'S HAMMER!!!

NOW ALL I NEED DO IS SLITHER UP THE SIDE OF THE BUILDING AT SNAKE-LIKE SPEED...!
MR. HYDE SAID TO EXECUTE "PLAN B"! THAT MEANS WE'LL LURE THOR TO ANOTHER PLACE WHERE THE ODDS WILL BE IN OUR FAVOR!!

WE'VE PLANNED TOO WELL TO BE FRUSTRATED NOW! NO MATTER WHAT MOVE THOR MAKES, WE'LL KNOW HOW TO BEAT HIM!

THEY WERE RIGHT! YOU COULDN'T FOLLOW BOTH OF THEM! THEY GOT AWAY!!
IT WAS ONLY A TEMPORARY VICTORY FOR THEM! REMAIN HERE TILL DR. BLAKE RETURNS FOR YOU...

...AS FOR ME, I'LL FOLLOW THE TRAIL OF MR. HYDE! SOONER OR LATER, HE'LL LEAD ME TO THE COBRA, AND THEN I'LL HAVE THEM BOTH AGAIN!

IT SEEMS I CAN NEVER GIVE UP THE ROLE OF THOR!! NOT SO LONG AS MENACES LIKE HYDE AND THE COBRA WALK THE EARTH!!

MEANWHILE, DOWN BELOW...
HE'S COMING AFTER ME AGAIN!! BUT THIS TIME, I'LL KNOW WHAT TO DO! IT'S LUCKY I PREPARED A SECOND PLAN FOR DEALING WITH HIM!!

THIS TIME I WANT THOR TO FOLLOW ME! BUT I MUST MAKE SURE HE DOESN'T CATCH UP WITH ME TILL I REACH MY DESTINATION!
AUTO JUNK YARD

THIS SMALL ULTRA-WAVE TRANSMITTER WHICH I HAD CONCEALED BENEATH MY CLOAK WILL ATTRACT THE METAL IN HIS HAMMER! MY SECOND TRAP CAN'T FAIL!

HYDE IS MAKING CERTAIN THAT I DON'T LOSE HIM! HE MUST HAVE A TRAP PREPARED FOR ME!
BUT THE GOD OF THUNDER FEARS NO TRAPS!

HERE HE COMES! NOW I'LL JUST SCATTER THESE METAL HEAPS BEHIND ME TO SLOW HIM UP LONG ENOUGH FOR ME TO REACH MY GOAL!!

BLAST IT! HE'S FASTER THAN I THOUGHT! BUT IT DOESN'T MATTER-- I'M ALMOST THERE!

HYDE'S RUSHING INTO THE COLOSSEUM! IT'S JAMMED WITH PEOPLE ATTENDING THE "HEAVY MACHINERY SHOW"!! I'VE GOT TO MAKE SURE THAT NO INNOCENT BYSTANDERS ARE INJURED IN THE NEXT FATAL MOMENTS!
MACHINE SHOW

HE MUST HAVE KNOWN I WOULDN'T DARE THROW MY LETHAL HAMMER WITH THIS HELPLESS CROWD MILLING ABOUT!! BUT IF HE COUNTED ON THAT TO SAVE HIM, I'LL PROVE HOW DANGEROUSLY WRONG HE WAS!
LOOK! UP THERE! IT'S THOR-- THE THUNDER GOD!!
SAY! THEY SPARED NO EXPENSE TO MAKE THIS A BANG-UP EXHIBITION!! WHAT A CLEVER STUNT!!

BUT THE ASTONISHED SPECTATORS ARE SOON TO LEARN THAT WHAT THEY ARE WITNESSING IS FAR FROM A "PUBLICITY STUNT"!!
I WAS SURE THOR WOULDN'T USE HIS HAMMER AT SUCH CLOSE QUARTERS!! AND THAT GIVES ME THE ADVANTAGE!
I CAN'T LET THESE INNOCENT PEOPLE BE MENACED BY THAT SAVAGE BRUTE!! BUT NEITHER CAN I YIELD TO HIM-- HE MUST BE STOPPED, WHILE THERE'S STILL TIME!
BUT HE'S TURNING ALL HIS SUPER-STRENGTH AGAINST ME!!

FOR MR. HYDE DOESN'T CARE WHAT DAMAGE HE DOES-- OR WHO GETS INJURED!!
SURRENDER TO ME, THOR!! IF YOU DON'T WANT ME TO TURN THIS PLACE INTO A SHAMBLES, GIVE UP!

I'VE NO OTHER CHOICE-- I HAVE TO USE MY POWER DEFENSIVELY... UNTIL I CAN THINK OF A PLAN!

HEAR ME, HYDE! IT IS I WHO CALL ON YOU TO SURRENDER! YOU CANNOT INJURE ME --BUT IF I SHOULD REACH YOU--
THOR DIDN'T SUSPECT THAT I'D BE HERE, TOO! I'LL SEE TO IT THAT HE NEVER DOES REACH HYDE!!

I HAVE LONG KNOWN THAT NOTHING HUMAN CAN LIFT THOR'S ACCURSED HAMMER! BUT--
--I SUSPECT THAT SOMETHING WHICH IS NOT HUMAN--IF IT HAS ENOUGH POWER--CAN DO WHAT NO LIVING BEING CAN DO!!

HAH! I WAS RIGHT! THIS ATOMIC-POWERED HYDRAULIC HOIST HAS ENOUGH POWER TO LIFT ANYTHING!!!
MY HAMMER!!

THE MACHINE DEPOSITED THE HAMMER WITHIN ITS STORAGE COMPARTMENT! HOW CAN I EVER REACH IT WITHIN SIXTY SECONDS???
18

FOR IF IT IS OUT OF MY GRASP FOR MORE THAN ONE MINUTE, I CEASE BEING THOR, AND REVERT BACK TO THE MORTAL DON BLAKE!!
NOW, THUNDER GOD--WITHOUT YOUR HAMMER, THE COBRA AND I ARE MORE THAN A MATCH FOR YOU!

LITTLE DO THEY DREAM HOW RIGHT THEY ARE!! WITHIN A FEW SECONDS, LAME, POWERLESS DR. BLAKE WILL BE FACING TWO OF THE WORST MENACES ON EARTH!!
THE END

WE TOLD YOU THIS WAS A DOUBLE-LENGTH MARVEL MASTERPIECE, AND WE MEANT IT! NEXT ISH WILL FEATURE THE CONCLUSION OF THIS TALE, IN ONE OF THE MOST SPECTACULAR BATTLES OF ALL! SO, DON'T MISS THE FINAL 18-PAGER IN THOR #106-- WE PROMISE IT'S WORTH WAITING FOR!!

TALES of ASGARD HOME OF THE MIGHTY NORSE GODS
"WHEN HEIMDALL FAILED!"
ALTHOUGH I AM KING OF THE STORM GIANTS, I CANNOT ATTACK ASGARD AS LONG AS THE EVER-VIGILANT HEIMDALL GUARDS THEIR RAINBOW BRIDGE! IT IS IMPOSSIBLE, NEDRA!
NO, KING BRIMER! THERE IS A WAY TO GET PAST HEIMDALL! AND I KNOW WHAT IT IS!
WRITTEN BY....... STAN LEE
ILLUSTRATED BY... JACK KIRBY
INKING... GEO. BELL
LETTERING... ART SIMEK

HOW, NEDRA?? HEIMDALL HEARS EVERYTHING! HE SEES EVERYTHING! HE NEVER SLEEPS! NOTHING CAN ESCAPE HIS NOTICE!!
YOU FORGET, MY LORD! YOU FORGET THE AIR CREATURES --THE ONES WE CALL VANNA! WATCH-- I SHALL SUMMON ONE! THE VANNA SHALL DO OUR BIDDING!!

HEAR ME, VANNA-- WHEREVER YOU MAY BE! QUEEN NEDRA COMMANDS YOU TO APPEAR! YOU MAY NOT DISOBEY MY COMMAND!! YOU MUST HEED THE ORDERS OF QUEEN NEDRA!!
I HEAR THEE, MY QUEEN! AND I OBEY!

ONLY YOU, CREATURE OF AIR, CAN MAKE YOURSELF A PART OF THE SILENT BREEZE, SO THAT NONE CAN SEE OR HEAR YOU! I ORDER YOU TO DO SO-- TO SPY UPON ASGARD FOR ME!
YOUR WISH IS MY COMMAND, GREAT QUEEN! I SHALL STEAL PAST HEIMDALL LIKE A WRAITH, AND LEARN ALL OF ASGARD'S SECRETS FOR YOU! THERE IS NOTHING I WOULD NOT DO FOR QUEEN NEDRA!!

THEN GO!! IF YOU SUCCEED, YOU WILL BE RICHLY REWARDED! BUT NEVER FORGET WHAT MY PENALTY IS-- FOR FAILURE!!
I SHALL NOT FAIL, MY QUEEN! HEIMDALL WILL NEVER SUSPECT MY PRESENCE!

A SHORT TIME LATER, AT THE FABLED RAINBOW BRIDGE, THE ONLY ENTRANCE TO LEGENDARY ASGARD, WHERE STANDS THE LOYAL HEIMDALL...
THOUGH I SEE AND HEAR NOTHING, YET MY SENSES ARE SORELY TROUBLED, FOR I FEEL THE PRESENCE OF GRAVE DANGER!

THEN, SUDDENLY, FOR NO APPARENT REASON, THE GALLANT GUARDIAN SWINGS HIS MIGHTY SWORD AT WHAT SEEMS TO BE THE EMPTY AIR-- SWINGS, AND TOUCHES NOTHING!
WHAT IS HAPPENING TO ME?? AM I TAKING LEAVE OF MY SENSES??? WHAT POSSESSES ME TO FLAY THE EMPTY AIR WITH USELESS GESTURES!

NEVER HAVE I FELT THIS WAY BEFORE!! NEVER SO UNCERTAIN-- SO TROUBLED!! HAVE I BEEN AT MY POST TOO LONG?? CAN IT BE THAT I AM NO LONGER WORTHY OF GUARDING THE ALL-IMPORTANT RAINBOW BRIDGE??

AND WITHIN THE TOWERING GATES OF ASGARD ITSELF...
I WILL BE RICHLY REWARDED WHEN I REPORT BACK TO QUEEN NEDRA AND TELL ALL ABOUT THE DEFENSES OF ASGARD!

HOW EASY IT IS FOR ME TO COUNT THE WARRIORS ODIN HAS UNDER HIS COMMAND --TO LEARN THEIR STRENGTHS AND WEAKNESSES!!

I CAN EVEN ENTER THE ROYAL CHAMBER OF ODIN HIMSELF-- AND ALL BECAUSE THE USELESS HEIMDALL FAILED TO STOP ME!!
NOBLE ODIN, I BRING WORD FROM HEIMDALL! HE SAYS WE MUST BE ALERT! THOUGH HE HAS SEEN NOTHING, HE SUSPECTS GREAT DANGER IS NEAR US!
SO SPEAKS TRUST-WORTHY HEIMDALL?? THEN WE MUST HEED HIS WORDS!!

LET ALL BE SILENT! LET ALL BE MOTIONLESS! AS LORD OF ASGARD, MY POWERS ARE SUPREME! I SHALL EXERT THEM TO THEIR FULLEST!!
SOFTLY! SOFTLY! HEIMDALL SPOKE THE TRUTH! THERE IS A PRESENCE HERE! AND IN THE NAME OF ASGARD -- I COMMAND IT TO SHOW ITSELF!! ODIN MUST BE OBEYED!!
I MUST FLEE-- BUT--I CANNOT!!

SEE, MY LORD!! IT IS ONE OF THE VANNA-- ONE OF THE ENCHANTED AIR CREATURES!! YOU HAVE CAUGHT THE UNCATCHABLE!!!
SET ME FREE, LORD ODIN! I HAVE DONE NO WRONG!
SILENCE!! HOLD YOUR TONGUE IN THE IMPERIAL PRESENCE, DECEITFUL ONE!!

LATER, HEIMDALL IS SUMMONED TO THE THRONE ROOM OF ODIN--
YOU HAVE CAPTURED A VANNA, MY LORD! THEN TRULY HAVE I FAILED MY TRUST!! FOR HE ENTERED ASGARD WITHOUT MY KNOWLEDGE!
THAT'S RIGHT, GREAT ODIN! PUNISH HEIMDALL --NOT ME! I DID YOU A FAVOR! I PROVED HE IS NOT WORTHY TO GUARD THE RAINBOW BRIDGE!

YOU SHALL BE PUNISHED, FALSE-TONGUED ONE! ODIN CAN SEE THRU YOUR WEB OF LIES! BUT, MY DEALINGS WITH YOU CAN WAIT! FIRST, I MUST GIVE HEIMDALL HIS DUE...
DO WITH ME AS YOU WISH, NOBLE LORD! BUT NO PUNISHMENT YOU METE OUT TO ME CAN BE AS PAINFUL AS THE REGRET I FEEL IN MY HEART FOR MY FAILURE!

RISE, GALLANT HEIMDALL! YOU HAVE NOT FAILED! SO LOYAL IS YOUR HEART, THAT YOU SENSED THE EVIL VANNA ALTHOUGH YOU COULD NOT SEE HIM! AND SO HONORABLE IS YOUR SOUL THAT YOU REPORTED YOUR FEARS TO ME, ALTHOUGH YOU KNEW OTHERS MIGHT SCORN YOU FOR FEARING THE UNSEEN!
RETURN TO YOUR POST, HEIMDALL, AND KNOW THAT YOU HOLD A PLACE IN THE HEART OF ODIN SECOND ONLY TO THOR HIMSELF!

AND AS THE MIGHTY LEGIONS OF ODIN SET OUT ACROSS THE RAINBOW BRIDGE ON THEIR JOURNEY TO THE LAND OF THE FROST GIANTS, THEY ARE SECURE IN THE KNOWLEDGE THAT HEIMDALL REMAINS! HEIMDALL, WHOSE AWESOME PRESENCE GUARANTEES THAT ASGARD SHALL STILL BE SAFE TILL THEY RETURN!!
The End

PERSONAL NOTE: STAN LEE AND JACK KIRBY WANT TO THANK THE COUNTLESS READERS WHO HAVE FLOODED THEM WITH LETTERS IN PRAISE OF *TALES OF ASGARD!* WE APPRECIATE YOUR ENTHUSIASM AND PROMISE TO CONTINUE WITH TALES SUCH AS THESE!! TALES FOUND ONLY WITHIN THE PAGES OF *THE MIGHTY THOR!!*

JOURNEY INTO MYSTERY
WITH
THE MIGHTY
THOR
APPROVED BY THE COMICS CODE AUTHORITY
IND.
MARVEL COMICS GROUP 12¢
106 JULY
HOW CAN THOR HOPE TO DEFEAT Mr. HYDE AND THE COBRA AFTER THEY'VE TAKEN HIS MIGHTY HAMMER FROM HIM ?
THE THUNDER GOD STRIKES BACK!
OUR PLEDGE TO YOU: IF YOU DON'T LIKE THIS EPIC BATTLE... ...YOU MIGHT ENJOY "MILLIE the MODEL"!

THE MIGHTY THOR
THE COBRA and MR. HYDE FEEL THOR'S MIGHTY RAGE, WHEN "THE THUNDER GOD STRIKES BACK!"
CONCLUDED FROM LAST ISSUE!
MY ENCHANTED HAMMER IS SOMEWHERE INSIDE THAT COMPLEX MACHINE! WITHOUT IT, I'LL TURN INTO THE MORTAL DON BLAKE WITHIN SIXTY SECONDS, AND BE AT THE MERCY OF HYDE AND THE COBRA!!
WRITTEN FAIRLY WELL BY STAN LEE
DRAWN NOT TOO BADLY BY JACK KIRBY
INKED KINDA NICE BY CHIC STONE
LETTERED PRETTY FAIR BY ART SIMEK
X-704
1

EDITOR'S NOTE: IF YOU MISSED THE PRECEDING ISSUE OF THE MIGHTY THOR, SHAME ON YOU! NOW, OUT OF THE KINDNESS OF OUR HEARTS, WE PRESENT A BRIEF SUMMARY TO BRING YOU UP TO DATE-- BUT DON'T LET IT HAPPEN AGAIN!!
LITTLE DREAMING THAT MR. HYDE AND THE COBRA WERE HEADING HIS WAY, DR. DON BLAKE LOCKED HIS MYSTICAL CANE INSIDE A STEEL CABINET IN HIS OFFICE.
WITHOUT MY CANE I CANNOT TURN INTO THOR AGAIN! PERHAPS I CAN LEARN TO GIVE UP MY OTHER IDENTITY FOREVER!
FOR, ONLY BY FORSAKING MY ROLE AS THUNDER GOD WILL I BE ABLE TO MARRY JANE FOSTER, THE GIRL I LOVE!
BUT, AFTER BEING ATTACKED BY THE TWO SUPER-MENACES, AND FINDING JANE'S LIFE AT STAKE, DON BLAKE HAS TO REGAIN HIS WALKING STICK AGAIN...
IF YOU VALUE THIS FEMALE'S LIFE, TELL US HOW TO FIND THOR!
VERY WELL! BREAK OPEN THAT CABINET AND TAKE THE CANE YOU'LL FIND INSIDE!
THEN, TELLING THE DEADLY DUO TO STOMP THE CANE ONCE UPON THE FLOOR, AND TO WATCH THE WINDOW FOR THE ARRIVAL OF THOR, THE LAME DOCTOR HOLDS HIS BREATH --- WAITING FOR THE IMPACT!
AS SOON AS THE CANE IS STRUCK, I'LL TURN INTO THOR!
AT THAT INSTANT, THE CANE WILL BE TRANSFORMED INTO MY HAMMER, AND FLY TO MY HAND!
HE STRUCK IT!! NOW, I PRAY IT WILL ALL HAPPEN SO FAST, THEY WON'T REALIZE THAT BLAKE AND THOR ARE ONE AND THE SAME!!!
TURN AND FACE ME! I AM THE ONE YOU SEEK!!
BLAKE DECEIVED YOU! HE SUMMONED ME AND THEN FLED WHILE YOU ALL WERE FACING THE WINDOW!!
THE THUNDER GOD'S DESPERATE PLAN SUCCEEDED! BUT, EVEN MIGHTY THOR COULD NOT BE IN TWO PLACES AT ONCE, AND, MOVING WITH INCREDIBLE SPEED, THE COBRA AND MR. HYDE MANAGE TO ESCAPE...
HOW CAN ANYONE CATCH ME WHEN I CAN MOVE WITH THE SPEED OF A HUMAN SERPENT?!!
ALTHOUGH HYDE IS SLOWER, HIS FLYING FOE ALLOWS HIM TO KEEP GOING...
MR. HYDE IS UP TO SOMETHING! IF I GIVE HIM ENOUGH ROPE, HE MAY LEAD ME TO THE COBRA!!
2

FINALLY, THE TRAIL LEADS TO A HEAVY-DUTY MACHINE EXHIBIT AT NEW YORK'S COLOSSEUM WHERE THE COBRA AND HYDE SPRING THEIR TRAP--
YOU DID IT, COBRA! YOU MANAGED TO GRAB HIS ACCURSED HAMMER WITH THAT GRAPPLING MACHINE!!

AND SO WE RETURN TO THE PRESENT-- AND TO THOR'S DESPERATE PLIGHT...
OUR GAMBLE PAID OFF! EVEN THOUGH NOTHING HUMAN CAN LIFT YOUR HAMMER, WE GUESSED THAT SOMETHING NOT HUMAN--SUCH AS A MACHINE--COULD DO IT!!
AND NOW YOU MUST FACE US--WITHOUT YOUR GREATEST WEAPON! THIS TIME, THUNDER GOD, WE SHALL BE THE VICTORS!!
I CAN ONLY REMAIN THOR FOR ONE MINUTE WITHOUT MY HAMMER!

SO I HAVEN'T A SECOND TO SPARE!!
EVEN WITHOUT MY HAMMER, HAVE YOU FORGOTTEN THE POWER OF THOR???

POWER WHICH ENABLES ME TO LIFT A SECTION OF THIS STEEL FLOORING AS THOUGH IT'S MADE OF PAPER!

LOOK OUT!! HE'S FLINGING US AWAY LIKE TOYS!!
WHY DIDN'T YOU GRAB HIM WHEN YOU HAD THE CHANCE??!

THAT WILL GIVE ME THE BREATHING SPACE I NEED! NOW TO LOSE MYSELF IN THE CROWD!!
ONLY SECONDS TO GO! BUT WHEN I CHANGE TO BLAKE AGAIN--NONE MUST SEE ME!

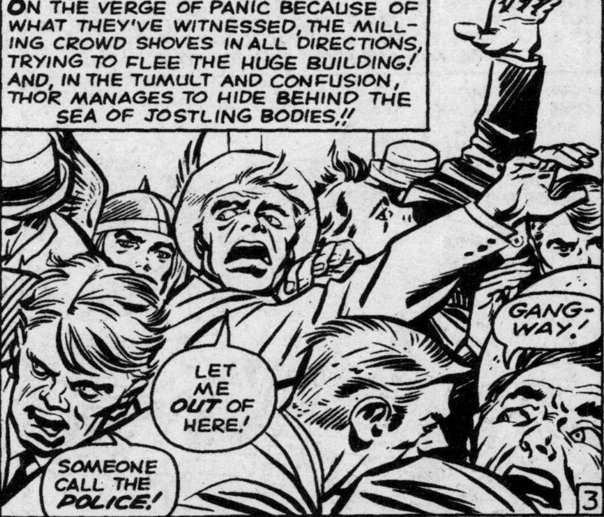
ON THE VERGE OF PANIC BECAUSE OF WHAT THEY'VE WITNESSED, THE MILLING CROWD SHOVES IN ALL DIRECTIONS, TRYING TO FLEE THE HUGE BUILDING! AND, IN THE TUMULT AND CONFUSION, THOR MANAGES TO HIDE BEHIND THE SEA OF JOSTLING BODIES!!
GANG-WAY!
LET ME OUT OF HERE!
SOMEONE CALL THE POLICE!

SO INTENT UPON ESCAPE IS THE MILLING THRONG, THAT NONE STOP TO OBSERVE THE BLINDING PHENOMINON THAT OCCURS IN THEIR MIDST--!
HURRY! GET TO THE EXIT!!
LOOK OUT! WATCH WHERE YOU'RE GOING!! OHH!

AND, SECONDS LATER, NO ONE NOTICES ONE NEW FACE IN THE CROWD... THE FACE OF DON BLAKE!

LUCKILY, MY SECRET IDENTITY IS STILL SAFE BUT, THE WORST IS YET TO COME!

I'VE GOT TO FIND A WAY TO RETRIEVE MY HAMMER FROM INSIDE THAT HUGE GRAPPLING MACHINE--FOR WITHOUT IT, HYDE AND THE COBRA CAN'T BE STOPPED!

MEANTIME WITHIN THE GIANT MACHINE, THOR'S HAMMER HAS TURNED BACK TO A SIMPLE WALKING STICK ONCE MORE, AS IT SILENTLY LIES NEXT TO A VAST COMPLEX OF COGS, AND GEARS--SEPARATED FROM ITS RIGHTFUL OWNER BY INCHES OF POWERFUL STEEL SHIELDING!!

AND, WITHIN THE EXHIBITION HALL, THE SEARCH FOR THOR CONTINUES--!!

OUT OF MY WAY--ALL OF YOU!!

THOR MUST STILL BE HERE!! ALL THE DOORS ARE BOLTED! HE CAN'T HAVE ESCAPED!!

AND, IN HIS OWN SERPENTINE WAY, THE COBRA ALSO SEARCHES FOR HIS ELUSIVE ENEMY--!
N-NOBODY'S SAFE HERE! THE COBRA AND MR. HYDE ARE EVERYWHERE!!
I'LL FIND HIM YET! NO MATTER WHERE HE IS, THOR CAN'T ESCAPE ME MUCH LONGER!

MEANTIME, LEARNING OF THE UNCANNY EVENTS TAKING PLACE AT THE MACHINERY SHOW, HEAVILY-ARMED UNITS OF THE POLICE RIOT SQUAD RACE TO THE SCENE!
WE'VE GOT TO MAKE SURE THAT NO INNOCENT PEOPLE ARE INJURED!!
RRRRRRRRRRRR
POLICE

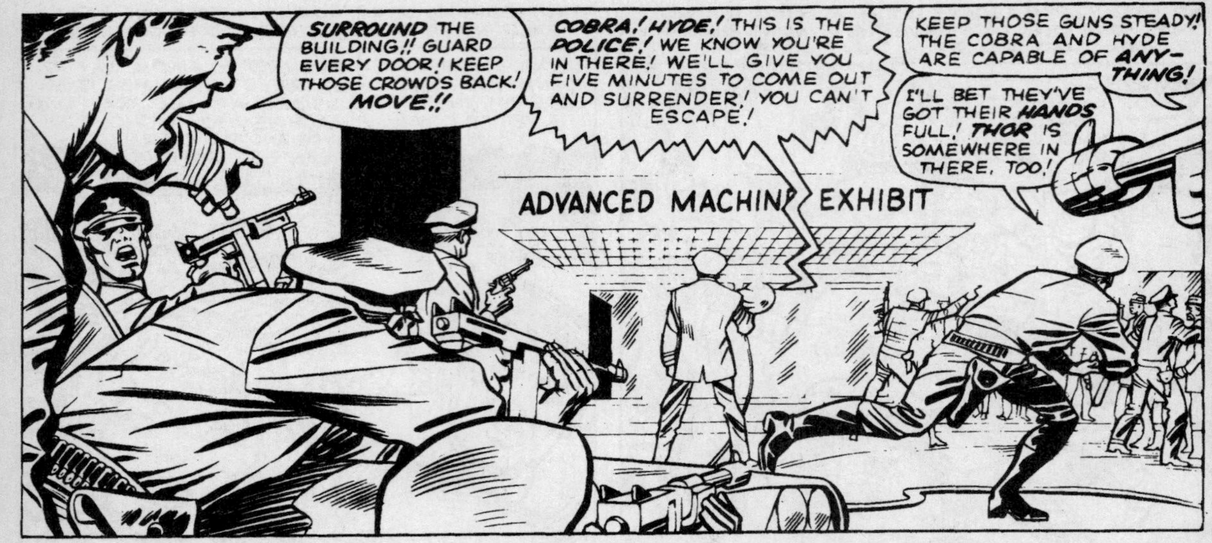
SURROUND THE BUILDING!! GUARD EVERY DOOR! KEEP THOSE CROWDS BACK! MOVE!!
COBRA! HYDE! THIS IS THE POLICE! WE KNOW YOU'RE IN THERE! WE'LL GIVE YOU FIVE MINUTES TO COME OUT AND SURRENDER! YOU CAN'T ESCAPE!
KEEP THOSE GUNS STEADY! THE COBRA AND HYDE ARE CAPABLE OF ANYTHING!
I'LL BET THEY'VE GOT THEIR HANDS FULL! THOR IS SOMEWHERE IN THERE, TOO!
ADVANCED MACHIN EXHIBIT

AND, INSIDE THE BESIEGED BUILDING, MR. HYDE LIFTS A BROADCASTER THE WAY A CHILD MIGHT LIFT A TOY--!
GIVE ME THAT MICROPHONE!! I'LL USE IT TO MAKE MYSELF HEARD ABOVE THE CROWD!!
S-SURE!! TAKE IT! KEEP IT!! B-BE MY GUEST!!

HYDE, WHAT DO WE DO NOW? THE POLICE HAVE THE BUILDING SURROUNDED--AND WE'VE STILL FOUND NO TRACE OF THE THUNDER GOD!! WE CAN'T KEEP AN ENTIRE CITY AT BAY!
STOP YOUR SNIVELLING, COBRA!! THOR IS HERE SOMEWHERE, AND WE'VE GOT TO FIND HIM! AFTER HE'S BEEN DISPOSED OF, THE REST WILL BE EASY!

IT'S HOPELESS! THERE'S NO WAY I CAN REACH INTO THE MACHINE FOR MY CANE!!
THOR COULD RIP THIS THING APART WITH ONE HAND, BUT DON BLAKE HASN'T A CHANCE!

THE GRAPPLER IS SO WELL MADE, THERE ARE NO WEAK SECTIONS-- NO LOOSE JOINTS THAT I CAN POSSIBLY PRY APART!!

IT'S HOPELESS! NOTHING SHORT OF A MIRACLE CAN TRANSFORM ME INTO THOR AGAIN!!

AND YET, MIRACLES SOMETIMES DO HAPPEN!!
HEY, QUIT SHOVIN'! YOU'RE NOT GOIN' ANYWHERE!
WHAT'S THE HURRY, SKINNY? WE'RE ALL IN THE SAME BOAT HERE!!

THEN, SUDDENLY...
THOR! SHOW YOURSELF, OR I ATTACK THE CROWD!
THIS IS MY LAST WARNING!

AND THEN, SLOWLY, QUIETLY, AS THE CROWD STARES IN MUTE DISBELIEF, ONE FIGURE STEPS FORWARD -- THE FIGURE OF DON BLAKE -- THE LAME DOCTOR WHO SEEMS TO BE BETRAYING THE THUNDER GOD!!
I TOLD YOU ONCE BEFORE HOW TO FIND THOR, AND YOU LET HIM ESCAPE! I'LL DO IT AGAIN, BUT THIS TIME HOLD ON TO HIM!!
YOU!!

NO! YOU MUSTN'T DO IT!! YOU CAN'T SACRIFICE THOR!! WE'RE NOT AFRAID!!
THEY DON'T REALIZE I'M TRYING TO SAVE THOR --AND I CAN'T EXPLAIN!
YOU CRUMMY COWARD!! THE POLICE WILL SAVE US SOON! HYDE'S ONLY BLUFFING! LET THOR STAY HIDDEN!!

QUIET, ALL OF YOU!! THE NEXT ONE TO SPEAK WILL FEEL THE ANGER OF MR. HYDE!!

NOW TALK, BLAKE! TELL US WHAT WE WANT TO KNOW!
I'LL TELL YOU ON ONE CONDITION! MY ANTIQUE CANE ACCIDENTALLY GOT CAUGHT WITHIN THE GRAPPLER MACHINE! FIRST GET IT FOR ME!
HAH! THAT WILL BE CHILD'S PLAY FOR ONE WITH MY STRENGTH!
6

NEVER MIND YOUR STRENGTH, HYDE! THIS IS A JOB FOR ME!
I'LL SHOW YOU WHAT THE COBRA CAN DO! I CAN SLITHER IN ANYWHERE!

MAKE IT FAST, COBRA! I'M NOT INTERESTED IN DEMONSTRATIONS! I WANT THOR!!!

THIS BETTER NOT BE A TRICK, BLAKE! IF YOU DON'T PRODUCE THOR WHEN HE BRINGS YOU YOUR CANE, IT'LL BE YOUR FINISH!

SO FAR, HYDE HAS TRIED TO RUN THE WHOLE SHOW! IT'S ABOUT TIME I PROVED THAT THE COBRA CAN DO ANYTHING HE CAN DO-- AND DO IT EASIER!!

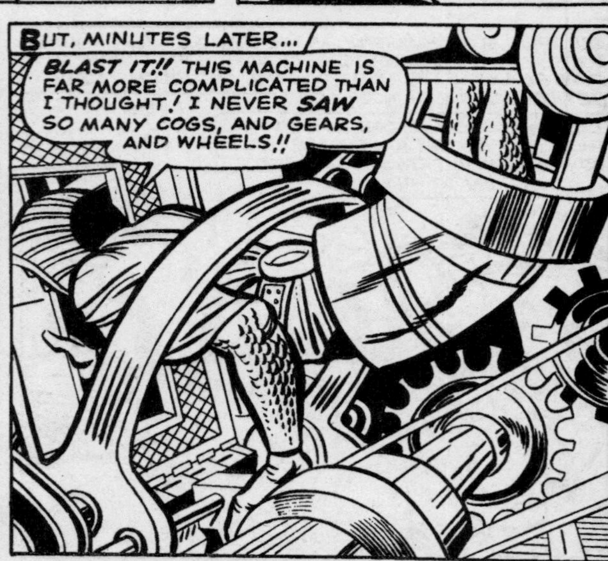
BUT, MINUTES LATER...
BLAST IT!! THIS MACHINE IS FAR MORE COMPLICATED THAN I THOUGHT! I NEVER SAW SO MANY COGS, AND GEARS, AND WHEELS!!

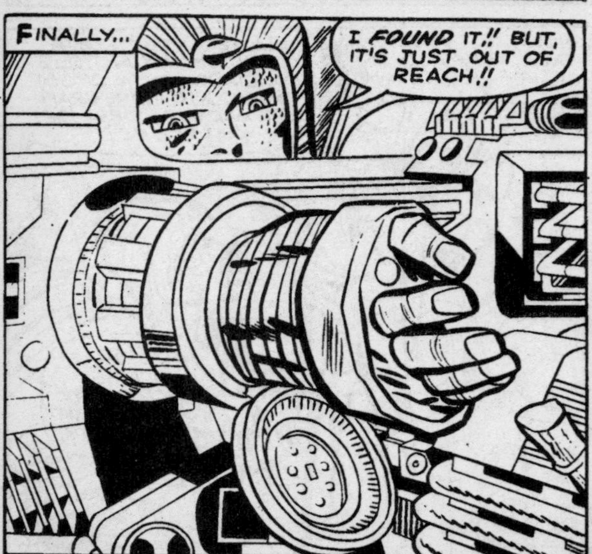
FINALLY...
I FOUND IT!! BUT, IT'S JUST OUT OF REACH!!

AND SO, A SHORT TIME LATER...
YOU BONELESS INCOMPETENT!! YOU FAILED!! YOU KNOW HOW I DESPISE FAILURE!!
IT WASN'T MY FAULT, HYDE!! I MANAGED TO FIND THE CANE-- BUT I JUST COULDN'T REACH IT!
NOW HYDE IS MY LAST HOPE! HE'S GOT TO GET IT!!

WITH A SAVAGE SNARL, THE BRUTAL BESTIAL CREATURE LUNGES AT THE MACHINE, AND THEN...
I'LL DO IT MY WAY-- THE ONLY WAY-- WITH RAW STRENGTH!!

IT'S GOT TO BE IN HERE SOMEWHERE, AND I'LL JUST KEEP RIPPING THE PIECES APART UNTIL--AHHH!
I'VE GOT IT!!

THERE, YOU WRETCHED WEAKLING!! THERE'S YOUR BLASTED CANE!! NOW TELL ME WHERE TO FIND THOR BEFORE I DECIDE TO ATTACK YOU NEXT!

BUT, NO SOONER DOES HE GRASP THE PRECIOUS OBJECT, THEN DON BLAKE SUDDENLY LIMPS INTO THE STARTLED CROWD...
COME BACK!! I'LL DESTROY YOU FOR THIS!!

SEEING THE ENRAGED HYDE RUSHING FORWARD, THE TERRIFIED CROWD BOLTS IN PANIC, IGNORING BLAKE...
HYDE IS COMING!! RUN!!
AT LAST I HAVE MY CHANCE!

...MY CHANCE ONCE AGAIN TO TURN INTO...

...THE MIGHTY THOR!!!

SEEING THE VENGEFUL THUNDER GOD, THE ASTONISHED CROWD STOPS IN ITS TRACKS, AS THOR'S DEEP VOICE RUMBLES THRU THE VAST HALL...
MAKE WAY!!
THE THUNDER GOD IS HERE!!

HYDE! HYDE! DON'T LEAVE ME!! I NEED YOU!! HE'S COMING AFTER ME!!
SHUT UP, YOU COWARD! KEEP HIM OCCUPIED WHILE I FIGURE OUT HOW TO TO WORK THIS GIANT SPRAYER MACHINE!!

BUT HE'S TOO STRONG!! I CAN'T KEEP DODGING HIS HAMMER!

IT WAS YOUR FAULT, HYDE--YOU GOT ME INTO THIS!! YOU CAN'T DESERT ME NOW!

HYDE CAN'T SAVE YOU NOW, COBRA! NOTHING CAN--NOT WHILE MY HAMMER FLIES STRAIGHT AND TRUE!!

YEOWWW! IT'S IMPOSSIBLE!! HE MANAGED TO HOOK HIS HAMMER'S THONG ONTO MY FOOT! IT'S PULLING ME TOWARDS HIM!

WITH YOU OUT OF THE WAY, I'LL BE ABLE TO TURN MY ATTENTION TO HYDE! YOU WERE MERELY HIS CAT'S PAW--HE IS THE MORE DANGEROUS OF THE TWO!!

THOR--LOOK OUT! MR. HYDE HAS MANAGED TO START THE GIANT SPRAYER!! IT CAN BUILD UP ENOUGH AIR PRESSURE TO DEMOLISH A STONE WALL!!
EVERYONE TAKE COVER!! NO MERE MACHINE, NO MATTER HOW POWERFUL, SHALL DEFEAT ME AGAIN!!

HAH! THE PURPOSE OF THIS MACHINE IS TO SPRAY ENOUGH PAINT TO COVER AN ENTIRE BUILDING IN SECONDS! BUT, BY CONCENTRATING THE BLAST OF AIR, I CAN TURN IT INTO AN ALL-POWERFUL WEAPON!

WELL, THUNDER GOD?? WHAT USE ARE YOUR BRAVE WORDS AND EMPTY THREATS NOW?? MR. HYDE IS STILL YOUR MASTER!!

BUT THEN, FLYING INTO A FIT OF RAGE SUCH AS FEW MORTALS HAVE EVER WITNESSED, THE MIGHTY THOR SLAMS HIS HAMMER INTO THE HEAVY OAK FLOORING, ANCHORING HIMSELF TO THE SPOT!
THE TIME FOR WORDS IS PAST!! MY POWER SHALL NOW SPEAK FOR ME!

THOR'S GODLIKE WRATH FLOWS DOWN INTO HIS HAMMER, CAUSING IT TO GLOW WITH NAKED ENERGY--ENERGY WHICH TRAVELS THRU THE WOODEN FLOOR LIKE LIGHTNING...

...UNTIL IT STRIKES THE GIGANTIC SPRAYER, SHORT-CIRCUITING THE MACHINE, AND SENDING THE EVIL CREATURE WHO HAD OPERATED IT SPRAWLING ACROSS THE HALL!!!
10

THEN, SEIZING THE COBRA AGAIN, THOR HURLS HIM INTO THE FLEEING MR. HYDE, STOPPING THE ARCH-VILLAIN IN HIS TRACKS!!
WHY SUCH HASTE, HYDE?? I'VE ONLY BEGUN TO FIGHT!!

WHILE OUTSIDE THE EXHIBITION HALL...
THE FIVE MINUTES ARE UP, MEN!! BREAK INTO THE HALL!!
LET'S GO!!

THE SOUND OF SPLINTERING TIMBERS!! THE POLICE ARE CRASHING IN!
THOR IS FAR STRONGER THAN I DREAMED!! I'VE NO CHANCE ALONE AGAINST HIM! I'VE GOT TO ESCAPE-- BEFORE THE POLICE REACH ME!!

NOW-- WHILE THOR'S HEAD IS TURNED! HE DOESN'T SUSPECT I HAVE ANOTHER IDENTITY! IF ONLY I CAN DRINK MY PRECIOUS POTION IN TIME!!

ONE MORE SECOND IS ALL I NEED!!

IT'S DONE!

BY THE TIME THOR REACHES THE SPOT, MR. HYDE IS GONE-- REPLACED BY THE ORDINARY-LOOKING FIGURE OF CALVIN ZABO...
GOOD! THE COBRA SLOWED HIM DOWN JUST LONG ENOUGH FOR ME TO MAKE MY TRANSFORMATION UNSEEN!
STEP ASIDE, FOLKS! LET US THRU!
YOU'RE JUST IN TIME, OFFICER!! THOR CAUGHT THE COBRA! THEY'RE IN THAT DIRECTION!!
LET'S GO, BOYS! AND KEEP YOUR EYES OPEN FOR MR. HYDE!
THEN, AS THE POLICE REACH THE SPOT AND TAKE OVER...
STOP SQUIRMING, COBRA! YOU'RE NOT GOIN' ANYWHERE!
EXCEPT TO JAIL, THAT IS!
WHERE COULD HYDE HAVE DISAPPEARED TO??
YOU WON'T BE ABLE TO HOLD ME! I'LL ESCAPE SOMEHOW! MR. HYDE WILL COME BACK FOR ME! YOU'LL SEE!
LET'S HOPE HE DOES! WE'VE GOT ANOTHER CELL WAITING FOR HIM!
TOO BAD, COBRA! YOU'VE SERVED YOUR PURPOSE! I'M THRU WITH YOU! HOW LUCKY FOR ME THAT NO ONE, NOT EVEN THOR SUSPECTS THAT MR. HYDE IS ALSO CALVIN ZABO!!
THOR MAY THINK I'VE FLED, BUT I'M NOT FINISHED WITH HIM YET!
CONGRATULATIONS, THOR! YOU PUT UP A MAGNIFICENT FIGHT!
OH, WAIT TILL THE GIRLS BACK HOME HEAR THAT I WAS CLOSE ENOUGH TO TOUCH THE MIGHTY THOR!!
ANY STATEMENT TO MAKE FOR THE PRESS, THOR?
NO! NONE!
I'LL FOLLOW HIM AND WAIT UNTIL I GET HIM ALONE!

I KNOW I CAN BEAT THOR IN A HAND-TO-HAND FIGHT, IF I CAN JUST TEAR THAT HAMMER OF HIS AWAY FROM HIM!
HYDE IS SOMEWHERE NEAR! I CAN ALMOST SENSE HIS EVIL PRESENCE!!

HE WALKED RIGHT PAST ME, NOT SUSPECTING A THING! BUT HOW COULD HE SUSPECT?? HE'S LOOKING FOR THE UGLY MR. HYDE!

AND, NOW THAT HE'S ALONE IN A QUIET SECTION OF TOWN, HE'S ABOUT TO FIND MR. HYDE--SOONER THAN HE THINKS!!

AND SO, FAREWELL ONCE AGAIN TO THE UNSUCCESSFUL, SECOND-RATE SCIENTIST NAMED CALVIN ZABO...

THE IDENTITY OF ZABO SERVES ONLY ONE PURPOSE--AS THE PERFECT HIDING PLACE FOR THE GREATEST CRIMINAL OF ALL TIME--

--THE MAN WITHOUT A CONSCIENCE--WITHOUT MERCY!! THE NIGHT PROWLER WITH THE STRENGTH OF A DOZEN NORMAL HUMANS--THE MYSTERIOUS MR. HYDE!!!

THERE!! I TURN MY JACKET INSIDE OUT AND MY TRANSFORMATION IS COMPLETE!!
AND NOW FOR MY GREATEST VICTORY--

--THE COMPLETE DESTRUCTION OF MY HATED ENEMY--THOR!!

ALL I NEED DO IS SEND THAT ACCURSED HAMMER FLYING FROM HIS HAND!

HAH! THANKS TO MY GREAT STRENGTH, I DID IT!
HYDE!!

ARGHH! I DIDN'T FORCE IT FAR ENOUGH!! IT'S ALMOST WITHIN HIS REACH!!
AGAIN I'VE SIXTY SECONDS TO REGAIN MY MALLET!!

BUT THIS TIME, THE THUNDER GOD MAKES A STARTLING DECISION...
LET IT LAY!! IF I CANNOT DEFEAT THIS EVIL BEING BARE-HANDED WITHIN ONE MINUTE, I AM NOT WORTHY OF THE NAME THOR!!

NEVER HAVE I DESPISED A FOE AS MUCH AS YOU! NEVER HAVE I BEEN SO EAGER TO FEEL MY AVENGING FISTS LASH OUT AND FIND THEIR MARK!!!
AND NEVER HAVE YOU BEEN BEATEN AS I'M GOING TO BEAT YOU NOW!!
14

AND SO, AS THE SECONDS TICK RELENTLESSLY BY, THE TWO TITANS CLASH!!!

YOU BOAST OF HAVING THE STRENGTH OF MANY MEN!! THEREFORE I NEED NOT SHRINK FROM USING SOME OF MY OWN SUPER POWER!!

FIVE SECONDS HAVE ALREADY ELAPSED! I MUST BE CAREFUL NOT TO LOSE COUNT!!

YOU CAN'T STOP HYDE WITH ONE SINGLE BLOW!!!
ALL YOU'VE DONE IS GIVEN ME A WEAPON!!

TRULY YOUR STRENGTH IS A THING TO MARVEL AT!! BUT--ONLY FOR A HUMAN!!

HUMAN YOU CALL ME??! I'LL SHOW YOU HOW MUCH MORE THAN HUMAN I REALLY AM!!
WHAT A PITY THAT SUCH SUPERB STRENGTH SHOULD BE HOUSED IN SO EVIL A BODY!

TALK! TALK! TALK! THAT'S ALL YOU DO! I'LL LET MY FISTS DO MY FIGHTING FOR ME!!
TWENTY SECONDS HAVE ELAPSED!! I MUST SPEED UP THE PACE NOW!!

OF THE MANY FOES I HAVE BATTLED--EVEN INCLUDING THE CRAFTY LOKI, YOU ARE THE MOST COMPLETELY EVIL-- THE MOST THOROUGHLY WICKED OF ALL!!

THE MOST TOTALLY UNDESERVING OF MERCY!!
NO! IT ISN'T POSSIBLE!! NOBODY CAN FIGHT LIKE THAT!!

THE MIGHTY THOR CAN!!!

SEIZING THAT CEMENT STAIR STANCHION WILL DO YOU NO GOOD, HYDE!!
STAY BACK!! KEEP AWAY FROM ME!

IT'S IMPOSSIBLE!! NOTHING HUMAN COULD STOP SHORT SO FAST!!
YOU FORGET, HYDE--THE THUNDER GOD IS FAR MORE THAN HUMAN!!

FORTY SECONDS!! THE MARGIN FOR ERROR IS GROWING TOO NARROW! I MUST END THIS--NOW!
YOU HAVE HAD YOUR LAST CHANCE, HYDE!! YOUR TIME HAS RUN OUT!

NO! I WON'T BE BEATEN! I WON'T!!
THE CHOICE IS NO LONGER YOURS, EVIL ONE!

FORTY FIVE SECONDS!! ONLY FIFTEEN SECONDS LEFT!!

IT COULD ONLY HAVE ENDED LIKE THIS, MORTAL!!

AND NOW, I CAN SULLY MY HANDS ON YOU NO LONGER! BUT THERE ARE OTHERS BETTER ABLE TO FINISH THE JOB...
FIFTY SECONDS!! NOT A SECOND TO SPARE!!

LET THESE WORDS REMAIN WITH YOU ALWAYS, HYDE!! IF EVER YOU APPEAR AGAIN TO MENACE MAN-KIND, THOR WILL BE THERE, TOO!! AND NOW--FAREWELL!

LOOK!! FLYING RIGHT TOWARDS US--IT'S HYDE!!
FIVE SECONDS LEFT TO RETRIEVE MY HAMMER!!

LET ME GRASP THEE, MY BELOVED URU MALLET! LET ME FEEL THY HEFT! TOGETHER, WE ARE AS NOBLE ODIN WOULD WILL IT--INVINCIBLE!!

WELL DONE, THOR!
GUARD HIM CAREFULLY, CAPTAIN! I FEEL THERE IS MUCH ABOUT MR. HYDE THAT WE DO NOT SUSPECT!

WHERE DID HE COME FROM? WHERE DID HE GET HIS STRENGTH?? WHAT IS HIS TRUE PURPOSE? SOMEDAY WE SHALL LEARN!

BUT, FOR THE PRESENT, I MUST RETURN TO MY OTHER EXISTENCE, AS DR. DON BLAKE... AND ONCE AGAIN BEHOLD THE FACE OF THE GIRL I LOVE!

A SHORT TIME LATER, A WEARY YOUNG DOCTOR OPENS THE DOOR TO HIS OUTER OFFICE...
HELLO, JANE! I'VE RETURNED!
AND, WITH THE CAPTURE OF THE COBRA AND MR. HYDE, THE CITIZENS OF OUR CITY CAN ONCE MORE RELAX AND...
SHE DOESN'T HEAR ME! SHE'S WATCHING THE LATE HOUR NEWS...

BUT THEN, AS JANE SWITCHES OFF THE SET, AND TURNS...
I RETURNED AS SOON AS I COULD, JANE...
YOU!! HOW CAN YOU STAND THERE--HOW CAN YOU LOOK ME IN THE EYE--AFTER WHAT YOU'VE DONE??!! I HEARD ABOUT IT ON THE NEWS!!

I HEARD HOW YOU BETRAYED THOR--TOLD MR. HYDE WHERE TO FIND HIM, IN ORDER TO INSURE YOUR OWN SAFETY!! TO THINK THAT I ONCE--ONCE THOUGHT I LOVED YOU!! -SOB-
JANE! MY DARLING--WAIT! LET ME EXPLAIN--!

SHE'S GONE! BUT WHAT ELSE COULD I EXPECT! A GIRL LIKE JANE COULD NEVER LOVE A COWARD! AND THAT'S WHAT SHE THINKS I AM!
AS THOR, I AM FORBIDDEN TO LOVE A MORTAL GIRL!! AND NOW--EVEN AS DON BLAKE, I HAVE LOST THE GIRL I DESIRE!
SLAM

THUS, EVEN IN VICTORY, I FIND DEFEAT! IS LONELINESS AND SORROW THE PRICE I MUST EVER PAY FOR BEING --THOR, THE GOD OF THUNDER ??!
THE END

DON'T MISS NEXT ISSUE'S FULL-LENGTH THOR THRILLER, STARRING THE MOST NOBLE, THE MOST DRAMATIC SUPER-HERO IN ALL THE WORLD!

TALES of ASGARD
HOME OF THE MIGHTY NORSE GODS!
THE MARVEL COMICS GROUP PROUDLY ANNOUNCES THE START OF A NEW BIOGRAPHY IN DEPTH...
BALDER
WRITTEN WITH PASSION BY: STAN LEE
DRAWN WITH PAGEANTRY BY: JACK KIRBY
INKED WITH POWER BY: VINCE COLLETTA
LETTERED WITH PRIDE BY: ART SIMEK
"THE BRAVE"
YOU SUMMONED ME, SIRE?
I DID! STEP FORWARD, BALDER--INTO THE PRESENCE OF ODIN!
X-718
1

YESTERDAY, DURING THE FINAL BATTLE BETWEEN MY WARRIORS AND THE DEADLY STORM GIANTS, YOU DESERTED THE FIGHT WHEN WE PURSUED THEM BACK TO THEIR LAND! HAVE YOU AN EXPLANATION FOR ME, BALDER?
YES, SIRE! I SAW A BIRD FALL FROM ITS NEST, AND I TURNED TO PLACE IT BACK WITH ITS MOTHER!

WHAT??! YOU DARE GIVE ODIN SO LAME AN EXCUSE?!! FOR THAT, YOU SHALL FACE THE TEST OF MORTAL DEATH!
NO, SIRE! HAVE MERCY! BALDER'S COURAGE HAS BEEN PROVED A THOUSAND-FOLD! WE BESEECH THEE--!!
STAY YOUR TONGUES, MY FRIENDS! I HAVE NO CHOICE BUT TO DO AS ODIN COMMANDS!

MY LORD-- HEAR OUR PETITION! WE BEG THEE NOT TO SLAY BRAVE BALDER!
TAKE THE LIFE OF ONE OF US INSTEAD!
SILENCE! ODIN HAS SPOKEN! MY LAW MAY NOT BE DEFIED-- BY GODLING, OR MORTAL!

AS FAMED FOR HIS TERRIBLE ANGER AND SWIFT PUNISHMENT, AS HIS INSCRUTIBLE WISDOM, MIGHTY ODIN HAS BALDER BROUGHT TO THE AREA OF EXECUTION...
I STAND READY TO ACCEPT WHATEVER MY LORD ODIN DECREES!

I CANNOT BEAR TO WATCH THIS SIGHT! FOR TRULY, BRAVE BALDER IS THE MOST BELOVED OF ALL THE GODLINGS OF ASGARD!
SOUND THE TRUMPETS! LET THE SENTENCE BE CARRIED OUT!
AS YOU COMMAND, SIRE!

WITH A GRIEVING HEART, THE STEADY-ARMED ***TYR***, MASTER ARCHER OF ASGARD, PREPARES TO CARRY OUT THE AWESOME COMMAND OF ODIN!

ONLY THE IMPERIAL COMMAND OF ODIN HIMSELF COULD MAKE ME DO THIS TRAGIC THING!

BUT, AT THE EXACT SPLIT-SECOND THAT TYR RELEASES HIS FATAL ARROW, A SHARP-EYED HAWK SWOOPS DOWN FROM THE CLOUDLESS SKY, AND...

...SEIZES THE SPEEDING ARROW IN ITS POWERFUL TALONS--MERE INCHES SHORT OF ITS UNFLINCHING TARGET!!

BRAVE BALDER HAS BEEN ***SAVED!!!***
EVEN THE DEADLY ***HAWK***, THAT MERCILESS BIRD OF PREY, FELT LOVE IN ITS HEART FOR NOBLE BALDER!

BUT THE ORDEAL OF BALDER IS NOT YET ENDED!! AT A COMMAND FROM ODIN, HIS BROTHER HONIR, CHAMPION SPEAR THROWER OF ASGARD, PICKS UP HIS TRUEST SHAFT...
I COMMAND THEE, HONIR!! LET YOUR WEAPON FLY STRAIGHT AND TRUE!!
I CAN DO NAUGHT BUT OBEY THE SOVEREIGN WE SERVE!

THIS IS A BLACK DAY FOR ASGARD!! NOW BALDER IS TRULY DOOMED!!

BUT AGAIN A SEEMING MIRACLE OCCURS! BEFORE THE HURTLING WEAPON CAN FIND ITS MARK, A STRONG-LIMBED PLANT SHOOTS UP FROM THE GROUND IN FRONT OF THE IMMOBILE GODLING!

THE SPEAR CANNOT REACH ITS TARGET!
ONCE AGAIN BRAVE BALDER IS SAVED!!!

THOR, MY NOBLE SON--SYMBOL OF ALL THAT'S BEST AMONG MAN AND GODLING--GRASP THY HAMMER!!
I CANNOT DISOBEY THEE, MY FATHER! BUT IN MY HEART I PRAY FOR ANOTHER MIRACLE TO SAVE THE COURAGEOUS BALDER!

THEN, AS THE STEEL-SINEWED ARM OF MIGHTY THOR RAISES HIS INVINCIBLE HAMMER--AND AS BALDER STANDS FIRM--NEITHER FALTERING NOR FLINCHING--THE HAND OF ODIN REACHES OUT...

ENOUGH!! THE TEST IS **ENDED!!** STEP FORWARD, BALDER! STEP FORWARD AND HEED THE WORDS OF ODIN...!

IT WAS **I** WHO SUMMONED THE HAWK--**I** WHO CALLED FORTH THE PLANT! FOR I HAVE A **GIFT** FOR THEE, BRAVE BALDER--THE GIFT OF **INVINCIBILITY!** THE GIFT WHICH CAN ONLY BE WON THRU TRIAL AND TEST! FROM THIS DAY HENCE, **NOTHING** CAN HARM THEE!
ALL HAIL TO **ODIN,** WISEST OF THE WISE!
HAIL TO BALDER THE BRAVE!
5

NOW FOR AGES TO COME, THE BELOVED BALDER WILL BE LIVING PROOF THAT THE BRAVEST ARE THE GENTLEST! LET GODLING AND HUMAN ALIKE NEVER FORGET THAT THERE IS ONE WHO IS **INVINCIBLE**--AND YET, FOR ALL HIS POWER, HIS HEART FEELS LOVE FOR THE HUMBLEST AND THE WEAKEST OF CREATURES!
THIS DAY MOST OF ALL, MY FATHER, I AM PROUD TO BE THE SON OF NOBLE ODIN!

BUT, EVEN AS **ACHILLES** HAD HIS VULNERABLE HEEL, SO DOES BRAVE **BALDER** HAVE ONE POINT OF VULNERABILITY! DON'T MISS OUR SECOND EPISODE NEXT ISSUE, BROUGHT TO YOU, AS ALWAYS, IN THE MAGNIFICENT MARVEL MANNER!

THE END

JOURNEY INTO MYSTERY
WITH
THE MIGHTY THOR
APPROVED BY THE COMICS CODE AUTHORITY
IND.
MARVEL COMICS GROUP 12¢
107 AUG
ALSO FEATURING: TALES OF ASGARD!
NEW! DIFFERENT! SEEMINGLY UNBEATABLE! YOU AND THOR ARE ABOUT TO MEET:
"The GREY GARGOYLE!"

THE MIGHTY THOR
"WHEN THE GREY GARGOYLE STRIKES!"
SETTLE BACK IN A COZY COMFORTABLE CHAIR... BE SURE YOU WON'T BE INTERRUPTED FOR A WHILE... AND PLEASE DON'T READ THIS IF YOU'RE IN A HURRY... BECAUSE YOU'RE REALLY GOING TO ENJOY THIS ONE!
YOUNG AND OLD, BIG AND SMALL, MIGHTY THOR HAS FOUGHT THEM ALL! BUT, THIS TIME HE COMES UP AGAINST A FANTASTIC FOE WHOSE POWER MIGHT EVEN DESTROY THE THUNDER GOD HIMSELF! WE THINK YOU'LL FLIP OVER OUR NEWEST SINISTER STAR... THE GREY GARGOYLE!
WRITTEN BY: STAN LEE, WHO NEEDS THE MONEY
DRAWN BY: JACK KIRBY, WHO ENJOYS THE PRACTICE
INKED BY: CHIC STONE, WHO LOVES THE PUBLICITY
LETTERED BY: ART SIMEK, WHOEVER HE IS!
X-725 1

THE INNER OFFICE OF DR. DON BLAKE IS EMPTY NOW! THE LAST PATIENT HAS DEPARTED, AND THE BROODING PHYSICIAN IS WRAPPED UP IN HIS OWN TROUBLED THOUGHTS...
IT SEEMS I'M NEVER TO FIND THE HAPPINESS I SEEK! AS THOR, GOD OF THUNDER, MY FATHER, ODIN, FORBIDS ME TO MARRY JANE FOSTER BECAUSE THE THUNDER GOD MAY NOT MARRY A MORTAL!

AND, AS DON BLAKE, JANE FOSTER HAS NOTHING BUT LOATHING FOR ME, SINCE SHE THINKS THAT I BETRAYED THOR TO THE COBRA AND MR. HYDE IN ORDER TO SAVE MYSELF!*
...AND THERE IS NO WAY I CAN CONVINCE HER HOW WRONG SHE IS WITHOUT REVEALING THAT DR. BLAKE AND MIGHTY THOR ARE ONE AND THE SAME MAN!!
* REFER TO THOR #105-- "THE THUNDER GOD STRIKES BACK!"--EDITOR.

IT'S TOO BIG A PROBLEM FOR ME TO SOLVE! I DON'T KNOW WHAT TO DO! BUT, IF DON BLAKE CAN'T FIND THE ANSWER--

--PERHAPS THERE IS ONE WHO CAN--

NOW, AS THE GOD OF THUNDER--AS AN IMMORTAL OF ASGARD, THOR, SON OF ODIN, MAY BE ABLE TO FIND AN ANSWER!

BUT, AT THAT MOMENT, THE DOOR TO THE OUTER OFFICE OPENS WIDE, AND...
THOR!! WHA-WHAT ARE YOU DOING HERE!?
JANE! I THOUGHT SHE HAD GONE FOR THE DAY!! I'LL HAVE TO THINK FAST!

I CAME TO FIND BLAKE! I'VE BEEN TOLD HE TRIED TO BETRAY ME TO TWO OF MY FOES! WHERE IS HE? SPEAK, WOMAN!!
I-I DON'T KNOW! HE MUST HAVE LEFT--BY HIS PRIVATE DOOR! HE'S NOT HERE!
2

BUT, THOR-- YOU MUSTN'T SEEK REVENGE! I'M SURE HE MEANT NO HARM! AFTER ALL, HE'S ONLY HUMAN--AND HE MUST HAVE BEEN FRIGHTENED--CONFUSED--

EVEN THOUGH HE'S NOT HEROIC AS YOU--HE'S GOOD--AND KIND--AND--I CAN'T HELP MYSELF--NO MATTER WHAT HE'S DONE--I LOVE HIM!
YOU--STILL LOVE HIM??

WITHOUT ANOTHER WORD--NOT TRUSTING HIMSELF TO SPEAK--NOT TRUSTING HIMSELF TO BETRAY THE ECSTASY IN HIS HEART THE MIGHTY THUNDER GOD TURNS AND STEPS OUT UPON THE WINDOW LEDGE WITH ONE EASY STRIDE! AND THEN...
THOR--WAIT! WHAT ARE YOU GOING TO DO??
DO NOT WORRY! I SHALL NOT HARM THE MAN YOU LOVE--I PROMISE!

THEN, WITH A BLINDING BURST OF SPEED, THOR HURLS HIMSELF INTO THE SKY, HIS HEART BURSTING WITH JOY, HIS VERY LUNGS ACHING TO CRY OUT IN SHEER HAPPINESS!
SHE LOVES ME! SHE LOVES ME!

ONCE HE IS SAFELY OUT OF SIGHT OF JANE FOSTER, THE GOD OF THUNDER PUTS ON A SHOW OF EXHUBERANCE SUCH AS NO MAN HAS EVER WITNESSED BEFORE!
SHE LOVES ME!!

FOR, WHILE THE JOY OF A MORTAL IN LOVE CAN BE A WONDERFUL THING, THE ELATION OF A GOD IS A SIGHT TO MARVEL AT!!
SHE WILL BE MINE! SOME HOW, SOME WAY, I'LL WIN HER!

I'M IN LOVE--EVEN AS YOU ARE!
DO YOU HEAR??? THOR IS IN LOVE!!

AND THEN, IN ONE FINAL BURST OF UNRESTRAINED ENTHUSIASM, THE LIGHT-HEARTED THUNDER GOD DOES A PINWHEEL AROUND AN INCOMING TRANS-ATLANTIC JET WHICH IS PREPARING TO LAND AT J.F.K. INTERNATIONAL AIRPORT...

BUT, WITHIN THE GIANT SHIP, THERE IS ONE WHOSE HEART IS ***NOT*** FILLED WITH GOOD CHEER -- ONE WHOSE COLD BALEFUL EYE WATCHES THE MIGHTY IMMORTAL FLY OFF -- AS HIS BRAIN HATCHES ONE OF THE MOST VILLAINOUS PLOTS OF ALL TIMES!

IT'S THOR!! THE ONE I'VE TRAVELLED HALF-WAY AROUND THE GLOBE TO FIND! THE ONE I MUST DEFEAT, IN ORDER TO ATTAIN MY GREAT GOAL!!

SECONDS LATER, LIKE A ROARING STEEL GOLIATH, THE SPEEDING JET MAKES A FLAWLESS LANDING, RIGHT ON SCHEDULE!

BUT THEN, WHEN THE DOOR SWINGS OPEN, AND THE STEWARD WAITS BELOW FOR THE USUAL RUSH OF PASSENGERS, ONLY ***ONE MAN*** SLOWLY EMERGES...

WH-WHERE ARE THE OTHERS, SIR?
YOU WILL FIND THEM INSIDE!

AND INDEED THEY ***ARE*** FOUND WITHIN THE SHIP -- BUT IN A CONDITION NO PASSENGERS AND CREW HAVE EVER BEEN FOUND IN ***BEFORE!!*** WITH STARK DISBELIEF IN HIS EYES, THE STEWARD EXCLAIMS INCREDULOUSLY...

I- I MUST BE DREAMING! THEY'VE ALL TURNED TO-- STONE!

AND, IN A TAXICAB, MAKING ITS WAY THRU THE CROWDED CITY'S TRAFFIC...

BY THE TIME THE STONE SPELL WEARS OFF THEM AND THEY ARE ABLE TO ACCUSE ME, I'LL BE SAFELY HIDDEN AMONG THE TEEMING MILLIONS OF THE CITY!

"I CAN STILL HARDLY BELIEVE THAT IT ALL HAPPENED SO QUICKLY! IT SEEMS LIKE ONLY YESTERDAY THAT I WAS AN UNKNOWN YOUNG CHEMIST IN PARIS..."
THERE IS SOMETHING WRONG WITH THIS MIXTURE! IT HAS TURNED BLUE INSTEAD OF RED!
DUVAL! HAVE YOU FINISHED THAT SOLUTION YET?? THE INSTITUTE DIRECTOR IS WAITING FOR THE RESULT!
I'M SORRY, SIR! IT WILL TAKE A FEW MOMENTS LONGER! A STRANGE, FOREIGN SUBSTANCE SEEMS TO HAVE AFFECTED THE MIXTURE!
THEN, AFTER HIS SUPERIOR HAS LEFT...
HOW MUCH LONGER MUST I TAKE ORDERS LIKE A MERE LACKEY?? PAUL DUVAL IS MEANT FOR GREATER THINGS!
OHH! I HAVE CARELESSLY SPILLED THE POTION ON MY HAND!
IT IS INCREDIBLE!! IT FEELS LIKE LIQUID FIRE! IT SEEMS TO HAVE A LIFE OF ITS OWN!
WHAT HAVE I DONE?? WHAT IS HAPPENING TO MY HAND??
NO! IT ISN'T POSSIBLE! IT CAN'T BE! THE FINGERS ARE TURNING INTO STONE!!
IT'S THE STRANGE SUBSTANCE IN THE MIXTURE!! IT GAVE THE LIQUID A POWER I NEVER SUSPECTED! BUT NOW-- MON DIEU!!
MY OTHER HAND HAS TURNED TO STONE-- MERELY BY TOUCHING IT!
WHAT WILL HAPPEN TO ME?? WHERE WILL IT END?? I'VE BECOME A FREAK-- A STRANGE, INHUMAN TYPE OF BEING! HOW CAN I GO OUT IN PUBLIC?? HOW CAN I FACE THE WORLD??
BUT THEN...
WAIT! I-I'VE TOUCHED MY FACE--!! NO! OH, NO!
IT'S TRUE!! WHATEVER I TOUCH, WITH MY HAND OF STONE--THAT ALSO TURNS INTO LIVING STONE!! WHAT MANNER OF MADNESS IS THIS??!
5

"I REMEMBER HOW I THEN TESTED MY **STONE SPELL** BY TOUCHING **ANOTHER** MAN IN THE STREET! IT WORKED ON OTHERS AS WELL AS ON MYSELF!"

A MOMENT AGO HE WAS **HUMAN**!! **NOW** HE'S A THING OF **STONE**!

A MAN MERELY **TOUCHED** HIM, AND NOW-- **LOOK**!

"THEN, I REALIZED MY STONE SPELL ENABLED ME TO ACCOMPLISH ALMOST **ANYTHING**! ALL I NEEDED DO, TO ROB A STORE, WAS **TOUCH** THE PROPRIETOR!"

DO NOT FEAR, MY FRIEND! MY STONE SPELL LASTS FOR ONLY AN HOUR! SIXTY SECONDS FROM NOW YOU WILL BE NORMAL AGAIN-- THOUGH CONSIDERABLY **POORER**!

"I TURNED MY POWER TO BIGGER AND BIGGER CRIMES--ALWAYS WITH THE SAME RESULT!"

THE VAULT IS **EMPTY**! THE GUARD HAS TURNED TO **STONE**!

NATIONAL BANK

"BUT EVEN THE WEALTH I HAD ACCUMULATED BROUGHT ME NO SATISFACTION--"

BAH! THESE BAUBLES ARE MEANINGLESS! SOONER OR LATER THE POLICE WILL TRACK THEM DOWN AND SEIZE THEM!

THERE MUST BE SOMETHING **GREATER** I CAN STRIVE FOR!

"AND THEN, READING ABOUT **THOR** IN THE PAPER, I FOUND WHAT I HAD BEEN SEEKING--"

OF **COURSE**! THAT'S THE **ONE** THING THAT MATTERS! THE ONE THING I CAN ACCOMPLISH WITH MY AWESOME STONE SPELL! I SHALL STEAL THOR'S POWER OF **IMMORTALITY**!

FINAL

PARIS ~ POST

FINAL

THOR'S HAMMER FLATTENS COBRA AND MISTER HYDE IN RUNNING BATTLE!

ANOTHER CRIME WAVE STOPPED BY ALLEGEDLY IMMORTAL ADVENTURER!

IF THOR TRULY **IS** IMMORTAL, HIS POWER MUST COME FROM HIS ENCHANTED **HAMMER**! SOMEHOW I MUST WIN IT **FROM** HIM!
HERE'S THE CENTER OF TOWN, LIKE YOU ASKED, PAL!

SLOWLY, MENACINGLY, THE COLD-EYED PASSENGER REMOVES HIS GLOVE...
I AM **NOT** YOUR PAL!

AND THEN, AT A TOUCH OF HIS GREY, STONE-HARD FINGERS...
NOW! YOU WILL REMAIN THIS WAY FOR **ONE HOUR**! IN THAT TIME, **THOR** IS SURE TO LEARN WHAT HAS HAPPENED AND COME TO INVESTIGATE! AND THEN-- I SHALL **STRIKE**!

MINUTES AFTER THE WORDS LEAVE DUVAL'S MERCILESS LIPS...

BULLETIN!! AUTHORITIES ARE MYSTIFIED OVER A PLANELOAD OF STONE PASSENGERS WHICH LANDED A FEW MINUTES AGO AT J.F.K. INTERNATIONAL AIRPORT! AND, JUST SECONDS AGO, A STONE TAXI DRIVER WAS FOUND AT THE CORNER OF 53RD AND MADISON...

THAT RADIO REPORT!! WHAT CAN IT MEAN??

THE MAYOR HAS CALLED UPON ALL CITIZENS TO REMAIN CALM--NOT TO PANIC--UNTIL A THOROUGH INVESTIGATION CAN BE MADE--

I MUST GET THERE AT ONCE!!

I'VE GOTTEN USED TO SEEIN' PIGEONS AT MY WINDOW LEDGE--BUT WHO EVER EXPECTED HIM??!

I'M JUST IN TIME!

WHAT NUT WOULD DRESS A STONE STATUE LIKE A CAB DRIVER, AND PUT HIM IN A TAXI??

SEARCH ME! I JUST HOPE HE IS ONLY A STATUE!!

HEY, CHARLIE--LOOK WHO'S HERE! WHAT DO YOU MAKE OF THIS, THOR?
IN VIEW OF WHAT HAPPENED AT THE AIRPORT, IT BEARS CLOSE STUDY! IT IS TOO LIFELIKE!

OFFICER, WITH THE AUTHORITY VESTED IN ME BY THE AVENGERS, I REQUEST PERMISSION TO TAKE THAT STONE FIGURE TO DR. DON BLAKE FOR DETAILED EXAMINATION!
THE AVENGERS HAVE TOP FEDERAL PRIORITY, SO HE'S ALL YOURS, BIG FELLOW!

EASILY CARRYING THE HEAVY STONE FIGURE TO DON BLAKE'S OFFICE, THE MIGHTY THUNDER GOD THEN CHANGES BACK TO THE LAME PHYSICIAN AND SUMMONS HIS LOVELY NURSE...
DOCTOR BLAKE!! WHAT IS IT??
I'LL EXPLAIN LATER, JANE! BRING ME MY MEDICAL BAG AND ADMIT NO PATIENTS FOR THE REST OF THE DAY!
I WAS RIGHT! THERE IS A HEARTBEAT-- ALTHOUGH IT'S SO FAINT AS TO BE ALMOST INAUDIBLE!
THAT STONE MAN! HE MUST HAVE SOMETHING IN COMMON WITH THOSE FIGURES FOUND AT THE AIRPORT! BUT THE LATEST BULLETIN SAID THEY HAVE TURNED BACK TO NORMAL AGAIN!

I BELIEVE HE WILL TURN BACK TO NORMAL IN A MATTER OF MINUTES, ALSO! HIS CONDITION NOW IS SIMILAR TO A MAN WHO'S BEEN IN A DEEP FREEZE AND IS STARTING TO THAW OUT!
BUT WHAT COULD HAVE CAUSED SUCH A FANTASTIC CONDITION??
I DON'T KNOW, JANE--BUT I WON'T REST UNTIL I'VE FOUND THE ANSWER!

MEANWHILE, IN A NEARBY HOTEL ROOM, PAUL DUVAL BEGINS TO DON A STRANGE COSTUME... AS HE PREPARES TO EXECUTE ONE OF THE MOST DARING PLANS EVER CONCEIVED!
STANDING IN THE STREET NEAR THE TAXI, NO ONE NOTICED ME AS I OBSERVED THE ENTIRE THING!

FOR WHY SHOULD ANYONE NOTICE THE ORDINARY FORM OF PAUL DUVAL?? I WAS JUST ONE OF THE CROWD!
BUT NOW, BY REMOVING MY PROTECTIVE GLOVE, AND TOUCHING MY STONE HAND TO THE REST OF MY BODY, I SHALL CEASE BEING PAUL DUVAL FOR THE NEXT HOUR...

AND INSTEAD, THE GREY GARGOYLE SHALL MAKE HIS FIRST PUBLIC APPEARANCE AS I GO TO THE PLACE WHERE I SAW THOR FLY WITH THE STONE TAXI DRIVER!
8

EFFORTLESSLY, EASILY, WITHOUT THE SLIGHTEST HESITATION, THE GREY GARGOYLE SCALES THE WALL OF HIS BUILDING...
MY STONE FINGERS ARE SO POWERFUL, THAT IT'S AN EASY MATTER FOR ME TO SCALE ANY WALL MERELY BY TEARING OUT CHUNKS OF THE MASONRY TO GRIP ONTO!

THEN, MOVING MENACINGLY FROM ROOFTOP TO ROOFTOP, HE REACHES THE MIDTOWN OFFICE OF DR. DON BLAKE...

I'M GLAD I SENT JANE HOME EARLY! I WANT TO GIVE THIS STRANGE CASE MY FULL ATTENTION!
NOW TO WAIT FOR THOR TO RETURN!

WHA-?? ANOTHER STONE FIGURE! BUT--YOU CAN MOVE! YOU'RE DIFFERENT!
VERY PERCEPTIVE OF YOU, DOCTOR! BUT YOU CANNOT SUSPECT HOW DIFFERENT THE GREY GARGOYLE REALLY IS!

BEFORE YOU ENTERTAIN ANY FOOLISH NOTIONS SUCH AS TRYING TO SUMMON THE POLICE, LET ME SHOW YOU THE EXTENT OF MY POWER! SEE HOW I FOLD A PAPER AIRPLANE!..
I'LL HEAR HIM OUT! I MUST LEARN WHAT HIS PURPOSE IS!

NOW, MERELY BY TOUCHING IT TO THE EXPOSED PALM OF MY HAND, I TURN IT INTO A THING OF STONE!

SO YOU SEE, DOCTOR, ANYTHING CAN BECOME A DANGEROUS WEAPON IN THE HANDS OF THE GREY GARGOYLE!!

IF YOU POSSESS SUCH INCREDIBLE POWER, THEN YOU'RE THE ONE RESPONSIBLE FOR TURNING THOSE PEOPLE INTO STONE FIGURES!!

BUT OF COURSE! I HAVE NO REASON TO DENY IT! NO ONE IS POWERFUL ENOUGH TO MAKE ME ACCOUNT FOR MY DEEDS!
NOT EVEN MIGHTY THOR-- WHOM I SHALL DEFEAT COMPLETELY AS SOON AS HE RETURNS HERE! WAIT! COME BACK!
I'VE GOT TO GET AWAY LONG ENOUGH TO CHANGE TO THOR WITHOUT HIM SEEING ME!

DESPITE HIS LAMENESS, THE VALIANT DOCTOR MANAGES TO MAKE IT TO THE ELEVATOR BEFORE THE HEAVIER, SLOWER GREY GARGOYLE CAN REACH HIM...
YOU CAN'T ESCAPE ME! THE INDICATOR WILL TELL ME WHERE THE ELEVATOR HAS GONE, AND I'LL COME AFTER YOU!
THAT'S WHAT I WANT! FOR, BY THEN-- I'LL BE THOR!

FINALLY, AS HE REACHES THE ROOF...
I'VE GOT TO LEARN WHY HE WANTS TO FIND AND DEFEAT THOR! AND THERE'S ONLY ONE WAY TO DO IT--

LIKE THIS!!

AND NOW, THE GREY GARGOYLE WILL GET HIS WISH!

THAT SOUND! LIKE SOMEONE CHIPPING AWAY AT THE SIDE OF THE BUILDING!
THOR! IT'S YOU!! NOW TO SEIZE YOUR HAMMER --AND THEN DESTROY YOU!
YOU THINK SUCH A TASK IS AS SIMPLE AS YOU MAKE IT SOUND?? YOU SHALL NOT TURN ME TO STONE!

SO! YOU KNOW OF MY POWER! THEN YOU SHOULD KNOW I CANNOT BE DEFEATED!
AND ONCE I POSSESS YOUR ENCHANTED HAMMER, IMMORTALITY SHALL BE MINE!
10

AHHH! IT IS MY HAMMER YOU WANT! VERY WELL-- YOU SHALL HAVE IT!

YOU SAY YOU CANNOT BE DEFEATED?? LET THIS PUT THE LIE TO YOUR WORDS!!

I KNOW THAT A MERE FALL WILL NOT STOP SO POWERFUL A CREATURE, BUT I SHALL GIVE HIM NO REST UNTIL HE BEGS FOR MERCY!

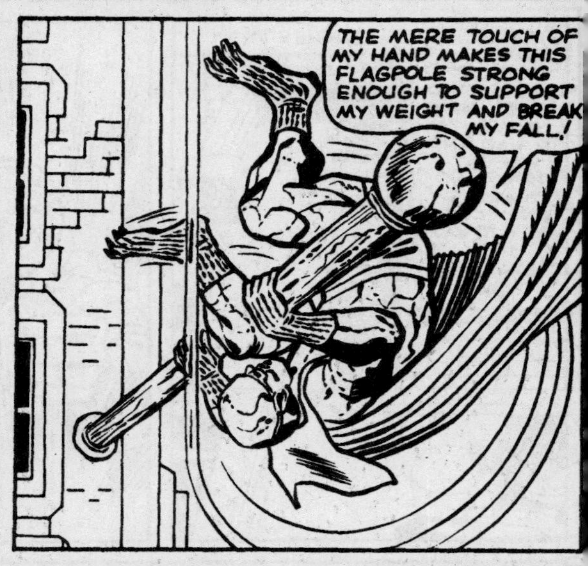
THE MERE TOUCH OF MY HAND MAKES THIS FLAGPOLE STRONG ENOUGH TO SUPPORT MY WEIGHT AND BREAK MY FALL!

BUT THOR IS EVEN MIGHTIER THAN I HAD THOUGHT! I MUST BE MORE CAREFUL NEXT TIME!

HE'S AFTER ME AGAIN! SUCH SPEED-- SUCH POWER!! I MUST BE CLEVER-- RUTHLESS-- IF I AM TO TRIUMPH!
MARVEL OIL

BY STRIKING MY STONE HANDS TOGETHER, THEY'LL ACT LIKE FLINT, CAUSING THE GAS FUMES IN THIS SERVICE STATION TO IGNITE!
HE'S ALMOST UPON ME! NOW, IF I CAN TIME THIS JUST RIGHT, THE ENSUING EXPLOSION WILL CATCH HIM JUST WHEN HE LEASTS EXPECTS IT!! --NOW!!

WHOOM!

HE'S STUNNED! IT WAS EASIER THAN I DARED TO HOPE!
AND NOW, AT LAST--THOR'S HAMMER SHALL BE MINE--AND WITH IT, THE GREATEST GIFT OF ALL TIME--THE GIFT OF--IMMORTALITY!!!

BUT, ALTHOUGH THE GREY GARGOYLE CAN LIFT THE HANDLE OF THOR'S ENCHANTED MALLET, WHEN HE TRIES TO LIFT THE MIGHTY HAMMER HEAD OFF THE GROUND, HE LEARNS TO HIS AMAZEMENT...
WITH ALL MY SUPER-HUMAN STRENGTH, I CAN'T LIFT IT A HAIRSBREADTH OFF THE GROUND!! IT'S AS THOUGH IT'S WELDED TO THE CEMENT!

BUT THEN, QUICKLY RECOVERING FROM THE EFFECTS OF THE UNEXPECTED EXPLOSION, AND SEEING HIS HAMMER BEING GRASPED BY ANOTHER, THE ANGRY THUNDER GOD MAKES HIS FIRST MISTAKE...
YOU DARE PROFANE MY BELOVED HAMMER WITH YOUR EVIL GRASP??!!
THIS IS MY CHANCE!! HE'S CLOSE ENOUGH FOR ME TO TOUCH HIM!

MOVING WITH SURPRISING SPEED FOR ONE SO HEAVY, THE GREY GARGOYLE LASHES OUT, TOUCHING THE ASTONISHED IMMORTAL WITH HIS NAKED PALM!!

I'VE **DONE** IT! I'VE **BEATEN** YOU! YOU'VE TURNED TO MOTIONLESS **STONE!**

BUT, AT THAT MOMENT, A SPECIAL POLICE DETAIL REACHES THE SCENE, ARMED WITH PORTABLE FLAME-THROWERS!

THERE HE **IS!!**

TURN THE FLAME-THROWERS ON HIM! THEY'RE THE ONLY THINGS THAT MIGHT **STOP** HIM! FLAME CAN TURN STONE TO **LAVA!**

BUT FAST THOUGH THE OFFICERS ARE, THE AWESOME GREY GARGOYLE IS EVEN FASTER--UTILIZING HIS AMAZING CLIMBING ABILITY, HE SCAMPERS UP THE SIDE OF A BUILDING, HIGHER THAN THE FLAME-THROWERS CAN REACH!

HE'S GETTING **AWAY!**

QUICK! THROW A CORDON AROUND THE NEIGHBOR-HOOD!

AND, AS THE POLICE MOVE SPEEDILY TO CUT OFF THE GREY GARGOYLE'S ESCAPE, THEY FAIL TO NOTICE THE HANDSOME, SEEMINGLY-LIFELESS FIGURE WHO, STANDING OFF-BALANCE, BEGINS TO SLOWLY TOPPLE TO THE GROUND...

CIRCLE THE BLOCK!! SPREAD OUT! **ON THE DOUBLE!**

BUT, AS THE STONE FIGURE OF THOR STRIKES THE CEMENT BELOW HIM, HIS ENCHANTED **HAMMER** ALSO STRIKES THE GROUND-- AND, AT THAT SPLIT-SECOND...

...THE MOST DRAMATIC CHANGE IN ALL ADVENTUREDOM TAKES PLACE ONCE MORE! FOR, NO STONE SPELL, NO EARTHLY POWER, CAN PREVENT THE URU HAMMER FROM WEAVING ITS ENCHANTMENT AS ODIN HAD SO ORDAINED, MANY MANY CENTURIES AGO!

I'M **DON BLAKE** AGAIN!! AND, WHEN MY PHYSICAL SELF CHANGED--WHEN MY ENTIRE NUCLEAR AND MOLECULAR CELL STRUCTURE WAS ALTERED--THE STONE SPELL **ALSO** FADED INTO OBLIVION!!

I'M FLESH AND BLOOD ONCE MORE! I CAN **MOVE!**

I MUST RETURN TO MY OFFICE-- I NEED TIME TO THINK-- TO PLAN! THE GREY GARGOYLE IS PERHAPS THE MOST DANGEROUS FOE I'VE EVER BATTLED!

THE GARGOYLE'S SPELL LASTS FOR TWENTY-FOUR HOURS! SO, I DARE NOT CHANGE BACK TO THOR DURING THAT TIME, OR I'LL RETURN TO STONE AGAIN!

BUT I CAN'T STAY HERE AND DO NOTHING! THE GARGOYLE MUST BE HIDING NOW, GLOATING OVER HIS VICTORY! I'VE GOT TO FIND A WAY TO MAKE HIM SHOW HIMSELF AGAIN-- I MUST LEARN MORE ABOUT HIM!

MOMENTS LATER, THE LAME PHYSICIAN PHONES A FRIEND WHO MANAGES A TV NEWSREEL COMPANY...
--AND IF YOU DO AS I SAY, I PROMISE YOU THE SCOOP OF THE CENTURY! TONY STARK HAS THE DEVICE YOU NEED-- TELL HIM THE CODE WORD I GAVE YOU, AND HE'LL LEND IT TO YOU!*
IT'S A DEAL, DOC! YOU'VE NEVER STEERED ME WRONG BEFORE! I'LL DO IT!
GLOBE
*THUS DO THE AVENGERS AID EACH OTHER IN EVERY WAY POSSIBLE! TONY STARK IS, OF COURSE, THE INVENTIVE GENIUS WHOSE OTHER IDENTITY IS THAT OF IRON MAN!

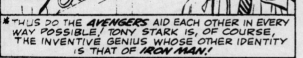

A SHORT TIME LATER, A T.V. 3-D-TYPE PROJECTOR, CONTAINING CERTAIN MODIFICATIONS INVENTED BY TONY STARK, IS MOUNTED ON A FAST-MOVING MOTOR CYCLE...
EVERYTHING IS SET, JUST AS YOU ASKED, DOC!
FINE! NOW I'LL TAKE TV SHOTS OF WHATEVER HAPPENS, AND THE FILM WILL BE YOURS!
ABG NEWS

IT'S WORKING PERFECTLY! ANYONE SEEING THE IMAGE PROJECTED IN FRONT OF ME WOULD SWEAR THAT THE REAL THOR IS RACING THRU THE STREETS AT BREAKNECK SPEED!

SOONER OR LATER, NO MATTER WHERE HE IS, THE GARGOYLE WILL HAVE TO NOTICE THIS!
THANKS TO STARK'S GENIUS, I CAN CONTROL THE ACTIONS OF THE PROJECTED IMAGE--MAKING IT MOVE LIKE A LIVING BEING! LUCKY FOR US THAT STARK IS A FRIEND OF IRON MAN!*
*RESPECTING EACH OTHER'S SECRETS, NONE OF THE AVENGERS ARE AWARE OF THE OTHERS' TRUE IDENTITIES!

FINALLY, THE INTENDED QUARRY SEES THE BAIT!
THOR!! BUT HOW DID THE SPELL WEAR OFF SO QUICKLY?

IT WORKED!! THERE'S THE GREY GARGOYLE!!

NOW I MUST MAKE NO SLIP-UP! I'LL RACE THRU THE STREETS, MAKING IT SEEM THAT THOR IS TRYING TO DODGE THE GARGOYLE!

THINKING THE LIFE-LIKE IMAGE IS THE REAL THUNDER GOD, THE STONE MENACE PURSUES IT, UNAWARE OF THE MOTORCYCLE SPEEDING BELOW!
HE'S RUNNING AWAY FROM ME! HE'S AFRAID OF ME! HE KNOWS I'M MORE POWERFUL!

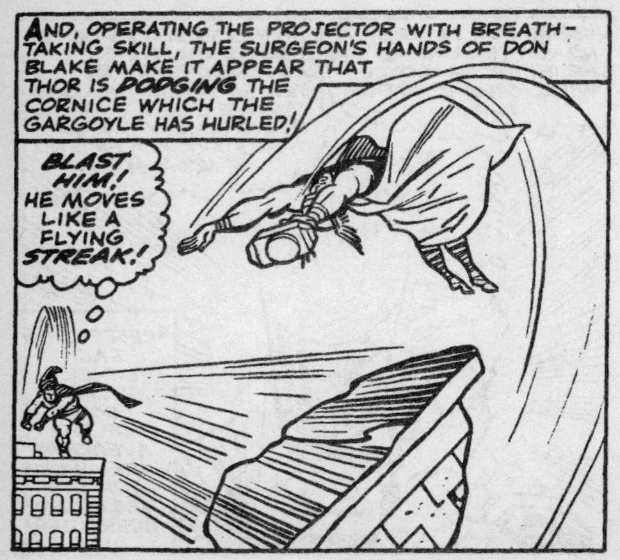
AND, OPERATING THE PROJECTOR WITH BREATH-TAKING SKILL, THE SURGEON'S HANDS OF DON BLAKE MAKE IT APPEAR THAT THOR IS DODGING THE CORNICE WHICH THE GARGOYLE HAS HURLED!
BLAST HIM! HE MOVES LIKE A FLYING STREAK!

SO FAR, SO GOOD! BUT THIS IS ONLY THE BEGINNING! NOW I'VE GOT TO TAKE THE OFFENSIVE!

THOR IS HURLING HIS HAMMER AT ME! THE FOOL! HE DOESN'T REALIZE IT'S THE ONE THING I WANT!

I'LL CATCH IT, AND IT WILL BE MINE FOREVER!
ONLY MY STONE HANDS HAVE THE STRENGTH TO STOP THAT MIGHTY WEAPON!

AM I GOING MAD?? IT PASSED RIGHT THRU ME!

NOW IT'S TURNING IN MID-AIR, HEADING BACK TOWARDS THE THUNDER GOD!

HE'S RETRIEVING IT AGAIN! BUT WAIT! SOMETHING IS WRONG HERE!

HOW DID THOR REMAIN IN THE AIR WITHOUT HOLDING HIS HAMMER?? HE CANNOT FLY BY HIMSELF! THERE IS MORE TO THIS THAN MEETS THE EYE!
16

SUDDENLY, THE GARGOYLE GLANCES BELOW, NOTICING THE SPEEDING CYCLIST WITH THE STRANGE PROJECTOR! QUICKLY PUTTING TWO AND TWO TOGETHER, HE PLUNGES TO THE STREET--

WHATEVER THE EXPLANATION IS, IT MUST LIE WITH THAT MOTORCYCLE RIDER!

HE'S *ON* TO ME! THIS IS THE *SHOWDOWN!*

I'LL CATCH HIM AND DRAG THE TRUTH OUT OF --*WAIT!* THAT FACE!! IT'S THE *DÖCTOR*-- DON BLAKE!!

THE *HUDSON RIVER* IS JUST AHEAD! NOW, IF I CAN TIME THIS JUST RIGHT....!

CRASH

I *DID* IT!! HE COULDN'T STOP IN TIME!! WITHIN SECONDS I'LL HAVE *WON*-- OR IT WILL BE MY *FINISH!*

YOU CAN'T ESCAPE ME *THAT* EASILY! I CAN FOLLOW YOU *ANYWHERE!*

BUT, THE GREY GARGOYLE'S REACH FALLS INCHES SHORT OF THE VALIANT PHYSICIAN, AND BOTH FALL INTO THE DARK, MURKY WATERS...

ONE THING I DIDN'T REALIZE-- IT'S HARD TO KEEP AFLOAT-- MY STONE BODY IS TOO HEAVY!! THAT SHIP!! ITS WAKE IS PULLING ME OUT TO SEA!!

MINUTES LATER, UNABLE TO FIGHT AGAINST THE PULL OF HIS ABNORMALLY HEAVY WEIGHT, THE GREY GARGOYLE BEGINS TO SINK-- DEEPER, AND DEEPER--
IT WILL BE AT LEAST A HALF HOUR BEFORE I CHANGE BACK TO NORMAL AGAIN! BUT, IF I'VE SUNK TOO LOW BY THEN--I'LL NEVER BE ABLE TO REACH THE SURFACE!

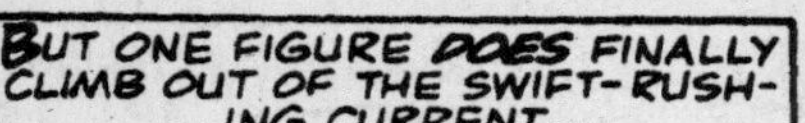

BUT ONE FIGURE DOES FINALLY CLIMB OUT OF THE SWIFT-RUSHING CURRENT...

IT'S OVER!! HE'S BEATEN!

THE GREY GARGOYLE FINALLY FOUND THE IMMORTALITY HE WANTED--AT THE BOTTOM OF THE SEA!

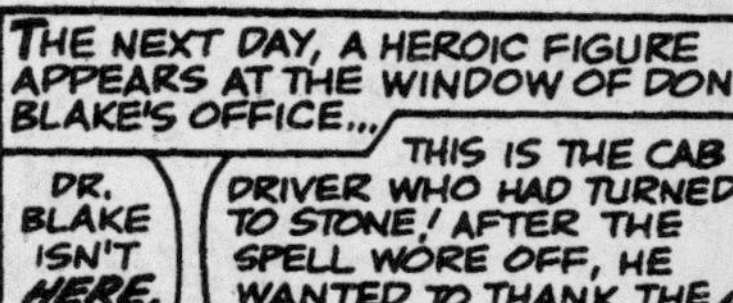

THE NEXT DAY, A HEROIC FIGURE APPEARS AT THE WINDOW OF DON BLAKE'S OFFICE...

DR. BLAKE ISN'T HERE, THOR!
THIS IS THE CAB DRIVER WHO HAD TURNED TO STONE! AFTER THE SPELL WORE OFF, HE WANTED TO THANK THE DOCTOR!
WHERE IS BLAKE?

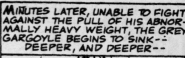

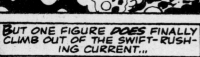

HE'S HOME, RESTING! AS YOU CAN SEE, YOU'RE NOT THE ONLY HERO AROUND HERE!

HMMM... PERHAPS BLAKE IS BRAVER THAN I HAD THOUGHT!

DAILY ...

DARING PHYSICIAN RIDS CITY OF GREY GARGOYLE MENACE

18

YOU CAN SAY THAT AGAIN, MISTER! ANYONE AS POWERFUL AS YOU CAN BE A REAL RIP-SNORTER--BUT YOU GOTTA HAND IT TO THAT SPUNKY LAME DOCTOR!
PERHAPS THERE IS TRUTH IN WHAT YOU SAY! MORE TRUTH THAN YOU EVEN SUSPECT!
NOW WHAT DOES HE MEAN BY THAT?

THEN, WITHOUT ANOTHER WORD, THE MIGHTY THOR, HIS HEART SINGING, TURNS AND HURLS HIMSELF INTO THE BLUE--!!

THOR BATTLES AGAINST HIS OWN ALLIES IN AVENGERS #7, NOW ON SALE! ALSO, DON'T MISS OUR NEXT GREAT ISSUE OF THOR, IN WHICH THE SON OF ODIN MEETS A SURPRISE GUEST STAR!! SEE YOU THEN!

THE END

Tales of ASGARD
HOME OF THE MIGHTY NORSE GODS
OUR LEGENDARY TALE BEGINS WHEN EVIL LOKI VOWS:
"BALDER MUST DIE!"
LAST ISSUE, WE SAW ODIN GIVE BRAVE BALDER THE GIFT OF INVULNERABILITY! BALDER, THE LOYAL! BALDER, THE GENTLE! BALDER, THE PROTECTOR, THE PROTECTOR OF ALL OF NATURE'S LIVING CREATURES!
THE SIMPERING, SOFT-HEARTED BALDER BECOMES ODIN'S FAVORITE, NEXT TO THE ACCURSED THOR! BUT NOT FOR LONG! I SHALL FIND A WAY TO DESTROY HIM!
WRITTEN AND DRAWN BY THE PRIZE-WINNING TEAM OF:
STAN (THE MAN) LEE
and
JACK (KING) KIRBY
INKED BY: VINCE COLLETTA
LETTERING: ART SIMEK
AS THE INNOCENT GODLING SINGS A REFRAIN TO HIS FRIENDS IN THE FOREST, LITTLE DOES HE DREAM THAT LOKI HAS VOWED HIS DEATH!
X-738
1

SEE HIM FUSSING OVER THE BRAIN-LESS BIRDS AND BEASTS, SECURE IN THE KNOWLEDGE THAT ODIN HAS MADE HIM INVINCIBLE! BUT I'LL FIND SOME WAY TO STRIKE AT HIM! LOKI, GOD OF MISCHIEF, CANNOT BEAR TO SEE ONE SO HAPPY AND CONTENTED!
THE NORN QUEEN, MISTRESS OF MAGIC, IS SURE TO KNOW A MYSTIC SPELL WHICH CAN HELP ME DESTROY THE BRAVE BALDER!
THERE SHE IS NOW, PRACTICING HER MAGICAL CHANTS --WEAVING HER WEB OF SORCERY!
LOKI!! THE EVIL ONE! BEGONE! THE NORN QUEEN HAS NO USE FOR SUCH AS YOU!
SILENCE, FEMALE! YOUR FEELINGS ARE OF NO IMPORTANCE TO THE SON OF ODIN! I HAVE A TASK FOR YOU!
NO! I SHALL NOT SERVE YOU! YOU ARE THE EMBODIMENT OF ALL THAT IS EVIL--ALL THAT IS SINISTER!!
I DEEPLY APPRECIATE YOUR COMPLIMENT! AND NOW, HEAR MY WISHES--HEAR THE WISHES OF THE GOD OF MISCHIEF, FOR I AM TRULY YOUR MASTER!
2

I CANNOT REFUSE!! ONLY THE OTHER GODS OF ASGARD THEMSELVES ARE EQUAL TO YOU IN POWER!
SO! NOW HEAR MY WORDS! EVERY LIVING THING HAS PLEDGED TO PROTECT BALDER-- ODIN HAS MADE HIM INVINCIBLE! AND YET, HE MUST HAVE FORGOTTEN SOMETHING!! HAS HE?? HAS HE??
YES!! THERE IS ONE LIVING THING WHICH ODIN OVERLOOKED!! THE TINY MISTLETOE MADE NO SUCH PLEDGE!

HAH! THAT WAS THE KNOWLEDGE I SOUGHT!! NOW, ALL I NEED DO IS FIND ONE SMALL CLUMP OF MISTLETOE...

...AND, WITH IT, I SHALL REMOVE THE UNSUSPECTING BALDER FROM HIS PLACE IN ODIN'S HEART-- FOREVER!

WITHIN MINUTES, THE GLOATING LOKI ORDERS ONE OF HIS SLAVE TROLLS TO FASHION A BLOW-GUN AND A DART OUT OF THE MISTLETOE...

REMEMBER, CLEVER ONE-- IT MUST BE CAPABLE OF PIERCING THE VERY ARMOR WHICH BALDER WEARS!

FEAR NOT, LOKI! IT SHALL BE!

THE NEXT DAY, AS BALDER THE BRAVE JOUSTS ON THE COMBAT PRACTICE FIELD, AN EVIL FIGURE WATCHES, WAITING FOR THE RIGHT MOMENT--TO STRIKE!
I WILL ONLY HAVE ONE CHANCE-- SO I MUST NOT FAIL ON MY FIRST TRY!

TO PREVENT SUSPICION FROM FALLING UPON ME, I MUST MAKE IT LOOK LIKE SOME SORT OF BATTLE ACCIDENT!

AFTER LONG, TENSE MOMENTS OF PATIENT OBSERVING, LOKI FINALLY GETS HIS OPPORTUNITY, AS BRAVE BALDER STUMBLES IN AN EFFORT TO AVOID STEPPING UPON A NEARBY CATERPILLAR!

NOW!!

BUT, BEFORE THE FATAL MISSILE CAN BE EJECTED, THE ENTIRE BLOW GUN ERUPTS INTO FLAME AND FALLS FROM LOKI'S STARTLED FINGERS!!
WHAT ACCURSED WITCHERY IS THIS??!

IT IS I WHO AM RESPONSIBLE, EVIL ONE! YOU MADE ONE CARELESS MISTAKE--YOU FORGOT THAT ODIN HAD PLEDGED ALL WHO LIVE TO GUARD BALDER'S LIFE--AND I, TOO, TOOK THAT SOLEMN PLEDGE!
BLAST YOU, FEMALE!! YOU HAVEN'T HEARD THE LAST OF THIS!!

KEEP STIRRING YOUR WITCHES' BREW, MY AGED ONE! THE NEXT TIME LOKI RETURNS, THE NORN QUEEN SHALL BE ***READY*** FOR HIM!!

AND SO WE LEAVE LOKI WITH HIS SINISTER THOUGHTS AND MENACING PLANS! BUT, NO MATTER HOW WELL THE GOD OF MISCHIEF MAY PLAN, HE IS DESTINED EVER TO LEARN THAT FATE SAVES HER SMILE FOR THE NOBLE SOUL AND THE PURE IN HEART!
THOUGH DANGER MAY LURK IN THE SHADOWS AROUND ME, I FEAR IT NOT! FOR I AM ARMED WITH TRUST, AND FORTIFIED WITH FAITH!
The END

NEXT ISSUE... PREPARE YOURSELF FOR A NEVER-TO-BE FORGOTTEN EXPERIENCE AS WE TAKE YOU ON A STARTLING JOURNEY TO-- ***THE LAND OF THE TROLLS!!!***

JOURNEY INTO MYSTERY
WITH
THE MIGHTY THOR
APPROVED BY THE COMICS CODE AUTHORITY
IND.
MARVEL COMICS GROUP 12¢
108 SEPT.
the MIGHTY THOR, POSSIBLY THE HANDSOMEST, MOST NOBLE SUPER-HERO OF ALL TIME!
SEE THOR BATTLE LOKI, PRINCE OF EVIL, FOR THE LIFE OF LOVELY JANE FOSTER.
ALSO FEATURING: TALES OF ASGARD! "TRAPPED BY THE TROLLS!"
GUEST STARRING THE WORLD'S MOST MYSTERIOUS MORTAL: Dr. STRANGE, MASTER OF BLACK MAGIC!

THE MIGHTY THOR!
"AT THE MERCY OF LOKI, PRINCE OF EVIL!"
WHAT IS THIS? THE MIGHTY THUNDER GOD THREATENING THE PEOPLE OF NEW YORK WITH HIS HAMMER?? THERE MUST BE A REASON! BUT WHAT??
GUEST-STARRING: DOCTOR STRANGE, MASTER OF BLACK MAGIC!
WRITTEN BY.......STAN LEE, THE IDOL OF MILLIONS!
ILLUSTRATED BY...JACK KIRBY, THE TOAST OF THE TOWN!
INKED BY..........CHIC STONE, THE MAN OF THE HOUR!
LETTERED BY......ART SIMEK, THE PEOPLE'S CHOICE!
X-749
1

WHILE THE ONLOOKERS WATCH IN MUTE, UNCOMPREHENDING AWE, THE MIGHTY THOR SLAMS HIS ENCHANTED HAMMER DOWN UPON THE PAVEMENT WITH AN IMPACT FELT HALFWAY ACROSS THE STATE!!
WHOOM!
MOVING AT THE ALMOST INDESCRIBABLE SPEED OF SOUND, THE FORCE OF IMPACT TRAVELS DOWN UNDER THE ROADBED FOR MILES IN A PREDETERMINED DIRECTION, UNTIL--
--IT REACHES ONE CERTAIN STREET CORNER--A CORNER WHICH THOR HAD SEEN WHILE FLYING ABOVE THE CITY, BUT WHICH HE KNEW HE COULD NEVER REACH IN TIME!
BILLY! LOOK OUT FOR THAT RUNAWAY TRUCK!!
AT THAT SPLIT-SECOND, THE VIBRATION OF THOR'S HAMMER BLAST REACHES THE SPOT, CAUSING THE CAREENING, DRIVERLESS TRUCK TO LITERALLY JUMP INTO THE AIR, MISSING THE BOY WHO HAD BEEN IN ITS PATH!!
THE EVENT YOU HAVE JUST WITNESSED ACTUALLY TOOK PLACE IN THE TOTAL ELAPSED TIME OF ONE AND ONE-FIFTH SECONDS--TIME ENOUGH FOR THE TRIGGER-FAST MIND OF THE THUNDER GOD TO PLAN AND EXECUTE HIS LIFE-SAVING ACTION!
IT IS FORTUNATE I WAS ABLE TO ACT IN TIME! BETTER A BROKEN PAVEMENT THAN AN INJURED HUMAN BEING!
AT ANY RATE, I SHALL REIMBURSE THE CITY FOR THE DAMAGE I'VE DONE BY USING THE EMERGENCY FUND WHICH THE AVENGERS KEEP FOR SUCH A PURPOSE!*
WE SHOULD HAVE KNOWN THAT THOR HAD A REASON FOR USING THAT HAMMER OF HIS! BOY! WHAT A COP ON THE BEAT HE'D MAKE!
*THOR IS, OF COURSE, ONE OF THE MEMBERS OF THE WORLD-FAMOUS AVENGERS!--EDITORS.
2

MINUTES LATER, THE MOST DRAMATIC, MOST HEROIC, MOST NOBLE OF ALL COSTUMED ADVENTURERS IS AGAIN HURTLING THRU THE CITY, EVER ALERT--EVER VIGILANT--

--AND ONCE AGAIN HE SENSES ANOTHER LIVING BEING IN DIRE NEED OF HELP!
I SEEM TO FEEL A THOUGHT REACHING OUT--CALLING ME--IN DESPERATION...

FOLLOWING THE MENTAL SUMMONS, THOR CAREENS INTO THE GREENWICH VILLAGE RETREAT OF THE MAN KNOWN AS DOCTOR STRANGE, MASTER OF BLACK MAGIC!
WHAT HAS HAPPENED HERE??
THOR-- I SENSED YOUR PRESENCE--KNEW YOU'D COME--

YOU ARE ILL!! FEVERISH! YOU NEED MEDICAL ATTENTION!
TOO WEAK TO CALL A DOCTOR-- A DEADLY ENEMY OF MINE--MORDO--TRIED TO USE MAGIC SPELL ON CITY --ONLY WAY TO STOP HIM WAS BY STRONGER SPELL--I DROVE MORDO BACK TO THE SHADOWS--THE CITY IS SAFE--BUT--SPELL WAS TOO STRONG--WEAKENED ME--UHHHH--
HE'S LOST CONSCIOUS-NESS--!

WITHOUT A MOMENT'S HESITATION, THE MIGHTY THOR RUSHES TO THE PHONE AND CALLS CITY HOSPITAL...
SEND AN AMBULANCE RIGHT AWAY! IT'S A PATIENT OF DR. DON BLAKE!

THE AMBULANCE WILL BE HERE WITHIN MINUTES! HE IS TOO WEAK FOR ME TO CARRY THRU THE AIR! HE NEEDS A STRETCHER!

AND WHEN THE ATTENDANTS GET HERE--

--THEY WILL BE MET BY DR. BLAKE!! I HEAR THE SIRENS *NOW*!
WHEEEEE

A QUARTER OF AN HOUR LATER, IN THE OPERATING ROOM OF CITY HOSPITAL, DON BLAKE FIGHTS A BATTLE AS DIFFICULT AS ANY HE HAS EVER FOUGHT IN HIS OTHER IDENTITY AS *THOR*, GOD OF THUNDER!!

NO DRUGS KNOWN TO MODERN MEDICINE CAN COUNTERACT THE EFFECTS OF THE *SPELL* WHICH WEAKENED HIM! ONLY THE FACT THAT I CAN DRAW UPON THE UNEARTHLY KNOWLEDGE OF *THOR* CAN SAVE HIS LIFE!

OXYGE

BUT THEN, AT THE MOST CRUCIAL MOMENT OF THE DELICATE OPERATION, DON BLAKE HEARS A CALL-- A CALL WHICH CAN BE HEARD BY HIS EARS ALONE-- FROM THE PLACE KNOWN AS--ASGARD!!
HEAR ME...MY SON...
NO!! NOT NOW!! I CAN'T STOP NOW!!

AND IN THE HOME OF THE GODS-- SO FAR FROM US THAT IT IS IMPOSSIBLE TO DESCRIBE THE DISTANCE IN EARTHLY TERMS-- ODIN, LORD OF ASGARD, ONCE AGAIN SUMMONS HIS SON--THOR!!
WHY DOES THOR NOT REPLY TO ME?? HE KNOWS THAT NONE MAY IGNORE A SUMMONS FROM ODIN-- NOT EVEN THE SON WHOM I HOLD SO DEAR!

HE HAS NOT ANSWERED! BY ALL THE FURIES, I'LL HOLD HIM ACCOUNTABLE FOR THIS!! THERE IS NO TIME TO FIND HIM NOW, FOR I MUST LEAD MY WARRIORS INTO BATTLE-- BUT WHEN I RETURN-- THE THUNDER GOD SHALL FEEL MY WRATH!!!

SO GREAT IS ODIN'S ANGER--SO VIOLENT HIS RAGE--THAT THE VERY POWER OF HIS EMOTION CAUSES A SUDDEN ELECTRICAL STORM TO ERUPT OVER THE AREA HE CONCENTRATED UPON--

--A STORM WHICH SUDDENLY AFFECTS THE LIGHTING IN THE OPERATING ROOM OF CITY HOSPITAL!
THE POWER IS FAILING!!
WE CAN'T STOP NOW!!

BUT THEN, THE COOL COMMANDING VOICE OF DR. BLAKE CUTS THRU THE SUDDEN PANIC WITH THE IRON RING OF AUTHORITY!
CUT IN EMERGENCY LIGHTS! REMAIN WHERE YOU ARE!

I'M GOING TO SAVE THIS MAN--NO MATTER WHAT!

WHILE, NOT SUSPECTING THE REASON FOR THOR'S FAILURE TO ANSWER HIS SUMMONS, A RAGING, WRATHFUL ODIN RACES INTO BATTLE WITH BUT ONE BURNING THOUGHT IN MIND--!
WHEN I RETURN, THOR SHALL ANSWER TO ME!! EVEN THOUGH HE BE MY FAVORED SON--
--ONLY ONE MAY BE LORD OF ASGARD, AND THAT ONE IS-- AND EVER SHALL BE--ODIN!!

BUT A PAIR OF CRUEL, UNBLINKING EYES WATCH THE NOBLE ODIN'S DEPARTURE WITH GRIM SATISFACTION --THE EYES OF THOR'S ARCH-ENEMY-- LOKI, GOD OF EVIL!

SUDDENLY, THE CRAFTY IMMORTAL TRANSFORMS HIMSELF INTO A TINY BEE...
NOW, AT LAST, I CAN ATTEMPT WHAT I NEVER DARED DO WHILE ODIN WAS NEAR--!

HEIMDALL, GUARDIAN OF THE RAINBOW BRIDGE, WHOSE EYES ARE KEENEST IN THE UNIVERSE, WOULD NEVER DREAM OF SUSPECTING A PASSING BEE...
..AND THUS I RETURN TO EARTH!!

A SHORT TIME LATER, IN A PRIVATE HOSPITAL ROOM...
YOU SAVED MY LIFE, DOCTOR BLAKE! YOU SHALL NOT FIND ME WANTING IN GRATITUDE!
TO A PHYSICIAN, THE SAVING OF A LIFE IS ITS OWN REWARD, SIR!

I UNDERSTAND, DOCTOR --BUT PLEASE REMEMBER --I AM NOT WITHOUT CERTAIN POWERS OF MY OWN...
...IF I CAN EVER BE OF SERVICE TO YOU, YOU MUST GIVE ME THE OPPORTUNITY TO REPAY YOU, IN SOME SMALL MEASURE!
I SHALL, DR. STRANGE --AND THANK YOU!
6

LATER, UPON HIS RETURN TO HIS OFFICE, THE LAME PHYSICIAN SEES AN ELDERLY MAN IN THE WAITING ROOM, HOLDING A CANE SIMILAR TO BLAKE'S OWN...
THIS GENTLEMAN HAS BEEN WAITING FOR YOU, DR. BLAKE!
IT'S PAST MY OFFICE HOURS, NURSE FOSTER--BUT, IF IT'S IMPORTANT...

IT IS IMPORTANT, DR. BLAKE! IT'S MY LEG! YOU'VE GOT TO--OHH! THE PAIN IS SO UNBEARABLE I CAN HARDLY STAND!!
EASY THERE! DON'T STRAIN YOURSELF! LET ME HELP YOU!

OH, I DROPPED MY CANE--!
ALLOW ME TO GET IT FOR YOU, DOCTOR!

HERE YOU ARE! I NOTICE THAT YOU ARE LAME, ALSO!
YES--IT'S FROM AN OLD INJURY! AND NOW, MY NURSE WILL HELP YOU INTO THE EXAMINING ROOM!

THAT WON'T BE NECESSARY, DOCTOR! I FEEL BETTER ALREADY! I DON'T EVEN NEED MY CANE!
HE'S NOT LAME ANY MORE! HE STRAIGHTENED HIMSELF UPRIGHT--!!
WAIT! WHAT ARE YOU DOING--??!

YOU'LL RECEIVE YOUR ANSWER IN A MOMENT!
IN FACT, I BELIEVE YOU'RE BEGINNING TO SUSPECT THE TRUTH NOW!
THAT SUDDEN MIST--THE HAZE--YOU'RE NO ORDINARY AILING PATIENT! YOU'RE--!
7

OF COURSE! YOUR OLD FRIEND, LOKI, AT YOUR SERVICE!! I'VE COME TO END OUR RIVALRY ONCE AND FOR ALL--BY DEFEATING YOU FOREVER!
MY "SLUMBER MIST" HAS PUT YOUR NURSE MERCIFULLY TO SLEEP--SO THAT WE SHALL NOT BE DISTURBED!

HMMM--I WAS NEVER AWARE HOW LOVELY SHE IS--FOR A MORTAL!
STAY BACK---! DON BLAKE IS NO MATCH FOR THE MIGHTY LOKI!
IN ORDER TO THOROUGHLY ENJOY MY VICTORY, I SHALL NOT DESTROY YOU NOW--I PREFER TO TOY WITH YOU FOR A WHILE!

YOU ARROGANT FOOL! HAVE YOU FORGOTTEN HOW EASILY I CAN TURN INTO THOR?? ALL I NEED DO IS STAMP MY ENCHANTED WALKING STICK--
STAMP IT, THEN! THERE IS NONE TO STOP YOU!

BUT FOR THE FIRST TIME WITHIN BLAKE'S MEMORY...
I'VE LOST MY POWER!!

WHO IS THE FOOL NOW, MY WITLESS FOE?? THAT IS THE FIRST PART OF MY CUNNING PLAN--

IT WAS YOUR CANE I THREW OUT OF THE WINDOW--NOT MINE!
AND SO I WIN THE FIRST JOUST--AS I SHALL WIN EVERY FOLLOWING ONE--UNTIL I HAVE VANQUISHED YOU FOREVER!

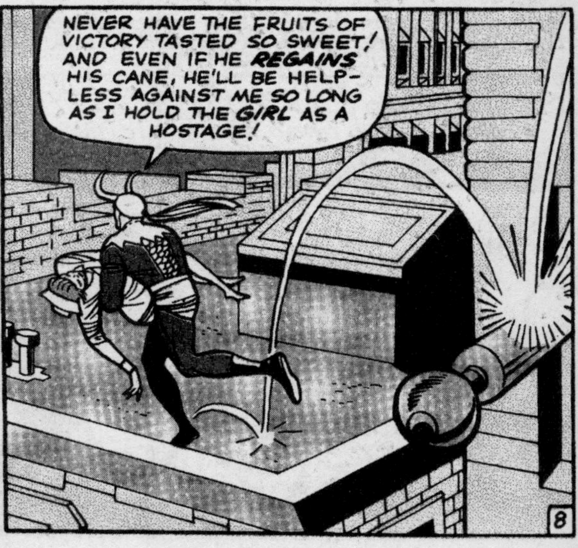
NEVER HAVE THE FRUITS OF VICTORY TASTED SO SWEET! AND EVEN IF HE REGAINS HIS CANE, HE'LL BE HELPLESS AGAINST ME SO LONG AS I HOLD THE GIRL AS A HOSTAGE!
8

HE'S RUN OFF WITH JANE!! AND I'M POWERLESS AGAINST HIM UNLESS I CAN RETRIEVE MY WALKING STICK!!

IN A MAD, FRANTIC FRENZY, THE VALIANT DOCTOR SCRAMBLES DOWN THE STAIRS, EVEN THOUGH EACH STEP IS SHEER AGONY TO HIS LAME, ACHING LEG...
EVERY SECOND COUNTS! I DARE NOT EVEN STOP TO WAIT FOR THE ELEVATOR! I MUST FIND MY CANE!

BUT UPON BREATHLESSLY REACHING THE STREET...
IT'S GONE!!

DESPERATE, DON BLAKE USES THE ONE SUPERNATURAL ABILITY HE POSSESSES IN HIS MORTAL FORM...
I'LL MENTALLY CONTACT ASGARD!! I MUST BEG ODIN'S HELP!

BUT THE HALLS OF ODIN'S PALACE ARE EMPTY!! THERE ARE NONE TO RECEIVE THE URGENT MENTAL SUMMONS!!
--ODIN--MY FATHER--ODIN---

NOT KNOWING THAT ODIN AND HIS COURT HAVE GONE OFF TO BATTLE, THE BITTERLY DISAPPOINTED PHYSICIAN REACHES A FALSE CONCLUSION...
ODIN HAS IGNORED ME! HE'S FORSAKEN ME! WHATEVER I DO--I MUST DO ALONE, AS THE MORTAL DON BLAKE!

AND THEN, SUDDENLY, THE LAME DOCTOR REMEMBERS SOMETHING--AND, WITHOUT A SECOND'S HESITATION, HE HAILS A PASSING CAB--
CITY GENERAL HOSPITAL--AND STEP ON IT!!
IN THIS TRAFFIC?? YOU'D GET THERE FASTER ON A POGO STICK! BUT I'LL DO THE BEST I CAN!

DESPITE THE HEAVY TRAFFIC, THE DRIVER MAKES RECORD TIME, SPURRED ON BY BLAKE'S URGING, UNTIL...
BLAKE!! WHAT'S WRONG??
DR. STRANGE--YOU TOLD ME TO CONTACT YOU IF I EVER NEEDED HELP! I-I DIDN'T THINK IT WOULD HAPPEN SO SOON, BUT I NEED YOU!

I CAN'T TELL YOU TOO MUCH-- BUT MY WALKING STICK IS GONE! I MUST FIND IT! IT'S A MATTER OF LIFE AND DEATH!
YOU NEED EXPLAIN NO MORE! YOUR MOTIVES ARE YOUR OWN AFFAIR! I CAN SENSE HOW DESPERATE YOU ARE! STAND BACK-- DO NOT BE SHOCKED BY WHAT YOU ARE ABOUT TO SEE!

THEN, BEFORE THE STARTLED EYES OF DON BLAKE, DR. STRANGE'S BODY SEEMS TO GO LIMP IN ITS WHEELCHAIR AS HIS ECTOPLASMIC FORM FLOATS OUT OF ITS MORTAL SHELL...
WAIT UNTIL I CONTACT YOU!

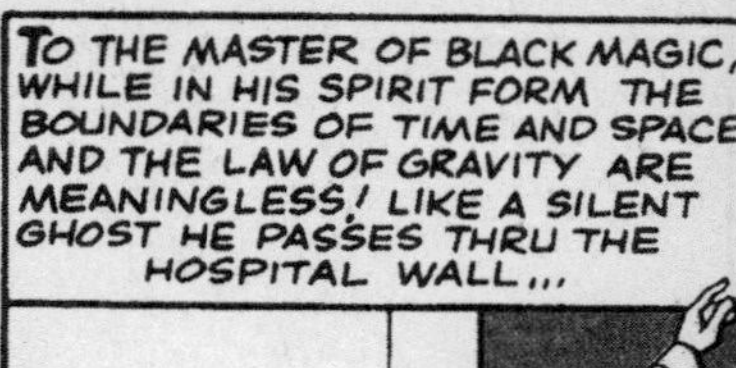
TO THE MASTER OF BLACK MAGIC, WHILE IN HIS SPIRIT FORM THE BOUNDARIES OF TIME AND SPACE AND THE LAW OF GRAVITY ARE MEANINGLESS! LIKE A SILENT GHOST HE PASSES THRU THE HOSPITAL WALL...

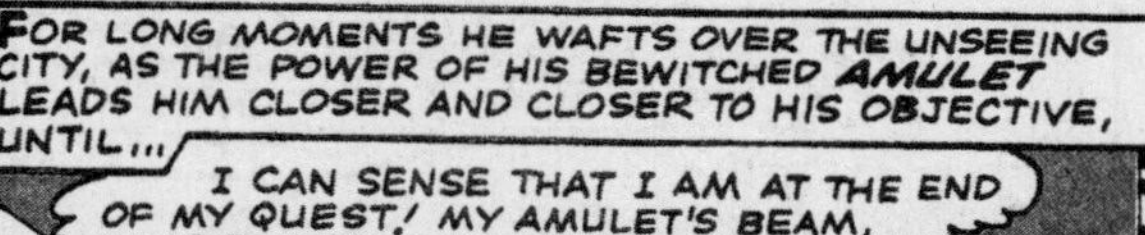
FOR LONG MOMENTS HE WAFTS OVER THE UNSEEING CITY, AS THE POWER OF HIS BEWITCHED AMULET LEADS HIM CLOSER AND CLOSER TO HIS OBJECTIVE, UNTIL...

I CAN SENSE THAT I AM AT THE END OF MY QUEST! MY AMULET'S BEAM, INVISIBLE TO HUMAN EYES, IS MOVING SLOWLY TO MY RIGHT, AND TURNING DOWNWARD...

WITH THE SPEED OF THOUGHT, THE HOVERING APPARITION RETURNS TO HIS MORTAL FORM AND TELLS DON BLAKE WHAT HE HAS FOUND! AND THEN, MINUTES LATER...
STRANGE WAS RIGHT! THOSE VAGRANTS HAVE FOUND MY CANE-- THEY'RE USING IT AS A FISHING ROD! IT MUSTN'T FALL INTO THE WATER--!!!
STOP! BE CAREFUL OF THAT CANE! IT'S MINE! I MUST HAVE IT BACK!

HEY, LEGGO! YOU SOME KINDA NUT OR SOMETHIN'?? I FOUND THIS STICK AND I'M KEEPIN' IT!
I'LL TAKE CARE OF THAT TROUBLE-MAKER, CHARLIE!
THEY DON'T UNDER-STAND! THEY'RE SPOILING FOR A FIGHT! I'VE GOT TO THINK OF SOMETHING!

BUT, AT THAT VERY INSTANT, THE TWO VAGRANTS SEE ANOTHER FORM NEAR THEM--A FLOATING, ETHEREAL, GHOSTLIKE FORM! AND THEN...
LET'S GET OUTTA HERE, CHARLIE!! THE PLACE IS HAUNTED!!
HE CAN HAVE HIS BLASTED CANE! I AIN'T CARRYIN' ANYTHING THAT'LL SLOW ME DOWN WHEN I RUN!

AND MINUTES LATER...
HE'S BEGINNING TO FADE AWAY! HE'S RETURNING TO HIS PHYSICAL FORM, BACK AT THE HOSPITAL! HE CAN'T HELP ME ANY LONGER!

NOW THERE'S ONLY ONE WHO CAN HELP ME--ONLY ONE WHO CAN FIND LOKI--AND RESCUE JANE FOSTER FROM HIM--

WHEREVER YOU ARE, LOKI--IN WHATEVER PART OF THE KNOWN UNIVERSE--LOOK TO YOUR DEFENSES!! FOR NOTHING CAN SAVE YOU NOW--FROM THE VENGEANCE OF THOR!!

I NEED HEIGHT!! I'LL SCAN THE CITY FROM HIGH ABOVE--NOTHING THAT MOVES BELOW WILL ESCAPE THE THUNDER GOD'S NOTICE!!

MEANWHILE, IN ASGARD, ODIN AND HIS VICTORIOUS LEGIONS RETURN, FLUSHED WITH VICTORY...
AND NOW TO RETURN TO THE MATTER OF THOR!!

DONNING HIS ROBE OF CONQUEST, THE NOBLE LORD OF ASGARD SENDS A MENTAL CALL THRU THE ENDLESS GALAXIES--FAR OUT INTO SPACE--TOWARDS THE PLANET EARTH...
PERHAPS I WAS TOO HARSH WITH THOR! HE MAY HAVE HAD REASON FOR NOT RESPONDING BEFORE! I'LL GIVE HIM A CHANCE TO EXPLAIN...
11

BUT ONCE AGAIN, AN IRONIC MISUNDERSTANDING OCCURS BETWEEN ODIN AND THE MIGHTY THOR...
THOR! WE HAVE MUCH TO DISCUSS!!
NOT SO, FATHER! THE TIME FOR TALK IS PAST!
YOU DID NOT SEE FIT TO ANSWER WHEN I NEEDED YOU --AND NOW THE NEED EXISTS NO MORE!!

WHATEVER MUST NOW BE DONE, SHALL BE DONE--AND DONE BY THOR, GOD OF THUNDER--AND BY THOR ALONE!

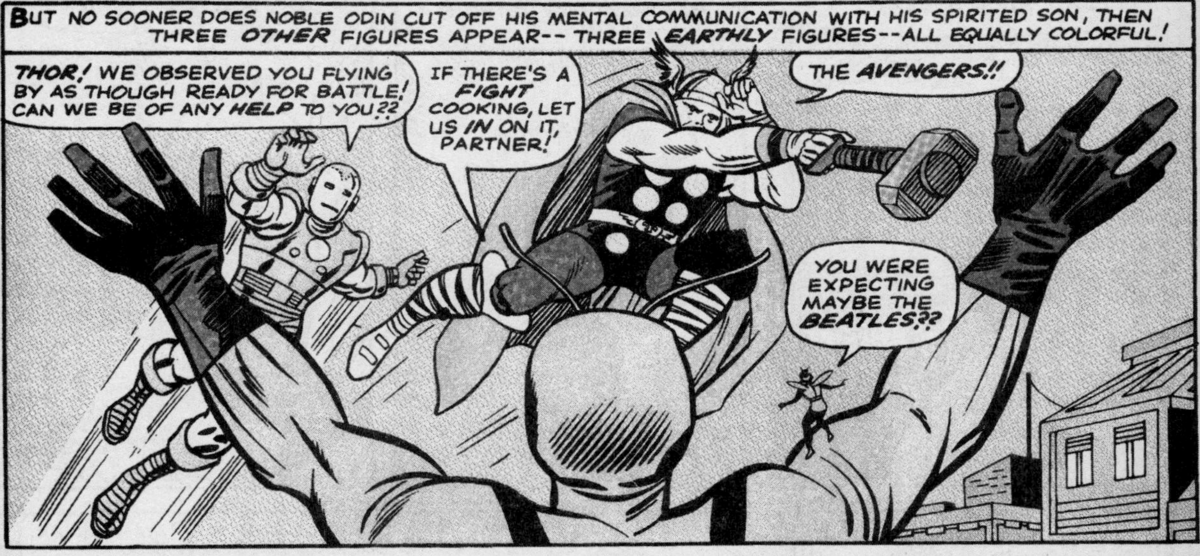
BUT NO SOONER DOES NOBLE ODIN CUT OFF HIS MENTAL COMMUNICATION WITH HIS SPIRITED SON, THEN THREE OTHER FIGURES APPEAR-- THREE EARTHLY FIGURES--ALL EQUALLY COLORFUL!
THOR! WE OBSERVED YOU FLYING BY AS THOUGH READY FOR BATTLE! CAN WE BE OF ANY HELP TO YOU??
IF THERE'S A FIGHT COOKING, LET US IN ON IT, PARTNER!
THE AVENGERS!!
YOU WERE EXPECTING MAYBE THE BEATLES??

MY FIGHT IS A PERSONAL ONE--I DESIRE NO ASSISTANCE! THIS IS NOT A CASE FOR THE AVENGERS!!
ARE YOU SURE, PAL? YOU WOULDN'T BE KEEPING A GOOD FIGHT TO YOURSELF, WOULD YOU?

I HAVE NO MORE TO SAY ABOUT THE MATTER! THE SUBJECT IS CLOSED! NOW STAND ASIDE, ALL OF YOU!
OKAY! OKAY! BE CAREFUL WITH THAT CLOBBER-STICK OF YOURS, THOR! THAT THING REALLY BLOWS UP A STORM!
12

WOW! LOOK AT HIM GO!
WHOEVER IT IS THAT HE'S AFTER, I'M SURE GLAD THAT I'M NOT IN THAT FELLA'S SHOES!
I AM GRATEFUL FOR THEIR SUPPORT, BUT THEY WOULD BE NO MATCH FOR IMMORTAL LOKI!

IN ORDER TO FIND MY CUNNING FOE, I MUST REACH THE HIGHEST POINT IN THE CITY!

ALL THE GODS OF ASGARD EMIT AN AURA OF FREE-FLOWING ELECTRONS FROM THEIR PERSON...

...AN AURA WHICH ONLY ANOTHER IMMORTAL CAN DETECT--AS MY HAMMER NOW DETECTS LOKI'S!!

BUT IT IS NOT THROWING BACK A BEAM TO INDICATE WHERE THE AURA COMES FROM!

THAT MEANS THERE IS SOME SORT OF OBSTRUCTION BLOCKING THE PATH OF THE FREE-FLOWING ELECTRONS!!
THUS, I SHALL GO HIGHER --TO THE EDGE OF THE UNIVERSE IF NEED BE-- UNTIL I CAN LOCATE THE EVIL LOKI!

AHH! NOW I HAVE FOUND HIM!! MY HAMMER IS HURLING BACK AN ELECTRON BEAM-- STRAIGHT INTO THE HEART OF A SECTION OF THE ADIRONDACK MOUNTAINS!!
13

NOW NOTHING CAN SAVE MY EVIL HALF-BROTHER--FOR I FINALLY SEE HIM, UP AHEAD!!
BUT JANE IS NOT WITH HIM! THAT MEANS THERE IS YET ONE MORE THING I MUST DO--!

IN A SPLIT SECOND, THE MIGHTY THUNDER GOD CONJURES UP A MENTAL IMAGE OF THE MASTER OF BLACK MAGIC--
DR. STRANGE! THOUGH YOU CANNOT SEE ME, I HAVE A REQUEST TO MAKE OF YOU--IN THE NAME OF DON BLAKE!
STATE IT, AND I SHALL COMPLY!

THE GIRL HE LOVES IS IN MORTAL DANGER--BUT YOU CAN HELP HER--THRU THE POWER OF YOUR SORCERY! HEED ME WELL, MAN OF MYSTERY...

THEN, HAVING TRANSMITTED HIS MESSAGE TO DR. STRANGE, THOR BREAKS CONTACT AND GIRDS HIMSELF FOR BATTLE AGAINST HIS MOST POWERFUL FOE--!!
DEFEND YOURSELF, EVIL ONE!! IF YOU CAN!!
THOR!! YOU RETRIEVED YOUR CANE!!

STAY BACK, ACCURSED BROTHER!! THE GIRL YOU CHERISH IS MY PRISONER--IN LIMBO!! ONLY I CAN SAVE HER! IF ANY HARM COMES TO ME--!!
SHE WILL NOT ENTER INTO THIS! SO, SAVE YOUR BREATH FOR BATTLE--YOU SHALL NEED IT!

A MIGHTY ATTACK, THOR--BUT REMEMBER, MY SPEED IS THAT OF A GOD--MY POWER IS AT LEAST THE EQUAL OF YOURS!

IF YOU ARE SO CONFIDENT, LOKI, WHY DO I SEE FEAR GLOWING IN YOUR EYES??
YOU KNOW THE MOMENT OF RECKONING IS AT HAND!

NO! YOU CAN'T BEAT ME AGAIN-- YOU CAN'T!! FOR AGES I'VE HATED YOU-- ENVIED YOU-- SWORN TO DESTROY YOU!! AND I WILL-- I WILL!!
NEVER, EVIL ONE!! NOT WHILE A BREATH OF LIFE REMAINS WITHIN ME!

THEN I'LL SNUFF THAT BREATH OF LIFE OUT OF YOU-- SOMEHOW!!

UNHAND MY HAMMER!! HOW DARE YOU PROFANE IT WITH YOUR VILE TOUCH!!

BAH!! I SNEER AT YOUR BUMBLING BRUTE STRENGTH!! SEE HOW MY SUPERIOR CUNNING CAN PLACE VICTORY WITHIN MY GRASP!!
YOU THINK TO BEAT ME WITH SO SIMPLE A MOVE??

NOT AS SIMPLE AS YOU THINK, THUNDER GOD!! I HAD A TRAP PREPARED IN THE GROUND FOR JUST SUCH AN EMERGENCY!
15

AND NOW-- BEFORE YOU CAN FREE YOURSELF, I SHALL MAKE YOU PAY THE PRICE FOR DEFYING LOKI!! I SHALL PROJECT MY POWER DEEP INTO LIMBO-- AND IT WILL SPELL THE END OF JANE FOSTER!
LOKI!--IF ANY HARM COMES TO THAT GIRL--YOU'LL SPEND ALL OF ETERNITY REGRETTING IT!

YOUR EMPTY THREATS DO NOT BOTHER ME! AND NOW--I SHALL BRIDGE THE DIMENSIONS--
--IF I CANNOT HARM YOU, HARMING THE GIRL YOU LOVE IS THE SECOND BEST THING!

THERE!! WHILE YOU FUME HELPLESSLY IN THE TRAP I SET FOR YOU-- I HAVE CONTACTED THE EXACT SPOT IN LIMBO WHERE JANE FOSTER IS IMPRISONED! ALL I NEED DO IS HURL ONE PSYCHIC BOLT--LIKE THIS--!

WAIT! WHAT MANNER OF SORCERY IS THIS?? MY PSYCHIC BOLT CANNOT REACH HER! SHE IS SAFELY ENSCONCED BEHIND A MYSTIC FORCE FIELD!! BUT--HOW??!

FOR THE ANSWER TO LOKI'S STARTLED QUESTION, LET US PEER INTO A DARKENED HOSPITAL ROOM, WHERE WE FIND...
THE POWER OF MY AMULET IS PROTECTING THE GIRL... BUT FOR HOW LONG??

I DO NOT KNOW WHAT SUPER-NATURAL FORCE I AM BATTLING, THOUGH IT IS THE MOST POWERFUL, THE MOST AWESOME I HAVE EVER ENCOUNTERED!

BUT, DESPITE THE GRUELLING STRAIN, THE MASTER OF BLACK MAGIC HOLDS FAST--AND FINALLY THE BATTLE ENDS, AS LOKI STOPS HIS MENTAL ASSAULT UPON THE GIRL...
I--DID AS BLAKE REQUESTED!! THE GIRL-- IS SAFE!!
16

AND THE REASON LOKI HAS CEASED TO BATTER AGAINST THE STRANGE FORCE FIELD IS--HE HEARS HIS MIGHTY ADVERSARY SLOWLY REACHING THE TOP OF THE SEEMINGLY ESCAPE-PROOF TRAP HE HAD FALLEN INTO--
THOUGH THE PIT IS TOO NARROW FOR ME TO SWING MY HAMMER ENOUGH TO FLY OUT, I AM ABLE TO PROP MYSELF AGAINST THE SLIPPERY SIDES, AND INCH UPWARD BY SHEER BRUTE STRENGTH--!

--AND NOW, I CAN SWING MY HAMMER --FASTER--AND HARDER THAN EVER BEFORE!!
BLAST YOU, THOR!! DOES NOTHING STOP YOU FOR GOOD?? THOUGH YOU ARE ONE OF THE IMMORTALS, I'LL FIND A WAY TO SLAY YOU YET--IF IT'S THE LAST THING I DO!

BUT THEN THE SOUND OF THOR'S CRASHING, CAREENING, THUNDERING HAMMER DROWNS OUT LOKI'S THREATS--AS IT BLASTS THRU THE FOREST LIKE A LIVING THING!!

CAN'T MOVE!! CAN'T SEE!! FLYING CHIPS AND SPLINTERS ALL AROUND ME--KEEPING ME OFF-BALANCE!!

RETURN TO ME, MY ENCHANTED MALLET! I'VE ONLY SECONDS IN WHICH TO ACT--WHILE LOKI IS DAZED AND CONFUSED!

AND THERE, IN THE LONELY ADIRONDACK FOREST, LOKI FINALLY FEELS THE FULL FORCE OF ONE OF THE MOST POWERFUL BLOWS IN THE UNIVERSE--THE PULVERIZING KNOCKOUT PUNCH OF THE MIGHTY THOR!

THOUGH THAT AWESOME BLOW WOULD HAVE SHATTERED A SMALL MOUNTAIN, IT ONLY DAZES THE POWERFUL LOKI--BUT THAT IS ENOUGH TO ACHIEVE THOR'S OBJECTIVE--!
FREE JANE FOSTER FROM LIMBO--OR FEEL MY WRATH AGAIN!!
NO! ENOUGH--ENOUGH!

AND THEN, AT A MENTAL COMMAND BY THE EVIL LOKI...
THERE! SHE'S BACK! NOW ARE YOU SATISFIED??

BUT AS THOR MOMENTARILY RELEASES HIS GRIP...
AS FOR ME, I AM NOT YET SATISFIED!

IF MY OWN STRENGTH WAS NOT ENOUGH TO VANQUISH YOU-- I'LL BEAT YOU WITH MY SPELLS! FOR IN WIZARDRY, I AM EASILY YOUR SUPERIOR!!
BUT EVEN AS LOKI SPEAKS, A SMALL WHITE CLOUD GETS CLOSER AND CLOSER TO HIM, EVER INCREASING IN SIZE, UNTIL--

--A MIGHTY MAILED ARM APPEARS THRU THE BILLOWING MIST, SEIZING THE STARTLED IMMORTAL IN AN UNBREAKABLE GRIP--!!

LOKI!! YOU ARE WANTED!!
WHA--??!

NO! DON'T-- NOT YET! I MIGHT HAVE BEATEN HIM IF I HAD MORE TIME!

YOUR TIME HAS ALMOST RUN OUT, EVIL ONE! ODIN COMMANDED ME TO BRING YOU TO HIM--AND HE GAVE MY ARM ENOUGH POWER TO HOLD YOU NO MATTER HOW YOU STRUGGLE TO BREAK FREE!

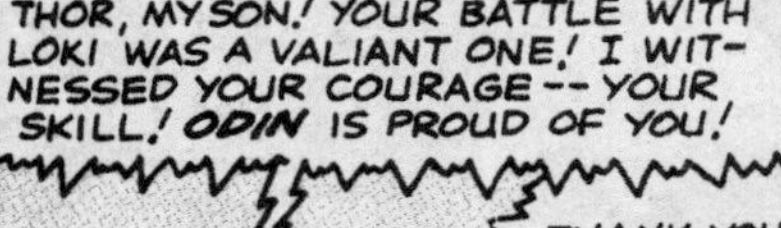

THOR, MY SON! YOUR BATTLE WITH LOKI WAS A VALIANT ONE! I WITNESSED YOUR COURAGE -- YOUR SKILL! ODIN IS PROUD OF YOU!

THANK YOU, NOBLE FATHER! AND I APOLOGIZE FOR MY INTEMPERATE BEHAVIOR TOWARDS YOU EARLIER! BUT NOW, I MUST RETURN THE GIRL BEFORE SHE AWAKENS!

STILL HE LOVES THE MORTAL GIRL-- THE FEMALE HE CAN NEVER BE PERMITTED TO MARRY! WHAT AM I TO DO WITH MY STRONG-WILLED SON??

IMMEDIATELY FOLLOWING IS ANOTHER MAGNIFICENTLY ILLUSTRATED TALE OF ASGARD --DON'T MISS IT! AND DON'T MISS THE NEXT ISH OF THOR FOR STILL ANOTHER EXAMPLE OF COMIC MAGAZINE ARTISTRY CARRIED TO THE HIGHEST DEGREE!!

THE END

Tales of ASGARD HOME OF THE MIGHTY NORSE GODS!
"TRAPPED BY the TROLLS!"
BEHOLD! A WEARY TRAVELER APPEARS AT THE COURT OF SINDRI, KING OF THE DWARFS! FINALLY, THE STRANGER SPEAKS--
OH, MIGHTY KING SINDRI... I HAVE LOST MY WAY! I BEG SHELTER FROM THE STORM OUTSIDE!
YOU SEEK SHELTER? SO BE IT! YOU SHALL FIND IT HERE!
HAH! IF THE FOOL STRANGER BELIEVES KING SINDRI, IT WILL COST HIM HIS LIFE!
FANTASTICALLY WRITTEN BY STAN LEE
FAITHFULLY DRAWN BY: JACK KIRBY
FABULOUSLY INKED BY: VINCE COLLETTA
FINALLY LETTERED BY: ART SIMEK
1

THE UNSUSPECTING STRANGER HAS ARRIVED AT THE RIGHT TIME! I PROMISED TO SEND ANOTHER SLAVE TO THE TROLLS TODAY--AS PART OF THE PRICE I PAY TO KEEP THEM FROM ATTACKING MY KINGDOM!

SUDDENLY, A TRAP DOOR OPENS BENEATH THE STRANGER'S FEET. AND...
I'VE BEEN TRICKED! I'M FALLING!

GO, WITLESS TRAVELER! PLUNGE DOWNWARD--TO THE LAND OF THE TROLLS--WHOM YOU WILL SERVE FOREVERMORE!

HAH! HERE IS THE HOSTAGE SINDRI PROMISED US!
HE SEEMS STRONG AND WELL-FORMED! HE WILL MAKE A GOOD LABORER FOR US!

DISDAINFULLY, THE SAVAGE TROLLS CARRY THEIR MOTIONLESS CAPTIVE DEEP INTO THE INTERIOR OF THEIR UNDERGROUND KINGDOM, THRU WINDING CAVERNS AND TWISTING TUNNELS, UNTIL...

TO THE *WAITING CHAMBER* WITH HIM!

...REACHING A DARK, MURKY CHAMBER, THEY CHAIN THE HAPLESS PRISONER TO THE WALL, AS HE NOTICES ANOTHER CAPTIVE FROM ASGARD CHAINED NEARBY...
MY HEART IS HEAVY AT THE SIGHT OF ANOTHER WHOM THE EVIL TROLLS HAVE CAPTURED!

DO NOT DESPAIR, *MAN OF ASGARD!* WHILE LIFE REMAINS, HOPE CAN TRULY NEVER PERISH!
BRAVE WORDS, RECKLESS STRANGER! BUT *NONE* CAN ESCAPE THE TROLLS! OUR PLIGHT IS HOPELESS!

BUT--WHAT IS *THAT??* YOU HAVE LOOSED THAT SACK WHICH YOU CARRIED --AND AS IT STRIKES THE FLOOR, I SEE A *HAMMER* CONTAINED WITHIN!

MEANWHILE, A SHORT DISTANCE AWAY, THE CRUEL TROLL OVERSEERS DEMAND MORE AND MORE LABOR FROM THEIR HELPLESS SERFS...
FASTER, MEN OF ASGARD! WORK, OR PERISH! NONE CAN SAVE YOU ONCE YOU HAVE FALLEN VICTIM TO THE TROLLS!

YOU LIE, WICKED ONE! THEIR MOMENT OF RESCUE IS HERE! NOW YOU SHALL PAY FOR YOUR HEARTLESS OPPRESSION! BY ASGARD, HOW YOU SHALL PAY!
IT IS THOR-- THE YOUNG THUNDER GOD!
HE FREED HIMSELF BY THE POWER OF HIS HAMMER! NEVER HAVE I SEEN SUCH MIGHT--SUCH MAJESTY! NOTHING THAT LIVES CAN DEFY THE SON OF NOBLE ODIN!

AS IF TO PUNCTUATE THOSE DRAMATIC WORDS, THOR SWINGS HIS MIGHTY MALLET BUT ONCE, AND THE VERY HEAVENS SEEM TO POUR FORTH A SURGE OF NAKED FORCE SUCH AS NO LIVING EYES HAVE EVER WITNESSED BEFORE!

THEN, A SECOND SWING OF THE AWESOME HAMMER CAUSES THE VERY AIR TO VIBRATE WITH SUCH UNIMAGINABLE ENERGY THAT THE PRISONERS' CHAINS ARE SHATTERED INTO NOTHINGNESS!
NOW ATTACK, MEN OF ASGARD! SHOW THE EVIL TROLLS HOW FREE MEN FIGHT! FOR VENGEANCE SHALL BE OURS THIS DAY!

BUT, EVEN AS THEIR PULSE-POUNDING WAR CRIES REVERBERATE THRU THE DANK, WINDING TUNNELS, THE CHARGING WARRIORS CAN FIND NO FURTHER TRACE OF THEIR ONCE-PROUD CAPTORS!
THEY HAVE FLED BEFORE US! THE COWARDLY TYRANTS FEAR TO MEET US IN EQUAL BATTLE! BUT THE WRATH OF THOR IS NOT SO EASILY DEFIED!
TO THE SURFACE, MY BRETHREN!

RETURN NOW TO YOUR HOMES AND YOUR LOVED ONES! I STILL HAVE ONE MORE TASK TO PERFORM!
WE WERE FOOLS TO ABANDON HOPE! WE SHOULD HAVE KNOWN THAT ODIN WOULD NOT FORSAKE US! WE SHOULD HAVE KNOWN THAT HE WOULD SEND MIGHTY THOR TO SET US FREE!

LATER, AFTER ALL HAVE DEPARTED, ONE LONE FIGURE STANDS ATOP THE ENTRANCE TO THE TROLL KINGDOM, AND WITH ONE LAST BLOW OF HIS ENCHANTED HAMMER, SEALS THE OPENING FOREVER!
NEVERMORE SHALL MEN MAKE SLAVES OF OTHERS! NOT IN ASGARD--NOT ON EARTH--NOT ANY PLACE WHERE THE HAMMER OF THOR CAN BE SWUNG--OR WHERE MEN OF GOOD FAITH HOLD FREEDOM DEAR!
THE END
ANOTHER MIGHTY EPIC OF DRAMA AND DARING NEXT ISSUE AS THOR HIMSELF IS BANISHED FROM ASGARD! DON'T DARE MISS IT--YOU KNOW HOW SENSITIVE STAN AND JACK ARE!

JOURNEY INTO MYSTERY
WITH
THE MIGHTY
THOR
APPROVED BY THE COMICS CODE AUTHORITY
IND.
MARVEL COMICS GROUP 12¢
109 OCT.
FEATURING the MENACE of...
MAGNETO,
MOST POWERFUL OF THE EVIL MUTANTS!

THE MIGHTY THOR! "WHEN MAGNETO* STRIKES!"
WRITTEN BY: STAN LEE, THE MONARCH OF THE MARVEL AGE, AT THE PINNACLE OF HIS POWER!
ILLUSTRATED BY: JACK KIRBY, THE PRINCE OF PAGEANTRY, AT THE HEIGHT OF HIS TITANIC TALENT!
INKED BY: CHIC STONE, THE DEAN OF LINE DESIGN, AT THE PEAK OF HIS PROWESS!
LETTERED BY: S. ROSEN, THE SULTAN OF SPELL-ING, AT THE LITTLE TABLE IN HIS STUDIO!
* BY SPECIAL ARRANGEMENT WITH THE PUBLISHERS OF X-MEN MAGAZINE! (NAMELY... OURSELVES!)
LIKE IT, THOR? IT'S ONE OF OUR LEADING EXHIBITS FOR THE PROPOSED "HALL OF HEROES" AT THE FAIR!
I AM DEEPLY TOUCHED! I SHALL ALWAYS STRIVE TO BE WORTHY OF SO GREAT AN HONOR!
MIGHTY THOR
OUR EPIC TALE BEGINS AT THE SITE OF THE WORLD'S FAIR, WHERE THE DYNAMIC THUNDER GOD VIEWS THE SCULPTURE FOR A NEW EXHIBITION! A PEACEFUL SCENE, PERHAPS... BUT ONE WHICH GIVES NO HINT OF THE FANTASTIC EVENTS WHICH ARE SOON TO FOLLOW...!!
X-789

AND HERE WE HAVE ADDITIONAL PIECES OF SCULPTURE, ALL BASED UPON SOME OF THE MOST DRAMATIC ADVENTURERS IN THE WORLD TODAY! YOU WILL NOTICE THE FANTASTIC FOUR, YOUR FELLOW AVENGERS, AND, IN THE NEXT ROOM, WE HAVE SPIDER MAN, DAREDEVIL, AND THE X-MEN!
A TRULY IMPOSING ARRAY! YOU HAVE CHOSEN WELL, SIR!

I SINCERELY HOPE YOU WILL BE ABLE TO ATTEND THE OPENING CEREMONIES WHEN THE PAVILLION IS COMPLETE, THOR!
I SHALL DO MY BEST! THANK YOU FOR THIS PREVIEW TOUR... AND FAREWELL!

MOMENTS LATER, THE MIGHTY THUNDER GOD HURTLES THROUGH THE SKY AT BLINDING SPEED AS HE HEADS FOR THE MEDICAL OFFICE OF DR. DON BLAKE..
I WOULD HAVE LIKED TO REMAIN LONGER, BUT I HAVE OTHER DUTIES WHICH MUST NOW BE PERFORMED IN MY MORTAL GUISE!

THE CITY BELOW IS QUIET... PEACEFUL! I PRAY IT SHALL REMAIN THUS!

BUT, HOW DIFFERENT WOULD THE HANDSOME IMMORTAL'S THOUGHTS BE IF HE COULD SEE THE STRANGE, CAMOU-FLAGED SUBMERSIBLE FORT WHICH EVEN NOW QUIETLY APPROACHES NEW YORK'S UNSUSPECTING HARBOR!
ALL ENGINES HALT! WE ARE WITHIN RANGE!
I SHALL TAKE OVER THE CONTROLS PERSONALLY NOW! STAND ASIDE!

AHH! JUST AS I THOUGHT! THE MENTAL EMANATIONS ARE STRONGER THAN EVER! THAT MEANS I'M GETTING CLOSER TO THE X-MEN!
I HAVE LONG SUSPECTED THAT THEY WERE BASED SOMEWHERE IN THE METROPOLITAN AREA... AND NOW I AM CERTAIN!!

NO, YOUR EYES DO NOT DECEIVE YOU! YOU ARE GAZING AT THE DREAD MAGNETO, LEADER OF THE EVIL MUTANTS, ONE OF THE STRANGEST BANDS OF ARCH-MENACES THE WORLD HAS EVER KNOWN!
TOAD! HOW DARE YOU INTERRUPT MY MUSINGS?!!
MASTER... LOOK! A SEA MONSTER HAS BROKEN INTO OUR SHIP!

WITLESS FOOL!! IT IS MERELY ONE OF MASTERMIND'S INSIPID ILLUSIONS!!
HE FOOLED ME AGAIN! ONE OF THESE DAYS HE'LL PAY FOR THAT!! I'LL SHOW HIM!

HAVE YOU NO BETTER WAY TO SPEND YOUR TIME THAN TORMENTING THE DIM-WITTED TOAD?
FORGIVE ME, MAGNETO! BUT IT GETS SO BORING COOPED UP HERE, DAY AFTER DAY!

YOUR DAYS OF BOREDOM HAVE COME TO AN END! I HAVE A TASK FOR ALL OF YOU! ACCORDING TO MY CALCULATIONS, THE X-MEN ARE HIDDEN SOMEWHERE WITHIN A FIFTY MILE AREA! YOUR ORDERS ARE... FIND THEM!
QUICKSILVER! YOU AND YOUR SISTER WILL ACCOMPANY MASTERMIND AND THE TOAD! I SHALL STAY BEHIND TO PLAN OUR STRATEGY WHEN OUR ENEMIES HAVE BEEN TRACKED DOWN!
VERY WELL, MAGNETO!

IT WILL BE A RELIEF TO GET AWAY FROM THAT EVIL CREATURE FOR A WHILE! IF ONLY MASTERMIND AND THE TOAD WEREN'T COMING WITH US!
JUST WAIT, WANDA! I'LL TELL MAGNETO WHAT YOU SAID!
SILENCE! NO HARM SHALL COME TO MY SISTER WHILE I LIVE!
NOW GO! DO NOT RETURN UNTIL YOU HAVE FOUND THE X-MEN!!
SOME-DAY YOU'LL REGRET THOSE WORDS, MY HAUGHTY BEAUTY!
3.

HOW THEY DESPISE EACH OTHER! IT IS ONLY MY WILL, MY POWER, THAT KEEPS THEM WORKING AS A TEAM!
BUT I ASK NOT FOR FRIENDSHIP, OR LOVE! ALL I DEMAND IS FEAR, AND BLIND OBEDIENCE! FOR I AM MAGNETO... MIGHTIEST OF ALL THE MUTANTS!

AND NOW I SHALL EXPERIMENT WITH MY MATCHLESS MAGNETIC POWERS... THE POWERS THAT WILL SOMEDAY MAKE ME THE RULER OF ALL THE INFERIOR HOMO SAPIENS!

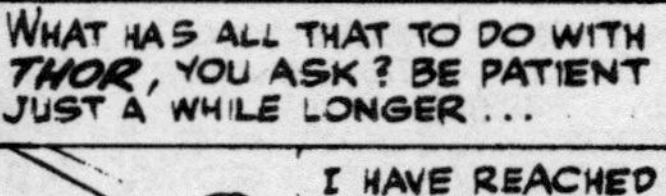
WHAT HAS ALL THAT TO DO WITH THOR, YOU ASK? BE PATIENT JUST A WHILE LONGER...

I HAVE REACHED MY DESTINATION! NOW, ONLY ONE THING REMAINS!

IT IS TIME FOR MIGHTY THOR TO DEPART TEMPORARILY FROM THIS MORTAL VALE...

...AND TO BE REPLACED BY DR. DON BLAKE, WHO HAS A MEDICAL PRACTICE THAT MUST NOT BE NEGLECTED!

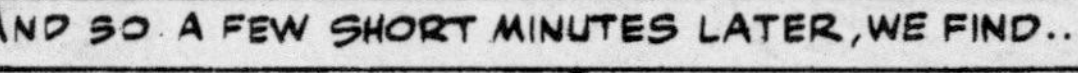
AND SO A FEW SHORT MINUTES LATER, WE FIND...

NEXT TIME YOU THROW A FOOTBALL, TOMMY, DON'T SNAP YOUR ARM... USE A SMOOTH FOLLOW THROUGH!
YOU'LL GET MORE POWER AND YOU WON'T SPRAIN YOUR ARM!
THANKS, DOC! I'LL REMEMBER!

HOW DID YOU BECOME SUCH AN AUTHORITY ON FOOTBALL, DOCTOR? I NEVER KNEW...
HOLD IT, JANE!! LOOK AT THE INSTRUMENTS!! WHAT'S HAPPENING??!
4.

--EVEN IN THE STREET! ALL SORTS OF METALLIC OBJECTS... FLOATING CRAZILY BY... AS THOUGH THEY'RE ON INVISIBLE STRINGS!!
I DON'T UNDERSTAND! IT HAPPENED SO SUDDENLY!! WHAT DOES IT MEAN??
I DON'T KNOW, JANE! I HAVEN'T ANY IDEA!
NO, DR. DON BLAKE HAS NO IDEA.. BUT, THE PART OF ME WHICH IS THE MIGHTY THOR KNOWS THAT SOME SUPER-NATURAL FORCE IS AT WORK...AND ITS PURPOSES CAN ONLY BE EVIL ONES!!
THE UN-BELIEVABLE PHENOMENON LASTS ONLY A FEW SECONDS... BUT, IN THAT TIME, IT SEEMS AS THOUGH A GIGANTIC, INVISIBLE MAGNET IS WREAKING HAVOC ON THE STARTLED CITY!
SEA FOOD
ROGERS
RESTAURANT
SOMETHING IS LIFTING THE CAR! WE'RE FLOATING IN THE AIR!
IT'S NOT ONLY US! LOOK DOWN BELOW...THAT MOTOR-CYCLE... TRASH CANS... LAMPPOSTS... EVERYTHING METAL!! THE WORLD'S GONE MAD!!
K-1351

BUT, AS SUDDENLY AS IT BEGAN, THE AMAZING PHENOMENON ABRUPTLY ENDS! INSTANTANEOUSLY, EVERYTHING RETURNS TO NORMAL, AS MOST OF THE DAZED OBSERVERS BELIEVE THEY WERE VICTIMS OF SOME SORT OF MASS DELUSION ...
PERHAPS WE'VE BEEN WORKING TOO HARD... IMAGINING THINGS!
I WOULDN'T BE TOO SURPRISED!
IT'S LUCKY THE HUMAN BRAIN ALWAYS FINDS EXCUSES FOR INEXPLICABLE EVENTS!
AW, IT WAS PROBABLY JUST SOME KINDA FREAK ELECTRICAL STORM OR SOMETHING!

THAT'S THE LAST PATIENT FOR TODAY, JANE! IF ANY OTHERS ARRIVE, REFER THEM TO DR. CARLSON! I'M GOING TO LEAVE NOW!
DONALD BLAKE!! HAVE YOU FORGOTTEN THAT WE HAVE A DINNER DATE TONIGHT??
OMIGOSH! I DID FORGET! BUT I'VE GOT TO INVESTIGATE WHAT JUST HAPPENED!

PLEASE FORGIVE ME, JANE DEAR! I'M AFRAID THE EVENTS OF THE PAST FEW MINUTES HAVE RATHER UNNERVED ME! I FEEL RATHER ILL! LET'S HAVE DINNER TOMORROW, INSTEAD!
OF COURSE, DOCTOR! WE WOULDN'T WANT YOU TO INCONVENIENCE YOURSELF, WOULD WE?

BUT, A FEW MOMENTS LATER...
POOR JANE! SHE'S HURT... AND DISAPPOINTED IN ME!
IF ONLY I WERE FREE TO TELL HER THE TRUTH!! HOW I PRAY THAT SOME DAY NOBLE ODIN WILL GIVE ME THAT RIGHT...!!

AHH! I HAVE FOUND WHAT I SEEK! A FLOW OF MAGNETIC FORCE... ATTRACTING THE ENCHANTED URU METAL OF MY HAMMER!

IT IS LEADING ME IRRESISTIBLY TOWARDS THAT LARGE PIECE OF FLOATING DRIFTWOOD!
THERE MUST BE FAR MORE TO IT THAN MEETS THE EYE!
6.

THEN, STANDING ATOP ONE OF THE STURDY BRANCHES, THE DETERMINED THUNDER GOD FINDS...
MY SUSPICIONS WERE CORRECT! THERE IS SOME SORT OF *PERISCOPE* CONCEALED WITHIN THIS LIMB!

WHATEVER STRANGE POWER IS BEHIND THE INCREDIBLE OCCURANCE I HAVE WITNESSE THE ANSWER IS CERTAIN TO BE FOUND DOWN *THERE!*

THEN, USING HIS ENCHANTED HAMMER LIKE A BATTERING RAM, THE MIGHTY IMMORTAL SOON REACHES THE HEART OF THE UNDERSEA CRAFT...

WHOOM!
WHO DARES?!

I DARE!!
A COSTUMED INTRUDER!! WHO *ARE* YOU??
THOR, OF ASGARD! NOW, STATE *YOUR* NAME!

I AM... *MAGNETO,* MOST POWER-FUL OF *HOMO SUPERIORS!*
AT A GESTURE FROM THE POWER-FUL MUTANT, THE PONDEROUS IRON DOOR RISES FROM THE FLOOR AND SMASHES ITSELF AGAINST THE WALL WITH INCREDIBLE FORCE!

YOU THINK TO IMPRESS ME WITH SUCH AN EXHIBITION? MY POWER IS BEYOND HUMAN COMPREHENSION!
STOP! THERE IS NO NEED FOR US TO BATTLE!

ONLY ANOTHER MUTANT WOULD HAVE THE POWER TO FIND ME HERE! THAT MEANS WE SHOULD BE ALLIES!!
EXPLAIN YOURSELF, MASKED ONE! I SHALL HEAR YOU OUT!

STEP INTO THIS CHAMBER! SEE THE TREASURES I POSSESS! WITH NO MORE EFFORT THAN LIFTING A FINGER, I CAN OBTAIN THE WEALTH OF NATIONS... THE PRIZES OF THE WORLD!
WHAT HAVE SUCH IRRELEVANCIES TO DO WITH ME?!

I SEE THAT YOU ARE NOT EASILY IMPRESSED!
THIS IS WHAT IT HAS TO DO WITH YOU... JOIN MY MUTANT BROTHERHOOD... PLEDGE ALLEGIANCE TO MAGNETO... AND YOU SHALL SHARE MY TRIUMPH WHEN I CONQUER THE HUMAN RACE!

ARROGANT VILLAIN!! THOR IS NO EVIL MUTANT! I AM THE SON OF ODIN, SWORN PROTECTOR OF THE HUMAN RACE!
SO BE IT, FOOL! I OFFERED YOU GREATNESS, BUT YOU CHOSE DEFEAT!

THEN, BEFORE THE ANGRY THUNDER GOD CAN MOVE, THE MUTANT MASTER OF MAGNETISM DRAWS THE STEEL FLOORING UP AROUND HIM...

THERE IS NO MIDDLE GROUND, LONG-HAIRED ONE! THOSE WHO DO NOT SWEAR ALLEGIANCE TO MAGNETO MUST BE ***DESTROYED!***

FAREWELL, SO-CALLED PRINCE OF ASGARD! YOU HAVE MADE YOUR CHOICE... THOUGH IT GRIEVES ME TO DO THIS, FOR WE MIGHT HAVE BEEN MOST POWERFUL ALLIES!

YOU COUNT YOUR VICTORY TOO SOON, BRAGGART!

THE MIGHTY ***THOR*** IS NOT SO EASILY DISPOSED OF!!
CLANG!

STOP!!! I ALLOWED YOU TO DEMONSTRATE YOUR POWER!! NOW IT IS TIME FOR YOU TO WITNESS ***MINE!!***

WHAT SORCERY IS THIS?? WHEREVER I GO, THAT ACCURSED HAMMER FOLLOWS!!

BUT NOTHING CAN GET PAST MY MAGNETIC REPELLOR FIELD!

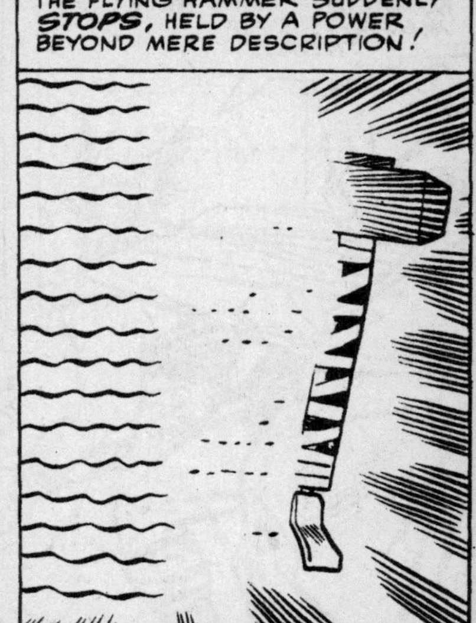
AND, JUST AS MAGNETO SAYS, THE FLYING HAMMER SUDDENLY STOPS, HELD BY A POWER BEYOND MERE DESCRIPTION!

THEN, THOR MAKES HIS FIRST MISTAKE! CAUGHT UP IN THE WHITE HEAT OF BATTLE, HE FORGETS HIS HAMMER AS HE LUNGES AT HIS FOE...!!
I NEED NO ENCHANTED MALLET TO DEAL WITH THE LIKES OF YOU!
THAT GRASP... IT'S LIKE AN IRON VISE...!!

...BUT EVEN IRON MUST GIVE WAY TO THE IRRESISTIBLE FORCE OF MAGNETISM, WHEN USED BY THE MASTER OF SUCH POWER!

FAREWELL, THOR!! WITHIN SECONDS, MY FAST-MOVING, MAGNETICALLY-POWERED STEEL WALLS WILL CLOSE IN ON YOU, UNTIL YOU ARE NO MORE THAN A FLEETING MEMORY IN THE MINDS OF MEN!

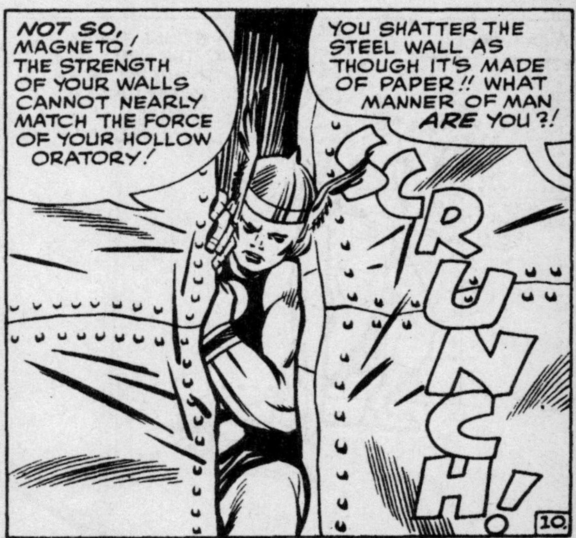
NOT SO, MAGNETO! THE STRENGTH OF YOUR WALLS CANNOT NEARLY MATCH THE FORCE OF YOUR HOLLOW ORATORY!
YOU SHATTER THE STEEL WALL AS THOUGH IT'S MADE OF PAPER!! WHAT MANNER OF MAN ARE YOU?!
SCRUNCH!
10

I AM MORE THAN MAN, MAGNETO... MORE THAN MUTANT! I AM THOR!!
AND NO MATTER HOW MANY WALLS YOU PUT BETWEEN US, YOU CANNOT ESCAPE ME!

BUT, THEN, SIXTY SECONDS AFTER HE HAS HURLED HIS HAMMER, THOR REALIZES THE GRAVE MISTAKE HE HAS MADE! FOR, WITHOUT THE ENCHANTED URU MALLET, IN THE SPACE OF ONE FULL MINUTE HE AGAIN REVERTS TO THE MORTAL FORM OF DR. DON BLAKE!
I'VE BEEN UNPARDONABLY CARELESS! WHAT CAN I DO NOW? WHAT CHANCE DOES THE LAME DR. BLAKE HAVE AGAINST MAGNETO??

I'VE GOT TO RUN... HIDE SOMEWHERE... STALL FOR TIME... UNTIL I CAN THINK!!

BUT, I CAN'T!! THERE'S NO PLACE TO GO! I'M TRAPPED!

AT THE SAME INSTANT THAT I CHANGED TO DR. DON BLAKE, MY HAMMER MUST HAVE CHANGED TO BLAKE'S ORDINARY-LOOKING CANE! BUT, HOW CAN I GET IT?? IT'S IN THE OTHER CHAMBER, BEHIND THIS STEEL WALL!!

MEANWHILE...
NOT A SOUND FROM BEHIND THE WALL!! HE'S TRYING TO TRICK ME... PREPARING A TRAP!

HE'S WAITING FOR ME TO OPEN THE DOOR... BUT I'M TOO CLEVER! I WON'T OPEN IT!!
WHAT IS THIS? A SIMPLE WALKING-STICK! WHERE COULD IT HAVE COME FROM??

BAH! NO TIME TO WORRY ABOUT THAT NOW! I'LL ATTACK THOR MAGNETICALLY, RIGHT THROUGH THE WALL!!

RIVETS! FLYING OFF THE WALL LIKE BULLETS! IF ONE HITS ME, I'M FINISHED!

UGHHH! THE GRILL FELL FROM THE CEILING! MAGNETO IS CAUSING THIS TO HAPPEN... IT'S THAT UNCANNY POWER OF HIS!

I HAVEN'T A CHANCE! I'LL... WAIT! THERE'S ONE PLACE... BACK TO THE INNER CHAMBER, THROUGH THE WALL WHICH THOR HAD OPENED!

LATER, WHEN MAGNETO FINALLY DARES TO ENTER THE SEALED ROOM...
THOR IS GONE! IT WAS NOT A TRAP! BUT... WHAT IS HE UP TO??

HE CANNOT HIDE FROM ME! I'LL FOLLOW HIS PROGRESS BY THIS SCHEMATIC RADAR! THERE... I SEE HIS BLIP NOW!
12.

AND SO, STILL THINKING HE IS BATTLING THOR HIMSELF, MAGNETO CONTINUES ATTACKING FROM A SAFE DISTANCE, USING HIS MAGNETIC POWER...
NO MATTER WHERE I RUN, I'M STOPPED AT EVERY TURN!
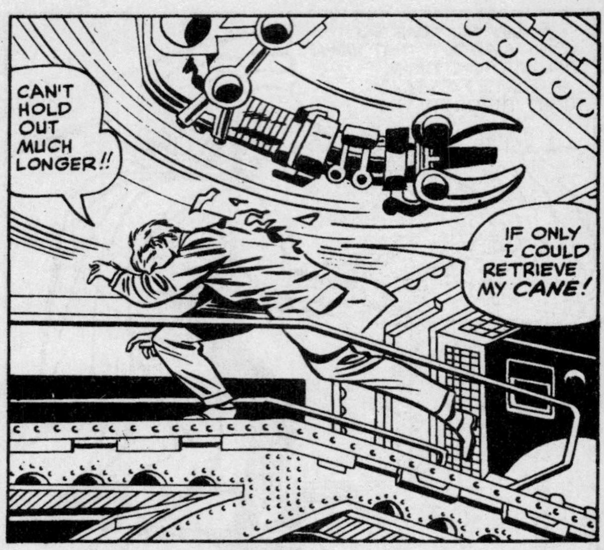
CAN'T HOLD OUT MUCH LONGER!!
IF ONLY I COULD RETRIEVE MY CANE!

TOO WEAK...TOO TIRED TO RUN ANY MORE!! LEG IS THROBBING...HEAD IS SPINNING...

BUT, JUST AS MAGNETO PREPARES FOR THE FINAL ONSLAUGHT...
BEEP! BEEP!
MY TELEVISION ALARM! I'M BEING SUMMONED!

MASTERMIND!! DID YOU HAVE TO DISTURB ME NOW??
YES! WE FOUND THE X-MEN!

WELL!? WHY BOTHER WITH THE ALARM SYSTEM!? RETURN TO BASE AND GIVE ME THE INFORMATION!
BUT... WE'RE IN A JAM! THEY FOUND US, TOO! THEY'RE HOT ON OUR TRAIL!
YOU SHOULDN'T HAVE TOLD HIM! THE MASTER WILL PUNISH US ALL!

YOU BUMBLING INCOMPETENT! CAN YOU ACCOMPLISH NOTHING WITHOUT ME??
RUN! THE X-MEN ARE LESS THAN HALF A MILE AWAY!
TELL US, MAGNETO! WHAT SHALL WE DO??

STOP SNIVELLING, AND GIVE ME YOUR EXACT LOCATION!!
YES! YES... I WILL!!

WE'RE NEAR THE 12TH STREET DOCKS, AT THE SOUTHEAST CORNER!! YOU MUST COME SOON!!
A SOUND! BEHIND ME! IT MUST BE THOR!
WAIT THERE! HOLD THEM AT BAY TILL I JOIN YOU!

THERE HE IS! BUT... WHY WOULD THE MIGHTY THOR BOTHER TO PICK UP A MERE WALKING STICK??

A SPLIT-SECOND LATER, ALTHOUGH HE CANNOT POSSIBLY COMPREHEND THE TRUTH, MAGNETO GETS HIS ANSWER!!
WHA... WHAT CAN THIS BE?!
14.

THE TIME FOR *TALK* IS PAST, EVIL ONE! *NOW* YOU FACE THE HAMMER OF THOR!!

MY MAGNETIC FORCE FIELD CAN SHIELD ME FROM THE *FIRST* FEW BLOWS... BUT IT CAN'T HOLD OFF SUCH INDESCRIBABLE POWER MUCH LONGER!

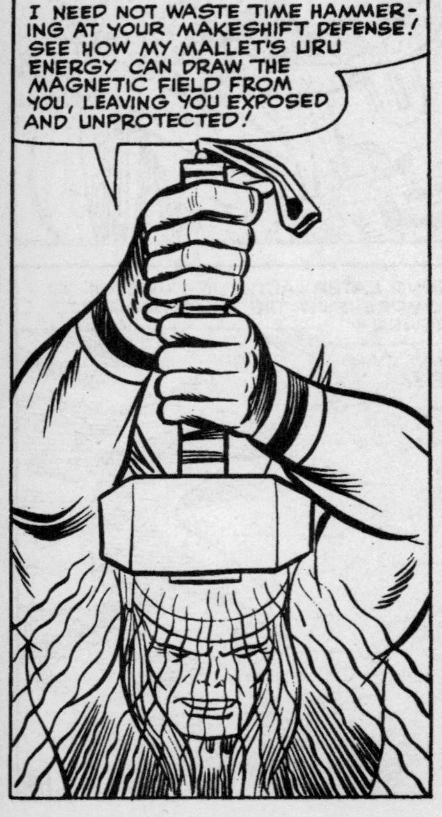

I NEED NOT WASTE TIME HAMMERING AT YOUR MAKESHIFT DEFENSE! SEE HOW MY MALLET'S URU ENERGY CAN DRAW THE MAGNETIC FIELD FROM YOU, LEAVING YOU EXPOSED AND UNPROTECTED!

WHAT SAY YOU *NOW*, MAGNETO? WHERE ARE THE BOASTFUL WORDS OF THE MUTANT WHO PLANS TO CONQUER THE HUMAN RACE?

THROUGHOUT HISTORY, THERE HAVE BEEN *MANY* WHO FELT THEY WERE SUPERIOR TO MANKIND... BUT ALWAYS THEY WERE DESTROYED... WHILE HUMANITY ENDURES!

NONE MAY STRIKE MAGNETO AND LIVE TO TELL OF IT!! AND YOU, ACCURSED THOR, SHALL BE NO EXCEPTION!!

HE DROPPED THROUGH A TRAP DOOR!!
IS THIS HOW TO PUNISH THOR, EVIL BRAGGART?? BY FLEEING FROM HIM??

HE DOESN'T SUSPECT MY REAL MOTIVE! HE'S TRYING TO PRY THE DOOR OPEN, AS I HOPED HE WOULD!
HE'LL BE DOWN HERE IN A MOMENT...!!

BUT, IN PLACE OF MAGNETO, HE'LL FIND A THERMO-NUCLEAR PROTON BOMB AWAITING HIM!

THAT BOMB WILL NEVER HURT ANYONE, MAGNETO!!
ICE FORMING AROUND THE MECHANISM!!
IT CAN ONLY MEAN ONE THING...

EXACTLY, MAGNETO!!
THE X-MEN HAVE FOUND YOU!!
I'VE GOT TO REACH MY MAGNI-SUB! ...I CAN STILL ESCAPE!!
18.

SECONDS LATER, PEERING THROUGH A PLEXIGLASS VIEWPORT, THE MIGHTY THUNDER GOD IS SURPRISED TO SEE...
MAGNETO!! FLEEING IN A ONE-MAN SUB!

BUT WHAT IS THAT STRANGE CRAFT PURSUING HIM?? IT SEEMS TO BE MARKED ONLY WITH... AN X!!
X

THERE MUST BE AN ESCAPE HATCH OF SOME SORT BELOW!!
WHOOM!!

A BOMB!! THAT'S HOW HE INTENDED TO DEFEAT ME!! BUT IT'S FROZEN INTO USELESSNESS NOW!

I'M NOT FULLY CERTAIN WHAT TRANSPIRED IN THE PLACE BELOW, BUT, OF ONE THING I AM CERTAIN... THE LAIR OF MAGNETO IS A PLACE OF EVIL...

AND, BY THE POWER OF THE STORM... BY THE FURY OF THE ELEMENTS, IT MUST BE DESTROYED!!
THE THUNDER GOD HAS SO ORDAINED!!
BAROOM!

I SUSPECT IT WAS NOT FROM ME THAT MAGNETO FLED! THERE WERE OTHERS... OTHERS HE FEARED EVEN MORE! SOME DAY I SHALL LEARN THE TRUTH!

MEANWHILE, A SMALL ONE-MAN SUB LIES SILENT IN THE MURKY DARKNESS OF THE DEEP... PROTECTED FROM DETECTION BY A THICK INVISIBLE COATING OF MAGNETIC FORCE!!
I'M SAFE AT LAST! THE X-MEN CANNOT PENETRATE MY MAGNETIC BLANKET TO LOCATE ME!!

THEN, LONG MINUTES LATER...
THEY OUTSMARTED MY INEPT ALLIES! THEY MUST HAVE TRACED ME THROUGH MASTER-MIND'S RADIO BEAM!..BUT IT AVAILED THEM NOTHING!

I SHALL NOW REJOIN QUICK-SILVER AND THE OTHERS! THIS IS BUT A TEMPORARY DEFEAT! SOONER OR LATER, ULTIMATE VICTORY WILL BE MINE!!
IT CANNOT BE OTHERWISE! I WAS BORN TO RULE MANKIND!

A SHORT TIME LATER...
HELLO! ANY-BODY HOME?
WELL! DOCTOR BLAKE! HOW HEROIC OF YOU TO VENTURE OUTDOORS ON SUCH A WINDY NIGHT!

JANE, DARLING... DID ANYONE EVER TELL YOU THAT SARCASM DOESN'T BECOME YOU? LIPS LIKE YOURS WERE MEANT ONLY TO WHISPER SWEET NOTHINGS!!
IF YOU THINK YOU CAN BREAK A DATE WITH ME, AND MAKE UP FOR IT WITH A LITTLE SWEET TALK...
...YOU'RE ABSOLUTELY RIGHT!

LOOK AT YOU! YOU'RE THIN AS A RAIL! I'LL BET YOU HAVEN'T EVEN EATEN TODAY!
WELL, I...EH... WAS RATHER BUSY!

MMM! I NEVER KNEW HAM AND CHEESE COULD TASTE SO GOOD! DID I EVER TELL YOU YOU'RE WONDERFUL?
NOT OFTEN ENOUGH, YOU SILLY GOOP! HERE...HAVE A GLASS OF MILK!

WILL HE EVER SAY THE WORDS I'M LONGING TO HEAR? I JUST KNOW HE NEEDS ME TO LOOK AFTER HIM! HE'S SO DEAR... SO TRUSTING... SO LIKE A HELPLESS LITTLE BOY!
THE END

IT'S EXTREMELY DOUBTFUL WHETHER MAGNETO WOULD AGREE WITH LOVELY JANE FOSTER... BUT THEN, HE SAW DON BLAKE IN A SOME-WHAT DIFFERENT ASPECT! BE WITH US AGAIN, NEXT ISSUE, FOR MORE DAZZLING THRILLS WITH THE MOST DRAMATIC SUPER-HERO THE WORLD HAS EVER KNOWN! TILL THEN, MAY THE EYES OF ASGARD WATCH OVER YOU!

TALES OF ASGARD
HOME OF THE MIGHTY NORSE GODS!
FOR DARING TO FIGHT A DUEL AGAINST MY WISHES, YOU MUST ACCEPT MY PUNISHMENT! EVEN THE SON OF ODIN MAY NOT DISOBEY AN IMPERIAL COM-MAND! AND SO I ORDER YOU TO BE...
"BANISHED FROM ASGARD!"
The TIME: YEARS AGO, WHEN THOR WAS NOT YET 20! The PLACE: ASGARD!
PRESENTED BY THE GREATEST NAMES IN ILLO-DRAMATICS:
STAN LEE, Author
JACK KIRBY, Illustrator
VINCE COLLETTA, Delineator
SAM ROSEN, Letterer
LIVING PROOF OF THE TITANIC TALENT WHICH HAS MADE THIS SERIES SUCH A SMASHING SUCCESS!
Another MIGHTY MARVEL Saga of Epic Adventure and Powerful Pageantry!
X-781

SIRE! WE BEG YOU TO RECONSIDER YOUR VERDICT!
AT A TIME LIKE THIS, WHEN THE MOUNTAIN GIANTS ARE AT WAR WITH ASGARD, WE NEED THE MIGHTY HAMMER OF THOR!
SILENCE! JUSTICE IS JUSTICE! I WILL HEAR NO MORE!

BUT, EVEN SO HALLOWED A PLACE AS ASGARD IS NOT WITHOUT ITS TRAITORS! ONE SUCH CONSCIENCE-LESS CREATURE IS... ARKIN, THE WEAK, COUSIN OF EVIL LOKI!
SO! THOR HAS BEEN BANISHED FROM ASGARD! THAT MEANS HE WILL HAVE TO RIDE THE MOUNTAIN ROAD ALONE!
THIS NEWS MAY SERVE TO SOFTEN THE HEART OF THE MOUNTAIN QUEEN TOWARDS ME... I MUST TELL HER WITHOUT DELAY!

LONG HAVE I LOVED KNORDA, NORMAL-SIZED QUEEN OF THE MOUNTAIN GIANTS... BUT LONG HAS SHE SPURNED MY HEART!
BUT, WHEN I BRING HER MY TIDINGS SHE WILL SEE THAT ARKIN IS NOT WEAK! PERHAPS SHE WILL FIND ME WORTHY OF HER LOVE!

AND SO, ON A DESOLATE MOUNTAIN RIDGE, JUST OUTSIDE THE FABLED LAND OF ASGARD...
THE NEWS YOU BROUGHT MAY MEAN THE DEATH KNELL OF ASGARD! DO YOU REALIZE THE EXTENT OF THE TREASON YOU HAVE COMMITTED, ARKIN??
YES, BEAUTIFUL QUEEN! BUT IT MATTERS NOT, SO LONG AS YOU LOOK WITH FAVOR UPON YOUR ADORING SLAVE!

TIME ENOUGH TO DISCUSS SUCH MATTERS LATER! NOW I MUST ACT! FIRST, WE SHALL DISPOSE OF THOR... AND THEN... ALL ASGARD SHALL BE OURS!
I CARE NOT WHAT FATE BEFALLS THE SON OF ODIN... NOR THE LAND OF ASGARD! I CARE ONLY TO WIN THE HEART OF QUEEN KNORDA!
LATER, THE MIGHTIEST WARRIOR THE WORLD HAS EVER KNOWN SLOWLY RIDES ALONG THE MOUNTAIN ROAD WHICH LEADS AWAY FROM THE LAND OF HIS BIRTH...
THE TRAIL I FOLLOW IS FRAUGHT WITH DANGER... BUT AN IMMORTAL OF ASGARD MUST SHOW NO FEAR! NO MATTER WHAT BEFALLS, I AM THOR, SON OF NOBLE ODIN!
THEN, SUDDENLY, WITHOUT WARNING... THE GRAVEST DANGER OF ALL APPEARS, AS A HEAVILY-ARMED BAND OF MOUNTAIN GIANTS ATTACKS THE LONE WARRIOR IN AN AWESOME ASSAULT FROM AMBUSH!
RIDE, MY POWERFUL LEGIONS! SHOW THE BRASH YOUNG THUNDER GOD NO MERCY! ASGARD MUST BE MINE!

BUT, NOT FOR *NAUGHT* HAS THE PROWESS AND DARING OF *THOR* LIVED IN LEGEND FOR ALL THESE AGES! FEARLESSLY, AS THOUGH FOLLOWED BY HIS OWN LOYAL LEGIONS... THE GOLDEN-HAIRED IMMORTAL THUNDERS THROUGH A NARROW CANYON PASS... HIS SMALLER STEED RACING LIKE THE WIND WHILE HIS LARGER PURSUERS SLOW DOWN IN ORDER TO ENTER!

YOU CANNOT ESCAPE US, PUNY ONE! THE MORE YOU FLEE, THE SWEETER WILL BE THE FRUITS OF OUR ULTIMATE VICTORY!

NOW HE IS TRULY TRAPPED! HE HAS LED US INTO A WALLED-IN VALLEY, FROM WHICH THERE CAN BE NO ESCAPE!

STOP HIM... BEFORE HE ENTERS THE MOUTH OF THAT SMALL CAVE! WE CANNOT FOLLOW IN SO LIMITED A SPACE!
BAH! IT MATTERS NOT! IF HE REMAINS WITHIN, WE SHALL STARVE HIM OUT! PANIC HAS MADE A FOOL OF THE SMALL ONE!

BUT, THE GLOATING MOUNTAIN GIANTS MIGHT NOT FEEL SO CONFIDENT IF THEY COULD LOOK WITHIN THE CAVE, AND SEE...

THIS NARROW TUNNEL IS JUST WIDE ENOUGH TO ALLOW MY STALLION AND ME TO REACH THE TOP OF THE CANYON!

AND THEN ...
YOUR PLAN *WORKED,* NOBLE FATHER! THE MOUNTAIN GIANTS ARE TRAPPED IN THE VALLEY BELOW!
WELL DONE, MY SON! YOU HAVE BROUGHT A GREAT VICTORY TO ASGARD THIS DAY!

I *SUSPECTED* THAT THERE WAS A *TRAITOR* IN OUR MIDST... WHICH IS WHY I TOLD *NONE* THAT YOUR BANISHMENT WAS JUST A RUSE! AND OUR SCHEME WORKED! I SEE HIM BELOW, WITH THE TRAPPED QUEEN KNORDA... IT IS ARKIN, THE WEAK!
HIS LOVE FOR KNORDA CAUSED HIM TO BETRAY HIS OWN LAND! AND NOW, IN A SENSE, HE HAS ACHIEVED HIS DESIRE... HE SHALL BE WITH THE ONE HE LOVES FOREVER ... IN *CAPTIVITY!*

KNORDA, I DID NOT REALIZE... I COULD NOT SUSPECT THAT IT WAS ALL A TRAP, STAGED BY ODIN! KNORDA... YOU MUST LISTEN...!
SILENCE, WEAK ONE! WE HAVE NO MORE TO SAY TO EACH OTHER... EVER AGAIN!!
ACCEPT MY SWORD, ODIN! I ACKNOWLEDGE MY DEFEAT, AND BEG THAT YOU BE GENEROUS IN VICTORY!

THE END

THUS, THE WARRIORS OF ASGARD ADD ANOTHER VICTORY TO THEIR GLORIOUS HISTORY! BUT, NEXT ISSUE, BE PREPARED FOR A SURPRISE! FOR YOU WILL READ THE NEVER-BEFORE-REVEALED ACCOUNT OF THE TIME ODIN *LOST* A CRUCIAL BATTLE... THE TIME HIS LEGIONS WERE FORCED TO ACCEPT *DEFEAT!* AND NOW, UNTIL WE MEET AGAIN, MAY THE BLESSINGS OF ASGARD BE SHOWERED UPON YOU!

JOURNEY INTO MYSTERY
WITH
THE MIGHTY THOR
APPROVED BY THE COMICS CODE AUTHORITY
IND.
MARVEL COMICS GROUP 12¢
110 NOV.
SEE: MIGHTY THOR BATTLING AGAINST THE LEGIONS OF ASGARD!
IN WHICH THE DESPERATE THUNDER GOD FINDS...
"EVERY HAND AGAINST HIM!"
SEE:
THE MYSTERIOUS MR. HYDE!
THE SERPENTINE COBRA!
THE SINISTER LOKI!
THE NOBLE ODIN!

THE MIGHTY THOR!
BACK AGAIN... MORE DANGEROUS THAN EVER!
THE COBRA and MR. HYDE!
"EVERY HAND AGAINST HIM!"
THERE IS AN AURA OF EVIL OVER THE CITY! I CAN SENSE IT! IT IS HIDING... WAITING TO STRIKE!
ALSO FEATURING: THE INHUMAN VILLAINY OF LOKI!
SPECTACULARLY WRITTEN BY: STAN LEE
MAGNIFICENTLY DRAWN BY: JACK KIRBY
POWERFULLY INKED BY: CHIC STONE
EVENTUALLY LETTERED BY: ART SIMEK
X-811
1

I HAVE SEARCHED FOR HOURS, BUT I CANNOT PINPOINT THE EXACT LOCATION OF THE MENACE WHICH IS LYING IN WAIT...

AND YET, I FEEL ITS PRESENCE AS A MORTAL CAN FEEL THE BITING STING OF A SUMMER STORM!
AND, WHENEVER IT STRIKES, THOR SHALL BE READY!!

FAR BELOW, IN A SHADOWY ALLEY, WE FIND...
YOU WOULD NOT GLIDE SO CONFIDENTLY BY, THUNDER GOD, IF YOU KNEW YOUR ARCH ENEMY LOKI WAS ON EARTH ONCE MORE!

BUT NO EARTHLING MUST SUSPECT THE TRUE IDENTITY OF THE GOD OF EVIL! AND SO...

--BY THE MERE POWER OF A RANDOM THOUGHT, I CHANGE MY APPEARANCE INTO THAT OF A MEASLY, EARTH-BOUND MORTAL!

ONCE AGAIN I SHALL USE OTHERS TO SERVE ME IN MY NEVER-ENDING BATTLE AGAINST THE ACCURSED THOR! THE ONES I SEEK ARE WITHIN THOSE WALLS!
14 PRECINCT
14th PRECINCT

MINUTES LATER...
YOU WANT TO PAY THE BAIL FOR THE COBRA AND MISTER HYDE?? LOOK, FELLA, THE REASON THEY'RE STILL BEHIND BARS IS-- THE JUDGE SET THE AMOUNT AT HALF A MILLION DOLLARS!
RELEASE THEM! I HAVE THE CASH RIGHT HERE!

MEANWHILE...
I CAN SEARCH NO LONGER! I MUST RETURN TO MY OFFICE, AS DR. DON BLAKE...!

BUT, I SHALL STAND READY TO BECOME THE GOD OF THUNDER AGAIN AT A MOMENT'S NOTICE!

SLOWLY, SILENTLY, THE LAME DR. BLAKE ENTERS HIS OFFICE FROM THE LEDGE OUTSIDE--THE LEDGE UPON WHICH THE MIGHTIEST AVENGER OF ALL HAD STOOD BUT SECONDS BEFORE!
NOW TO PRETEND I HAVEN'T EVER LEFT!
NURSE FOSTER--SEND IN THE FIRST PATIENT, PLEASE!

UNLOCKING HIS DOOR FROM THE INSIDE, DR. BLAKE BUSIES HIMSELF WITH HIS INSTRUMENTS, AS HIS LOVELY NURSE ENTERS...
YOU COMPLETED YOUR RESEARCH JUST IN TIME, DOCTOR! MR. PERKINS JUST ARRIVED FOR HIS YEARLY CHECKUP!
GOOD! I'LL SEE HIM NOW!
E
BGLW
YOPH

BUT, BEFORE SUMMONING THE WAITING PATIENT, JANE FOSTER TENDERLY CUPS DR. BLAKE'S CHIN IN HER HAND, AS SHE SOFTLY SAYS...
YOU'RE LOOKING PALE, DON! I HOPE YOU'RE NOT DRIVING YOURSELF TOO HARD!
DON'T WORRY, DEAR--I'M FEELING ALRIGHT!

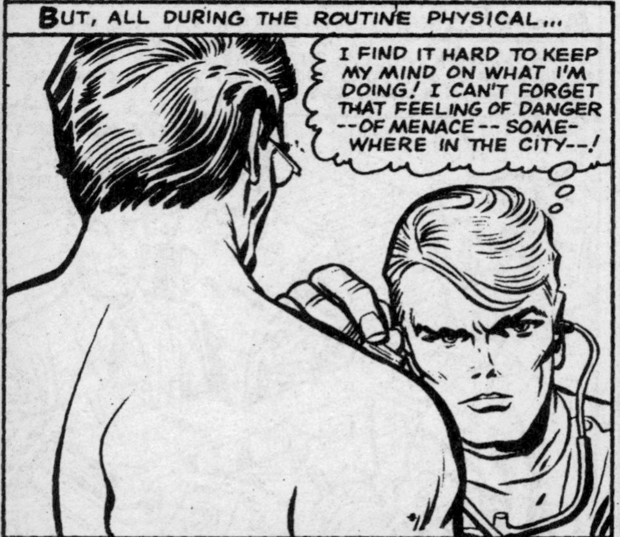
BUT, ALL DURING THE ROUTINE PHYSICAL...
I FIND IT HARD TO KEEP MY MIND ON WHAT I'M DOING! I CAN'T FORGET THAT FEELING OF DANGER--OF MENACE--SOMEWHERE IN THE CITY--!

AND, IN A LOCKED HOTEL ROOM ON THE OTHER SIDE OF TOWN...
WHY DID YOU PAY A HALF MILLION DOLLARS TO FREE US??
WHO ARE YOU? WHAT ARE YOU AFTER?

MY OBJECTIVES, GENTLEMEN, ARE NOT TOO DIFFERENT FROM YOURS! I AM AFTER RE-VENGE!! REVENGE ON A MUTUAL ENEMY! AND YOU SHALL HELP ME TO GET IT! FOR THOR IS AN EMEMY OF YOURS, AS WELL AS MINE!
SO! THOR IS YOUR ENEMY, TOO, EH? I THINK IT'S TIME YOU TOLD US WHO YOU ARE-- AND I MEAN NOW!
VERY WELL! I'VE NO REASON TO CONCEAL MY IDENTITY FROM YOU--

STRONG AS YOU BOTH ARE, YOUR STRENGTH IS NOTHING TO MINE! EVIL AS YOU BOTH ARE, YOUR EVILNESS IS NOTHING TO MINE!
FOR I AM-- LOKI!! I AM HALF-BROTHER TO THOR HIMSELF!!

THOR HAS BEATEN YOU IN THE PAST BECAUSE HIS POWER WAS GREATER THAN YOURS! BUT NOW, BY MEANS OF CHARMS AND SPELLS WHICH ONLY I POSSESS, I AM INCREASING YOUR POWER--DOUBLING IT!
NOW IF YOU WORK TOGETHER, YOUR COMBINED POWERS MAY EVEN EXCEED HIS! BUT YOU MUST OBEY MY ORDERS TO THE LETTER!!
YOUR FIRST TASK IS TO CAPTURE A NURSE! SHE IS JANE FOSTER, THE ONE WHO WORKS FOR DR. DON BLAKE! NOW GO!

ALTHOUGH LOKI KNOWS THAT THOR AND DON BLAKE ARE ONE AND THE SAME, HE MAY NEVER REVEAL THAT FACT TO ANY MORTAL, DUE TO AN UNALTER-ABLE EDICT OF LORD ODIN HIMSELF!
HOW CAN WE DEFEAT THOR BY CAPTURING THE NURSE OF THE LAME WEAKLING DOCTOR?
I DON'T KNOW--BUT LOOK HOW LOKI INCREASED OUR POWERS!! AS FAR AS I'M CONCERNED, WHATEVER HE SAYS GOES!!
4

NOT SO FAST, HYDE! WE DON'T WANT TO BE SEEN! IF SOMEONE SHOULD WARN THOR--!
BAH! THOR CAN DO NOTHING! I CAN FEEL INCREASED STRENGTH SURGING THRU ME-- NO ONE CAN STAND IN MY WAY!

HOLY SMOKE!! LOOK OUT, YOU NUTS!! I CAN'T STOP IN TIME!!
MR. HYDE STEPS ASIDE FOR NOTHING!
M-MISTER HYDE??!

WHOOM!
H-HE STOPPED A SPEEDING 4-TON CAR LIKE IT WAS A FEATHER!

LATER, AFTER DR. BLAKE'S LAST PATIENT HAS DEPARTED...
I GUESS YOU CAN GO HOME NOW, JANE! I WON'T BE NEEDING YOU ANY MORE TODAY!
YOU MIGHT NEED ME IF YOU SUDDENLY DECIDED TO TAKE A GIRL OUT TO DINNER THOUGH!!

THEN, SUDDENLY-- WITHOUT ANY WARNING--!!
DON! HELP!!
JANE! WHO-- IT'S THE COBRA!!
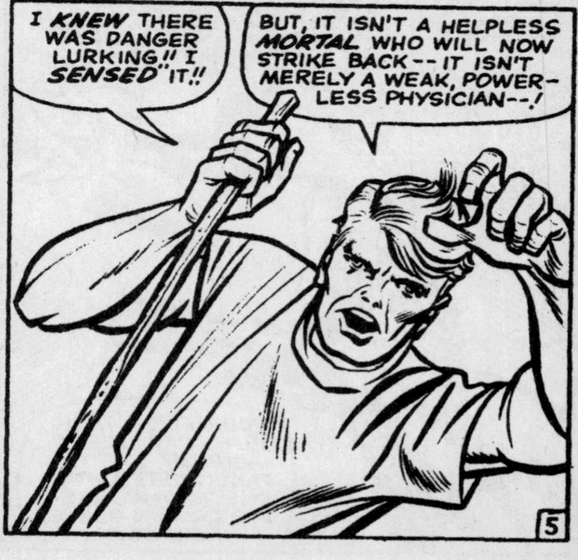
I KNEW THERE WAS DANGER LURKING!! I SENSED IT!!
BUT, IT ISN'T A HELPLESS MORTAL WHO WILL NOW STRIKE BACK-- IT ISN'T MERELY A WEAK, POWERLESS PHYSICIAN--!

THERE IS NO PLACE WHERE THE COBRA CAN HIDE THAT THOR CAN'T FIND HIM.!!

AFTER THE WAY I DEFEATED HIM LAST TIME, HOW DOES HE DARE STRIKE THUS AGAIN??
THERE HE IS-- ON THE STREET BELOW ME! I'LL HAVE HIM IN SECONDS!

BUT BEFORE THE ASGARD IMMORTAL CAN REACH THE SCENE...
HE SLITHERED UNDER THAT PARKED TAXI! SOMEONE IS WAITING FOR HIM--IT'S HYDE!!
HYDE-- TAKE HER!!
HAH! JUST IN TIME!

SO! MY INFORMATION WAS CORRECT! CAPTURING THIS PUNY FEMALE WAS ENOUGH TO BRING YOU TO ME!
NOW STAY BACK! COME NO FURTHER--NOT IF YOU VALUE HER LIFE!!
DO NOT HARM THE GIRL! I MAKE NO MOVE!

I'VE WAITED A LONG TIME FOR THIS VICTORY OVER YOU--AND I DON'T WANT IT TO END TOO SOON! I WANT TO ENJOY IT! SO, WE SHALL TAKE THE GIRL WITH US, TO MAKE SURE YOU DO AS WE COMMAND!!
AS YOU COMMAND? WHAT DO YOU MEAN?

MEET US AGAIN ON THIS SAME CORNER IN EXACTLY 24 HOURS!!
AT THAT TIME, YOU'LL SURRENDER YOUR HAMMER TO US, AND I'LL FINISH YOU OFF FOREVER! AND NOW, YOU HAVE 24 HOURS TO WORRY--AND TO BE POWER-LESS TO DO ANYTHING!! HOW SWEET IS THE FRUIT OF VICTORY!
JANE!! DON'T LOSE HEART!! I'LL SAVE YOU--SOMEHOW!!
6

STAY WHERE YOU ARE, THUNDER GOD! FOLLOW US-- AND THE GIRL IS FINISHED!
LOKI WAS RIGHT! THOR MUST LOVE THIS FEMALE! SO LONG AS SHE IS OUR PRISONER, HE IS BEATEN!

THAT EVIL DUO IS CAPABLE OF ANYTHING! I DARE NOT FOLLOW! I CANNOT GAMBLE WITH JANE FOSTER'S LIFE!!
BUT-- HOW COULD THEY HAVE KNOWN TO CAPTURE JANE?? NO ONE ON EARTH KNEW THAT I'M THE ONE WHO LOVES HER!!

BUT, AT THAT MOMENT, IN A PLACE NOT ON EARTH-- IN ASGARD, HOME OF THE LEGENDARY NORSE GODS, WE FIND...
SEE HOW COWARDLY THOR HAS GROWN! SEE HOW HE ALLOWED THOSE TWO MENACES TO ESCAPE, OH, NOBLE ODIN!
I THANK YOU FOR ADVISING ME TO VIEW MY SON ON THE PLANET EARTH, LOKI! ALTHOUGH, SUCH A SORRY SPECTACLE MAKES ME SAD OF HEART!

I PLANNED IT PERFECTLY! ODIN DOES NOT SUSPECT WHY THOR ALLOWED THEM TO ESCAPE! THIS WILL BE MY GREATEST TRIUMPH!
I MUST MAKE MY DIS- PLEASURE KNOWN TO THOR! HE MUST BE AWARE OF MY ANGER!

SINCE WHEN DOES THE SON OF ODIN LET EVILDOERS ESCAPE HIS VENGEANCE??
MOST NOBLE ODIN!!
THEY LEFT ME NO CHOICE, FATHER! THE LIFE OF JANE FOSTER WAS AT STAKE!!

AGAIN YOUR FORBIDDEN LOVE FOR THAT MORTAL FEMALE HAS CAUSED YOU TO SHIRK YOUR DUTY!!
THIS TIME THERE IS NO FORGIVENESS IN MY HEART! THIS TIME I ORDER YOU BANISHED FROM ASGARD!

SECONDS LATER...
STRANGE! THERE'S NOT A CLOUD IN THE SKY-- AND YET, I COULD HAVE SWORN I HEARD A DEAFENING THUNDERCLAP!
LOOK! IT'S THOR! WHAT HAPPENED TO HIM?
BACK! STAND NO ONE APPROACH ME!

I SUDDENLY REALIZE WHO MY TRUE FOE IS!! AT LAST MY EYES ARE OPENED!
I SHOULD HAVE SUSPECTED SOONER! THERE IS ONLY ONE WHO KNOWS OF THE LOVE THOR FEELS FOR JANE FOSTER! ONLY ONE WHO COULD BE BEHIND HYDE AND THE COBRA--!

ONLY MY EVIL ARCH-ENEMY-- MY HALF-BROTHER--LOKI!

BUT THIS TIME HE HAS GONE TOO FAR! THIS TIME NOTHING SHALL SAVE HIM FROM MY VENGEANCE!!
HIS ENTIRE BEING CONSUMED WITH AN INDESCRIBABLE RAGE, THE VENGEANCE-SEEKING THUNDER GOD STORMS ACROSS THE ENCHANTED RAINBOW BRIDGE WHICH LINKS EARTH WITH ASGARD!

UNTIL, FINALLY...
HEIMDALL!! STAND ASIDE!
HALT, SON OF ODIN! KNOW YOU THAT YOUR FATHER HAS BANISHED THEE FROM THIS LAND! YOU MAY NOT PASS!

I WARN YOU, HEIMDALL-- I WILL NOT BE STOPPED!!
THE WILL OF ODIN IS SUPREME! SHOULDER TO SHOULDER HAVE WE FOUGHT IN THE PAST, MIGHTY THOR-- I HAVE NO WISH TO HARM THEE NOW!! BUT STOP YOU I MUST!
AND I SHALL DO IT THUS-- WITH THE BLUE FLAME FROM COUNTLESS COSMIC SUNS!!

NEVER! MY URU HAMMER SHALL ABSORB THE FLAMES--CONVERTING THEM TO RAW POWER BOLTS WHICH IT HURLS BACK AT THEE!

THE LEGENDS HAVE IT THAT THOR CAN NEVER BE STOPPED!! BUT, SO LONG AS BREATH REMAINS WITHIN ME, MY SWORD SHALL FIGHT TO UPHOLD ODIN'S LAW--NO MATTER WHAT THE ODDS!!

I WOULD SOONER GIVE UP MY LIFE THAN INJURE LOYAL HEIMDALL --BUT I MUST REACH LOKI!!
AS GOD OF THUNDER --SOVEREIGN OF THE STORM-- I HAVE ONE FINAL WEAPON--!!

NOW STAND ASIDE, GUARDIAN OF THE GATES!! EVEN YOU CANNOT HOLD BACK THE WINDS OF A THOUSAND WORLDS!!

AND SO, BLINDED WITH RAGE, LIVID WITH ANGER, SEETHING WITH AN UNQUENCHABLE THIRST FOR VENGEANCE, THE MIGHTIEST WARRIOR THE WORLD HAS EVER KNOWN SMASHES INTO THE ENCHANTED REALM OF ASGARD--
I MUST FIND LOKI!! NO POWER IN THE UNIVERSE SHALL STOP ME UNTIL I DO!!
ALL OUR WEAPONS--ALL OUR NUMBERS ARE POWERLESS TO HALT THE RAMPAGING THUNDER GOD!!
SEND WORD TO NOBLE ODIN!! HIS SON SCATTERS US LIKE LEAVES IN THE STORM!
BACK!! BACK--OR ANSWER TO THE FURY OF MY HAMMER!!
10

FINALLY, THE THUNDER GOD REACHES HIS OBJECTIVE -- THE GREAT HALL OF THE CASTLE ITSELF!!
TURN, LOKI!! TURN, AND FACE THE ONE YOU SHALL NEVER DEFEAT!!

IT WAS YOU WHO TOLD THE COBRA AND MR. HYDE TO CAPTURE JANE FOSTER!! IT COULD ONLY HAVE BEEN YOU! ADMIT IT, THOU BASEST OF VILLAINS!!
NEVER! I ADMIT NOTHING!

YOU CANNOT THREATEN ME, HALF-BROTHER! WERE I FOOLHARDY ENOUGH TO FIGHT YOU, I KNOW YOU WOULD LASH OUT LIKE A THOUSAND DEMONS-- BUT, YOU CANNOT STRIKE AT ONE WHO STANDS QUIETLY BEFORE YOU! YOUR STUPID HONOR WOULD NOT PERMIT IT!
TAKE HEED, EVIL ONE!! I HAVE MY BREAKING POINT!!

YES--I CAN SEE THAT YOU MIGHT LOSE CONTROL --YOU MIGHT STRIKE OUT AT ME! AND SO, ALTHOUGH I STILL ADMIT NOTHING, I DO HAVE THE POWER TO CONJURE UP A VISION--
THERE! THAT IS WHERE YOU WILL FIND SHE WHOM YOU SEEK!
A LONELY ESTATE ON THE JERSEY HIGH-LANDS!

MY FIRST CONCERN IS TO FREE THE GIRL BEFORE ANY HARM CAN COME TO HER!
BUT THEN, HATED ONE, I SHALL RETURN-- AND YOU WILL PAY FOR WHAT YOU HAVE DONE! NOTHING WILL SAVE YOU!
YOUR WORDS IMPRESS ME NOT, THUNDER GOD! MY SHREWD-NESS AND CUNNING WILL EVER BE MORE THAN A MATCH FOR YOUR BLUNDER-ING BRUTE STRENGTH!

BUT THEN, BEFORE ANOTHER WORD CAN BE SAID-- ODIN'S ANGRY BELLOW FILLS THE GREAT CHAMBER--
THOR!! YOU DARED FORCE YOUR WAY BACK TO ASGARD?? YOU DARED COME HERE AGAINST MY IMPERIAL COMMAND??

IS THERE NO LIMIT TO YOUR DEFIANCE?? WILL YOU FORCE ME TO DO BATTLE WITH MY OWN SON??!
HAIL, ODIN, LORD OF ASGARD!!
A THOUSAND PARDONS, NOBLE FATHER! BUT, I DID WHAT HAD TO BE DONE!

THERE IS MUCH EVIL AFOOT ON EARTH, FATHER! MY FIRST DUTY IS TO CRUSH THE EVILDOER! IT WAS YOU YOURSELF WHO TAUGHT ME THAT!
THE SHARPNESS OF YOUR TONGUE MATCHES THE STRENGTH OF YOUR LIMBS! SPEAK ON!
AN INNOCENT LIFE DEPENDED UPON MY FINDING LOKI, NOBLE LORD! I COULD NOT SHIRK THAT TASK!
WORDS! NAUGHT BUT HOLLOW WORDS!

NO MORE! I HAVE HEARD ENOUGH! BACK TO EARTH WITH YOU! I SHALL SUSPEND MY JUDGEMENT TILL YOU RETURN! BEGONE!!

FASTER THAN THE SPEED OF THOR'S OWN ENCHANTED HAMMER -- THE POWER OF ODIN'S MERE WILL SENDS HIS DEFIANT SON BACK TO EARTH IN A FRACTION OF A MICRO-SECOND!!

SO AWESOME IS ODIN'S POWER -- SO SUBJECT TO HIS WILL ARE ALL THE FORCES OF NATURE ITSELF -- THAT THOR LANDS UPON HIS BELOVED PLANET WITHIN SIGHT OF THE DESTINATION HE SEEKS!!
ON THAT HILLTOP -- THE HOUSE WHEREIN JANE IS HELD CAPTIVE!

AND, INSIDE...
HE'S COMING! HE FOUND US!!
I EXPECTED THIS! BUT HE DOES NOT EXPECT THAT OUR HOUSE IS READY FOR HIM!
12

AND THEN...
I MUST FIND WHERE JANE IS IMPRISONED -- AND THEN RESCUE HER BEFORE SHE CAN BE HARMED! THE HOUSE IS QUIET-- SOMEHOW TOO QUIET!

BUT, SUDDENLY...
IT'S A TRAP! THE WALLS ARE REVERSING THEMSELVES-TURNING INSIDE OUT!!

THEY'RE CLOSING IN ON ME!!! BUT NOTHING CAN CRUSH MY URU HAMMER!!

AND NOTHING CAN KEEP THOR FROM THE WOMAN HE LOVES!!

SOMETHING SLITHERED PAST ME--ALMOST TOO FAST TO SEE! IT'S THE COBRA!!
LOKI MUST HAVE INCREASED HIS POWER--HE WAS NEVER THAT FAST BEFORE!

MISSED HIM! HE'S ESCAPING THRU THAT TRAPDOOR! BUT--WHAT DID HE DROP BEHIND HIM--?

A TEAR GAS GRENADE!!
THE BLINDING, CHOKING FUMES ARE SOMETHING WHICH ALL MY MIGHT CANNOT PROTECT ME FROM!

THEN, AS THOR COVERS HIS HEAD WITH HIS SILKEN CAPE TO KEEP OUT THE TEAR GAS FUMES, A SAVAGE FIGURE, WEARING A GAS-MASK, LEAPS TO THE ATTACK!
NOW, THUNDER GOD-- WE MEET TO FIGHT ON MY TERMS!!
IT'S HYDE!

UNNHH! THE FORCE OF HIS COWARDLY BLOW WAS STRONGER THAN I EXPECTED! IT CAUSED ME TO DROP MY HAMMER! HIS STRENGTH, TOO, HAS BEEN DOUBLED! THIS ALSO MUST BE LOKI'S DOING!!

DESPERATELY CLUTCHING TO KEEP HIS BALANCE, THE STEEL-MUSCLED FINGERS OF THE THUNDER GOD RIP A GRID RIGHT OUT OF THE WALL BEHIND HIM...

BUT, UNWITTINGLY, THE MIGHTY THOR HAS EXPOSED A LIVE PIPE WHICH IGNITES WITH THE THICK TEAR GAS FUMES, CAUSING A DEAFENING EXPLOSION--

AND, WHEN THE SMOKE HAS FINALLY CLEARED...
MY GAS MASK SAVED ME FROM THE DEADLY FUMES! BUT, WHAT OF THOR?

I'VE DONE IT! I'VE WON AT LAST! I'VE SLAIN THE ACCURSED THOR!!

WITH A FIENDISH CHORTLE, THE MACABRE MR. HYDE RUSHES OFF TO TELL THE NEWS TO HIS REPTILIAN PARTNER, LITTLE DREAMING THAT FUMES WHICH WOULD KILL A DOZEN HUMANS CAN ONLY TEMPORARILY STUN THE MIGHTY THOR!
I'VE LOST THE ELEMENT OF SURPRISE!! NOW I MUST REACH JANE-- EVERY SECOND COUNTS!!

AND THEN, THE STARTLED THUNDER GOD FINDS WHAT HE SEEKS SOONER THAN HE EXPECTED-
SOMETHING LYING THERE --IN THE RUBBLE!
IT'S--JANE!! SHE WAS TRAPPED IN THE EXPLOSION!!

BUT, THOUGH THE SON OF ODIN WAS MERELY STUNNED, JANE FOSTER IS BUT A FRAIL MORTAL. AND SO--
SHE'S BARELY BREATHING!!

WITH HANDS THAT CAN SHATTER A TWO-TON BOULDER, MIGHTY THOR GENTLY LIFTS THE MOTIONLESS GIRL, AND--THE PART OF HIM WHICH IS DR. BLAKE SOON REALIZES--
HER CONDITION IS CRITICAL! SHE IS DYING!

FORGOTTEN HIS ENEMIES-- FORGETTING THE DANGERS THAT AWAIT HIM--THE HEAVY-HEARTED IMMORTAL SILENTLY PLACES THE INJURED GIRL UPON A COUCH...

HER PULSE--IT'S GROWING WEAKER!! SHE CAN'T LAST MORE THAN A FEW MORE MINUTES!!
JANE--MY DARLING!! YOU CAN'T DIE--YOU MUSTN'T--JANE! JANE!!

THEN, THE ANGUISHED WARRIOR RAISES HIS EYES TO THE HEAVENS, AND CRIES OUT--
IN THE NAME OF ASGARD --DO NOT LET THIS FEMALE PERISH!! HEAR MY WORDS, OH POWERS THAT BE!
15

MEANWHILE, FLUSHED WITH VICTORY, HYDE AND THE COBRA RUSH BACK TO THE SCENE OF CARNAGE...
YOU THINK I LIED, DO YOU?? COME! I'LL SHOW YOU WHERE THOR FELL!
FOOL! THOR CANNOT BE SLAIN SO EASILY!

WAIT! YOU SERPENTINE FREAK! I DARE NOT TURN MY BACK ON YOU! YOU GO FIRST!
HAH! FOR ALL YOUR BRUTAL STRENGTH YOU STILL FEAR ME! GOOD! THAT IS HOW I WANT IT!

AND NOW, WE SHALL SEE IF YOU HAVE TRULY DEFEATED THE MIGHTY THOR!
THANKS TO THE INCREASED POWER LOKI HAS GIVEN US, WE CAN CONQUER ANY ENEMY! IF WE STAND TOGETHER, THE WORLD CAN BE OURS!

AND, JUST BEYOND THE DOOR...
IT'S NO USE! SHE'S SINKING FAST! WITH ALL MY POWER --ALL MY STRENGTH --THERE'S NOTHING I CAN DO!!
AND NOW I HEAR FOOTSTEPS-- HYDE AND THE COBRA ARE RETURNING!!
BUT WAIT! THERE IS STILL ONE CHANCE!!

BY SWINGING MY HAMMER IN A PRESCRIBED MANNER, I HAVE THE POWER TO CIRCUMVENT TIME ITSELF-- FOR TIME IS BUT ANOTHER DIMENSION!!
THUS I SHALL CREATE A TIME WARP--ONE WHICH WILL ENVELOP THIS ENTIRE HOUSE!!

TRUE TO HIS WORD, THE VALIANT IMMORTAL MAKES THE VERY FABRIC OF TIME ITSELF STAND STILL IN THE AREA SURROUNDING THE LONELY HOUSE!!
I'VE DONE IT! FROM THIS INSTANT ON, IN THIS VERY PLACE, THERE IS NO TIME!
16

AND, THAT MEANS JANE FOSTER WILL REMAIN ALIVE! FOR, TO HER, THERE WILL BE NO MORE FLEETING SECONDS, EACH ONE MAKING HER WEAKER THAN THE LAST!
LOOK! THOR STILL LIVES!
BAH! BUT NOT FOR LONG!!

SLEEP, MY BELOVED! NOW MUST I TURN FROM YOU, AND DO BATTLE ONCE AGAIN!
THE END

NEXT ISSUE BRINGS THE STARTLING CLIMAX OF THIS EPIC TALE, AS THOR BATTLES MORE SAVAGELY, MORE POWERFULLY THAN EVER BEFORE! AS SURELY AS ODIN IS LORD OF ASGARD, YOU WILL NEVER FORGET THOR'S COMING BATTLE WITH HYDE AND THE COBRA!

Tales of ASGARD
HOME OF THE MIGHTY NORSE GODS!
the DEFEAT OF ODIN!
THE ENEMY APPROACHES, SIRE!
IN WHICH NOBLE ODIN, LORD OF ASGARD, MONARCH OF THE LEGENDARY NORSE GODS, SUFFERS HIS FIRST DEFEAT!! OR--DOES HE??
WARRIORS, ASSEMBLE! PREPARE FOR BATTLE!
ANOTHER TOWERING TRIUMPH BY MARVEL'S TALENTED TITANIC TEAM:
STAN LEE WRITER
JACK KIRBY ILLUSTRATOR
VINCE COLLETTA DELINEATOR
ART SIMEK LETTERER
X-814
1

RAMPOK THE REBEL IS DEAD!! RAMPOK, THE KING WHO HAS DARED TO DEFY THE RULE OF ODIN FOR AGES! RAMPOK, THE KING WHOSE LEGIONS HAVE LONG BEEN AT WAR WITH ASGARD! AND NOW, RAMPOK'S SON, PRINCE RIVVAK, TAKES UP THE BATTLE...!
WE SHALL ATTACK THE ARMY OF PRINCE RIVVAK HEAD ON! AT MY COMMAND, WE SHALL CHARGE ACROSS THE BOILING PLAIN!!
BUT, MOST HONORED FATHER, WHY ATTACK THEM WHERE THEY ARE STRONGEST?? WHY NOT STRIKE AT THEIR FLANK?
SILENCE!! I HAVE SPOKEN!

SEE THEM WAITING ACROSS THE BOILING PLAIN! THEY THINK I HAVE NOT THE COURAGE TO CROSS IT IN FRONTAL ASSAULT!! WELL, RIVVAK HAS MUCH TO LEARN!!

AND WHAT OF YOUNG PRINCE RIVVAK, FACING HIS FIRST BATTLE AS LEADER OF HIS LEGIONS?
OUR PRINCE IS ASHEN PALE! METHINKS HE HAS NO STOMACH FOR YON COMING BATTLE!
I AM SICK WITH FEAR AT THE THOUGHT OF FACING ODIN'S WARRIORS!! AND YET, I MUST NOT SHIRK MY DUTY!
OFFICERS! OUR TRIAL IS AT HAND!

DIRECT YOUR MEN TO STATION THEMSELVES IN BATTLE FORMATION!
METHINKS HIS VOICE SHOWS SIGNS OF FALTERING!
CAN ONE SO YOUNG-- ONE SO UNSURE --LEAD US AGAINST SO MIGHTY A FOE??
AND YET, WE HAVE NO CHOICE! WE MUST OBEY THE YOUTHFUL RIVVAK, NO MATTER WHAT THE COST!

AND THEN, A ROARING, EAR-SPLITTING, REVERBERATING CRY RINGS OUT FROM THE ARMY OF ASGARD AS PRINCE RIVVAK AND HIS WARRIORS PREPARE TO MEET THE MOST POWERFUL LEGIONS OF ALL TIME!

ATTACK!

FORWARD!! FOR ASGARD!!

AND, ACROSS THE VAST BOILING PLAIN...
LANCES AT THE READY!! CHARGE!

BUT, BEFORE THE TWO ARMIES CAN MEET, THE SEETHING POTHOLES BENEATH THEIR FEET SUDDENLY ERUPT, AS GIGANTIC FLAMING GEYSERS SHOOT SKYWARD!
LOOK TO YOUR STEEDS, MEN OF ASGARD!! THEY HAVE NOT BEEN TINGED WITH IMMORTALITY, AS WE HAVE! THE FLAMES MUST NOT TOUCH THEM!

THE FIERY GEYSERS SHOOT UPWARD WHEREVER WE RIDE --AS THOUGH THEY HAVE WILLS OF THEIR OWN!
BUT NONE APPEAR BENEATH THE ADVANCING WARRIORS OF RIVVAK!

NO WEAPONS IN THE UNIVERSE CAN TURN BACK OUR CHARGE-- BUT WE DARE NOT ENDANGER OUR VALIANT STEEDS WITH THESE BLAZING GEYSERS!!
TRUMPETER!! FOR THE FIRST TIME SINCE THE DAWN OF MAN--SOUND THE RETREAT!!

ALMOST UNABLE TO BELIEVE THEIR EARS, THE STARTLED LEGIONS OF ODIN RESPOND TO THE GRIM TRUMPET CALL, WHEELING ABOUT IN THEIR TRACKS AND RETREATING TOWARDS ASGARD!!

WHILE THE YOUNG PRINCE, FLUSHED WITH TRIUMPH, PURSUES THEM TO THE EDGE OF THE FLAMING GEYSERS!
FLEE, SOLDIERS OF ASGARD! EVEN NATURE CONSPIRES AGAINST YOU!!
NEVER AGAIN SHALL I TREMBLE WITH FEAR BEFORE AN ENEMY! FOR NOW I KNOW THAT NO ONE IS UN-BEATABLE! THERE IS NO BATTLE THAT CANNOT BE WON!

HAIL TO THE FEARLESS RIVVAK!! HAIL OUR PRINCE!!
RIVVAK THE FEARLESS HAS TURNED BACK MIGHTY ODIN!!
MY MEN ACCLAIM ME! HENCE-FORTH I SHALL BE KNOWN AS *THE FEARLESS!*

MEANWHILE, WHAT OF THE HEAVY-HEARTED, RETREATING WARRIORS OF ASGARD...?
NOBLE FATHER, ONE SIMPLE SPELL FROM YOUR LIPS WOULD HAVE STILLED THE FLAMING GEYSERS! ONE SUDDEN COMMAND WOULD HAVE LED OUR CHARGE *AROUND* THE BLAZING PLAIN! AND YET--!
AND YET, I CHOSE *NOT* TO UTTER SUCH A COMMAND! FOR REMEMBER, MY VALIANT SON, I AM *ODIN*, THE ALL-POWERFUL!! BUT, I AM *ALSO* ODIN, THE *ALL-WISE!* THE BATTLE ENDED AS I *WISHED* IT TO END!

THERE MUST *ALWAYS* BE THOSE WITH THE FIRE OF REBELLION IN THEIR BLOOD! THERE MUST *ALWAYS* BE THOSE WHO WILL DARE TO FIGHT AN UNBEATABLE ENEMY! ONLY THUS CAN THE RACE OF MAN REMAIN STRONG AND FEARLESS!
I THINK I BEGIN TO UNDERSTAND, FATHER!
5

IT IS *GOOD* THAT THE LEGENDS WILL SAY A DAY THERE WAS WHEN *ODIN* HIMSELF RETREATED!
FOR MEN MUST NEVER FEEL A CAUSE IS HOPE-LESS--MEN MUST NEVER FEEL AN ENEMY CANNOT BE BEATEN!
I PRAY THAT MEN WILL ONE DAY ACCLAIM YOUR *WISDOM* AS THEY DO YOUR POWER, MY MOST NOBLE FATHER!
THE END

AND SO WE LEARN THAT THERE ARE *MANY* WAYS TO WIN A VICTORY--MANY WAYS TO ACHIEVE A GOAL! IN THE CASE OF ODIN, LORD OF ASGARD, HIS GOAL WAS HELPING MANKIND, AND ONLY THE TRULY STRONG, ONLY THE TRULY COURAGEOUS, WILL DARE TO *LOSE* A BATTLE--IN ORDER TO GAIN A TRIUMPH! NOW, UNTIL OUR NEXT EPIC OF ASGARD, MAY THE WISDOM OF ODIN BE SHOWERED UPON THEE!

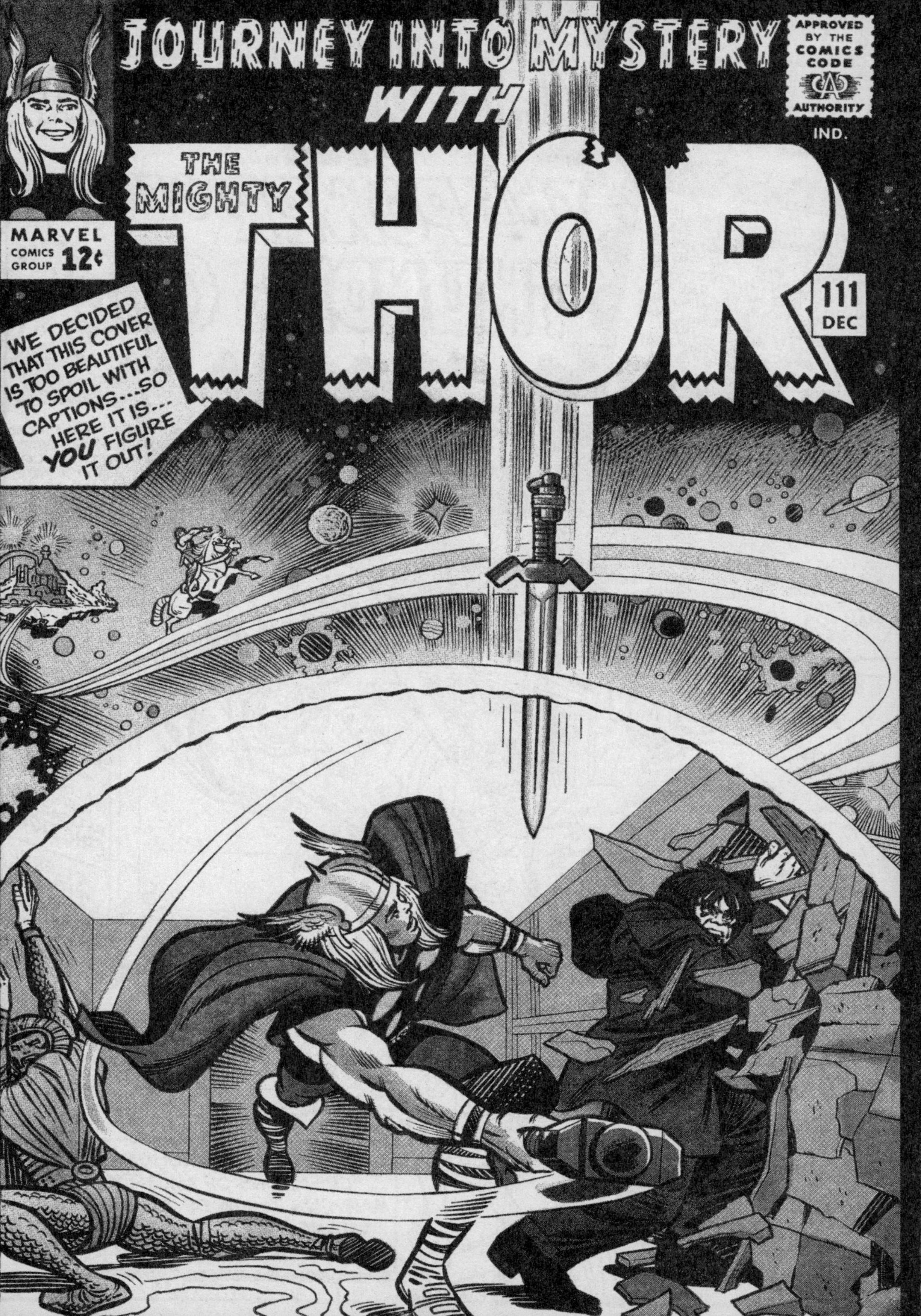

JOURNEY INTO MYSTERY
WITH
THE MIGHTY
THOR
APPROVED BY THE COMICS CODE AUTHORITY
IND.
MARVEL COMICS GROUP 12¢
111 DEC
WE DECIDED THAT THIS COVER IS TOO BEAUTIFUL TO SPOIL WITH CAPTIONS...SO HERE IT IS... YOU FIGURE IT OUT!

THE MIGHTY THOR
THE MYSTERIOUS Mr. HYDE and THE SERPENTINE COBRA FEEL... "THE POWER OF THE THUNDER GOD!"
WE FIND IT HARD TO BELIEVE THAT ANYONE WOULD EVER KNOWINGLY MISS AN ISSUE OF THOR! BUT, FOR THE FEW UNFORTUNATES WHO MIGHT NOT HAVE SEEN OUR PREVIOUS MEMORABLE TALE, WE'LL EXPLAIN THAT THOR HAS BEEN LURED TO A SPECIALLY-PREPARED "HOUSE OF TRAPS" BY MR. HYDE AND THE COBRA! FINDING HIS BELOVED JANE DYING, THOR SAVES HER TEMPORARILY BY CAUSING TIME TO STAND STILL WITHIN THE GLOOMY HOUSE, AND THEN...
LOOK! IT'S THOR! HE STILL LIVES!
BUT NOT FOR LONG, HYDE! NOT SINCE LOKI MADE US AS POWERFUL AS HE!
HYDE! COBRA! BY ASGARD, YOU SHALL PAY FOR THIS!
WRITTEN WITH THE MASTERY OF STAN LEE
ILLUSTRATED WITH THE GENIUS OF JACK KIRBY
DELINEATED WITH THE DELICACY OF CHIC STONE
LETTERED WITH THE INDIA INK OF ARTIE SIMEK
ONE OF THE PROUDEST CREATIONS OF MIGHTY MARVEL'S TEAM OF TALENTED TITANS! AN ADVENTURE DRENCHED WITH GLORY!
1

IN TRUTH, YOU ARE FAR STRONGER THAN I REMEMBER YOU! BUT IT SHALL AVAIL YOU NOTHING! NO POWER ON EARTH CAN EQUAL THAT OF THOR'S!
NOT ALONE PERHAPS, BUT WORKING TOGETHER, THE COBRA AND I CAN DESTROY YOU!

WE'RE TOO STRONG--TOO FAST! NO SOONER CAN YOU STRIKE ONE OF US, THAN THE OTHER IS UPON YOU--LIKE THIS!
FIE! YOU ARE SPEAKING TO ONE WHO HAS BESTED THE STORM GIANTS OF ASGARD--THE TROLLS OF THE NETHER WORLDS!
AFTER HIM, HYDE! EVEN WITH MY NEW AND GREATER POWER, I CANNOT FACE HIS THUNDERING HAMMER!

TOGETHER, HYDE AND THE COBRA ARE FAR STRONGER THAN I DARE TO ADMIT! EVEN WITH MY ENCHANTED HAMMER, I CANNOT HOLD THEM OFF MUCH LONGER! YET, THEY MUST BE STOPPED!

THIS IS ONLY A TEMPORARY MEASURE--YET, IT WILL GIVE ME TIME TO THINK--TO PLAN--!
LET THE WINDS AT MY COMMAND--THE MIGHTY GALE, THE IRRESISTIBLE STORM--LASH OUT WITH SAVAGE FURY!
THIS WON'T HELP YOU, THOR! YOU CAN'T KEEP IT UP FOREVER!

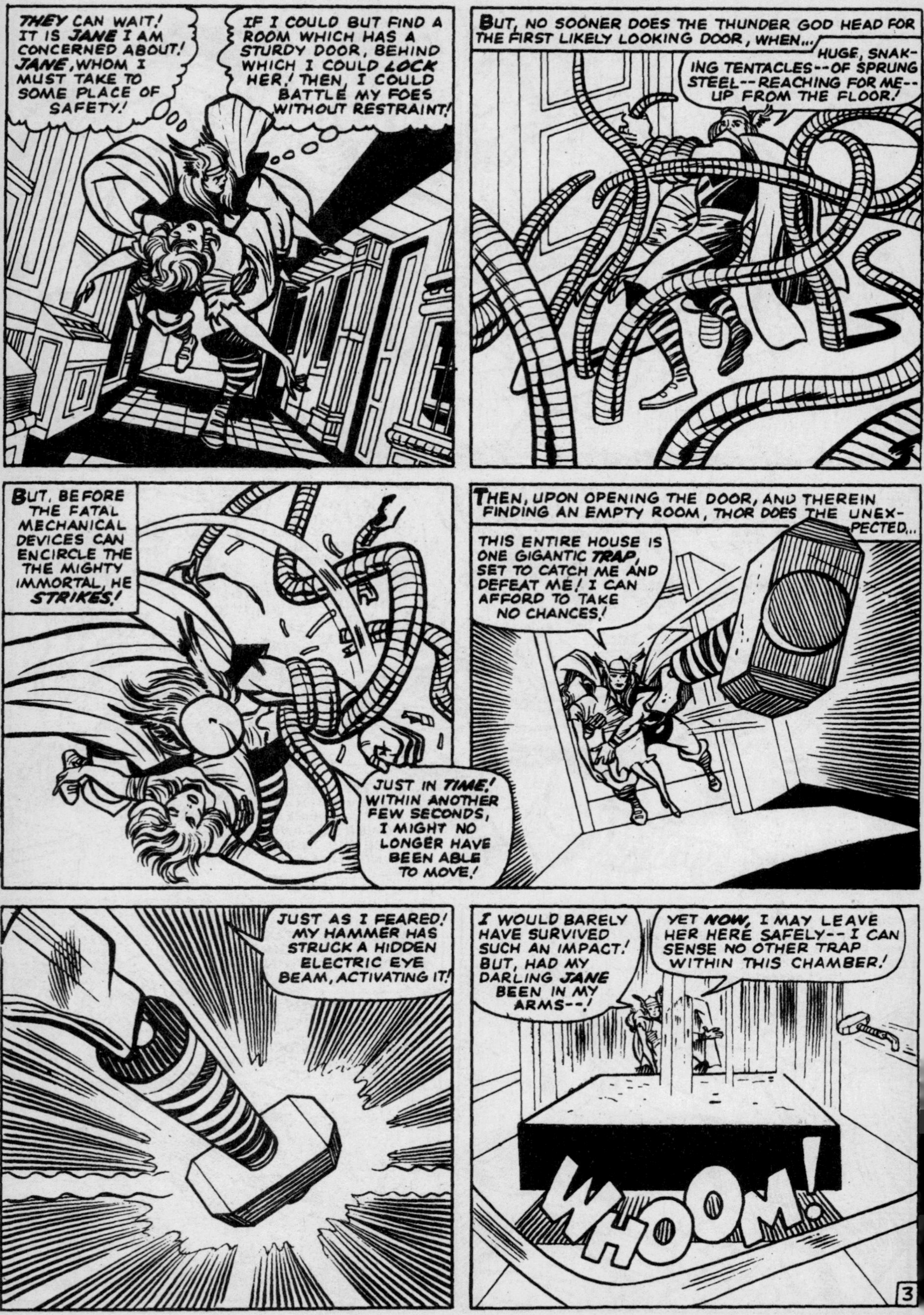

THEY CAN WAIT! IT IS JANE I AM CONCERNED ABOUT! JANE, WHOM I MUST TAKE TO SOME PLACE OF SAFETY!

IF I COULD BUT FIND A ROOM WHICH HAS A STURDY DOOR, BEHIND WHICH I COULD LOCK HER! THEN, I COULD BATTLE MY FOES WITHOUT RESTRAINT!

BUT, NO SOONER DOES THE THUNDER GOD HEAD FOR THE FIRST LIKELY LOOKING DOOR, WHEN...

HUGE, SNAKING TENTACLES--OF SPRUNG STEEL--REACHING FOR ME--UP FROM THE FLOOR!

BUT, BEFORE THE FATAL MECHANICAL DEVICES CAN ENCIRCLE THE THE MIGHTY IMMORTAL, HE STRIKES!

JUST IN TIME! WITHIN ANOTHER FEW SECONDS, I MIGHT NO LONGER HAVE BEEN ABLE TO MOVE!

THEN, UPON OPENING THE DOOR, AND THEREIN FINDING AN EMPTY ROOM, THOR DOES THE UNEXPECTED...

THIS ENTIRE HOUSE IS ONE GIGANTIC TRAP, SET TO CATCH ME AND DEFEAT ME! I CAN AFFORD TO TAKE NO CHANCES!

JUST AS I FEARED! MY HAMMER HAS STRUCK A HIDDEN ELECTRIC EYE BEAM, ACTIVATING IT!

I WOULD BARELY HAVE SURVIVED SUCH AN IMPACT! BUT, HAD MY DARLING JANE BEEN IN MY ARMS--!
YET NOW, I MAY LEAVE HER HERE SAFELY--I CAN SENSE NO OTHER TRAP WITHIN THIS CHAMBER!
WHOOM!

SLEEP, MY DEAREST ONE! SLEEP IN SAFETY, WHILE I GO TO DO BATTLE WITH THOSE WHO WOULD DESTROY US!

BUT, EVEN IF I DEFEAT HYDE AND THE COBRA, WHAT OF JANE? SHE IS BUT SECONDS AWAY FROM DEATH--AND I CANNOT CAUSE TIME TO STAND STILL IN THIS HOUSE FOREVER!

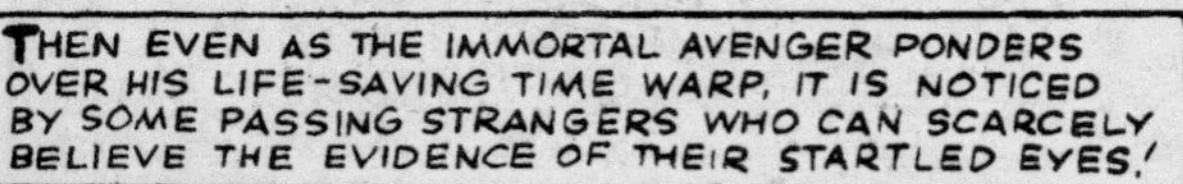
THEN EVEN AS THE IMMORTAL AVENGER PONDERS OVER HIS LIFE-SAVING TIME WARP, IT IS NOTICED BY SOME PASSING STRANGERS WHO CAN SCARCELY BELIEVE THE EVIDENCE OF THEIR STARTLED EYES!

LOOK! WHAT IN THE NAME OF HEAVEN IS THAT??!

IT LOOKS LIKE SOME KINDA BREEZE, SPINNING AROUND THAT HOUSE! BUT--HOW COME WE CAN SEE IT?? I--I WONDER WHAT IT FEELS LIKE??
HOLD IT! DON'T TOUCH IT, CHARLIE--IT MIGHT BE DANGEROUS!
HERE--I'LL TAKE THIS ROCK AND THROW IT TOWARDS THE HOUSE, AND WE'LL SEE WHAT HAPPENS!

HOLY COW! AS SOON AS IT HIT THAT--THAT--WHAT EVER IT IS--IT STOPPED IN MID-AIR! IT'S JUST FLOATING THERE!
IT'S SCARY! IT'S LIKE THAT HOUSE DOESN'T BELONG TO THIS DIMENSION, OR TO THIS TIME!
I'VE SEEN ENOUGH! I'M GETTING OUT OF HERE--WHILE I STILL CAN!

AND, IN FAR-OFF, LEGENDARY ASGARD, ANOTHER WATCHES ALSO...
STRANGE EVENTS TRANSPIRE BELOW!
BUT, LORD ODIN SHALL NOT INTERFERE!
4

TOO MANY TIMES HAVE I ORDERED THOR TO GIVE UP THE EARTH GIRL-- THE MORTAL FEMALE WHOM AN IMMORTAL OF ASGARD MAY NEVER MARRY! YET, HE HAS DEFIED ME! AND, ALAS, THE LIVING *HEART* IS ONE THING EVEN *ODIN* HAS NO POWER TO CONTROL!

FOR *LOVE* IS THE UNIVERSAL *EQUALIZER!* IT STRIKES MORTAL AND IMMORTAL ALIKE--AND NONE CAN CHANGE IT TILL IT RUNS ITS COURSE!

POOR, UNHAPPY THOR! IF ONLY ODIN WOULD PERMIT HIM TO MARRY THE MORTAL GIRL!

MAY I SOOTHE THY TROUBLED BREAST WITH A BALLAD, NOBLE LORD?

IF IT PLEASE THEE, BRAVE BALDER--FOR IN TRUTH I AM SORELY VEXED!

I SING OF ANCIENT TIMES, AND OF THE LOVE OF A WARRIOR FOR A MAIDEN FAIR...

SOON, CAUGHT UNDER THE SUBTLE SPELL OF BALDER'S BALLAD, ODIN THINKS BACK--BACK TO HIS *OWN* YOUNGER DAYS...

STATELY WAS SHE, AND LIKE UNTO A GODDESS! IN ALL OF ASGARD, THERE WAS NONE SO FAIR--NONE SO BE-LOVED OF THE WARRIOR WHOM OTHERS CALLED --*ODIN!*

"AND YET, THEIR MARRIAGE COULD NEVER BE--FOR IT WAS *FORBIDDEN!* BUT ODIN WOULD NEVER GIVE UP--NOT EVEN AFTER HE AND HIS LOVED ONE TOOK THEIR LAST RIDE OVER THE ENCHANTED CHASM TOGETHER, LO THOSE MANY AGES AGO!"
YOUR BALLAD BRINGS BACK MEMORIES I HAVE TRIED TO KEEP HIDDEN FOR CENTURIES! AND YET, NOW THAT I THINK BACK--
BALDER! YOU DARE TRY TO *TRICK* THE NOBLE ODIN?!!
LOKI! YOU *HEARD?*
OF *COURSE* I HEARD! YOU SEEK TO SOFTEN ODIN'S HEART TOWARDS THE EARTH GIRL! HOW LUCKY I ARRIVED IN TIME TO WARN MY LIEGE!

MEANWHILE, BACK ON EARTH, WITH A COLD, GNAWING FURY RAGING IN HIS SOUL, A VENGEFUL THOR PREPARES TO BATTLE TILL THE DEATH IF NEED BE!
HYDE! COBRA! SHOW YOURSELVES! THE THUNDER GOD CALLS!

WE'VE BEEN WAITING, THOR! HA! EVEN YOUR SPEED CANNOT MATCH THE COBRA'S!
GLOAT WHILE YOU MAY, EVIL ONES! YOUR RETRIBUTION IS TRULY CLOSE AT HAND!

ALL YOU CAN DO IS TALK TO KEEP YOUR NERVE UP!
YOU KNOW YOU HAVEN'T A CHANCE BETWEEN THE TWO OF US! 'SPECIALLY SINCE WE'RE MANY TIMES STRONGER THAN BEFORE!

NEVER HAVE I FACED SUCH EVIL INCARNATE! NEVER HAVE I BEEN SO ANXIOUS TO STRIKE OUT AT IT, DRIVE IT FROM THE FACE OF THE EARTH! ATTACK ME AT WILL-- I'LL CRUSH YOU BOTH!

STAND BACK, COBRA! I'VE WAITED TOO LONG FOR THIS PERFECT CHANCE!
NO! I'LL GET HIM FIRST! HE'S MINE! MY HATRED IS GREATER THAN YOURS!

I SAID BACK, YOU SLITHERING FOOL! THE FIRST BLOW MUST BE MINE!
I'VE WARNED YOU NOT TO TRY TO GIVE ME ORDERS, HYDE!
6

YOUR STRENGTH NO LONGER HOLDS ME IN AWE OF YOU, FOR I AM NOW EQUALLY STRONG!

YOU BRAINLESS DOLT! WHAT ARE YOU DOING?? THOR IS THE ENEMY! IT IS THOR WE MUST DEFEAT!

MY SENTIMENTS EXACTLY! AND SINCE YOU'RE SO EAGER TO LAND THE FIRST BLOW, I'LL GIVE YOU THE CHANCE! THERE!

WHOOM!

NOW! THAT SHOULD STOP YOUR BRAGGING! HE HURLED YOU BACK LIKE A BEANBAG! YOU NEED ME, HYDE--AND DON'T EVER FORGET IT!

I'VE GOT TO ESCAPE! THESE MISSILES WILL EXPLODE IN SECONDS!
AND THEY CONTAIN A POISON GAS FOR WHICH THERE IS NO KNOWN ANTIDOTE!

THEN, AT THE LAST SPLIT SECOND, THE SERPENTINE COBRA FINDS A WAY TO SAFETY WHICH ONLY HIS OWN AMAZING BODY COULD TAKE ADVANTAGE OF!
AN AIR-CONDITIONING DUCT! JUST WHAT I NEED TO SLITHER THRU!

MEANTIME...
LET THE COBRA DO AS HE PLEASES--I'LL STILL RELY ON MY OWN GREAT STRENGTH, AND MY BURNING HATRED--TO FINISH YOU OFF FOREVER!
SO BE IT! WHATEVER FATE BEFALLS, YOU HAVE BROUGHT IT DOWN UPON YOUR OWN HEAD, EVIL ONE!

BUT THEN, HYDE IS THE FIRST TO DETECT THE PRESENCE OF THE DEADLY WAFTING POISON GAS!
THE COBRA'S GAS--DRIFTING THIS WAY! I'VE GOT TO FLEE! I'LL LEAVE THOR BEHIND!

LIKE A HUMAN BATTERING RAM, THE HUNCHED, GNARLED, MALEVOLENT FIGURE CRASHES THRU A PLASTER WALL, AS THE DRAMATIC GOD OF THUNDER SLOWLY LIFTS HIS CAPE TO HIS FACE...
THINK YOU THAT THOR CANNOT DETECT A POISONOUS VAPOR?? BUT, MY FLOWING CAPE GIVES ME WHAT LITTLE PROTECTION I MAY NEED!

AND, IT IS TIME THAT YOU LEARN THERE IS NO ESCAPE FROM THE VENGEANCE OF THOR!

MEANWHILE, IN ASGARD, LORDLY ODIN FINALLY REACHES A MOMENTOUS DECISION...
ALTHOUGH THOR MAY NOT TAKE THE EARTH GIRL FOR HIS BRIDE, STILL I SHALL TRY TO SAVE HER FROM DEATH--BECAUSE OF MY LOVE FOR MY WARRIOR SON!
BY ALL THE PLANETS, THIS IS A DISAPPOINT-MENT TO ME!

LOKI! BY MY IMPERIAL COMMAND, YOU ARE ORDERED TO DELIVER THIS MESSAGE TO HARDOL, THE MYSTIC HEALER WHO LIVES BEYOND THE MOLTEN CHASM! HE WILL FIND A REMEDY FOR THE ONE CALLED JANE!
THE WORD OF ODIN IS THE LAW SUPREME! I SHALL OBEY AT ONCE, NOBLE ONE!

FOR ONCE, I SPOKE WITH COMPLETE TRUTH! THE WORD OF ODIN IS INDEED THE LAW WHEREVER IT IS SPOKEN OR HEARD!
BUT, STILL THE GIRL SHALL DIE--FOR LAWS HAVE BEEN KNOWN TO BE BROKEN!

BUT, NO SOONER DOES THOR'S AGELESS ARCH-ENEMY TURN ABOUT, THEN HE SEES...
I'LL DELIVER THAT MESSAGE, CRAFTY ONE!
WE KNOW THEE TOO WELL TO HAVE IT OTHERWISE!
MEANTIME, YOU SHALL STAY WITH US!
CAN IT BE?? MY OWN PEERS TURNING AGAINST ME!
NOT SO, LOKI! WE ARE NOT THY PEERS! FOR NONE CAN MATCH THEE IN VILLAINY, OR IN DECEIT!

AND SO, BALDER THE BRAVE, BALDER THE BOLD, BALDER, THE TRUE AND LOYAL COMRADE OF THOR, RIDES UNHESITATINGLY ACROSS THE SAVAGE AND WILD CHASM...
I DARE NOT FAIL--FOR IT WOULD MEAN THE LIFE OF SHE WHOM MY DEAREST FRIEND HOLDS EVER IN HIS HEART!

WHILE LOKI, NEVER FAR FROM THE WATCHFUL EYE OF ONE OF ASGARD'S IMMORTAL WARRIORS, SCANS THE DISTANT HORIZON WITH A GRIM, SEETHING HATRED IN HIS SOUL...!
I HAVEN'T LOST YET! MANY ARE THE DANGERS BETWEEN BALDER AND HIS GOAL, AND EVEN THE BOLD ONE IS NOT INFALLIBLE!

AND, THE SINISTER LOKI KNOWS WELL WHEREOF HE SPEAKS! FOR, THE TRAIL WHICH BALDER MUST FOLLOW, IS FRAUGHT WITH COUNTLESS PERILS...
STEADY, MY FAITHFUL STEED! ONE MISSTEP WILL PLUNGE US INTO THE SWAMPS OF ENDLESS FLAME!

THEN, FINALLY PASSING THE FIERY SWAMP, BALDER SEES A MORE FRIGHTENING, MORE INDESCRIBABLE DANGER...
UP AHEAD! THE ONE WHOSE NAME IS USED TO FRIGHTEN CHILDREN! THE PHANTOM WHOSE VERY TOUCH MEANS DEATH! AND IT IS TOO LATE TO AVOID HIM!

BUT, LET US AGAIN RETURN TO THE MIGHTY THOR, AS HE CALMLY PURSUES THE HORRIBLE MR. HYDE...
THERE IS NO PLACE ON EARTH, OR ANY-WHERE, THAT YOU MAY ESCAPE TO WHEN THOR FOLLOWS!
WORDS! WORDS! WHO CARES FOR WORDS?!! MY BRUTAL STRENGTH AND MY CRAFTINESS WILL WIN IN THE END!

HAH! YOU DIDN'T EXPECT ME TO TURN AND ATTACK YOU SO SOON, DID YOU?!!
YOUR HAMMER IS YOUR GREATEST WEAPON! BUT IT WON'T HELP YOU IF I CAN KEEP YOU FROM CATCHING IT! AND KEEP YOU I WILL!!

IF I CAN KEEP HIM FROM TURNING--KEEP HIM FROM SEEING THE RAY I'M PUSHING HIM INTO--I'LL DEFEAT HIM YET!
I PREPARED IT DAYS AGO--AS MY FINAL, MOST POWERFUL TRAP! IT WILL NOT FAIL ME!

BUT, THOR IS TOO BATTLE-WISE, TOO ALERT, NOT TO SUSPECT THE IMMINENT DANGER...
ANOTHER TRAP! A BLAST RAY, SHOOTING OUT FROM THE WALL! BUT, BY DROPPING IN TIME, I CAN HURL HYDE INTO ITS PATH!
IT MUST TRULY HAVE BEEN A STAGGERING BLOW--EVEN THE MIGHTY HYDE IS STIFF AS A BOARD!
BUT STILL HE LIVES--ALTHOUGH IT WILL BE MANY DAYS BEFORE HE IS FIT TO FIGHT AGAIN!
I SHALL LEAVE HIM THERE WHILE I SEEK THE COBRA!
FOR, SO LONG AS THE SERPENTINE ONE IS FREE, MY VICTORY OVER HYDE HAS NO MEANING!
CRUNCH!
FIRST, I MUST LEARN WHAT I CAN OF THE DEADLY RAY...!
JUST AS I THOUGHT--AN INVOLVED, COMPLEX SYSTEM OF ELECTRONIC COMPONENT PARTS!
LUCKILY, MY MONTHS OF ASSOCIATION WITH IRON MAN IN THE AVENGERS HAS GIVEN ME MUCH KNOWLEDGE OF SUCH EARTHLY THINGS...!
--KNOWLEDGE WHICH WILL ENABLE ME TO MODIFY THIS SYSTEM FOR MY OWN UNIQUE PURPOSE!
11

THERE! HOW AMUSED THE IMMORTALS OF ASGARD WOULD BE TO SEE THE THUNDER GOD CHANGING WIRING LIKE AN EARTHBOUND ELECTRICIAN!

MINUTES LATER, A HIGH-TENSION SUPERCHARGED ELECTRICAL EFFECT COURSES THRU THE ENTIRE HOUSE, SENDING TINGLY WAVES OF ELECTRIC ENERGY THRU EVERY NOOK AND CRANNY...

--EVEN TO THE AREA WHERE HIDES THE COBRA!
WHAT MADNESS IS THIS?? SHOCK WAVES--STRIKING ME FROM NOWHERE!

UNABLE TO BEAR THE PAINFUL PRODDING, THE SERPENTINE MENACE SPEEDS THRU THE INTERIOR OF THE BUILDING'S POWER PLANT LIKE A RUN-AWAY THUNDERBOLT!!

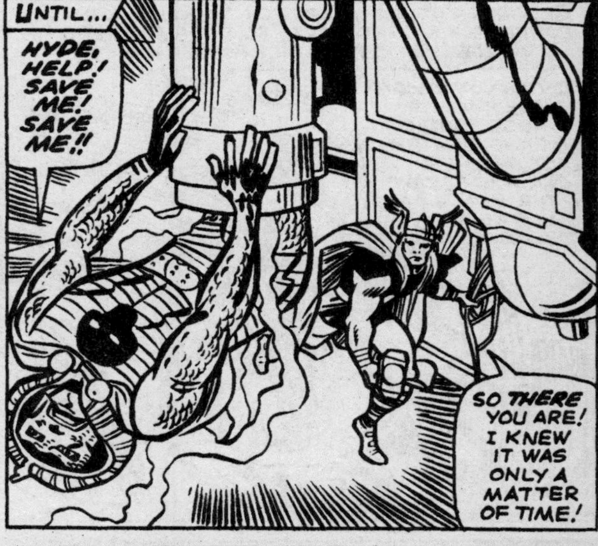
UNTIL...
HYDE, HELP! SAVE ME! SAVE ME!!
SO THERE YOU ARE! I KNEW IT WAS ONLY A MATTER OF TIME!

REALIZING THE THUNDER GOD HAS TRICKED HIM OUT OF HIDING, THE WILY COBRA TRIES TO FLEE--BUT HIS LIMBS ARE STILL TOO WEAK...
ALTHOUGH YOUR HEART IS EVIL ENOUGH...

...NEITHER YOU NOR HYDE HAVE THE WIT NOR CUNNING FOR TRUE ARCH-VILLAINY!
BUT I CAN DALLY NO LONGER WITH SUCH AS THESE--I MUST RETURN TO MY LOVED ONE AND PONDER HER FATE!

STILL SHE LIVES! BUT, ONLY SO LONG AS TIME STANDS STILL CAN I FORESTALL THE FINAL TRAGEDY!
EVEN THE MEDICAL KNOWLEDGE I POSSESS AS DR. DON BLAKE CANNOT SAVE THE GIRL I LOVE! NOR CAN ALL THE POWER OF THOR RESTORE THE BLOOM TO THAT POOR, MORTAL FLESH!

IF I REMOVE THE TIME WARP WHICH ENGULFS THIS HOUSE, THEN JANE FOSTER WILL SURELY DIE!
YET, I CANNOT CONTINUE IT INDEFINITELY! FOR IT WILL CAUSE TOO GREAT A TEMPORAL DISPLACEMENT THRUOUT THE KNOWN UNIVERSE!

AND, EVEN AS THE HEARTSICK THUNDER GOD PONDERS HIS NEXT MOVE, SO DOES BALDER THE BRAVE DESPERATELY PONDER HIS--!
I CANNOT AVOID THEE, PHANTOM WHOSE TOUCH MEANS DEATH-- BUT NEITHER CAN YOU ESCAPE THE BLADE OF BALDER!

HAVE AT YOU, CREATURE FROM A FOREIGN UNIVERSE! THY ATOMS ARE ALIEN MATTER --AS ARE THE ATOMS OF MY SWORD TO THEE!

AND THERE, AT THE EDGE OF THE LEGENDARY MOLTEN CHASM, BALDER'S DESPERATE GAMBLE BEARS FRUIT! THE INSTANT HIS SWORD TOUCHES THE PHANTOM OF DEATH, THE TWO ALIEN OBJECTS, UNABLE TO EXIST IN THE SAME SPATIAL SPHERE, REACH INSTANT CRITICAL MASS...

I'VE DESTROYED HIM!! BY THE SHINING MOONS OF ASGARD, THE PHANTOM IS NO MORE!!
MY SWORD, FORGED BY ODIN'S HANDS, WAS THE STRONGEST! IT SURVIVED WHILE THE PHANTOM PERISHED!

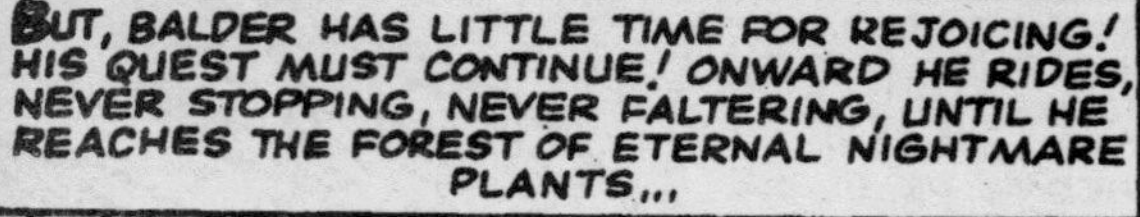
BUT, BALDER HAS LITTLE TIME FOR REJOICING! HIS QUEST MUST CONTINUE! ONWARD HE RIDES, NEVER STOPPING, NEVER FALTERING, UNTIL HE REACHES THE FOREST OF ETERNAL NIGHTMARE PLANTS...

SUDDENLY REALIZING THE GRAVE DANGER, BALDER QUICKLY COVERS HIS STEED'S HEAD WITH HIS OWN GREATCAPE! THEN, WITH ONLY HIS SUPERB STAMINA AND RESOLVE TO SUSTAIN HIM, HE CROSSES THE FATAL PLAIN...
I MUST NOT WEAKEN! I DARE NOT SHUT MY EYES, LEST THE ETERNAL SLEEP DESCEND UPON ME!

BUT, NO SOONER HAS HE SURVIVED THAT AWE-SOME MENACE, THEN HE FINDS...
THE VALLEY OF SWORDS LIES AHEAD! NO ASGARDIAN HAS EVER SAFELY TRAVERSED THOSE UPTURNED BLADES BEFORE!

BUT, THOR, WHOM MY HEART HOLDS AS DEAR AS MY LIEGE, IS IN GRAVE NEED! I SHALL NOT FAIL HIM!
THUS, HAVING RIPPED HIS GREATCAPE TO SHREDS AND TIED LARGE FLAT ROCKS TO HIS STALLION'S HOOVES WITH THE FRAG-MENTS, THE BRAVE BALDER ONCE AGAIN OVERCOMES A SEEMINGLY INSURMOUNT-ABLE OBSTACLE!

UNTIL AT LAST, THE FINAL DANGER HAS BEEN MET AND VANQUISHED...
ONLY YOUR GREAT SPEED, MY FAITHFUL MOUNT, HAVE ENABLED US TO SAFELY CROSS THE VALLEY OF AVALANCHES!! AND NOW-- OUR GOAL IS IN SIGHT--!

WHO APPROACHES THE HOME OF HARDOL, THE HEALER??
BALDER DOES, AT THE BEHEST OF NOBLE ODIN!
THEN COME FORTH, BRAVE ONE, AND STATE YOUR REQUEST!
14

MEANWHILE, UNAWARE OF BALDER'S HEROIC ERRAND, THE MIGHTY THOR MAKES A HEART-RENDING DECISION...
I MUST LIFT THE TIME WARP! I DARE CONTINUE IT NO LONGER! I HAVE NOT THE RIGHT!
JANE, MY MOST DEARLY BELOVED-- IS THIS THE PRICE YOU MUST PAY FOR HAVING WON THE LOVE OF A GOD? IS THIS WHAT THOR, SON OF ODIN, HAS DONE TO YOU??

WHEN THE TIME WARP IS LIFTED, ADORED ONE, I SHALL AGAIN BECOME DR. BLAKE --AND I SHALL TRY TO SAVE YOU WITH EVERY OUNCE OF SKILL AND STRENGTH THAT I POSSESS...! AND, IF I FAIL-- THEN WE BOTH SHALL DIE--!

FOR, MY HEART WILL EVERMORE BE NAUGHT BUT A COLD, WITHERED EMBER IF I SHOULD LOSE THEE!
AND NOW, I DO WHAT I MUST! MAY ASGARD LOOK UPON THEE WITH FAVOR, JANE FOSTER!

ONCE AGAIN THE MIGHTY HAMMER SWINGS, AND ONCE AGAIN NORMAL TIME BEGINS TO ENVELOP THE HOUSE AS THE TIME WARP FADES INTO THE NOTHINGNESS FROM WHENCE IT CAME...

BUT THEN, IN THE SPACE OF ONE SINGLE HEART-BEAT...
BY THE GODS!! IT IS THE GLISTENING SWORD OF BALDER!!

THERE IS A VIAL ATTACHED-- AND A BRIEF NOTE! CAN THIS BE THE MIRACLE FOR WHICH I DARED NOT EVEN HOPE???

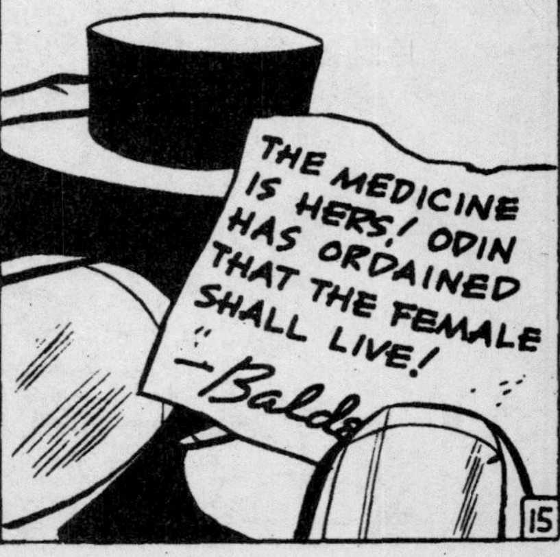
HARDLY TRUSTING HIMSELF TO BELIEVE IT-- HIS EYES MISTING UP WITH TEARS OF GRATITUDE, THE MIGHTY THOR READS THE BRIEF NOTE, HIS SOUL SINGING WITHIN HIM!!
THE MEDICINE IS HERS! ODIN HAS ORDAINED THAT THE FEMALE SHALL LIVE!
—Balder

THE WARP HAS ONLY BEEN LIFTED FOR A FEW SPLIT-SECONDS!! I CAN STILL REACH JANE IN *TIME!*
I **MUST** REACH HER!! I **MUST!!**

MY DARLING-- YOU CAN'T HEAR ME--CAN'T SEE ME--BUT LET YOUR **HEART** KNOW THAT YOUR LOVED ONE IS HERE--WITH THESE WORDS FOR YOU--
YOU WILL **LIVE,** MY BELOVED! YOU WILL SEE MANY DAWNS, MANY SUNSETS, AND PERHAPS, ODIN WILLING, WE'LL ONE DAY SHARE THEM TOGETHER!

AND, AS THE LIFE SLOWLY RETURNS TO THE SLEEPING GIRL, THE SWORD OF BALDER BEGINS TO RISE...

HIGHER AND HIGHER IT GOES, ITS SPEED INCREASING WITH EACH PASSING SECOND...

...UNTIL IT REACHES ITS MASTER WHO WAITS ON THE RAINBOW BRIDGE!
MY MISSION IS ENDED! THE GIRL LIVES!

AND, BACK ON THAT SMALL, SEEMINGLY INSIGNIFICANT PLANET, WHICH SPINS ETERNALLY IN THE GLITTERING COSMOS MAN CALLS THE UNIVERSE...

THOR! WHAT HAPPENED?? I SEEM TO HAVE HAD --SOME AWFUL NIGHTMARE--!
IT IS ENDED, LOVELY ONE! YOU MUST REST NOW--

THEN, AFTER BESTOWING THE PRICELESS GIFT OF PEACEFUL SLEEP UPON THE MORTAL GIRL, THE THUNDER GOD RAISES HIS EYES TO ASGARD--

HAIL, NOBLE ODIN! THY UNDESERVING SON GIVES THEE THANKS!!

GENTLY, THE MIGHTY IMMORTAL LIFTS THE SLEEPING GIRL! THEN, HE SLOWLY TURNS HIS BACK UPON HIS DEFEATED FOES, AND UPON THE HOUSE OF DARKNESS, AS HE WALKS INTO THE SHINING LIGHT OF MORNING!

REMEMBER: YOU NEED NOT BE AN IMMORTAL TO ENJOY THESE COLORFUL, THRILLING TALES! EVEN IF YOU'RE A MERE HUMAN BEING, WE HOPE YOU'LL BE WITH US AGAIN NEXT ISSUE, BUT WHILE WE'RE WAITING --LET'S TURN TO OUR **TALE OF ASGARD** WHICH FOLLOWS...

Tales of ASGARD HOME OF THE MIGHTY NORSE GODS!
"The SECRET of SIGURD!"
RETURNING FROM A SPECIAL MISSION FOR ODIN, WE FIND THOR, LOKI, AND BALDER! SOON, LOKI SLYLY SUGGESTS THEY TAKE A SHORT-CUT THRU THE FORBIDDEN FOREST OF THE MYSTERIOUS SIGURD... AND THUS BEGINS OUR TENSE, GRIPPING DRAMA....!
STOP! YOU MAY COME NO FURTHER!! I AM SIGURD..., AND THIS FOREST IS MINE!
SIGURD!
PERHAPS HE KNOWS NOT WHO WE ARE!
HE SEEMS EAGER FOR THE THRILL OF BATTLE!
SUPERBLY WRITTEN BY STAN LEE
SUPREMELY DRAWN BY JACK KIRBY
SAVAGELY INKED BY VINCE COLLETTA
SAGATIOUSLY LETTERED BY ARTIE SIMEK

FULL WELL DO I KNOW WHO YOU ARE! YOU BE THREE GODLINGS FROM FABLED ASGARD!
BUT THAT MATTERS NOT TO SIGURD! I CAN DEFEAT ANY OR ALL OF YOU!
METHINKS THE MAN IS BEREFT OF HIS SENSES!
BAH! ONLY WEAKLINGS MAKE IDLE BOASTS SUCH AS HIS! I SAY THE CREATURE IS NO MATCH FOR YOU, THOR!
BE THAT AS IT MAY! I HAVE NO DESIRE TO ENGAGE IN NEEDLESS COMBAT!
I'VE HEARD OF SIGURD! THERE IS SOME STRANGE SECRET ABOUT HIM--BUT I CAN-NOT REMEMBER WHAT IT IS!
GODLINGS OF ASGARD--BAH! YOU ARE COWARDS ALL! NONE OF YOU DARES TO BATTLE THE POWERFUL SIGURD!
STAY YOUR TONGUE, RECKLESS ONE! NONE MAY SPEAK THUS OF THE SUBJECTS OF ODIN--NOT WHILE THOR LIVES!
THIS IS YOUR CHANCE, THOR! MAKE HIM REGRET HIS RASH, INSULTING WORDS!
LOKI SEEMS STRANGELY ANXIOUS FOR THOR TO BATTLE SIGURD!! I WONDER WHY??
NOW, SIGURD! WE SHALL SEE WHO THE COWARD IS!

BE FOREWARNED, SIGURD -- I AM THOR, SON OF NOBLE ODIN!
AND I AM SIGURD, POSSESSOR OF THE GREAT SECRET POWER!
SECRET POWER?

NO POWER CAN SAVE YOUR WAR CLUB FROM BEING SHATTERED BY MY ENCHANTED HAMMER!

I BID THEE YIELD, SIGURD!
FOR TRULY, I HAVE NO WISH TO DO THEE HARM!

YOUTHFUL FOOL! SIGURD YIELDS TO NO ONE! IT IS YOU WHO SHALL TASTE THE BITTER DREGS OF DEFEAT!
HE SEEMS STRONGER NOW THAN BEFORE I STRUCK HIM! BUT-- HOW CAN THAT BE?
DO NOT FORGET, GODLING-- I POSSESS THE SECRET POWER!

I NEED NOT USE MY HAMMER TO DISPOSE OF YOU! MY LIMBS ALONE SHALL SUFFICE!
IF ONLY I KNEW WHAT SECRET POWER IT IS THAT HE POSSESSES!

IT IS IMPOSSIBLE!! NONE CAN RISE SO QUICKLY AFTER BEING STRUCK BY THE FISTS OF THOR!
SIGURD CAN!!

AND SO THE BATTLE RAGES, WITH MIGHTY THOR FIGHTING AS VALIANTLY AS EVER, BUT TO NO AVAIL! FOR, EACH TIME SIGURD IS BEATEN TO THE GROUND, HE RISES AGAIN, STRONGER THAN BEFORE!
SOONER OR LATER, THUNDER GOD, YOU MUST SURELY TIRE--
--WHILE I GROW STRONGER WITH EACH PASSING MINUTE!

IT LOOKS AS THOUGH THOR HAS FINALLY MET HIS MATCH, BALDER!
AND YOU ACT AS THOUGH YOU'RE PLEASED! IN FACT, YOU SUGGESTED TAKING THIS TRAIL THRU SIGURD'S FOREST! AND YOU-- WAIT! NOW I REMEMBER WHAT SIGURD'S SECRET POWER IS!!!

THOR--HEED MY WORDS! SIGURD IS THE SON OF THE EARTH SPRITES! EACH TIME HIS BODY STRIKES THE GROUND, THEY GIVE IT NEW AND GREATER STRENGTH!
SO! THAT IS THE SECRET OF SIGURD!
BUT KNOWING IT WILL DO YOU NO GOOD, THUNDER GOD! YOU CANNOT PREVENT ME FROM CONSTANTLY INCREASING MY STRENGTH BY CONTACT WITH THE GROUND!

WISE ODIN HAS TOLD ME MANY TIMES--THE TRUE WARRIOR FIGHTS WITH HIS BRAIN AS MUCH AS WITH HIS SINEWS! AND SO SHALL THOR!
HAVE YOU TAKEN LEAVE OF YOUR SENSES?? WHY DO YOU PLACE YOUR ACCURSED HAMMER WITHIN MY BELT??

THIS IS WHY, EVIL ONE! IT WILL TAKE BUT ONE FULL SWING TO CAUSE YOUR BELT TO SNAP AND SEND YOU INTO SPACE--WHERE THERE WILL BE NO GROUND FOR YOUR FEET TO TOUCH!
WHEN YOU REACH THE DESERTED ASTEROID I HAVE AIMED YOU AT, YOU WILL BE MASTER OF ALL YOU SURVEY--BUT NEVER WILL YOU MENACE EITHER HUMAN OR GODLING AGAIN!
5.

YOU SEEM DISAPPOINTED, CLEVER LOKI! CAN IT BE THAT YOU EXPECTED A SOMEWHAT DIFFERENT RESULT?
NOT AT ALL, MIGHTY HALF-BROTHER! I REJOICE WITH YOU IN YOUR MOMENT OF TRIUMPH!
I PRAY THAT THOR NEVER TURNS HIS BACK ON LOKI, FOR THE EVIL ONE'S HATRED IS ALMOST BEYOND UNDERSTANDING!
THE END

YES, FOR AGES THE MENACE OF LOKI HAS BEEN THE GOLDEN HAIRED GOD'S CHIEF CONCERN--FOR LOKI EVER HAS BEEN, AND EVER WILL BE--ONE OF THE MOST POWERFUL OF ALL THE IMMORTALS! BUT, POWERFUL THOUGH HE IS, MIGHTY THOR HAS ALWAYS BEEN HIS MASTER, AND IN THE NAME OF ODIN, WE PRAY HE REMAINS SO TILL THE END OF TIME!

JOURNEY INTO MYSTERY
WITH
THE MIGHTY
THOR
APPROVED BY THE COMICS CODE AUTHORITY
IND.
MARVEL COMICS GROUP 12¢
112 JAN
THE EPIC BATTLE OF THE AGE!
THE MIGHTY THUNDER GOD! VS. THE INCREDIBLE HULK!
HERE IT IS! THE BATTLE YOU'VE BEEN WAITING FOR!
ANOTHER ALL-TIME GREAT FROM MIGHTY MARVEL, POWERHOUSE of IDEAS!

THE MIGHTY THOR
BATTLES THE INCREDIBLE
HULK!
A STAN LEE-JACK KIRBY MARVEL MASTERWORK!
INKING BY CHIC STONE LETTERING BY S. ROSEN
THOSE YOUNGSTERS SEEM TO BE ARGUING ABOUT WHO IS... STRONGER... THE HULK... OR MYSELF!
THOR IS STRONGER THAN ANYBODY!
YEAH? TAKE AWAY THOR'S HAMMER AND WHAT HAVE YOU GOT?
YAY, HULK!
AW, THOR COULD MOP UP THE PLACE WITH THAT DUMB HULK!
DUMB, HUH? SO, HOW COME NOBODY'S EVER LICKED 'IM?
THOR IS THE GREATEST!
NO ONE CAN BEAT OL' GREEN-SKIN!

WOW-EEE! THIS IS TOO GOOD TO BE TRUE! IT'S THOR HIMSELF!!
NOW WE'LL SETTLE THIS! WE'LL ASK HIM!
I COULD NOT HELP OVERHEARING THE TOPIC YOU WERE DISCUSSING!
NO SENSE ASKIN' THOR! NATURALLY HE'LL SAY THAT HE'S THE STRONGEST!

I HEARD WHAT YOU SAID! KNOW YOU ALL THAT THE SON OF ODIN SPEAKS ONLY THE TRUTH!
S-SURE, THOR! NO OFFENSE MEANT... HONEST!
BUT WHAT ABOUT THE HULK? IS HE STRONGER THAN YOU ARE...OR WHAT??

SOMETIMES BRUTE STRENGTH ALONE IS NOT THE IMPORTANT THING!
AW, C'MON! THAT'S NO ANSWER! WHO'S THE STRONGEST?
MAYBE HE DOESN'T WANT TO TELL US!

NO! I SHALL TELL YOU! HARKEN...
THERE WAS A TIME THAT I FOUGHT THE HULK! PARTS OF THAT BATTLE ARE NOW IN THE PUBLIC RECORD... WHILE PARTS ARE NOT!
THAT'S RIGHT! I REMEMBER...IT WAS MONTHS AGO ...YOU WERE WITH THE REST OF THE AVENGERS..!

"YES! WE WERE IN A CAVE IN GIBRALTAR...PURSUING BOTH SUB-MARINER AND THE HULK!"*
CAREFUL!! THEY MUST BE WAITING... DIRECTLY AHEAD OF US!!
*SEE AVENGERS #3...STAN.

"AND, IRON MAN'S WARNING WAS WELL-ADVISED! FOR, DIRECTLY ABOVE US..."
ONCE THEY COME CLOSER, THE HIGH, PIERCING BLAST OF THIS MODIFIED AIR RAID ALARM WILL DESTROY ANY LIVING BEINGS IT IS DIRECTED AT!!
BAH!! WHO CARES ABOUT THAT?? I JUST WANT TO GET MY HANDS ON THEM!!

"BUT, LUCKILY, THE 12-FOOT TALL GIANT-MAN SAW THEM IN TIME...!"
YOU'RE TOO LITTLE TO BE PLAYIN' WITH SUCH DANGEROUS TOYS, FELLA!
WELL DONE, GIANT-MAN!

"AH, YES... I STILL REMEMBER IT ALL CLEARLY...!"
UGHHH!
HANG ON, PARTNER! MY TRANSISTOR-POWERED ARMOR WILL GET HIM!!
I'VE BEEN WAITIN' FOR A CHANCE TO GET AT YOU!! AND NOW...!!
BACK, RAMPAGING ONE! BACK, I SAY!
THOUGH YOU ARE TWICE MY SIZE, MY STRENGTH IS STILL GREATER THAN YOURS!

GOSH, THOR, MOST OF THAT WAS IN THE PAPERS... BUT IT'S MORE EXCITING TO HEAR IT FROM YOU!
BUT, WHAT HAPPENED NEXT?? ACCORDING TO THE PAPERS, SUB-MARINER AND THE HULK JUST KINDA RAN OFF! I'LL BET THERE WAS MORE TO THE FIGHT THAN THAT!

YES! THERE WAS MUCH MORE! THERE WAS A BATTLE BETWEEN THE HULK AND ME... WHICH NO ONE ELSE KNEW ABOUT!
3.

"IT HAPPENED AT THE HEIGHT OF THE BATTLE... WHILE MY FELLOW AVENGERS WERE TRYING TO FIND A WAY TO STOP PRINCE NAMOR WITHOUT ACTUALLY INJURING HIM! THE *HULK* AND I WERE ALL BUT FORGOTTEN IN THE SHADOWS ..."

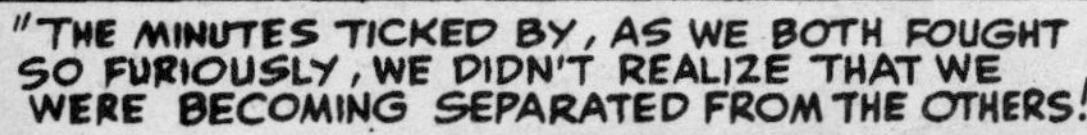

"THE MINUTES TICKED BY, AS WE BOTH FOUGHT SO FURIOUSLY, WE DIDN'T REALIZE THAT WE WERE BECOMING SEPARATED FROM THE OTHERS!"

WHOOOM!

"NEVER HAD I SEEN SUCH RAGE, SUCH FURY, IN ANY LIVING BEING!! THE HULK FOUGHT LIKE A DEMON POSSESSED... ACTUALLY TEARING OFF SECTIONS OF THE CAVE WALL ITSELF IN A DESPERATE ATTEMPT TO TRAP ME!!"
I'LL SMASH YOU LIKE A WORM!! YOU CAN'T DEFEAT ME!! I'M THE HULK!! I'M THE HULK!!
SCRUNCH!

YOU THINK YOUR STRENGTH IMPRESSES ME?? YOU ARE BUT THE HULK... YET I... I AM THOR... OF ASGARD!!

"BY MERELY WHIRLING MY ENCHANTED HAMMER AT A CERTAIN PRESCRIBED SPEED, I CAUSED A DIMENSION DISRUP-TION, MAKING IT IMPOSSIBLE FOR THE HULK TO BREAK THROUGH...!"
CAN'T PUSH FORWARD ANY FURTHER... NO MATTER WHAT I DO!!

"THEN, WITHIN MY DIMENSION DISRUPTION, A PLAN BEGAN TO TAKE SHAPE IN MY MIND...!"
OF ALL THOSE WHO WALK THE EARTH, ONLY THE STRENGTH OF THE HULK SEEMS TO MATCH MY OWN!
NOW I SHALL PROVE WHICH OF US IS TRULY THE STRONGER!

"AND SO, UTILIZING THE SECRETS OF THE ANCIENT NORSE GODS, I SENT A MESSAGE THROUGH THE INFINITE VOID... PAST THE RAINBOW BRIDGE ITSELF... TO ASGARD!"

"AND, NOBLE ODIN, ON A DISTANT HUNTING EXPEDITION, HEARD MY SUMMONS... AND MADE REPLY!!"
WHAT DOES MY FIRST-BORN SON DESIRE OF HIS ROYAL FATHER?
DIRECT YOUR THOUGHTS TO ASGARD, GOD OF THUNDER... AND I SHALL HEAR THEM!
5.

MOST NOBLE FATHER, I CRAVE FIVE MINUTES DURING WHICH I MAY RETAIN MY POWER WITHOUT MY HAMMER!
FOR I WOULD TEST MY STRENGTH AGAINST A MIGHTY ENEMY IN A HAND-TO-HAND BATTLE!
SO BE IT, MY SON!

AND, FOR THE NEXT FIVE MINUTES, YOUR HAMMER SHALL LOSE ITS MAGICAL FORCE! YOU NOW FACE YOUR FOE MAN-TO-MAN ... WITH NO ENCHANTED POWER!

THEN I HAVE NO FURTHER NEED OF MY MALLET!! SO, I SHALL HURL IT AWAY! IT SHALL BE MY RAW MUSCLE POWER AGAINST THAT OF THE HULK!

"BUT, WITH ONE INCREDIBLE LEAP, THE HULK LANDED IN FRONT OF THE FLYING HAMMER, WITH OUTSTRETCHED HANDS... !"
HAH!! AT LAST I'LL GET YOUR HAMMER AWAY FROM YOU! ONLY THE HULK COULD CATCH IT LIKE THIS!

I'M STRONGER THAN EVER! I COULDN'T LIFT YOUR HAMMER BEFORE... BUT NOW I CAN!
HE DOESN'T KNOW HE CAN LIFT IT ONLY BECAUSE ITS MAGIC POWER IS GONE FOR THE NEXT FIVE MINUTES!

AND NOW, I'LL SNAP IT IN TWO... JUST AS I CAN DO TO YOU... ANY TIME I FEEL LIKE IT!
WITHOUT ITS ENCHANTMENT, MY MALLET MIGHT BE DESTROYED! I CAN'T LET THAT HAPPEN....IT WAS A GIFT FROM ODIN!
6.

"SEEING ME LUNGE FORWARD AT HIM MADE THE HULK FORGET ABOUT SNAPPING THE HAMMER AS HE SWUNG IT AT ME INSTEAD!"
GIVE ME THAT HAMMER!!
BROOM

THOUGH IT HAS NO POWER NOW... IT HAS BEEN AT MY SIDE THROUGH TOO MANY BATTLES FOR ME TO ALLOW IT TO BE DESTROYED!

THERE IT IS! I'VE GOT TO GET IT OUT OF THE HULK'S REACH!
"BUT, I HAD NOT COUNTED ON THE HULK'S ALMOST-MIRACULOUS ABILITY TO BOUNCE BACK FROM A FALL...!"

HOLD IT, THUNDER GOD! YOU'RE NOT GOIN' ANY-WHERE...!

...UNLESS I SEND YOU THERE!
KA-POW!

YOU HAVE FLOORED THE SON OF ODIN! I CANNOT REMEMBER THE LAST TIME SUCH A FEAT HAS BEEN ACCOMPLISHED!
HE HAS NOT TAKEN HIS EYES FROM MY HAMMER! STILL HE HOPES TO DESTROY IT! I MUST MOVE WITH BLINDING SPEED!

THOUGH THERE MAY BE SOME QUESTION ABOUT WHICH OF US IS THE STRONGER... THERE CAN BE NO DOUBT AS TO WHO HAS THE GREATER SPEED!

AND NOW, GARGANTUAN ONE... I HAVE SHEATHED MY HAMMER! THE ONLY WAY YOU CAN SEIZE IT IS BY DEFEATING ME!

I CAN DEFEAT ANYTHING THAT LIVES!! I AM THE HULK!
HE IS TEARING THAT LONG-HIDDEN WORLD WAR II MINE FROM ITS CACHE WITHIN THE WALL! HIS FINGERS ARE LIKE TEN IRON CROWBARS!

HERE, GOD OF THUNDER!! HERE'S SOME MAN-MADE THUNDER FOR YOU!!
HIS LIVID RAGE... HIS INDESCRIBABLE FURY IS BEYOND COMPREHENSION!! NEVER HAVE I SEEN SUCH POWER IN MORTAL LIMBS!!

WHOOM!

I HAVE WEAKENED YOU!! BUT I CAN'T GET WEAK!! I GROW STRONGER EVERY MINUTE!! STRONGER! STRONGER! STRONGER! STRONG ENOUGH TO CRUSH EVEN YOU!!

IT'LL TAKE JUST ONE BLOW TO... HUH??! WHERE DID HE GO??
ZIZZ
I HAVE EVADED YOUR BLOW, VIOLENT ONE! AND NOW...

...WE SHALL SEE HOW WELL YOU CAN FACE THE WRATH OF THOR!!
THWUP!

I HAVE LISTENED TO YOUR BOASTFUL THREATS!! I HAVE SUFFERED THE INDIGNITY OF YOUR SAVAGE, POUNDING BLOWS!!
AND NOW, MY PATIENCE IS AT AN END!!

NOW, YOU SHALL LEARN THAT THERE IS POWER BEYOND THE POWER THAT LIES WITHIN YOUR SINEWS!

THERE IS MORE TO STRENGTH THAN SIZE ALONE!!
BAM!

"AGAIN AND AGAIN MY OWN THUNDERING FIST LASHED OUT, BATTERING THE DAZED, ROARING GIANT WHO HAD NEVER BEFORE FELT SUCH MIGHTY, PUNISHING BLOWS!!"
WHOOM!

"THEN, I PAUSED... TO SEE WHAT EFFECT MY BLOWS HAD UPON THE INCREDIBLE ONE... AND THAT WAS MY BIGGEST MISTAKE..."
ARGHH!
AND STILL HE STANDS!!
"...FOR, IT GAVE HIM TIME ENOUGH TO REACH OUT WITH HIS ENORMOUS, CLUTCHING HANDS, UNTIL.."
I'VE GOT YOU, THUNDER GOD!!
I WAS A FOOL TO PAUSE! NOW I'M IN THE GRIP OF ONE WHO CAN CRUSH GRANITE BLOCKS WITH HIS TITANIC FINGERS!!

"WHILE, IN DISTANT ASGARD, THE MOST NOBLE ODIN WATCHED US WITH EVER-INCREASING INTEREST!"
MY SON FIGHTS VALIANTLY, AS AN IMMORTAL SHOULD... AGAINST A MOST AWESOME FOE!!

NEVER HAVE I SEEN HIM SC CLOSE TO DEFEAT! NEVER HAS HE FACED A MORTAL OF SUCH INCOMPREHENSIBLE POWER!

IF HE IS TO TRIUMPH, IT MUST BE SOON! HIS ALLOTTED FIVE MINUTES ARE RAPIDLY FLEETING... AND I MUST DO NOTHING TO AFFECT THE BATTLE'S FINAL OUTCOME!

HAH!! FEEL THE POWER OF THE HULK!! DOWN... BOW DOWN TO YOUR MASTER!!
THOR BOWS TO NO ONE!! I SHALL SHOW YOU NOW WHAT STRENGTH REALLY IS!!

NO! NO! IT CAN'T BE!! YOU CAN'T LIFT ME OFF MY FEET! I'M BIGGER THAN YOU!... I'M THE HULK!!
I KNOW WHO YOU ARE!! I'VE KNOWN MANY LIKE YOU, THROUGH-OUT THE AGES!! THOUGH THE NAMES MAY CHANGE.. THE POWER AND THE FURY ARE ALWAYS PRESENT!!

...THE BLIND, SENSELESS RAGE ...THE NEED TO LASH OUT...TO STRIKE AND DESTROY... THE BELIEF THAT YOUR RAW POWER CAN SMASH ANY OBSTACLE ... I KNOW YOU, HULK! I'VE, ALWAYS KNOWN YOUR BREED!

"SUDDENLY, I REALIZED MY FIVE MINUTES HAD ALMOST EXPIRED! THE UNEXPECTED THOUGHT CAUSED ME TO RELAX MY MUSCLES INVOLUNTARI-LY... AND, IN THAT SPLIT-SECOND, THE HULK PLUMMETTED DOWN AGAIN!!"
NOW THERE'LL BE NO MORE WORDS!!
UHHH...!!
12.

I MUST NEVER FORGET... WITH A FOE SUCH AS THE HULK, I CANNOT RELAX MY VIGIL FOR A SECOND!! THERE CAN BE NO RESPITE... NO QUARTER ASKED, NOR GIVEN!
THERE'S GOT BE A WAY TO SMASH YOU! AND I'LL FIND IT, DO YOU HEAR!?? THE HULK WILL FIND IT!

WHITTT!
I MUST STOP MY FLIGHT! I'LL DO IT WITH THE IMPACT OF MY OWN TWO HANDS!

"BUT, SO VIOLENT, SO THUNDEROUS WAS THE FORCE I EXERTED, THAT THE VERY ATOMIC FABRIC OF THE STONES THEMSELVES GAVE WAY, CAUSING A CHAIN REACTION WHICH AFFECTED THE ENTIRE SUBTERRANEAN TUNNEL...!!"
BAROOOOMM!
THE ENTIRE TUNNEL IS ABOUT TO CAVE IN!! I EXERTED TOO MUCH FORCE!!

"I SHALL ALWAYS REMEMBER THE SIGHT OF HIS FACE AT THAT MOMENT... THE DAZED, UNCOMPREHENDING LOOK... EXPRESSING SHOCK, SURPRISE, BEWILDERMENT... EVERYTHING EXCEPT... FEAR!"
NO! NO! IT CAN'T END LIKE THIS! I WON'T LET IT!! NO!!!

"NOR DID I DESIRE SUCH AN END!! IT WAS TOO INCONCLUSIVE..TOO FRUSTRATING!! FRANTICALLY I RUSHED TO THE SPOT WHERE I HAD LAST SEEN MY INCREDIBLE FOE...!!"
I MUST FIND HIM! I MUST PUT AN END TO THIS CHARADE, ONCE AND FOREVER!
13.

"THEN, WITH A BLAZING FURY, WITH A BLIND RAGE WHICH ALMOST EQUALLED THE HULK'S, I STRUCK OUT... SHATTERING EVERYTHING IN MY PATH... DETERMINED TO FIND THE GREEN-SKINNED GIANT WHO CONTINUED TO DEFY ME!"
BLAM!
THOOOM!
KRAK!
"UNTIL, I FINALLY FOUND..."
A ROUGH-HEWN HOLE BENEATH THE RUBBLE! THE HULK HAS DUG HIS WAY OUT WITH HIS OWN BARE HANDS!!
PERHAPS HE HAS NOT YET GONE TOO FAR!! THERE MAY STILL BE TIME TO FIND HIM!!
CRUNCH!
SKRAK!
"AND, AT THAT MOMENT..."
ONLY SCANT SECONDS REMAIN!
AND I CANNOT GIVE MY SON MORE TIME THAN THE AMOUNT HE REQUESTED!
I HAVE WITNESSED ENOUGH! THERE SHALL BE NO FINAL DECISION THIS DAY!
BUT, ONE GOOD PURPOSE SHALL HAVE BEEN SERVED! THE GOD OF THUNDER WILL, FROM THIS MOMENT FORTH, HAVE GREATER KNOWLEDGE OF THE MEANING OF... HUMILITY!
"WHILE, BACK ON EARTH, I FINALLY EMERGED FROM THE DESERTED TUNNEL, ONLY TO SEE...!"
CAN'T CONTINUE BATTLE! MUST REPAIR CHEST DEVICE! IF TRANSISTORS STOP... I'M DOOMED!
SUB-MARINER! ..ESCAPING!!
14.

"SO INTENT WAS I UPON STOPPING THE MENACING MONARCH OF THE SEA, THAT I FAILED TO HEAR THE HEAVY BREATHING OF THE CREATURE WHO STOLE UP BEHIND ME . . . !"

I'LL PROVE ONCE AND FOR ALL HOW OVER-RATED YOU ARE, YOU COSTUMED CLOWN!

"AND, ONCE AGAIN, I WAS HELD IN A GRIP SO POWERFUL, THAT NO HUMAN WORDS CAN ADEQUATELY DESCRIBE IT!!"

NOW *NOTHING* CAN STOP ME FROM GETTING YOUR HAMMER!!

"BUT, AT THAT VERY SECOND, THE FIVE FATAL MINUTES EXPIRED . . . AND MY ENCHANTED MALLET PROVED MORE THAN *ANY* MORTAL COULD HANDLE!"

TO YOUR *MASTER*, MY URU HAMMER!!

"ONCE AGAIN I WAS THOR, GOD OF THUNDER, SON OF ODIN, IMMORTAL OF ASGARD!! YEA, MIGHTY THOR, AT THE PEAK OF ALL MY POWER!!"
GOSH, THOR . . . YOU HAVEN'T SAID ANYTHING FOR MINUTES!! WHAT HAPPENED NEXT??
HE'S JUST SITTING THERE . . . AS THOUGH HIS THOUGHTS ARE A MILLION MILES AWAY!!
THEY PROBABLY ARE! WHAT ABOUT THE REST OF THAT FIGHT, THOR?
THE FIGHT . . . ?
15.

THERE IS NOTHING MORE TO TELL...!
THE HULK SEEMS TO HAVE VANISHED! I FOUND NO FURTHER TRACE OF HIM, UNTIL... BUT, THAT IS ANOTHER TALE!
BUT, YOU STILL HAVEN'T TOLD US... WHO'S THE STRONGEST!

I CAN ONLY GUESS AT THE ANSWER... BUT I CAN OFFER NO PROOF!
THEREFORE, I SHALL SAY NOTHING! FOR THE GOD OF THUNDER DOES NOT SCATTER HIS WORDS RASHLY TO THE WIND!

BUT, I LEAVE YOU WITH THIS THOUGHT... IT IS NOT THE ONE POSSESSING THE GREATEST POWER WHO IS IMPORTANT!! IT IS THE ONE WHO USES HIS POWER WISELY... IN THE CAUSE OF JUSTICE!

FOR, THE LESSON I HAVE LEARNED IS ONE I SHALL NEVER FORGET! STRENGTH ALONE IS MEANINGLESS! WITHOUT VIRTUE, IT IS AN EMPTY SHELL!
I PRAY THE HULK SOMEDAY LEARNS THAT LESSON... WHEREVER HE MAY BE!

AND, DAYS LATER, IN A LONELY DESERT AREA OF THE GREAT SOUTHWEST, THE STRONGEST MORTAL CREATURE ON EARTH SHUFFLES FORTH, LOST IN HIS OWN DARK, CLOUDED THOUGHTS...!
I MUST FIND THOR SOMEDAY! AND I MUST CRUSH HIM!! AS ONLY I CAN!

BUT, WHERE THE THUNDER GOD IS GENTLE, THE HULK IS SAVAGE! WHERE THOR IS THOUGHTFUL, THE HULK IS FILLED WITH FRENZY!
NOTHING CAN STAND IN MY WAY! NOTHING CAN DEFY MY MIGHT!

ONLY IN ONE WAY ARE THEY SIMILAR... THE POWER OF EACH IS BEYOND DESCRIPTION... BEYOND MERE HUMAN COMPREHENSION!!

SOMEDAY WE'LL MEET AGAIN... AND THOR WILL BE SMASHED... FOREVER!

AND, IN TRUTH, THEY SHALL MEET AGAIN! PERHAPS NOT THIS MONTH... PERHAPS NOT NEXT... BUT, MEET THEY SHALL! AND, WHEN THAT EPIC CONFRONTATION TAKES PLACE, WE SHALL BRING YOU EVERY PULSE-POUNDING INCIDENT... AS YOU HAVE COME TO EXPECT IN THIS, THE MARVEL AGE OF COMICS!!

THE START OF A NEW MARVEL BIOGRAPHY-IN-DEPTH...
Tales of Asgard
HOME OF THE MIGHTY NORSE GODS!
"THE COMING OF LOKI!"

AGES AGO, WHEN THE UNIVERSE WAS YOUNG, AND ASGARD WAS A'BORNING, NOBLE ODIN WAS COMPELLED TO BATTLE A MYRIAD HOST OF FOES IN ORDER TO SECURE HIS RIGHTFUL REIGN!

ONE SUCH FOE WAS THE TITANIC *LAUFEY,* KING OF THE GIANT WARRIORS OF JOTUNHEIM...

ASGARD MUST BE *MINE!* YIELD, ODIN... AND PERHAPS I SHALL ALLOW YOU TO LIVE IN BONDAGE!

ODIN YIELDS TO *NO* ONE! LET THE BATTLE BEGIN!

MAJESTICALLY WRITTEN BY: STAN LEE

MAGNIFICENTLY DRAWN BY: JACK KIRBY

MASTERFULLY INKED BY: VINCE COLLETTA

MAGNANIMOUSLY LETTERED BY: ARTIE SIMEK

IT WILL TAKE NO MORE THAN ONE BLOW OF MY THUNDERING WAR CLUB TO--HOLD, ODIN! STAND YOUR GROUND AND FIGHT!
I STAND MY GROUND! BUT YOUR MOVEMENTS ARE CLUMSY--YOUR ARM IS SLOW!

HOWEVER, LAUFEY'S POUNDING WAR CLUB EVENTUALLY DOES FIND ITS TARGET, AS DOES ODIN'S LEGENDARY HAMMER--AND THE BATTLE IS ON, AS THE VERY PEAKS OF JOTUNHEIM RING WITH THE SOUND OF THE EPIC DUEL!

I NO LONGER HEAR YOUR EMPTY BOASTS, KING OF JOTUNHEIM! DOES THE POWER OF MY HAMMER SURPRISE YOU??
AYE, BEARDED ONE! BUT YOUR VALOR IS WASTED UPON A BATTLE YOU CAN NEVER HOPE TO WIN!

KNOW YOU, THIS LAND IS MINE! SEE HOW I ALMOST CAUSED YOU TO STEP ON A FATAL POTHOLE WHICH POURS FORTH COSMIC FLAME!
HIS WORDS RING TRUE! IN THIS ALIEN LAND, THE ADVANTAGE IS HIS--UNLESS I CAN ACHIEVE VICTORY WITHIN MINUTES!

ENOUGH OF THIS USELESS DUEL! LET THE DECISION BE NOW! HAVE YOU FORGOTTEN, SAVAGE LAUFEY, A HAMMER CAN BE THROWN AS WELL AS SWUNG??!
MY WAR CLUB-- SHATTERED!

SEEING THEIR MONARCH'S WEAPON SO EASILY DESTROYED, THE GIANT WARRIORS OF JOTUNHEIM BELLOW IN UNCONTROLLABLE RAGE, AS THEY BREAK RANKS, HUNGERING TO JOIN THE BATTLE!

DEATH TO ALL THE MINIONS OF ASGARD! THEY MUST BE CRUSHED FOR THE GLORY OF JOTUNHEIM!
WE CAN REMAIN INACTIVE NO LONGER! OUR WARLORD IS DEFENSELESS! WE MUST FIGHT AT THE SIDE OF LAUFEY!
STRIKE FOR JOTUNHEIM! SLAY THE WARRIORS OF ASGARD!

THEN, SOUNDING THEIR EAR-SHATTERING WAR CRY, PLACING A POWERFUL BATTLE-SWORD IN THE EAGER HAND OF LAUFEY, THE ENTIRE ASSEMBLED FIGHTING FORCE OF JOTUNHEIM SURGES FORWARD LIKE AN IRRESISTIBLE LIVING TIDAL WAVE...!

YOUR SWORD, MY KING! MAY IT POINT THE WAY TO VICTORY!

TO MY SIDE, WARRIORS OF ASGARD! LET THE STRENGTH OF OUR LIMBS, THE POWER OF OUR ARMS, DRIVE BACK THE HORDES OF LAUFEY!

THERE ARE NO EARTHLY WORDS WHICH CAN ADEQUATELY DESCRIBE A BATTLE SUCH AS THIS! SO WE, POOR MORTALS, WILL NOT EVEN ATTEMPT SUCH A DESCRIPTION! WE SHALL MERELY ALLOW THE SCENE TO SPEAK FOR ITSELF!

TO FOES SUCH AS THESE-- IN A CONFLICT SUCH AS THIS-TIME HAS LITTLE OR NO MEANING! IT MIGHT BE MINUTES, HOURS, OR DAYS--BUT FINALLY, THE COURAGE AND THE SKILL OF ODIN'S LEGIONS SERVE TO DRIVE BACK LAUFEY'S BEATEN WARRIORS, IN ONE OF THE GREATEST VICTORIES IN THE ANNALS OF ASGARD!

FLEE! WE CAN FIGHT NO LONGER! THE CAUSE IS LOST! ODIN HAS TRIUMPHED AGAIN!
NO! I ORDER DEATH TO THOSE WHO SURRENDER! WE SHALL REGROUP AT MY CASTLE, AND ATTACK AGAIN--WHEN THEY LEAST SUSPECT IT!

BUT ODIN, EVER VIGILANT, EVER OMNIPOTENT, HAS HEARD LAUFEY'S DESPERATE CRY, AND SO A NEW ORDER IS ISSUED BY THE MIGHTY MONARCH...!
AFTER THEM! THE REIGN OF LAUFEY MUST BE ENDED FOREVER! SO LONG AS HE IS KING OF JOTUNHEIM, OUR VICTORY WILL NEVER BE COMPLETE!

BUT, LAUFEY'S COURAGE IS A MATCH FOR HIS AMBITION--AND HE CHOOSES DEATH AT THE HANDS OF HIS ENEMY RATHER THAN THE IGNOMINY OF SURRENDER!
ENOUGH! LET THE FIGHTING CEASE! THE WARLORD OF JOTUNHEIM IS SLAIN!
SOMETHING LIVES WITHIN THAT BUNDLE! OPEN IT, THAT I MAY BEHOLD ITS CONTENT!
I HEAR A FAINT WHIMPERING CRY! METHINKS, MY LORD, THERE IS AN INFANT CHILD WITHIN!
OF COURSE! IT IS LOKI, SON OF LAUFEY! THE CHILD HE KEPT HIDDEN, FOR HIS HEART WAS FILLED WITH SHAME THAT LOKI WAS NOT BORN A GIANT, AS WERE THE OTHER OFFSPRING OF JOTUNHEIM!
LOKI! THE VERY NAME HAS A RING OF EVIL--A TINGE OF FOREBODING TO IT!
MAYHAP! BUT STILL HE IS A REGAL PRINCE, SON OF A KINGLY FATHER! I MUST ACCORD HIM HIS RIGHTFUL DUE!
5
HEAR ME, LEGIONS OF ASGARD! FROM THIS MOMENT HENCE, I PROCLAIM LOKI: SON OF ODIN, HALF-BROTHER TO MY WELL-BELOVED THOR! FOR BETTER OR FOR WORSE, LOKI IS FOREVERMORE AN IMMORTAL OF ASGARD! THIS HAVE I PROCLAIMED! SO BE IT!
MANY ARE THE LEGENDS OF LOKI'S BIRTH--BUT THIS IS ONE WE FAVOR! HOWEVER, WE HAVE MERELY SCRATCHED THE SURFACE--WE HAVE BARELY BEGUN THIS DRAMATIC BIOGRAPHY-IN-DEPTH! IN FORTHCOMING ISSUES, WE SHALL TRACE LOKI'S EARLY CHILDHOOD--AND YOU SHALL RELIVE THE LEGENDARY PAST WITH LOKI AND WITH US! IN THE WORDS OF NOBLE ODIN--SO BE IT!
THE END

HOLDS
THE
THOR"

A MARVEL MASTERWORK PiN-UP

May the eyes of Asgard
Smile down on thee---
Thor

x-811

A MARVEL MASTERWORK PIN-UP

Loki

THE EVIL ONE!

THOR'S ETERNAL ENEMY!

THOR

Real name: Thor
Occupation: (as Thor) Warrior, adventurer, (as Sigurd Jarlson) Construction worker, (as Donald Blake) Physician, surgeon
Identity: Thor's identities as Blake and Jarlson are secret. The general populace of Earth knows of Thor's existence, but most do not believe he is the god who was worshipped by the Norsemen.
Legal status: Prince of Asgard, honorary citizen of the United States of America with no criminal record
Other current aliases: Sigurd Jarlson, the God of Thunder
Former aliases: Donald Blake, Donner, possibly Siegmund and Siegfried
Place of birth: A cave somewhere in Norway
Marital status: Single
Known relatives: Odin (father), Jord (Gaea, mother), Frigga (adoptive mother), Loki (adoptive brother), Vidar (half-brother), Buri (Tiwaz, great-grandfather), Bor (grandfather, possibly deceased), Vili, Ve (uncles, presumed deceased), Sigyn (former sister-in-law)
Group affiliation: East Coast Avengers, Gods of Asgard
Base of operations: Asgard, New York City
First appearance: JOURNEY INTO MYSTERY #83
Origin: JOURNEY INTO MYSTERY #83, THOR #159, THOR ANNUAL #11
History: Thor is the bloodson of Odin, lord of the gods of Asgard, and Jord, who is also known as Gaea, the elder goddess of the Earth (see *Asgard, Asgardians, Gaea, Odin*). Odin sought to father a son whose power would derive from Earth as well as Asgard, and hence he sought to mate with Jord. Odin created a cave in Norway where Jord gave birth to Thor. Months after the infant Thor was weaned, Odin brought him to Asgard to be raised. From that time on-

der his hammer to him, and then sent him to Earth in the mortal guise of a crippled young medical student named Donald Blake, stripped of his memory of his true identity.

As Blake Thor learned the value of humble perseverence in dealing with his injured leg, and he came to care for the sick and dying, first as a medical student, and later as a successful physician. After leaving medical school, Blake opened a private practice in New York, and quickly gained renown as a great surgeon.

After Thor had spent ten years in the role of Blake, Odin planted within Blake's mind the suggestion to take a vacation in Norway. There Blake encountered a party of alien Kronans, also known as the Stone Men from Saturn (see *Alien Races: Kronans*). Blake fled from the Kronans into a cavern, the very same one that had served as Thor's birthplace millennia ago, where Odin had left Thor's hammer in the enchanted form of a wooden cane. Trapped in the cavern by a great boulder, Blake struck the boulder with the cane in frustrated anger, and was transformed back into his true godly form of Thor. As Thor he escaped the cavern and drove off the Kronans.

At first Thor still had no memory of his past life as an Asgardian god, although as months passed, more of his memories returned. Finally, a few years later, Odin revealed to him the false nature of the Blake identity and the reason for it.

Thor maintained his Blake identity on Earth and continued his medical practice. Part of his affinity for Earth was his subconscious realization that his maternal heritage was on this world. The other part was simply his love for humanity and his need to experience those things that only mortals could know. Thor came to divide his time between Earth and Asgard, and does so to this day.

For years Thor was in love with Jane Foster, who worked as a nurse for Blake. Odin disapproved of Thor's love for this mortal, but eventually the romance between Thor and Foster came to an end, and Thor renewed his past relationship with Sif. That relationship has suffered strains in recent years, and it is unclear what path it may take in the future.

Thor was a founding member of the team of superhuman champions known as the Avengers, and has continued to serve with the team from time to time through the present.

Recently Thor gave up his identity as Don Blake. In fact, Odin transferred the enchantment enabling Thor to change into mortal form and back from Thor's hammer to that of his ally and alien counterpart, Beta Ray Bill (see *Beta Ray Bill*). With the aid of Nick Fury, Public Director of SHIELD, Thor has adopted a new "secret identity," that of construction worker Sigurd Jarlson (see *Fury, Nick; SHIELD*). Thor does not actually become a mortal in his Jarlson identity; he simply dresses as a normal contemporary Earthman and wears glasses.

Lately, Thor has grown a beard to conceal the terrible scars left on his face due to wounds inflicted by the Asgardian death goddess Hela (see *Hela*). It is not known if these scars will ever completely heal and fade.

After Odin disappeared during his battle with Surtur, the people of Asgard wished to make Thor, Odin's designated heir, their new ruler (see *Surtur*). Unwilling to give up his guardianship of Earth or his life of adventure, at least not yet, Thor declined the offer and instead nominated his friend Balder the Brave to be Asgard's ruler (see *Balder*). Balder now rules until such time as Odin returns or Thor himself claims the throne.

Height: 6′ 6″
Weight: 640 lbs.
Eyes: Blue
Hair: Blond
Strength level: Thor possesses Class 100 strength, enabling him to lift (press) over 100 tons. Thor's strength is doubled when he wears his enchanted belt of strength.
Known superhuman powers: Thor possesses the superhuman physical attributes of an Asgardian, but as the son of Odin, lord of the Asgardians, and Jord, elder goddess of the Earth, his strength, endurance, and resistance to injury are greater than those of the vast majority of his race. Like all Asgardians Thor is extremely long-lived (although not immortal like the Olympians), superhumanly strong (the average Asgardian male can lift about 30 tons over his head; Thor can lift over 100 tons above his own), is immune to all Earthly diseases, and is resistant to conventional injury. (Asgardian flesh and bone is about three times as dense as similar human tissue, contributing to the Asgardians' superhuman strength and weight.) Thor's Asgardian metabolism gives him far greater than human endurance at all physical activites.

Abilities: Trained in the arts of war, Thor is a superbly skilled warrior, highly preficient in hand-to-hand combat, swordsmanship, and hammer throwing.

Due to his years as Donald Blake, Thor has considerable expertise in medicine.

Weapons: Thor's principal weapon is the enchanted hammer named Mjolnir, one of the most formidable weapons known to man or god. Forged out of the mystical metal uru, whose chief properties are durability and ability to maintain enchantment, the hammer is two feet long and its handle is wrapped in leather which terminates in a thong. Besides being a nearly indestructible throwing weapon, the hammer has been given six enchantments by Odin by augment its physical qualities.

The first enchantment is that no living being can lift the hammer from the ground unless he or she is worthy. Hence, so far as is known, only Odin, Thor, and Beta Ray Bill are able to lift Mjolnir. Apparently no one without superhuman strength can lift the hammer, whether he or she is worthy or not.

The second enchantment causes the hammer to return to the exact spot from which it is thrown after striking its target.

The third enchantment enables the hammer's wielder to summon the elements of storm (wind, rain, thunder, lightning, and so forth) by stamping its handle twice upon the ground and willing it to do so. Thor can also project various forms of mystical energy from the hammer without striking it on the ground.

The fourth enchantment enables the hammer to open interdimensional portals, allowing its wielder to travel to other dimensions, such as from Earth to Asgard. (It is not known how Thor locates the dimension to which he wishes to travel.)

The fifth enchantment, bestowed on the hammer by Odin in recent times, enabled Thor to transform into the mortal Don Blake, by stamping the hammer once upon the ground and willing the change to occur. When Thor became Blake, Mjolnir became a gnarled wooden cane. By stamping the cane upon the ground once and willing the change to occur, Blake could turn himself back to his godly form of Thor, and the cane would again become the hammer. When the hammer was in the form of a cane, anyone could lift it. A provision of the enchantment required that the hammer could not be out of Thor's hand forover 60 seconds while he was on Earth without his spontaneous reversion to his mortal self.

Most of the fifth enchantment has been transferred to the hammer of Beta Ray Bill. However, enough of the fifth enchantment remains in Thor's hammer so that by stamping his hammer, he can instantaneously transform his Thor costume into Sigurd Jarlson's clothing, or vice versa. The hammer itself does not change form.

The hammer has had one enchantment that has been rescinded. Formerly the hammer could be swung in such a way as to generate chronal displacement inertia, enabling its wielder to travel through time. Most of this property, which is separate from the hammer's power to traverse dimensions, was removed by Immortus, and Thor himself recently apparently exhausted whatever time-traveling power Mjolnir had remaining (see *Immortus*).

By throwing the hammer and grasping its leather thong, Thor can magically propel himself through the air in the semblance of flight. Just as the hammer can magically change its course in order to return to his hand when he throws it, so can it be influenced by its wielder to change its course while it is in his grasp in flight. The precise manner in which Thor "steers" his hammer while in flight is not known, nor is the precise speed and distance Thor can attain with a single throw. Thor has been observed to be able to attain escape velocity from Earth's gravity with a single throw and to overtake space vessels.

Paraphernalia: Thor possesses an enchanted belt of strength which doubles his strength while he wears it. However, Thor feels physically drained after wearing the belt of strength.

Thor sometimes wears a pair of strong iron gauntlets.

Transportation: Thor drives a chariot-like vehicle pulled by two large enchanted goats, Toothgnasher and Toothgrinder. These two goats possess unusually high intelligence, can run at incredible speed on land and in the air, and can traverse dimensional barriers.

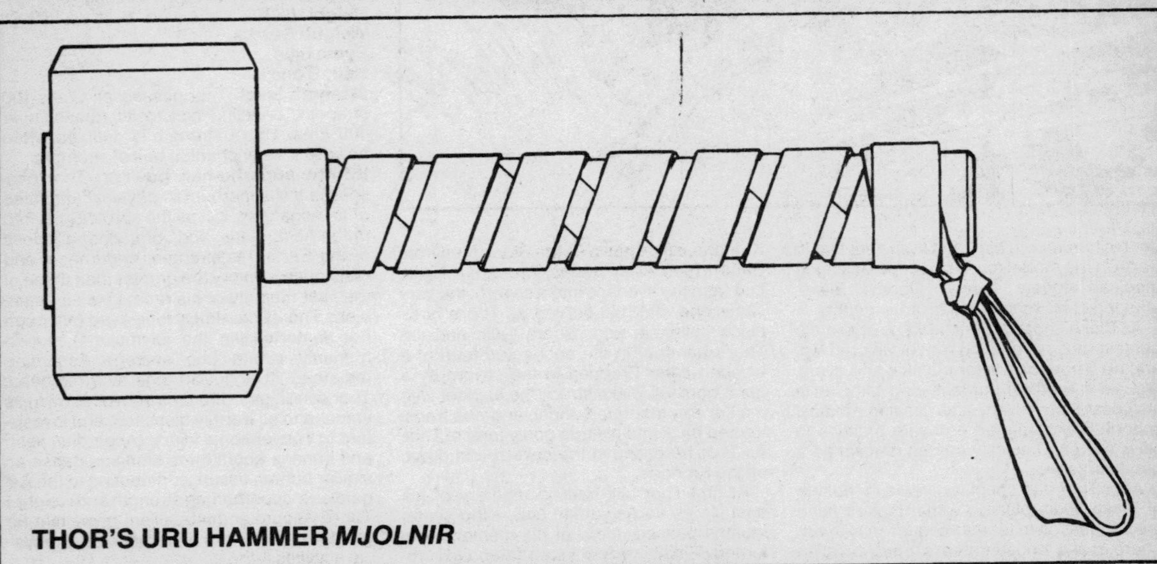

THOR'S URU HAMMER *MJOLNIR*

ward Odin's wife, the goddess Frigga, acted as Thor's mother. Not until recent years did Thor learn that Jord was his mother.

A severed eye of Odin once grew to great size, achieved sentience, and informed Thor that another Thor had existed before the current Thor's birth. This previous Thor was also the son of Odin, but had red hair, not blond hair like the current Thor. This previous Thor is said to have killed the Midgard Serpent, and to have been killed himself by the dying monster's venom, at Ragnarok, the destruction of a previous version of Asgard (see *Appendix: Midgard Serpent*). Odin himself was killed, but a new Odin appeared in the place of several gods who survived Ragnarok, and it was this new Odin who fathered the current version of Thor.

Possibly these previous versions of Odin and Thor were earlier physical incarnations of the Odin and Thor of today. However, this account of Thor's origin by the severed eye of Odin may very well be entirely false. The eye's motives for constructing such a story, if it is false, are unknown.

The young Thor was raised alongside Loki, who had been adopted by Odin after Loki's father, the Frost Giant Laufey, had been killed in battle (see *Loki*). From childhood Loki was jealous of Thor, and his hatred of Thor grew over the years to a wish to destroy him. Thus began Loki's enmity for Thor, which persists to this day.

When Thor was eight, Odin sent him to Nidalvellir, the land of the dwarves, to bid the dwarves Brokk and Eitri to create three treasures for Asgard's ruler. Among the three treasures that Brokk and Eitri created was the uru hammer Mjolnir (although Loki sabotaged the creation of the hammer so that its handle was made too short). Odin bestowed various enchantments upon the hammer, including one that made it impossible for anyone to lift it except someone who was truly worthy of wielding it. Odin then declared that he was reserving the use of Mjolnir for Thor, who would receive it on the day that great deeds of selfless valor had proved him worthy of it.

For years Thor strove to become strong and worthy enough to wield the hammer, and was responsible for many heroic deeds. Finally, when Thor was sixteen, Odin presented him with the hammer, declaring he was indeed worthy of it. Thor became Asgard's greatest warrior.

Before Thor was twenty, he had fallen in love with the goddess Sif (see *Sif*). However, at some point their romance came to an end, although they have renewed it in recent years.

Sometime in the 9th Century A.D. Thor journeyed to Earth for the first time and promoted his worship among the Vikings. Both the Norsemen and the Germans, who called him Donner, came to worship Thor and other Asgardians. Thor actively encouraged the adolation of his Viking worshippers for years, and also encouraged them to find glory in battle. But finally, Thor discovered that a party of his Viking worshippers had slaughtered the inhabitants of a Christian monastery. Shocked, realizing that some of his more zealous worshippers were committing atrocities like this one in his name, Thor withdrew from Earthly activities altogether, and allowed the worship of the gods of Asgard to die out.

According to the severed eye of Odin, Odin himself later caused Thor to live on Earth in the mortal guises of the Germanic heroes Siegmund and his son, Siegfriend. In these two roles, Thor played a major role in Odin's efforts to regain the dangerously powerful Ring of the Nibelung. Siegmund was killed by the warrior Hunding, but Thor was reborn as Siegfriend, the son of Siegmund and his lover Sieglinde. Siegfriend took possession of the Ring after killing the giant Fafnir, who guarded it in the guise of a dragon. (This Fafnir is not to be confused with the dragon Fafnir whom Thor has fought in recent years. See *Deceased: Fafnir*). Siegfriend then fell in love with the Valkyrie Brunnhilde, but was murdered by Hagen, the son of Alberich, the dwarf who had created the Ring and placed a curse upon it (see *Valkyrie*). Odin, however, resurrected Siegfried as Thor, who again had his full godly powers, but wiped out Thor's memory of his two mortal identities. It is unclear how much, if any, of this account by Odin's severed eye is true.

Thor led an active, adventurous life in Asgard, doing battle with Frost Giants and other enemies of the realm. But Odin grew increasingly dissatisfied with Thor's headstrong behavior and excessive pride. On one occasion Thor violated a truce between the Asgardians and the Frost Giants, thereby nearly starting a war. Finally, while Thor was engaged in a brawl in an Asgardian tavern, Odin summoned him to his presence. Odin had decided that it was time Thor learned humility. Odin had Thor surren-